P9-ANZ-729

GOLDSMITH

GOLDSMITH

SELECTED WORKS

Chosen by Richard Garnett

HARVARD UNIVERSITY PRESS

Cambridge Massachusetts

1967

First published 1950
Second impression 1967

Printed in Great Britain

CONTENTS

INTRODUCTION

"Mr. Posterity," wrote Goldsmith in 1765, despairing of appreciation from anyone else, "Sir, Nine hundred and ninety-nine years after the sight hereof, pay the bearer, or order, a thousand pound's worth of praise, free from all deductions whatsoever, it being a commodity that will then be very serviceable to him."

This bill has long since been honoured; I shall therefore confine myself to a few remarks about the present selection of his works. It does not claim to be representative; for with so excellent and so copious a writer as Goldsmith, there is no room for anything second-rate, and this means that works of certain kinds must go almost unrepresented.

Goldsmith's reputation rests on a comparatively small amount of his work: *The Vicar of Wakefield*, the two plays, the poems and a few essays. But most of his writings were compilations, such as *The Roman History*, *The Grecian History*, *An History of England in a Series of Letters from a Nobleman to his Son*, *An History of the Earth and Animated Nature* and *Poems for Young Ladies*; notices of books and plays in the *Monthly* and the *Critical Review*; and ephemeral publications, such as *The Mystery Revealed; Containing a Series of Transactions and Authentic Testimonials respecting the supposed Cock-Lane Ghost* and the *Memoirs of M. de Voltaire*.

When I had included the novel and the plays, almost all the poems (the only notable omissions being the two oratorios and a long translation of Vida's *Scacchiae Ludus* which may not be Goldsmith's), a generous selection of his essays and four of his letters, little space remained. Of his compilations, *An History of the Earth and Animated Nature* seemed to me the most undeservedly neglected and the most quotable. I preferred to represent the biographies by the best of them, *The Life of Richard Nash*, rather than by snippets of several. None of Goldsmith's criticism is outstanding—he was an original in his character, not in his ideas—but the most valuable is what he discloses about himself in *An Enquiry into the Present State of Polite Learning in Europe*, where he throws off the scholar's cap and gown and reveals a starving poet bitterly conscious of the world's indifference to his merits. His notices in the Reviews and, indeed, the lofty opening of *An Enquiry* itself are, in comparison, too impersonal to be distinguished from the ruck of contemporary criticism. Moreover the chapters of *An Enquiry* included here are not only conspicuously better than the rest of the book but are more or less complete in themselves. I was particularly sorry to exclude that delightful children's book, *The History of Little Goody Two-Shoes*; but even if Goldsmith's authorship were not extremely dubious, it was far too long.

Selecting the essays was complicated by their peculiar repetitiveness. Most of them were written in a hurry when he was pressed for money, and he did not find invention easy. It was his nature to cling to his earliest opinions and cherish the phrases in which he first expressed them. Thus he tended to repeat himself. The same sentence, or even paragraph, often recurs over a space of many years.

Goldsmith, moreover, would frequently republish an earlier essay, adapting it to serve a somewhat different purpose. Essays from *The Bee* as well as from the *Public Ledger* were included in *The Citizen of the World*, and almost all the *Essays* of 1765 had previously appeared in periodicals. When Goldsmith came to make new use of his old essays he revised or rewrote them. Some of his verbal corrections are undoubted improvements; but the essays as a whole are apt to suffer. He wrote the first version while he was still unknown. It is usually fresh and spontaneous. He often did not make the revision until after many years had passed, by which time he was a literary figure and no longer had the freedom of anonymity. The end of *A City Night-Piece* and much of *A Reverie in the Boar's-*

head-tavern in Eastcheap (too long, unfortunately, to be included here) are unnecessarily bowdlerised in the final version. And what was particular and personal is apt to become generalised, self-conscious, and sometimes even self-important.

Thus, on their merits rather than on any literary principle, I have usually preferred the first texts of essays which were revised after a lapse of many years. On the other hand, where a work was corrected almost immediately after publication, or continuously revised at short intervals over a period of several years, I have preferred the later text. The additions in the second edition of *The Life of Richard Nash* are as good as anything in the first; the revisions in the second edition of *The Vicar of Wakefield* seem to me improvements; and when Goldsmith made alterations to his poems they were almost always for the better. There is a short textual and general note prefixed to each work in this edition. The editorial footnotes are enclosed in square brackets, to distinguish them from Goldsmith's own.

Having chosen the text I have edited it as little as possible. A few general typographical changes have been made; the short s has been substituted for the long one; Greek contractions have been expanded; and, to save space, the speech-headings of *She Stoops to Conquer*, which were originally centred above the speeches, have been brought down and run into the first line. Indisputable misprints have been corrected; and where the punctuation is so faulty as to obscure the sense it has been emended; I have not attempted to standardise the varied conventions of printing direct speech; but where a question mark is used to indicate an ejaculation that is in no sense a question, it has been replaced by an exclamation mark. I hope that by reproducing Goldsmith's text with almost all its native imperfections some of the original flavour has been retained.

Finally I have various acknowledgments to make. For

many of the footnotes I am indebted to the wisdom and learning of previous editors, and to none more than Austin Dobson. I wish particularly to thank Miss Katharine C. Balderston of Wellesley College for help and advice and for kindly allowing me to use the text of her *Collected Letters of Oliver Goldsmith*, for which acknowledgment is also due to the Syndics of the Cambridge University Press. I must also thank Mr. D. M. Low for providing most of the translations and references for the classical quotations, Sir John Murray for his kindness in letting me examine his unique copy of *Edwin and Angelina*, Captain R. A. Anslow for information about racehorses, Mr. John Hayward for a multitude of small favours, and Mr. Alan Turing for having interested me in the properties of toadstools.

RICHARD GARNETT

March 1950

CHRONOLOGICAL TABLE

? 1730	(10 *November*) Birth of Oliver Goldsmith, fifth child of the Rev. Charles Goldsmith, Rector of Kilkenny West in Ireland.
c. 1737–44	At school at Elphin, Athlone and Edgeworthstown.
1745	(11 *June*) Entered Trinity College, Dublin.
1747	Death of his father. (*May*) Involved in a college riot.
1749	(27 *February*) Admitted to a B.A. degree.
1750–2	Idled in Ireland trying, without success, to go to America, to study law and to take holy orders.
1753	Studied medicine at Edinburgh.
1754	Imprisoned (? for debt). (*April*) Went to Leyden to study medicine.
1755	(*February*) Left Leyden; probably at Padua for six months; then wandered penniless through Northern Italy, Switzerland and France.
1756	(1 *February*) Landed at Dover. Worked as an apothecary's assistant and as an usher.
1757	(*April*) Began writing for the *Monthly Review*.
1758	(*February*) Publication of his translation of *The Memoirs of a Protestant*. (*Late in the year*) Moved to Green Arbour Court. (21 *December*) Failed to qualify as a hospital mate.
1759	(2 *April*) Publication of *An Enquiry*. (6 *October*–24 *November*) Publication of *The Bee*. Met Smollett and Newbery.
1760	(24 *January*) Publication of first *Chinese Letter*. Moved to 6 Wine Office Court.
1761	Editor of *Lady's Magazine*. (31 *May*) First visited by Johnson.
1762	(1 *May*) Publication of *The Citizen of the World*. (14 *October*) Publication of *The Life of Richard Nash*. (28 *October*) Sold a third share in *The Vicar of Wakefield*. (*Christmas*) Moved to Islington.
1763	(*Christmas*) Moved to the Temple.
1764	(*Spring*) Became an habitué of the Ivy Lane Club. (29 *March*) Returned to Islington. (26 *June*) Publication of *History of England*. (19 *December*) Publication of *The Traveller*.
1765	(4 *June*) Publication of *Essays*. Private edition of *Edwin and Angelina*. Unsuccessful attempt to practise medicine.

1766	(12 *March*) Publication of *The Vicar of Wakefield.* Compiled *History of Philosophy* and *Poems for Young Ladies.* (*Winter*) Wrote *The Good Natur'd Man.*
1767	(*July*) Living at Garden Court. Refused to become Sandwich's political propagandist.
1768	(29 *January*) First night of *The Good Natur'd Man.* Moved to 2 Brick Court, Middle Temple. (*Summer*) Compiled *The Roman History.*
1770	(9 *January*) Elected Professor of Ancient History to the Royal Academy. (26 *May*) Publication of *The Deserted Village.* (*July*) Visit to Paris with the Hornecks.
1771	(*Spring*) Wrote *The Haunch of Venison.* (*Late Summer*) Wrote *She Stoops to Conquer.*
1773	(15 *March*) First night of *She Stoops to Conquer.*
1774	Wrote *Retaliation.* (25 *March*) Taken seriously ill; refused medical attention, relying on "Dr. James's powder." (4 *April*) Died at 2 Brick Court, Middle Temple.

PROSE

[1] ["Hope on ye wretched, and beware ye happy!" the motto at the end of Burton's *Anatomy of Melancholy*.]

THE VICAR
OF
WAKEFIELD

A TALE

SUPPOSED TO BE
WRITTEN BY
HIMSELF

Sperate miseri, cavete fœlices.[1]

The Vicar of Wakefield was first published on 12 March, 1766, with the imprint, *Salisbury: Printed by B. Collins, for F. Newbery, in Pater-Noster-Row, London.* But there is good reason to think that it was written four years earlier. There are several different accounts of the circumstances in which the manuscript was sold to the bookseller. Boswell's version is as follows:

> Mrs. Piozzi and Sir John Hawkins have strangely mis-stated the history of Goldsmith's situation and Johnson's friendly interference, when this novel was sold. I shall give it authentically from Johnson's own exact narration:
>
> "I received one morning a message from poor Goldsmith that he was in great distress, and, as it was not in his power to come to me, begging that I would come to him as soon as possible. I sent him a guinea, and promised to come to him directly. I accordingly went as soon as I was drest, and found that his landlady had arrested him for his rent, at which he was in a violent passion. I perceived that he had already changed my guinea, and had got a bottle of Madeira and a glass before him. I put the cork into the bottle, desired he would be calm, and began to talk to him of the means by which he might be extricated. He then told me that he had a novel ready for the press, which he produced to me. I looked into it, and saw its merit; told the landlady I should soon return, and having gone to a bookseller, sold it for sixty pounds. I brought Goldsmith the money, and he discharged his rent, not without rating his landlady in a high tone for having used him so ill."

Mrs. Piozzi, Sir John Hawkins and Richard Cumberland give substantially similar accounts, though they differ in some important details. I can find no reference to *The Vicar of Wakefield* in the *Index to the Private Papers of James Boswell from Malahide Castle.* There is, however, one other piece of indisputable and important evidence. Charles Welsh discovered an entry in the account books of Benjamin Collins, the Salisbury printer; it reads:

> *Vicar of Wakefield*, 2 vols. 12mo., 1/3rd. B. Collins, Salisbury, bought of Dr. Goldsmith, the author, October 28, 1762, £21.

In other words, Collins bought a third share in *The Vicar of Wakefield* from Goldsmith for twenty-one pounds. This would make the total value of the book sixty guineas, which agrees tolerably well with Johnson's sixty pounds. But exactly what Johnson's transaction was, with which bookseller it was made, and how it is to be reconciled with the deal with Collins, are problems which remain unsolved. There is too much evidence, most of it conflicting, to be included here.[1]

On 31 May, 1766, a second edition was published in which Goldsmith made a great many minor revisions. He does not appear to have corrected any of the other three editions published during his lifetime. The text of the second edition is therefore used here.

The Vicar of Wakefield did not become really popular, nor particularly profitable to its publishers, until six or seven years after Goldsmith's death.

[1] The reader will find it set out in full in Mr. Oswald Doughty's admirable introduction to *The Vicar of Wakefield* (Scholartis Press, 1928).

ADVERTISEMENT

THERE are an hundred faults in this Thing, and an hundred things might be said to prove them beauties. But it is needless. A book may be amusing with numerous errors, or it may be very dull without a single absurdity. The hero of this piece unites in himself the three greatest characters upon earth; he is a priest, an husbandman, and the father of a family. He is drawn as ready to teach, and ready to obey, as simple in affluence, and majestic in adversity. In this age of opulence and refinement whom can such a character please? Such as are fond of high life, will turn with disdain from the simplicity of his country fire-side. Such as mistake ribaldry for humour, will find no wit in his harmless conversation; and such as have been taught to deride religion, will laugh at one whose chief stores of comfort are drawn from futurity.

OLIVER GOLDSMITH

CONTENTS OF THE FIRST VOLUME

CONTENTS OF THE SECOND VOLUME

VOLUME I

THE VICAR OF WAKEFIELD

CHAPTER I

The description of the family of Wakefield; in which a kindred likeness prevails as well of minds as of persons.

I WAS ever of opinion, that the honest man who married and brought up a large family, did more service than he who continued single, and only talked of population. From this motive, I had scarce taken orders a year before I began to think seriously of matrimony, and chose my wife as she did her wedding gown, not for a fine glossy surface, but such qualities as would wear well. To do her justice, she was a good-natured notable woman; and as for breeding, there were few country ladies who could shew more. She could read any English book without much spelling; but for pickling, preserving, and cookery, none could excel her. She prided herself also upon being an excellent contriver in house-keeping; tho' I could never find that we grew richer with all her contrivances.

However, we loved each other tenderly, and our fondness encreased as we grew old. There was in fact nothing that could make us angry with the world or each other. We had an elegant house, situated in a fine country, and a good neighbourhood. The year was spent in moral or rural amusements; in visiting our rich neighbours, and relieving such as were poor. We had no revolutions to fear, nor fatigues to undergo; all our adventures were by the fire-side, and all our migrations from the blue bed to the brown.

As we lived near the road, we often had the traveller or stranger visit us to taste our gooseberry wine, for which we had great reputation; and I profess with the veracity of an historian, that I never knew one of them find fault with it.

Our cousins too, even to the fortieth remove, all remembered their affinity, without any help from the herald's office, and came very frequently to see us. Some of them did us no great honour by these claims of kindred; as we had the blind, the maimed, and the halt amongst the number. However, my wife always insisted that as they were the same *flesh and blood*, they should sit with us at the same table. So that if we had not very rich, we generally had very happy friends about us; for this remark will hold good thro' life, that the poorer the guest, the better pleased he ever is with being treated: and as some men gaze with admiration at the colours of a tulip, or the wing of a butterfly, so I was by nature an admirer of happy human faces. However, when any one of our relations was found to be a person of very bad character, a troublesome guest, or one we desired to get rid of, upon his leaving my house, I ever took care to lend him a riding coat, or a pair of boots, or sometimes an horse of small value, and I always had the satisfaction of finding he never came back to return them. By this the house was cleared of such as we did not like; but never was the family of Wakefield known to turn the traveller or the poor dependant out of doors.

Thus we lived several years in a state of much happiness, not but that we sometimes had those little rubs which Providence sends to enhance the value of its favours. My orchard was often robbed by school-boys, and my wife's custards plundered by the cats or the children. The 'Squire would sometimes fall asleep in the most pathetic parts of my sermon, or his lady return my wife's civilities at church with a mutilated curtesy. But we soon got over the uneasiness caused by such accidents, and usually in three or four days began to wonder how they vext us.

My children, the offspring of temperance, as they were educated without softness, so they were at once well formed and healthy; my sons hardy and active, my daughters beautiful and blooming. When I stood in the midst of the little circle, which promised to be the supports of my declining age, I could not avoid repeating the famous story of Count Abensberg, who, in Henry II's progress through Germany, while other courtiers came with their treasures, brought his thirty-two children, and presented them to his sovereign as the most valuable offering he had to bestow. In this manner, though I had but six, I considered them as a very valuable present made to my country, and consequently looked upon it as my debtor. Our eldest son was named George, after his uncle, who left us ten thousand pounds. Our second child, a girl, I intended to call after her aunt Grissel; but my wife, who during her pregnancy had been reading romances, insisted upon her being called Olivia. In less than another year we had another daughter, and now I was determined that Grissel should be her name; but a rich relation taking a fancy to stand godmother, the girl was, by her directions, called Sophia; so that we had two romantic names in the family; but I solemnly protest I had no hand in it. Moses was our next, and after an interval of twelve years, we had two sons more.

It would be fruitless to deny my exultation when I saw my little ones about me; but the vanity and the satisfaction of my wife were even greater than mine. When our visitors would say, "Well, upon my word, Mrs. Primrose, you have the finest children in the whole country."—"Ay, neighbour," she would answer, "they are as heaven made them, handsome enough, if they be good enough; for handsome is that handsome does." And then she would bid the girls hold up their heads; who, to conceal nothing, were certainly very handsome. Mere outside is so very trifling a circumstance with me, that I should scarce have remembered to mention it, had it not been a general topic of conversation in the country. Olivia, now about eighteen, had that luxuriancy of beauty with which painters generally draw Hebe; open, sprightly, and commanding. Sophia's features were not so striking at first; but often did more certain execution; for they were soft, modest, and alluring. The one vanquished by a single blow, the other by efforts successfully repeated.

The temper of a woman is generally formed from the turn of her features, at least it was so with my daughters. Olivia wished for many lovers, Sophia to secure one. Olivia was often affected from too great a desire to please. Sophia even represt excellence from her fears to offend. The one entertained me with her vivacity when I was gay, the other with her sense when I was serious. But these qualities were never carried to excess in either, and I have often seen them exchange characters for a whole day together. A suit of mourning has transformed my coquet into a prude, and a new set of ribbands has given her younger sister more than natural vivacity. My eldest son George was bred at Oxford, as I intended him for one of the learned professions. My second boy Moses, whom I designed for business, received a sort of miscellaneous education at home. But it is needless to attempt describing the particular characters of young people that had seen but very little of the world. In short, a family likeness prevailed through all, and properly speaking, they had but one character, that of being all equally generous, credulous, simple, and inoffensive.

CHAPTER II

Family misfortunes. The loss of fortune only serves to encrease the pride of the worthy.

THE temporal concerns of our family were chiefly committed to my wife's management, as to the spiritual I took them entirely under my own direction. The profits of my living, which amounted to but thirty-five pounds a year, I made over to the orphans and widows of the clergy of our diocese; for having a sufficient fortune of my own, I was careless of temporalities, and felt a secret pleasure in doing my duty without reward. I also set a resolution of keeping no curate, and of being acquainted with every man in the parish, exhorting the married men to temperance, and the bachelors to matrimony; so that in a few years it was a common saying, that there were three strange wants at Wakefield, a parson wanting pride, young men wanting wives, and ale-houses wanting customers.

Matrimony was always one of my favourite topics, and I wrote several sermons to prove its happiness: but there was a peculiar tenet which I made a point of supporting; for I maintained with Whiston,[1] that it was unlawful for a priest of the church of England, after the death of his first wife, to take a second, or to express it in one word, I valued myself upon being a strict monogamist.

I was early initiated into this important dispute, on which so many laborious volumes have been written. I published some tracts upon the subject myself, which, as they never sold, I have the consolation of thinking are read only by the happy *Few*. Some of my friends called this my weak side; but alas! they had not like me made it the subject of long contemplation. The more I reflected upon it, the more important it appeared. I even went a step beyond Whiston in displaying my principles: as he had engraven upon his wife's tomb that she was the *only* wife of William Whiston; so I wrote a similar epitaph for my wife, though still living, in which I extolled her prudence, œconomy, and obedience till death; and having got it copied fair, with an elegant frame, it was placed over the chimney-piece, where it answered several very useful purposes. It admonished my wife of her duty to me, and my fidelity to her; it inspired her with a passion for fame, and constantly put her in mind of her end.

It was thus, perhaps, from hearing marriage so often recommended, that my eldest son, just upon leaving college, fixed

[1] [William Whiston (1667–1752), an eccentric divine, minor mathematician and astrologer. Goldsmith appears to be the only authority for the anecdote about his wife's epitaph.]

his affections upon the daughter of a neighbouring clergyman, who was a dignitary in the church, and in circumstances to give her a large fortune: but fortune was her smallest accomplishment. Miss Arabella Wilmot was allowed by all (except my two daughters) to be completely pretty. Her youth, health, and innocence, were still heightened by a complexion so transparent, and such an happy sensibility of look, as even age could not gaze on with indifference. As Mr. Wilmot knew that I could make a very handsome settlement on my son, he was not averse to the match; so both families lived together in all that harmony which generally precedes an expected alliance. Being convinced by experience that the days of courtship are the most happy of our lives, I was willing enough to lengthen the period; and the various amusements which the young couple every day shared in each other's company, seemed to encrease their passion. We were generally awaked in the morning by music, and on fine days rode a hunting. The hours between breakfast and dinner the ladies devoted to dress and study: they usually read a page, and then gazed at themselves in the glass, which even philosophers might own often presented the page of greatest beauty. At dinner my wife took the lead; for as she always insisted upon carving every thing herself, it being her mother's way, she gave us upon these occasions the history of every dish. When we had dined, to prevent the ladies leaving us, I generally ordered the table to be removed; and sometimes, with the music master's assistance, the girls would give us a very agreeable concert. Walking out, drinking tea, country dances, and forfeits, shortened the rest of the day, without the assistance of cards, as I hated all manner of gaming, except backgammon, at which my old friend and I sometimes took a two-penny hit. Nor can I here pass over an ominous circumstance that happened the last time we played together; I only wanted to fling a quatre, and yet I threw deuce ace five times running.

Some months were elapsed in this manner, till at last it

was thought convenient to fix a day for the nuptials of the young couple, who seemed earnestly to desire it. During the preparations for the wedding, I need not describe the busy importance of my wife, nor the sly looks of my daughters: in fact, my attention was fixed on another object, the completing a tract which I intended shortly to publish in defence of my favourite principle. As I looked upon this as a master-piece both for argument and style, I could not in the pride of my heart avoid shewing it to my old friend Mr. Wilmot, as I made no doubt of receiving his approbation; but not till too late I discovered that he was most violently attached to the contrary opinion, and with good reason; for he was at that time actually courting a fourth wife. This, as may be expected, produced a dispute attended with some acrimony, which threatened to interrupt our intended alliance: but on the day before that appointed for the ceremony, we agreed to discuss the subject at large.

It was managed with proper spirit on both sides: he asserted that I was heterodox, I retorted the charge: he replied, and I rejoined. In the mean time, while the controversy was hottest, I was called out by one of my relations, who, with a face of concern, advised me to give up the dispute, at least till my son's wedding was over. "How," cried I, "relinquish the cause of truth, and let him be an husband, already driven to the very verge of absurdity. You might as well advise me to give up my fortune as my argument." "Your fortune," returned my friend, "I am now sorry to inform you, is almost nothing. The merchant in town, in whose hands your money was lodged, has gone off, to avoid a statute of bankruptcy, and is thought not to have left a shilling in the pound. I was unwilling to shock you or the family with the account till after the wedding: but now it may serve to moderate your warmth in the argument; for, I suppose, your own prudence will enforce the necessity of dissembling at least till your son has the young lady's fortune secure."—"Well," returned I, "if what you tell me be true, and if I am to be a beggar, it shall never make me a rascal, or induce me to disavow my principles. I'll go this moment and inform the company of my circumstances; and as for the argument, I even here retract my former concessions in the old gentleman's favour, nor will allow him now to be an husband in any sense of the expression."

It would be endless to describe the different sensations of both families when I divulged the news of our misfortune; but what others felt was slight to what the lovers appeared to endure. Mr. Wilmot, who seemed before sufficiently inclined to break off the match, was by this blow soon determined: one virtue he had in perfection, which was prudence, too often the only one that is left us at seventy-two.

CHAPTER III

A migration. The fortunate circumstances of our lives are generally found at last to be of our own procuring.

THE only hope of our family now was, that the report of our misfortunes might be malicious or premature: but a letter from my agent in town soon came with a confirmation of every particular. The loss of fortune to myself alone would have been trifling; the only uneasiness I felt was for my family, who were to be humble without an education to render them callous to contempt.

Near a fortnight had passed before I attempted to restrain their affliction; for premature consolation is but the remembrancer of sorrow. During this interval, my thoughts were employed on some future means of supporting them; and at last a small Cure of fifteen pounds a year was offered me in a distant neighbourhood, where I could still enjoy my principles without molestation. With this proposal I joyfully closed, having determined to encrease my salary by managing a little farm.

Having taken this resolution, my next care was to get together the wrecks of my fortune; and all debts collected and paid, out of fourteen thousand pounds we had but four hundred remaining. My chief attention therefore was now to bring down the pride of my family to their circumstances; for I well knew that aspiring beggary is wretchedness itself. "You cannot be ignorant, my children," cried I, "that no prudence of ours could have prevented our late misfortune; but prudence may do much in disappointing its effects. We are now poor, my fondlings, and wisdom bids us conform to our humble situation. Let us then, without repining, give up those splendours with which numbers are wretched, and seek in humbler circumstances that peace with which all may be happy. The poor live pleasantly without our help, why then should not we learn to live without theirs. No, my children, let us from this moment give up all pretensions to gentility; we have still enough left for happiness if we are wise, and let us draw upon content for the deficiencies of fortune."

As my eldest son was bred a scholar, I determined to send him to town, where his abilities might contribute to our support and his own. The separation of friends and families is, perhaps, one of the most distressful circumstances attendant on penury. The day soon arrived on which we were to disperse for the first time. My son, after taking leave of his mother and the rest, who mingled their tears with their kisses, came to ask a blessing from me. This I gave him from my heart, and which, added to five guineas, was all the patrimony I had now to bestow. "You are going, my boy," cried I, "to London on foot, in the manner Hooker, your great ancestor, travelled there before you. Take from me the same horse that was given him by the good bishop Jewel,[1] this staff, and take this book

[1] ["And at the Bishops parting with him, the Bishop gave him good Counsel, and his Benediction, but forgot to give him money; which when the Bishop had considered, he sent a Servant in all haste to call *Richard* back to him, and at

too, it will be your comfort on the way: these two lines in it are worth a million; *I have been young, and now am old; yet never saw I the righteous man forsaken, or his seed begging their bread.*[1] Let this be your consolation as you travel on. Go, my boy, whatever be thy fortune let me see thee once a year; still keep a good heart, and farewell." As he was possest of integrity and honour, I was under no apprehensions from throwing him naked into the amphitheatre of life; for I knew he would act a good part whether vanquished or victorious.

His departure only prepared the way for our own, which arrived a few days afterwards. The leaving a neighbourhood in which we had enjoyed so many hours of tranquillity, was not without a tear, which scarce fortitude itself could suppress. Besides, a journey of seventy miles to a family that had hitherto never been above ten from home, filled us with apprehension, and the cries of the poor, who followed us for some miles, contributed to encrease it. The first day's journey brought us in safety within thirty miles of our future retreat, and we put up for the night at an obscure inn in a village by the way. When we were shewn a room, I desired the landlord, in my usual way, to let us have his company, with which he complied, as what he drank would encrease the bill next morning. He knew, however, the whole neighbourhood to which I was removing, particularly 'Squire Thornhill, who was to be my landlord, and who lived within a few miles of the place. This gentleman he described as one who desired to know little more of the world than its pleasures, being particularly remarkable for his attachment to the fair sex. He observed that no virtue was able to resist his arts and assiduity, and that scarce a farmer's daughter within ten miles round but what had found

---

Richards return, the Bishop said to him, *Richard, I sent for you back to lend you a horse, which hath carried me many a Mile, and I thank God with much ease*; and presently delivered into his hand a Walking-staff, with which he professed he had travelled through many parts of *Germany*." Izaak Walton's *Life of Hooker*.]

[1] [*Psalms*, 37. 25.]

him successful and faithless. Though this account gave me some pain, it had a very different effect upon my daughters, whose features seemed to brighten with the expectation of an approaching triumph, nor was my wife less pleased and confident of their allurements and virtue. While our thoughts were thus employed, the hostess entered the room to inform her husband, that the strange gentleman, who had been two days in the house, wanted money, and could not satisfy them for his reckoning. "Want money!" replied the host, "that must be impossible; for it was no later than yesterday he paid three guineas to our beadle to spare an old broken soldier that was to be whipped through the town for dog-stealing." The hostess, however, still persisting in her first assertion, he was preparing to leave the room, swearing that he would be satisfied one way or another, when I begged the landlord would introduce me to a stranger of so much charity as he described. With this he complied, shewing in a gentleman who seemed to be about thirty, drest in cloaths that once were laced. His person was well formed, and his face marked with the lines of thinking. He had something short and dry in his address, and seemed not to understand ceremony, or to despise it. Upon the landlord's leaving the room, I could not avoid expressing my concern to the stranger at seeing a gentleman in such circumstances, and offered him my purse to satisfy the present demand. "I take it with all my heart, Sir," replied he, "and am glad that a late oversight in giving what money I had about me, has shewn me, that there are still some men like you. I must, however, previously entreat being informed of the name and residence of my benefactor, in order to repay him as soon as possible." In this I satisfied him fully, not only mentioning my name and late misfortunes, but the place to which I was going to remove. "This," cried he, "happens still more luckily than I hoped for, as I am going the same way myself, having been detained here two days by the floods, which, I hope, by to-morrow will be found passable." I testified the pleasure I should have in his company, and my wife and daughters joining in entreaty, he was prevailed upon to stay supper. The stranger's conversation, which was at once pleasing and instructive, induced me to wish for a continuance of it; but it was now high time to retire and take refreshment against the fatigues of the following day.

The next morning we all set forward together: my family on horseback, while Mr. Burchell, our new companion, walked along the foot-path by the road-side, observing, with a smile, that as we were ill mounted, he would be too generous to attempt leaving us behind. As the floods were not yet subsided, we were obliged to hire a guide, who trotted on before, Mr. Burchell and I bringing up the rear. We lightened the fatigues of the road with philosophical disputes, which he seemed to understand perfectly. But what surprised me most was, that though he was a money-borrower, he defended his opinions with as much obstinacy as if he had been my patron. He now and then also informed me to whom the different seats belonged that lay in our view as we travelled the road. "That," cried he, pointing to a very magnificent house which stood at some distance, "belongs to Mr. Thornhill, a young gentleman who enjoys a large fortune, though entirely dependant on the will of his uncle, Sir William Thornhill, a gentleman, who content with a little himself, permits his nephew to enjoy the rest, and chiefly resides in town." "What!" cried I, "is my young landlord then the nephew of a man whose virtues, generosity, and singularities are so universally known? I have heard Sir William Thornhill represented as one of the most generous, yet whimsical, men in the kingdom; a man of consummate benevolence."—"Something, perhaps, too much so," replied Mr. Burchell, "at least he carried benevolence to an excess when young; for his passions were then strong, and as they all were upon the side of virtue, they led it up to a romantic extreme. He early began to aim at the qualifications of the soldier and scholar;

was soon distinguished in the army, and had some reputation among men of learning. Adulation ever follows the ambitious; for such alone receive most pleasure from flattery. He was surrounded with crowds, who shewed him only one side of their character; so that he began to lose a regard for private interest in universal sympathy. He loved all mankind; for fortune prevented him from knowing that there were rascals. Physicians tell us of a disorder in which the whole body is so exquisitely sensible, that the slightest touch gives pain: what some have thus suffered in their persons, this gentleman felt in his mind. The slightest distress, whether real or fictitious, touched him to the quick, and his soul laboured under a sickly sensibility of the miseries of others. Thus disposed to relieve, it will be easily conjectured, he found numbers disposed to solicit: his profusions began to impair his fortune, but not his good-nature; that, indeed, was seen to encrease as the other seemed to decay: he grew improvident as he grew poor; and though he talked like a man of sense, his actions were those of a fool. Still, however, being surrounded with importunity, and no longer able to satisfy every request that was made him, instead of *money* he gave *promises*. They were all he had to bestow, and he had not resolution enough to give any man pain by a denial. By this he drew round him crowds of dependants, whom he was sure to disappoint; yet wished to relieve. These hung upon him for a time, and left him with merited reproaches and contempt. But in proportion as he became contemptible to others, he became despicable to himself. His mind had leaned upon their adulation, and that support taken away, he could find no pleasure in the applause of his heart, which he had never learnt to reverence. The world now began to wear a different aspect; the flattery of his friends began to dwindle into simple approbation. Approbation soon took the more friendly form of advice, and advice when rejected produced their reproaches. He now therefore found that such friends as benefits had gathered round him, were little estimable: he now found that a man's own heart must be ever given to gain that of another. I now found, that—that—I forget what I was going to observe: in short, Sir, he resolved to respect himself, and laid down a plan of restoring his falling fortune. For this purpose, in his own whimsical manner, he travelled through Europe on foot, and now, though he has scarce attained the age of thirty, his circumstances are more affluent than ever. At present, his bounties are more rational and moderate than before; but still he preserves the character of an humourist, and finds most pleasure in eccentric virtues."

My attention was so much taken up by Mr. Burchell's account, that I scarce looked forward as we went along, till we were alarmed by the cries of my family, when turning, I perceived my youngest daughter in the midst of a rapid stream, thrown from her horse, and struggling with the torrent. She had sunk twice, nor was it in my power to disengage myself in time to bring her relief. My sensations were even too violent to permit my attempting her rescue: she must have certainly perished had not my companion, perceiving her danger, instantly plunged in to her relief, and, with some difficulty, brought her in safety to the opposite shore. By taking the current a little farther up, the rest of the family got safely over; where we had an opportunity of joining our acknowledgments to her's. Her gratitude may be more readily imagined than described: she thanked her deliverer more with looks than with words, and continued to lean upon his arm, as if still willing to receive assistance. My wife also hoped one day to have the pleasure of returning his kindness at her own house. Thus, after we were refreshed at the next inn, and had dined together, as Mr. Burchell was going to a different part of the country, he took leave; and we pursued our journey. My wife observing as we went, that she liked him extremely, and protesting, that if he had birth and fortune to entitle him to match into such a family as our's, she knew no man she would sooner fix upon. I could not but smile to hear her talk in this lofty strain: but I was never much displeased with those harmless delusions that tend to make us more happy.

CHAPTER IV

A proof that even the humblest fortune may grant happiness, which depends not on circumstance, but constitution.

THE place of our retreat was in a little neighbourhood, consisting of farmers, who tilled their own grounds, and were equal strangers to opulence and poverty. As they had almost all the conveniencies of life within themselves, they seldom visited towns or cities in search of superfluity. Remote from the polite, they still retained the primæval simplicity of manners; and frugal by habit, they scarce knew that temperance was a virtue. They wrought with chearfulness on days of labour; but observed festivals as intervals of idleness and pleasure. They kept up the Christmas carol, sent true love-knots on Valentine morning, eat pancakes on Shrovetide, shewed their wit on the first of April, and religiously cracked nuts on Michaelmas eve. Being apprized of our approach, the whole neighbourhood came out to meet their minister, drest in their finest cloaths, and preceded by a pipe and tabor: A feast also was provided for our reception, at which we sate chearfully down; and what the conversation wanted in wit, was made up in laughter.

Our little habitation was situated at the foot of a sloping hill, sheltered with a beautiful underwood behind, and a pratling river before; on one side a meadow, on the other a green. My farm consisted of about twenty acres of excellent land, having given an hundred pound for my predecessor's good-will. Nothing could exceed the neatness of my little enclosures: the elms and hedge-rows appearing with inexpressible beauty. My house consisted of but one story, and was covered with thatch, which gave it an air of great snugness;

the walls on the inside were nicely white-washed, and my daughters undertook to adorn them with pictures of their own designing. Though the same room served us for parlour and kitchen, that only made it the warmer. Besides, as it was kept with the utmost neatness, the dishes, plates, and coppers, being well scoured, and all disposed in bright rows on the shelves, the eye was agreeably relieved, and did not want richer furniture. There were three other apartments, one for my wife and me, another for our two daughters, within our own, and the third, with two beds, for the rest of the children.

The little republic to which I gave laws, was regulated in the following manner: by sun-rise we all assembled in our common apartment; the fire being previously kindled by the servant. After we had saluted each other with proper ceremony, for I always thought fit to keep up some mechanical forms of good breeding, without which freedom ever destroys friendship, we all bent in gratitude to that Being who gave us another day. This duty being performed, my son and I went to pursue our usual industry abroad, while my wife and daughters employed themselves in providing breakfast, which was always ready at a certain time. I allowed half an hour for this meal, and an hour for dinner; which time was taken up in innocent mirth between my wife and daughters, and in philosophical arguments between my son and me.

As we rose with the sun, so we never pursued our labours after it was gone down, but returned home to the expecting family; where smiling looks, a neat hearth, and pleasant fire, were prepared for our reception. Nor were we without guests: sometimes farmer Flamborough, our talkative neighbour, and often the blind piper, would pay us a visit, and taste our gooseberry wine; for the making of which we had lost neither the receipt nor the reputation. These harmless people had several ways of being good company; while one played, the other would sing some soothing ballad, Johnny Armstrong's last good night, or the cruelty of Barbara Allen. The night was concluded in the manner we began the morning, my youngest boys being appointed to read the lessons of the day, and he that read loudest, distinctest, and best, was to have an half-penny on Sunday to put into the poor's box.

When Sunday came, it was indeed a day of finery, which all my sumptuary edicts could not restrain. How well so ever I fancied my lectures against pride had conquered the vanity of my daughters; yet I still found them secretly attached to all their former finery: they still loved laces, ribbands, bugles and catgut; my wife herself retained a passion for her crimson paduasoy, because I formerly happened to say it became her.

The first Sunday in particular their behaviour served to mortify me: I had desired my girls the preceding night to be drest early the next day; for I always loved to be at church a good while before the rest of the congregation. They punctually obeyed my directions; but when we were to assemble in the morning at breakfast, down came my wife and daughters, drest out in all their former splendour: their hair plaistered up with pomatum, their faces patched to taste, their trains bundled up into an heap behind, and rustling at every motion. I could not help smiling at their vanity, particularly that of my wife, from whom I expected more discretion. In this exigence, therefore, my only resource was to order my son, with an important air, to call our coach. The girls were amazed at the command; but I repeated it with more solemnity than before. —"Surely, my dear, you jest," cried my wife; "we can walk it perfectly well: we want no coach to carry us now."—"You mistake, child," returned I, "we do want a coach; for if we walk to church in this trim, the very children in the parish will hoot after us."—"Indeed," replied my wife, "I always imagined that my Charles was fond of seeing his children neat and handsome about him."—"You may be as neat as you please," interrupted I, "and I shall love you the better for it; but all this is not neatness, but frippery. These rufflings, and pinkings, and patchings, will only make us hated by all the wives of all our neighbours. No, my children," continued I, more gravely, "those gowns may be altered into something of a plainer cut; for finery is very unbecoming in us, who want the means of decency. I do not know whether such flouncing and shredding is becoming even in the rich, if we consider, upon a moderate calculation, that the nakedness of the indigent world may be cloathed from the trimmings of the vain."

This remonstrance had the proper effect; they went with great composure, that very instant, to change their dress; and the next day I had the satisfaction of finding my daughters, at their own request, employed in cutting up their trains into Sunday waistcoats for Dick and Bill, the two little ones, and what was still more satisfactory, the gowns seemed improved by this curtailing.

CHAPTER V

A new and great acquaintance introduced. *What we place most hopes upon, generally proves most fatal.*

At a small distance from the house my predecessor had made a seat, overshaded by an hedge of hawthorn and honeysuckle. Here, when the weather was fine and our labour soon finished, we usually sat together, to enjoy an extensive landscape, in the calm of the evening. Here too we drank tea, which now was become an occasional banquet; and as we had it but seldom, it diffused a new joy, the preparations for it being made with no small share of bustle and ceremony. On these occasions, our two little ones always read for us, and they were regularly served after we had done. Sometimes, to give a variety to our amusements, the girls sung to the guitar; and while they thus formed a little concert, my wife and I would stroll down the sloping field, that was embellished with bluebells and centaury, talk of our children with rapture, and enjoy the breeze that wafted both health and harmony.

In this manner we began to find that every situation in life may bring its own peculiar pleasures: every morning waked us to a repetition of toil; but the evening repaid it with vacant hilarity.

It was about the beginning of autumn, on a holiday, for I kept such as intervals of relaxation from labour, that I had drawn out my family to our usual place of amusement, and our young musicians began their usual concert. As we were thus engaged, we saw a stag bound nimbly by, within about twenty paces of where we were sitting, and by its panting, it seemed prest by the hunters. We had not much time to reflect upon the poor animal's distress, when we perceived the dogs and horsemen come sweeping along at some distance behind, and making the very path it had taken. I was instantly for returning in with my family; but either curiosity or surprize, or some more hidden motive, held my wife and daughters to their seats. The huntsman, who rode foremost, past us with great swiftness, followed by four or five persons more, who seemed in equal haste. At last, a young gentleman of more genteel appearance than the rest, came forward, and for a while regarding us, instead of pursuing the chace, stopt short, and giving his horse to a servant who attended, approached us with a careless superior air. He seemed to want no introduction, but was going to salute my daughters as one certain of a kind reception; but they had early learnt the lesson of looking presumption out of countenance. Upon which he let us know that his name was Thornhill, and that he was owner of the estate that lay for some extent round us. He again, therefore, offered to salute the female part of the family; and such was the power of fortune and fine cloaths, that he found no second repulse. As his address, though confident, was easy, we soon became more familiar; and perceiving musical instruments lying near, he begged to be favoured with a song. As I did not approve of such disproportioned acquaintances, I winked upon my daughters in order to prevent their compliance;

but my hint was counteracted by one from their mother; so that with a chearful air they gave us a favourite song of Dryden's. Mr. Thornhill seemed highly delighted with their performance and choice, and then took up the guitar himself. He played but very indifferently; however, my eldest daughter repaid his former applause with interest, and assured him that his tones were louder than even those of her master. At this compliment he bowed, which she returned with a curtesey. He praised her taste, and she commended his understanding: an age could not have made them better acquainted. While the fond mother, too, equally happy, insisted upon her landlord's stepping in, and tasting a glass of her gooseberry. The whole family seemed earnest to please him: my girls attempted to entertain him with topics they thought most modern, while Moses, on the contrary, gave him a question or two from the ancients, for which he had the satisfaction of being laughed at:[1] my little ones were no less busy, and fondly stuck close to the stranger. All my endeavours could scarce keep their dirty fingers from handling and tarnishing the lace on his cloaths, and lifting up the flaps of his pocket holes, to see what was there. At the approach of evening he took leave; but not till he had requested permission to renew his visit, which, as he was our landlord, we most readily agreed to.

As soon as he was gone, my wife called a council on the conduct of the day. She was of opinion, that it was a most fortunate hit; for that she had known even stranger things at last brought to bear. She hoped again to see the day in which we might hold up our heads with the best of them; and concluded, she protested she could see no reason why the two Miss Wrinklers should marry great fortunes, and her children get none. As this last argument was directed to me, I protested I could see no reason for it neither, nor why Mr. Simpkins

[1] [The first edition continued "for he always ascribed to his wit that laughter which was lavished at his simplicity." This was probably cut out because Goldsmith found it said of himself.]

got the ten thousand pound prize in the lottery, and we sate down with a blank. "I protest, Charles," cried my wife, "this is the way you always damp my girls and me when we are in Spirits. Tell me, Sophy, my dear, what do you think of our new visitor? Don't you think he seemed to be good-natured?" —"Immensely so, indeed, mamma," replied she. "I think he has a great deal to say upon every thing, and is never at a loss; and the more trifling the subject, the more he has to say."— "Yes," cried Olivia, "he is well enough for a man; but for my part, I don't much like him, he is so extremely impudent and familiar; but on the guitar he is shocking." These two last speeches I interpreted by contraries. I found by this, that Sophia internally despised, as much as Olivia secretly admired him.—"Whatever may be your opinions of him, my children," cried I, "to confess a truth, he has not prepossest me in his favour. Disproportioned friendships ever terminate in disgust; and I thought, notwithstanding all his ease, that he seemed perfectly sensible of the distance between us. Let us keep to companions of our own rank. There is no character more contemptible than a man that is a fortune-hunter; and I can see no reason why fortune-hunting women should not be contemptible too. Thus, at best, we shall be contemptible if his views are honourable; but if they be otherwise! I should shudder but to think of that! It is true, I have no apprehensions from the conduct of my children, but I think there are some from his character."—I would have proceeded, but for the interruption of a servant from the 'Squire, who, with his compliments, sent us a side of venison, and a promise to dine with us some days after. This well-timed present pleaded more powerfully in his favour, than any thing I had to say could obviate. I therefore continued silent, satisfied with just having pointed out danger, and leaving it to their own discretion to avoid it. That virtue which requires to be ever guarded, is scarce worth the centinel.

CHAPTER VI

The happiness of a country fire-side.

As we carried on the former dispute with some degree of warmth, in order to accommodate matters, it was universally agreed, that we should have a part of the venison for supper, and the girls undertook the task with alacrity. " I am sorry," cried I, "that we have no neighbour or stranger to take part in this good cheer; feasts of this kind acquire a double relish from hospitality."—"Bless me," cried my wife, "here comes our good friend Mr. Burchell, that saved our Sophia, and that run you down fairly in the argument."—"Confute me in argument, child!" cried I. "You mistake there, my dear. I believe there are but few that can do that: I never dispute your abilities at making a goose-pye, and I beg you'll leave argument to me."—As I spoke, poor Mr. Burchell entered the house, and was welcomed by the family, who shook him heartily by the hand, while little Dick officiously reached him a chair.

I was pleased with the poor man's friendship for two reasons; because I knew that he wanted mine, and I knew him to be friendly as far as he was able. He was known in our neighbourhood by the character of the poor Gentleman that would do no good when he was young, though he was not yet thirty. He would at intervals talk with great good sense; but in general he was fondest of the company of children, whom he used to call harmless little men. He was famous, I found, for singing them ballads, and telling them stories; and seldom went out without something in his pockets for them, a piece of ginger-bread, or an halfpenny whistle. He generally came for a few days into our neighbourhood once a year, and lived upon the neighbours hospitality. He sate down to supper among us, and my wife was not sparing of her gooseberry wine. The tale went round; he sung us old songs, and gave the children the story of the Buck of Beverland, with the history of Patient Grissel, the adventures of Catskin, and then Fair Rosamond's bower. Our cock, which always crew at eleven, now told us it was time for repose; but an unforeseen difficulty started about lodging the stranger: all our beds were already taken up, and it was too late to send him to the next alehouse. In this dilemma, little Dick offered him his part of the bed, if his brother Moses would let him lie with him; "And I," cried Bill, "will give Mr. Burchell my part, if my sisters will take me to theirs."—"Well done, my good children," cried I, "hospitality is one of the first christian duties. The beast retires to his shelter, and the bird flies to its nest; but helpless man can only find refuge from his fellow creature. The greatest stranger in this world, was he that came to save it. He never had an house, as if willing to see what hospitality was left remaining amongst us. Deborah, my dear," cried I to my wife, "give those boys a lump of sugar each, and let Dick's be the largest, because he spoke first."

In the morning early I called out my whole family to help at saving an aftergrowth of hay, and our guest offering his assistance, he was accepted among the number. Our labours went on lightly, we turned the swath to the wind, I went foremost, and the rest followed in due succession. I could not avoid, however, observing the assiduity of Mr. Burchell in assisting my daughter Sophia in her part of the task. When he had finished his own, he would join in her's, and enter into a close conversation: but I had too good an opinion of Sophia's understanding, and was too well convinced of her ambition, to be under any uneasiness from a man of broken fortune. When we were finished for the day, Mr. Burchell was invited as on the night before; but he refused, as he was to lie that night at a neighbour's, to whose child he was carrying a whistle. When gone, our conversation at supper turned upon our late unfortunate guest. "What a strong instance," said I, "is that poor man of the miseries attending a youth of levity and extravagance. He by no means wants sense, which only serves to aggravate his former folly. Poor forlorn creature, where are now the revellers, the flatterers, that he could once inspire and command! Gone, perhaps, to attend the bagnio pander, grown rich by his extravagance. They once praised him, and now they applaud the pander: their former raptures at his wit, are now converted into sarcasms at his folly: he is poor, and perhaps deserves poverty; for he has neither the ambition to be independent, nor the skill to be useful." Prompted perhaps by some secret reasons, I delivered this observation with too much acrimony, which my Sophia gently reproved. "Whatsoever his former conduct may be, pappa, his circumstances should exempt him from censure now. His present indigence is a sufficient punishment for former folly; and I have heard my pappa himself say, that we should never strike our unnecessary blow at a victim over whom providence holds the scourge of its resentment."—"You are right, Sophy," cried my son Moses, "and one of the antients finely represents so malicious a conduct, by the attempts of a rustic to flay Marsyas, whose skin, the fable tells us, had been wholly stript off by another. Besides I don't know if this poor man's situation be so bad as my father would represent it. We are not to judge of the feelings of others by what we might feel if in their place. However dark the habitation of the mole to our eyes, yet the animal itself finds the apartment sufficiently lightsome. And to confess a truth, this man's mind seems fitted to his station; for I never heard any one more sprightly than he was to-day, when he conversed with you."—This was said without the least design, however it excited a blush, which she strove to cover by an affected laugh, assuring him, that she scarce took any notice of what he said to her; but that she believed he might once have been a very fine gentleman. The readiness with which she undertook to vindicate herself, and her blushing, were symptoms I did not internally approve; but I represt my suspicions.

As we expected our landlord the next day, my wife went to

make the venison pasty; Moses sate reading, while I taught the little ones: my daughters seemed equally busy with the rest; and I observed them for a good while cooking something over the fire. I at first supposed they were assisting their mother; but little Dick informed me in a whisper, that they were making a *wash* for the face. Washes of all kinds I had a natural antipathy to; for I knew that instead of mending the complexion they spoiled it. I therefore approached my chair by sly degrees to the fire, and grasping the poker, as if it wanted mending, seemingly by accident, overturned the whole composition, and it was too late to begin another.

CHAPTER VII

A town wit described. The dullest fellows may learn to be comical for a night or two.

WHEN the morning arrived on which we were to entertain our young landlord, it may be easily supposed what provisions were exhausted to make an appearance. It may also be conjectured that my wife and daughters expanded their gayest plumage upon this occasion. Mr. Thornhill came with a couple of friends, his chaplain and feeder.[1] The servants, who were numerous, he politely ordered to the next ale-house: but my wife, in the triumph of her heart, insisted on entertaining them all; for which, by the bye, our family was pinched for three weeks after. As Mr. Burchell had hinted to us the day before, that he was making some proposals of marriage to Miss Wilmot, my son George's former mistress, this a good deal damped the heartiness of his reception: but accident, in some measure, relieved our embarrassment; for one of the company happening to mention her name, Mr.

[1] [Not the same person as the chaplain, since he is the second of the "couple of friends." Dobson suggested "feeder of hounds." The *Oxford English Dictionary* explains the word in this context as "crammer, tutor."]

Thornhill observed with an oath, that he never knew any thing more absurd than calling such a fright a beauty: "For, strike me ugly," continued he, "if I should not find as much pleasure in choosing my mistress by the information of a lamp under the clock of St. Dunstan's." At this he laughed, and so did we:—the jests of the rich are ever successful. Olivia too could not avoid whispering, loud enough to be heard, that he had an infinite fund of humour.

After dinner, I began with my usual toast, the Church; for this I was thanked by the chaplain, as he said the church was the only mistress of his affections.—"Come tell us honestly, Frank," said the 'Squire, with his usual archness, "suppose the church, your present mistress, drest in lawn sleeves, on one hand, and Miss Sophia, with no lawn about her, on the other, which would you be for?" "For both, to be sure," cried the chaplain.—"Right, Frank," cried the 'Squire; "for may this glass suffocate me but a fine girl is worth all the priestcraft in the creation. For what are tythes and tricks but an imposition, all a confounded imposture, and I can prove it."—"I wish you would," cried my son Moses, "and I think," continued he, "that I should be able to answer you."—"Very well, Sir," cried the 'Squire, who immediately smoaked him, and winking on the rest of the company, to prepare us for the sport, "if you are for a cool argument upon that subject, I am ready to accept the challenge. And first, whether are you for managing it analogically, or dialogically?" "I am for managing it rationally," cried Moses, quite happy at being permitted to dispute. "Good again," cried the 'Squire; "and firstly, of the first. I hope you'll not deny that whatever is, is. If you don't grant me that, I can go no further." —"Why," returned Moses, "I think I may grant that, and make the best of it."—"I hope too," returned the other, "you'll grant that a part is less than the whole."—"I grant that too," cried Moses, "it is but just and reasonable."—"I hope," cried the 'Squire, "you will not deny, that the two angles of a triangle are equal to two right ones."—"Nothing can be plainer," returned t'other, and looked round with his usual importance.—"Very well," cried the 'Squire, speaking very quick, "the premises being thus settled, I proceed to observe, that the concatenation of self existences, proceeding in a reciprocal duplicate ratio, naturally produce a problematical dialogism, which in some measure proves that the essence of spirituality may be referred to the second predicable."—"Hold, hold," cried the other, "I deny that: Do you think I can thus tamely submit to such heterodox doctrines?" —"What!" replied the 'Squire, as if in a passion, "not submit! Answer me one plain question: Do you think Aristotle right when he says, that relatives are related?" "Undoubtedly," replied the other. "If so then," cried the 'Squire, "answer me directly to what I propose: Whether do you judge the analytical investigation of the first part of my enthymem deficient secundum quoad, or quoad minus, and give me your reasons: give me your reasons, I say, directly."—"I protest," cried Moses, "I don't rightly comprehend the force of your reasoning; but if it be reduced to one simple proposition, I fancy it may then have an answer."—"O, Sir," cried the 'Squire, "I am your most humble servant, I find you want me to furnish you with argument and intellects too. No, Sir, there I protest you are too hard for me." This effectually raised the laugh against poor Moses, who sate the only dismal figure in a groupe of merry faces: nor did he offer a single syllable more during the whole entertainment.

But though all this gave me no pleasure, it had a very different effect upon Olivia, who mistook it for humour, though but a mere act of the memory. She thought him therefore a very fine gentleman; and such as consider what powerful ingredients a good figure, fine cloaths, and fortune are in that character, will easily forgive her. Mr. Thornhill, notwithstanding his real ignorance, talked with ease, and could expatiate upon the common topics of conversation with fluency. It is not surprising then that such talents should win the affections of a girl, who by education was taught to value an appearance in herself, and consequently to set a value upon it in another.

Upon his departure, we again entered into a debate upon the merits of our young landlord. As he directed his looks and conversation to Olivia, it was no longer doubted but that she was the object that induced him to be our visitor. Nor did she seem to be much displeased at the innocent raillery of her brother and sister upon this occasion. Even Deborah herself seemed to share the glory of the day, and exulted in her daughter's victory as if it were her own. "And now, my dear," cried she to me, "I'll fairly own, that it was I that instructed my girls to encourage our landlord's addresses. I had always some ambition, and you now see that I was right; for who knows how this may end?" "Ay, who knows that indeed," answered I, with a groan: "for my part I don't much like it; and I could have been better pleased with one that was poor and honest, than this fine gentleman with his fortune and infidelity; for depend on't, if he be what I suspect him, no free-thinker shall ever have a child of mine."

"Sure, father," cried Moses, "you are too severe in this; for heaven will never arraign him for what he thinks, but for what he does. Every man has a thousand vicious thoughts, which arise without his power to suppress. Thinking freely of religion may be involuntary with this gentleman: so that allowing his sentiments to be wrong, yet as he is purely passive in his assent, he is no more to be blamed for his errors than the governor of a city without walls for the shelter he is obliged to afford an invading enemy."

"True, my son," cried I; "but if the governor invites the enemy there, he is justly culpable. And such is always the case with those who embrace error. The vice does not lie in assenting to the proofs they see; but in being blind to many of the proofs that offer. So that, though our erroneous opinions be involuntary when formed, yet as we have been wilfully corrupt, or very negligent in forming them, we deserve punishment for our vice, or contempt for our folly."

My wife now kept up the conversation, though not the argument: she observed, that several very prudent men of our acquaintance were free-thinkers, and made very good husbands; and she knew some sensible girls that had skill enough to make converts of their spouses: "And who knows, my dear," continued she, "what Olivia may be able to do. The girl has a great deal to say upon every subject, and to my knowledge is very well skilled in controversy."

"Why, my dear, what controversy can she have read?" cried I. "It does not occur to me that I ever put such books into her hands: you certainly over-rate her merit."—"Indeed, pappa," replied Olivia, "she does not: I have read a great deal of controversy. I have read the disputes between Thwackum and Square;[1] the controversy between Robinson Crusoe and Friday the savage, and I am now employed in reading the controversy in Religious courtship."[2]—"Very well," cried I, "that's a good girl, I find you are perfectly qualified for making converts, and so go help your mother to make the gooseberry-pye."

CHAPTER VIII

An amour, which promises little good fortune, yet may be productive of much.

THE next morning we were again visited by Mr. Burchell, though I began, for certain reasons, to be displeased with the frequency of his return; but I could not refuse him my company and fire-side. It is true his labour more than requited his entertainment; for he wrought among us with vigour, and either in the meadow or at the hay-rick, put himself fore-

[1] [In *Tom Jones*.] [2] [The third volume of Defoe's *Family Instructor*.]

most. Besides, he had always something amusing to say that lessened our toil, and was at once so out of the way, and yet so sensible, that I loved, laughed at, and pitied him. My only dislike arose from an attachment he discovered to my daughter: he would, in a jesting manner, call her his little mistress, and when he bought each of the girls a set of ribbands, her's was the finest. I knew not how, but he every day seemed to become more amiable, his wit to improve, and his simplicity to assume the superior airs of wisdom.

Our family dined in the field, and we sate, or rather reclined, round a temperate repast, our cloth spread upon the hay, while Mr. Burchell gave chearfulness to the feast. To heighten our satisfaction two blackbirds answered each other from opposite hedges, the familiar redbreast came and pecked the crumbs from our hands, and every sound seemed but the echo of tranquillity. "I never sit thus," says Sophia, "but I think of the two lovers, so sweetly described by Mr. Gay,[1] who were struck dead in each other's arms. There is something so pathetic in the description, that I have read it an hundred times with new rapture."—"In my opinion," cried my son, "the finest strokes in that description are much below those in the Acis and Galatea of Ovid. The Roman poet understands the use of *contrast* better, and upon that figure artfully managed all strength in the pathetic depends."—"It is remarkable," cried Mr. Burchell, "that both the poets you mention have equally contributed to introduce a false taste into their respective countries, by loading all their lines with epithet. Men of little genius found them most easily imitated in their defects, and English poetry, like that in the latter empire of Rome, is nothing at present but a combination of luxuriant images, without plot or connexion; a string of epithets that improve the sound, without carrying on the sense. But perhaps, Madam, while I thus reprehend others, you'll think it just that I should give them an opportunity to

[1] [In a letter to Mr. Fortescue, 9 August, 1718.]

retaliate, and indeed I have made this remark only to have an opportunity of introducing to the company a ballad, which, whatever be its other defects, is I think at least free from those I have mentioned."

A BALLAD[1]

"Turn, gentle hermit of the dale,
And guide my lonely way,
To where yon taper cheers the vale,
With hospitable ray.

"For here, forlorn and lost I tread,
With fainting steps and slow;
Where wilds immeasurably spread,
Seem lengthening as I go."

"Forbear, my son," the hermit cries,
"To tempt the dangerous gloom;
For yonder faithless phantom flies
To lure thee to thy doom.

[1] [The earliest text of this ballad is a privately printed duodecimo: *Edwin and Angelina. A Ballad. By Mr. Goldsmith. Printed for the Amusement of the Countess of Northumberland* (1765). The unique copy in the possession of Sir John Murray was recently brought to light by Mr. John Hayward (see his *A Catalogue of English Poetry*, Cambridge University Press.) Goldsmith thoroughly revised the poem, omitting some stanzas and rewriting others, in the first edition of *The Vicar of Wakefield*, 1766. In the second edition he revised it yet again, introducing new readings, but occasionally reverting to the 1765 text. All subsequent editions of *The Vicar of Wakefield* and the poems derive from the second edition. But Goldsmith's anthology, *Poems for Young Ladies, In Three Parts, Devotional, Moral and Entertaining*, 1767, which opens its "Moral" section with the poem, follows the 1765 text, making only a few minor corrections and adding one stanza from the later version.

In July, 1767, Kenrick (see *Retaliation*, p. 634) in the *St. James's Chronicle* accused Goldsmith of plagiarising Percy's *Friar of Orders Gray*. Both poems were probably founded on a traditional ballad, *The Gentle Herdsman*.]

"Here to the houseless child of want,
My door is open still;
And tho' my portion is but scant,
I give it with good will.

"Then turn to-night, and freely share
Whate'er my cell bestows;
My rushy couch, and frugal fare,
My blessing and repose.

"No flocks that range the valley free,
To slaughter I condemn:
Taught by that power that pities me,
I learn to pity them.

"But from the mountain's grassy side
A guiltless feast I bring;
A scrip with herbs and fruits supply'd,
And water from the spring.

"Then, pilgrim, turn, thy cares forego;
All earth-born cares are wrong:
Man wants but little here below,
Nor wants that little long."

Soft as the dew from heav'n descends,
His gentle accents fell:
The modest stranger lowly bends,
And follows to the cell.

Far in a wilderness obscure
The lonely mansion lay,
A refuge to the neighbouring poor
And strangers led astray.

No stores beneath its humble thatch
  Requir'd a master's care;
The wicket opening with a latch,
  Receiv'd the harmless pair.

And now when busy crowds retire
  To take their evening rest,
The hermit trimm'd his little fire,
  And cheer'd his pensive guest;

And spread his vegetable store,
  And gayly prest, and smil'd,
And skill'd in legendary lore,
  The lingering hours beguil'd.

Around in sympathetic mirth
  Its tricks the kitten tries,
The cricket chirrups in the hearth;
  The crackling faggot flies.

But nothing could a charm impart
  To sooth the stranger's woe;
For grief was heavy at his heart,
  And tears began to flow.

His rising cares the hermit spy'd,
  With answering care opprest:
"And whence, unhappy youth," he cry'd,
  "The sorrows of thy breast?

"From better habitations spurn'd,
  Reluctant dost thou rove;
Or grieve for friendship unreturn'd,
  Or unregarded love?

"Alas! the joys that fortune brings
Are trifling, and decay;
And those who prize the paltry things,
More trifling still than they.

"And what is friendship but a name,
A charm that lulls to sleep;
A shade that follows wealth or fame,
But leaves the wretch to weep?

"And love is still an emptier sound,
The modern fair one's jest,
On earth unseen, or only found
To warm the turtle's nest.

"For shame, fond youth, thy sorrows hush,
And spurn the sex," he said:
But, while he spoke, a rising blush
His love-lorn guest betray'd.

Surpriz'd he sees new beauties rise
Swift mantling to the view,
Like colours o'er the morning skies,
As bright, as transient too.

The bashful look, the rising breast,
Alternate spread alarms,
The lovely stranger stands confest
A maid in all her charms.

And "ah, forgive a stranger rude,
A wretch forlorn," she cry'd,
"Whose feet unhallowed thus intrude
Where heaven and you reside.

"But let a maid thy pity share,
  Whom love has taught to stray;
Who seeks for rest, but finds despair
  Companion of her way.

"My father liv'd beside the Tyne,
  A wealthy lord was he;
And all his wealth was mark'd as mine,
  He had but only me.

"To win me from his tender arms,
  Unnumber'd suitors came;
Who prais'd me for imputed charms,
  And felt or feign'd a flame.

"Each hour a mercenary crowd
  With richest proffers strove:
Amongst the rest young Edwin bow'd,
  But never talk'd of love.

"In humble simplest habit clad,
  No wealth nor power had he;
Wisdom and worth were all he had,
  But these were all to me.

["And when, beside me in the dale,
  He caroll'd lays of love,
His breath lent fragrance to the gale.
  And music to the grove.][1]

"The blossom opening to the day,
  The dews of heaven refin'd,
Could nought of purity display
  To emulate his mind.

[1] [This stanza does not appear in *The Vicar of Wakefield.* It was written some years afterwards and first printed in the *Miscellaneous Works*, 1801.]

"The dew, the blossom on the tree,
With charms inconstant shine;
Their charms were his, but woe to me,
Their constancy was mine.

"For still I try'd each fickle art,
Importunate and vain;
And while his passion touch'd my heart,
I triumph'd in his pain.

"Till quite dejected with my scorn,
He left me to my pride;
And sought a solitude forlorn,
In secret where he died.

"But mine the sorrow, mine the fault,
And well my life shall pay,
I'll seek the solitude he sought,
And stretch me where he lay—

"And there forlorn despairing hid,
I'll lay me down and die:
'Twas so for me that Edwin did,
And so for him will I."

"Forbid it, heaven!" the hermit cry'd,
And clasp'd her to his breast:
The wondering fair one turn'd to chide,
'Twas Edwin's self that prest.

"Turn, Angelina, ever dear,
My charmer, turn to see,
Thy own, thy long-lost Edwin here,
Restor'd to love and thee.

"Thus let me hold thee to my heart,
And ev'ry care resign:
And shall we never, never part,
My life,—my all that's mine.

"No, never, from this hour to part,
We'll live and love so true;
The sigh that rends thy constant heart,
Shall break thy Edwin's too."

While this ballad was reading, Sophia seemed to mix an air of tenderness with her approbation. But our tranquillity was soon disturbed by the report of a gun just by us, and immediately after a man was seen bursting through the hedge, to take up the game he had killed. This sportsman was the 'Squire's chaplain, who had shot one of the blackbirds that so agreeably entertained us. So loud a report, and so near, startled my daughters; and I could perceive that Sophia in the fright had thrown herself into Mr. Burchell's arms for protection. The gentleman came up, and asked pardon for having disturbed us, affirming that he was ignorant of our being so near. He therefore sate down by my youngest daughter, and sportsman like, offered her what he had killed that morning. She was going to refuse, but a private look from her mother soon induced her to correct the mistake, and accept his present, though with some reluctance. My wife, as usual, discovered her pride in a whisper, observing, that Sophy had made a conquest of the chaplain, as well as her sister had of the 'Squire. I suspected, however, with more probability, that her affections were placed upon a different object. The chaplain's errand was to inform us, that Mr. Thornhill had provided music and refreshments, and intended that night giving the young ladies a ball by moon-light, on the grass-plot before our door. "Nor can I deny," continued he, "but I have an interest in being first to deliver this message, as I expect for my reward to be honoured with Miss Sophy's hand as a partner." To this my girl replied, that she should have no objection, if she could do it with honour: "But here," continued she, "is a gentleman," looking at Mr. Burchell, "who has been my companion in the task for the day, and it is fit he should share in its amusements." Mr. Burchell returned her a compliment for her intentions; but resigned her up to the chaplain, adding that he was to go that night five miles, being invited to an harvest supper. His refusal appeared to me a little extraordinary, nor could I conceive how so sensible a girl as my youngest, could thus prefer a man of broken fortunes to one whose expectations were much greater. But as men are most capable of distinguishing merit in women, so the ladies often form the truest judgments of us. The two sexes seem placed as spies upon each other, and are furnished with different abilities, adapted for mutual inspection.

CHAPTER IX

Two ladies of great distinction introduced. Superior finery ever seems to confer superior breeding.

Mr. Burchell had scarce taken leave, and Sophia consented to dance with the chaplain, when my little ones came running out to tell us that the 'Squire was come, with a crowd of company. Upon our return, we found our landlord with a couple of under gentlemen and two young ladies richly drest, whom he introduced as women of very great distinction and fashion from town. We happened not to have chairs enough for the whole company; but Mr. Thornhill immediately proposed that every gentleman should sit in a lady's lap. This I positively objected to, notwithstanding a look of disapprobation from my wife. Moses was therefore dispatched to borrow a couple of chairs; and as we were in want of ladies to make up a set at country dances, the two gentlemen went with him in quest of a couple of partners. Chairs and partners were soon provided. The gentlemen returned with my neighbour Flamborough's rosy daughters, flaunting with red top-knots, but an unlucky circumstance was not adverted to; though the Miss Flamboroughs were reckoned the very best dancers in the parish, and understood the jig and the round-about to perfection; yet they were totally unacquainted with country dances. This at first discomposed us: however, after a little shoving and dragging, they at last went merrily on. Our music consisted of two fiddles, with a pipe and tabor. The moon shone bright, Mr. Thornhill and my eldest daughter led up the ball, to the great delight of the spectators; for the neighbours hearing what was going forward, came flocking about us. My girl moved with so much grace and vivacity, that my wife could not avoid discovering the pride of her heart, by assuring me, that though the little chit did it so cleverly, all the steps were stolen from herself. The ladies of the town strove hard to be equally easy, but without success. They swam, sprawled, languished, and frisked; but all would not do: the gazers indeed owned that it was fine; but neighbour Flamborough observed, that Miss Livy's feet seemed as pat to the music as its echo. After the dance had continued about an hour, the two ladies, who were apprehensive of catching cold, moved to break up the ball. One of them, I thought, expressed her sentiments upon this occasion in a very coarse manner, when she observed, that by the *living jingo, she was all of a muck of sweat.* Upon our return to the house, we found a very elegant cold supper, which Mr. Thornhill had ordered to be brought with him. The conversation at this time, was more reserved than before. The two ladies threw my girls quite into the shade; for they would talk of nothing but high life, and high lived company; with other fashionable topics, such as pictures, taste, Shakespear, and the musical glasses. 'Tis true they once or twice mortified us sensibly by slipping out an oath; but that appeared to me as the surest symptom of their distinction, (tho' I am since informed that swearing is perfectly unfashionable.) Their finery, however, threw a veil over any grossness in their conversation. My daughters seemed to regard their superior accomplishments with envy; and what appeared amiss was ascribed to tip-top quality breeding. But the condescension of the ladies was still superior to their accomplishments. One of them observed, that had Miss Olivia seen a little more of the world, it would greatly improve her. To which the other added, that a single winter in town would make her little Sophia quite another thing. My wife warmly assented to both; adding, that there was nothing she more ardently wished than to give her girls a single winter's polishing. To this I could not help replying, that their breeding was already superior to their fortune; and that greater refinement would only serve to make their poverty ridiculous, and give them a taste for pleasures they had no right to possess.—"And what pleasures," cried Mr. Thornhill, "do they not deserve to possess, who have so much in their power to bestow? As for my part," continued he, "my fortune is pretty large, love, liberty, and pleasure are my maxims; but curse me if a settlement of half my estate could give my charming Olivia pleasure, it should be hers; and the only favour I would ask in return would be to add myself to the benefit." I was not such a stranger to the world as to be ignorant that this was the fashionable cant to disguise the insolence of the basest proposal; but I made an effort to suppress my resentment. "Sir," cried I, "the family which you now condescend to favour with your company, has been bred with as nice a sense of honour as you. Any attempts to injure that, may be attended with very dangerous consequences. Honour, Sir, is our only possession at present, and of that last treasure we must be particularly careful."—I was soon sorry for the warmth with which I had spoken this, when the young gentleman, grasping my hand, swore he commended my spirit, though he disapproved my suspicions. "As to your present hint," continued he, "I protest nothing was farther from my heart than such a thought. No, by all that's tempting, the virtue that will stand a regular siege was never to my taste; for all my amours are carried by a coup de main."

The two ladies, who affected to be ignorant of the rest, seemed highly displeased with this last stroke of freedom, and began a very discreet and serious dialogue upon virtue: in this my wife, the chaplain, and I soon joined; and the 'Squire himself was at last brought to confess a sense of sorrow for his former excesses. We talked of the pleasures of temperance, and of the sun-shine in the mind unpolluted with guilt. I was so well pleased, that my little ones were kept up beyond the usual time to be edified by so much good conversation. Mr. Thornhill even went beyond me, and demanded if I had any objection to giving prayers. I joyfully embraced the proposal, and in this manner the night was passed in the most comfortable way, till at last the company began to think of returning. The ladies seemed very unwilling to part with my daughters; for whom they conceived a particular affection, and joined in a request to have the pleasure of their company home. The 'Squire seconded the proposal, and my wife added her entreaties: the girls too looked upon me as if they wished to go. In this perplexity I made two or three excuses, which my daughters as readily removed; so that at last I was obliged to give a peremptory refusal; for which we had nothing but sullen looks and short answers the whole day ensuing.

CHAPTER X

The family endeavours to cope with their betters. The miseries of the poor when they attempt to appear above their circumstances.

I NOW began to find that all my long and painful lectures upon temperance, simplicity, and contentment, were entirely disregarded. The distinctions lately paid us by our betters awaked that pride which I had laid asleep, but not removed. Our windows again, as formerly, were filled with washes for the neck and face. The sun was dreaded as an enemy to the skin without doors, and the fire as a spoiler of the complexion within. My wife observed, that rising too early would hurt her daughters' eyes, that working after dinner would redden their noses, and she convinced me that the hands never looked so white as when they did nothing. Instead therefore of finishing George's shirts, we now had them new modelling their old gauzes, or flourishing upon catgut. The poor Miss Flamboroughs, their former gay companions, were cast off as mean acquaintance, and the whole conversation ran upon high life and high lived company, with pictures, taste, Shakespear, and the musical glasses.

But we could have borne all this, had not a fortune-telling gypsey came to raise us into perfect sublimity. The tawney sybil no sooner appeared, than my girls came running to me for a shilling a piece to cross her hand with silver. To say the truth, I was tired of being always wise, and could not help gratifying their request, because I loved to see them happy. I gave each of them a shilling; though, for the honour of the family, it must be observed, that they never went without money themselves, as my wife always generously let them have a guinea each, to keep in their pockets; but with strict injunctions never to change it. After they had been closetted up with the fortune-teller for some time, I knew by their looks, upon their returning, that they had been promised something great.—"Well, my girls, how have you sped? Tell me, Livy, has the fortune-teller given thee a pennyworth?"—"I protest, pappa," says the girl, "I believe she deals with some body that's not right; for she positively declared, that I am to be married to a 'Squire in less than a twelvemonth!"—"Well, now, Sophy, my child," said I, "and what sort of a husband are you to have?" "Sir," replied she, "I am to have a Lord soon after my sister has married the 'Squire."—"How," cried I, "is that all you are to have for your two shillings! Only a Lord and a 'Squire for two shillings! You fools, I could have promised you a Prince and a Nabob for half the money."

This curiosity of theirs, however, was attended with very serious effects: we now began to think ourselves designed by the stars to something exalted, and already anticipated our future grandeur.

It has been a thousand times observed, and I must observe it once more, that the hours we pass with happy prospects in view, are more pleasing than those crowned with fruition. In the first case we cook the dish to our own appetite; in the latter nature cooks it for us. It is impossible to repeat the train of agreeable reveries we called up for our entertainment. We looked upon our fortunes as once more rising; and as the whole parish asserted that the 'Squire was in love with my daughter, she was actually so with him; for they persuaded her into the passion. In this agreeable interval, my wife had the most lucky dreams in the world, which she took care to tell us every morning, with great solemnity and exactness. It was one night a coffin and cross bones, the sign of an approaching wedding: at another time she imagined her daughter's pockets filled with farthings, a certain sign of their being shortly stuffed with gold. The girls themselves had their omens. They felt strange kisses on their lips; they saw rings in the candle, purses[1] bounced from the fire, and true love-knots lurked in the bottom of every tea-cup.

Towards the end of the week we received a card from the town ladies; in which, with their compliments, they hoped to see all our family at church the Sunday following. All Saturday morning I could perceive, in consequence of this, my wife and daughters in close conference together, and now and then glancing at me with looks that betrayed a latent plot. To be

[1] [Small live coals bursting out of the fire. A round "purse" was an omen of money and a long "coffin" a portent of death.]

sincere, I had strong suspicions that some absurd proposal was preparing for appearing with splendor the next day. In the evening they began their operations in a very regular manner, and my wife undertook to conduct the siege. After tea, when I seemed in spirits, she began thus.—"I fancy, Charles, my dear, we shall have a great deal of good company at our church to-morrow."—"Perhaps we may, my dear," returned I; "though you need be under no uneasiness about that, you shall have a sermon whether there be or not."—"That is what I expect," returned she; "but I think, my dear, we ought to appear there as decently as possible, for who knows what may happen?" "Your precautions," replied I, "are highly commendable. A decent behaviour and appearance in church is what charms me. We should be devout, and humble, chearful and serene." —"Yes," cried she, "I know that; but I mean we should go there in as proper a manner as possible; not altogether like the scrubs about us." "You are quite right, my dear," returned I, "and I was going to make the very same proposal. The proper manner of going is, to go there as early as possible, to have time for meditation before the service begins."— "Phoo, Charles," interrupted she, "all that is very true; but not what I would be at. I mean, we should go there genteelly. You know the church is two miles off, and I protest I don't like to see my daughters trudging up to their pew all blowzed and red with walking, and looking for all the world as if they had been winners at a smock race. Now, my dear, my proposal is this: there are our two plow horses, the Colt that has been in our family these nine years, and his companion Blackberry, that has scarce done an earthly thing for this month past. They are both grown fat and lazy. Why should not they do something as well as we? And let me tell you, when Moses has trimmed them a little, they will cut a very tolerable figure."

To this proposal I objected, that walking would be twenty times more genteel than such a paltry conveyance, as Blackberry was wall-eyed, and the Colt wanted a tail: that they had never been broke to the rein; but had an hundred vicious tricks; and that we had but one saddle and pillion in the whole house. All these objections, however, were over-ruled; so that I was obliged to comply. The next morning I perceived them not a little busy in collecting such materials as might be necessary for the expedition; but as I found it would be a business of time, I walked on to the church before, and they promised speedily to follow. I waited near an hour in the reading desk for their arrival; but not finding them come as expected, I was obliged to begin, and went through the service, not without some uneasiness at finding them absent. This was encreased when all was finished, and no appearance of the family. I therefore walked back by the horse-way, which was five miles round, though the foot-way was but two, and when got about half-way home, perceived the procession marching slowly forward towards the church; my son, my wife, and the two little ones exalted upon one horse, and my two daughters upon the other. I demanded the cause of their delay; but I soon found by their looks they had met with a thousand misfortunes on the road. The horses had at first refused to move from the door, till Mr. Burchell was kind enough to beat them forward for about two hundred yards with his cudgel. Next the straps of my wife's pillion broke down, and they were obliged to stop to repair them before they could proceed. After that, one of the horses took it into his head to stand still, and neither blows nor entreaties could prevail with him to proceed. It was just recovering from this dismal situation that I found them; but perceiving every thing safe, I own their present mortification did not much displease me, as it would give me many opportunities of future triumph, and teach my daughters more humility.

CHAPTER XI

The family still resolve to hold up their heads.

MICHAELMAS eve happening on the next day, we were invited to burn nuts and play tricks at neighbour Flamborough's. Our late mortifications had humbled us a little, or it is probable we might have rejected such an invitation with contempt: however, we suffered ourselves to be happy. Our honest neighbour's goose and dumplings were fine, and the lamb's-wool,[1] even in the opinion of my wife, who was a connoisseur, was excellent. It is true, his manner of telling stories was not quite so well. They were very long, and very dull, and all about himself, and we had laughed at them ten times before: however, we were kind enough to laugh at them once more.

Mr. Burchell, who was of the party, was always fond of seeing some innocent amusement going forward, and set the boys and girls to blind man's buff. My wife too was persuaded to join in the diversion, and it gave me pleasure to think she was not yet too old. In the mean time, my neighbour and I looked on, laughed at every feat, and praised our own dexterity when we were young. Hot cockles succeeded next, questions and commands followed that, and last of all, they sate down to hunt the slipper. As every person may not be acquainted with this primæval pastime, it may be necessary to observe, that the company at this play plant themselves in a ring upon the ground, all, except one who stands in the middle, whose business it is to catch a shoe, which the company shove about under their hams from one to another, something like a weaver's shuttle. As it is impossible, in this case, for the lady who is up to face all the company at once, the great beauty of the play lies in hitting her a thump with the heel of the shoe on that side least capable of making a defence. It was in this manner that my eldest daughter was hemmed in,

[1] [A drink made with warm spiced ale and roast apples.]

and thumped about, all blowzed, in spirits, and bawling for fair play, fair play, with a voice that might deafen a ballad singer, when confusion on confusion, who should enter the room but our two great acquaintances from town, Lady Blarney and Miss Carolina Wilelmina Amelia Skeggs![1] Description would but beggar, therefore it is unnecessary to describe this new mortification. Death! To be seen by ladies of such high breeding in such vulgar attitudes! Nothing better could ensue from such a vulgar play of Mr. Flamborough's proposing. We seemed struck to the ground for some time, as if actually petrified with amazement.

The two ladies had been at our house to see us, and finding us from home, came after us hither, as they were uneasy to know what accident could have kept us from church the day before. Olivia undertook to be our prolocutor, and delivered the whole in a summary way, only saying, "We were thrown from our horses." At which account the ladies were greatly concerned; but being told the family received no hurt, they were extremely glad; but being informed that we were almost killed by the fright, they were vastly sorry; but hearing that we had a very good night, they were extremely glad again. Nothing could exceed their complaisance to my daughters; their professions the last evening were warm, but now they were ardent. They protested a desire of having a more lasting acquaintance. Lady Blarney was particularly attached to Olivia; Miss Carolina Wilelmina Amelia Skeggs (I love to give the whole name) took a greater fancy to her sister. They supported the conversation between themselves, while my daughters sate silent, admiring their exalted breeding. But as every reader, however beggarly himself, is fond of high-lived dialogues, with anecdotes of Lords, Ladies, and Knights of the Garter, I must beg leave to give him the concluding part of the present conversation.

"All that I know of the matter," cried Miss Skeggs, "is this,

[1] [A near namesake of Beau Tibbs's daughter (see p. 398).]

that it may be true, or may not be true: but this I can assure your Ladyship, that the whole rout was in amaze; his Lordship turned all manner of colours, my Lady fell into a sound; but Sir Tomkyn, drawing his sword, swore he was hers to the last drop of his blood."

"Well," replied our Peeress, "this I can say, that the Duchess never told me a syllable of the matter, and I believe her Grace would keep nothing a secret from me. This you may depend on as fact, that the next morning my Lord Duke cried out three times to his valet de chambre, Jernigan, Jernigan, Jernigan, bring me my garters."

But previously I should have mentioned the very impolite behaviour of Mr. Burchell, who, during this discourse, sate with his face turned to the fire, and at the conclusion of every sentence would cry out *fudge*, an expression which displeased us all, and in some measure damped the rising spirit of the conversation.

"Besides, my dear Skeggs," continued our Peeress, "there is nothing of this in the copy of verses that Dr. Burdock made upon the occasion." *Fudge!*

"I am surprised at that," cried Miss Skeggs; "for he seldom leaves any thing out, as he writes only for his own amusement. But can your Ladyship favour me with a sight of them?" *Fudge!*

"My dear creature," replied our Peeress, "do you think I carry such things about me? Though they are very fine to be sure, and I think myself something of a judge; at least I know what pleases myself. Indeed I was ever an admirer of all Dr. Burdock's little pieces; for except what he does, and our dear Countess at Hanover-Square, there's nothing comes out but the most lowest stuff in nature; not a bit of high life among them." *Fudge!*

"Your Ladyship should except," says t'other, "your own things in the Lady's Magazine.[1] I hope you'll say there's

[1] [Which Goldsmith had edited.]

nothing low lived there? But I suppose we are to have no more from that quarter?" *Fudge!*

"Why, my dear," says the Lady, "you know my reader and companion has left me, to be married to Captain Roach, and as my poor eyes won't suffer me to write myself, I have been for some time looking out for another. A proper person is no easy matter to find, and to be sure thirty pounds a year is a small stipend for a well bred girl of character, that can read, write, and behave in company; as for the chits about town, there is no bearing them about one." *Fudge!*

"That I know," cried Miss Skeggs, "by experience. For of the three companions I had this last half year, one of them refused to do plain-work an hour in the day, another thought twenty-five guineas a year too small a salary, and I was obliged to send away the third, because I suspected an intrigue with the chaplain. Virtue, my dear Lady Blarney, virtue is worth any price; but where is that to be found?" *Fudge!*

My wife had been for a long time all attention to this discourse; but was particularly struck with the latter part of it. Thirty pounds and twenty-five guineas a year made fifty-six pounds five shillings English money, all which was in a manner going a-begging, and might easily be secured in the family. She for a moment studied my looks for approbation; and, to own a truth, I was of opinion, that two such places would fit our two daughters exactly. Besides, if the 'Squire had any real affection for my eldest daughter, this would be the way to make her every way qualified for her fortune. My wife therefore was resolved that we should not be deprived of such advantages for want of assurance, and undertook to harangue for the family. "I hope," cried she, "your Ladyships will pardon my present presumption. It is true we have no right to pretend to such favours; but yet it is natural for me to wish putting my children forward in the world. And I will be bold to say my two girls have had a pretty good education, and capacity, at least the country can't shew better. They can read, write, and cast accompts; they understand their needle, breadstitch, cross and change, and all manner of plain-work; they can pink, point, and frill; and know something of music; they can do up small cloaths, work upon catgut; my eldest can cut paper, and my youngest has a very pretty manner of telling fortunes upon the cards." *Fudge!*

When she had delivered this pretty piece of eloquence, the two ladies looked at each other a few minutes in silence, with an air of doubt and importance. At last Miss Carolina Wilelmina Amelia Skeggs condescended to observe, that the young ladies, from the opinion she could form of them from so slight an acquaintance, seemed very fit for such employments: "But a thing of this kind, Madam," cried she, addressing my spouse, "requires a thorough examination into characters, and a more perfect knowledge of each other. Not, Madam," continued she, "that I in the least suspect the young ladies virtue, prudence and discretion; but there is a form in these things, Madam, there is a form."

My wife approved her suspicions very much, observing that she was very apt to be suspicious herself; but referred her to all the neighbours for a character: but this our Peeress declined as unnecessary, alledging that her cousin Thornhill's recommendation would be sufficient, and upon this we rested our petition.

CHAPTER XII

Fortune seems resolved to humble the family of Wakefield. Mortifications are often more painful than real calamities.

WHEN we returned home, the night was dedicated to schemes of future conquest. Deborah exerted much sagacity in conjecturing which of the two girls was likely to have the best place, and most opportunities of seeing good company. The only obstacle to our preferment was in obtaining the 'Squire's recommendation; but he had already shewn us too many instances of his friendship to doubt of it now. Even in bed my wife kept up the usual theme: "Well, faith, my dear Charles, between ourselves, I think we have made an excellent day's work of it."—"Pretty well," cried I, not knowing what to say.—"What only pretty well!" returned she. "I think it is very well. Suppose the girls should come to make acquaintances of taste in town! This I am assured of, that London is the only place in the world for all manner of husbands. Besides, my dear, stranger things happen every day: and as ladies of quality are so taken with my daughters, what will not men of quality be! Entre nous, I protest I like my Lady Blarney vastly, so very obliging. However, Miss Carolina Wilelmina Amelia Skeggs has my warm heart. But yet, when they came to talk of places in town, you saw at once how I nailed them. Tell me, my dear, don't you think I did for my children there?"—"Ay," returned I, not knowing well what to think of the matter, "heaven grant they may be both the better for it this day three months!" This was one of those observations I usually made to impress my wife with an opinion of my sagacity; for if the girls succeed, then it was a pious wish fulfilled; but if any thing unfortunate ensued, then it might be looked upon as a prophecy. All this conversation, however, was only preparatory to another scheme, and indeed I dreaded as much. This was nothing less than, that as we were now to hold up our heads a little higher in the world, it would be proper to sell the Colt, which was grown old, at a neighbouring fair, and buy us an horse that would carry single or double upon an occasion, and make a pretty appearance at church or upon a visit. This at first I opposed stoutly; but it was as stoutly defended. However, as I weakened, my antagonists gained strength, till at last it was resolved to part with him.

As the fair happened on the following day, I had intentions of going myself; but my wife persuaded me that I had got a cold, and nothing could prevail upon her to permit me from home. "No, my dear," said she, "our son Moses is a discreet boy, and can buy and sell to very good advantage; you know all our great bargains are of his purchasing. He always stands out and higgles, and actually tires them till he gets a bargain."

As I had some opinion of my son's prudence, I was willing enough to entrust him with this commission; and the next morning I perceived his sisters mighty busy in fitting out Moses for the fair; trimming his hair, brushing his buckles, and cocking his hat with pins. The business of the toilet being over, we had at last the satisfaction of seeing him mounted upon the Colt, with a deal box before him to bring home groceries in. He had on a coat made of that cloth they call thunder and lightning, which, though grown too short, was much too good to be thrown away. His waistcoat was of a gosling green, and his sisters had tied his hair with a broad black ribband. We all followed him several paces from the door, bawling after him, good luck, good luck, till we could see him no longer.

He was scarce gone, when Mr. Thornhill's butler came to congratulate us upon our good fortune, saying, that he overheard his young master mention our names with great commendation.

Good fortune seemed resolved not to come alone. Another footman from the same family followed, with a card for my daughters, importing, that the two ladies had received such pleasing accounts from Mr. Thornhill of us all, that, after a few previous enquiries, they hoped to be perfectly satisfied. "Ay," cried my wife, "I now see it is no easy matter to get into the families of the great; but when one once gets in, then, as Moses says, one may go sleep." To this piece of humour, for she intended it for wit, my daughters assented with a loud laugh of pleasure. In short, such was her satisfaction at this message, that she actually put her hand in her pocket, and gave the messenger seven-pence halfpenny.

This was to be our visiting-day. The next that came was Mr. Burchell, who had been at the fair. He brought my little ones a pennyworth of gingerbread each, which my wife undertook to keep for them, and give them by letters at a time. He brought my daughters also a couple of boxes, in which they might keep wafers, snuff, patches, or even money, when they got it. My wife was usually fond of a weesel skin purse, as being the most lucky; but this by the bye. We had still a regard for Mr. Burchell, though his late rude behaviour was in some measure displeasing; nor could we now avoid communicating our happiness to him, and asking his advice: although we seldom followed advice, we were all ready enough to ask it. When he read the note from the two ladies, he shook his head, and observed, that an affair of this sort demanded the utmost circumspection.—This air of diffidence highly displeased my wife. "I never doubted, Sir," cried she, "your readiness to be against my daughters and me. You have more circumspection than is wanted. However, I fancy when we come to ask advice, we shall apply to persons who seem to have made use of it themselves."—"Whatever my own conduct may have been, Madam," replied he, "is not the present question; though as I have made no use of advice myself, I should in conscience give it to those that will." As I was apprehensive this answer might draw on a repartee, making up by abuse what it wanted in wit, I changed the subject, by seeming to wonder what could keep our son so long at the fair, as it was now almost nightfall.—"Never mind our son," cried my wife, "depend upon it he knows what he is about. I'll warrant we'll never see him sell his hen of a rainy day. I have seen him buy such bargains as would amaze one. I'll tell you a good story about that, that will make you split your sides with laughing.—But as I live, yonder comes Moses, without an horse, and the box at his back."

As he spoke, Moses came slowly on foot, and sweating under the deal box, which he had strapt round his shoulders like a pedlar.—"Welcome, welcome, Moses; well, my boy, what have you brought us from the fair?"—"I have brought you myself," cried Moses, with a sly look, and resting the box on the dresser.—"Ay, Moses," cried my wife, "that we know, but where is the horse?" "I have sold him," cried Moses, "for three pounds five shillings and two-pence."—"Well done, my good boy," returned she, "I knew you would touch them off. Between ourselves, three pounds five shillings and two-pence is no bad day's work. Come, let us have it then."—"I have brought back no money," cried Moses again. "I have laid it all out in a bargain, and here it is," pulling out a bundle from his breast: "here they are; a groce of green spectacles, with silver rims and shagreen cases."—"A groce of green spectacles!" repeated my wife in a faint voice. "And you have parted with the Colt, and brought us back nothing but a groce of green paltry spectacles!"—"Dear mother," cried the boy, "why won't you listen to reason? I had them a dead bargain, or I should not have bought them. The silver rims alone will sell for double the money."—"A fig for the silver rims," cried my wife, in a passion: "I dare swear they won't sell for above half the money at the rate of broken silver, five shillings an ounce."—"You need be under no uneasiness," cried I, "about selling the rims; for they are not worth six-pence, for I perceive they are only copper varnished over."—"What," cried my wife, "not silver, the rims not silver!" "No," cried I, "no more silver than your sauce-pan."—"And so," returned she, "we have parted with the Colt, and have only got a groce of green spectacles, with copper rims and shagreen cases! A murrain take such trumpery. The blockhead has been imposed upon, and should have known his company better."—"There, my dear," cried I, "you are wrong, he should not have known them at all."—"Marry, hang the ideot," returned she, "to bring me such stuff; if I had them, I would throw them in the fire." "There again you are wrong, my dear," cried I; "for though they be copper, we will keep them by us, as copper spectacles, you know, are better than nothing."

By this time the unfortunate Moses was undeceived. He now saw that he had indeed been imposed upon by a prowling sharper, who, observing his figure, had marked him for an easy prey. I therefore asked the circumstances of his deception. He sold the horse, it seems, and walked the fair in search of another. A reverend looking man brought him to a tent, under pretence of having one to sell. "Here," continued Moses, "we met another man, very well drest, who desired to borrow twenty pounds upon these, saying, that he wanted money, and would dispose of them for a third of the value. The first gentleman, who pretended to be my friend, whispered me to buy them, and cautioned me not to let so good an offer pass. I sent for Mr. Flamborough, and they talked him up as finely as they did me, and so at last we were persuaded to buy the two groce between us."

CHAPTER XIII

Mr. Burchell is found to be an enemy; for he has the confidence to give disagreeable advice.

OUR family had now made several attempts to be fine; but some unforeseen disaster demolished each as soon as projected. I endeavoured to take the advantage of every disappointment, to improve their good sense in proportion as they were frustrated in ambition. "You see, my children," cried I, "how little is to be got by attempts to impose upon the world, in coping with our betters. Such as are poor and will associate with none but the rich, are hated by those they avoid, and despised by those they follow. Unequal combinations are always disadvantageous to the weaker side: the rich having the pleasure, and the poor the inconveniencies that result from them. But come, Dick, my boy, and repeat the fable you were reading to-day, for the good of the company."

"Once upon a time," cried the child, "a Giant and a Dwarf were friends, and kept together. They made a bargain that they would never forsake each other, but go seek adventures. The first battle they fought was with two Saracens, and the Dwarf, who was very courageous, dealt one of the champions a most angry blow. It did the Saracen but very little injury, who lifting up his sword, fairly struck off the poor Dwarf's arm. He was now in a woeful plight; but the Giant coming to his assistance, in a short time left the two Saracens dead on the plain, and the Dwarf cut off the dead man's head out of spite. They then travelled on to another adventure. This was against three bloody-minded Satyrs, who were carrying away a damsel in distress. The Dwarf was not quite so fierce now as before; but for all that, struck the first blow, which was returned by another, that knocked out his eye: but the Giant was soon up with them, and had they not fled, would certainly have killed them every one. They were all very joyful for this victory, and the damsel who was relieved fell in love with the Giant, and married him. They now travelled far, and farther than I can tell, till they met with a company of robbers. The Giant, for the first time, was foremost now; but the Dwarf was not far behind. The battle was stout and long. Wherever the Giant came all fell before him; but the Dwarf had like to have been killed more than once. At last the victory declared for the two adventurers; but the Dwarf lost his leg. The Dwarf had now lost an arm, a leg, and an eye, while the Giant was without a single wound. Upon which he cried out to his little companion, My little heroe, this is glorious sport; let us get one victory more, and then we shall have honour for ever.—No, cries the Dwarf, who was by this time grown wiser, no, I declare off; I'll fight no more: for I find in every battle that you get all the honour and rewards, but all the blows fall upon me."

I was going to moralize this fable, when our attention was called off to a warm dispute between my wife and Mr. Burchell, upon my daughters intended expedition to town. My wife very strenuously insisted upon the advantages that would result from it. Mr. Burchell, on the contrary, dissuaded her with great ardor, and I stood neuter. His present dissuasions seemed but the second part of those which were received with so ill a grace in the morning. The dispute grew high, while poor Deborah, instead of reasoning stronger, talked louder, and at last was obliged to take shelter from a defeat in clamour. The conclusion of her harangue, however, was highly displeasing to us all: she knew, she said, of some who had their own secret reasons for what they advised; but, for her part, she wished such to stay away from her house for the future.—"Madam," cried Burchell, with looks of great composure, which tended to enflame her the more, "as for secret reasons, you are right: I have secret reasons, which I forbear to mention, because you are not able to answer those of which I make no secret: but I find my visits here are become troublesome; I'll take my leave therefore now, and perhaps come once more to take a final farewel when I am quitting the country." Thus saying, he took up his hat, nor could the attempts of Sophia, whose looks seemed to upbraid his precipitancy, prevent his going.

When gone, we all regarded each other for some minutes with confusion. My wife, who knew herself to be the cause, strove to hide her concern with a forced smile, and an air of assurance, which I was willing to reprove: "How, woman," cried I to her, "is it thus we treat strangers? Is it thus we return their kindness? Be assured, my dear, that these were the harshest words, and to me the most unpleasing that ever escaped your lips!"—"Why would he provoke me then?" replied she; "but I know the motives of his advice perfectly well. He would prevent my girls from going to town, that he may have the pleasure of my youngest daughter's company here at home. But, whatever happens, she shall chuse better company than such low-lived fellows as he."—"Low-lived, my dear, do you call him?" cried I; "it is very possible we may mistake this man's character: for he seems upon some occasions the most finished gentleman I ever knew.—Tell me, Sophia, my girl, has he ever given you any secret instances of his attachment?"—"His conversation with me, Sir," replied my daughter, "has ever been sensible, modest, and pleasing. As to aught else, no, never. Once indeed, I remember to have heard him say he never knew a woman who could find merit in a man that seemed poor." "Such, my dear," cried I, "is the common cant of all the unfortunate or idle. But I hope you have been taught to judge properly of such men, and that it would be even madness to expect happiness from one who has been so very bad an œconomist of his own. Your mother and I have now better prospects for you. The next winter, which you will probably spend in town, will give you opportunities of making a more prudent choice."

What Sophia's reflections were upon this occasion, I can't pretend to determine; but I was not displeased at the bottom that we were rid of a guest from whom I had much to fear. Our breach of hospitality went to my conscience a little: but I quickly silenced that monitor by two or three specious reasons, which served to satisfy and reconcile me to myself. The pain which conscience gives the man who has already done wrong, is soon got over. Conscience is a coward, and those faults it has not strength enough to prevent, it seldom has justice enough to accuse.

CHAPTER XIV

Fresh mortifications, or a demonstration that seeming calamities may be real blessings.

THE journey of my daughters to town was now resolved upon, Mr. Thornhill having kindly promised to inspect their conduct himself, and inform us by letter of their behaviour.

But it was thought indispensably necessary that their appearance should equal the greatness of their expectations, which could not be done without expence. We debated therefore in full council what were the easiest methods of raising money, or, more properly speaking, what we could most conveniently sell. The deliberation was soon finished, it was found that our remaining horse was utterly useless for the plow, without his companion, and equally unfit for the road, as wanting an eye; it was therefore determined that we should dispose of him for the purposes above mentioned, at the neighbouring fair, and, to prevent imposition, that I should go with him myself. Though this was one of the first mercantile transactions of my life, yet I had no doubt about acquitting myself with reputation. The opinion a man forms of his own prudence is measured by that of the company he keeps; and as mine was mostly in the family way, I had conceived no unfavourable sentiments of my worldly wisdom. My wife, however, next morning, at parting, after I had got some paces from the door, called me back, to advise me, in a whisper, to have all my eyes about me.

I had, in the usual forms, when I came to the fair, put my horse through all his paces; but for some time had no bidders. At last a chapman approached, and, after he had for a good while examined the horse round, finding him blind of one eye, he would have nothing to say to him: a second came up; but observing he had a spavin, declared he would not take him for the driving home: a third perceived he had a windgall, and would bid no money: a fourth knew by his eye that he had the botts: a fifth wondered what a plague I could do at the fair with a blind, spavined, galled hack, that was only fit to be cut up for a dog kennel. By this time I began to have a most hearty contempt for the poor animal myself, and was almost ashamed at the approach of every customer; for though I did not entirely believe all the fellows told me; yet I reflected that the number of witnesses was a strong presumption they were right, and St. Gregory, upon good works, professes himself to be of the same opinion.

I was in this mortifying situation, when a brother clergyman, an old acquaintance, who had also business at the fair, came up, and shaking me by the hand, proposed adjourning to a public-house and taking a glass of whatever we could get. I readily closed with the offer, and entering an ale-house, we were shewn into a little back room, where there was only a venerable old man, who sat wholly intent over a large book, which he was reading. I never in my life saw a figure that prepossessed me more favourably. His locks of silver grey venerably shaded his temples, and his green old age seemed to be the result of health and benevolence. However, his presence did not interrupt our conversation; my friend and I discoursed on the various turns of fortune we had met: the Whistonian controversy, my last pamphlet, the archdeacon's reply, and the hard measure that was dealt me. But our attention was in a short time taken off by the appearance of a youth, who, entering the room, respectfully said something softly to the old stranger. "Make no apologies, my child," said the old man; "to do good is a duty we owe to all our fellow creatures: take this, I wish it were more; but five pounds will relieve your distress, and you are welcome." The modest youth shed tears of gratitude, and yet his gratitude was scarce equal to mine. I could have hugged the good old man in my arms, his benevolence pleased me so. He continued to read, and we resumed our conversation, until my companion, after some time, recollecting that he had business to transact in the fair, promised to be soon back; adding, that he always desired to have as much of Dr. Primrose's company as possible. The old gentleman, hearing my name mentioned, seemed to look at me with attention, for some time, and when my friend was gone, most respectfully demanded if I was any way related to the great Primrose, that courageous monogamist, who had been the bulwark of the church. Never did my heart feel sincerer rapture than at that moment. "Sir," cried I, "the applause of so good a man, as I am sure you are, adds to that happiness in my breast which your benevolence has already excited. You behold before you, Sir, that Doctor Primrose, the monogamist, whom you have been pleased to call great. You here see that unfortunate Divine, who has so long, and it would ill become me to say successfully, fought against the deuterogamy of the age." "Sir," cried the stranger, struck with awe, "I fear I have been too familiar; but you'll forgive my curiosity, Sir: I beg pardon." "Sir," cried I, grasping his hand, "you are so far from displeasing me by your familiarity, that I must beg you'll accept my friendship, as you already have my esteem."—"Then with gratitude I accept the offer," cried he, squeezing me by the hand, "thou glorious pillar of unshaken orthodoxy; and do I behold"——I here interrupted what he was going to say; for though, as an author, I could digest no small share of flattery, yet now my modesty would permit no more. However, no lovers in romance ever cemented a more instantaneous friendship. We talked upon several subjects: at first I thought he seemed rather devout than learned, and began to think he despised all human doctrines as dross. Yet this no way lessened him in my esteem; for I had for some time begun privately to harbour such an opinion myself. I therefore took occasion to observe, that the world in general began to be blameably indifferent as to doctrinal matters, and followed human speculations too much—"Ay, Sir," replied he, as if he had reserved all his learning to that moment, "Ay, Sir, the world is in its dotage, and yet the cosmogony or creation of the world has puzzled philosophers of all ages. What a medley of opinions have they not broached upon the creation of the world? Sanconiathon, Manetho, Berosus, and Ocellus Lucanus, have all attempted it in vain. The latter has these words, *Anarchon ara kai atelutaion to pan*, which imply that all things have neither beginning nor end. Manetho also, who lived about the time of Nebuchadon-

Asser, Asser being a Syriac word usually applied as a sirname to the kings of that country, as Teglat Phael-Asser, Nabon-Asser, he, I say, formed a conjecture equally absurd; for as we usually say, *ek to biblion kubernetes*, which implies that books will never teach the world; so he attempted to investigate—— But, Sir, I ask pardon, I am straying from the question."— That he actually was; nor could I for my life see how the creation of the world had any thing to do with the business I was talking of; but it was sufficient to shew me that he was a man of letters, and I now reverenced him the more. I was resolved therefore to bring him to the touchstone; but he was too mild and too gentle to contend for victory. Whenever I made any observation that looked like a challenge to controversy, he would smile, shake his head, and say nothing; by which I understood he could say much, if he thought proper. The subject therefore insensibly changed from the business of antiquity to that which brought us both to the fair; mine I told him was to sell an horse, and very luckily, indeed, his was to buy one for one of his tenants. My horse was soon produced, and in fine we struck a bargain. Nothing now remained but to pay me, and he accordingly pulled out a thirty pound note, and bid me change it. Not being in a capacity of complying with his demand, he ordered his footman to be called up, who made his appearance in a very genteel livery. "Here, Abraham," cried he, "go and get gold for this; you'll do it at neighbour Jackson's, or any where." While the fellow was gone, he entertained me with a pathetic harangue on the great scarcity of silver, which I undertook to improve, by deploring also the great scarcity of gold; so that by the time Abraham returned, we had both agreed that money was never so hard to be come at as now. Abraham returned to inform us, that he had been over the whole fair and could not get change, though he had offered half a crown for doing it. This was a very great disappointment to us all; but the old gentleman having paused a little, asked me if I knew one

Solomon Flamborough in my part of the country: upon replying that he was my next door neighbour, "If that be the case then," returned he, "I believe we shall deal. You shall have a draught upon him, payable at sight; and let me tell you he is as warm a man as any within five miles round him. Honest Solomon and I have been acquainted for many years together. I remember I always beat him at three jumps; but he could hop upon one leg farther than I." A draught upon my neighbour was to me the same as money; for I was sufficiently convinced of his ability: the draught was signed and put into my hands, and Mr. Jenkinson, the old gentleman, his man Abraham, and my horse, old Blackberry, trotted off very well pleased with each other.

After a short interval, being left to reflection, I began to recollect that I had done wrong in taking a draught from a stranger, and so prudently resolved upon following the purchaser, and having back my horse. But this was now too late: I therefore made directly homewards, resolving to get the draught changed into money at my friend's as fast as possible. I found my honest neighbour smoking his pipe at his own door, and informing him that I had a small bill upon him, he read it twice over. "You can read the name, I suppose," cried I, "Ephraim Jenkinson." "Yes," returned he, "the name is written plain enough, and I know the gentleman too, the greatest rascal under the canopy of heaven. This is the very same rogue who sold us the spectacles. Was he not a venerable looking man, with grey hair, and no flaps to his pocket-holes? And did he not talk a long string of learning about Greek and cosmogony, and the world?" To this I replied with a groan. "Aye," continued he, "he has but that one piece of learning in the world, and he always talks it away whenever he finds a scholar in company: but I know the rogue, and will catch him yet."

Though I was already sufficiently mortified, my greatest struggle was to come, in facing my wife and daughters. No truant was ever more afraid of returning to school, there to behold the master's visage, than I was of going home. I was determined, however, to anticipate their fury, by first falling into a passion myself.

But, alas! upon entering, I found the family no way disposed for battle. My wife and girls were all in tears, Mr. Thornhill having been there that day to inform them, that their journey to town was entirely over. The two ladies having heard reports of us from some malicious person about us, were that day set out for London. He could neither discover the tendency, nor the author of these, but whatever they might be, or whoever might have broached them, he continued to assure our family of his friendship and protection. I found, therefore, that they bore my disappointment with great resignation, as it was eclipsed in the greatness of their own. But what perplexed us most was to think who could be so base as to asperse the character of a family so harmless as ours, too humble to excite envy, and too inoffensive to create disgust.

CHAPTER XV

All Mr. Burchell's villainy at once detected. The folly of being over-wise.

THAT evening and a part of the following day was employed in fruitless attempts to discover our enemies: scarce a family in the neighbourhood but incurred our suspicions, and each of us had reasons for our opinion best known to ourselves. As we were in this perplexity, one of our little boys, who had been playing abroad, brought in a letter-case, which he found on the green. It was quickly known to belong to Mr. Burchell, with whom it had been seen, and, upon examination, contained some hints upon different subjects; but what particularly engaged our attention was a sealed note, superscribed, *the copy of a letter to be sent to the ladies at Thornhill-*

castle. It instantly occurred that he was the base informer, and we deliberated whether the note should not be broke open. I was against it; but Sophia, who said she was sure that of all men he would be the last to be guilty of so much baseness, insisted upon its being read. In this she was seconded by the rest of the family, and, at their joint solicitation, I read as follows:

"Ladies,
The bearer will sufficiently satisfy you as to the person from whom this comes: one at least the friend of innocence, and ready to prevent its being seduced. I am informed for a truth, that you have some intention of bringing two young ladies to town, whom I have some knowledge of, under the character of companions. As I would neither have simplicity imposed upon, nor virtue contaminated, I must offer it as my opinion, that the impropriety of such a step will be attended with dangerous consequences. It has never been my way to treat the infamous or the lewd with severity; nor should I now have taken this method of explaining myself, or reproving folly, did it not aim at guilt. Take therefore the admonition of a friend, and seriously reflect on the consequences of introducing infamy and vice into retreats where peace and innocence have hitherto resided."

Our doubts were now at an end. There seemed indeed something applicable to both sides in this letter, and its censures might as well be referred to those to whom it was written, as to us; but the malicious meaning was obvious, and we went no farther. My wife had scarcely patience to hear me to the end, but railed at the writer with unrestrained resentment. Olivia was equally severe, and Sophia seemed perfectly amazed at his baseness. As for my part, it appeared to me one of the vilest instances of unprovoked ingratitude I had met with. Nor could I account for it in any other manner than by imputing it to his desire of detaining my youngest daughter in the country, to have the more frequent opportunities of an interview. In this manner we all sate ruminating upon schemes of vengeance, when our other little boy came running in to tell us that Mr. Burchell was approaching at the other end of the field. It is easier to conceive than describe the complicated sensations which are felt from the pain of a recent injury, and the pleasure of approaching vengeance. Tho' our intentions were only to upbraid him with his ingratitude; yet it was resolved to do it in a manner that would be perfectly cutting. For this purpose we agreed to meet him with our usual smiles, to chat in the beginning with more than ordinary kindness, to amuse him a little; and then in the midst of the flattering calm to burst upon him like an earthquake, and overwhelm him with the sense of his own baseness. This being resolved upon, my wife undertook to manage the business herself, as she really had some talents for such an undertaking. We saw him approach, he entered, drew a chair, and sate down.—"A fine day, Mr. Burchell."—"A very fine day, Doctor; though I fancy we shall have some rain by the shooting of my corns."—"The shooting of your horns," cried my wife in a loud fit of laughter, and then asked pardon for being fond of a joke.—"Dear madam," replied he, "I pardon you with all my heart; for I protest I should not have thought it a joke had you not told me."—"Perhaps not, Sir," cried my wife, winking at us, "and yet I dare say you can tell us how many jokes go to an ounce."—"I fancy, madam," returned Burchell, "you have been reading a jest book this morning, that ounce of jokes is so very good a conceit; and yet, madam, I had rather see half an ounce of understanding."—"I believe you might," cried my wife, still smiling at us, though the laugh was against her; "and yet I have seen some men pretend to understanding that have very little."—"And no doubt," replied her antagonist, "you have known ladies set up for wit that had none."—I quickly began to find that my wife was likely to gain but little at this business; so I resolved to treat him in a style of more severity myself. "Both wit and understanding," cried I, "are trifles without integrity; it is that which gives value to every character. The ignorant peasant, without fault, is greater than the philosopher with many; for what is genius or courage without an heart? *An honest man is the noblest work of God.*"

"I always held that hackney'd maxim of Pope," returned Mr. Burchell, "as very unworthy a man of genius, and a base desertion of his own superiority. As the reputation of books is raised not by their freedom from defect, but the greatness of their beauties; so should that of men be prized not for their exemption from fault, but the size of those virtues they are possessed of. The scholar may want prudence, the statesman may have pride, and the champion ferocity; but shall we prefer to these the low mechanic, who laboriously plods on through life, without censure or applause? We might as well prefer the tame correct paintings of the Flemish school to the erroneous, but sublime animations of the Roman pencil."

"Sir," replied I, "your present observation is just, when there are shining virtues and minute defects; but when it appears that great vices are opposed in the same mind to as extraordinary virtues, such a character deserves contempt."

"Perhaps," cried he, "there may be some such monsters as you describe, of great vices joined to great virtues; yet in my progress through life, I never yet found one instance of their existence: on the contrary, I have ever perceived, that where the mind was capacious, the affections were good. And indeed Providence seems kindly our friend in this particular, thus to debilitate the understanding where the heart is corrupt, and diminish the power where there is the will to do mischief. This rule seems to extend even to other animals: the little vermin race are ever treacherous, cruel, and cowardly, whilst those endowed with strength and power are generous, brave, and gentle."

"These observations sound well," returned I, "and yet it

would be easy this moment to point out a man," and I fixed my eye stedfastly upon him, "whose head and heart form a most detestable contrast. Ay, Sir," continued I, raising my voice, "and I am glad to have this opportunity of detecting him in the midst of this fancied security. Do you know this, Sir, this pocket-book?"—"Yes, Sir," returned he, with a face of impenetrable assurance, "that pocket-book is mine, and I am glad you have found it."—"And do you know," cried I, "this letter? Nay, never falter, man; but look me full in the face: I say, do you know this letter?"—"That letter,"—returned he, "yes, it was I that wrote that letter."—"And how could you," said I, "so basely, so ungratefully presume to write this letter?"—"And how came you," replied he, with looks of unparalleled effrontery, "so basely to presume to break open this letter? Don't you know, now, I could hang you all for this? All that I have to do is to swear at the next justice's, that you have been guilty of breaking open the lock of my pocket-book, and so hang you all up at his door." This piece of unexpected insolence raised me to such a pitch, that I could scarce govern my passion. "Ungrateful wretch, begone, and no longer pollute my dwelling with thy baseness. Begone, and never let me see thee again: go from my doors, and the only punishment I wish thee, is an alarmed conscience, which will be a sufficient tormentor!" so saying, I threw him his pocket-book, which he took up with a smile, and shutting the clasps with the utmost composure, left us, quite astonished at the serenity of his assurance. My wife was particularly enraged that nothing could make him angry, or make him seem ashamed of his villainies: "My dear," cried I, willing to calm those passions that had been raised too high among us, "we are not to be surprised that bad men want shame; they only blush at being detected in doing good, but glory in their vices.

"Guilt and Shame, says the allegory, were at first companions, and in the beginning of their journey inseparably kept together. But their union was soon found to be disagreeable and inconvenient to both; Guilt gave Shame frequent uneasiness, and Shame often betrayed the secret conspiracies of Guilt. After long disagreement, therefore, they at length consented to part for ever. Guilt boldly walked forward alone to overtake Fate, that went before in the shape of an executioner: but Shame being naturally timorous, returned back to keep company with Virtue, which, in the beginning of their journey, they had left behind. Thus, my children, after men have travelled through a few stages in vice, shame forsakes them, and returns back to wait upon the few virtues they have still remaining."

CHAPTER XVI

The family use art, which is opposed with still greater.

WHATEVER might have been Sophia's sensations, the rest of the family was easily consoled for Mr. Burchell's absence by the company of our landlord, whose visits now became more frequent and longer. Though he had been disappointed in procuring my daughters the amusements of the town, as he designed, he took every opportunity of supplying them with those little recreations which our retirement would admit of. He usually came in the morning, and while my son and I followed our occupations abroad, he sat with the family at home, and amused them by describing the town, with every part of which he was particularly acquainted. He could repeat all the observations that were retailed in the atmosphere of the play-houses, and had all the good things of the high wits by rote long before they made way into the jest-books. The intervals between conversation were employed in teaching my daughters piquet, or sometimes in setting my two little ones to box to make them *sharp*, as he called it: but the hopes of having him for a son-in-law, in some measure blinded us to all his imperfections. It must be owned that my wife laid a thousand schemes to entrap him, or, to speak it more tenderly, used every art to magnify the merit of her daughter. If the cakes at tea eat short and crisp, they were made by Olivia; if the gooseberry wine was well knit, the gooseberries were of her gathering: it was her fingers which gave the pickles their peculiar green; and in the composition of a pudding, it was her judgment that mix'd the ingredients. Then the poor woman would sometimes tell the 'Squire, that she thought him and Olivia extremely of a size, and would bid both stand up to see which was tallest. These instances of cunning, which she thought impenetrable, yet which every body saw through, were very pleasing to our benefactor, who gave every day some new proofs of his passion, which though they had not arisen to proposals of marriage, yet we thought fell but little short of it; and his slowness was attributed sometimes to native bashfulness, and sometimes to his fear of offending his uncle. An occurrence, however, which happened soon after, put it beyond a doubt, that he designed to become one of our family; my wife even regarded it as an absolute promise.

My wife and daughters happening to return a visit to neighbour Flamborough's found that family had lately got their pictures drawn by a limner, who travelled the country, and took likenesses for fifteen shillings a head. As this family and ours had long a sort of rivalry in point of taste, our spirit took the alarm at this stolen march upon us, and notwithstanding all I could say, and I said much, it was resolved that we should have our pictures done too. Having, therefore, engaged the limner, for what could I do? our next deliberation was to shew the superiority of our taste in the attitudes. As for our neighbour's family, there were seven of them, and they were drawn with seven oranges, a thing quite out of taste, no variety in life, no composition in the world. We desired to have something in a brighter style, and after many debates, at length came to a unanimous resolution of being drawn together, in one large historical family piece. This would be cheaper, since one frame would serve for all, and it would be infinitely more genteel; for all families of any taste were now drawn in the same manner. As we did not immediately recollect an historical subject to hit us, we were contented each with being drawn as independent historical figures. My wife desired to be represented as Venus, and the painter was desired not to be too frugal of his diamonds in her stomacher and hair. Her two little ones were to be as Cupids by her side, while I, in my gown and band, was to present her with my books on the Whistonian controversy. Olivia would be drawn as an Amazon, sitting upon a bank of flowers, drest in a green Joseph,[1] richly laced with gold, and a whip in her hand. Sophia was to be a shepherdess, with as many sheep as the painter could put in for nothing; and Moses was to be drest out with an hat and white feather. Our taste so much pleased the 'Squire, that he insisted on being put in as one of the family in the character of Alexander the great, at Olivia's feet. This was considered by us all as an indication of his desire to be introduced into the family, nor could we refuse his request. The painter was therefore set to work, and as he wrought with assiduity and expedition, in less than four days the whole was compleated. The piece was large, and it must be owned he did not spare his colours; for which my wife gave him great encomiums. We were all perfectly satisfied with his performance; but an unfortunate circumstance had not occurred till the picture was finished, which now struck us with dismay. It was so very large that we had no place in the house to fix it. How we all came to disregard so material a point is inconceivable; but certain it is, we had been all greatly remiss. The picture, therefore, instead of gratifying our vanity, as we hoped, leaned, in a most mortifying manner, against the kitchen wall, where the canvas was stretched and painted much too large to be got through any of the doors, and the

[1] [A long riding cloak, chiefly worn by women.]

jest of all our neighbours. One compared it to Robinson Crusoe's long-boat, too large to be removed; another thought it more resembled a reel in a bottle; some wondered how it could be got out, but still more were amazed how it ever got in.

But though it excited the ridicule of some, it effectually raised more malicious suggestions in many. The 'Squire's portrait being found united with ours, was an honour too great to escape envy. Scandalous whispers began to circulate at our expence, and our tranquillity was continually disturbed by persons who came as friends to tell us what was said of us by enemies. These reports we always resented with becoming spirit; but scandal ever improves by opposition.

We once again therefore entered into a consultation upon obviating the malice of our enemies, and at last came to a resolution which had too much cunning to give me entire satisfaction. It was this: as our principal object was to discover the honour of Mr. Thornhill's addresses, my wife undertook to sound him, by pretending to ask his advice in the choice of an husband for her eldest daughter. If this was not found sufficient to induce him to a declaration, it was then resolved to terrify him with a rival. To this last step, however, I would by no means give my consent, till Olivia gave me the most solemn assurances that she would marry the person provided to rival him upon this occasion, if he did not prevent it, by taking her himself. Such was the scheme laid, which though I did not strenuously oppose, I did not entirely approve.

The next time, therefore, that Mr. Thornhill came to see us, my girls took care to be out of the way, in order to give their mamma an opportunity of putting her scheme in execution; but they only retired to the next room, from whence they could over-hear the whole conversation: My wife artfully introduced it, by observing, that one of the Miss Flamboroughs was like to have a very good match of it in Mr. Spanker. To this the 'Squire assenting, she proceeded to remark, that they who had warm fortunes were always sure of getting good husbands; "But heaven help," continued she, "the girls that have none. What signifies beauty, Mr. Thornhill? or what signifies all the virtue, and all the qualifications in the world, in this age of self-interest? It is not, what is she? but what has she? is all the cry."

"Madam," returned he, "I highly approve the justice, as well as the novelty, of your remarks, and if I were a king, it should be otherwise. It should then, indeed, be fine times with the girls without fortunes: our two young ladies should be the first for whom I would provide."

"Ah, Sir!" returned my wife, "you are pleased to be facetious: but I wish I were a queen, and then I know where my eldest daughter should look for an husband. But now, that you have put it into my head, seriously, Mr. Thornhill, can't you recommend me a proper husband for her? She is now nineteen years old, well grown and well educated, and, in my humble opinion, does not want for parts."

"Madam," replied he, "if I were to chuse, I would find out a person possessed of every accomplishment that can make an angel happy. One with prudence, fortune, taste, and sincerity, such, Madam, would be, in my opinion, the proper husband." "Ay, Sir," said she, "but do you know of any such person?" —"No, Madam," returned he, "it is impossible to know any person that deserves to be her husband: she's too great a treasure for one man's possession: she's a goddess. Upon my soul, I speak what I think, she's an angel."—"Ah, Mr. Thornhill, you only flatter my poor girl: but we have been thinking of marrying her to one of your tenants, whose mother is lately dead, and who wants a manager: you know whom I mean, farmer Williams; a warm man, Mr. Thornhill, able to give her good bread; and who has several times made her proposals:" (which was actually the case) "but, Sir," concluded she, "I should be glad to have your approbation of our choice."— "How, Madam," replied he, "my approbation! My approbation of such a choice! Never. What! Sacrifice so much beauty, and sense, and goodness, to a creature insensible of the blessing! Excuse me, I can never approve of such a piece of injustice! And I have my reasons!"—"Indeed, Sir," cried Deborah, "if you have your reasons, that's another affair; but I should be glad to know those reasons."—"Excuse me, madam," returned he, "they lie too deep for discovery:" (laying his hand upon his bosom) "they remain buried, rivetted here."

After he was gone, upon general consultation, we could not tell what to make of these fine sentiments. Olivia considered them as instances of the most exalted passion; but I was not quite so sanguine: it seemed to me pretty plain, that they had more of love, than matrimony in them: yet, whatever they might portend, it was resolved to prosecute the scheme of farmer Williams, who, from my daughter's first appearance in the country, had paid her his addresses.

CHAPTER XVII

Scarce any virtue found to resist the power of long and pleasing temptation.

As I only studied my child's real happiness, the assiduity of Mr. Williams pleased me, as he was in easy circumstances, prudent, and sincere. It required but very little encouragement to revive his former passion; so that in an evening or two he and Mr. Thornhill met at our house, and surveyed each other for some time with looks of anger: but Williams owed his landlord no rent, and little regarded his indignation. Olivia, on her side, acted the coquet to perfection, if that might be called acting which was her real character, pretending to lavish all her tenderness on her new lover. Mr. Thornhill appeared quite dejected at this preference, and with a pensive air took leave, though I own it puzzled me to find him so much in pain as he appeared to be, when he had it in his power so easily to remove the cause, by declaring an honourable passion. But whatever uneasiness he seemed to endure, it could easily be perceived that Olivia's anguish was still greater. After any of these interviews between her lovers, of which there were several, she usually retired to solitude, and there indulged her grief. It was in such a situation I found her one evening, after she had been for some time supporting a fictitious gayety.—"You now see, my child," said I, "that your confidence in Mr. Thornhill's passion was all a dream: he permits the rivalry of another, every way his inferior, though he knows it lies in his power to secure you to himself by a candid declaration."—"Yes, pappa," returned she, "but he has his reasons for this delay: I know he has. The sincerity of his looks and words convince me of his real esteem. A short time, I hope, will discover the generosity of his sentiments, and convince you that my opinion of him has been more just than yours."—"Olivia, my darling," returned I, "every scheme that has been hitherto pursued to compel him to a declaration, has been proposed and planned by yourself, nor can you in the least say that I have constrained you. But you must not suppose, my dear, that I will ever be instrumental in suffering his honest rival to be the dupe of your ill-placed passion. Whatever time you require to bring your fancied admirer to an explanation shall be granted; but at the expiration of that term, if he is still regardless, I must absolutely insist that honest Mr. Williams shall be rewarded for his fidelity. The character which I have hitherto supported in life demands this from me, and my tenderness, as a parent, shall never influence my integrity as a man. Name then your day, let it be as distant as you think proper, and in the mean time take care to let Mr. Thornhill know the exact time on which I design delivering you up to another. If he really loves you, his own good sense will readily suggest that there is but one method alone to prevent his losing you for ever."—This proposal, which she could not avoid considering as perfectly just, was readily agreed to. She again renewed her most positive promise of marrying Mr. Williams, in case of the other's insensibility; and at the next opportunity, in Mr. Thornhill's presence, that day month was fixed upon for her nuptials with his rival.

Such vigorous proceedings seemed to redouble Mr. Thornhill's anxiety: but what Olivia really felt gave me some uneasiness. In this struggle between prudence and passion, her vivacity quite forsook her, and every opportunity of solitude was sought, and spent in tears. One week passed away; but Mr. Thornhill made no efforts to restrain her nuptials. The succeeding week he was still assiduous; but not more open. On the third he discontinued his visits entirely, and instead of my daughter testifying any impatience, as I expected, she seemed to retain a pensive tranquillity, which I looked upon as resignation. For my own part, I was now sincerely pleased with thinking that my child was going to be secured in a continuance of competence and peace, and frequently applauded her resolution, in preferring happiness to ostentation.

It was within about four days of her intended nuptials, that my little family at night were gathered round a charming fire, telling stories of the past, and laying schemes for the future. Busied in forming a thousand projects, and laughing at whatever folly came uppermost, "Well, Moses," cried I, "we shall soon, my boy, have a wedding in the family; what is your opinion of matters and things in general?"—"My opinion, father, is that all things go on very well; and I was just now thinking, that when sister Livy is married to farmer Williams, we shall then have the loan of his cyder-press and brewing tubs for nothing."—"That we shall, Moses," cried I, "and he will sing us Death and the Lady to raise our spirits into the bargain."—"He has taught that song to our Dick," cried Moses; "and I think he goes through it very prettily."—"Does he so?" cried I, "then let us have it: where's little Dick? let him up with it boldly."—"My brother Dick," cried Bill my youngest, "is just gone out with sister Livy; but Mr. Williams has taught me two songs, and I'll sing them for you, pappa. Which song do you chuse, *the dying Swan*, or the *Elegy on the death of a mad dog?*" "The elegy, child, by all means," said I; "I never heard that yet; and Deborah, my life, grief you know is dry, let us have a bottle of the best gooseberry wine, to keep up our spirits. I have wept so much at all sorts of elegies of late, that without an enlivening glass I am sure this will overcome me; and Sophy, love, take your guitar, and thrum in with the boy a little."

AN ELEGY ON THE DEATH OF A MAD DOG

Good people all, of every sort,
  Give ear unto my song;
And if you find it wond'rous short,
  It cannot hold you long.

In Isling town there was a man,
  Of whom the world might say,
That still a godly race he ran,
  Whene'er he went to pray.

A kind and gentle heart he had,
  To comfort friends and foes;
The naked every day he clad,
  When he put on his cloaths.

And in that town a dog was found,
  As many dogs there be,
Both mungrel, puppy, whelp and hound,
  And curs of low degree.

This dog and man at first were friends;
  But when a pique began,
The dog, to gain some private ends,
  Went mad and bit the man.

Around from all the neighbouring streets,
The wondering neighbours ran,
And swore the dog had lost his wits,
To bite so good a man.

The wound it seem'd both sore and sad,
To every christian eye;
And while they swore the dog was mad,
They swore the man would die.

But soon a wonder came to light,
That shew'd the rogues they lied,
The man recovered of the bite,
The dog it was that dy'd.

"A very good boy, Bill, upon my word, and an elegy that may truly be called tragical. Come, my children, here's Bill's health, and may he one day be a bishop."

"With all my heart," cried my wife; "and if he but preaches as well as he sings, I make no doubt of him. The most of his family, by the mother's side, could sing a good song: it was a common saying in our country, that the family of the Blenkinsops could never look straight before them, nor the Hugginsons blow out a candle; that there were none of the Grograms but could sing a song, or of the Marjorams but could tell a story."—"However that be," cried I, "the most vulgar ballad of them all generally pleases me better than the fine modern odes, and things that petrify us in a single stanza; productions that we at once detest and praise. Put the glass to your brother, Moses. The great fault of these elegiasts is, that they are in despair for griefs that give the sensible part of mankind very little pain. A lady loses her muff, her fan, or her lapdog, and so the silly poet runs home to versify the disaster."

"That may be the mode," cried Moses, "in sublimer compositions; but the Ranelagh songs that come down to us are perfectly familiar, and all cast in the same mold: Colin meets Dolly, and they hold a dialogue together; he gives her a ſairing to put in her hair, and she presents him with a nosegay; and then they go together to church, where they give good advice to young nymphs and swains to get married as fast as they can."

"And very good advice too," cried I, "and I am told there is not a place in the world where advice can be given with so much propriety as there; for, as it persuades us to marry, it also furnishes us with a wife; and surely that must be an excellent market, my boy, where we are told what we want, and supplied with it when wanting."

"Yes, Sir," returned Moses, "and I know but of two such markets for wives in Europe,—Ranelagh in England, and Fontarabia in Spain. The Spanish market is open once a year, but our English wives are saleable every night."

"You are right, my boy," cried his mother, "Old England is the only place in the world for husbands to get wives."—"And for wives to manage their husbands," interrupted I. "It is a proverb abroad, that if a bridge were built across the sea, all the ladies of the Continent would come over to take pattern from ours; for there are no such wives in Europe as our own. But let us have one bottle more, Deborah, my life, and Moses give us a good song. What thanks do we not owe to heaven for thus bestowing tranquillity, health, and competence. I think myself happier now than the greatest monarch upon earth. He has no such fire-side, nor such pleasant faces about it. Yes, Deborah, we are now growing old; but the evening of our life is likely to be happy. We are descended from ancestors that knew no stain, and we shall leave a good and virtuous race of children behind us. While we live they will be our support and our pleasure here, and when we die they will transmit our honour untainted to posterity. Come, my son, we wait for a song; let us have a chorus. But where is my darling Olivia? That little cherub's voice is always sweetest in the concert."—Just as I spoke Dick came running in, "O pappa, pappa, she is gone from us, she is gone from us, my sister Livy is gone from us for ever."—"Gone, child!"—"Yes, she is gone off with two gentlemen in a post chaise, and one of them kissed her, and said he would die for her; and she cried very much, and was for coming back; but he persuaded her again, and she went into the chaise, and said, O, what will my poor pappa do when he knows I am undone!"—"Now, then," cried I, "my children, go and be miserable; for we shall never enjoy one hour more. And O may heaven's everlasting fury light upon him and his! Thus to rob me of my child! And sure it will, for taking back my sweet innocent that I was leading up to heaven. Such sincerity as my child was possest of. But all our earthly happiness is now over! Go, my children, go, and be miserable and infamous; for my heart is broken within me!"—"Father," cried my son, "is this your fortitude?"—"Fortitude, child! Yes, he shall see I have fortitude! Bring me my pistols. I'll pursue the traitor. While he is on earth I'll pursue him. Old as I am, he shall find I can sting him yet. The villain! the perfidious villain."—I had by this time reached down my pistols, when my poor wife, whose passions were not so strong as mine, caught me in her arms. "My dearest, dearest husband," cried she, "the bible is the only weapon that is fit for your old hands now. Open that, my love, and read our anguish into patience, for she has vilely deceived us."—"Indeed, Sir," resumed my son, after a pause, "your rage is too violent and unbecoming. You should be my mother's comforter, and you encrease her pain. It ill suited you and your reverend character thus to curse your greatest enemy: you should not have curst him, villain as he is."—"I did not curse him, child, did I?"—"Indeed, Sir, you did; you curst him twice."—"Then may heaven forgive me and him if I did. And now, my son, I see it was more than human benevolence that first taught us to bless our enemies! Blest be his holy name for all the good he hath given, and for all that he hath taken away. But it is not, it is not a small distress that can wring tears from these old eyes, that have not wept for so many years. My Child!—To undo my darling! May confusion seize!——Heaven forgive me, what am I about to say! You may remember, my love, how good she was, and how charming; till this vile moment all her care was to make us happy. Had she but died! But she is gone, the honour of our family contaminated, and I must look out for happiness in other worlds than here. But my child, you saw them go off: perhaps he forced her away? If he forced her, she may yet be innocent."—"Ah no, Sir!" cried the child; "he only kissed her, and called her his angel, and she wept very much, and leaned upon his arm, and they drove off very fast."—"She's an ungrateful creature," cried my wife, who could scarce speak for weeping, "to use us thus. She never had the least constraint put upon her affections. The vile strumpet has basely deserted her parents without any provocation, thus to bring your grey hairs to the grave, and I must shortly follow."

In this manner that night, the first of our real misfortunes, was spent in the bitterness of complaint, and ill supported sallies of enthusiasm. I determined, however, to find out our betrayer, wherever he was, and reproach his baseness. The next morning we missed our wretched child at breakfast, where she used to give life and chearfulness to us all. My wife, as before, attempted to ease her heart by reproaches. "Never," cried she, "shall that vilest stain of our family again darken those harmless doors. I will never call her daughter more. No, let the strumpet live with her vile seducer: she may bring us to shame, but she shall never more deceive us."

"Wife," said I, "do not talk thus hardly: my detestation of her guilt is as great as yours; but ever shall this house and this heart be open to a poor returning repentant sinner. The sooner she returns from her transgression, the more welcome shall she be to me. For the first time the very best may err; art may persuade, and novelty spread out its charm. The first fault is the child of simplicity; but every other the offspring of guilt. Yes, the wretched creature shall be welcome to this heart and this house, tho' stained with ten thousand vices. I will again hearken to the music of her voice, again will I hang fondly on her bosom, if I find but repentance there. My son, bring hither my bible and my staff; I will pursue her, wherever she is, and tho' I cannot save her from shame, I may prevent the continuance of iniquity."

CHAPTER XVIII

The pursuit of a father to reclaim a lost child to virtue.

THO' the child could not describe the gentleman's person who handed his sister into the post chaise, yet my suspicions fell entirely upon our young landlord, whose character for such intrigues was but too well known. I therefore directed my steps towards Thornhill-castle, resolving to upbraid him, and, if possible, to bring back my daughter: but before I had reached his seat, I was met by one of my parishioners, who said he saw a young lady resembling my daughter in a post chaise with a gentleman, whom, by the description, I could only guess to be Mr. Burchell, and that they drove very fast. This information, however, did by no means satisfy me. I therefore went to the young 'Squire's, and though it was yet early, insisted upon seeing him immediately: he soon appeared with the most open familiar air, and seemed perfectly amazed at my daughter's elopement, protesting upon his honour that he was quite a stranger to it. I now therefore condemned my former suspicions, and could turn them only on Mr. Burchell, who I recollected had of late several private conferences with her: but the appearance of another witness left me no room to doubt his villany, who averred, that he and my daughter were actually gone towards the wells, about thirty miles off, where there was a great deal of company. Being driven to that state of mind in which we are more ready to act precipitately than to reason right, I never debated with myself whether these accounts might not have been given by persons purposely placed in my way, to mislead me, but resolved to pursue my daughter and her fancied deluder thither. I walked along with earnestness, and enquired of several by the way; but received no accounts, till entering the town, I was met by a person on horseback, whom I remembered to have seen at the 'Squire's, and he assured me, that if I followed them to the races, which were but thirty miles farther, I might depend upon overtaking them; for he had seen them dance there the night before, and the whole assembly seemed charmed with my daughter's performance. Early the next day I walked forward to the races, and about four in the afternoon I came upon the course. The company made a very brilliant appearance, all earnestly employed in one pursuit, that of pleasure; how different from mine, that of reclaiming a lost child to virtue! I thought I perceived Mr. Burchell at some distance from me; but, as if he dreaded an interview, upon my approaching him, he mixed among a crowd, and I saw him no more. I now reflected that it would be to no purpose to continue my pursuit farther, and resolved to return home to an innocent family, who wanted my assistance. But the agitations of my mind, and the fatigue I had undergone, threw me into a fever, the symptoms of which I perceived before I came off the course. This was another unexpected stroke, as I was more than seventy miles distant from home: however, I retired to a little ale-house by the road-side, and in this place, the usual retreat of indigence and frugality, I laid me down patiently to wait the issue of my disorder. I languished here for near three weeks; but at last my constitution prevailed, though I was unprovided with money to defray the expenses of my entertainment. It is possible the anxiety from this last circumstance alone might have brought on a relapse, had I not been supplied by a traveller, who stopt to take a cursory refreshment. This person was no other than the philanthropic book-seller in St. Paul's Church-yard,[1] who has written so many little books for children: he called himself their friend; but he was the friend of all mankind. He was no sooner alighted, but he was in haste to be gone; for he was ever on business of the utmost importance, and was at that time actually compiling materials for the history of one Mr. Thomas Trip.[2] I immediately recollected this good-natured man's red pimpled face; for he had published for me against the Deuterogamists of the age, and from him I borrowed a few pieces to be paid at my return. Leaving the inn, therefore, as I was yet but weak, I resolved to return home by easy journies of ten miles a day. My health and usual tranquillity were almost restored, and I now condemned that pride which had made me refractory to the hand of correction. Man little knows what calamities are beyond his patience to bear till he tries them; as in ascending the heights of ambition, which look bright from below, every step we rise shews us some new and gloomy prospect of hidden disappointment: so in our descent from the summits of pleasure, though the vale of misery below may appear at first dark and gloomy, yet the busy mind, still attentive to its own amusement, finds as we descend something to flatter and to please. Still as we approach, the darkest objects appear to brighten, and the mental eye becomes adapted to its gloomy situation.

I now proceeded forward, and had walked about two hours, when I perceived what appeared at a distance like a waggon, which I was resolved to overtake; but when I came up with it, found it to be a strolling company's cart, that was carrying their scenes and other theatrical furniture to the next village, where they were to exhibit. The cart was attended only by

[1] [John Newbery, the father of Francis Newbery who published *The Vicar of Wakefield.*]

[2] [Sometimes attributed to Goldsmith.]

the person who drove it, and one of the company, as the rest of the players were to follow the ensuing day. Good company upon the road, says the proverb, is the shortest cut, I therefore entered into conversation with the poor player; and as I once had some theatrical powers myself, I disserted on such topics with my usual freedom: but as I was pretty much unacquainted with the present state of the stage, I demanded who were the present theatrical writers in vogue, who the Drydens and Otways of the day.—"I fancy, Sir," cried the player, "few of our modern dramatists would think themselves much honoured by being compared to the writers you mention. Dryden and Row's manner, Sir, are quite out of fashion; our taste has gone back a whole century, Fletcher, Ben Johnson, and all the plays of Shakespear, are the only things that go down."—"How," cried I, "is it possible the present age can be pleased with that antiquated dialect, that obsolete humour, those over-charged characters, which abound in the works you mention?"—"Sir," returned my companion, "the public think nothing about dialect, or humour, or character; for that is none of their business, they only go to be amused, and find themselves happy when they can enjoy a pantomime, under the sanction of Johnson's or Shakespear's name."—"So then, I suppose," cried I, "that our modern dramatists are rather imitators of Shakespear than of nature."—"To say the truth," returned my companion, "I don't know that they imitate any thing at all; nor indeed does the public require it of them: it is not the composition of the piece, but the number of starts and attitudes that may be introduced into it that elicits applause. I have known a piece, with not one jest in the whole, shrugged into popularity, and another saved by the poet's throwing in a fit of the gripes. No, Sir, the works of Congreve and Farquhar have too much wit in them for the present taste; our modern dialect is much more natural."

By this time the equipage of the strolling company was

arrived at the village, which, it seems, had been apprised of our approach, and was come out to gaze at us; for my companion observed, that strollers always have more spectators without doors than within. I did not consider the impropriety of my being in such company till I saw a mob gather about me. I therefore took shelter, as fast as possible, in the first alehouse that offered, and being shewn into the common room, was accosted by a very well-dressed gentleman, who demanded whether I was the real chaplain of the company, or whether it was only to be my masquerade character in the play. Upon informing him of the truth, and that I did not belong in any sort to the company, he was condescending enough to desire me and the player to partake in a bowl of punch, over which he discussed modern politics with great earnestness and interest. I set him down in my own mind for nothing less than a parliament-man at least; but was almost confirmed in my conjectures, when upon asking what there was in the house for supper, he insisted that the player and I should sup with him at his house, with which request, after some entreaties, we were prevailed on to comply.

CHAPTER XIX

The description of a person discontented with the present government, and apprehensive of the loss of our liberties.

THE house where we were to be entertained, lying at a small distance from the village, our inviter observed, that as the coach was not ready, he would conduct us on foot, and we soon arrived at one of the most magnificent mansions I had seen in that part of the country. The apartment into which we were shewn was perfectly elegant and modern; he went to give orders for supper, while the player, with a wink, observed that we were perfectly in luck. Our entertainer soon returned, an elegant supper was brought in, two or three ladies in easy dishabile were introduced, and the conversation began with some sprightliness. Politics, however, were the subject on which our entertainer chiefly expatiated; for he asserted that liberty was at once his boast and his terror. After the cloth was removed, he asked me if I had seen the last Monitor, to which replying in the negative, "What, nor the Auditor, I suppose?" cried he. "Neither, Sir," returned I. "That's strange, very strange," replied my entertainer. "Now, I read all the politics that come out. The Daily, the Public, the Ledger, the Chronicle, the London Evening, the Whitehall Evening, the seventeen magazines, and the two Reviews; and though they hate each other, I love them all. Liberty, Sir, liberty is the Briton's boast, and by all my coal mines in Cornwall, I reverence its guardians." "Then it is to be hoped," cried I, "you reverence the king." "Yes," returned my entertainer, "when he does what we would have him; but if he goes on as he has done of late, I'll never trouble myself more with his matters. I say nothing. I think only. I could have directed some things better. I don't think there has been a sufficient number of advisers: he should advise with every person willing to give him advice, and then we should have things done in anotherguess manner."

"I wish," cried I, "that such intruding advisers were fixed in the pillory. It should be the duty of honest men to assist the weaker side of our constitution, that sacred power that has for some years been every day declining, and losing its due share of influence in the state. But these ignorants still continue the same cry of liberty, and if they have any weight, basely throw it into the subsiding scale."

"How," cried one of the ladies, "do I live to see one so base, so sordid, as to be an enemy to liberty, and a defender of tyrants? Liberty, that sacred gift of heaven, that glorious privilege of Britons!"

"Can it be possible," cried our entertainer, "that there should be any found at present advocates for slavery? Any who are for meanly giving up the privileges of Britons? Can any, Sir, be so abject?"

"No, Sir," replied I, "I am for liberty, that attribute of Gods! Glorious liberty! that theme of modern declamation. I would have all men kings. I would be a king myself. We have all naturally an equal right to the throne: we are all originally equal. This is my opinion, and was once the opinion of a set of honest men who were called Levellers. They tried to erect themselves into a community, where all should be equally free. But, alas! it would never answer; for there were some among them stronger, and some more cunning than others, and these became masters of the rest; for as sure as your groom rides your horses, because he is a cunninger animal than they, so surely will the animal that is cunninger or stronger than he, sit upon his shoulders in turn. Since then it is entailed upon humanity to submit, and some are born to command, and others to obey, the question is, as there must be tyrants, whether it is better to have them in the same house with us, or in the same village, or still farther off, in the metropolis. Now, Sir, for my own part, as I naturally hate the face of a tyrant, the farther off he is removed from me, the better pleased am I. The generality of mankind also are of my way of thinking, and have unanimously created one king, whose election at once diminishes the number of tyrants, and puts tyranny at the greatest distance from the greatest number of people. Now the great who were tyrants themselves before the election of one tyrant, are naturally averse to a power raised over them, and whose weight must ever lean heaviest on the subordinate orders. It is the interest of the great, therefore, to diminish kingly power as much as possible; because whatever they take from that, is naturally restored to themselves; and all they have to do in the state, is to undermine the single tyrant, by which they resume their primæval authority. Now the state may be so circumstanced, or its laws may be so disposed, or its men of opulence so minded, as all to conspire in carrying on this business of undermining monarchy. For, in the first place, if the circumstances of our state be such, as to favour the accumulation of wealth, and make the opulent still more rich, this will encrease their ambition. An accumulation of wealth, however, must necessarily be the consequence, when as at present more riches flow in from external commerce than arise from internal industry: for external commerce can only be managed to advantage by the rich, and they have also at the same time all the emoluments arising from internal industry: so that the rich, with us, have two sources of wealth, whereas the poor have but one. For this reason, wealth, in all commercial states, is found to accumulate, and all such have hitherto in time become aristocratical. Again, the very laws also of this country may contribute to the accumulation of wealth; as when by their means the natural ties that bind the rich and poor together are broken, and it is ordained, that the rich shall only marry with the rich; or when the learned are held unqualified to serve their country as counsellors merely from a defect of opulence, and wealth is thus made the object of a wise man's ambition; by these means, I say, and such means as these, riches will accumulate. Now the possessor of accumulated wealth, when furnished with the necessaries and pleasures of life, has no other method to employ the superfluity of his fortune but in purchasing power. That is, differently speaking, in making dependants, by purchasing the liberty of the needy or the venal, of men who are willing to bear the mortification of contiguous tyranny for bread. Thus each very opulent man generally gathers round him a circle of the poorest of the people; and the polity abounding in accumulated wealth, may be compared to a Cartesian system, each orb with a vortex of its own. Those, however, who are willing to move in a great man's vortex, are only such as must be slaves, the rabble of mankind, whose souls and whose education are adapted to servitude, and who know nothing of liberty except the name.

But there must still be a large number of the people without the sphere of the opulent man's influence, namely, that order of men which subsists between the very rich and the very rabble; those men who are possest of too large fortunes to submit to the neighbouring man in power, and yet are too poor to set up for tyranny themselves. In this middle order of mankind are generally to be found all the arts, wisdom, and virtues of society. This order alone is known to be the true preserver of freedom, and may be called the People. Now it may happen that this middle order of mankind may lose all its influence in a state, and its voice be in a manner drowned in that of the rabble: for if the fortune sufficient for qualifying a person at present to give his voice in state affairs, be ten times less than was judged sufficient upon forming the constitution, it is evident that great numbers of the rabble will thus be introduced into the political system, and they ever moving in the vortex of the great, will follow where greatness shall direct. In such a state, therefore, all that the middle order has left, is to preserve the prerogative and privileges of the one principal governor with the most sacred circumspection. For he divides the power of the rich, and calls off the great from falling with tenfold weight on the middle order placed beneath them. The middle order may be compared to a town of which the opulent are forming the siege, and which the governor from without is hastening the relief. While the besiegers are in dread of an enemy over them, it is but natural to offer the townsmen the most specious terms; to flatter them with sounds, and amuse them with privileges; but if they once defeat the governor from behind, the walls of the town will be but a small defence to its inhabitants. What they may then expect, may be seen by turning our eyes to Holland, Genoa, or Venice where the laws govern the poor, and the rich govern the law. I am then for, and would die for, monarchy, sacred monarchy; for if there be any thing sacred amongst men, it must be the anointed SOVEREIGN of his people, and every diminution of his power in war, or in peace, is an infringement upon the real liberties of the subject. The sounds of liberty, patriotism, and Britons, have already done *much*, it is to be hoped that the true sons of freedom will prevent their ever doing more. I have known many of those pretended champions for liberty in my time, yet do I not remember one that was not in his heart and in his family a tyrant."

My warmth I found had lengthened this harangue beyond the rules of good breeding: but the impatience of my entertainer, who often strove to interrupt it, could be restrained no longer. "What," cried he, "then I have been all this while entertaining a Jesuit in parson's cloaths; but by all the coal mines of Cornwall, out he shall pack, if my name be Wilkinson." I now found I had gone too far, and asked pardon for the warmth with which I had spoken. "Pardon," returned he in a fury; "I think such principles demand ten thousand pardons. What, give up liberty, property, and, as the Gazetteer says, lie down to be saddled with wooden shoes! Sir, I insist upon your marching out of this house immediately, to prevent worse consequences, Sir, I insist upon it." I was going to repeat my remonstrances; but just then we heard a footman's rap at the door, and the two ladies cried out, "As sure as death there is our master and mistress come home." It seems my entertainer was all this while only the butler, who, in his master's absence, had a mind to cut a figure, and be for a while the gentleman himself; and, to say the truth, he talked politics as well as most country gentlemen do. But nothing could now exceed my confusion upon seeing the gentleman, and his lady enter, nor was their surprize, at finding such company and good cheer, less than ours. "Gentlemen," cried the real master of the house, to me and my companion, "my wife and I are your most humble servants; but I protest this is so unexpected a favour, that we almost sink under the obligation." However unexpected our company might be to them, theirs, I am sure, was still more so to us, and I was struck dumb with the apprehensions of my own absurdity, when whom should I next see enter the room but my dear Miss Arabella Wilmot, who was formerly designed to be married to my son George; but whose match was broken off, as already related. As soon as she saw me, she flew to my arms with the utmost joy. "My dear sir," cried she, "to what happy accident is it that we owe so unexpected a visit? I am sure my uncle and aunt will be in raptures when they find they have the good Dr. Primrose for their guest." Upon hearing my name, the old gentleman and lady very politely stepped up, and welcomed me with most cordial hospitality. Nor could they forbear smiling upon being informed of the nature of my present visit: but the unfortunate butler, whom they at first seemed disposed to turn away, was, at my intercession, forgiven.

Mr. Arnold and his lady, to whom the house belonged now, insisted upon having the pleasure of my stay for some days, and as their niece, my charming pupil, whose mind, in some measure, had been formed under my own instructions, joined in their entreaties, I complied. That night I was shewn to a magnificent chamber, and the next morning early miss Wilmot desired to walk with me in the garden, which was decorated in the modern manner. After some time spent in pointing out the beauties of the place, she enquired, with seeming unconcern, when last I had heard from my son George. "Alas! Madam," cried I, "he has now been near three years absent, without ever writing to his friends or me. Where he is I know not; perhaps I shall never see him or happiness more. No, my dear Madam, we shall never more see such pleasing hours as were once spent by our fire-side at Wakefield. My little family are now dispersing very fast, and poverty has brought not only want, but infamy upon us." The good-natured girl let fall a tear at this account; but as I saw her possessed of too much sensibility, I forbore a more minute detail of our sufferings. It was, however, some consolation to me to find that time had made no alteration in her affections, and that she had rejected several matches that had been made her since our leaving her part of the country. She led me round all the extensive improvements of the place, pointing to the several walks and arbours, and at the same time catching from every object a hint for some new question relative to my son. In this manner we spent the forenoon, till the bell summoned us in to dinner, where we found the manager of the strolling company that I mentioned before, who was come to dispose of tickets for the Fair Penitent,[1] which was to be acted that evening, the part of Horatio by a young gentleman who had never appeared on any stage. He seemed to be very warm in the praises of the new performer, and averred, that he never saw any who bid so fair for excellence. Acting, he observed, was not learned in a day; "But this gentleman," continued he, "seems born to tread the stage. His voice, his figure, and attitudes, are all admirable. We caught him up accidentally in our journey down." This account, in some measure, excited our curiosity, and, at the entreaty of the ladies, I was prevailed upon to accompany them to the play-house, which was no other than a barn. As the company with which I went was incontestably the chief of the place, we were received with the greatest respect, and placed in the front seat of the theatre; where we sate for some time with no small impatience to see Horatio make his appearance. The new performer advanced at last, and let parents think of my sensations by their own, when I found it was my unfortunate son. He was going to begin, when, turning his eyes upon the audience, he perceived Miss Wilmot and me, and stood at once speechless and immoveable. The actors behind the scene, who ascribed this pause to his natural timidity, attempted to encourage him; but instead of going on, he burst into a flood of tears, and retired off the stage. I don't know what were my feelings on this occasion; for they succeeded with too much rapidity for description: but I was soon awaked from this disagreeable

[1] [A tragedy by Nicholas Rowe.]

reverie by Miss Wilmot, who, pale and with a trembling voice, desired me to conduct her back to her uncle's. When got home, Mr. Arnold, who was as yet a stranger to our extraordinary behaviour, being informed that the new performer was my son, sent his coach, and an invitation, for him; and as he persisted in his refusal to appear again upon the stage, the players put another in his place, and we soon had him with us. Mr. Arnold gave him the kindest reception, and I received him with my usual transport; for I could never counterfeit false resentment. Miss Wilmot's reception was mixed with seeming neglect, and yet I could perceive she acted a studied part. The tumult in her mind seemed not yet abated; she said twenty giddy things that looked like joy, and then laughed loud at her own want of meaning. At intervals she would take a sly peep at the glass, as if happy in the consciousness of unresisted beauty, and often would ask questions, without giving any manner of attention to the answers.

VOLUME II

CHAPTER I

The history of a philosophic vagabond, pursuing novelty, but losing content.

After we had supped, Mrs. Arnold politely offered to send a couple of her footmen for my son's baggage, which he at first seemed to decline; but upon her pressing the request, he was obliged to inform her, that a stick and wallet were all the movable things upon this earth that he could boast of. "Why, aye my son," cried I, "you left me but poor, and poor I find you are come back; and yet I make no doubt you have seen a great deal of the world."—"Yes, Sir," replied my son, "but travelling after fortune, is not the way to secure her; and, indeed, of late, I have desisted from the pursuit."—"I fancy, Sir," cried Mrs. Arnold, "that the account of your adventures would be amusing: the first part of them I have often heard from my niece; but could the company prevail for the rest, it would be an additional obligation."—"Madam," replied my son, "I promise you the pleasure you have in hearing, will not be half so great as my vanity in repeating them, and yet in the whole narrative I can scarce promise you one adventure, as my account is rather of what I saw than what I did. The first misfortune of my life, which you all know, was great; but though it distrest, it could not sink me. No person ever had a better knack at hoping than I. The less kind I found fortune at one time, the more I expected from her another, and being now at the bottom of her wheel, every new revolution might lift, but could not depress me. I proceeded, therefore, towards London in a fine morning, no way uneasy about to-morrow, but chearful as the birds that carolled by the road, and comforted myself with reflecting, that London was the mart where abilities of every kind were sure of meeting distinction and reward.

"Upon my arrival in town, Sir, my first care was to deliver your letter of recommendation to our cousin, who was himself in little better circumstances than I. My first scheme, you know, Sir, was to be usher at an academy,[1] and I asked his advice on the affair. Our cousin received the proposal with a true Sardonic grin. Aye, cried he, this is indeed a very pretty career, that has been chalked out for you. I have been an usher at a boarding school myself; and may I die by an anodine necklace,[2] but I had rather be an under turnkey in Newgate. I was up early and late: I was brow-beat by the master, hated for my ugly face by the mistress, worried by the boys within, and never permitted to stir out to meet civility abroad. But are you sure you are fit for a school? Let me examine you a little. Have you been bred apprentice to the business? No. Then you won't do for a school. Can you dress the boys hair? No. Then you won't do for a school. Have you had the small-pox? No. Then you won't do for a school. Can you lie three in a bed? No. Then you will never do for a school. Have you got a good stomach? Yes. Then you will by no means do for a school. No, Sir, if you are for a genteel easy profession, bind yourself seven years an apprentice to turn a cutler's wheel; but avoid a school by any means. Yet come, continued he, I see you are a lad of spirit and some learning, what do you think of commencing author, like me? You have read in books, no doubt, of men of genius starving at the trade: At present I'll shew you forty very dull fellows about town that live by it in opulence. All honest joggtrot men, who go on smoothly and dully, and write history and politics, and are praised: men, Sir, who, had they been bred coblers, would all their lives have only mended shoes, but never made them.

"Finding that there was no great degree of gentility affixed to the character of an usher, I resolved to accept his proposal; and having the highest respect for literature, hailed the antiqua mater of Grubstreet with reverence. I thought it my glory to pursue a track which Dryden and Otway trod before me. I considered the goddess of this region as the parent

[1] As Goldsmith had been. Much of this chapter is autobiographical.]
[2] [*i.e.*, a hangman's halter.]

of excellence; and however an intercourse with the world might give us good sense, the poverty she granted I supposed to be the nurse of genius! Big with these reflections, I sate down, and finding that the best things remained to be said on the wrong side, I resolved to write a book that should be wholly new. I therefore drest up three paradoxes with some ingenuity. They were false, indeed, but they were new. The jewels of truth have been so often imported by others, that nothing was left for me to import but some splendid things that at a distance looked every bit as well. Witness you powers what fancied importance sate perched upon my quill while I was writing. The whole learned world, I made no doubt, would rise to oppose my systems; but then I was prepared to oppose the whole learned world. Like the porcupine I sate self collected, with a quill pointed against every opposer."

"Well said, my boy," cried I, "and what subject did you treat upon? I hope you did not pass over the importance of Monogamy. But I interrupt, go on; you published your paradoxes; well, and what did the learned world say to your paradoxes?"

"Sir," replied my son, "the learned world said nothing to my paradoxes; nothing at all, Sir. Every man of them was employed in praising his friends and himself, or condemning his enemies; and unfortunately, as I had neither, I suffered the cruellest mortification, neglect.

"As I was meditating one day in a coffee-house on the fate of my paradoxes, a little man happening to enter the room, placed himself in the box before me, and after some preliminary discourse, finding me to be a scholar, drew out a bundle of proposals, begging me to subscribe to a new edition he was going to give to the world of Propertius, with notes. This demand necessarily produced a reply that I had no money; and that concession led him to enquire into the nature of my expectations. Finding that my expectations were just as great as my purse, I see, cried he, you are unacquainted with the town. I'll teach you a part of it. Look at these proposals, upon these very proposals I have subsisted very comfortably for twelve years. The moment a nobleman returns from his travels, a Creolian arrives from Jamaica, or a dowager from her country seat, I strike for a subscripton. I first besiege their hearts with flattery, and then pour in my proposals at the breach. If they subscribe readily the first time, I renew my request to beg a dedication fee. If they let me have that, I smite them once more for engraving their coat of arms at the top. Thus, continued he, I live by vanity, and laugh at it. But between ourselves, I am now too well known, I should be glad to borrow your face a bit: a nobleman of distinction has just returned from Italy; my face is familiar to his porter; but if you bring this copy of verses, my life for it you succeed, and we divide the spoil."

"Bless us, George," cried I, "and is this the employment of poets now! Do men of their exalted talents thus stoop to beggary! Can they so far disgrace their calling, as to make a vile traffic of praise for bread?"

"O no, Sir," returned he, "a true poet can never be so base; for wherever there is genius there is pride. The creatures I now describe are only beggars in rhyme. The real poet, as he braves every hardship for fame, so he is equally a coward to contempt, and none but those who are unworthy protection condescend to solicit it.

"Having a mind too proud to stoop to such indignities, and yet a fortune too humble to hazard a second attempt for fame, I was now obliged to take a middle course, and write for bread. But I was unqualified for a profession where mere industry alone was to ensure success. I could not suppress my lurking passion for applause; but usually consumed that time in efforts after excellence which takes up but little room, when it should have been more advantageously employed in the diffusive productions of fruitful mediocrity. My little piece would therefore come forth in the mist of periodical publication, unnoticed and unknown. The public were more importantly employed than to observe the easy simplicity of my style, or the harmony of my periods. Sheet after sheet was thrown off to oblivion. My essays were buried among the essays upon liberty, eastern tales, and cures for the bite of a mad dog; while Philautos, Philalethes, Phileleutheros and Philanthropos, all wrote better, because they wrote faster, than I.

"Now, therefore, I began to associate with none but disappointed authors, like myself, who praised, deplored, and despised each other. The satisfaction we found in every celebrated writer's attempts, was inversely as their merits. I found that no genius in another could please me. My unfortunate paradoxes had entirely dried up that source of comfort. I could neither read nor write with satisfaction; for excellence in another was my aversion, and writing was my trade.

"In the midst of these gloomy reflections, as I was one day sitting on a bench in St. James's Park, a young gentleman of distinction, who had been my intimate acquaintance at the university, approached me. We saluted each other with some hesitation, he almost ashamed of being known to one who made so shabby an appearance, and I afraid of a repulse. But my suspicions soon vanished; for Ned Thornhill was at the bottom a very good natured fellow."

"What did you say, George?" interrupted I. "Thornhill, was not that his name? It can certainly be no other than my landlord."—"Bless me," cried Mrs. Arnold, "is Mr. Thornhill so near a neighbour of yours? He has long been a friend in our family, and we expect a visit from him shortly."

"My friend's first care," continued my son, "was to alter my appearance by a very fine suit of his own cloaths, and then I was admitted to his table upon the footing of half friend, half underling. My business was to attend him at auctions, to put him in spirits when he sate for his picture, to take the left hand in his chariot when not filled by another, and to assist at tattering a kip,[1] as the phrase was, when he had a mind for a frolic. Besides this, I had twenty other little employments in the family. I was to do many small things without bidding; to carry the cork screw; to stand godfather to all the butler's children; to sing when I was bid; to be never out of humour; always to be humble, and, if I could, to be very happy.

"In this honourable post, however, I was not without a rival. A captain of marines, who was formed for the place by nature, opposed me in my patron's affections. His mother had been laundress to a man of quality, and thus he early acquired a taste for pimping and pedigree. As this gentleman made it the study of his life to be acquainted with lords, though he was dismissed from several for his stupidity; yet he found many of them who were as dull as himself, that permitted his assiduities. As flattery was his trade, he practised it with the easiest address imaginable; but it came aukward and stiff from me; and as every day my patron's desire of flattery encreased, so every hour being better acquainted with his defects, I became more unwilling to give it. Thus I was once more fairly going to give up the field to the captain, when my friend found occasion for my assistance. This was nothing less than to fight a duel for him, with a gentleman whose sister it was pretended he had used ill. I readily complied with his request, and though I see you are displeased at my conduct, yet as it was a debt indispensably due to friendship, I could not refuse. I undertook the affair, disarmed my antagonist, and soon after had the pleasure of finding that the lady was only a woman of the town, and the fellow her bully and a sharper. This piece of service was repaid with the warmest professions of gratitude; but as my friend was to leave town in a few days, he knew no other method of serving me, but by recommending me to his uncle Sir William Thornhill, and another nobleman of great distinction, who enjoyed a post under the government.

[1] [Beating up a brothel.]

When he was gone, my first care was to carry his recommendatory letter to his uncle, a man whose character for every virtue was universal, yet just. I was received by his servants with the most hospitable smiles; for the looks of the domestics ever transmit their master's benevolence. Being shewn into a grand apartment, where Sir William soon came to me, I delivered my message and letter, which he read, and after pausing some minutes, Pray, Sir, cried he, inform me what you have done for my kinsman, to deserve this warm recommendation? But I suppose, Sir, I guess your merits, you have fought for him; and so you would expect a reward from me, for being the instrument of his vices. I wish, sincerely wish, that my present refusal may be some punishment for your guilt; but still more, that it may be some inducement to your repentance.—The severity of this rebuke I bore patiently, because I knew it was just. My whole expectations now, therefore, lay in my letter to the great man. As the doors of the nobility are almost ever beset with beggars, all ready to thrust in some sly petition, I found it no easy matter to gain admittance. However, after bribing the servants with half my worldly fortune, I was at last shewn into a spacious apartment, my letter being previously sent up for his lordship's inspection. During this anxious interval I had full time to look round me. Every thing was grand, and of happy contrivance; the paintings, the furniture, the gildings, petrified me with awe, and raised my idea of the owner. Ah, thought I to myself, how very great must the possessor of all these things be, who carries in his head the business of the state, and whose house displays half the wealth of a kingdom: sure his genius must be unfathomable! During these awful reflections I heard a step come heavily forward. Ah, this is the great man himself! No, it was only a chambermaid. Another foot was heard soon after. This must be He! No, it was only the great man's valet de chambre. At last his lordship actually made his appearance. Are you, cried he, the bearer of this here letter? I answered with a bow. I learn by this, continued he, as how that—— But just at that instant a servant delivered him a card, and without taking farther notice, he went out of the room, and left me to digest my own happiness at leisure. I saw no more of him, till told by a footman that his lordship was going to his coach at the door. Down I immediately followed, and joined my voice to that of three or four more, who came, like me, to petition for favours. His lordship, however, went too fast for us, and was gaining his Chariot door with large strides, when I hallowed out to know if I was to have any reply. He was by this time got in, and muttered an answer, half of which only I heard, the other half was lost in the rattling of his chariot wheels. I stood for some time with my neck stretched out, in the posture of one that was listening to catch the glorious sounds, till looking round me, I found myself alone at his lordship's gate.

"My patience," continued my son, "was now quite exhausted: stung with the thousand indignities I had met with, I was willing to cast myself away, and only wanted the gulph to receive me. I regarded myself as one of those vile things that nature designed should be thrown by into her lumber room, there to perish in obscurity. I had still, however, half a guinea left, and of that I thought nature herself should not deprive me: but in order to be sure of this, I was resolved to go instantly and spend it while I had it, and then trust to occurrences for the rest. As I was going along with this resolution, it happened that Mr. Crispe's office seemed invitingly open, to give me a welcome reception. In this office Mr. Crispe kindly offers all his majesty's subjects a generous promise of 30 l. a year, for which promise all they give in return is their liberty for life, and permission to let him transport them to America as slaves. I was happy at finding a place where I could lose my fears in desperation, and entered this cell, for it had the appearance of one, with the devotion of a monastic. Here I found a number of poor creatures, all in circumstances like myself, expecting the arrival of Mr. Crispe, presenting a true epitome of English impatience. Each untractable soul at variance with fortune, wreaked her injuries on their own hearts: but Mr. Crispe at last came down, and all our murmurs were hushed. He deigned to regard me with an air of peculiar approbation, and indeed he was the first man who for a month past had talked to me with smiles. After a few questions, he found I was fit for every thing in the world. He paused a while upon the properest means of providing for me, and slapping his forehead, as if he had found it, assured me, that there was at that time an embassy talked of from the synod of Pensylvania to the Chickasaw Indians, and that he would use his interest to get me made secretary. I knew in my own heart that the fellow lied, and yet his promise gave me pleasure, there was something so magnificent in the sound. I fairly, therefore, divided my half-guinea, one-half of which went to be added to his thirty thousand pound, and with the other half I resolved to go to the next tavern, to be there more happy than he.

"As I was going out with that resolution, I was met at the door by the captain of a ship, with whom I had formerly some little acquaintance, and he agreed to be my companion over a bowl of punch. As I never chose to make a secret of my circumstances, he assured me that I was upon the very point of ruin, in listening to the office-keeper's promises; for that he only designed to sell me to the plantations. But, continued he, I fancy you might, by a much shorter voyage, be very easily put into a genteel way of bread. Take my advice. My ship sails to-morrow for Amsterdam; what if you go in her as a passenger? The moment you land all you have to do is to teach the Dutchmen English, and I'll warrant you'll get pupils and money enough. I suppose you understand English, added he, by this time, or the deuce is in it. I confidently assured him of that; but expressed a doubt whether the Dutch would be willing to learn English. He affirmed with an oath that they were fond of it to distraction; and upon that affirmation I agreed with his proposal, and embarked the next day to teach the Dutch English in Holland. The wind was fair, our voyage short, and after having paid my passage with half my moveables, I found myself, fallen as from the skies, a stranger in one of the principal streets of Amsterdam. In this situation I was unwilling to let any time pass unemployed in teaching. I addressed myself therefore to two or three of those I met, whose appearance seemed most promising; but it was impossible to make ourselves mutually understood. It was not till this very moment I recollected, that in order to teach the Dutchmen English, it was necessary that they should first teach me Dutch. How I came to overlook so obvious an objection, is to me amazing; but certain it is I overlooked it.

"This scheme thus blown up, I had some thoughts of fairly shipping back to England again; but happening into company with an Irish student, who was returning from Louvain, our conversation turning upon topics of literature, (for by the way it may be observed, that I always forgot the meanness of my circumstances when I could converse upon such subjects) from him I learned that there were not two men in his whole university who understood Greek. This amazed me. I instantly resolved to travel to Louvain, and there live by teaching Greek; and in this design I was heartened by my brother student, who threw out some hints that a fortune might be got by it.

"I set boldly forward the next morning. Every day lessened the burthen of my moveables, like Æsop and his basket of bread; for I paid them for my lodgings to the Dutch as I travelled on. When I came to Louvain, I was resolved not to go sneaking to the lower professors, but openly tendered my talents to the principal himself. I went, had admittance, and offered him my service as a master of the Greek language, which I had been told was a desideratum in this university. The principal seemed at first to doubt of my abilities; but of these I offered to convince him, by turning a part of any Greek author he should fix upon into Latin. Finding me perfectly earnest in my proposal, he addressed me thus: You see me, young man, continued he, I never learned Greek, and I don't find that I have ever missed it. I have had a doctor's cap and gown without Greek: I have ten thousand florins a year without Greek; I eat heartily without Greek; and in short, continued he, as I don't know Greek, I do not believe there is any good in it.

"I was now too far from home to think of returning; so I resolved to go forward. I had some knowledge of music, with a tolerable voice, and now turned what was once my amusement into a present means of subsistence. I passed among the harmless peasants of Flanders, and among such of the French as were poor enough to be very merry; for I ever found them sprightly in proportion to their wants. Whenever I approached a peasant's house, towards night-fall, I played one of my most merry tunes, and that procured me not only a lodging, but subsistence for the next day. I once or twice attempted to play for people of fashion; but they always thought my performance odious, and never rewarded me even with a trifle. This was to me the more extraordinary, as whenever I used in better days to play for company, when playing was my amusement, my music never failed to throw them into raptures, and the ladies especially; but as it was now my only means, it was received with contempt; a proof how ready the world is to under rate those talents by which a man is supported.

"In this manner, I proceeded to Paris, with no design but just to look about me, and then to go forward. The people of Paris are much fonder of strangers that have money, than of those that have wit. As I could not boast much of either, I was no great favourite. After walking about the town four or five days, and seeing the outsides of the best houses, I was preparing to leave this retreat of venal hospitality, when passing through one of the principal streets, whom should I meet but our cousin, to whom you first recommended me. This meeting was very agreeable to me, and I believe not displeasing to him. He enquired into the nature of my journey to Paris, and informed me of his own business there, which was to collect pictures, medals, intaglios, and antiques of all kinds, for a gentleman in London, who had just stept into taste and a large fortune. I was the more surprised at seeing our cousin pitched upon for this office, as he himself had often assured me he knew nothing of the matter. Upon asking how he had been taught the art of a connoscento so very suddenly, he assured me that nothing was more easy. The whole secret consisted in a strict adherence to two rules: the one always to observe, that the picture might have been better if the painter had taken more pains; and the other, to praise the works of Pietro Perugino. But, says he, as I once taught you how to be an author in London, I'll now undertake to instruct you in the art of picture buying at Paris.

"With this proposal I very readily closed, as it was living, and now all my ambition was to live. I went therefore to his lodgings, improved my dress by his assistance, and after some time, accompanied him to auctions of pictures, where the English gentry were expected to be purchasers. I was not a little surprised at his intimacy with people of the best fashion, who referred themselves to his judgment, upon every picture or medal, as an unerring standard of taste. He made very good use of my assistance upon these occasions; for when asked his opinion, he would gravely take me aside, and ask mine, shrug, look wise, return, and assure the company, that he could give no opinion upon an affair of so much importance. Yet there was sometimes an occasion for a more supported assurance. I remember to have seen him, after giving his opinion that the colouring of a picture was not mellow enough, very deliberately take a brush with brown varnish, that was accidentally lying by, and rub it over the piece with great composure before all the company, and then ask if he had not improved the tints.

"When he had finished his commission in Paris, he left me strongly recommended to several men of distinction, as a person very proper for a travelling tutor; and after some time I was employed in that capacity by a gentleman who brought his ward to Paris, in order to set him forward on his tour through Europe. I was to be the young gentleman's governor, but with a proviso that he should always be permitted to govern himself. My pupil in fact understood the art of guiding, in money concerns, much better than I. He was heir to a fortune of about two hundred thousand pounds, left him by an uncle in the West-Indies; and his guardians, to qualify him for the management of it, had bound him apprentice to an attorney. Thus avarice was his prevailing passion: all his questions on the road were how money might be saved; which was the least expensive course of travel; whether any thing could be bought that would turn to account when disposed of again in London. Such curiosities on the way as could be seen for nothing he was ready enough to look at; but if the sight of them was to be paid for, he usually asserted that he had been told they were not worth seeing. He never paid a bill that he would not observe, how amazingly expensive travelling was, and all this tho' he was not yet twenty-one. When arrived at Leghorn, as we took a walk to look at the port and shipping, he enquired the expense of the passage by sea home to England. This he was informed was but a trifle, compared to his returning by land, he was therefore unable to withstand the temptation; so paying me the small part of my salary that was due, he took leave, and embarked with only one attendant for London.

"I now therefore was left once more upon the world at large; but then it was a thing I was used to. However my skill in music could avail me nothing in a country where every peasant was a better musician than I; but by this time I had acquired another talent, which answered my purpose as well, and this was a skill in disputation. In all the foreign universities and convents, there are upon certain days philosophical theses maintained against every adventitious disputant; for which, if the champion opposes with any dexterity, he can claim a gratuity in money, a dinner, and a bed for one night. In this manner therefore I fought my way towards England, walked along from city to city, examined mankind more nearly, and, if I may so express it, saw both sides of the picture. My remarks, however, are but few: I found that monarchy was the best government for the poor to live in, and commonwealths for the rich. I found that riches in general were in every country another name for freedom; and that no man is so fond of liberty himself as not to be desirous of subjecting the will of some individuals in society to his own.

"Upon my arrival in England I resolved to pay my respects first to you, and then to enlist as a volunteer in the first expedition that was going forward; but on my journey down my resolutions were changed, by meeting an old acquaintance, who I found belonged to a company of comedians, that were going to make a summer campaign in the country. The company seemed not much to disapprove of me for an associate. They all, however, apprized me of the importance of the task at which I aimed; that the public was a many headed monster, and that only such as had very good heads could please it: that acting was not to be learnt in a day; and that without some traditional shrugs, which had been on the stage, and only on the stage, these hundred years, I could never pretend to please. The next difficulty was in fitting me with parts, as almost every character was in keeping. I was driven for some time from one character to another, till at last Horatio was fixed upon, which the presence of the present company has happily hindered me from acting."

CHAPTER II

The short continuance of friendship amongst the vicious, which is coeval only with mutual satisfaction.

My son's account was too long to be delivered at once, the first part of it was begun that night, and he was concluding the rest after dinner the next day, when the appearance of Mr. Thornhill's equipage at the door seemed to make a pause in the general satisfaction. The butler, who was now become my friend in the family, informed me with a whisper, that the 'Squire had already made some overtures to Miss Wilmot, and that her aunt and uncle seemed highly to approve the match. Upon Mr. Thornhill's entering, he seemed, at seeing my son and me, to start back; but I readily imputed that to surprize, and not displeasure. However, upon our advancing to salute him, he returned our greeting with the most apparent candour; and after a short time his presence served only to encrease the general good humour.

After tea he called me aside, to enquire after my daughter; but upon my informing him that my enquiry was unsuccessful, he seemed greatly surprised; adding, that he had been since frequently at my house, in order to comfort the rest of my family, whom he left perfectly well. He then asked if I had communicated her misfortune to Miss Wilmot, or my son; and upon my replying that I had not told them as yet, he greatly approved my prudence and precaution, desiring me by all means to keep it a secret: "For, at best," cried he, "it is but divulging one's own infamy; and perhaps Miss Livy may not be so guilty as we all imagine." We were here interrupted by a servant, who came to ask the 'Squire in, to stand up at country dances; so that he left me quite pleased with the interest he seemed to take in my concerns. His addresses, however, to Miss Wilmot, were too obvious to be mistaken: and yet she seemed not perfectly pleased, but bore them rather in compliance to the will of her aunt, than from real inclination. I had even the satisfaction to see her lavish some kind looks upon my unfortunate son, which the other could neither extort by his fortune nor assiduity. Mr. Thornhill's seeming composure, however, not a little surprised me: we had now continued here a week, at the pressing instances of Mr. Arnold; but each day the more tenderness Miss Wilmot shewed my son, Mr. Thornhill's friendship seemed proportionably to encrease for him.

He had formerly made us the most kind assurances of using his interest to serve the family; but now his generosity was not confined to promises alone: the morning I designed for my departure, Mr. Thornhill came to me with looks of real pleasure, to inform me of a piece of service he had done for his friend George. This was nothing less than his having procured him an ensign's commission in one of the regiments that was going to the West Indies, for which he had promised but one hundred pounds, his interest having been sufficient to get an abatement of the other two. "As for this trifling piece of service," continued the young gentleman, "I desire no other reward but the pleasure of having served my friend; and as for the hundred pound to be paid, if you are unable to raise it yourselves, I will advance it, and you shall repay me at your leisure." This was a favour we wanted words to express our sense of: I readily therefore gave my bond for the money, and testified as much gratitude as if I never intended to pay.

George was to depart for town the next day to secure his commission, in pursuance of his generous patron's directions, who judged it highly expedient to use dispatch, lest in the mean time another should step in with more advantageous proposals. The next morning, therefore, our young soldier was early prepared for his departure, and seemed the only person among us that was not affected by it. Neither the fatigues and dangers he was going to encounter, nor the friends and mistress, for Miss Wilmot actually loved him, he was leaving behind, any way damped his spirits. After he had taken leave of the rest of the company, I gave him all I had, my blessing. "And now, my boy," cried I, "thou art going to fight for thy country, remember how thy brave grandfather fought for his sacred king, when loyalty among Britons was a virtue. Go, my boy, and imitate him in all but his misfortunes, if it was a misfortune to die with Lord Falkland. Go, my boy, and if you fall, though distant, exposed and unwept by those that love you, the most precious tears are those with which heaven bedews the unburied head of a soldier."

The next morning I took leave of the good family, that had been kind enough to entertain me so long, not without several expressions of gratitude to Mr. Thornhill for his late bounty. I left them in the enjoyment of all that happiness which affluence and good breeding procure, and returned towards home, despairing of ever finding my daughter more, but sending a sigh to heaven to spare and to forgive her. I was now come within about twenty miles of home, having hired an horse to carry me, as I was yet but weak, and comforted myself with the hopes of soon seeing all I held dearest upon earth. But the night coming on, I put up at a little public house by the road side, and asked for the landlord's company over a pint of wine. We sate beside his kitchen fire, which was the best room in the house, and chatted on politics and the news of the country. We happened, among other topics, to talk of young 'Squire Thornhill, who the host assured me was hated as much as his uncle Sir William, who sometimes came down to the country, was loved. He went on to observe, that he made it his whole study to betray the daughters of such as received him to their houses, and after a fortnight or three weeks possession, turned them out unrewarded and abandoned to the world. As we continued our discourse in this manner, his wife, who had been out to get change, returned, and perceiving that her husband was enjoying a pleasure in which she was not a sharer, she asked him, in an angry tone, what he did there, to which he only replied, in an ironical way, by drinking her health. "Mr. Symmonds," cried she, "you use me very ill, and I'll bear it no longer. Here three parts of the business is left for me to do, and the fourth left unfinished; while you do nothing but soak with the guests all day long, whereas if a spoonful of liquor were to cure me of a fever, I never touch a drop." I now found what she would be at, and immediately poured her out a glass, which she received with a curtesy, and drinking towards my good health, "Sir," resumed she, "it is not so much for the value of the liquor I am angry, but one cannot help it, when the house is going out of the windows. If the customers or guests are to be dunned, all the burthen lies upon my back, he'd as lief eat that glass as budge after them himself. There now above stairs, we have a young woman who has come to take up her lodgings here, and I don't believe she has got any money by her over-civility. I am certain she is very slow of payment, and I wish she were put in mind of it."—"What signifies minding her," cried the host, "if she be slow, she is sure."—"I don't know that," replied the wife; "but I know that I am sure she has been here a fortnight, and we have not yet seen the cross of her money."—"I suppose, my dear," cried he, "we shall have it all in a lump."—"In a lump!" cried the other, "I hope we may get it any way; and that I am resolved we will this very night, or out she tramps, bag and baggage."—"Consider, my dear," cried the husband, "she is a gentlewoman, and deserves more respect."—"As for the matter of that," returned the hostess, "gentle or simple, out she shall pack with a sassarara.[1] Gentry may be good things where they take; but for my part I never saw much good of them at the sign of the Harrow."—Thus saying, she ran up a narrow flight of stairs, that went from the kitchen to a room over-head, and I soon perceived by the loudness of her voice, and the bitterness of her reproaches, that no money was to be had from her lodger. I could hear her remonstrances very distinctly: "Out I say, pack out this

[1] [With a vengeance. Apparently a corruption of *certiorari*.]

moment, tramp thou infamous strumpet, or I'll give thee a mark thou won't be the better for these three months. What! you trumpery, to come and take up an honest house, without cross or coin to bless yourself with; come along I say."—"O dear madam," cried the stranger, "pity me, pity a poor abandoned creature for one night, and death will soon do the rest."—I instantly knew the voice of my poor ruined child Olivia. I flew to her rescue, while the woman was dragging her along by her hair, and I caught the dear forlorn wretch in my arms.—"Welcome, any way welcome, my dearest lost one, my treasure, to your poor old father's bosom. Though the vicious forsake thee, there is yet one in the world that will never forsake thee; tho' thou hadst ten thousand crimes to answer for, he will forget them all."—"O my own dear,"—for minutes she could do more—"my own dearest good papa! Could angels be kinder! How do I deserve so much! The villain, I hate him and myself to be a reproach to such goodness. You can't forgive me. I know you cannot."—"Yes, my child, from my heart I do forgive thee! Only repent, and we both shall yet be happy. We shall see many pleasant days yet, my Olivia."—"Ah! never, sir, never. The rest of my wretched life must be infamy abroad and shame at home. But, alas! papa, you look much paler than you used to do. Could such a thing as I am give you so much uneasiness? Sure you have too much wisdom to take the miseries of my guilt upon yourself."—"Our wisdom, young woman," replied I.—"Ah, why so cold a name, papa?" cried she. "This is the first time you ever called me by so cold a name."—"I ask pardon, my darling," returned I; "but I was going to observe, that wisdom makes but a slow defence against trouble, though at last a sure one." The landlady now returned to know if we did not chuse a more genteel apartment, to which assenting, we were shewn a room where we could converse more freely. After we had talked ourselves into some degree of tranquillity, I could not avoid desiring some account of the gradations that led to her present wretched situation. "That villain, sir," said she, "from the first day of our meeting, made me honourable, though private, proposals."

"Villain indeed!" cried I: "and yet it in some measure surprizes me, how a person of Mr. Burchell's good sense and seeming honour could be guilty of such deliberate baseness, and thus step into a family to undo it."

"My dear papa," returned my daughter, "you labour under a strange mistake, Mr. Burchell never attempted to deceive me. Instead of that he took every opportunity of privately admonishing me against the artifices of Mr. Thornhill, who I now find was even worse than he represented him."—"Mr. Thornhill," interrupted I; "can it be?"—"Yes, Sir," returned she, "it was Mr. Thornhill who seduced me, who employed the two ladies, as he called them, but who, in fact, were abandoned women of the town, without breeding or pity, to decoy us up to London. Their artifices, you may remember would have certainly succeeded, but for Mr. Burchell's letter, who directed those reproaches at them, which we all applied to ourselves. How he came to have so much influence as to defeat their intentions, still remains a secret to me; but I am convinced he was ever our warmest, sincerest friend."

"You amaze me, my dear," cried I; "but now I find my first suspicions of Mr. Thornhill's baseness were too well grounded: but he can triumph in security; for he is rich, and we are poor. But tell me, my child, sure it was no small temptation that could thus obliterate all the impressions of such an education, and so virtuous a disposition as thine?"

"Indeed, Sir," replied she, "he owes all his triumph to the desire I had of making him, and not myself, happy. I knew that the ceremony of our marriage, which was privately performed by a popish priest, was no way binding, and that I had nothing to trust to but his honour."—"What," interrupted I, "and were you indeed married by a priest, and in orders?"—"Indeed, Sir, we were," replied she, "though we were both sworn to conceal his name."—"Why then, my child, come to my arms again, and now you are a thousand times more welcome than before; for you are now his wife to all intents and purposes; nor can all the laws of man, though written upon tables of adamant, lessen the force of that sacred connexion."

"Alas, Papa," replied she, "you are but little acquainted with his villainies: he has been married already, by the same priest, to six or eight wives more, whom, like me, he has deceived and abandoned."

"Has he so?" cried I, "then we must hang the priest, and you shall inform against him to-morrow."—"But, Sir," returned she, "will that be right, when I am sworn to secrecy?" —"My dear," I replied, "if you have made such a promise, I cannot, nor will I tempt you to break it. Even though it may benefit the public, you must not inform against him. In all human institutions a smaller evil is allowed to procure a greater good; as in politics, a province may be given away to secure a kingdom; in medicine, a limb may be lopt off to preserve the body. But in religion the law is written, and inflexible, *never* to do evil. And this law, my child, is right: for otherwise, if we commit a smaller evil, to procure a greater good, certain guilt would be thus incurred, in expectation of contingent advantage. And though the advantage should certainly follow, yet the interval between commission and advantage, which is allowed to be guilty, may be that in which we are called away to answer for the things we have done, and the volume of human actions is closed for ever. But I interrupt you, my dear; go on."

"The very next morning," continued she, "I found what little expectations I was to have from his sincerity. That very morning he introduced me to two unhappy women more, whom, like me, he had deceived, but who lived in contented prostitution. I loved him too tenderly to bear such rivals in his affections, and strove to forget my infamy in a tumult of pleasures. With this view, I danced, dressed, and talked; but still was unhappy. The gentlemen who visited there told me every moment of the power of my charms, and this only contributed to encrease my melancholy, as I had thrown all their power quite away. Thus each day I grew more pensive, and he more insolent, till at last the monster had the assurance to offer me to a young Baronet of his acquaintance. Need I describe, Sir, how his ingratitude stung me. My answer to this proposal was almost madness. I desired to part. As I was going he offered me a purse; but I flung it at him with indignation, and burst from him in a rage, that for a while kept me insensible of the miseries of my situation. But I soon looked round me, and saw myself a vile, abject, guilty thing, without one friend in the world to apply to. Just in that interval, a stage coach happening to pass by, I took a place, it being my only aim to be driven at a distance from a wretch I despised and detested. I was set down here, where, since my arrival, my own anxiety, and this woman's unkindness, have been my only companions. The hours of pleasure that I have passed with my mamma and sister, now grow painful to me. Their sorrows are much; but mine is greater than theirs; for mine are mixed with guilt and infamy."

"Have patience, my child," cried I, "and I hope things will yet be better. Take some repose to-night, and to-morrow I'll carry you home to your mother and the rest of the family, from whom you will receive a kind reception. Poor woman, this has gone to her heart: but she loves you still, Olivia, and will forget it."

CHAPTER III

Offences are easily pardoned where there is love at bottom.

THE next morning I took my daughter behind me, and set out on my return home. As we travelled along, I strove, by every persuasion, to calm her sorrows and fears, and to arm her with resolution to bear the presence of her offended mother. I took every opportunity, from the prospect of a fine country, through which we passed, to observe how much kinder heaven was to us, than we to each other, and that the misfortunes of nature's making were very few. I assured her, that she should never perceive any change in my affections, and that during my life, which yet might be long, she might depend upon a guardian and an instructor. I armed her against the censures of the world, shewed her that books were sweet unreproaching companions to the miserable, and that if they could not bring us to enjoy life, they would at least teach us to endure it.

The hired horse that we rode was to be put up that night at an inn by the way, within about five miles from my house, and as I was willing to prepare my family for my daughter's reception, I determined to leave her that night at the inn, and to return for her, accompanied by my daughter Sophia, early the next morning. It was night before we reached our appointed stage: however, after seeing her provided with a decent apartment, and having ordered the hostess to prepare proper refreshments, I kissed her, and proceeded towards home. And now my heart caught new sensations of pleasure the nearer I approached that peaceful mansion. As a bird that had been frighted from its nest, my affections out-went my haste, and hovered round my little fire-side, with all the rapture of expectation. I called up the many fond things I had to say, and anticipated the welcome I was to receive. I already felt my wife's tender embrace, and smiled at the joy of my little ones. As I walked but slowly, the night wained apace. The labourers of the day were all retired to rest; the lights were out in every cottage; no sounds were heard but of the shrilling cock, and the deep-mouthed watch-dog, at hollow distance. I approached my abode of pleasure, and before I was within a furlong of the place, our honest mastiff came running to welcome me.

It was now near mid-night that I came to knock at my door:

all was still and silent; my heart dilated with unutterable happiness, when, to my amazement, I saw the house bursting out in a blaze of fire, and every aperture red with conflagration! I gave a loud convulsive outcry, and fell upon the pavement insensible. This alarmed my son, who had till this been asleep, and he perceiving the flames, instantly waked my wife and daughter, and all running out, naked, and wild with apprehension, recalled me to life with their anguish. But it was only to objects of new terror; for the flames had, by this time, caught the roof of our dwelling, part after part continuing to fall in, while the family stood, with silent agony, looking on, as if they enjoyed the blaze. I gazed upon them, and upon it by turns, and then looked round me for my two little ones; but they were not to be seen. O misery! "Where," cried I, "where are my little ones?"—"They are burnt to death in the flames," says my wife calmly, "and I will die with them."—That moment I heard the cry of the babes within, who were just awaked by the fire, and nothing could have stopped me. "Where, where are my children?" cried I, rushing through the flames, and bursting the door of the chamber in which they were confined, "Where are my little ones?"—"Here, dear papa, here we are," cried they together, while the flames were just catching the bed where they lay. I caught them both in my arms, and snatched them through the fire as fast as possible, while just as I was got out, the roof sunk in. "Now," cried I, holding up my children, "now let the flames burn on, and all my possessions perish. Here they are, I have saved my treasure. Here, my dearest, here are our treasures, and we shall yet be happy." We kissed our little darlings a thousand times, they clasped us round the neck, and seemed to share our transports, while their mother laughed and wept by turns.

I now stood a calm spectator of the flames, and after some time, began to perceive that my arm to the shoulder was scorched in a terrible manner. It was therefore out of my power to give my son any assistance, either in attempting to save our goods, or preventing the flames spreading to our corn. By this time, the neighbours were alarmed, and came running to our assistance; but all they could do was to stand, like us, spectators of the calamity. My goods, among which were the notes I had reserved for my daughters fortunes, were entirely consumed, except a box, with some papers, that stood in the kitchen, and two or three things more of little consequence, which my son brought away in the beginning. The neighbours contributed, however, what they could to lighten our distress. They brought us cloaths, and furnished one of our out-houses with kitchen utensils; so that by daylight we had another, though a wretched, dwelling to retire to. My honest next neighbour, and his children, were not the least assiduous in providing us with every thing necessary, and offering whatever consolation untutored benevolence could suggest.

When the fears of my family had subsided, curiosity to know the cause of my long stay began to take place; having therefore informed them of every particular, I proceeded to prepare them for the reception of our lost one, and though we had nothing but wretchedness now to impart, I was willing to procure her a welcome to what we had. This task would have been more difficult but for our recent calamity, which had humbled my wife's pride, and blunted it by more poignant afflictions. Being unable to go for my poor child myself, as my arm grew very painful, I sent my son and daughter, who soon returned, supporting the wretched delinquent, who had not the courage to look up at her mother, whom no instructions of mine could persuade to a perfect reconciliation; for women have a much stronger sense of female error than men. "Ah, madam," cried her mother, "this is but a poor place you are come to after so much finery. My daughter Sophy and I can afford but little entertainment to persons who have kept company only with people of distinction. Yes,

Miss Livy, your poor father and I have suffered very much of late; but I hope heaven will forgive you."—During this reception, the unhappy victim stood pale and trembling, unable to weep or to reply; but I could not continue a silent spectator of her distress, wherefore assuming a degree of severity in my voice and manner, which was ever followed with instant submission, "I entreat, woman, that my words may be now marked once for all: I have here brought you back a poor deluded wanderer; her return to duty demands the revival of our tenderness. The real hardships of life are now coming fast upon us, let us not therefore encrease them by dissention among each other. If we live harmoniously together, we may yet be contented, as there are enough of us to shut out the censuring world, and keep each other in countenance. The kindness of heaven is promised to the penitent, and let ours be directed by the example. Heaven, we are assured, is much more pleased to view a repentant sinner, than ninety-nine persons who have supported a course of undeviating rectitude. And this is right; for that single effort by which we stop short in the down-hill path to perdition, is itself a greater exertion of virtue, than an hundred acts of justice."

CHAPTER IV

None but the guilty can be long and completely miserable.

SOME assiduity was now required to make our present abode as convenient as possible, and we were soon again qualified to enjoy our former serenity. Being disabled myself from assisting my son in our usual occupations, I read to my family from the few books that were saved, and particularly from such, as, by amusing the imagination, contributed to ease the heart. Our good neighbours too came every day with the kindest condolence, and fixed a time in which they were all to assist at repairing my former dwelling. Honest farmer

Williams was not last among these visitors; but heartily offered his friendship. He would even have renewed his addresses to my daughter; but she rejected them in such a manner as totally represt his future solicitations. Her grief seemed formed for continuing, and she was the only person of our little society that a week did not restore to chearfulness. She now lost that unblushing innocence which once taught her to respect herself, and to seek pleasure by pleasing. Anxiety now had taken strong possession of her mind, her beauty began to be impaired with her constitution, and neglect still more contributed to diminish it. Every tender epithet bestowed on her sister brought a pang to her heart and a tear to her eye; and as one vice, though cured, ever plants others where it has been, so her former guilt, though driven out by repentance, left jealousy and envy behind. I strove a thousand ways to lessen her care, and even forgot my own pain in a concern for her's, collecting such amusing passages of history, as a strong memory and some reading could suggest. "Our happiness, my dear," I would say, "is in the power of one who can bring it about a thousand unforeseen ways, that mock our foresight. If example be necessary to prove this, I'll give you a story, my child, told us by a grave, though sometimes a romancing, historian.

"Matilda was married very young to a Neapolitan nobleman of the first quality, and found herself a widow and a mother at the age of fifteen. As she stood one day caressing her infant son in the open window of an apartment, which hung over the river Volturna, the child, with a sudden spring, leaped from her arms into the flood below, and disappeared in a moment. The mother, struck with instant surprize, and making an effort to save him, plunged in after; but, far from being able to assist the infant, she herself with great difficulty escaped to the opposite shore, just when some French soldiers were plundering the country on that side, who immediately made her their prisoner.

"As the war was then carried on between the French and Italians with the utmost inhumanity, they were going at once to perpetrate those two extremes, suggested by appetite and cruelty. This base resolution, however, was opposed by a young officer, who, though their retreat required the utmost expedition, placed her behind him, and brought her in safety to his native city. Her beauty at first caught his eye, her merit soon after his heart. They were married; he rose to the highest posts; they lived long together, and were happy. But the felicity of a soldier can never be called permanent: after an interval of several years, the troops which he commanded having met with a repulse, he was obliged to take shelter in the city where he had lived with his wife. Here they suffered a siege, and the city at length was taken. Few histories can produce more various instances of cruelty, than those which the French and Italians at that time exercised upon each other. It was resolved by the victors, upon this occasion, to put all the French prisoners to death; but particularly the husband of the unfortunate Matilda, as he was principally instrumental in protracting the siege. Their determinations were, in general, executed almost as soon as resolved upon. The captive soldier was led forth, and the executioner, with his sword, stood ready, while the spectators in gloomy silence awaited the fatal blow, which was only suspended till the general, who presided as judge, should give the signal. It was in this interval of anguish and expectation, that Matilda came to take her last farewell of her husband and deliverer, deploring her wretched situation, and the cruelty of fate, that had saved her from perishing by a premature death in the river Volturna, to be the spectator of still greater calamities. The general, who was a young man, was struck with surprize at her beauty, and pity at her distress; but with still stronger emotions when he heard her mention her former dangers. He was her son, the infant for whom she had encountered so much danger. He acknowledged her at once as his mother, and fell at her feet.

The rest may be easily supposed: the captive was set free, and all the happiness that love, friendship, and duty could confer on each, were united."

In this manner I would attempt to amuse my daughter; but she listened with divided attention; for her own misfortunes engrossed all the pity she once had for those of another, and nothing gave her ease. In company she dreaded contempt; and in solitude she only found anxiety. Such was the colour of her wretchedness, when we received certain information, that Mr. Thornhill was going to be married to Miss Wilmot, for whom I always suspected he had a real passion, though he took every opportunity before me to express his contempt both of her person and fortune. This news only served to encrease poor Olivia's affliction; such a flagrant breach of fidelity, was more than her courage could support. I was resolved, however, to get more certain information, and to defeat, if possible, the completion of his designs, by sending my son to old Mr. Wilmot's, with instructions to know the truth of the report, and to deliver Miss Wilmot a letter, intimating Mr. Thornhill's conduct in my family. My son went, in pursuance of my directions, and in three days returned, assuring us of the truth of the account; but that he had found it impossible to deliver the letter, which he was therefore obliged to leave, as Mr. Thornhill and Miss Wilmot were visiting round the country. They were to be married, he said, in a few days, having appeared together at church the Sunday before he was there, in great splendour, the bride attended by six young ladies, and he by as many gentlemen. Their approaching nuptials filled the whole country with rejoicing, and they usually rode out together in the grandest equipage that had been seen in the country for many years. All the friends of both families, he said, were there, particularly the 'Squire's uncle, Sir William Thornhill, who bore so good a character. He added, that nothing but mirth and feasting were going forward; that all the country praised the young bride's beauty, and the bridegroom's fine person, and that they were immensely fond of each other; concluding, that he could not help thinking Mr. Thornhill one of the most happy men in the world.

"Why let him if he can," returned I: "but, my son, observe this bed of straw, and unsheltering roof; those mouldering walls, and humid floor; my wretched body thus disabled by fire, and my children weeping round me for bread; you have come home, my child, to all this, yet here, even here, you see a man that would not for a thousand worlds exchange situations. O, my children, if you could but learn to commune with your own hearts, and know what noble company you can make them, you would little regard the elegance and splendours of the worthless. Almost all men have been taught to call life a passage, and themselves the travellers. The similitude still may be improved when we observe that the good are joyful and serene, like travellers that are going towards home; the wicked but by intervals happy, like travellers that are going into exile."

My compassion for my poor daughter, overpowered by this new disaster, interrupted what I had further to observe. I bade her mother support her, and after a short time she recovered. She appeared from that time more calm, and I imagined had gained a new degree of resolution: but appearances deceived me; for her tranquillity was the languor of over-wrought resentment. A supply of provisions, charitably sent us by my kind parishioners, seemed to diffuse new chearfulness among the rest of the family, nor was I displeased at seeing them once more sprightly and at ease. It would have been unjust to damp their satisfactions, merely to condole with resolute melancholy, or to burthen them with a sadness they did not feel. Thus, once more, the tale went round and the song was demanded, and chearfulness condescended to hover round our little habitation.

CHAPTER V

Fresh calamities.

THE next morning the sun arose with peculiar warmth for the season; so that we agreed to breakfast together on the honey-suckle bank: where, while we sate, my youngest daughter, at my request, joined her voice to the concert on the trees about us. It was in this place my poor Olivia first met her seducer, and every object served to recall her sadness. But that melancholy, which is excited by objects of pleasure, or inspired by sounds of harmony, sooths the heart instead of corroding it. Her mother too upon this occasion, felt a pleasing distress, and wept, and loved her daughter as before. "Do, my pretty Olivia," cried she, "let us have that little melancholy air your pappa was so fond of, your sister Sophy has already obliged us. Do child, it will please your old father." She complied in a manner so exquisitely pathetic as moved me.

When lovely woman stoops to folly,
And finds too late that men betray,
What charm can sooth her melancholy,
What art can wash her guilt away?

The only art her guilt to cover,
To hide her shame from every eye,
To give repentance to her lover,
And wring his bosom—is to die.

As she was concluding the last stanza, to which an interruption in her voice from sorrow gave peculiar softness, the appearance of Mr. Thornhill's equipage at a distance alarmed us all, but particularly encreased the uneasiness of my eldest daughter, who, desirous of shunning her betrayer, returned to the house with her sister. In a few minutes he was alighted from his chariot, and making up to the place where I was still sitting, enquired after my health with his usual air of familiarity. "Sir," replied I, "your present assurance only serves to aggravate the baseness of your character; and there was a time when I would have chastised your insolence, for presuming thus to appear before me. But now you are safe; for age has cooled my passions, and my calling restrains them."

"I vow, my dear sir," returned he, "I am amazed at all this; nor can I understand what it means! I hope you don't think your daughter's late excursion with me had any thing criminal in it."

"Go," cried I, "thou art a wretch, a poor, pitiful wretch, and every way a liar; but your meanness secures you from my anger! Yet, sir, I am descended from a family that would not have borne this!—And so, thou vile thing, to gratify a momentary passion, thou hast made one poor creature wretched for life, and polluted a family that had nothing but honour for their portion."

"If she or you," returned he, "are resolved to be miserable, I cannot help it. But you may still be happy; and whatever opinion you may have formed of me, you shall ever find me ready to contribute to it. We can marry her to another in a short time, and what is more, she may keep her lover beside; for I protest I shall ever continue to have a true regard for her."

I found all my passions alarmed at this new degrading proposal; for though the mind may often be calm under great injuries, little villainy can at any time get within the soul, and sting it into rage.—"Avoid my sight, thou reptile," cried I, "nor continue to insult me with thy presence. Were my brave son at home, he would not suffer this; but I am old, and disabled, and every way undone."

"I find," cried he, "you are bent upon obliging me to talk in a harsher manner than I intended. But as I have shewn you what may be hoped from my friendship, it may not be improper to represent what may be the consequences of my resentment. My attorney, to whom your late bond has been transferred, threatens hard, nor do I know how to prevent the course of justice, except by paying the money myself, which, as I have been at some expenses lately, previous to my intended marriage, is not so easy to be done. And then my steward talks of driving for the rent: it is certain he knows his duty; for I never trouble myself with affairs of that nature. Yet still I could wish to serve you, and even to have you and your daughter present at my marriage, which is shortly to be solemnized with Miss Wilmot: it is even the request of my charming Arabella herself, whom I hope you will not refuse."

"Mr. Thornhill," replied I, "hear me once for all: as to your marriage with any but my daughter, that I never will consent to; and though your friendship could raise me to a throne, or your resentment sink me to the grave, yet would I despise both. Thou hast once wofully, irreparably, deceived me. I reposed my heart upon thine honour, and have found its baseness. Never more, therefore, expect friendship from me. Go, and possess what fortune has given thee, beauty, riches, health, and pleasure. Go, and leave me to want, infamy, disease, and sorrow. Yet humbled as I am, shall my heart still vindicate its dignity, and though thou hast my forgiveness, thou shalt ever have my contempt."

"If so," returned he, "depend upon it you shall feel the effects of this insolence, and we shall shortly see which is the fittest object of scorn, you or me."—Upon which he departed abruptly.

My wife and son, who were present at this interview, seemed terrified with the apprehension. My daughters also, finding that he was gone, came out to be informed of the result of our conference which, when known, alarmed them not less than the rest. But as to myself, I disregarded the utmost stretch of his malevolence: he had already struck the blow, and now I stood prepared to repel every new effort.

Like one of those instruments used in the art of war, which, however thrown, still presents a point to receive the enemy.

We soon, however, found that he had not threatened in vain; for the very next morning his steward came to demand my annual rent, which, by the train of accidents already related, I was unable to pay. The consequence of my incapacity was his driving my cattle that evening, and their being appraised and sold the next day for less than half their value. My wife and children now therefore entreated me to comply upon any terms, rather than incur certain destruction. They even begged of me to admit his visits once more, and used all their little eloquence to paint the calamities I was going to endure: The terrors of a prison in so rigorous a season as the present, with the danger that threatened my health from the late accident that happened by the fire. But I continued inflexible.

"Why, my treasures," cried I, "why will you thus attempt to persuade me to the thing that is not right! My duty has taught me to forgive him; but my conscience will not permit me to approve. Would you have me applaud to the world what my heart must internally condemn? Would you have me tamely sit down and flatter our infamous betrayer; and to avoid a prison continually suffer the more galling bonds of mental confinement! No, never. If we are to be taken from this abode, only let us hold to the right, and wherever we are thrown, we can still retire to a charming apartment, when we can look round our own hearts with intrepidity and with pleasure!"

In this manner we spent that evening. Early the next morning, as the snow had fallen in great abundance in the night, my son was employed in clearing it away, and opening a passage before the door. He had not been thus engaged long, when he came running in, with looks all pale, to tell us that two strangers, whom he knew to be officers of justice, were making towards the house.

Just as he spoke they came in, and approaching the bed where I lay, after previously informing me of their employment and business, made me their prisoner, bidding me prepare to go with them to the county gaol, which was eleven miles off.

"My friends," said I, "this is severe weather in which you have come to take me to a prison; and it is particularly unfortunate at this time, as one of my arms has lately been burnt in a terrible manner, and it has thrown me into a slight fever, and I want cloaths to cover me, and I am now too weak and old to walk far in such deep snow: but if it must be so——"

I then turned to my wife and children, and directed them to get together what few things were left us, and to prepare immediately for leaving this place. I entreated them to be expeditious, and desired my son to assist his elder sister, who, from a consciousness that she was the cause of all our calamities, was fallen, and had lost anguish in insensibility. I encouraged my wife, who, pale and trembling, clasped our affrighted little ones in her arms, that clung to her bosom in silence, dreading to look round at the strangers. In the mean time my youngest daughter prepared for our departure, and as she received several hints to use dispatch, in about an hour we were ready to depart.

CHAPTER VI

No situation, however wretched it seems, but has some sort of comfort attending it.

We set forward from this peaceful neighbourhood, and walked on slowly. My eldest daughter being enfeebled by a slow fever, which had begun for some days to undermine her constitution, one of the officers, who had an horse, kindly took her behind him; for even these men cannot entirely divest themselves of humanity. My son led one of the little ones by the hand, and my wife the other, while I leaned upon my youngest girl, whose tears fell, not for her own but my distresses.

We were now got from my late dwelling about two miles, when we saw a croud running and shouting behind us, consisting of about fifty of my poorest parishioners. These, with dreadful imprecations, soon seized upon the two officers of justice, and swearing they would never see their minister go to gaol while they had a drop of blood to shed in his defence, were going to use them with great severity. The consequence might have been fatal, had I not immediately interposed, and with some difficulty rescued the officers from the hands of the enraged multitude. My children, who looked upon my delivery now as certain, appeared transported with joy, and were incapable of containing their raptures. But they were soon undeceived, upon hearing me address the poor deluded people, who came, as they imagined, to do me service.

"What! my friends," cried I, "and is this the way you love me! Is this the manner you obey the instructions I have given you from the pulpit! Thus to fly in the face of justice, and bring down ruin on yourselves and me! Which is your ringleader? Shew me the man that has thus seduced you. As sure as he lives he shall feel my resentment. Alas! my dear deluded flock, return back to the duty you owe to God, to your country, and to me. I shall yet perhaps one day see you in greater felicity here, and contribute to make your lives more happy. But let it at least be my comfort when I pen my fold for immortality, that not one here shall be wanting."

They now seemed all repentance, and melting into tears, came one after the other to bid me farewell. I shook each tenderly by the hand, and leaving them my blessing, proceeded forward without meeting any farther interruption. Some hours before night we reached the town, or rather village; for it consisted but of a few mean houses, having lost all its former opulence, and retaining no marks of its ancient superiority but the gaol.

Upon entering, we put up at an inn, where we had such refreshments as could most readily be procured, and I supped with my family with my usual chearfulness. After seeing them properly accommodated for that night, I next attended the sheriff's officers to the prison, which had formerly been built for the purposes of war, and consisted of one large apartment, strongly grated, and paved with stone, common to both felons and debtors at certain hours in the four and twenty. Besides this, every prisoner had a separate cell, where he was locked in for the night.

I expected upon my entrance to find nothing but lamentations, and various sounds of misery; but it was very different. The prisoners seemed all employed in one common design, that of forgetting thought in merriment or clamour. I was apprized of the usual perquisite required upon these occasions, and immediately complied with the demand, though the little money I had was very near being all exhausted. This was immediately sent away for liquor, and the whole prison was soon filled with riot, laughter, and prophaneness.

"How," cried I to myself, "shall men so very wicked be chearful, and shall I be melancholy! I feel only the same confinement with them, and I think I have more reason to be happy."

With such reflections I laboured to become chearful; but chearfulness was never yet produced by effort, which is itself painful. As I was sitting therefore in a corner of the gaol, in a pensive posture, one of my fellow prisoners came up, and sitting by me, entered into conversation. It was my constant rule in life never to avoid the conversation of any man who seemed to desire it: for if good, I might profit by his instruction; if bad, he might be assisted by mine. I found this to be a knowing man, of strong unlettered sense; but a thorough knowledge of the world, as it is called, or more properly speaking, of human nature on the wrong side. He asked me if I had taken care to provide myself with a bed, which was a circumstance I had never once attended to.

"That's unfortunate," cried he, "as you are allowed here nothing but straw, and your apartment is very large and cold. However you seem to be something of a gentleman, and as I have been one myself in my time, part of my bed-cloaths are heartily at your service."

I thanked him, professing my surprize at finding such humanity in a gaol in misfortunes; adding, to let him see that I was a scholar, "That the sage ancient seemed to understand the value of company in affliction, when he said, Ton kosman aire, ei dos ton etairon; and in fact," continued I, "what is the world if it affords only solitude?"

"You talk of the world, Sir," returned my fellow prisoner; "*the world is in its dotage, and yet the cosmogony or creation of the world has puzzled the philosophers of every age. What a medley of opinions have they not broached upon the creation of the world. Sanconiathon, Manetho, Berosus and Ocellus Lucanus have all attempted it in vain. The latter has these words, Anarchon ara kai atelutaion to pan, which implies*"—"I ask pardon, Sir," cried I, "for interrupting so much learning; but I think I have heard all this before. Have I not had the pleasure of once seeing you at Welbridge fair, and is not your name Ephraim Jenkinson?" At this demand he only sighed. "I suppose you must recollect," resumed I, "one Doctor Primrose, from whom you bought a horse?"

He now at once recollected me; for the gloominess of the place and the approaching night had prevented his distinguishing my features before.—"Yes, Sir," returned Mr. Jenkinson, "I remember you perfectly well; I bought an horse, but forgot to pay for him. Your neighbour Flamborough is the only prosecutor I am any way afraid of at the next assizes: for he intends to swear positively against me as a coiner. I am heartily sorry, Sir, I ever deceived you, or indeed any man;

for you see," continued he, shewing his shackles, "what my tricks have brought me to."

"Well, sir," replied I, "your kindness in offering me assistance, when you could expect no return, shall be repaid with my endeavours to soften or totally suppress Mr. Flamborough's evidence, and I will send my son to him for that purpose the first opportunity; nor do I in the least doubt but he will comply with my request; and as to my own evidence, you need be under no uneasiness about that."

"Well, sir," cried he, "all the return I can make shall be yours. You shall have more than half my bed-cloaths to night, and I'll take care to stand your friend in the prison, where I think I have some influence."

I thanked him, and could not avoid being surprised at the present youthful change in his aspect; for at the time I had seen him before he appeared at least sixty.—"Sir," answered he, "you are little acquainted with the world; I had at that time false hair, and have learnt the art of counterfeiting every age from seventeen to seventy. Ah sir, had I but bestowed half the pains in learning a trade, that I have in learning to be a scoundrel, I might have been a rich man at this day. But rogue as I am, still I may be your friend, and that perhaps when you least expect it."

We were now prevented from further conversation, by the arrival of the gaoler's servants, who came to call over the prisoners' names, and lock up for the night. A fellow also, with a bundle of straw for my bed attended, who led me along a dark narrow passage into a room paved like the common prison, and in one corner of this I spread my bed, and the cloaths given me by my fellow prisoner; which done, my conductor, who was civil enough, bade me a good-night. After my usual meditations, and having praised my heavenly corrector, I laid myself down and slept with the utmost tranquillity till morning.

CHAPTER VII

A reformation in the gaol. To make laws complete, they should reward as well as punish.

THE next morning early I was awakened by my family, whom I found in tears at my bed side. The gloomy strength of every thing about us, it seems, had daunted them. I gently rebuked their sorrow, assuring them I had never slept with greater tranquillity, and next enquired after my eldest daughter, who was not among them. They informed me that yesterday's uneasiness and fatigue had increased her fever, and it was judged proper to leave her behind. My next care was to send my son to procure a room or two to lodge the family in, as near the prison as conveniently could be found. He obeyed; but could only find one apartment, which was hired at a small expence, for his mother and sisters, the gaoler with humanity consenting to let him and his two little brothers lie in the prison with me. A bed was therefore prepared for them in a corner of the room, which I thought answered very conveniently. I was willing however previously to know whether my little children chose to lie in a place which seemed to fright them upon entrance.

"Well," cried I, "my good boys, how do you like your bed? I hope you are not afraid to lie in this room, dark as it appears."

"No, papa," says Dick, "I am not afraid to lie any where where you are."

"And I," says Bill, who was yet but four years old, "love every place best that my papa is in."

After this, I allotted to each of the family what they were to do. My daughter was particularly directed to watch her declining sister's health; my wife was to attend me; my little boys were to read to me: "And as for you, my son," continued I, "it is by the labour of your hands we must all hope to be supported. Your wages, as a day-labourer, will be full sufficient, with proper frugality, to maintain us all, and comfortably too. Thou art now sixteen years old, and hast strength, and it was given thee, my son, for very useful purposes: for it must save from famine your helpless parents and family. Prepare then this evening to look out for work against to morrow, and bring home every night what money you earn, for our support."

Having thus instructed him, and settled the rest, I walked down to the common prison, where I could enjoy more air and room. But I was not long there when the execrations, lewdness, and brutality that invaded me on every side, drove me back to my apartment again. Here I sate for some time, pondering upon the strange infatuation of wretches, who finding all mankind in open arms against them, were labouring to make themselves a future and a tremendous enemy.

Their insensibility excited my highest compassion, and blotted my own uneasiness from my mind. It even appeared a duty incumbent upon me to attempt to reclaim them. I resolved therefore once more to return, and in spite of their contempt to give them my advice, and conquer them by perseverance. Going therefore among them again, I informed Mr. Jenkinson of my design, at which he laughed heartily, but communicated it to the rest. The proposal was received with the greatest good-humour, as it promised to afford a new fund of entertainment to persons who had now no other resource for mirth, but what could be derived from ridicule or debauchery.

I therefore read them a portion of the service with a loud unaffected voice, and found my audience perfectly merry upon the occasion. Lewd whispers, groans of contrition burlesqued, winking and coughing, alternately excited laughter. However, I continued with my natural solemnity to read on, sensible that what I did might amend some, but could itself receive no contamination from any.

After reading, I entered upon my exhortation, which was

rather calculated at first to amuse them than to reprove. I previously observed, that no other motive but their welfare could induce me to this; that I was their fellow prisoner, and now got nothing by preaching. I was sorry, I said, to hear them so very prophane; because they got nothing by it, but might lose a great deal: "For be assured, my friends," cried I, "for you are my friends, however the world may disclaim your friendship, though you swore twelve thousand oaths in a day, it would not put one penny in your purse. Then what signifies calling every moment upon the devil, and courting his friendship, since you find how scurvily he uses you. He has given you nothing here, you find, but a mouthful of oaths and an empty belly; and by the best accounts I have of him, he will give you nothing that's good hereafter.

"If used ill in our dealings with one man, we naturally go elsewhere. Were it not worth your while then, just to try how you may like the usage of another master, who gives you fair promises at least to come to him. Surely, my Friends, of all stupidity in the world, his must be greatest, who after robbing an house, runs to the thieftakers for protection. And yet how are you more wise? You are all seeking comfort from one that has already betrayed you, applying to a more malicious being than any thieftaker of them all; for they only decoy, and then hang you; but he decoys and hangs, and what is worst of all, will not let you loose after the hangman has done."

When I had concluded, I received the compliments of my audience, some of whom came and shook me by the hand, swearing that I was a very honest fellow, and that they desired my further acquaintance. I therefore promised to repeat my lecture next day, and actually conceived some hopes of making a reformation here; for it had ever been my opinion, that no man was past the hour of amendment, every heart lying open to the shafts of reproof, if the archer could but take a proper aim. When I had thus satisfied my mind, I went back to my apartment, where my wife prepared a frugal meal, while Mr. Jenkinson begged leave to add his dinner to ours, and partake of the pleasure, as he was kind enough to express it, of my conversation. He had not yet seen my family, for as they came to my apartment by a door in the narrow passage, already described, by this means they avoided the common prison. Jenkinson at the first interview therefore seemed not a little struck with the beauty of my youngest daughter, which her pensive air contributed to heighten, and my little ones did not pass unnoticed.

"Alas, Doctor," cried he, "these children are too handsome and too good for such a place as this!"

"Why, Mr. Jenkinson," replied I, "thank heaven, my children are pretty tolerable in morals, and if they be good, it matters little for the rest."

"I fancy, sir," returned my fellow prisoner, "that it must give you great comfort to have this little family about you."

"A comfort, Mr. Jenkinson," replied I, "yes it is indeed a comfort, and I would not be without them for all the world; for they can make a dungeon seem a palace. There is but one way in this life of wounding my happiness, and that is by injuring them."

"I am afraid then, sir," cried he, "that I am in some measure culpable; for I think I see here" (looking at my son Moses) "one that I have injured, and by whom I wish to be forgiven."

My son immediately recollected his voice and features, though he had before seen him in disguise, and taking him by the hand, with a smile forgave him. "Yet," continued he, "I can't help wondering at what you could see in my face, to think me a proper mark for deception."

"My dear sir," returned the other, "it was not your face, but your white stockings and the black ribband in your hair, that allured me. But no disparagement to your parts, I have deceived wiser men than you in my time; and yet, with all my tricks, the blockheads have been too many for me at last."

"I suppose," cried my son, "that the narrative of such a life as yours must be extremely instructive and amusing."

"Not much of either," returned Mr. Jenkinson. "Those relations which describe the tricks and vices only of mankind, by increasing our suspicion in life, retard our success. The traveller that distrusts every person he meets, and turns back upon the appearance of every man that looks like a robber, seldom arrives in time at his journey's end.

"Indeed I think from my own experience, that the knowing one is the silliest fellow under the sun. I was thought cunning from my very childhood; when but seven years old the ladies would say that I was a perfect little man; at fourteen I knew the world, cocked my hat, and loved the ladies; at twenty, though I was perfectly honest, yet every one thought me so cunning, that not one would trust me. Thus I was at last obliged to turn sharper in my own defence, and have lived ever since, my head throbbing with schemes to deceive, and my heart palpitating with fears of detection. I used often to laugh at your honest simple neighbour Flamborough, and one way or another generally cheated him once a year. Yet still the honest man went forward without suspicion, and grew rich, while I still continued tricksy and cunning, and was poor, without the consolation of being honest. However," continued he, "let me know your case, and what has brought you here; perhaps, though I have not skill to avoid a gaol myself, I may extricate my friends."

In compliance with his curiosity, I informed him of the whole train of accidents and follies that had plunged me into my present troubles, and my utter inability to get free.

After hearing my story, and pausing some minutes, he slapt his forehead, as if he had hit upon something material, and took his leave, saying he would try what could be done.

CHAPTER VIII

The same subject continued.

THE next morning I communicated to my wife and children the scheme I had planned of reforming the prisoners, which they received with universal disapprobation, alledging the impossibility and impropriety of it; adding, that my endeavours would no way contribute to their amendment, but might probably disgrace my calling.

"Excuse me," returned I, "these people, however fallen, are still men, and that is a very good title to my affections. Good counsel rejected returns to enrich the giver's bosom; and though the instruction I communicate may not mend them, yet it will assuredly mend myself. If these wretches, my children, were princes, there would be thousands ready to offer their ministry; but, in my opinion, the heart that is buried in a dungeon is as precious as that seated upon a throne. Yes, my treasures, if I can mend them I will; perhaps they will not all despise me. Perhaps I may catch up even one from the gulph, and that will be great gain; for is there upon earth a gem so precious as the human soul?"

Thus saying, I left them, and descended to the common prison, where I found the prisoners very merry, expecting my arrival; and each prepared with some gaol trick to play upon the doctor. Thus, as I was going to begin, one turned my wig awry, as if by accident, and then asked my pardon. A second, who stood at some distance, had a knack of spitting through his teeth, which fell in showers upon my book. A third would cry amen in such an affected tone as gave the rest great delight. A fourth had slyly picked my pocket of my spectacles. But there was one whose trick gave more universal pleasure than all the rest; for observing the manner in which I had disposed my books on the table before me, he very dexterously displaced one of them, and put an obscene jest-book of his own in the place. However I took no notice of all that this mischievous group of little beings could do; but went on, perfectly sensible that what was ridiculous in my attempt, would excite mirth only the first or second time, while what was serious would be permanent. My design succeeded, and, in less than six days some were penitent, and all attentive.

It was now that I applauded my perseverance and address, at thus giving sensibility to wretches divested of every moral feeling, and now began to think of doing them temporal services also, by rendering their situation somewhat more comfortable. Their time had hitherto been divided between famine and excess, tumultuous riot and bitter repining. Their only employment was quarrelling among each other, playing at cribbage, and cutting tobacco stoppers. From this last mode of idle industry I took the hint of setting such as chose to work at cutting pegs for tobacconists and shoemakers, the proper wood being bought by a general subscription, and when manufactured, sold by my appointment; so that each earned something every day: a trifle indeed, but sufficient to maintain him.

I did not stop here, but instituted fines for the punishment of immorality, and rewards for peculiar industry. Thus, in less than a fortnight, I had formed them into something social and humane, and had the pleasure of regarding myself as a legislator, who had brought men from their native ferocity into friendship and obedience.

And it were highly to be wished, that legislative power would thus direct the law rather to reformation than severity. That it would seem convinced that the work of eradicating crimes is not by making punishments familiar, but formidable. Then instead of our present prisons, which find or make men guilty, which enclose wretches for the commission of one crime, and return them, if returned alive, fitted for the perpetration of thousands; we should see, as in other parts of Europe, places of penitence and solitude, where the accused might be attended by such as could give them repentance if guilty, or new motives to virtue if innocent. And this, but not the increasing punishments, is the way to mend a state: nor can I avoid even questioning the validity of that right which social combinations have assumed of capitally punishing offences of a slight nature. In cases of murder their right is obvious, as it is the duty of us all, from the law of self-defence, to cut off that man who has shewn a disregard for the life of another. Against such, all nature rises in arms; but it is not so against him who steals my property. Natural law gives me no right to take away his life, as by that the horse he steals is as much his property as mine. If then I have any right, it must be from a compact made between us, that he who deprives the other of his horse shall die. But this is a false compact; because no man has a right to barter his life, no more than to take it away, as it is not his own. And beside, the compact is inadequate, and would be set aside even in a court of modern equity, as there is a great penalty for a very trifling convenience, since it is far better that two men should live, than that one man should ride. But a compact that is false between two men, is equally so between an hundred, or an hundred thousand; for as ten millions of circles can never make a square, so the united voice of myriads cannot lend the smallest foundation to falsehood. It is thus that reason speaks, and untutored nature says the same thing. Savages that are directed by natural law alone are very tender of the lives of each other; they seldom shed blood but to retaliate former cruelty.

Our Saxon ancestors, fierce as they were in war, had but few executions in times of peace; and in all commencing governments that have the print of nature still strong upon them, scarce any crime is held capital.

It is among the citizens of a refined community that penal laws, which are in the hands of the rich, are laid upon the poor. Government, while it grows older, seems to acquire the moroseness of age; and as if our property were become dearer in proportion as it increased, as if the more enormous our wealth, the more extensive our fears, all our possessions are paled up with new edicts every day, and hung round with gibbets to scare every invader.

I cannot tell whether it is from the number of our penal laws, or the licentiousness of our people, that this country should shew more convicts in a year, than half the dominions of Europe united. Perhaps it is owing to both; for they mutually produce each other. When by indiscriminate penal laws a nation beholds the same punishment affixed to dissimilar degrees of guilt, from perceiving no distinction in the penalty, the people are led to lose all sense of distinction in the crime, and this distinction is the bulwark of all morality: thus the multitude of laws produce new vices, and new vices call for fresh restraints.

It were to be wished then that power, instead of contriving new laws to punish vice, instead of drawing hard the cords of society till a convulsion come to burst them, instead of cutting away wretches as useless, before we have tried their utility, instead of converting correction into vengeance, it were to be wished that we tried the restrictive arts of government, and made law the protector, but not the tyrant of the people. We should then find that creatures, whose souls are held as dross, only wanted the hand of a refiner; we should then find that wretches, now stuck up for long tortures, lest luxury should feel a momentary pang, might, if properly treated, serve to sinew the state in times of danger; that, as their faces are like ours, their hearts are so too; that few minds are so base as that perseverance cannot amend; that a man may see his last crime without dying for it; and that very little blood will serve to cement our security.

CHAPTER IX

Happiness and misery rather the result of prudence than of virtue in this life. Temporal evils or felicities being regarded by heaven as things merely in themselves trifling and unworthy its care in the distribution.

I HAD now been confined more than a fortnight, but had not since my arrival been visited by my dear Olivia, and I greatly longed to see her. Having communicated my wishes to my wife, the next morning the poor girl entered my apartment, leaning on her sister's arm. The change which I saw in her countenance struck me. The numberless graces that once resided there were now fled, and the hand of death seemed to have molded every feature to alarm me. Her temples were sunk, her forehead was tense, and a fatal paleness sat upon her cheek.

"I am glad to see thee, my dear," cried I; "but why this dejection, Livy? I hope, my love, you have too great a regard for me, to permit disappointment thus to undermine a life which I prize as my own. Be chearful, child, and we may yet see happier days."

"You have ever, sir," replied she, "been kind to me, and it adds to my pain, that I shall never have an opportunity of sharing that happiness you promise. Happiness, I fear, is no longer reserved for me here; and I long to be rid of a place where I have only found distress. Indeed, Sir, I wish you would make a proper submission to Mr. Thornhill; it may, in some measure, induce him to pity you, and it will give me relief in dying."

"Never, child," replied I, "never will I be brought to acknowledge my daughter a prostitute; for though the world may look upon your offence with scorn, let it be mine to regard it as a mark of credulity, not of guilt. My dear, I am no way miserable in this place, however dismal it may seem, and be assured that while you continue to bless me by living, he shall never have my consent to make you more wretched by marrying another."

After the departure of my daughter, my fellow-prisoner, who was by at this interview, sensibly enough expostulated on my obstinacy, in refusing a submission, which promised to give me freedom. He observed, that the rest of my family was not to be sacrificed to the peace of one child alone, and she the only one who had offended me. "Beside," added he, "I don't know if it be just thus to obstruct the union of man and wife, which you do at present, by refusing to consent to a match you cannot hinder, but may render unhappy."

"Sir," replied I, "you are unacquainted with the man that oppresses us. I am very sensible that no submission I can make could procure me liberty even for an hour. I am told that even in this very room a debtor of his, no later than last year, died for want. But though my submission and approbation could transfer me from hence to the most beautiful apartment he is possessed of; yet I would grant neither, as something whispers me, that it would be giving a sanction to adultery. While my daughter lives, no other marriage of his shall ever be legal in my eye. Were she removed, indeed, I should be the basest of men, from any resentment of my own, to attempt putting asunder those who wish for an union. No, villain as he is, I should then wish him married, to prevent the consequences of his future debaucheries. But now should I not be the most cruel of all fathers, to sign an Instrument which must send my child to the grave, merely to avoid a prison myself; and thus to escape one pang, break my child's heart with a thousand?"

He acquiesced in the justice of this answer, but could not avoid observing, that he feared my daughter's life was already too much wasted to keep me long a prisoner. "However," continued he, "though you refuse to submit to the nephew, I hope you have no objections to laying your case before the uncle, who has the first character in the kingdom for every thing that is just and good. I would advise you to send him a letter by the post, intimating all his nephew's ill usage, and my life for it, that in three days you shall have an answer." I thank'd him for the hint, and instantly set about complying; but I wanted paper, and unluckily all our money had been laid out that morning in provisions, however, he supplied me.

For the three ensuing days I was in a state of anxiety, to know what reception my letter might meet with; but in the mean time was frequently solicited by my wife to submit to any conditions rather than remain here, and every hour received repeated accounts of the decline of my daughter's health. The third day and the fourth arrived, but I received no answer to my letter: the complaints of a stranger against a favourite nephew, were no way likely to succeed; so that these hopes soon vanished like all my former. My mind, however, still supported itself, though confinement and bad air began to make a visible alteration in my health, and my arm that had suffered in the fire, grew worse. My children, however, sate by me, and while I was stretched on my straw, read to me by turns, or listened and wept at my instructions. But my daughter's health declined faster than mine; every message from her contributed to encrease my apprehensions and pain. The fifth morning after I had written the letter which was sent to sir William Thornhill, I was alarmed with an account that she was speechless. Now it was, that confinement was truly painful to me; my soul was bursting from its prison to be near the pillow of my child, to comfort, to strengthen her, to receive her last wishes, and teach her soul the way to heaven! Another account came. She was expiring, and yet I was debarred the small comfort of weeping by her. My fellow prisoner, some time after, came with the last account. He bade me be patient. She was dead!——The next morning he returned, and found me with my two little ones, now my only companions, who were using all their innocent efforts to comfort me. They entreated to read to me, and bade me not to cry, for I was now too old to weep. "And is not my sister an angel, now, pappa," cried the eldest, "and why then are you sorry for her? I wish I were an angel out of this frightful place, if my pappa were with me." "Yes," added my youngest darling, "Heaven, where my sister is, is a finer place than this, and there are none but good people there, and the people here are very bad."

Mr. Jenkinson interrupted their harmless prattle, by observing that now my daughter was no more, I should seriously think of the rest of my family, and attempt to save my own life, which was every day declining, for want of necessaries and wholesome air. He added, that it was now incumbent on me to sacrifice any pride or resentment of my own, to the welfare of those who depended on me for support; and that I was now, both by reason and justice, obliged to try to reconcile my landlord.

"Heaven be praised," replied I, "there is no pride left me now. I should detest my own heart, if I saw either pride or resentment lurking there. On the contrary, as my oppressor has been once my parishioner, I hope one day to present him up an unpolluted soul at the eternal tribunal. No, sir, I have no resentment now, and though he has taken from me what I held dearer than all his treasures, though he has wrung my heart, for I am sick almost to fainting, very sick, my fellow prisoner, yet that shall never inspire me with vengeance. I am now willing to approve his marriage, and if this submission can do him any pleasure, let him know, that if I have done him any injury, I am sorry for it." Mr. Jenkinson took pen and ink, and wrote down my submission nearly as I have exprest it, to which I signed my name. My son was employed to carry the letter to Mr. Thornhill, who was then at his seat in the country. He went, and, in about six hours returned with a verbal answer. He had some difficulty, he said, to get a sight of his landlord, as the servants were insolent and suspicious; but he accidentally saw him as he was going out upon business, preparing for his marriage, which was to be in three days. He continued to inform us, that he stept up in the humblest manner, and delivered the letter, which, when Mr. Thornhill had read, he said that all submission was now too late and unnecessary; that he had heard of our application to his uncle, which met with the contempt it deserved; and as for the rest, that all future applications should be directed to his attorney, not to him. He observed, however, that as he had a very good opinion of the discretion of the two young ladies, they might have been the most agreeable intercessors.

"Well, sir," said I to my fellow prisoner, "you now discover the temper of the man that oppresses me. He can at once be facetious and cruel; but let him use me as he will, I shall soon be free, in spite of all his bolts to restrain me. I am now drawing towards an abode that looks brighter as I approach it: this expectation cheers my afflictions, and though I leave an helpless family of orphans behind me, yet they will not be utterly forsaken; some friend, perhaps, will be found to assist them for the sake of their poor father, and some may charitably relieve them for the sake of their heavenly Father."

Just as I spoke, my wife, whom I had not seen that day before, appeared with looks of terror, and making efforts, but unable to speak. "Why, my love," cried I, "why will you thus encrease my afflictions by your own? what though no submissions can turn our severe master, though he has doomed me to die in this place of wretchedness, and though we have lost a darling child, yet still you will find comfort in your other children when I shall be no more." "We have indeed lost," returned she, "a darling child. My Sophia, my dearest, is gone, snatched from us, carried off by ruffians!" "How, madam," cried my fellow prisoner, "miss Sophia carried off by villains, sure it cannot be?"

She could only answer with a fixed look and a flood of tears. But one of the prisoners' wives, who was present, and came in with her, gave us a more distinct account: she informed us that as my wife, my daughter, and herself, were taking a walk together on the great road a little way out of the village, a post-chaise and pair drove up to them and instantly stopt. Upon which a well drest man, but not Mr. Thornhill, stepping out, clasped my daughter round the waist, and forcing her in, bid the postillion drive on, so that they were out of sight in a moment.

"Now," cried I, "the sum of my miseries is made up, nor is it in the power of any thing on earth to give me another pang. What! not one left! not to leave me one! the monster! the child that was next my heart! she had the beauty of an angel, and almost the wisdom of an angel. But support that woman, nor let her fall. Not to leave me one!"—"Alas, my husband," said my wife, "you seem to want comfort even more than I. Our distresses are great; but I could bear this and more, if I saw you but easy. They may take away my children, and all the world, if they leave me but you."

My Son, who was present, endeavoured to moderate our grief; he bade us take comfort, for he hoped that we might still have reason to be thankful.—"My child," cried I, "look round the world, and see if there be any happiness left me now. Is not every ray of comfort shut out; while all our bright prospects only lie beyond the grave!"—"My dear father," returned he, "I hope there is still something that will give you an interval of satisfaction; for I have a letter from my brother George."—"What of him, child," interrupted I, "does he know our misery? I hope my boy is exempt from any part of what his wretched family suffers?"—"Yes, sir," returned he, "he is perfectly gay, chearful, and happy. His letter brings nothing but good news; he is the favourite of his colonel, who promises to procure him the very next lieutenancy that becomes vacant!"

"And are you sure of all this," cried my wife, "are you sure that nothing ill has befallen my boy?"—"Nothing indeed, madam," returned my son; "you shall see the letter, which will give you the highest pleasure; and if any thing can procure you comfort, I am sure that will." "But are you sure," still repeated she, "that the letter is from himself, and that he is really so happy?"—"Yes, Madam," replied he, "it is certainly his, and he will one day be the credit and the support of our family!"—"Then I thank providence," cried she, "that my last letter to him has miscarried. Yes, my dear," continued she, turning to me, "I will now confess, that though the hand of heaven is sore upon us in other instances, it has been favourable here. By the last letter I wrote my son, which was in the bitterness of anger, I desired him, upon his mother's blessing, and if he had the heart of a man, to see justice done his father and sister, and avenge our cause. But thanks be to him that directs all things, it has miscarried, and I am at rest." "Woman, cried I, "thou hast done very ill, and at another time my reproaches might have been more severe. Oh! what a tremendous gulph hast thou escaped, that would have buried both thee and him in endless ruin. Providence, indeed, has here been kinder to us than we to ourselves. It has reserved that son to be the father and protector of my children when I shall be away. How unjustly did I complain of being stript of every comfort, when still I hear that he is happy and insensible of our afflictions; still kept in reserve to support his widowed mother, and to protect his brothers and sisters. But what sisters has he left, he has no sisters now, they are all gone, robbed from me, and I am undone."—"Father," interrupted my son, "I beg you will give me leave to read his letter, I know it will please you." Upon which, with my permission, he read as follows:

Honoured Sir,

I have called off my imagination a few moments from the pleasures that surround me, to fix it upon objects that are still more pleasing, the dear little fire-side at home. My fancy draws that harmless groupe as listening to every line of this with great composure. I view those faces with delight which never felt the deforming hand of ambition or distress! But whatever your happiness may be at home, I am sure it will be some addition to it, to hear that I am perfectly pleased with my situation, and every way happy here.

Our regiment is countermanded, and is not to leave the kingdom; the colonel, who professes himself my friend, takes me with him to all companies where he is acquainted, and after my first visit, I generally find myself received with encreased respect upon repeating it. I danced last night with lady G—, and could I forget you know whom, I might be perhaps successful. But it is my fate still to remember others, while I am myself forgotten by most of my absent friends, and in this number, I fear, Sir, that I must consider you; for I have long expected the pleasure of a letter from home to no purpose. Olivia and Sophia too, promised to write, but seem to have forgotten me. Tell them they are two arrant little baggages, and that I am at this moment in a most violent passion with them: yet still, I know not how, tho' I want to bluster a little, my heart is respondent only to softer emotions. Then tell them, sir, that after all, I love them affectionately, and be assured of my ever remaining

Your dutiful son.

"In all our miseries," cried I, "what thanks have we not to return, that one at least of our family is exempted from what we suffer. Heaven be his guard, and keep my boy thus happy to be the support of his widowed mother, and the father of these two babes, which is all the patrimony I can now bequeath him. May he keep their innocence from the temptations of want, and be their conductor in the paths of honour." I had scarce said these words, when a noise, like that of a tumult, seemed to proceed from the prison below; it died away soon after, and a clanking of fetters was heard along the passage that led to my apartment. The keeper of the prison entered, holding a man all bloody, wounded and fettered with the heaviest irons. I looked with compassion on the wretch as he approached me, but with horror when I found it was my own son.—"My George! My George! and do I behold thee thus. Wounded! Fettered! Is this thy happiness! Is this the manner you return to me? O that this sight could break my heart at once and let me die!"

"Where, sir, is your fortitude?" returned my son with an intrepid voice. "I must suffer, my life is forfeited, and let them take it."

I tried to restrain my passion for a few minutes in silence, but I thought I should have died with the effort.—"O my boy, my heart weeps to behold thee thus, and I cannot, cannot help it. In the moment that I thought thee blest, and prayed for thy safety, to behold thee thus again! Chained, wounded. And yet the death of the youthful is happy. But I am old, a very old man, and have lived to see this day. To see my children all untimely falling about me, while I continue a wretched survivor in the midst of ruin! May all the curses that ever sunk a soul fall heavy upon the murderer of my children. May he live, like me, to see—"

"Hold, Sir," replied my son, "or I shall blush for thee. How, Sir, forgetful of your age, your holy calling, thus to arrogate the justice of heaven, and fling those curses upward that must soon descend to crush thy own grey head with destruction! No, Sir, let it be your care now to fit me for that vile death I must shortly suffer, to arm me with hope and resolution, to give me courage to drink of that bitterness which must shortly be my portion."

"My child, you must not die: I am sure no offence of thine can deserve so vile a punishment. My George could never be guilty of any crime to make his ancestors ashamed of him."

"Mine, Sir," returned my son, "is I fear, an unpardonable one. When I received my mother's letter from home, I immediately came down, determined to punish the betrayer of our honour, and sent him an order to meet me, which he answered, not in person, but by dispatching four of his domestics to seize me. I wounded one who first assaulted me, and I fear desperately; but the rest made me their prisoner. The coward is determined to put the law in execution against me; the proofs are undeniable; I have sent a challenge, and as I am the first transgressor upon the statute, I see no hopes of pardon. But you have often charmed me with your lessons of fortitude; let me now, Sir, find them in your example."

"And, my son, you shall find them. I am now raised above this world, and all the pleasures it can produce. From this moment I break from my heart all the ties that held it down to earth, and will prepare to fit us both for eternity. Yes, my son, I will point out the way, and my soul shall guide yours in the ascent, for we will take our flight together. I now see and am convinced you can expect no pardon here, and I can only exhort you to seek it at that greatest tribunal where we both shall shortly answer. But let us not be niggardly in our exhortation, but let all our fellow prisoners have a share: good gaoler, let them be permitted to stand here, while I attempt to improve them." Thus saying, I made an effort to rise from my straw, but wanted strength, and was able only to recline against the wall. The prisoners assembled according to my directions, for they loved to hear my counsel; my son and his mother supported me on either side; I looked and saw that none were wanting, and then addressed them with the following exhortation.

CHAPTER X

The equal dealings of providence demonstrated with regard to the happy and the miserable here below. That from the nature of pleasure and pain, the wretched must be repaid the balance of their sufferings in the life here-after.

MY friends, my children, and fellow sufferers, when I reflect on the distribution of good and evil here below, I find that much has been given man to enjoy, yet still more to suffer. Though we should examine the whole world, we shall not find one man so happy as to have nothing left to wish for; but we daily see thousands who by suicide shew us they have nothing left to hope. In this life then it appears that we cannot be entirely blest; but yet we may be completely miserable.

Why man should thus feel pain, why our wretchedness should be requisite in the formation of universal felicity, why, when all other systems are made perfect by the perfection of their subordinate parts, the great system should require for its perfection, parts that are not only subordinate to others, but imperfect in themselves? These are questions that never can be explained, and might be useless if known. On this subject providence has thought fit to elude our curiosity, satisfied with granting us motives to consolation.

In this situation, man has called in the friendly assistance of philosophy, and heaven seeing the incapacity of that to console him, has given him the aid of religion. The consolations of philosophy are very amusing, but often fallacious. It tells us that life is filled with comforts, if we will but enjoy them; and on the other hand, that though we unavoidably have miseries here, life is short, and they will soon be over. Thus do these consolations destroy each other; for if life is a place of comfort, its shortness must be misery, and if it be long, our griefs are protracted. Thus philosophy is weak; but religion comforts in an higher strain. Man is here, it tells us, fitting up his mind, and preparing it for another abode. When the good man leaves the body, and is all a glorious mind, he will find he has been making himself a heaven of happiness here, while the wretch that has been maimed and contaminated by his vices, shrinks from his body with terror, and finds that he has anticipated the vengeance of heaven. To religion then we must hold in every circumstance of life for our truest comfort; for if already we are happy, it is a pleasure to think that we can make that happiness unending; and if we are miserable, it is very consoling to think that there is a place of rest. Thus to the fortunate religion holds out a continuance of bliss, to the wretched a change from pain.

But though religion is very kind to all men, it has promised peculiar rewards to the unhappy; the sick, the naked, the houseless, the heavy-laden, and the prisoner, have ever most frequent promises in our sacred law. The author of our religion every where professes himself the wretch's friend, and unlike the false ones of this world, bestows all his caresses upon the forlorn. The unthinking have censured this as partiality, as a preference without merit to deserve it. But they never reflect that it is not in the power even of heaven itself to make the offer of unceasing felicity as great a gift to the happy as to the miserable. To the first eternity is but a single blessing, since at most it but encreases what they already possess. To the latter it is a double advantage; for it diminishes their pain here, and rewards them with heavenly bliss hereafter.

But providence is in another respect kinder to the poor than to the rich; for as it thus makes the life after death more desirable, so it smooths the passage there. The wretched have had a long familiarity with every face of terror. The man of sorrows lays himself quietly down, without possessions to regret, and but few ties to stop his departure: he feels only nature's pang in the final separation, and this is no way greater than he has often fainted under before; for after a certain degree of pain, every new breach that death opens in the constitution, nature kindly covers with insensibility.

Thus providence has given the wretched two advantages over the happy in this life, greater felicity in dying, and in heaven all that superiority of pleasure which arises from contrasted enjoyment. And this superiority, my friends, is no small advantage, and seems to be one of the pleasures of the poor man in the parable; for though he was already in heaven, and felt all the raptures it could give, yet it was mentioned as an addition to his happiness, that he had once been wretched and now was comforted; that he had known what it was to be miserable, and now felt what it was to be happy.

Thus, my friends, you see religion does what philosophy could never do: it shews the equal dealings of heaven to the happy and the unhappy, and levels all human enjoyments to nearly the same standard. It gives to both rich and poor the same happiness hereafter, and equal hopes to aspire after it; but if the rich have the advantage of enjoying pleasure here, the poor have the endless satisfaction of knowing what it was once to be miserable, when crowned with endless felicity hereafter; and even though this should be called a small advantage, yet being an eternal one, it must make up by duration what the temporal happiness of the great may have exceeded by intenseness.

These are therefore the consolations which the wretched have peculiar to themselves, and in which they are above the rest of mankind; in other respects they are below them. They who would know the miseries of the poor, must see life and endure it. To declaim on the temporal advantages they enjoy, is only repeating what none either believe or practise. The men who have the necessaries of living are not poor, and they who want them must be miserable. Yes, my friends, we must be miserable. No vain efforts of a refined imagination can sooth the wants of nature, can give elastic sweetness to the dank vapour of a dungeon, or ease to the throbbings of a broken heart. Let the philosopher from his couch of softness tell us that we can resist all these. Alas! the effort by which we resist them is still the greatest pain! Death is slight, and any man may sustain it; but torments are dreadful, and these no man can endure.

To us then, my friends, the promises of happiness in heaven should be peculiarly dear; for if our reward be in this life alone, we are then indeed of all men the most miserable. When I look round these gloomy walls, made to terrify, as well as to confine us; this light that only serves to shew the horrors of the place, those shackles that tyranny has imposed, or crime made necessary; when I survey these emaciated looks, and hear those groans, O, my friends, what a glorious exchange would heaven be for these! To fly through regions unconfined as air, to bask in the sunshine of eternal bliss, to carrol over endless hymns of praise, to have no master to threaten or insult us, but the form of Goodness himself for ever in our eyes; when I think of these things, death becomes the messenger of very glad tidings; when I think of these things, his sharpest arrow becomes the staff of my support; when I think of these things, what is there in life worth having? when I think of these things, what is there that should not be spurned away? kings in their palaces should groan for such advantages; but we, humbled as we are, should yearn for them.

And shall these things be ours? Ours they will certainly be if we but try for them; and what is a comfort, we are shut out from many temptations that would retard our pursuit. Only let us try for them, and they will certainly be ours, and what is still a comfort, shortly too; for if we look back on past life, it appears but a very short span, and whatever we may think of the rest of life, it will yet be found of less duration; as we grow older, the days seem to grow shorter, and our intimacy with time, ever lessens the perception of his stay. Then let us take comfort now, for we shall soon be at our journey's end; we shall soon lay down the heavy burthen laid by heaven upon us; and though death, the only friend of the wretched, for a little while mocks the weary traveller with the view, and like his horizon, still flies before him; yet the time will certainly and shortly come, when we shall cease from our toil; when the luxurious great ones of the world shall no more tread us to the earth; when we shall think with pleasure of our sufferings below; when we shall be surrounded with all our friends, or such as deserved our friendship; when our bliss shall be unutterable, and still, to crown all, unending.

CHAPTER XI

Happier prospects begin to appear. Let us be inflexible, and fortune will at last change in our favour.

When I had thus finished, and my audience was retired, the gaoler, who was one of the most humane of his profession, hoped I would not be displeased, as what he did was but his duty, observing that he must be obliged to remove my son into a stronger cell, but that he should be permitted to revisit me every morning. I thanked him for his clemency, and grasping my boy's hand, bade him farewell, and be mindful of the great duty that was before him.

I again, therefore, laid me down, and one of my little ones sate by my bedside reading, when Mr. Jenkinson entering, informed me that there was news of my daughter; for that she was seen by a person about two hours before, in a strange gentleman's company, and that they had stopt at a neighbouring village for refreshment, and seemed as if returning to town. He had scarcely delivered this news, when the gaoler came with looks of haste and pleasure, to inform me, that my daughter was found. Moses came running in a moment after, crying out that his Sister Sophy was below, and coming up with our old friend Mr. Burchell.

Just as he delivered this news, my dearest girl entered, and with looks almost wild with pleasure, ran to kiss me in a transport of affection. Her mother's tears and silence also shewed her pleasure.—"Here, pappa," cried the charming girl, "here is the brave man to whom I owe my delivery; to this gentleman's intrepidity I am indebted for my happiness and safety——" A kiss from Mr. Burchell, whose pleasure seemed even greater than hers, interrupted what she was going to add.

"Ah, Mr. Burchell," cried I, "this is but a wretched habitation you now find us in; and we are now very different from what you last saw us. You were ever our friend: we have long discovered our errors with regard to you, and repented of our ingratitude. After the vile usage you then received at my hands, I am almost ashamed to behold your face; yet I hope you'll forgive me, as I was deceived by a base ungenerous wretch, who, under the mask of friendship, has undone me."

"It is impossible," cried Mr. Burchell, "that I should forgive you, as you never deserved my resentment. I partly saw your delusion then, and as it was out of my power to restrain, I could only pity it!"

"It was ever my conjecture," cried I, "that your mind was noble; but now I find it so. But tell me, my dear child, how hast thou been relieved, or who the ruffians were who carried thee away?"

"Indeed, Sir," replied she, "as to the villain who carried me off, I am yet ignorant. For as my mamma and I were walking out, he came behind us, and almost before I could call for help, forced me into the post-chaise, and in an instant the horses drove away. I met several persons on the road, to whom I cried out for assistance; but they disregarded my entreaties. In the mean time, the ruffian himself used every art to hinder me from crying out: he flattered and threatened by turns, and swore that if I continued but silent, he intended no harm. In the mean time, I had broken the canvas that he had drawn up, and whom should I perceive at some distance but your old friend Mr. Burchell, walking along with his usual swiftness, with the great stick for which we used so much to ridicule him. As soon as we came within hearing, I called out to him by name, and entreated his help. I repeated my exclamations several times, upon which, with a very loud voice, he bid the postillion stop; but the boy took no notice, but drove on with still greater speed. I now thought he could never overtake us, when in less than a minute I saw Mr. Burchell come running up by the side of the horses, and with one blow knock the postillion to the ground. The horses when he was fallen soon stopt of themselves, and the ruffian stepping out, with oaths and menaces drew his sword, and ordered him at his peril to retire; but Mr. Burchell running up, shivered his sword to pieces, and then pursued him for near a quarter of a mile; but he made his escape. I was at this time come out myself, willing to assist my deliverer; but he soon returned to me in triumph. The postillion, who was recovered, was going to make his escape too; but Mr. Burchell ordered him at his peril to mount again, and drive back to town. Finding it impossible to resist, he reluctantly complied, though the wound he had received seemed, to me at least, to be dangerous. He continued to complain of the pain as we drove along, so that he at last excited Mr. Burchell's compassion, who, at my request, exchanged him for another at an inn where we called on our return."

"Welcome, then," cried I, "my child, and thou her gallant deliverer, a thousand welcomes. Though our chear is but wretched, yet our hearts are ready to receive you. And now, Mr. Burchell, as you have delivered my girl, if you think her a recompence she is yours; if you can stoop to an alliance with a family so poor as mine, take her, obtain her consent, as I know you have her heart, and you have mine. And let me tell you, Sir, that I give you no small treasure; she has been celebrated for beauty it is true, but that is not my meaning, I give you up a treasure in her mind."

"But, I suppose, Sir," cried Mr. Burchell, "that you are apprized of my circumstances, and of my incapacity to support her as she deserves?"

"If your present objection," replied I, "be meant as an evasion of my offer, I desist: but I know no man so worthy to deserve her as you; and if I could give her thousands, and thousands sought her from me, yet my honest brave Burchell should be my dearest choice."

To all this his silence alone seemed to give a mortifying refusal, and without the least reply to my offer, he demanded if we could not be furnished with refreshments from the next inn, to which being answered in the affirmative, he ordered them to send in the best dinner that could be provided upon such short notice. He bespoke also a dozen of their best wine; and some cordials for me. Adding, with a smile, that he would stretch a little for once, and though in a prison, asserted he was never better disposed to be merry. The waiter soon made his appearance with preparations for dinner, a table was lent us by the gaoler, who seemed remarkably assiduous, the wine was disposed in order, and two very well-dressed dishes were brought in.

My daughter had not yet heard of her poor brother's melancholy situation, and we all seemed unwilling to damp her chearfulness by the relation. But it was in vain that I attempted to appear chearful, the circumstances of my unfortunate son broke through all efforts to dissemble; so that I was at last obliged to damp our mirth by relating his misfortunes, and wishing that he might be permitted to share with us in this little interval of satisfaction. After my guests were recovered from the consternation my account had produced, I requested also that Mr. Jenkinson, a fellow prisoner, might be admitted, and the gaoler granted my request with an air of unusual submission. The clanking of my son's irons was no sooner heard along the passage, than his sister ran impatiently to meet him; while Mr. Burchell, in the mean time, asked me if my son's name were George; to which replying in the affirmative, he still continued silent. As soon as my boy entered the room, I could perceive he regarded Mr. Burchell with a look of astonishment and reverence. "Come on," cried I, "my son, though we are fallen very low, yet providence has been pleased to grant us some small relaxation from pain. Thy sister is restored to us, and there is her deliverer: to that brave man it is that I am indebted for yet having a daughter; give him, my boy, the hand of friendship, he deserves our warmest gratitude."

My son seemed all this while regardless of what I said, and

still continued fixed at a respectful distance.—"My dear brother," cried his sister, "why don't you thank my good deliverer? the brave should ever love each other."

He still continued his silence and astonishment, till our guest at last perceived himself to be known, and assuming all his native dignity, desired my son to come forward. Never before had I seen anything so truly majestic as the air he assumed upon this occasion. The greatest object in the universe, says a certain philosopher,[1] is a good man struggling with adversity; yet there is still a greater, which is the good man that comes to relieve it. After he had regarded my son for some time with a superior air, "I again find," said he, "unthinking boy, that the same crime"—— But here he was interrupted by one of the gaoler's servants, who came to inform us that a person of distinction, who had driven into town with a chariot and several attendants, sent his respects to the gentleman that was with us, and begged to know when he should think proper to be waited upon.—"Bid the fellow wait," cried our guest, "till I shall have leisure to receive him;" and then turning to my son, "I again find, Sir," proceeded he, "that you are guilty of the same offence for which you once had my reproof, and for which the law is now preparing its justest punishments. You imagine, perhaps, that a contempt for your own life, gives you a right to take that of another: but where, Sir, is the difference between a duellist who hazards a life of no value, and the murderer who acts with greater security? Is it any diminution of the gamester's fraud when he alleges that he has staked a counter?"

"Alas, Sir," cried I, "whoever you are, pity the poor misguided creature; for what he has done was in obedience to a deluded mother, who in the bitterness of her resentment required him upon her blessing to avenge her quarrel. Here, Sir, is the letter, which will serve to convince you of her imprudence, and diminish his guilt."

[1] [Seneca, *De Providentia*, 2.6.]

He took the letter, and hastily read it over. "This," says he, "though not a perfect excuse, is such a palliation of his fault, as induces me to forgive him. And now, Sir," continued he, kindly taking my son by the hand, "I see you are surprised at finding me here; but I have often visited prisons upon occasions less interesting. I am now come to see justice done a worthy man, for whom I have the most sincere esteem. I have long been a disguised spectator of thy father's benevolence. I have at his little dwelling enjoyed respect uncontaminated by flattery, and have received that happiness that courts could not give, from the amusing simplicity around his fire-side. My nephew has been apprised of my intentions of coming here, and I find is arrived; it would be wronging him and you to condemn him without examination: if there be injury, there shall be redress; and this I may say without boasting, that none have ever taxed the injustice of Sir William Thornhill."

We now found the personage whom we had so long entertained as an harmless amusing companion, was no other than the celebrated Sir William Thornhill, to whose virtues and singularities scarce any were strangers. The poor Mr. Burchell was in reality a man of large fortune and great interest, to whom senates listened with applause, and whom party heard with conviction; who was the friend of his country, but loyal to his king. My poor wife recollecting her former familiarity, seemed to shrink with apprehension; but Sophia, who a few moments before thought him her own, now perceiving the immense distance to which he was removed by fortune, was unable to conceal her tears.

"Ah, Sir," cried my wife, with a piteous aspect, "how is it possible that I can ever have your forgiveness; the slights you received from me the last time I had the honour of seeing you at our house, and the jokes which I audaciously threw out, these jokes, Sir, I fear can never be forgiven."

"My dear good lady," returned he with a smile, "if you

had your joke, I had my answer: I'll leave it to all the company if mine were not as good as yours. To say the truth, I know no body whom I am disposed to be angry with at present but the fellow who so frighted my little girl here. I had not even time to examine the rascal's person so as to describe him in an advertisement. Can you tell me, Sophia, my dear, whether you should know him again?"

"Indeed, Sir," replied she, "I can't be positive; yet now I recollect he had a large mark over one of his eye-brows."—"I ask pardon, madam," interrupted Jenkinson, who was by, "but be so good as to inform me if the fellow wore his own red hair?"—"Yes, I think so," cried Sophia. "And did your honour," continued he, turning to Sir William, "observe the length of his legs?"—"I can't be sure of their length," cried the Baronet, "but I am convinced of their swiftness; for he out-ran me, which is what I thought few men in the kingdom could have done."—"Please your honour," cried Jenkinson, "I know the man: it is certainly the same; the best runner in England; he has beaten Pinwire of Newcastle, Timothy Baxter is his name, I know him perfectly, and the very place of his retreat this moment. If your honour will bid Mr. Gaoler let two of his men go with me, I'll engage to produce him to you in an hour at farthest." Upon this the gaoler was called, who instantly appearing, Sir William demanded if he knew him. "Yes, please your honour," replied the gaoler, "I know Sir William Thornhill well, and every body that knows any thing of him, will desire to know more of him."—"Well then," said the Baronet, "my request is, that you will permit this man and two of your servants to go upon a message by my authority, and as I am in the commission of the peace, I undertake to secure you."—"Your promise is sufficient," replied the other, "and you may at a minute's warning send them over England whenever your honour thinks fit."

In pursuance of the gaoler's compliance, Jenkinson was despatched in search of Timothy Baxter, while we were amused with the assiduity of our youngest boy Bill, who had just come in and climbed up to Sir William's neck, in order to kiss him. His mother was immediately going to chastise his familiarity, but the worthy man prevented her; and taking the child, all ragged as he was, upon his knee, "What, Bill, you chubby rogue," cried he, "do you remember your old friend Burchell? and Dick too, my honest veteran, are you here, you shall find I have not forgot you." So saying, he gave each a large piece of gingerbread, which the poor fellows eat very heartily, as they had got that morning but a very scanty breakfast.

We now sate down to dinner, which was almost cold; but previously, my arm still continuing painful, Sir William wrote a prescription, for he had made the study of physic his amusement, and was more than moderately skilled in the profession: this being sent to an apothecary who lived in the place, my arm was dressed, and I found almost instantaneous relief. We were waited upon at dinner by the gaoler himself, who was willing to do our guest all the honour in his power. But before we had well dined, another message was brought from his nephew, desiring permission to appear, in order to vindicate his innocence and honour, with which request the Baronet complied, and desired Mr. Thornhill to be introduced.

CHAPTER XII

Former benevolence now repaid with unexpected interest.

MR. THORNHILL made his appearance with a smile, which he seldom wanted, and was going to embrace his uncle, which the other repulsed with an air of disdain. "No fawning, Sir, at present," cried the Baronet, with a look of severity, "the only way to my heart is by the road of honour; but here I only see complicated instances of falsehood, cowardice, and oppression. How is it, Sir, that this poor man, for whom I know you professed a friendship, is used thus hardly? His daughter vilely seduced, as a recompence for his hospitality, and he himself thrown into a prison perhaps but for resenting the insult? His son too, whom you feared to face as a man——"

"Is it possible, Sir," interrupted his nephew, "that my uncle should object that as a crime which his repeated instructions alone have persuaded me to avoid."

"Your rebuke," cried Sir William, "is just; you have acted in this instance prudently and well, though not quite as your father would have done: my brother indeed was the soul of honour; but thou—— yes you have acted in this instance perfectly right, and it has my warmest approbation."

"And I hope," said his nephew, "that the rest of my conduct will not be found to deserve censure. I appeared, Sir, with this gentleman's daughter at some places of public amusement; thus what was levity, scandal called by a harsher name, and it was reported that I had debauched her. I waited on her father in person, willing to clear the thing to his satisfaction, and he received me only with insult and abuse. As for the rest, with regard to his being here, my attorney and steward can best inform you, as I commit the management of business entirely to them. If he has contracted debts and is unwilling or even unable to pay them, it is their business to proceed in this manner, and I see no hardship or injustice in pursuing the most legal means of redress."

"If this," cried Sir William, "be as you have stated it, there is nothing unpardonable in your offence; and though your conduct might have been more generous in not suffering this gentleman to be oppressed by subordinate tyranny, yet it has been at least equitable."

"He cannot contradict a single particular," replied the 'Squire, "I defy him to do so, and several of my servants are ready to attest what I say. Thus, Sir," continued he, finding that I was silent, for in fact I could not contradict him, "thus,

Sir, my own innocence is vindicated; but though at your entreaty I am ready to forgive this gentleman every other offence, yet his attempts to lessen me in your esteem, excite a resentment that I cannot govern. And this too at a time when his son was actually preparing to take away my life; this, I say, was such guilt, that I am determined to let the law take its course. I have here the challenge that was sent me, and two witnesses to prove it; one of my servants has been wounded dangerously, and even though my uncle himself should dissuade me, which I know he will not, yet I will see public justice done, and he shall suffer for it.

"Thou monster," cried my wife, "hast thou not had vengeance enough already, but must my poor boy feel thy cruelty? I hope that good Sir William will protect us, for my son is as innocent as a child; I am sure he is, and never did harm to man."

"Madam," replied the good man, "your wishes for his safety are not greater than mine; but I am sorry to find his guilt too plain; and if my nephew persists——" But the appearance of Jenkinson and the gaoler's two servants now called off our attention, who entered, haling in a tall man, very genteelly drest, and answering the description already given of the ruffian who had carried off my daughter.—"Here," cried Jenkinson, pulling him in, "here we have him; and if ever there was a candidate for Tyburn, this is one."

The moment Mr. Thornhill perceived the prisoner, and Jenkinson, who had him in custody, he seemed to shrink back with terror. His face became pale with conscious guilt, and he would have withdrawn; but Jenkinson, who perceived his design, stopt him.—"What, 'Squire," cried he, "are you ashamed of your two old acquaintances, Jenkinson and Baxter? but this is the way that all great men forget their friends, though I am resolved we will not forget you. Our prisoner, please your honour," continued he, turning to Sir William, "has already confessed all. This is the gentleman reported to be so dangerously wounded: He declares that it was Mr. Thornhill who first put him upon this affair, that he gave him the cloaths he now wears to appear like a gentleman, and furnished him with the post-chaise. The plan was laid between them that he should carry off the young lady to a place of safety, and that there he should threaten and terrify her; but Mr. Thornhill was to come in in the mean time, as if by accident, to her rescue, and that they should fight awhile, and then he was to run off, by which Mr. Thornhill would have the better opportunity of gaining her affections himself under the character of her defender."

Sir William remembered the coat to have been frequently worn by his nephew, and all the rest the prisoner himself confirmed by a more circumstantial account; concluding, that Mr. Thornhill had often declared to him that he was in love with both sisters at the same time.

"Heavens," cried Sir William, "what a viper have I been fostering in my bosom! And so fond of public justice too as he seemed to be. But he shall have it; secure him, Mr. Gaoler—yet hold, I fear there is not legal evidence to detain him."

Upon this, Mr. Thornhill, with the utmost humility, entreated that two such abandoned wretches might not be admitted as evidences against him, but that his servants should be examined.—"Your servants!" replied Sir William, "wretch, call them yours no longer: but come let us hear what those fellows have to say, let his butler be called."

When the butler was introduced, he soon perceived by his former master's looks that all his power was now over. "Tell me," cried Sir William sternly, "have you ever seen your master and that fellow drest up in his cloaths in company together?" "Yes, please your honour," cried the butler, "a thousand times: he was the man that always brought him his ladies."—"How," interrupted young Mr. Thornhill, "this to my face!"—"Yes," replied the butler, "or to any man's face. To tell you a truth, Master Thornhill, I never either loved you or liked you, and I don't care if I tell you now a piece of my mind."—"Now then," cried Jenkinson, "tell his honour whether you know any thing of me." —"I can't say," replied the butler, "that I know much good of you. The night that gentleman's daughter was deluded to our house, you were one of them."—"So then," cried Sir William, "I find you have brought a very fine witness to prove your innocence: thou stain to humanity! to associate with such wretches!" (But continuing his examination) "You tell me, Mr. Butler, that this was the person who brought him this old gentleman's daughter?"—"No, please your honour," replied the butler, "he did not bring her, for the 'Squire himself undertook that business; but he brought the priest that pretended to marry them."—"It is but too true," cried Jenkinson, "I cannot deny it, that was the employment assigned me, and I confess it to my confusion."

"Good heavens!" exclaimed the Baronet, "how every new discovery of his villainy alarms me. All his guilt is now too plain, and I find his present prosecution was dictated by tyranny, cowardice and revenge; at my request, Mr. Gaoler, set this young officer, now your prisoner, free, and trust to me for the consequences. I'll make it my business to set the affair in a proper light to my friend the magistrate who has committed him. But where is the unfortunate young lady herself? let her appear to confront this wretch; I long to know by what arts he has seduced her. Entreat her to come in. Where is she?"

"Ah, Sir," said I, "that question stings me to the heart: I was once indeed happy in a daughter, but her miseries——" Another interruption here prevented me; for who should make her appearance but Miss Arabella Wilmot, who was next day to have been married to Mr. Thornhill. Nothing could equal her surprize at seeing Sir William and his nephew here before her; for her arrival was quite accidental. It happened that she and the old gentleman her father were passing through the town, on the way to her aunt's, who had insisted that her nuptials with Mr. Thornhill should be consummated at her house; but stopping for refreshment, they put up at an inn at the other end of the town. It was there from the window that the young lady happened to observe one of my little boys playing in the street, and instantly sending a footman to bring the child to her, she learnt from him some account of our misfortunes; but was still kept ignorant of young Mr. Thornhill's being the cause. Though her father made several remonstrances on the impropriety of going to a prison to visit us, yet they were ineffectual; she desired the child to conduct her, which he did, and it was thus she surprised us at a juncture so unexpected.

Nor can I go on, without a reflection on those accidental meetings, which, though they happen every day, seldom excite our surprize but upon some extraordinary occasion. To what a fortuitous concurrence do we not owe every pleasure and convenience of our lives. How many seeming accidents must unite before we can be clothed or fed. The peasant must be disposed to labour, the shower must fall, the wind fill the merchant's sail, or numbers must want the usual supply.

We all continued silent for some moments, while my charming pupil, which was the name I generally gave this young lady, united in her looks compassion and astonishment, which gave new finishings to her beauty. "Indeed, my dear Mr. Thornhill," cried she to the 'Squire, who she supposed was come here to succour and not to oppress us, "I take it a little unkindly that you should come here without me, or never inform me of the situation of a family so dear to us both: you know I should take as much pleasure in contributing to the relief of my reverend old master here, whom I shall ever esteem, as you can. But I find that, like your uncle, you take a pleasure in doing good in secret."

"He find pleasure in doing good!" cried Sir William, interrupting her. "No, my dear, his pleasures are as base as he is. You see in him, madam, as complete a villain as ever disgraced humanity. A wretch, who after having deluded this poor man's daughter, after plotting against the innocence of her sister, has thrown the father into prison, and the eldest son into fetters, because he had courage to face his betrayer. And give me leave, madam, now to congratulate you upon an escape from the embraces of such a monster."

"O goodness," cried the lovely girl, "how have I been deceived! Mr. Thornhill informed me for certain that this gentleman's eldest son, Captain Primrose, was gone off to America with his new-married lady."

"My sweetest miss," cried my wife, "he has told you nothing but falsehoods. My son George never left the kingdom, nor never was married. Tho' you have forsaken him, he has always loved you too well to think of any body else; and I have heard him say he would die a batchelor for your sake." She then proceeded to expatiate upon the sincerity of her son's passion, she set his duel with Mr. Thornhill in a proper light, from thence she made a rapid digression to the 'Squire's debaucheries, his pretended marriages, and ended with a most insulting picture of his cowardice.

"Good heavens!" cried Miss Wilmot, "how very near have I been to the brink of ruin! But how great is my pleasure to have escaped it! Ten thousand falsehoods has this gentleman told me! He had at last art enough to persuade me that my promise to the only man I esteemed was no longer binding, since he had been unfaithful. By his falsehoods I was taught to detest one equally brave and generous!"

But by this time my son was freed from the incumbrances of justice, as the person supposed to be wounded was detected to be an impostor. Mr. Jenkinson also, who had acted as his valet de chambre, had dressed up his hair, and furnished him with whatever was necessary to make a genteel appearance. He now therefore entered, handsomely drest in his regimentals, and, without vanity, (for I am above it) he appeared as handsome a fellow as ever wore a military dress. As he entered, he made Miss Wilmot a modest and distant bow, for he was not as yet acquainted with the change which the eloquence of his mother had wrought in his favour. But no decorums could restrain the impatience of his blushing mistress to be forgiven. Her tears, her looks, all contributed to discover the real sensations of her heart, for having forgotten her former promise, and having suffered herself to be deluded by an impostor. My son appeared amazed at her condescension, and could scarce believe it real.—"Sure, madam," cried he, "this is but delusion! I can never have merited this! To be blest thus is to be too happy."—"No, Sir," replied she, "I have been deceived, basely deceived, else nothing could have ever made me unjust to my promise. You know my friendship, you have long known it; but forget what I have done, and as you once had my warmest vows of constancy, you shall now have them repeated; and be assured that if your Arabella cannot be yours, she shall never be another's."—"And no other's you shall be," cried Sir William, "if I have any influence with your father."

This hint was sufficient for my son Moses, who immediately flew to the inn where the old gentleman was, to inform him of every circumstance that had happened. But in the mean time the 'Squire perceiving that he was on every side undone, now finding that no hopes were left from flattery or dissimulation, concluded that his wisest way would be to turn and face his pursuers. Thus laying aside all shame, he appeared the open hardy villain. "I find then," cried he, "that I am to expect no justice here; but I am resolved it shall be done me. You shall know, Sir," turning to Sir William, "I am no longer a poor dependant upon your favours. I scorn them. Nothing can keep Miss Wilmot's fortune from me, which, I thank her father's assiduity, is pretty large. The articles, and a bond for her fortune, are signed, and safe in my possession. It was her fortune, not her person, that induced me to wish for this match; and possessed of the one, let who will take the other."

This was an alarming blow: Sir William was sensible of the justice of his claims, for he had been instrumental in drawing up the marriage articles himself. Miss Wilmot therefore perceiving that her fortune was irretrievably lost, turning to my son, she asked if the loss of fortune could lessen her value to him. "Though fortune," said she, "is out of my power, at least I have my hand to give."

"And that, madam," cried her real lover, "was indeed all that you ever had to give; at least all that I ever thought worth the acceptance. And I now protest, my Arabella, by all that's happy, your want of fortune this moment encreases my pleasure, as it serves to convince my sweet girl of my sincerity."

Mr. Wilmot now entering, he seemed not a little pleased at the danger his daughter had just escaped, and readily consented to a dissolution of the match. But finding that her fortune, which was secured to Mr. Thornhill by bond, would not be given up, nothing could exceed his disappointment. He now saw that his money must all go to enrich one who had no fortune of his own. He could bear his being a rascal, but to want an equivalent to his daughter's fortune was wormwood. He sat therefore, for some minutes, employed in the most mortifying speculations, till Sir William attempted to lessen his anxiety.—"I must confess, Sir," cried he, "that your present disappointment does not entirely displease me. Your immoderate passion for wealth is now justly punished. But tho' the young lady cannot be rich, she has still a competence sufficient to give content. Here you see an honest young soldier, who is willing to take her without fortune; they have long loved each other, and for the friendship I bear his father, my interest shall not be wanting in his promotion. Leave then that ambition which disappoints you, and for once admit that happiness which courts your acceptance."

"Sir William," replied the old gentleman, "be assured I never yet forced her inclinations, nor will I now. If she still continues to love this young gentleman, let her have him with all my heart. There is still, thank heaven, some fortune left, and your promise will make it something more. Only let my old friend here (meaning me) give me a promise of settling six thousand pounds upon my girl, if ever he should come to his fortune, and I am ready this night to be the first to join them together."

As it now remained with me to make the young couple happy, I readily gave a promise of making the settlement he required, which, to one who had such little expectations as I, was no great favour. We had now therefore the satisfaction of seeing them fly into each other's arms in a transport. "After all my misfortunes," cried my son George, "to be thus rewarded! Sure this is more than I could ever have presumed to hope for. To be possessed of all that's good, and after such an interval of pain! My warmest wishes could never rise so high!"—"Yes, my George," returned his lovely bride, "now let the wretch take my fortune; since you are happy without it so am I. O what an exchange have I made from the basest of men to the dearest, best! Let him enjoy our fortune, I now can be happy even in indigence."—"And I promise you," cried the 'Squire, with a malicious grin, "that I shall be very happy with what you despise."—"Hold, hold, Sir," cried Jenkinson, "there are two words to that bargain. As for that lady's fortune, Sir, you shall never touch a single stiver of it. Pray your honour," continued he to Sir William, "can the 'Squire have this lady's fortune if he be married to another?"—"How can you make such a simple demand?" replied the Baronet, "undoubtedly he cannot."—"I am sorry for that," cried Jenkinson; "for as this gentleman and I have been old fellow sporters, I have a friendship for him. But I must declare, well as I love him, that his contract is not worth a tobacco stopper, for he is married already."—"You lie, like a rascal," returned the 'Squire, who seemed roused by this insult; "I never was legally married to any woman."—"Indeed, begging your honour's pardon," replied the other, "you were; and I hope you will shew a proper return of friendship to your own honest Jenkinson, who brings you a wife, and if the company restrains their curiosity a few minutes, they shall see her."—So saying he went off with his usual celerity, and left us all unable to form any probable conjecture as to his design.—"Ay let him go," cried the 'Squire; "whatever else I may have done I defy him there. I am too old now to be frightened with squibs."

"I am surprised," said the Baronet, "what the fellow can intend by this. Some low piece of humour I suppose!"—"Perhaps, Sir," replied I, "he may have a more serious meaning. For when we reflect on the various schemes this gentleman has laid to seduce innocence, perhaps some one more artful than the rest has been found able to deceive him. When we consider what numbers he has ruined, how many parents now feel with anguish the infamy and the contamination which he has brought into their families, it would not surprise me if some one of them——Amazement! Do I see my lost daughter! Do I hold her! It is, it is my life, my happiness. I thought thee lost, my Olivia, yet still I hold thee,—and still thou shalt live to bless me." The warmest transports of the fondest lover were not greater than mine when I saw him introduce my child, and held my daughter in my arms, whose silence only spoke her raptures. "And art thou returned to me, my darling," cried I, "to be my comfort in age!"—"That she is," cried Jenkinson; "and make much of her, for she is your own honourable child, and as honest a woman as any in the whole room, let the other be who she will. And as for you, 'Squire, as sure as you stand there, this young lady is your lawful wedded wife. And to convince you that I speak nothing but truth, here is the licence by which you were married together."—So saying, he put the licence into the

Baronet's hands, who read it, and found it perfect in every respect. "And now, gentlemen," continued he, "I find you are surprised at all this; but a few words will explain the difficulty. That there 'Squire of renown, for whom I have a great friendship, but that's between ourselves, has often employed me in doing odd little things for him. Among the rest he commissioned me to procure him a false licence and a false priest, in order to deceive this young lady. But as I was very much his friend, what did I do but went and got a true licence and a true priest, and married them both as fast as the cloth could make them. Perhaps you'll think it was generosity that made me do all this. But no. To my shame I confess it, my only design was to keep the licence and let the 'Squire know that I could prove it upon him whenever I thought proper, and so make him come down whenever I wanted money." A burst of pleasure now seemed to fill the whole apartment; our joy reached even to the common room, where the prisoners themselves sympathized,

And shook their chains
In transport and rude harmony.

Happiness was expanded upon every face, and even Olivia's cheek seemed flushed with pleasure. To be thus restored to reputation, to friends and fortune at once, was a rapture sufficient to stop the progress of decay and restore former health and vivacity. But perhaps among all there was not one who felt sincerer pleasure than I. Still holding the dear-loved child in my arms, I asked my heart if these transports were not delusion. "How could you," cried I, turning to Mr. Jenkinson, "how could you add to my miseries by the story of her death? But it matters not; my pleasure at finding her again, is more than a recompence for the pain."

"As to your question," replied Jenkinson, "that is easily answered. I thought the only probable means of freeing you from prison, was by submitting to the 'Squire, and consenting to his marriage with the other young lady. But these you had vowed never to grant while your daughter was living; there was therefore no other method to bring things to bear but by persuading you that she was dead. I prevailed on your wife to join in the deceit, and we have not had a fit opportunity of undeceiving you till now."

In the whole assembly now there only appeared two faces that did not glow with transport. Mr. Thornhill's assurance had entirely forsaken him: he now saw the gulph of infamy and want before him, and trembled to take the plunge. He therefore fell on his knees before his uncle, and in a voice of piercing misery implored compassion. Sir William was going to spurn him away, but at my request he raised him, and after pausing a few moments, "Thy vices, crimes and ingratitude," cried he, "deserve no tenderness; yet thou shalt not be entirely forsaken, a bare competence shall be supplied, to support the wants of life, but not its follies. This young lady, thy wife, shall be put in possession of a third part of that fortune which once was thine, and from her tenderness alone thou art to expect any extraordinary supplies for the future." He was going to express his gratitude for such kindness in a set speech; but the Baronet prevented him by bidding him not aggravate his meanness, which was already but too apparent. He ordered him at the same time to be gone, and from all his former domestics to chuse one such as he should think proper, which was all that should be granted to attend him.

As soon as he left us, Sir William very politely stept up to his new niece with a smile, and wished her joy. His example was followed by Miss Wilmot and her father; my wife too kissed her daughter with much affection, as, to use her own expression, she was now made an honest woman of. Sophia and Moses followed in turn, and even our benefactor Jenkinson desired to be admitted to that honour. Our satisfaction seemed scarce capable of increase. Sir William, whose greatest pleasure was in doing good, now looked round with a countenance open as the sun, and saw nothing but joy in the looks of all except that of my daughter Sophia, who, for some reasons we could not comprehend, did not seem perfectly satisfied. "I think now," cried he, with a smile, "that all the company, except one or two, seem perfectly happy. There only remains an act of justice for me to do. You are sensible, Sir," continued he, turning to me, "of the obligations we both owe Mr. Jenkinson. And it is but just we should both reward him for it. Miss Sophia will, I am sure, make him very happy, and he shall have from me five hundred pounds as her fortune, and upon this I am sure they can live very comfortably together. Come, Miss Sophia, what say you to this match of my making? Will you have him?"—My poor girl seemed almost sinking into her mother's arms at the hideous proposal. —"Have him, Sir!" cried she faintly. "No, Sir, never."—"What!" cried he again, "not have Mr. Jenkinson, your benefactor, a handsome young fellow, with five hundred pounds and good expectations!"—"I beg, Sir," returned she, scarce able to speak, "that you'll desist, and not make me so very wretched."—"Was ever such obstinacy known," cried he again, "to refuse a man whom the family has such infinite obligations to, who has preserved your sister, and who has five hundred pounds! What! not have him!"—"No, Sir, never!" replied she angrily, "I'd sooner die first."—"If that be the case then," cried he, "if you will not have him—I think I must have you myself." And so saying, he caught her to his breast with ardour. "My loveliest, my most sensible of girls," cried he, "how could you ever think your own Burchell could deceive you, or that Sir William Thornhill could ever cease to admire a mistress that loved him for himself alone? I have for some years sought for a woman, who a stranger to my fortune could think that I had merit as a man. After having tried in vain, even amongst the pert and ugly, how great at last must be my rapture to have made a conquest over such sense and such heavenly beauty." Then turning to Jenkinson,

"As I cannot, Sir, part with this young lady myself, for she has taken a fancy to the cut of my face, all the recompence I can make is to give you her fortune, and you may call upon my steward to-morrow for five hundred pounds." Thus we had all our compliments to repeat, and Lady Thornhill underwent the same round of ceremony that her sister had done before. In the mean time Sir William's gentleman appeared to tell us that the equipages were ready to carry us to the inn, where every thing was prepared for our reception. My wife and I led the van, and left those gloomy mansions of sorrow. The generous Baronet ordered forty pounds to be distributed among the prisoners, and Mr. Wilmot, induced by his example, gave half that sum. We were received below by the shouts of the villagers, and I saw and shook by the hand two or three of my honest parishioners, who were among the number. They attended us to our inn, where a sumptuous entertainment was provided, and coarser provisions distributed in great quantities among the populace.

After supper, as my spirits were exhausted by the alternation of pleasure and pain which they had sustained during the day, I asked permission to withdraw, and leaving the company in the midst of their mirth, as soon as I found myself alone, I poured out my heart in gratitude to the giver of joy as well as of sorrow, and then slept undisturbed till morning.

CHAPTER XIII

The Conclusion.

THE next morning as soon as I awaked, I found my eldest son sitting by my bedside, who came to encrease my joy with another turn of fortune in my favour. First having released me from the settlement that I had made the day before in his favour, he let me know that my merchant who had failed in town was arrested at Antwerp, and there had given up effects to a much greater amount than what was due to his creditors. My boy's generosity pleased me almost as much as this unlooked for good fortune. But I had some doubts whether I ought in justice to accept his offer. While I was pondering upon this, Sir William entered the room, to whom I communicated my doubts. His opinion was, that as my son was already possessed of a very affluent fortune by his marriage, I might accept his offer without any hesitation. His business, however, was to inform me that as he had the night before sent for the licences, and expected them every hour, he hoped that I would not refuse my assistance in making all the company happy that morning. A footman entered while we were speaking, to tell us that the messenger was returned, and as I was by this time ready, I went down, where I found the whole company as merry as affluence and innocence could make them. However, as they were now preparing for a very solemn ceremony, their laughter entirely displeased me. I told them of the grave, becoming and sublime deportment they should assume upon this mystical occasion, and read them two homilies and a thesis of my own composing, in order to prepare them. Yet they still seemed perfectly refractory and ungovernable. Even as we were going along to church, to which I led the way, all gravity had quite forsaken them, and I was often tempted to turn back in indignation. In church a new dilemma arose, which promised no easy solution. This was, which couple should be married first; my son's bride warmly insisted, that Lady Thornhill (that was to be) should take the lead; but this the other refused with equal ardour, protesting she would not be guilty of such rudeness for the world. The argument was supported for some time between both with equal obstinacy and good breeding. But as I stood still all this time with my book ready, I was at last quite tired of the contest, and shutting it, "I perceive," cried I, "that none of you have a mind to be married, and I think we had as good go back again; for I suppose there will be no business done here to-day."—This at once reduced them to reason. The Baronet and his Lady were first married, and then my son and his lovely partner.

I had previously that morning given orders that a coach should be sent for my honest neighbour Flamborough and his family, by which means, upon our return to the inn, we had the pleasure of finding the two Miss Flamboroughs alighted before us. Mr. Jenkinson gave his hand to the eldest, and my son Moses led up the other; (and I have since found that he has taken a real liking to the girl, and my consent and bounty he shall have whenever he thinks proper to demand them.) We were no sooner returned to the inn, but numbers of my parishioners, hearing of my success, came to congratulate me, but among the rest were those who rose to rescue me, and whom I formerly rebuked with such sharpness. I told the story to Sir William, my son-in-law, who went out and reproved them with great severity; but finding them quite disheartened by his harsh reproof, he gave them half a guinea a piece to drink his health and raise their dejected spirits.

Soon after this we were called to a very genteel entertainment, which was drest by Mr. Thornhill's cook. And it may not be improper to observe with respect to that gentleman, that he now resides, in quality of companion at a relation's house, being very well liked and seldom sitting at the side-table except when there is no room at the other; for they make no stranger of him. His time is pretty much taken up in keeping his relation, who is a little melancholy, in spirits, and in learning to blow the French horn. My eldest daughter, however, still remembers him with regret; and she has even told me, though I make a great secret of it, that when he reforms she may be brought to relent. But to return, for I am not apt to digress thus; when we were to sit down to dinner our ceremonies were going to be renewed. The question was, whether my eldest daughter, as being a matron, should not sit above the two young brides; but the debate was cut short by my son George, who proposed that the company should sit indiscriminately, every gentleman by his lady. This was received with great approbation by all, excepting my wife, who I could perceive was not perfectly satisfied, as she expected to have had the pleasure of sitting at the head of the table and carving all the meat for all the company. But notwithstanding this, it is impossible to describe our good humour. I can't say whether we had more wit among us now than usual; but I am certain we had more laughing, which answered the end as well. One jest I particularly remember, old Mr. Wilmot drinking to Moses, whose head was turned another way, my son replied, "Madam, I thank you." Upon which the old gentleman winking upon the rest of the company, observed that he was thinking of his mistress. At which jest I thought the two Miss Flamboroughs would have died with laughing. As soon as dinner was over, according to my old custom, I requested that the table might be taken away, to have the pleasure of seeing all my family assembled once more by a chearful fireside. My two little ones sat upon each knee, the rest of the company by their partners. I had nothing now on this side of the grave to wish for, all my cares were over, my pleasure was unspeakable. It now only remained that my gratitude in good fortune should exceed my former submission in adversity.

[1] ["I have a friendly feeling for philosophers; but for professors and schoolmasters I have none now, and may I never have any hereafter."]

[2] ["One could put up with it if our buildings were pulled down by men capable of building."]

SELECTIONS FROM

AN ENQUIRY

INTO THE PRESENT STATE OF POLITE LEARNING IN EUROPE

Ἐμοὶ πρὸς φιλοσοφούς ἐστι φιλία· πρὸς μέντοι σοφιστὰς ἢ γραμματιστας οὔτε νῦν ἐστι φιλία μήτε ὕστερόν ποτε γένοιτο.[1]

Tolerabile si Ædificia nostra diruerent Ædificandi capaces.[2]

An Enquiry into the Present State of Polite Learning in Europe, Goldsmith's first book, was published anonymously on 2 April, 1759. He was certainly writing it during the previous August (see Letter, p. 842). It was *Printed for R. and J. Dodsley, in Pall-Mall*, with a handsome title-page including a plate of the Temple of the Arts (inscribed ΤΩΝ ΧΑΡΙΤΩΝ). Apollo is shown supervising two amoretti, who are putting the finishing touches to the pediment, while Pan demolishes the back of the building with a pickaxe. *An Enquiry* suffered a vicious notice in the *Monthly Review*.

> Thus, notwithstanding our Author talks so familiarly of *us*, the great, and affects to be thought to stand in the rank of Patrons, we cannot help thinking that in more places than one he has betrayed, in himself, the man he so severely condemns for drawing his quill to take a purse. We are even so firmly convinced of this, that we dare put the question home to his conscience, whether he never experienced the unhappy situation he so feelingly describes in that of a Literary Understrapper?

The *Review* was, of course, quite right. Goldsmith was no detached scholar inquiring into polite learning; the opening chapters in which he makes an attempt at scholarship are flat and unconvincing. But he was well qualified to write about the plight of a bookseller's hack, if only because he was one; and the chapters printed here are the better for having been written from bitter experience.

A second edition, revised and rearranged, appeared in July, 1774, three months after his death. I have preferred the more outspoken text of the first edition.

AN ENQUIRY

INTO THE PRESENT STATE OF POLITE LEARNING IN EUROPE

CHAPTER IX

Of learning in Great Britain.

To acquire a character for learning among the English at present, it is necessary to know much more than is either important or useful. The absurd passion of being deemed profound, has done more injury to all kinds of science, than is generally imagined. Some thus exhaust their natural sagacity in exploring the intricacies of another man's thought, and have never found leisure to think for themselves; others have carried on learning from that stage, where the good sense of our ancestors have thought it too minute or too speculative to instruct or amuse. By the industry of such, the sciences which in themselves are easy of access, affright the learner with the severity of their appearance. He sees them surrounded with speculation and subtility, placed there by their professors as if with a view of deterring his approach. From hence it happens, that the generality of readers fly from the scholar to the compiler, who offers them a more safe and speedy conveyance.

From this fault also arises that mutual contempt between the scholar and the man of the world, of which every day's experience furnisheth instances.

The man of taste, however, stands neuter in this controversy, he seems placed in a middle station, between the world and the cell, between learning and common sense. He teaches the vulgar on what part of a character to lay the emphasis of praise, and the scholar where to point his application so as to deserve it. By his means, even the philosopher, acquires popular applause, and all that are truly great the admiration of posterity. By means of polite learning alone, the patriot and the hero, the man who praiseth virtue, and he who practices it, who fights successfully for his country, or who dies in its defence, become immortal.

Let none affect to despise future fame, the actions of even the lowest part of mankind testify a desire of this kind. Wealth, titles, and several paltry advantages, are secured for posterity, who can only give their applause in return. If all ranks, therefore, are inspired with this passion, how great should his encouragement be, who is capable of conferring it not only upon the most deserving, but even upon the age in which he lives?

Yet this honest ambition of being admired by posterity, cannot be gratified without continual efforts in the present age to deserve it. For if the rewards of genius are improperly directed; if those who are capable of supporting the honour of the times by their writings prefer opulence to fame; if the stage should be shut to writers of merit, and open only to interest or intrigue. If such should happen to be the vile complexion of the times, the very virtues of the age will be forgotten by posterity; and nothing remembered, except our filling a chasm in the registers of time, or having served to continue the species.

CHAPTER X

Of the encouragement of learning.

THERE is nothing authors are more apt to lament, than want of encouragement from the age. Whatever their differences in other respects may be, they are all ready to unite in this complaint, and each indirectly offers himself as an instance of the truth of his assertion.

The beneficed divine, whose wants are only imaginary, expostulates as bitterly as the poorest author, that ever snuffed his candle with finger and thumb. Should interest or good fortune, advance the divine to a bishopric, or the poor son of Parnassus into that place which the other has resign'd; both are authors no longer, the one goes to prayers once a day, kneels upon cushions of velvet, and thanks gracious heaven for having made the circumstances of all mankind so extremely happy; the other battens on all the delicacies of life, enjoys his wife and his easy chair, and sometimes, for the sake of conversation, deplores the luxury of these degenerate days.

All encouragements to merit are misapplied, which make the author too rich to continue his profession. There can be nothing more just than the old observation, that authors, like running horses, should be fed but not fattened. If we would continue them in our service, we should reward them with a little money and a great deal of praise, still keeping their avarice subservient to their ambition. Not that I think a writer incapable of filling an employment with dignity, I would only insinuate, that when made a bishop or statesman, he will continue to please us as a writer no longer. As to resume a former allusion, the running horse, when fattened, will still be fit for very useful purposes, though unqualified for a courser.

No nation gives greater encouragements to learning than we do; yet, at the same time, none are so injudicious in the application. We seem to confer them with the same view, that statesmen have been known to grant employments at court, rather as bribes to silence, than incentives to emulation.

Upon this principle, all our magnificent endowments of colleges are erroneous, and, at best, more frequently enrich the prudent than reward the ingenious. A lad whose passions are not strong enough in youth to mislead him from that path of science, which his tutors, and not his inclinations, have chalked out, by four or five years perseverance, may probably obtain every advantage and honour his college can bestow. I forget whether the simile has been used before, but I would compare the man, whose youth has been thus passed in the tranquility of dispassionate prudence, to liquors which never ferment, and consequently, continue always muddy. Passions may raise a commotion in the youthful breast, but they disturb only to refine it. However this be, mean talents are often rewarded in colleges, with an easy subsistence. The candidates for preferments of this kind, often regard their admission as a patent for future laziness; so that a life begun in studious labour, is often continued in luxurious affluence.

Among the universities abroad, I have ever observed their riches and their learning in a reciprocal proportion, their stupidity and pride encreasing with their opulence. Happening once in conversation with Gaubius[1] of Leyden, to mention the college of Edinburgh, he began by complaining that all the English students, which formerly came to his university, now went intirely there; and the fact surprized him more, as Leyden was now as well as ever furnished with masters excellent in their respective professions. He concluded by asking, if the professors of Edinburgh were rich. I reply'd, that the salary of a professor there seldom amounted to more than thirty pounds a year. Poor men, says he, I heartily wish they were better provided for, until they become rich, we can have no expectation of English students at Leyden.

Premiums also, proposed for literary excellence, when given as encouragements to boys may be useful, but when designed as rewards to men, are certainly misapplied. We have seldom seen a performance of any great merit, in consequence of rewards proposed in this manner. Who has ever observed a writer of any eminence, a candidate in so precarious a contest? The man who knows the real value of his own genius, will no more venture it upon an uncertainty, than he who knows the true use of a guinea, will stake it with a sharper by throwing a main.

[1] [Jérôme-David Gaubius (1705–80), "the chymicall Professor" at Leyden. See Letter, p. 840.]

Every encouragement given to stupidity, when known to be such, is also a negative insult upon genius. This appears in nothing more evident, than the undistinguished success of those who sollicit subscriptions. When first brought into fashion, subscriptions were conferred upon the ingenious alone, or those who were reputed such. But at present, we see them made a resource of indigence, and requested not as rewards of merit, but as a relief of distress. If tradesmen happen to want skill in conducting their own business, yet they are able to write a book; if mechanics want money, or ladies shame, they write books and solicit subscriptions. Scarce a morning passes, that proposals of this nature are not thrust into the half-opening doors of the rich, with, perhaps, a paltry petition, shewing the author's wants, but not his merits. I would not willingly prevent that pity which is due to indigence, but while the streams of liberality are thus diffused, they must in the end become proportionably shallow.

What then are the proper encouragements of genius? I answer, subsistence and respect, for these are rewards congenial to its nature. Every animal has an aliment peculiarly suited to its constitution. The heavy ox seeks nourishment from the earth; the light cameleon has been supposed to exist on air; a sparer diet even than this, will satisfy the man of true genius, for he makes a luxurious banquet on empty applause. It is this alone, which has inspired all that ever was truly great and noble among us. It is, as Cicero finely calls it the eccho of virtue. Avarice is the passion of inferior natures; money the pay of the common herd. The author who draws his quill merely to take a purse, no more deserves success than he who presents a pistol.

When the link between patronage and learning was entire, then all who deserved fame were in a capacity of attaining it. When the great Somers was at the helm, patronage was fashionable among our nobility. The middle ranks of mankind, who generally imitate the Great, then followed their example; and applauded from fashion, if not from feeling. I have heard an old poet[1] of that glorious age say, that a dinner with his lordship, has procured him invitations for the whole week following: that an airing in his patron's chariot, has supplied him with a citizen's coach on every future occasion. For who would not be proud to entertain a man who kept so much good company?

But this link now seems entirely broken. Since the days of a certain prime minister[2] of inglorious memory, the learned have been kept pretty much at a distance. A jockey, or a laced player, supplies the place of the scholar, poet, or the man of virtue. Those conversations, once the result of wisdom, wit, and innocence, are now turned to humbler topics, little more being expected from a companion than a laced coat, a pliant bow, and an immoderate friendship for—a well served table.

Wit, when neglected by the great, is generally despised by the vulgar. Those who are unacquainted with the world, are apt to fancy the man of wit, as leading a very agreeable life. They conclude, perhaps, that he is attended to with silent admiration, and dictates to the rest of mankind, with all the eloquence of conscious superiority. Very different is his present situation. He is called an author, and all know that an author is a thing only to be laughed at. His person, not his jest, becomes the mirth of the company. At his approach, the most fat unthinking face, brightens into malicious meaning. Even aldermen laugh, and revenge on him, the ridicule which was lavish'd on their forefathers.

Etiam victis redit in præcordia virtus,
Victoresque cadunt.[3]

It is indeed a reflection somewhat mortifying to the author, who breaks his ranks, and singles out for public favour to

[1] [Edward Young (1683–1765).] [2] [Sir Robert Walpole.]

[3] ["Even the conquered take fresh heart, and the conquerors fall." Virgil, *Æneid*, 2. 367.]

think that he must combat contempt, before he can arrive at glory. That he must expect to have all the fools of society united against him, before he can hope for the applause of the judicious. For this, however, he must prepare beforehand; as those who have no idea of the difficulty of his employment, will be apt to regard his inactivity as idleness, and not having a notion of the pangs of uncomplying thought in themselves, it is not to be expected they should have any desire of rewarding by respecting them in others.[1]

. . . .

Yet it were well, if none but the dunces of society, were combined to render the profession of an author ridiculous or unhappy. Men of the first eminence are often found to indulge this illiberal vein of raillery. Two contending writers often by the opposition of their wit, render their profession contemptible in the eyes of ignorants, who should have been taught to admire. Whatever the reader may think of himself, it is at least two to one, but he is a greater blockhead than the most scribling dunce he affects to despise.

The poet's poverty is a standing topic of contempt. His writing for bread is an unpardonable offence. Perhaps, of all mankind, an author, in these times, is used most hardly. We keep him poor, and yet revile his poverty. Like angry parents, who correct their children till they cry, and then correct them for crying, we reproach him for living by his wit, and yet allow him no other means to live.

His taking refuge in garrets and cellars, and living among vermin, have, of late been violently objected to him, and that by men, who I dare hope, are more apt to pity than insult his distress. Is poverty the writer's fault? No doubt, he knows how to prefer a bottle of champaign, to the nectar of the neighbouring alehouse, or a venison pasty to a

[1] [Here is omitted a long quotation from Voltaire, describing "the hardships a man must encounter, who writes for the public."]

plate of potatoes. Want of delicacy is not in him, but in us, who deny him the opportunity of making an elegant choice.

Wit certainly is the property of those who have it, nor should we be displeased if it is the only property a man sometimes has. We must not under-rate him who uses it for subsistence, and flies from the ingratitude of the age, even to a bookseller for redress. If the profession of an author is to be laughed at by stupids, it is certainly better sure to be contemptibly rich, than contemptibly poor. For all the wit that ever adorned the human mind, will at present no more shield the author's poverty from ridicule, than his high topped gloves conceal the unavoidable omissions of his laundress.

To be more serious, new fashions, follies, and vices, make new monitors necessary in every age. An author may be considered as a merciful substitute to the legislature; he acts not by punishing crimes, but preventing them; however virtuous the present age, there may be still growing employment for ridicule, or reproof, for persuasion, or satire. If the author be, therefore, still so necessary among us, let us treat him with proper consideration, as a child of the public, not a rent-charge on the community. And, indeed, a *child* of the public he is in all respects; for while so well able to direct others, how incapable is he frequently found of guiding himself. His simplicity exposes him to all the insidious approaches of cunning, his sensibility to the slightest invasions of contempt. Though possessed of fortitude to stand unmoved the expected bursts of an earthquake, yet of feelings so exquisitely poignant, as to agonize under the slightest disappointment. Broken rest, tasteless meals, and causeless anxiety, shorten his life, or render it unfit for active employment; prolonged vigils, and intense application still farther contract his span, and make his time glide insensibly away. Let us not then aggravate those natural inconveniencies by neglect; we have had sufficient instances of this kind already.

Sale, Savage, Amherst, More[1] will suffice for one age at least. But they are dead, and their sorrows are over. The neglected author of the Persian eclogues,[2] which, however inaccurate, excel any in our language, is still alive. Happy, if *insensible* of our neglect, not *raging* at our ingratitude. It is enough, that the age has already yielded instances of men pressing foremost in the lists of fame, and worthy of better times, schooled by continued adversity into an hatred of their kind, flying from thought to drunkenness, yielding to the united pressure of labour, penury, and sorrow, sinking unheeded, without one friend to drop a tear on their unattended obsequies, and indebted to charity for a grave among the dregs of mankind.

The author, when unpatronized by the Great, has naturally recourse to the bookseller. There cannot be, perhaps, imagined a combination more prejudicial to taste than this. It is the interest of the one to allow as little for writing, and of the other to write as much, as possible; accordingly, tedious compilations, and periodical magazines, are the result of their joint endeavours. In these circumstances, the author bids adieu to fame, writes for bread, and for that only. Imagination is seldom called in; he sits down to address the venal muse with the most phlegmatic apathy; and, as we are told of the Russian, courts his mistress by falling asleep in her lap. His reputation never spreads in a wider circle than that of the trade, who generally value him, not for the fineness of his compositions, but the quantity he works off in a given time.

A long habitude of writing for bread, thus turns the ambition of every author at last into avarice. He finds, that he has wrote many years, that the public are scarcely acquainted

[1] [George Sale (1697–1736), orientalist and translator of the *Koran*. Richard Savage (*d.* 1743), poet and dramatist. He lived in poverty and squalor, was arrested for a debt of £8 in January, 1743 and died six months later in prison, Johnson wrote his biography. Nicholas Amhurst (1697–1742), poet and satirist, political writer. Edward Moore (1712–57), fabulist and dramatist.]

[2] [William Collins (1721–59). He spent the last years of his life in madness, and died three months after *An Enquiry* was published.]

even with his name; he despairs of applause, and turns to profit, which invites him. He finds that money procures all those advantages, that respect, and that ease, which he vainly expected from fame. Thus the man, who under the protection of the Great, might have done honour to humanity, when only patronized by the bookseller, becomes a thing little superior to the fellow who works at the press.

Sint Mæcenates, non deerunt, Flacce, Marones.[1]

CHAPTER XI

Upon Criticism.

But there are still some men, whom fortune has blessed with affluence, to whom the muse pays her morning visit, not like a creditor, but a friend: to this happy few, who have leisure to polish what they write, and liberty to chuse their own subjects, I would direct my advice, which consists in a few words: *Write what you think, regardless of the critics.* To persuade to this, was the chief design of this essay. To break, or at least to loosen those bonds, first put on by caprice, and afterwards drawn hard by fashion, is my wish. I have assumed the critic only to dissuade from criticism.

There is scarce an error of which our present writers are guilty, that does not arise from this source. From this proceeds the affected obscurity of our odes, the tuneless flow of our blank verse, the pompous epithet, laboured diction, and every other deviation from common sense, which procures the poet the applause of the connoisseur; he is praised by all, read by a few, and soon forgotten.

There never was an unbeaten path trodden by the poet, that the critic did not endeavour to reclaim him, by calling his

[1] ["Grant us patrons like Mæcenas, Flaccus, and there will be no lack of Virgils." Martial, *Epigrams*, 8. 56. 5.]

attempt innovation. This might be instanced in Dante, who first followed nature, and was persecuted by the critics as long as he lived. Thus novelty, one of the greatest beauties in poetry, must be avoided, or the connoisseur will be displeased. It is one of the chief privileges, however, of genius, to fly from the herd of imitators by some happy singularity; for should he stand still, his heavy pursuers will at length come up, and fairly dispute the victory.

The ingenious Mr. Hogarth used to assert, that every one, except the connoisseur, was a judge of painting. The same may be asserted of writing; the public in general set the whole piece in the proper point of view; the critic lays his eye close to all its minutenesses, and condemns or approves in detail. And this may be the reason why so many writers at present, are apt to appeal from the tribunal of criticism to that of the people.

From a desire in the critic of grafting the spirit of ancient languages upon the English, has proceeded of late several disagreeable instances of pedantry. Among the number, I think we may reckon blank verse. Nothing but the greatest sublimity of subject can render such a measure pleasing; however, we now see it used upon the most trivial occasions; it has particularly found its way into our didactic poetry,[1] and is likely to bring that species of composition into disrepute, for which the English are deservedly famous.

Those who are acquainted with writing, know that our language runs almost naturally into blank verse. The writers of our novels, romances, and all of this class, who have no notion of stile, naturally hobble into this unharmonious

[1] [*E.g.*, Akenside's *Pleasures of the Imagination*, Armstrong's *Art of Preserving Health*, Dyer's *Fleece* and John Philips's *Cider*, of which last Johnson wrote:

> Contending angels may shake the regions of heaven in blank verse; but the flow of equal measures, and the embellishment of rhyme, must recommend to our attention the art of engrafting, and decide the merit of the *redstreak* and the *pearmain*.]

measure. If rhymes, therefore, be more difficult, for that very reason, I would have our poets write in rhyme. Such a restriction upon the thought of a good poet, often lifts and encreases the vehemence of every sentiment; for fancy, like a fountain, plays highest by diminishing the aperture. But rhymes, it will be said, are a remnant of monkish stupidity, an innovation upon the poetry of the ancients. They are but indifferently acquainted with antiquity, who make the assertion. Rhymes are probably of older date than either the Greek or Latin dactyl and spondé. The Celtic, which is allowed to be the first language spoken in Europe, has ever preserved them, as we may find in the Edda of Iceland, and the Irish carrols still sung among the original inhabitants of that island. Olaus Wormius gives us some of the Teutonic poetry in this way; and Pantoppidan, bishop of Bergen, some of the Norwegian; in short, this jingle of sounds is almost natural to mankind, at least, it is so to our language, if we may judge from many unsuccessful attempts to throw it off.

I should not have employed so much time in opposing this erroneous innovation, if it were not apt to introduce another in its train: I mean, a disgusting solemnity of manner into our poetry; and, as the prose writer has been ever found to follow the poet, it must consequently banish in both, all that agreeable trifling, which, if I may so express it, often deceives us into instruction. Dry reasoning, and dull morality, have no force with the wild fantastic libertine. He must be met with smiles, and courted with the allurements of gaiety. He must be taught to believe, that he is in pursuit of pleasure, and surprized into reformation. The finest sentiment, and the most weighty truth, may put on a pleasing face, and it is even virtuous to jest when serious advice must be disgusting. But instead of this, the most trifling performance among us now, assumes all the didactic stiffness of wisdom. The most diminutive son of fame, or of famine, has his *we* and his *us*, his *firstlys* and his *secondlys* as methodical, as if bound in cow-hide, and closed with clasps of brass. Were these Monthly Reviews and Magazines frothy, pert, or absurd, they might find some pardon; but to be dull and dronish, is an encroachment on the prerogative of a folio.

These pamphlets should be considered as pills to purge melancholly; they should be made up in our splenetic climate, to be taken as physic, and not so as to be used when we take it. Some such law should be enacted in the republic of letters, as we find take place in the house of commons. As no man there can shew his wisdom, unless first qualified by three hundred pounds a year, so none here should profess gravity, unless his work amounted to three hundred pages.

However, by the power of one single monosyllable, our critics have almost got the victory over humour amongst us. Does the poet paint the absurdities of the vulgar; then he is *low*: does he exaggerate the features of folly, to render it more thoroughly ridiculous, he is then very *low*. In short, they have proscribed the comic or satyrical muse from every walk but high life, which, though abounding in fools as well as the humblest station, is by no means so fruitful in absurdity. Among well-bred fools we may despise much, but have little to laugh at; nature seems to present us with an universal blank of silk, ribbands, smiles, and whispers; absurdity is the poet's game, and good breeding is the nice concealment of absurdities. The truth is, the critic generally mistakes humour for wit, which is a very different excellence. Wit raises human nature above its level; humour acts a contrary part, and equally depresses it. To expect exalted humour; is a contradiction in terms; and the critic, by demanding an impossibility from the comic poet, has, in effect, banished new comedy from the stage. But to put the same thought in a different light:

When an unexpected similitude in two objects strikes the imagination; in other words, when a thing is *wittily* expressed, all our pleasure turns into admiration of the artist, who had fancy enough to draw the picture. When a thing is *humourously* described, our burst of laughter proceeds from a very different cause; we compare the absurdity of the character represented with our own, and triumph in our conscious superiority. No natural defect can be a cause of laughter, because it is a misfortune to which ourselves are liable; a defect of this kind changes the passion to pity or horror; we only laugh at those instances of moral absurdity, to which we are conscious we ourselves are not liable. For instance, should I describe a man as wanting his nose, there is no humour in this, as it is an accident to which human nature is subject, and may be any man's case: but should I represent this man without his nose, as extremely curious in the choice of his snuff-box, we here see him guilty of an absurdity of which we imagine it impossible for ourselves to be guilty, and therefore applaud our own good sense on the comparison. Thus, then, the pleasure we receive from wit, turns on the admiration of another; that we feel from humour, centers in the admiration of ourselves. The poet, therefore, must place the object he would have the subject of humour in a state of inferiority; in other words, the subject of humour must be low.

The solemnity worn by many of our modern writers is, I fear, often the mask of dulness; for certain it is, it seems to fit every author who pleases to put it on. By the complexion of many of our late publications, one might be apt to cry out with Cicero, *Civem mehercule non puto esse qui his temporibus ridere possit.* On my conscience, I believe we have all forgot to laugh in these days. Such writers probably make no distinction between what is praised, and what is pleasing; between those commendations which the reader pays his own discernment, and those which are the genuine result of his sensations.

As our gentlemen writers have it therefore so much in their power to lead the taste of the times, they may now part with the inflated stile that has for some years been looked upon as fine writing, and which every young writer is now obliged to adopt, if he chuses to be read. They may now dispense with loaded epithet, and dressing up of trifles with dignity. For to use an obvious instance, it is not those who make the greatest noise with their wares in the streets, that have the most to sell. Let us, instead of writing finely, try to write naturally. Not hunt after lofty expressions to deliver mean ideas; nor be for ever gaping, when we only mean to deliver a whisper.

[1] [Like bees at large about the flowery fields,
So in our turn we sip of everything.
Lucretius, *De Rerum Naturae*, 3. 11.]

SELECTED ESSAYS FROM

THE BEE

BEING ESSAYS ON THE MOST INTERESTING SUBJECTS

Floriferis ut Apes in saltibus omnia libant,
Omnia Nos itidem.[1]

The first number of *The Bee*, Goldsmith's own weekly magazine, was published on Saturday, 6 October, 1759. Each number was a small octavo of sixteen pages, *Printed for J. Wilkie, at the Bible, in St. Paul's Church-Yard.* The price was threepence. Apart from four translations of Voltaire, and two, or possibly three, essays, everything in it was written by Goldsmith. At that time he was also contributing to *The Busy Body*, and the strain of turning out four or five essays and perhaps a poem each week began to tell after the fifth number. *The Bee* lasted only eight weeks. In December the separate weekly papers were bound up as a single volume and sold for two shillings and sixpence.

Goldsmith reprinted the *Introduction*, *On Dress* and *On the Use of Language* with many alterations in *Essays*, 1765, as Essays I, XV and V. *A City Night-Piece* was reprinted without its last paragraph as Letter CXVII of *The Citizen of the World.* In revising the text of these essays, Goldsmith corrected many faults and weeded out redundancies. Unfortunately he also removed anything that might be thought too low or to savour too much of a garret in Grub-street. The reference, for instance, to the Cat and Bag-pipes in St. Giles's is omitted. Where *The Bee* says simply:

> Jack Spindle and I were old acquaintance; but he's gone.

the later text has:

> These speculations bring to my mind the fate of a very good natured fellow, who is now no more.

And Jack becomes an anonymous friend throughout. The old gentleman of *On Dress* no longer tells his own story, but is described, quite unnecessarily, and then his account is quoted at length. I have therefore preferred the more direct text of *The Bee* to that of the *Essays*, even though in a few places, the last paragraph of the *Introduction* in particular, the later text is a definite improvement on the earlier. (See footnotes on pp. 231 and 233.)

The *Introduction* is taken from the first number; *On Dress* and *On Our Theatres*, from the second; *On the Use of Language*, from the third; *Miscellaneous* and *A City Night-Piece*, from the fourth; and *A Resverie*, from the fifth.

All the poems in *The Bee* except a Latin epigram are included in this edition (see pp. 639–43).

THE BEE

BEING ESSAYS ON THE MOST INTERESTING SUBJECTS

INTRODUCTION

THERE is not, perhaps, a more whimsically dismal figure in nature, than a man of real modesty who assumes an air of impudence; who, while his heart beats with anxiety, studies ease, and affects good humour. In this situation, however, a periodical writer often finds himself, upon his first attempt to address the public in form. All his power of pleasing is damped by solicitude, and his chearfulness dashed with apprehension. Impressed with the terrors of the tribunal before which he is going to appear, his natural humour turns to pertness, and for real wit he is obliged to substitute vivacity. His first publication draws a crowd, they part dissatisfied, and the author, never more to be indulged a favourable hearing, is left to condemn the indelicacy of his own address, or their want of discernment.

For my part, as I was never distinguished for address, and have often even blundered in making my bow, such bodings as these had like to have totally repressed my ambition. I was at a loss whether to give the public specious promises, or give none; whether to be merry or sad on this solemn occasion. If I should modestly decline all merit, it was too probable the hasty reader might have taken me at my word. If, on the other hand, like labourers in the Magazine trade, I had, with modest impudence, humbly presumed to promise an epitome of all the good things that ever were said or written, this might have disgusted those readers I most desire to please. Had I been merry, I might have been censured as *vastly low*; and had I been sorrowful, I might have been left to mourn in solitude and silence: In short, which ever way I turned, nothing presented but prospects of terror, despair, chandlers shops, and waste paper.

In this debate between fear and ambition, my publisher happening to arrive, interrupted for a while my anxiety. Perceiving my embarrassment about making my first appearance, he instantly offered his assistance and advice: "You must know, sir, says he, that the republic of letters is at present divided into three classes. One writer, for instance, excels at a plan, or a title-page, another works away the body of the book, and a third is a dab at an index. Thus a Magazine is not the result of any single man's industry; but goes through as many hands as a new pin, before it is fit for the public. I fancy, sir, continues he, I can provide an eminent hand, and upon moderate terms, to draw up a promising plan to smooth up our readers a little, and pay them, as colonel Charteris[1] paid his seraglio, at the rate of three halfpence in hand, and three shillings more in promises."

He was proceeding in his advice, which, however, I thought proper to decline, by assuring him, that as I intended to pursue no fixed method, so it was impossible to form any regular plan; determ.ned never to be tedious, in order to be logical, wherever pleasure presented, I was resolved to follow. Like

[1] [Francis Charteris (1669–1732), "a man infamous for all manner of vices," a swindler and a bawd, drummed out of two regiments for cheating and stealing, twice condemned for rape, but pardoned. At his funeral the people rioted, almost tore his corpse out of its coffin and flung "dead dogs &c." into the grave with it. Dr. Arbuthnot wrote a magnificent epitaph, beginning,

HERE continueth to rot
The Body of FRANCIS CHARTRES,
Who, with an INFLEXIBLE CONSTANCY,
and INIMITABLE UNIFORMITY of Life,
PERSISTED,
In spite of AGE and INFIRMITIES,
In the Practice of EVERY HUMAN VICE;
Excepting PRODIGALITY and HYPOCRISY:
His insatiable AVARICE exempted him from the first,
His matchless IMPUDENCE from the second.]

the Bee, which I had taken for the title of my paper, I would rove from flower to flower, with seeming inattention, but concealed choice, expatiate over all the beauties of the season, and make my industry my amusement.

This reply may also serve as an apology to the reader, who expects, before he sits down, a bill of his future entertainment. It would be improper to pall his curiosity by lessening his surprize, or anticipate any pleasure I am able to procure him, by saying what shall come next. Thus much, however, he may be assured of, that neither war nor scandal shall make any part of it. Homer finely imagines his deity turning away with horror from the prospect of a field of battle and seeking tranquility among a nation noted for peace and simplicity. Happy could any effort of mine, but for a moment, repress that savage pleasure some men find in the daily accounts of human misery! How gladly would I lead them from scenes of blood and altercation, to prospects of innocence and ease, where every breeze breathes health, and every sound is but the echo of tranquility.

But whatever the merit of his intentions may be, every writer is now convinced that he must be chiefly indebted to good fortune for finding readers willing to allow him any degree of reputation. It has been remarked, that almost every character which has excited either attention or praise, has owed part of its success to merit, and part to an happy concurrence of circumstances in its favour. Had Cæsar or Cromwell exchanged countries, the one might have been a serjeant, and the other an exciseman. So it is with wit, which generally succeeds more from being happily addressed, than from its native poignancy. A *bon mot*, for instance, that might be relished at White's, may lose all its flavour when delivered at the Cat and bag-pipes in St. Giles's. A jest calculated to spread at a gaming-table, may be received with a perfect neutrality of face should it happen to drop in a mackrel-boat. We have all seen dunces triumph in some companies, where men of real humour were disregarded, by a general combination in favour of stupidity. To drive the observation as far as it will go, should the labours of a writer who designs his performances for readers of a more refined appetite fall into the hands of a devourer of compilations, what can he expect but contempt and confusion. If his merits are to be determined by judges who estimate the value of a book from its bulk, or its frontispiece, every rival must acquire an easy superiority, who with persuasive eloquence promises four extraordinary pages of *letter press*, or three beautiful prints, curiously coloured from nature.

But to proceed; though I cannot promise as much entertainment, or as much elegance as others have done, yet the reader may be assured he shall have as much of both as I can. He shall, at least, find me alive while I study his entertainment; for I solemnly assure him, I was never yet possessed of the secret at once of writing and sleeping.

During the course of this paper, therefore, all the wit and learning I have, are heartily at his serviçe; which if, after so candid a confession he should, notwithstanding, still find intolerably dull, low, or sad stuff, this I protest is more than I know. I have a clear conscience, and am entirely out of the secret.

Yet I would not have him, upon the perusal of a single paper, pronounce me incorrigible; he may try a second, which, as there is a studied difference in subject and style, may be more suited to his taste; if this also fails, I must refer him to a third, or even to a fourth, in case of extremity: If he should still continue refractory, and find me dull to the last, I must inform him, with Bays[1] in the Rehearsal, that I think him a very odd kind of a fellow, and desire no more of his acquaintance.

It is with such reflections as these I endeavour to fortify myself against the future contempt or neglect of some readers,

[1] [The caricature of Dryden in Buckingham's play.]

and am prepared for their dislike by mutual recrimination. If such should impute dealing neither in battles nor scandal to me as a fault, instead of acquiescing in their censure, I must beg leave to tell them a story.

A traveller, in his way to Italy, happening to pass at the foot of the Alps, found himself at last in a country where the inhabitants had each a large excrescence depending from the chin, like the pouch of a monkey. This deformity, as it was endemic, and the people little used to strangers, it had been the custom, time immemorial, to look upon as the greatest ornament of the human visage. Ladies grew toasts from the size of their chins, and none were regarded as pretty fellows, but such whose faces were broadest at the bottom. It was Sunday, a country church was at hand, and our traveller was willing to perform the duties of the day. Upon his first appearance at the church door, the eyes of all were naturally fixed upon the stranger; but what was their amazement, when they found that he actually wanted that emblem of beauty, a pursed chin. This was a defect that not a single creature had sufficient gravity (though they were noted for being grave) to withstand. Stifled bursts of laughter, winks, and whispers circulated from visage to visage, and the prismatic figure of the stranger's face was a fund of infinite gaiety; even the parson, equally remarkable for his gravity and chin, could hardly refrain joining in the good humour. Our traveller could no longer patiently continue an object for deformity to point at. Good folks, said he, I perceive that I am the unfortunate cause of all this good humour. It is true, I may have faults in abundance, but I shall never be induced to reckon my want of a swelled face among the number.[1]

[1] [Altered in *Essays* to,

"Good folks," said he, "I perceive that I am a very ridiculous figure here, but I assure you am reckoned no way deformed at HOME."]

ON DRESS

FOREIGNERS observe that there are no ladies in the world more beautiful, or more ill dressed than those of England. Our countrywomen have been compared to those Pictures, where the face is the work of a Raphael; but the draperies thrown out by some empty pretender, destitute of taste, and entirely unacquainted with design.

If I were a poet, I might observe, on this occasion, that so much beauty set off with all the advantages of dress, would be too powerful an antagonist for the opposite sex, and therefore it was wisely ordered, that our ladies should want taste, lest their admirers should entirely want reason.

But to confess a truth, I do not find they have a greater aversion to fine cloaths than the women of any other country whatsoever. I can't fancy that a shopkeeper's wife in Cheapside has a greater tenderness for the fortune of her husband than a citizen's wife in Paris; or that miss in a boarding-school is more an oeconomist in dress than mademoiselle in a nunnery.

Although Paris may be accounted the soil in which almost every fashion takes its rise, its influence is never so general there as with us. They study there the happy method of uniting grace and fashion, and never excuse a woman for being aukwardly dressed, by saying her cloaths are made in the mode. A French woman is a perfect architect in dress; she never, with Gothic ignorance, mixes the orders; she never tricks out a squabby Doric shape, with Corinthian finery; or, to speak without metaphor, she conforms to general fashion, only when it happens not to be repugnant to private beauty.

Our ladies, on the contrary, seem to have no other standard for grace but the run of the town. If fashion gives the word, every distinction of beauty, complexion, or stature ceases. Sweeping trains, Prussian bonnets, and trollopees,[1] as like

[1] [Long loose gowns, also called "slammerkins."]

each other, as if cut from the same piece, level all to one standard. The mall, the gardens, and playhouses are filled with ladies in uniform, and their whole appearance shews as little variety or taste as if their cloaths were bespoke by the colonel of a marching regiment, or fancied by the same artist who dresses the three battalions of guards.

But not only ladies of every shape and complexion, but of every age too, are possessed of this unaccountable passion of dressing in the same manner. A lady of no quality can be distinguished from a lady of some quality only by the redness of her hands; and a woman of sixty, masked, might easily pass for her grand-daughter.[1] I remember, a few days ago, to have walked behind a damsel, tossed out in all the gaiety of fifteen; her dress was loose, unstudied, and seemed the result of conscious beauty. I called up all my poetry on this occasion, and fancied twenty Cupids prepared for execution in every folding of her white negligee. I had prepared my imagination for an angel's face; but what was my mortification to find that the imaginary goddess was no other than my cousin Hannah, four years older than myself, and I shall be sixty-two the twelfth of next November.

After the transports of our first salute were over, I could not avoid running my eye over her whole appearance. Her gown was of cambrick, cut short before, in order to discover an high-heeled shoe, which was buckled almost at the toe. Her cap, if cap it might be called that cap was none, consisted of a few bits of cambrick, and flowers of painted paper stuck

[1] [In *Essays* the rest of this paragraph was altered to,

> A friend of mine, a good-natured old man, amused me, the other day, with an account of his journey to the Mall. It seems, in his walk thither, he, for some time, followed a lady who, as he thought by her dress, was a girl of fifteen. It was airy, elegant, and youthful. My old friend had called up all his poetry on this occasion, and fancied twenty cupids prepared for execution in every folding of her white negligee. He had prepared his imagination for an angel's face; but what was his mortification to find that the imaginary goddess was no other than his cousin Hannah, some years older than himself.]

on one side of her head. Her bosom, that had felt no hand, but the hand of time, these twenty years, rose, suing, but in vain, to be pressed. I could, indeed, have wished her more than an handkerchief of Paris-net to shade her beauties; for, as Tasso says of the rose-bud, *Quanto si mostra men tanto e piu bella*, I should think her's most pleasing when least discovered.

As my cousin had not put on all this finery for nothing, she was at that time sallying out to the park, when I had overtaken her. Perceiving, however, that I had on my best wig, she offered, if I would 'squire her there, to send home the footman. Though I trembled for our reception in public, yet I could not, with any civility, refuse; so, to be as gallant as possible, I took her hand in my arm, and thus we marched on together.

When we made our entry at the Park, two antiquated figures, so polite and so tender as we seemed to be, soon attracted the eyes of the company. As we made our way among crowds who were out to show their finery as well as we, wherever we came I perceived we brought good humour in our train. The polite could not forbear smiling, and the vulgar broke out into a horse laugh at our grotesque figures. Cousin Hannah, who was perfectly conscious of the rectitude of her own appearance, attributed all this mirth to the oddity of mine; while I as cordially placed the whole to her account. Thus, from being two of the best-natured creatures alive, before we got half way up the mall, we both began to grow peevish, and, like two mice on a string, endeavoured to revenge the impertinence of others upon ourselves. "I am amazed, cousin Jeffery, says miss, that I can never get you to dress like a Christian. I knew we should have the eyes of the Park upon us, with your great wig so frizzed, and yet so beggarly, and your monstrous muff. I hate those odious muffs." I could have patiently borne a criticism on all the rest of my equipage; but, as I had always a peculiar veneration for my muff, I could not forbear being piqued a little; and throwing my eyes with a spiteful air on her bosom, "I could heartily wish, madam, replied I, that, for your sake, my muff was cut into a tippet."

As my cousin, by this time, was grown heartily ashamed of her gentleman usher, and as I was never very fond of any kind of exhibition myself, it was mutually agreed to retire, for a while, to one of the seats, and from that retreat remark on others as freely as they had remarked on us.

When seated we continued silent for some time, employed in very different speculations. I regarded the whole company now passing in review before me, as drawn out merely for my amusement. For my entertainment the beauty had all that morning been improving her charms, the beau had put on lace, and the young doctor a big wig, merely to please me. But quite different were the sentiments of cousin Hannah; she regarded every well-dressed woman as a victorious rival, hated every face that seemed dressed in good humour, or wore the appearance of greater happiness than her own. I perceived her uneasiness, and attempted to lessen it, by observing that there was no company in the Park to-day. To this she readily assented; "and yet, says she, it is full enough of scrubs of one kind or another." My smiling at this observation gave her spirits to pursue the bent of her inclination, and now she began to exhibit her skill in secret history, as she found me disposed to listen. "Observe, says she to me, that old woman in tawdry silk, and dressed out even beyond the fashion. That is miss Biddy Evergreen. Miss Biddy, it seems, has money, and as she considers that money was never so scarce as it is now, she seems resolved to keep what she has to herself. She is ugly enough, you see; yet, I assure you, she has refused several offers, to my own knowledge, within this twelvemonth, Let me see, three gentlemen from Ireland who study the law, two waiting captains, her doctor, and a Scotch preacher, who had like to have carried her off. All her time is passed between sickness and finery. Thus she spends the whole week in a close chamber, with no other company but her monkey, her apothecary, and cat, and comes dressed out to the Park every Sunday, to shew her airs, to get new lovers, to catch a new cold, and to make new work for the doctor.

"There goes Mrs. Roundabout, I mean the fat lady in the lutestring[1] trollopee. Between you and I, she is but a cutler's wife. See how she's dressed as fine as hands and pins can make her, while her two marriageable daughters, like bunters,[2] in stuff gowns, are now taking sixpennyworth of tea at the White-conduit-house. Odious puss, how she waddles along, with her train two yards behind her! She puts me in mind of my lord Bantam's Indian sheep, which are obliged to have their monstrous tails trundled along in a go-cart. For all her airs, it goes to her husband's heart to see four yards of good lutestring wearing against the ground, like one of his knives on a grindstone. To speak my mind, cousin Jeffery, I never liked tails; for suppose a young fellow should be rude, and the lady should offer to step back in a fright, instead of retiring, she treads upon her train, and falls fairly on her back; and then you know, cousin,—her cloaths may be spoiled.

"Ah! miss Mazzard! I knew we should not miss her in the Park; she in the monstrous Prussian bonnet. Miss, though so very fine, was bred a milliner, and might have had some custom if she had minded her business; but the girl was fond of finery, and instead of dressing her customers, laid out all her goods in adorning herself. Every new gown she put on impaired her credit; she still, however, went on, improving her appearance and lessening her little fortune, and is now, you see, become a belle and a bankrupt."

My cousin was proceeding in her remarks, which were interrupted by the approach of the very lady she had been so freely describing. Miss had perceived her at a distance, and

[1] [Lustrous bright silk.]

[2] [Women who lived by scavenging rags and bones in the streets.]

approached to salute her. I found, by the warmth of the two ladies protestations, that they had been long intimate esteemed friends and acquaintance. Both were so pleased at this happy rencounter, that they were resolved not to part for the day. So we all crossed the Park together, and I saw them into a hackney coach at the gate of St. James's. I could not, however, help observing, *That they are generally most ridiculous themselves, who are apt to see most ridicule in others.*

ON OUR THEATRES

MADEMOISELLE CLAIRON,[1] a celebrated actress at Paris, seems to me the most perfect female figure I have ever seen upon any stage. Not, perhaps, that nature has been more liberal of personal beauty to her, than some to be seen upon our theatres at home. There are actresses here who have as much of what connoisseurs call statuary grace, by which is meant elegance unconnected with motion, as she; but they all fall infinitely short of her, when the soul comes to give expression to the limbs, and animates every feature.

Her first appearance is excessively engaging; she never comes in staring round upon the company, as if she intended to count the benefits of the house, or at least to see, as well as be seen. Her eyes are always, at first, intently fixed upon the persons of the drama, and she lifts them by degrees, with enchanting diffidence, upon the spectators. Her first speech, or at least the first part of it, is delivered with scarce any motion of the arm; her hands and her tongue never set out together; but the one prepares us for the other. She sometimes begins with a mute, eloquent attitude; but never goes forward all at once with hands, eyes, head, and voice. This observation, though it may appear of no importance, should certainly be

[1] [Claire-Joseph-Hippolyte de Latude, (1723–1803).]

adverted to; nor do I see any one performer (Garrick only excepted) among us, that is not, in this particular, apt to offend. By this simple beginning she gives herself a power of rising in the passion of the scene. As she proceeds, every gesture, every look acquires new violence, till at last transported, she fills the whole vehemence of the part, and all the idea of the poet.

Her hands are not alternately stretched out, and then drawn in again, as with the singing women at Sadler's-wells; they are employed with graceful variety, and every moment please with new and unexpected eloquence. Add to this, that their motion is generally from the shoulder; she never flourishes her hands while the upper part of her arm is motionless, nor has she the ridiculous appearance, as if her elbows were pinned to her hips.

But of all the cautions to be given our rising actresses, I would particularly recommend it to them never to take notice of the audience, upon any occasion whatsoever; let the spectators applaud never so loudly, their praises should pass, except at the end of the epilogue, with seeming inattention. I can never pardon a lady on the stage who, when she draws the admiration of the whole audience, turns about to make them a low courtesy for their applause. Such a figure no longer continues Belvidera, but at once drops into Mrs. Cibber. Suppose a sober tradesman, who once a year takes his shilling's worth at Drury-lane, in order to be delighted with the figure of a queen, the queen of Sheba for instance, or any other queen: This honest man has no other idea of the great but from their superior pride and impertinence: Suppose such a man placed among the spectators, the first figure that presents on the stage is the queen herself, courtesying and cringing to all the company; how can he fancy her the haughty favourite of king Solomon the wise, who appears actually more submissive than the wife of his bosom. We are all tradesmen of a nicer relish in this respect, and such a conduct must disgust every spectator who loves to have the illusion of nature strong upon him.

Yet, while I recommend to our actresses a skilful attention to gesture, I would not have them study it in the looking-glass. This, without some precaution, will render their action formal; by too great an intimacy with this, they become stiff and affected. People seldom improve, when they have no other model but themselves to copy after. I remember to have known a notable performer of the other sex,[1] who made great use of this flattering monitor, and yet was one of the stiffest figures I ever saw. I am told his apartment was hung round with looking-glass, that he might see his person twenty times reflected upon entering the room; and I will make bold to say, he saw twenty very ugly fellows whenever he did so.

ON THE USE OF LANGUAGE

THE manner in which most writers begin their treatises on the Use of Language, is generally thus: "Language has been granted to man, in order to discover his wants and necessities, so as to have them relieved by society. Whatever we desire, whatever we wish, it is but to cloath those desires or wishes in words, in order to fruition; the principal use of language, therefore, say they, is to express our wants, so as to receive a speedy redress."

Such an account as this may serve to satisfy grammarians and rhetoricians well enough, but men who know the world, maintain very contrary maxims; they hold, and I think with some shew of reason, they hold that he who best knows how to conceal his necessities and desires, is the most likely person

[1] [Probably Thomas Sheridan, the father of Richard Brinsley Sheridan, who had been manager of the Smock Alley Theatre in Dublin when Goldsmith was a student there. The anecdote also occurs in Goldsmith's letter to Mrs. Jane Lawder of 15 August, 1758.]

to find redress, and that the true use of speech is not so much to express our wants as to conceal them.

When we reflect on the manner in which mankind generally confer their favours, we shall find that they who seem to want them least, are the very persons who most liberally share them. There is something so attractive in riches, that the large heap generally collects from the smaller; and the poor find as much pleasure in encreasing the enormous mass, as the miser, who owns it, sees happiness in its encrease. Nor is there in this any thing repugnant to the laws of true morality. Seneca himself allows, that in conferring benefits, the present should always be suited to the dignity of the receiver. Thus the rich receive large presents, and are thanked for accepting them. Men of middling stations are obliged to be content with presents something less, while the beggar, who may be truly said to want indeed, is well paid if a farthing rewards his warmest solicitations.

Every man who has seen the world, and has had his *ups and downs in life*, as the expression is, must have frequently experienced the truth of this doctrine, and must know that to have much, or to seem to have it, is the only way to have more. Ovid finely compares a man of broken fortune to a falling column; the lower it sinks, the greater weight it is obliged to sustain. Thus, when a man has no occasion to borrow, he finds numbers willing to lend him. Should he ask his friend to lend him an hundred pounds, it is possible, from the largeness of the demand, he may find credit for twenty; but should he humbly only sue for a trifle, it is two to one whether he might be trusted for two pence. A certain young fellow at George's, whenever he had occasion to ask his friend for a guinea, used to prelude his request as if he wanted two hundred, and talked so familiarly of large sums, that none could ever think he wanted a small one. The same gentleman, whenever he wanted credit for a new suit from his taylor, always made the proposal in laced cloaths; for he found by experience, that if he appeared shabby on these occasions, Mr. Lynch had taken an oath against trusting; or what was every bit as bad, his foreman was out of the way, and would not be at home these two days.

There can be no inducement to reveal our wants, except to find pity, and by this means relief; but before a poor man opens his mind in such circumstances, he should first consider whether he is contented to lose the esteem of the person he solicits, and whether he is willing to give up friendship only to excite compassion. Pity and friendship are passions incompatible with each other, and it is impossible that both can reside in any breast for the smallest space, without impairing each other. Friendship is made up of esteem and pleasure; pity is composed of sorrow and contempt: the mind may for some time fluctuate between them, but it never can entertain both together.

Yet let it not be thought that I would exclude pity from the human mind. There is scarce any who are not in some degree possessed of this pleasing softness; but it is at best but a short-lived passion, and seldom affords distress more than transitory assistance: With some it scarce lasts from the first impulse till the hand can be put into the pocket; with others it may continue for twice that space, and on some of extraordinary sensibility, I have seen it operate for half an hour. But, however, last as it will, it generally produces but beggarly effects; and where, from this motive we give an halfpenny, from others we give always pound. In great distress we sometimes, it is true, feel the influence of tenderness strongly; when the same distress solicits a second time, we then feel with diminished sensibility, but like the repetition of an eccho, every new impulse becomes weaker, till at last our sensations lose every mixture of sorrow, and degenerate into downright contempt.

Jack Spindle and I were old acquaintance; but he's gone. Jack was bred in a compting-house, and his father dying just as he was out of his time, left him an handsome fortune, and many friends to advise with. The restraint in which he had been brought up, had thrown a gloom upon his temper, which some regarded as an habitual prudence, and from such considerations, he had every day repeated offers of friendship. Those who had money, were ready to offer him their assistance that way; and they who had daughters, frequently, in the warmth of affection, advised him to marry. Jack, however, was in good circumstances; he wanted neither money, friends, nor a wife, and therefore modestly declined their proposals.

Some errors in the management of his affairs, and several losses in trade, soon brought Jack to a different way of thinking; and he at last thought it his best way to let his friends know that their offers were at length acceptable. His first address was therefore to a scrivener, who had formerly made him frequent offers of money and friendship, at a time when, perhaps, he knew those offers would have been refused.

Jack, therefore, thought he might use his old friend without any ceremony, and as a man confident of not being refused, requested the use of an hundred guineas for a few days, as he just then had an occasion for money. "And pray, Mr. Spindle, replied the scrivener, do you want all this money?"[1] "Want it, Sir, says the other, if I did not want it, I should not have asked it." "I am sorry for that, says the friend; for those who want money when they come to borrow, will want money when they should come to pay. To say the truth, Mr. Spindle, money is money now-a-days. I believe it is all sunk in the bottom of the sea, for my part; and he that has got a little, is a fool if he does not keep what he has got."

Not quite disconcerted by this refusal, our adventurer was resolved to apply to another, whom he knew to be the very best friend he had in the world. The gentleman whom he now addressed, received his proposal with all the affability that

[1] [This passage, down to "serve for all, you know," is closely paralleled in *The Citizen of the World* (see p. 340).]

could be expected from generous friendship. "Let me see, you want an hundred guineas; and pray, dear Jack, would not fifty answer?" "*If you have but fifty to spare, Sir, I must be contented.*" "Fifty to spare, I do not say that, for I believe I have but twenty about me." "*Then I must borrow the other thirty from some other friend.*" "And pray, replied the friend, would it not be the best way to borrow the whole money from that other friend, and then one note will serve for all, you know. Lord, Mr. Spindle, make no ceremony with me at any time; you know I'm your friend, and when you chuse a bit of dinner or so.——You, Tom, see the gentleman down. You won't forget to dine with us now and then. Your very humble servant."

Distressed, but not discouraged at this treatment, he was at last resolved to find that assistance from love, which he could not have from friendship. Miss Jenny Dismal had a fortune in her own hands, and she had already made all the advances that her sex's modesty would permit. He made his proposal, therefore with confidence, but soon perceived, *No bankrupt ever found the fair one kind.* Miss Jenny and Master Billy Galloon were lately fallen deeply in love with each other, and the whole neighbourhood thought it would soon be a match.

Every day now began to strip Jack of his former finery; his cloaths flew piece by piece to the pawnbroker's, and he seemed at length equipped in the genuine mourning of antiquity. But still he thought himself secure from starving, the numberless invitations he had received to dine, even after his losses, were yet unanswered; he was therefore now resolved to accept of a dinner because he wanted one; and in this manner he actually lived among his friends a whole week without being openly affronted. The last place I saw poor Jack was at the Rev. Dr. Gosling's. He had, as he fancied, just nicked the time, for he came in as the cloth was laying. He took a chair without being desired, and talked for some time without being attended to. He assured the company, that nothing procured so good an appetite as a walk to White Conduit-house, where he had been that morning. He looked at the table-cloth, and praised the figure of the damask; talked of a feast where he had been the day before, but that the venison was over done. All this, however, procured the poor creature no invitation, and he was not yet sufficiently hardened to stay without being asked; wherefore, finding the gentleman of the house insensible to all his fetches, he thought proper, at last, to retire, and mend his appetite by a walk in the Park.

You then, O ye beggars of my acquaintance, whether in rags or lace; whether in Kent-street or the Mall; whether at the Smyrna or St. Giles's, might I advise as a friend, never seem in want of the favour which you solicit. Apply to every passion but pity, for redress. You may find relief from vanity, from self-interest, or from avarice, but seldom from compassion. The very eloquence of a poor man is disgusting; and that mouth which is opened even for flattery, is seldom expected to close without a petition.

If then you would ward off the gripe of poverty, pretend to be a stranger to her, and she will at least use you with ceremony. Hear not my advice, but that of Offellus.[1] If you be caught dining upon a halfpenny porrenger of pease soup and potatoes, praise the wholesomeness of your frugal repast. You may observe, that Dr. Cheyne has prescribed pease broth for the gravel, hint that you are not one of those who are always making a god of your belly. If you are obliged to wear a flimsy stuff in the midst of winter, be the first to remark that stuffs are very much worn at Paris. If there be found some irreparable defects in any part of your equipage, which cannot be concealed by all the arts of sitting cross-legged, coaxing, or derning, say, that neither you nor Sampson Gideon[2] were ever very fond of dress. Or if you be a philo-

[1] [Horace, *Satires*, 2. 2. 2.]

[2] [A rich Jewish broker (1699–1762), equally notable for his wealth and his slovenly dress.]

sopher, hint that Plato and Seneca are the taylors you choose to employ; assure the company that men ought to be content with a bare covering, since what is now the pride of some, was formerly our shame. Horace will give you a Latin sentence fit for the occasion,

Toga quæ defendere frigus quamvis crassa queat.[1]

In short, however caught, do not give up, but ascribe to the frugality of your disposition what others might be apt to attribute to the narrowness of your circumstances, and appear rather to be a miser than a beggar. To be poor, and to seem poor, is a certain method never to rise. Pride in the great is hateful, in the wise it is ridiculous; *beggarly pride* is the only sort of vanity I can excuse.

MISCELLANEOUS

WERE I to measure the merit of my present undertaking by its success, or the rapidity of its sale, I might be led to form conclusions by no means favourable to the pride of an author. Should I estimate my fame by its extent, every News-Paper and every Magazine would leave me far behind. Their fame is diffused in a very wide circle, that of some as far as Islington, and some yet farther still; while mine, I sincerely believe, has hardly travelled beyond the sound of Bow-bell; and while the works of others fly like unpinioned swans, I find my own move as heavily as a new-plucked goose.

Still, however, I have as much pride as they who have ten times as many readers. It is impossible to repeat all the agreeable delusions in which a disappointed author is apt to find comfort. I conclude, that what my reputation wants in extent,

[1] ["And a cloak, however coarse, to keep out the cold." Horace, *Satires*, 1. 3. 14–15.]

is made up by its solidity. *Minus juvat Gloria lata quam magna.*[1] I have great satisfaction in considering the delicacy and discernment of those readers I have, and in ascribing my want of popularity to the ignorance or inattention of those I have not. All the world may forsake an author, but vanity will never forsake him.

Yet notwithstanding so sincere a confession, I was once induced to shew my indignation against the public, by discontinuing my endeavours to please; and was bravely resolved, like Raleigh, to vex them, by burning my manuscript in a passion.[2] Upon recollection, however, I considered what set or body of people would be displeased at my rashness. The sun, after so sad an accident, might shine next morning as bright as usual; men might laugh and sing the next day, and transact business as before, and not a single creature feel any regret but myself.

I reflected upon the story of a minister, who, in the reign of Charles II, upon a certain occasion, resigned all his posts, and retired into the country in a fit of resentment. But as he had not given the world entirely up with his ambition, he sent a messenger to town, to see how the courtiers would bear his resignation. Upon the messenger's return, he was asked whether there appeared any commotions at court? To which he replied, There were very great ones. "Ay, says the minister, I knew my friends would make a bustle; all petitioning the king for my restoration, I presume." "No, Sir, replied the messenger, they are only petitioning his majesty to be put in your place." In the same manner, should I retire

[1] ["A widespread reputation is of less value than a great one." Pliny, *Letters*, 4. 12. 7. (adapted).]

[2] ["His booke [the *History of the World*] sold very slowly at first, and the bookseller complayned of it, and told him that he should be a looser by it, which put Sir W. into a passion; and sayd that since the world did not understand it, they should not have his second part, which he tooke and threw into the fire, and burnt before his face." Aubrey's *Brief Lives*.
The story has since been discredited.]

in indignation, instead of having Apollo in mourning, or the Muses in a fit of the spleen; instead of having the learned world apostrophising at my untimely decease, perhaps all Grub-street might laugh at my fall, and self-approving dignity might never be able to shield me from ridicule. In short, I am resolved to write on, if it were only to spite them. If the present generation will not hear my voice, hearken, O posterity, to you I call, and from you I expect redress! What rapture will it not give to have the Scaligers, Daciers, and Warburtons of future times commenting with admiration upon every line I now write, working away those ignorant creatures who offer to arraign my merit with all the virulence of learned reproach. Ay, my friends, let them feel it; call names; never spare them; they deserve it all, and ten times more. I have been told of a critic, who was crucified, at the command of another, to the reputation of Homer. That, no doubt, was more than poetical justice, and I shall be perfectly content if those who criticise me are only clapped in the pillory, kept fifteen days upon bread and water, and obliged to run the gantlope through Pater-noster Row. The truth is, I can expect happiness from posterity either way. If I write ill, happy in being forgotten; if well, happy in being remembered with respect.

Yet, considering things in a prudential light, perhaps I was mistaken in designing my paper as an agreeable relaxation to the studious, or an help to conversation among the gay; instead of addressing it to such, I should have written down to the taste and apprehension of the many, and sought for reputation on the broad road. Literary fame I now find like religious, generally begins among the vulgar. As for the polite, they are so very polite, as never to applaud upon any account. One of these, with a face screwed up into affectation, tells you, that fools may *admire*, but men of sense only *approve*.[1] Thus, lest he should rise into rapture at any thing

[1] [Pope, *Essay on Criticism*, 391.]

new, he keeps down every passion but pride and self-importance; approves with phlegm, and the poor author is damned in the taking a pinch of snuff. Another has written a book himself, and being condemned for a dunce, he turns a sort of king's evidence in criticism, and now becomes the terror of every offender. A third, possessed of full-grown reputation, shades off every beam of favour from those who endeavour to grow beneath him, and keeps down that merit, which, but for his influence, might rise into equal eminence. While others, still worse, peruse old books for their amusement, and new books only to condemn; so that the public seem heartily sick of all but the business of the day, and read every thing new with as little attention as they examine the faces of the passing crowd.

From these considerations I was once determined to throw off all connexions with taste, and fairly address my countrymen in the same engaging style and manner with other periodical pamphlets, much more in vogue than probably mine shall ever be. To effect this, I had thoughts of changing the title into that of the ROYAL BEE, the ANTI-GALLICAN BEE, or the BEE'S MAGAZINE. I had laid in a proper stock of popular topicks, such as encomiums on the king of Prussia, invectives against the queen of Hungary and the French, the necessity of a militia, our undoubted sovereignty of the seas, reflections upon the present state of affairs, a dissertation upon liberty, some seasonable thoughts upon the intended bridge of Blackfriars,[1] and an address to Britons. The history of an old woman, whose teeth grew three inches long, an ode upon our victories, a rebus, an acrostic upon Miss Peggy P. and a journal of the

[1] [There was much controversy in the press whether the arches should be semicircular or elliptical. *Miscellaneous* appeared in *The Bee* of 27 October. Johnson wrote three letters to the *Daily Gazette*, on 1, 8 and 15 December, 1759, in which he supported his friend John Gwynn's semicircular arch against Robert Mylne, a Scot, whose elliptical one was eventually adopted when work was begun on the bridge in July, 1760. Mylne and Johnson later became fast friends.]

weather. All this, together with four extraordinary pages of *letter press*, a beautiful map of England, and two prints curiously coloured from nature, I fancied might touch their very souls. I was actually beginning an address to the people, when my pride at last overcame my prudence, and determined me to endeavour to please by the goodness of my entertainment, rather than by the magnificence of my sign.

The Spectator, and many succeeding essayists, frequently inform us of the numerous compliments paid them in the course of their lucubrations; of the frequent encouragements they met to inspire them with ardour, and increase their eagerness to please. I have received *my letters* as well as they; but alas! not congratulatory ones; not assuring me of success and favour; but pregnant with bodings that might shake even fortitude itself.

One gentleman assures me, he intends to throw away no more three-pences in purchasing the BEE; and what is still more dismal, he will not recommend me as a poor author wanting encouragement to his neighbourhood, which it seems is very numerous. Were my soul set upon three-pences, what anxiety might not such a denunciation produce. But such does not happen to be the present motive of publication! I write partly to shew my good-nature, and partly to shew my vanity; nor will I lay down the pen till I am satisfied one way or another.

Others have disliked the title and the motto of my paper, point out a mistake in the one, and assure me the other has been consigned to dulness by anticipation. All this may be true; *but what is that to me?* Titles and mottoes to books are like escutcheons and dignities in the hands of a king. The wise sometimes condescend to *accept* of them; but none but a fool will imagine them of any real importance. We ought to depend upon intrinsic merit, and not the slender helps of title. *Nam quæ non fecimus ipsi, vix ea nostra voco.*[1]

[1] ["I scarcely claim as mine what I have not achieved myself." Ovid.]

For my part, I am ever ready to mistrust a promising title, and have, at some expence, been instructed not to hearken to the voice of an advertisement, let it plead never so loudly, or never so long. A countryman coming one day to Smithfield, in order to take a slice of Bartholomew-fair, found a perfect shew before every booth. The drummer, the fire-eater, the wire-walker, and the salt-box were all employed to invite him in. *Just a going; the court of the king of Prussia in all his glory; pray, gentlemen, walk in and see.* From people who generously gave so much away, the clown expected a monstrous bargain for his money when he got in. He steps up, pays his sixpence, the curtain is drawn, when too late he finds that he had the best part of the shew for nothing at the door.

A CITY NIGHT-PIECE

Ille dolet vere qui sine teste dolet. MART.[1]

THE clock has struck two, the expiring taper rises and sinks in the socket, the watchman forgets the hour in slumber, the laborious and the happy are at rest, and nothing now wakes but guilt, revelry and despair. The drunkard once more fills the destroying bowl, the robber walks his midnight round, and the suicide lifts his guilty arm against his own sacred person.

Let me no longer waste the night over the page of antiquity, or the sallies of contemporary genius, but pursue the solitary walk, where vanity, ever changing, but a few hours past, walked before me, where she kept up the pageant, and now, like a froward child, seems hushed with her own importunities.

What a gloom hangs all around! the dying lamp feebly emits a yellow gleam, no sound is heard but of the chiming clock, or the distant watch-dog. All the bustle of human pride is forgotten, and this hour may well display the emptiness of human vanity.

[1] ["He truly grieves who grieves with none to spy.' *Epigrams*, I. 33. 4.]

There may come a time when this temporary solitude may be made continual, and the city itself, like its inhabitants, fade away, and leave a desart in its room.

What cities, as great as this, have once triumph'd in existence, had their victories as great as ours, joy as just, and as unbounded as we, and with short-sighted presumption, promised themselves immortality. Posterity can hardly trace the situation of some. The sorrowful traveller wanders over the awful ruins of others, and as he beholds, he learns wisdom, and feels the transience of every sublunary possession.

Here stood their citadel, but now grown over with weeds; there their senate-house, but now the haunt of every noxious reptile; temples and theatres stood here, now only an undistinguished heap of ruin. They are fallen, for luxury and avarice first made them feeble. The rewards of state were conferred on amusing, and not on useful members of society. Thus true virtue languished, their riches and opulence invited the plunderer, who, though once repulsed, returned again, and at last swept the defendants into undistinguished destruction.

How few appear in those streets, which but some few hours ago were crowded; and those who appear, no longer now wear their daily mask, nor attempt to hide their lewdness or their misery.

But who are those who make the streets their couch, and find a short repose from wretchedness at the doors of the opulent? These are strangers, wanderers, and orphans, whose circumstances are too humble to expect redress, and their distresses too great even for pity. Some are without the covering even of rags, and others emaciated with disease; the world seems to have disclaimed them; society turns its back upon their distress, and has given them up to nakedness and hunger. These poor shivering females, have once seen happier days, and been flattered into beauty. They have been prostituted to the gay luxurious villain, and are now turned out to meet the severity of winter in the streets. Perhaps now lying at the doors of their betrayers they sue to wretches whose hearts are insensible to calamity, or debauchees who may curse, but will not relieve them.

Why, why was I born a man, and yet see the sufferings of wretches I cannot relieve! Poor houseless creatures! the world will give you reproaches, but will not give you relief. The slightest misfortunes, the most imaginary uneasinesses of the rich, are aggravated with all the power of eloquence, and engage our attention; while you weep unheeded, persecuted by every subordinate species of tyranny, and finding enmity in every law.

Why was this heart of mine formed with so much sensibility! or why was not my fortune adapted to its impulse! Tenderness, without a capacity of relieving, only makes the heart that feels it more wretched than the object which sues for assistance.

But let me turn from a scene of such distress to the sanctified hypocrite, *who has been talking of virtue till the time of bed*, and now steals out, to give a loose to his vices under the protection of midnight; vices more attrocious, because he attempts to conceal them. See how he pants down the dark alley, and, with hastening steps, fears an acquaintance in every face. He has passed the whole day in company he hates, and now goes to prolong the night among company that as heartily hate him. May his vices be detected; may the morning rise upon his shame: yet I wish to no purpose; villainy, when detected, never gives up, but boldly adds impudence to imposture.

A RESVERIE

SCARCE a day passes in which we do not hear compliments paid to Dryden, Pope, and other writers of the last age, while not a month comes forward that is not loaded with invective against the writers of this. Strange, that our critics should be fond of giving their favours to those who are insensible of the obligation, and their dislike to these who, of all mankind, are most apt to retaliate the injury.

Even though our present writers had not equal merit with their predecessors, it would be politic to use them with ceremony. Every compliment paid them would be more agreeable, in proportion as they least deserved it. Tell a lady with an handsome face that she is pretty, she only thinks it her due; it is what she has heard a thousand times before from others, and disregards the compliment: but assure a lady, the cut of whose visage is something more plain, that she looks killing to-day, she instantly bridles up and feels the force of the well-timed flattery the whole day after. Compliments which we think are deserved, we only accept, as debts, with indifference; but those which conscience informs us we do not merit, we receive with the same gratitude that we do favours given away.

Our gentlemen, however, who preside at the distribution of literary fame, seem resolved to part with praise neither from motives of justice, or generosity; one would think, when they take pen in hand, that it was only to blot reputations, and to put their seals to the pacquet which consigns every new-born effort to oblivion.

Yet, notwithstanding the republic of letters hangs at present so feebly together; though those friendships which once promoted literary fame seem now to be discontinued; though every writer who now draws the quill seems to aim at profit, as well as applause, many among them are probably laying in stores for immortality, and are provided with a sufficient stock of reputation to last the whole journey.

As I was indulging these reflections, in order to eke out the present page, I could not avoid pursuing the metaphor, of going a journey, in my imagination, and formed the following Resverie, too wild for allegory, and too regular for a dream.

I fancied myself placed in the yard of a large inn, in which there were an infinite number of waggons and stage-coaches, attended by fellows who either invited the company to take their places, or were busied in packing their baggage. Each vehicle had its inscription, shewing the place of its destination. On one I could read, *The pleasure stage-coach*; on another, *The waggon of industry*; on a third, *The vanity whim*; and on a fourth, *The landau of riches*. I had some inclination to step into each of these, one after another; but I know not by what means I passed them by, and at last fixed my eye upon a small carriage, Berlin fashion, which seemed the most convenient vehicle at a distance in the world; and, upon my nearer approach, found it to be *The fame machine*.

I instantly made up to the coachman, whom I found to be an affable and seemingly good-natured fellow. He informed me, that he had but a few days ago returned from the temple of fame, to which he had been carrying Addison, Swift, Pope, Steele, Congreve, and Colley Cibber. That they made but indifferent company by the way, and that he once or twice was going to empty his berlin of the whole cargo: however, says he, I got them all safe home, with no other damage than a black eye, which Colley gave Mr. Pope, and am now returned for another coachful. "If that be all, friend, said I, and if you are in want of company, I'll make one with all my heart. Open the door; I hope the machine rides easy." "Oh! for that, sir, extremely easy." But still keeping the door shut, and measuring me with his eye, "Pray, sir, have you no luggage? You seem to be a good-natured sort of a gentleman; but I don't find you have got any luggage, and I never permit any to travel with me but such as have something valuable to pay for coach-hire." Examining my pockets, I own I was not a little disconcerted at this unexpected rebuff; but considering that I carried a number of the BEE under my arm, I was resolved to open it in his eyes, and dazzle him with the splendor of the page. He read the title and contents, however, without any emotion, and assured me he had never heard of it before. "In short, friend, said he, now losing all his former respect, you must not come in. I expect better passengers; but, as you seem an harmless creature, perhaps, if there be room left, I may let you ride a while for charity."

I now took my stand by the coachman at the door, and since I could not command a seat, was resolved to be as useful as possible, and earn by my assiduity, what I could not by my merit.

The next that presented for a place, was a most whimsical figure indeed.[1] He was hung round with papers of his own composing, not unlike those who sing ballads in the streets, and came dancing up to the door with all the confidence of instant admittance. The volubility of his motion and address prevented my being able to read more of his cargo than the word Inspector, which was written in great letters at the top of some of the papers. He opened the coach-door himself without any ceremony, and was just slipping in, when the coachman, with as little ceremony, pulled him back. Our figure seemed perfectly angry at this repulse, and demanded gentleman's satisfaction. "Lord, sir! replied the coachman, instead of proper luggage, by your bulk you seem loaded for a West-India voyage. You are big enough, with all your papers, to crack twenty stage-coaches. Excuse me, indeed, sir, for you must not enter." Our figure now began to expostulate; he assured the coachman, that though his baggage seemed so bulky, it was perfectly light, and that he would be contented with the smallest corner of room. But Jehu was inflexible, and the carrier of the inspectors was sent to dance back again, with all his papers fluttering in the wind. We expected to have no more trouble from this quarter, when, in a few minutes, the

[1] [John Hill, M.D. (1716?–75), an extremely prolific journalistic quack, who wrote the *Inspector* in the *London Daily Advertiser* (a list of his works occupies five columns of the *Dictionary of National Biography*). His writings range from *The Rout; a farce* to *Cautions against the immoderate use of snuff*. Garrick wrote an epigram on him,

> For farces and physic his equal there scarce is:
> His farces are physic, his physic a farce is.]

same figure changed his appearance, like harlequin upon the stage, and with the same confidence again made his approaches, dressed in lace, and carrying nothing but a nosegay.[1] Upon coming near, he thrust the nosegay to the coachman's nose, grasped the brass, and seemed now resolved to enter by violence. I found the struggle soon begin to grow hot, and the coachman, who was a little old, unable to continue the contest, so, in order to ingratiate myself, I stept in to his assistance, and our united efforts sent our literary Proteus, though worsted, unconquered still, clear off, dancing a rigadoon, and smelling to his own nosegay.

The person[2] who after him appeared as candidate for a place in the stage, came up with an air not quite so confident, but somewhat however theatrical; and, instead of entering, made the coachman a very low bow, which the other returned, and desired to see his baggage; upon which he instantly produced some farces, a tragedy, and other miscellany productions. The coachman, casting his eye upon the cargoe, assured him, at present he could not possibly have a place, but hoped in time he might aspire to one, as he seemed to have read in the book of nature, without a careful perusal of which none ever found entrance at the temple of fame. "What, (replied the disappointed poet) shall my tragedy, in which I have vindicated the cause of liberty and virtue!"——"Follow nature, (returned the other) and never expect to find lasting fame by topics which only please from their popularity. Had you been first in the cause of freedom, or praised in virtue more than an empty name,[3] it is possible you might have gained admit-

[1] [Hill was fond of fine clothes. He had published several books on botany and herbalism in 1759; hence the nosegay.]

[2] [Arthur Murphy (1727–1805).]

[3] [Goldsmith had reviewed Murphy's *Orphan of China* in the *Critical Review* of April, 1759, remarking,

> . . . the author has, perhaps, too frequently mentioned the word *virtue.* This expression . . . should be husbanded, . . . if repeated too often, it loses its cabalistic power, and at last degenerates into contempt.]

tance; but at present I beg, sir, you will stand aside for another gentleman whom I see approaching."

This was a very grave personage,[1] whom at some distance I took for one of the most reserved, and even disagreeable figures I had seen; but as he approached, his appearance improved, and when I could distinguish him thoroughly, I perceived, that, in spite of the severity of his brow, he had one of the most good-natured countenances that could be imagined. Upon coming to open the stage door, he lifted a parcel of folios into the seat before him, but our inquisitorial coachman at once shoved them out again. "What, not take in my dictionary! exclaimed the other in a rage." "Be patient, sir, (replyed the coachman) I have drove a coach, man and boy, these two thousand years; but I do not remember to have carried above one dictionary during the whole time. That little book which I perceive peeping from one of your pockets, may I presume to ask what it contains?" "A mere trifle, (replied the author) it is called the Rambler." "The Rambler! (says the coachman) I beg, sir, you'll take your place; I have heard our ladies in the court of Apollo frequently mention it with rapture; and Clio, who happens to be a little grave, has been heard to prefer it to the Spectator; though others have observed, that the reflections, by being refined, sometimes become minute."

This grave gentleman was scarce seated, when another,[2] whose appearance was something more modern, seemed willing to enter, yet afraid to ask. He carried in his hand a bundle of essays, of which the coachman was curious enough to inquire the contents. "These (replied the gentleman) are rhapsodies against the religion of my country." "And how can you expect to come into my coach, after thus chusing the wrong side of the question." "Ay, but I am right (replied the other;) and if you give me leave, I shall in a few minutes state

[1] [Johnson, whom Goldsmith had yet to meet when this was written.]

[2] [Hume, whose *History of the House of Tudor* had been published in 1758.]

the argument." "Right or wrong (said the coachman) he who disturbs religion, is a blockhead, and he shall never travel in a coach of mine." "If then (said the gentleman, mustering up all his courage) if I am not to have admittance as an essayist, I hope I shall not be repulsed as an historian; the last volume of my history met with applause." "Yes, (replied the coachman) but I have heard only the first approved at the temple of fame; and as I see you have it about you, enter without further ceremony." My attention was now diverted to a crowd, who were pushing forward a person[1] that seemed more inclined to the *stage coach of riches*; but by their means he was driven forward to the fame machine, which he, however, seemed heartily to despise. Impelled, however, by their sollicitations, he steps up, flourishing a voluminous history, and demanding admittance. "Sir, I have formerly heard your name mentioned (says the coachman) but never as an historian. Is there no other work upon which you may claim a place?" "None, replied the other, except a romance; but this is a work of too trifling a nature to claim future attention." "You mistake (says the inquisitor) a well-written romance is no such easy task as is generally imagined. I remember formerly to have carried Cervantes and Segrais, and if you think fit, you may enter." Upon our three literary travellers coming into the same coach, I listened attentively to hear what might be the conversation that passed upon this extraordinary occasion; when, instead of agreeable or entertaining dialogue, I found them grumbling at each other, and each seemed discontented with his companions. Strange! thought I to myself, that they who are thus born to enlighten the world, should still preserve the narrow prejudices of childhood, and, by disagreeing, make even the highest merit ridiculous. Were the learned and the wise to unite against the dunces of society, instead of sometimes siding into opposite parties with them, they might throw a lustre upon each other's reputation, and teach every rank of

[1] [Smollett, for whose *British Magazine* Goldsmith was shortly to write.]

subordinate merit, if not to admire, at least not to avow dislike.

In the midst of these reflections, I perceived the coachman, unmindful of me, had now mounted the box. Several were approaching to be taken in, whose pretensions I was sensible were very just, I therefore desired him to stop, and take in more passengers; but he replied, as he had now mounted the box, it would be improper to come down; but that he should take them all, one after the other, when he should return. So he drove away, and, for myself, as I could not get in, I mounted behind, in order to hear the conversation on the way.

To be continued.[1]

[1] [Unfortunately it never was.]

THE PROCEEDINGS OF PROVIDENCE VINDICATED

AN EASTERN TALE

The Proceedings of Providence vindicated, An Eastern Tale, was first printed in the *Royal Magazine, or Gentleman's Monthly Companion* for December, 1759. Goldsmith reprinted it, much revised and without the title, as Essay XVI in *Essays*, 1765. I have preferred this later text.

THE PROCEEDINGS OF PROVIDENCE VINDICATED

AN EASTERN TALE

WHERE Tauris lifts its head above the storm, and presents nothing to the sight of the distant traveller but a prospect of nodding rocks, falling torrents, and all the variety of tremendous nature; on the bleak bosom of this frightful mountain, secluded from society and detesting the ways of men, lived Asem the Manhater.

Asem had spent his youth with men; had shared in their amusements; and had been taught to love his fellow-creatures with the most ardent affection: but from the tenderness of his disposition, he exhausted all his fortune in relieving the wants of the distressed. The petitioner never sued in vain; the weary traveller never passed his door; he only desisted from doing good when he had no longer the power of relieving.

From a fortune thus spent in benevolence, he expected a grateful return from those he had formerly relieved; and made his application with confidence of redress: the ungrateful world soon grew weary of his importunity; for pity is but a short-lived passion. He soon, therefore, began to view mankind in a very different light from that in which he had before beheld them: he perceived a thousand vices he had never before suspected to exist: wherever he turned, ingratitude, dissimulation and treachery, contributed to increase his detestation of them. Resolved therefore to continue no longer in a world which he hated, and which repaid his detestation with contempt, he retired to this region of sterility, in order to brood over his resentment in solitude, and converse with the only honest heart he knew; namely, with his own.

A cave was his only shelter from the inclemency of the

weather; fruits gathered with difficulty from the mountain's side, his only food; and his drink was fetched with danger and toil from the headlong torrent. In this manner he lived, sequestered from society, passing the hours in meditation, and sometimes exulting that he was able to live independently of his fellow-creatures.

At the foot of the mountain, an extensive lake displayed its glassy bosom; reflecting, on its broad surface, the impending horrors of the mountain. To this capacious mirror he would sometimes descend, and, reclining on its steep banks, cast an eager look on the smooth expanse that lay before him. "How beautiful," he often cried, "is nature! how lovely, even in her wildest scenes! How finely contrasted is the level plain that lies beneath me, with yon awful pile that hides its tremendous head in clouds! But the beauty of these scenes is no way comparable with their utility, from hence an hundred rivers are supplied, which distribute health and verdure to the various countries through which they flow. Every part of the universe is beautiful, just, and wise, but man: vile man is a solecism in nature; the only monster in the creation. Tempests and whirlwinds have their use; but vicious, ungrateful man is a blot in the fair page of universal beauty. Why was I born of that detested species, whose vices are almost a reproach to the wisdom of the divine Creator! Were men entirely free from vice, all would be uniformity, harmony, and order. A world of moral rectitude, should be the result of a perfectly moral agent. Why, why then, O Alla! must I be thus confined in darkness, doubt, and despair!"

Just as he uttered the word Despair, he was going to plunge into the lake beneath him, at once to satisfy his doubts, and put a period to his anxiety; when he perceived a most majestic being walking on the surface of the water, and approaching the bank on which he stood. So unexpected an object at once checked his purpose; he stopped, contemplated, and fancied he saw something awful and divine in his aspect.

"Son of Adam," cried the genius, "stop thy rash purpose; the father of the faithful has seen thy justice, thy integrity, thy miseries, and hath sent me to afford and administer relief. Give me thine hand, and follow, without trembling, wherever I shall lead; in me behold the genius of conviction, kept by the great prophet, to turn from their errors those who go astray, not from curiosity, but a rectitude of intention. Follow me, and be wise."

Asem immediately descended upon the lake, and his guide conducted him along the surface of the water; till, coming near the centre of the lake, they both began to sink; the waters closed over their heads; they descended several hundred fathoms, till Asem, just ready to give up his life as inevitably lost, found himself with his celestial guide in another world, at the bottom of the waters, where human foot had never trod before. His astonishment was beyond description, when he saw a sun like that he had left, a serene sky over his head, and blooming verdure under his feet.

"I plainly perceive your amazement," said the genius; "but suspend it for a while. This world was formed by Alla, at the request, and under the inspection, of our great prophet, who once entertained the same doubts which filled your mind when I found you, and from the consequence of which you were so lately rescued. The rational inhabitants of this world are formed agreeable to your own ideas; they are absolutely without vice. In other respects it resembles your earth, but differs from it in being wholly inhabited by men who never do wrong. If you find this world more agreeable than that you so lately left, you have free permission to spend the remainder of your days in it; but permit me, for some time, to attend you, that I may silence your doubts, and make you better acquainted with your company and your new habitation."

"A world without vice! Rational beings without immorality!" cried Asem, in a rapture; "I thank thee, O Alla, who hast at length heard my petitions; this, this indeed will produce happiness, ecstasy, and ease. O for an immortality, to spend it among men who are incapable of ingratitude, injustice, fraud, violence, and a thousand other crimes, that render society miserable!"

"Cease thine acclamations," replied the genius. "Look around thee; reflect on every object and action before us, and communicate to me the result of thine observations. Lead wherever you think proper, I shall be your attendant and instructor." Asem and his companion travelled on in silence for some time, the former being entirely lost in astonishment; but, at last, recovering his former serenity, he could not help observing, that the face of the country bore a near resemblance to that he had left, except that this subterranean world still seemed to retain its primæval wildness.

"Here," cried Asem, "I perceive animals of prey, and others that seem only designed for their subsistence; it is the very same in the world over our heads. But had I been permitted to instruct our prophet, I would have removed this defect, and formed no voracious or destructive animals, which only prey on the other parts of the creation." "Your tenderness for inferior animals is, I find, remarkable," said the genius, smiling. "But, with regard to meaner creatures, this world exactly resembles the other; and, indeed, for obvious reasons: for the earth can support a more considerable number of animals, by their thus becoming food for each other, than if they had lived entirely on the vegetable productions. So that animals of different natures thus formed, instead of lessening their multitude, subsist in the greatest number possible. But let us hasten on to the inhabited country before us, and see what that offers for instruction."

They soon gained the utmost verge of the forest, and entered the country inhabited by men without vice; and Asem anticipated in idea the rational delight he hoped to experience in such an innocent society. But they had scarce left the confines of the wood, when they beheld one of the inhabitants flying with hasty steps, and terror in his countenance, from an army of squirrels that closely pursued him. "Heavens!" cried Asem, "why does he fly? What can he fear from animals so contemptible?" He had scarce spoke when he perceived two dogs pursuing another of the human species, who, with equal terror and haste, attempted to avoid them. "This," cried Asem to his guide, "is truly surprising; nor can I conceive the reason for so strange an action." "Every species of animals," replied the genius, "has of late grown very powerful in this country; for the inhabitants, at first, thinking it unjust to use either fraud or force in destroying them, they have insensibly increased, and now frequently ravage their harmless frontiers." "But they should have been destroyed," cried Asem; "you see the consequence of such neglect." "Where is then that tenderness you so lately expressed for subordinate animals?" replied the genius smiling: "you seem to have forgot that branch of justice." "I must acknowledge my mistake," returned Asem; "I am now convinced that we must be guilty of tyranny and injustice to the brute creation, if we would enjoy the world ourselves. But let us no longer observe the duty of man to these irrational creatures, but survey their connections with one another."

As they walked farther up the country, the more he was surprized to see no vestiges of handsome houses, no cities, nor any mark of elegant design. His conductor perceiving his surprize, observed, That the inhabitants of this new world were perfectly content with their antient simplicity; each had an house, which, though homely, was sufficient to lodge his little family; they were too good to build houses, which could only encrease their own pride, and the envy of the spectator; what they built was for convenience, and not for shew. "At least, then," said Asem, "they have neither architects, painters, or statuaries, in their society; but these are idle arts, and may be spared. However, before I spend much more time here, you should have my thanks for introducing me into the society of some of their wisest men: there is scarce any pleasure to me equal to a refined conversation; there is nothing of which I am so enamoured as wisdom." "Wisdom!" replied his instructor, "how ridiculous! We have no wisdom here, for we have no occasion for it; true wisdom is only a knowledge of our own duty, and the duty of others to us; but of what use is such wisdom here? each intuitively performs what is right in himself, and expects the same from others. If by wisdom you should mean vain curiosity and empty speculation, as such pleasures have their origin in vanity, luxury, or avarice, we are too good to pursue them." "All this may be right," says Asem; "but methinks I observe a solitary disposition prevail among the people; each family keeps separately within their own precincts, without society, or without intercourse." "That, indeed, is true," replied the other; "here is no established society; nor should there be any: all societies are made either through fear or friendship; the people we are among are too good to fear each other; and there are no motives to private friendship, where all are equally meritorious." "Well then," said the sceptic, "as I am to spend my time here, if I am to have neither the polite arts, nor wisdom, nor friendship, in such a world, I should be glad, at least, of an easy companion, who may tell me his thoughts, and to whom I may communicate mine." "And to what purpose should either do this?" says the genius: "flattery or curiosity are vicious motives, and never allowed of here; and wisdom is out of the question."

"Still, however," said Asem, "the inhabitants must be happy; each is contented with his own possessions, nor avariciously endeavours to heap up more than is necessary for his own subsistence: each has therefore leisure for pitying those that stand in need of his compassion." He had scarce spoken when his ears were assaulted with the lamentations of a wretch who sat by the way-side, and, in the most deplorable distress, seemed gently to murmur at his own misery. Asem immediately ran to his relief, and found him in the last stage of a consumption. "Strange," cried the son of Adam, "that men who are free from vice should thus suffer so much misery without relief!" "Be not surprized," said the wretch who was dying; "would it not be the utmost injustice for beings, who have only just sufficient to support themselves, and are content with a bare subsistence, to take it from their own mouths to put it into mine? They never are possessed of a single meal more than is necessary; and what is barely necessary cannot be dispensed with." "They should have been supplied with more than is necessary," cried Asem; "and yet I contradict my own opinion but a moment before: all is doubt, perplexity, and confusion. Even the want of ingratitude is no virtue here, since they never received a favour. They have, however, another excellence, yet behind; the love of their country is still, I hope, one of their darling virtues." "Peace, Asem," replied the guardian, with a countenance not less severe than beautiful, "nor forfeit all thy pretensions to wisdom; the same selfish motives by which we prefer our own interest to that of others, induce us to regard our country preferably to that of another. Nothing less than universal benevolence is free from vice, and that you see is practised here." "Strange!" cries the disappointed pilgrim, in an agony of distress; "what sort of a world am I now introduced to? There is scarce a single virtue, but that of temperance, which they practise; and in that they are no way superior to the very brute creation. There is scarce an amusement which they enjoy; fortitude, liberality, friendship, wisdom, conversation, and love of country, all are virtues entirely unknown here; thus it seems, that, to be unacquainted with vice is not to know virtue. Take me, O my genius, back to that very world which I have despised: a world which has Alla for its contriver is much more wisely formed than that which has been projected by Mahomet. Ingratitude, contempt, and hatred, I can now suffer, for perhaps I have deserved them. When I arraigned the wisdom of Providence, I only shewed my own ignorance; henceforth let me keep from vice myself, and pity it in others."

He had scarce ended, when the genius, assuming an air of terrible complacency, called all his thunders around him, and vanished in a whirlwind. Asem, astonished at the terror of the scene, looked for his imaginary world; when, casting his eyes around, he perceived himself in the very situation, and in the very place, where he first began to repine and despair; his right foot had been just advanced to take the fatal plunge, nor had it been yet withdrawn; so instantly did Providence strike the series of truths just imprinted on his soul. He now departed from the water-side in tranquility, and, leaving his horrid mansion, travelled to Segestan, his native city; where he diligently applied himself to commerce, and put in practice that wisdom he had learned in solitude. The frugality of a few years soon produced opulence; the number of his domestics increased; his friends came to him from every part of the city; nor did he receive them with disdain: and a youth of misery was concluded with an old age of elegance, affluence, and ease.

SELECTED LETTERS FROM

THE CITIZEN OF THE WORLD

OR

LETTERS FROM
A CHINESE PHILOSOPHER
RESIDING IN LONDON
TO
HIS FRIENDS IN
THE EAST

On 12 January, 1760, John Newbery started the *Public Ledger*; and on 24 January it contained the first of Goldsmith's *Chinese Letters*. They continued till 14 August, 1761.

The project was probably already in his mind when he wrote in 1758 to Robert Bryanton, "I shall soon make our Chinese talk like an Englishman." (See p. 842.) The *Chinese Letters* were very popular; this form of topical satire had already been well established, for instance by Horace Walpole's *Letter from Xo Ho, a Chinese Philosopher at London, to his friend, Lien Chi, at Peking*. But no one was better suited than Goldsmith to play the innocent abroad, and he exploits the situation with an irony that is never malicious. A remark of Voltaire's which Goldsmith had quoted in 1757 is pertinent to the *Chinese Letters*:

> The success of the Persian Letters [of Montesquieu] arose from the delicacy of their satire. That satire which in the mouth of an Asiatic is poignant, would lose all its force when coming from an European.

The *Chinese Letters* were assembled and published in two duodecimo volumes as *The Citizen of the World* on 1 May, 1762; it was *Printed for J. Newbery, at the Bible and Sun, in St. Paul's Church-yard. A City Night-Piece* was included from *The Bee*. Unfortunately it has not been possible to compare the text with that of the *Public Ledger*; and I have followed that of the first edition. *The Citizen of the World* is Goldsmith's longest original work and I have only been able to include about half of the letters here. It is only fair to tell the reader that my selection has not been altogether representative, as there is one class of letters, Lien Chi Altangi's moral injunctions to his son, which I have almost entirely excluded, for there was no room for them except at the expense of better material.

I have corrected the numbering of the letters in the first edition which was very faulty. The descriptive sub-titles were not at first printed at the head of each letter. They have been taken from the Table of Contents, which I have, for convenience, put before the letters instead of in its original place at the end.

Letters LIV, LV, LXIX, CVIII, CXIV and CXIX were subsequently reprinted by Goldsmith in *Essays*, 1765, as Essays X, XI, XIII, XVIII, XXIII, and XXIV. Letters XXIV and LXVIII were combined in Essay XX.

THE EDITOR'S PREFACE

THE schoolmen had formerly a very exact way of computing the abilities of their Saints or authors. Escobar, for instance, was said to have learning as five, genius as four, and gravity as seven. Caramuel was greater than he. His learning was as eight, his genius as six, and his gravity as thirteen.[1] Were I to estimate the merits of our Chinese Philosopher by the same scale, I would not hesitate to state his genius still higher; but as to his learning and gravity, these I think might safely be marked as nine hundred and ninety nine, within one degree of absolute frigidity.

Yet upon his first appearance here, many were angry not to find him as ignorant as a Tripoline ambassador, or an Envoy from Mujac. They were surprized to find a man born so far from London, that school of prudence and wisdom, endued even with a moderate capacity. They expressed the same surprize at his knowledge that the Chinese do at ours. **How comes it*, said they, *that the Europeans, so remote from China, think with so much justice and precision? They have never read our books, they scarcely know even our letters, and yet they talk and reason just as we do.* The truth is, the Chinese and we are pretty much alike. Different degrees of refinement, and not of distance, mark the distinctions among mankind. Savages of the most opposite climates, have all but one character of improvidence and rapacity; and tutored nations, however separate, make use of the very same methods to procure refined enjoyment.

The distinctions of polite nations are few; but such as are peculiar to the Chinese, appear in every page of the following

[1] [Antonio Escobar y Mendoza (1589–1669) and Jean de Lobkowitz, "Caramuel" (1606–82), Spanish theologians. Goldsmith had contributed a *Poetical Scale* on similar principles to the *Literary Magazine* of February, 1758.]

* Le Comte, Vol. 1. p. 210.

correspondence. The metaphors and allusions are all drawn from the East. Their formality our author carefully preserves. Many of their favourite tenets in morals are illustrated. The Chinese are always concise, so is he. Simple, so is he. The Chinese are grave and sententious, so is he. But in one particular, the resemblance is peculiarly striking: the Chinese are often dull; and so is he. Nor has my assistance been wanting. We are told in an old romance of a certain knight errant and his horse who contracted an intimate friendship. The horse most usually bore the knight, but, in cases of extraordinary dispatch, the knight returned the favour, and carried his horse. Thus in the intimacy between my author and me, he has usually given me a lift of his Eastern sublimity, and I have sometimes given him a return of my colloquial ease.

Yet it appears strange in this season of panegyric, when scarce an author passes unpraised either by his friends or himself, that such merit as our Philosopher's should be forgotten. While the epithets of ingenious, copious, elaborate, and refined, are lavished among the mob, like medals at a coronation, the lucky prizes fall on every side, but not one on him. I could on this occasion make myself melancholly, by considering the capriciousness of public taste, or the mutability of fortune; but during this fit of morality, lest my reader should sleep, I'll take a nap myself, and when I awake tell him my dream.

I imagined the Thames was frozen over, and I stood by its side. Several booths were erected upon the ice, and I was told by one of the spectators, that FASHION FAIR was going to begin. He added, that every author who would carry his works there, might probably find a very good reception. I was resolved however to observe the humours of the place in safety from the shore, sensible that ice was at best precarious, and having been always a little cowardly in my sleep.

Several of my acquaintance seemed much more hardy than I, and went over the ice with intrepidity. Some carried their works to the fair on sledges, some on carts, and those which were more voluminous, were conveyed in waggons. Their temerity astonished me. I knew their cargoes were heavy, and expected every moment they would have gone to the bottom. They all entered the fair, however, in safety, and each soon after returned to my great surprize, highly satisfied with his entertainment, and the bargains he had brought away.

The success of such numbers at last began to operate upon me. If these, cried I, meet with favour and safety, some luck may, perhaps, for once attend the unfortunate. I am resolved to make a new adventure. The furniture, frippery and fireworks of China, have long been fashionably bought up. I'll try the fair with a small cargoe of Chinese morality. If the Chinese have contributed to vitiate our taste, I'll try how far they can help to improve our understanding. But as others have driven into the market in waggons, I'll cautiously begin by venturing with a wheel-barrow. Thus resolved, I baled up my goods and fairly ventured; when, upon just entering the fair, I fancied the ice that had supported an hundred waggons before, cracked under me; and wheel-barrow and all went to the bottom.

Upon awaking from my reverie, with the fright, I cannot help wishing that the pains taken in giving this correspondence an English dress, had been employed in contriving new political systems, or new plots for farces. I might then have taken my station in the world, either as a poet or a philosopher; and made one in those little societies where men club to raise each others reputation. But at present I belong to no particular class. I resemble one of those solitary animals, that has been forced from its forest to gratify human curiosity. My earliest wish was to escape unheeded through life; but I have been set up for half-pence, to fret and scamper at the end of my chain. Tho' none are injured by my rage, I am naturally too savage to court any friends by fawning. Too obstinate to be taught new tricks; and too improvident to mind what may happen, I am appeased, though not contented. Too indolent for intrigue, and too timid to push for favour, I am—But what signifies what am I.

Ελπὶς καὶ συ τὺχη μέγα χαίρετε· τὸν λιμέν' εὗρον.
Οὐδὲν ἐμοὶ χ' ὑμῖν· παίζετε τοὺς μετ' ἐμέ.[1]

[1] [Greek Anthology (*Anth. Pal.* 9. 49.). The Dublin edition of 1769 first added a translation which may be by Goldsmith:

Fortune and Hope adieu! I see my Port,
Too long your dupe; be others now your Sport.]

TABLE OF CONTENTS

LETTERS
FROM A CITIZEN OF THE WORLD
TO HIS FRIENDS
IN THE EAST

LETTER I

Introduction. A character of the Chinese Philosopher.

To Mr. **** *Merchant in* London.

SIR, Amsterdam

YOURS of the 13th instant, covering two bills, one on Messrs. R. and D. value 478l. 10s. and the other on Mr.****, value 285l. duly came to hand, the former of which met with honour, but the other has been trifled with, and I am afraid will be returned protested.

The bearer of this is my friend, therefore let him be yours. He is a native of Honan in China, and one who did me signal services when he was a mandarine, and I a factor at Canton. By frequently conversing with English there, he has learned the language, though intirely a stranger to their manners and customs. I am told he is a philosopher, I am sure he is an honest man; that to you will be his best recommendation, next to the consideration of his being the friend of, Sir,

Yours, &c.

LETTER II

The arrival of the Chinese in London. His motives for the journey. Some description of the streets and houses.

From Lien Chi Altangi[1] *to* ****, *Merchant in* Amsterdam.

Friend of my heart, London

MAY *the wings of peace rest upon thy dwelling, and the shield of conscience preserve thee from vice and misery:* for all thy favours accept my gratitude and esteem, the only tributes a poor philosophic wanderer can return; sure fortune is resolved to make me unhappy, when she gives others a power of testifying their friendship by actions, and leaves me only words to express the sincerity of mine.

I am perfectly sensible of the delicacy by which you endeavour to lessen your own merit and my obligations. By calling your late instances of friendship only a return for former favours, you would induce me to impute to your justice what I owe to your generosity.

The services I did you at Canton, justice, humanity, and my office bade me perform; those you have done me since my arrival at Amsterdam, no laws obliged you to, no justice required, even half your favours would have been greater than my most sanguine expectations.

The sum of money therefore which you privately conveyed into my baggage, when I was leaving Holland, and which I was ignorant of till my arrival in London, I must beg leave to return. You have been bred a merchant, and I a scholar; You consequently love money better than I. You can find pleasure in superfluity, I am perfectly contented with what is sufficient; take therefore what is yours, it may give you some pleasure, even though you have no occasion to use it; my happiness it cannot improve, for I have already all that I want.

My passage by sea from Rotterdam to England, was more

[1] [Probably suggested by Horace Walpole's *Letter from Xo Ho, a Chinese Philosopher at London, to his friend Lien Chi, at Peking*, 1757.]

painful to me than all the journies I ever made on land. I have traversed the immeasurable wilds of Mogul Tartary; felt all the rigours of Siberian skies; I have had my repose an hundred times disturbed by invading savages, and have seen without shrinking the desert sands rise like a troubled ocean all around me; against these calamities I was armed with resolution; but in my passage to England, though nothing occurred that gave the mariners any uneasiness, yet to one who was never at sea before, all was subject of astonishment and terror. To find the land disappear, to see our ship mount the waves quick as an arrow from the Tartar bow, to hear the wind howling through the cordage, to feel a sickness which depresses even the spirits of the brave; these were unexpected distresses, and consequently assaulted me unprepared to receive them.

You men of Europe think nothing of a voyage by sea. With us of China, a man who has been from sight of land is regarded upon his return with admiration. I have known some provinces where there is not even a name for the ocean. What a strange people therefore am I got amongst, who have founded an empire on this unstable element, who build cities upon billows that rise higher than the mountains of Tipartala, and make the deep more formidable than the wildest tempest.

Such accounts as these, I must confess, were my first motives for seeing England. These induced me to undertake a journey of seven hundred painful days, in order to examine its opulence, buildings, sciences, arts and manufactures on the spot. Judge then how great is my disappointment on entering London, to see no signs of that opulence so much talked of abroad; wherever I turn, I am presented with a gloomy solemnity in the houses, the streets and the inhabitants; none of that beautiful gilding which makes a principal ornament in Chinese architecture. The streets of Nankin are sometimes strewed with gold leaf; very different are those of London; in the midst of their pavements, a great lazy puddle moves muddily along; heavy laden machines with wheels of unweildy thickness crowd up every passage; so that a stranger, instead of finding time for observation, is often happy if he has time to escape from being crushed to pieces.

The houses borrow very few ornaments from architecture; their chief decoration seems to be a paltry piece of painting, hung out at their doors or windows, at once a proof of their indigence and vanity. Their vanity, in each having one of those pictures exposed to public view; and their indigence, in being unable to get them better painted. In this respect, the fancy of their painters is also deplorable. Could you believe it? I have seen five black lions and three blue boars in less than a circuit of half a mile; and yet you know that animals of these colours are no where to be found except in the wild imaginations of Europe.

From these circumstances in their buildings, and from the dismal looks of the inhabitants, I am induced to conclude that the nation is actually poor; and that like the Persians, they make a splendid figure every where but at home. The proverb of Xixofou is, that a man's riches may be seen in his eyes; if we judge of the English by this rule, there is not a poorer nation under the sun.

I have been here but two days, so will not be hasty in my decisions; such letters as I shall write to Fipsihi in Moscow, I beg you'll endeavour to forward with all diligence; I shall send them open, in order that you may take copies or translations, as you are equally versed in the Dutch and Chinese languages. Dear friend, think of my absence with regret, as I sincerely regret yours; even while I write, I lament our separation. Farewell.

LETTER III

The description of London continued. The luxury of the English. Its benefits. The fine gentleman. The fine lady.

From Lien Chi Altangi, to the care of Fipsihi, resident in Moscow; to be forwarded by the Russian caravan to Fum Hoam,[1] *first president of the ceremonial academy at Pekin in China.*

THINK not, O thou guide of my youth, that absence can impair my respect, or interposing trackless desarts blot your reverend figure from my memory. The farther I travel I feel the pain of separation with stronger force, those ties that bind me to my native country, and you, are still unbroken. By every remove, I only drag a greater length of chain.

Could I find aught worth transmitting from so remote a region as this to which I have wandered, I should gladly send it; but instead of this, you must be contented with a renewal of my former professions, and an imperfect account of a people with whom I am as yet but superficially acquainted. The remarks of a man who has been but three days in the country can only be those obvious circumstances which force themselves upon the imagination: I consider myself here as a newly created Being introduced into a new world; every object strikes with wonder and surprise. The imagination still unsated, seems the only active principle of the mind. The most trifling occurrences give pleasure, till the gloss of novelty is worn away. When I have ceased to wonder, I may possibly grow wise; I may then call the reasoning principle to my aid, and compare those objects with each other, which were before examined without reflection.

Behold me then in London, gazing at the strangers, and they at me; it seems they find somewhat absurd in my figure; and had I been never from home it is possible I might find an infinite fund of ridicule in theirs; but by long travelling I am

[1] [Like Lien Chi this name is not original; *Chinese Tales; or, the Wonderful Adventures of the Mandarine Fum Hoam* had been published in 1725.]

taught to laugh at folly alone, and to find nothing truly ridiculous but villainy and vice.

When I had just quitted my native country, and crossed the Chinese wall, I fancied every deviation from the customs and manners of China was a departing from nature: I smiled at the blue lips and red foreheads of the Tonguese; and could hardly contain when I saw the Daures dress their heads with horns. The Ostiacs powdered with red earth; and the Calmuck beauties tricked out in all the finery of sheep-skin appeared highly ridiculous; but I soon perceived that the ridicule lay not in them but in me; that I falsely condemned others of absurdity, because they happened to differ from a standard originally founded in prejudice or partiality.

I find no pleasure therefore in taxing the English with departing from nature in their external appearance, which is all I yet know of their character; it is possible they only endeavour to improve her simple plan, since every extravagance in dress proceeds from a desire of becoming more beautiful than nature made us; and this is so harmless a vanity that I not only pardon but approve it: A desire to be more excellent than others is what actually makes us so, and as thousands find a livelihood in society by such appetites, none but the ignorant inveigh against them.

You are not insensible, most reverend Fum Hoam, what numberless trades, even among the Chinese, subsist by the harmless pride of each other. Your nose-borers, feet-swathers, tooth-stainers, eye brow pluckers, would all want bread, should their neighbours want vanity. These vanities, however, employ much fewer hands in China than in England; and a fine gentleman, or a fine lady, here dressed up to the fashion, seems scarcely to have a single limb that does not suffer some distortions from art.

To make a fine gentleman, several trades are required, but chiefly a barber: you have undoubtedly heard of the Jewish champion, whose strength lay in his hair: one would think that the English were for placing all wisdom there: To appear wise, nothing more is requisite here than for a man to borrow hair from the heads of all his neighbours, and clap it like a bush on his own: the distributors of law and physic stick on such quantities, that it is almost impossible, even in idea, to distinguish between the head and the hair.

Those whom I have been now describing, affect the gravity of the lion: those I am going to describe more resemble the pert vivacity of smaller animals. The barber, who is still master of the ceremonies, cuts their hair close to the crown; and then with a composition of meal and hog's lard, plaisters the whole in such a manner, as to make it impossible to distinguish whether the patient wears a cap or a plaister; but to make the picture more perfectly striking, conceive the tail of some beast, a greyhound's tail, or a pig's tail for instance, appended to the back of the head, and reaching down to that place where tails in other animals are generally seen to begin; thus betailed and bepowdered, the man of taste fancies he improves in beauty, dresses up his hard-featured face in smiles, and attempts to look hideously tender. Thus equipped, he is qualified to make love, and hopes for success more from the powder on the outside of his head, than the sentiments within.

Yet when I consider what sort of a creature the fine lady is, to whom he is supposed to pay his addresses, it is not strange to find him thus equipped in order to please. She is herself every whit as fond of powder, and tails, and hog's lard as he: to speak my secret sentiments, most reverend Fum, the ladies here are horridly ugly; I can hardly endure the sight of them; they no way resemble the beauties of China; the Europeans have a quite different idea of beauty from us; when I reflect on the small footed perfections of an Eastern beauty, how is it possible I should have eyes for a woman whose feet are ten inches long. I shall never forget the beauties of my native city of Nangfew. How very broad their faces; how very short their noses; how very little their eyes; how very thin their lips;

how very black their teeth; the snow on the tops of Bao is not fairer than their cheeks; and their eye-brows are small as the line by the pencil of Quamsi. Here a lady with such perfections would be frightful; Dutch and Chinese beauties indeed have some resemblance, but English women are entirely different; red cheeks, big eyes, and teeth of a most odious whiteness, are not only seen here, but wished for; and then they have such masculine feet, as actually serve *some* for walking!

Yet uncivil as nature has been, they seem resolved to outdo her in unkindness; they use white powder, blue powder, and black powder for their hair, and a red powder for the face on some particular occasions.

They like to have the face of various colours, as among the Tartars of Koreki, frequently sticking on, with spittle, little black patches on every part of it, except on the tip of the nose, which I have never seen with a patch. You'll have a better idea of their manner of placing these spots, when I have finished a map of an English face patch'd up to the fashion, which shall shortly be sent to encrease your curious collection of paintings, medals, and monsters.

But what surprizes more than all the rest, is, what I have just now been credibly informed by one of this country; "Most ladies here, says he, have two faces; one face to sleep in, and another to shew in company: the first is generally reserv'd for the husband and family at home, the other put on to please strangers abroad; the family face is often indifferent enough, but the out-door one looks something better; this is always made at the toilet, where the looking-glass, and toad-eater sit in council and settle the complexion of the day."

I can't ascertain the truth of this remark; however, it is actually certain, that they wear more cloaths within doors than without; and I have seen a lady who seem'd to shudder at a breeze in her own apartment, appear half naked in the streets. Farewell.

LETTER IV

English pride. Liberty. An instance of both. News papers. Politeness.

To the same.

THE English seem as silent as the Japonese, yet vainer than the inhabitants of Siam. Upon my arrival I attributed that reserve to modesty, which I now find has its origin in pride. Condescend to address them first, and you are sure of their acquaintance; stoop to flattery, and you conciliate their friendship and esteem. They bear hunger, cold, fatigue, and all the miseries of life without shrinking; danger only calls forth their fortitude; they even exult in calamity; but contempt is what they cannot bear. An Englishman fears contempt more than death; he often flies to death as a refuge from its pressure; and dies when he fancies the world has ceased to esteem him.

Pride seems the source not only of their national vices, but of their national virtues also. An Englishman is taught to love his king as his friend, but to acknowledge no other master than the laws which himself has contributed to enact. He despises those nations, who, that one may be free, are all content to be slaves; who first lift a tyrant into terror, and then shrink under his power as if delegated from heaven. Liberty is echoed in all their assemblies, and thousands might be found ready to offer up their lives for the sound, though perhaps not one of all the number understands its meaning. The lowest mechanic however looks upon it as his duty to be a watchful guardian of his country's freedom, and often uses a language that might seem haughty, even in the mouth of the great emperor who traces his ancestry to the moon.

A few days ago, passing by one of their prisons, I could not avoid stopping, in order to listen to a dialogue which I thought might afford me some entertainment. The conversation was carried on between a debtor through the grate of his prison, a porter, who had stopped to rest his burthen, and a soldier at the window. The subject was upon a threatened invasion from

France, and each seemed extreamly anxious to rescue his country from the impending danger. "*For my part*, cries the prisoner, *the greatest of my apprehensions is for our freedom; if the French should conquer, what would become of English liberty. My dear Friends, liberty is the Englishman's prerogative; we must preserve that at the expence of our lives, of that the French shall never deprive us; it is not to be expected that men who are slaves themselves would preserve our freedom should they happen to conquer:* Ay, slaves, cries the porter, they are all slaves, fit only to carry burthens every one of them. Before I would stoop to slavery, may this be my poison (and he held the goblet in his hand) may this be my poison—but I would sooner list for a soldier."

The soldier taking the goblet from his friend, with much awe fervently cried out, *It is not so much our liberties as our religion that would suffer by such a change: Ay, our religion, my lads. May the Devil sink me into flames*, (such was the solemnity of his adjuration) *if the French should come over, but our religion would be utterly undone.* So saying, instead of a libation, he applied the goblet to his lips, and confirmed his sentiments with a ceremony of the most persevering devotion.[1]

In short, every man here pretends to be a politician; even the fair sex are sometimes found to mix the severity of national altercation, with the blandishments of love, and often become conquerors by more weapons of destruction than their eyes.

This universal passion for politics is gratified by Daily Gazettes, as with us at China. But as in ours, the emperor en-

[1] [Possibly based on a similar dialogue in John Byrom's *Tom the Porter*, first printed in the *Chester Courant* of 25 November, 1746:

. . . The Soldier, touch'd a little with Surprise
To see his Friend's Indifference, replies:
"What you say *Tom*, I own, is very good,
But—OUR RELIGION!" and he d—n'd his Blood—
"What will become of OUR RELIGION?"—"True!"
Says the Jail-Bird; "and of OUR FREEDOM too?
If the PRETENDER," rapt he out, "comes on,
OUR LIBERTIES AND PROPERTIES are gone!"]

deavours to instruct his people, in theirs the people endeavour to instruct the administration. You must not, however, imagine, that they who compile these papers have any actual knowledge of the politics, or the government of a state; they only collect their materials from the oracle of some coffee-house, which oracle has himself gathered them the night before from a beau at a gaming-table, who has pillaged his knowledge from a great man's porter, who has had his information from the great man's gentleman, who has invented the whole story for his own amusement the night preceding.

The English in general seem fonder of gaining the esteem than the love of those they converse with: this gives a formality to their amusements; their gayest conversations have something too wise for innocent relaxation; though in company you are seldom disgusted with the absurdity of a fool; you are seldom lifted into rapture by those strokes of vivacity which give instant, though not permanent pleasure.

What they want, however, in gaiety, they make up in politeness. You smile at hearing me praise the English for their politeness: you who have heard very different accounts from the missionaries at Pekin, who have seen such a different behaviour in their merchants and seamen at home. But I must still repeat it, the English seem more polite than any of their neighbours: their great art in this respect lies in endeavouring, while they oblige, to lessen the force of the favour. Other countries are fond of obliging a stranger; but seem desirous that he should be sensible of the obligation. The English confer their kindness with an appearance of indifference, and give away benefits with an air as if they despised them.

Walking a few days ago between an English and a Frenchman into the suburbs of the city, we were overtaken by a heavy shower of rain. I was unprepared; but they had each large coats, which defended them from what seemed to me a perfect inundation. The Englishman seeing me shrink from the weather, accosted me thus: "*Psha, man, what dost shrink at? here, take this coat; I don't want it; I find it no way useful to me; I had as lief be without it.*" The Frenchman began to shew his politeness in turn. "*My dear friend,*" cries he, "*why wont you oblige me by making use of my coat; you see how well it defends me from the rain; I should not chuse to part with it to others, but to such a friend as you, I could even part with my skin to do him service.*"

From such minute instances as these, most reverend Fum Hoam, I am sensible your sagacity will collect instruction. The volume of nature is the book of knowledge; and he becomes most wise who makes the most judicious selection. Farewell.

LETTER V

English passion for politics. A specimen of a news paper. Characteristic of the manners of different countries.

To the same.

I HAVE already informed you of the singular passion of this nation for politics. An Englishman not satisfied with finding by his own prosperity the contending powers of Europe properly balanced, desires also to know the precise value of every weight in either scale. To gratify this curiosity, a leaf of political instruction is served up every morning with tea: When our politician has feasted upon this, he repairs to a coffee-house, in order to ruminate upon what he has read, and encrease his collection; from thence he proceeds to the ordinary, enquires what news, and treasuring up every acquisition there, hunts about all the evening in quest of more, and carefully adds it to the rest. Thus at night he retires home, full of the important advices of the day. When lo! awaking next morning, he finds the instructions of yesterday a collection of absurdity or palpable falshood. This, one would think, a mortifying repulse in the pursuit of wisdom; yet our politician no way discouraged, hunts on, in order to collect fresh materials, and in order to be again disappointed.

I have often admired the commercial spirit which prevails over Europe; have been surprised to see them carry on a traffic with productions, that an Asiatic stranger would deem entirely useless. It is a proverb in China, that an European suffers not even his spittle to be lost; the maxim, however, is not sufficiently strong; since they sell even their Lies to great advantage. Every nation drives a considerable trade in this commodity with their neighbours.

An English dealer in this way, for instance, has only to ascend to his work-house, and manufacture a turbulent speech averred to be spoken in the senate; or a report supposed to be dropt at court; a piece of scandal that strikes at a popular Mandarine; or a secret treaty between two neighbouring powers. When finished, these goods are baled up, and consigned to a factor abroad, who sends in return two battles, three sieges, and a shrewd letter filled with dashes —— blanks and stars **** of great importance.

Thus you perceive, that a single gazette is the joint manufacture of Europe; and he who would peruse it with a philosophical eye, might perceive in every paragraph something characteristick of the nation to which it belongs. A map does not exhibit a more distinct view of the boundaries and situation of every country, than its news does a picture of the genius, and the morals of its inhabitants. The superstition and erroneous delicacy of Italy, the formality of Spain, the cruelty of Portugal, the fears of Austria, the confidence of Prussia, the levity of France, the avarice of Holland, the pride of England, the absurdity of Ireland, and the national partiality of Scotland, are all conspicuous in every page.

But, perhaps, you may find more satisfaction in a real news paper, than in my description of one; I therefore send a specimen, which may serve to exhibit the manner of their being written, and distinguish the characters of the various nations which are united in its composition.

NAPLES. We have lately dug up here a curious Etruscan monument, broke in two in the raising. The characters are scarce visible; but *Nugosi*, the learned antiquary, supposes it to have been erected in honour of *Picus*, a Latin King, as one of the lines may be plainly distinguished to begin with a P. It is hoped this discovery will produce something valuable, as the literati of our twelve academies are deeply engaged in the disquisition.

PISA. Since father Fudgi, prior of St. Gilbert's, has gone to reside at Rome, no miracles have been performed at the shrine of St. Gilbert; the devout begin to grow uneasy, and some begin actually to fear that St. Gilbert has forsaken them with the reverend father.

LUCCA. The administrators of our serene republic, have frequent conferences upon the part they shall take in the present commotions of Europe. Some are for sending a body of their troops, consisting of one company of foot, and six horsemen, to make a diversion in favour of the empress-queen; others are as strenuous asserters of the Prussian interest: what turn these debates may take, time only can discover. However, certain it is, we shall be able to bring into the field at the opening of the next campaign, seventy-five armed men, a commander in chief, and two drummers of great experience.

SPAIN. Yesterday the new king shewed himself to his subjects, and after having staid half an hour in his balcony, retired to the royal apartment. The night concluded on this extraordinary occasion with illuminations, and other demonstrations of joy.

The queen is more beautiful than the rising sun, and reckoned one of the first wits in Europe: she had a glorious opportunity of displaying the readiness of her invention, and her skill in repartee lately at court. The duke of Lerma, coming up to her with a low bow and a smile, and presenting a nosegay set with diamonds, *Madam*, cries he, *I am your most obedient humble servant. Oh, Sir*, replies the queen, without any prompter, or the least hesitation, *I'm very proud of the very great honour you do me.* Upon which she made a low curtesy, and all the courtiers fell a laughing at the readiness and the smartness of her reply.

LISBON. Yesterday we had an *auto da fe*, at which were burned three young women accused of heresy, one of them of exquisite beauty; two Jews, and an old woman, convicted of being a witch: One of the friars, who attended this last, reports, that he saw the devil fly out of her at the stake in the shape of a flame of fire. The populace behaved on this occasion with great good humour, joy, and sincere devotion.

Our *merciful Sovereign* has been for some time past recovered of his fright: though so atrocious an attempt deserved to exterminate half the nation, yet he has been graciously pleased to spare the lives of his subjects, and not above five hundred have been broke upon the wheel, or otherwise executed upon this horrid occasion.

VIENNA. We have received certain advices that a party of twenty thousand Austrians, having attacked a much superior body of Prussians, put them all to flight, and took the rest prisoners of war.

BERLIN. We have received certain advices that a party of twenty thousand Prussians, having attacked a much superior body of Austrians, put them to flight, and took a great number of prisoners, with their military chest, cannon, and baggage.

Though we have not succeeded this campaign to our wishes; yet, when we think of him who commands us, we rest in security: while we sleep, our king is watchful for our safety.

PARIS. We shall soon strike a signal blow. We have seventeen flat-bottom'd boats at Havre. The people are in excellent spirits, and our ministers make no difficulty of raising the supplies.

We are all undone; the people are discontented to the last degree; the ministers are obliged to have recourse to the most rigorous methods to raise the expences of the war.

Our distresses are great; but madam Pompadour continues to supply our king, who is now growing old, with a fresh lady every night. His health, thank heaven, is still pretty well; nor is he in the least unfit, as was reported, for any kind of royal exercitation. He was so frighted at the affair of Damien,[1] that his physicians were apprehensive lest his reason should suffer, but that wretch's tortures soon composed the kingly terrors of his breast.

ENGLAND. Wanted an usher to an academy. *N.B.* He must be able to read, dress hair, and must have had the small pox.[2]

DUBLIN. We hear that there is a benevolent subscription on foot among the nobility and gentry of this kingdom, who are great patrons of merit, in order to assist Black and All Black,[3] in his contest with the Padderen mare.[4]

We hear from Germany that prince Ferdinand has gained a complete victory, and taken twelve kettle drums, five standards, and four waggons of ammunition prisoners of war.

EDINBURGH. We are positive when we say that Saunders M'Gregor, who was lately executed for horse-stealing, is not a Scotchman, but born in Carrickfergus. Farewell.

1 [Robert-François Damiens, a half-wit who suffered ghastly and elaborate torture before being put to death in March, 1757 for having tried to assassinate Louis XV. He is also mentioned in *The Traveller* (p. 601).]

2 [Goldsmith had been an usher, probably on similar qualifications.]

3 [Sir Ralph Gore's *Othello*, a famous racer and stud stallion, who won many races in Ireland, including a great match for 1,000 guineas at the Curragh in 1751.]

4 [Mr. Archbold's *Irish Lass* who won the Royal Plate at the Curragh in 1745 and 1748. Goldsmith was in Dublin on both occasions. He also refers to her in a letter to Daniel Hodson of 1757.]

From LETTER VI

Happiness lost, by seeking after refinement. The Chinese philosopher's disgraces.

Fum Hoam, first president of the ceremonial academy at Pekin, to Lien Chi Altangi, the discontented wanderer; by the way of Moscow.

IT IS with an heart full of sorrow, my dear Altangi, that I must inform you that what the world calls happiness must now be yours no longer. Our great emperor's displeasure at your leaving China, contrary to the rules of our government, and the immemorial custom of the empire, has produced the most terrible effects. Your wife, daughter, and the rest of your family have been seized by his order, and appropriated to his use; all except your son are now the peculiar property of him who possesses all; him I have hidden from the officers employed for this purpose; and even at the hazard of my life I have concealed him. The youth seems obstinately bent on finding you out, wherever you are; he is determined to face every danger that opposes his pursuit. Though yet but fifteen, all his father's virtues and obstinacy sparkle in his eyes, and mark him as one destined to no mediocrity of fortune.

You see, my dearest friend, what imprudence has brought thee to; from opulence, a tender family, surrounding friends, and your master's esteem, it has reduced thee to want, persecution; and still worse, to our mighty monarch's displeasure. Want of prudence is too frequently the want of virtue; nor is there on earth a more powerful advocate for vice than poverty. As I shall endeavour to guard thee from the one, so guard thyself from the other; and still think of me with affection and esteem. Farewell.

LETTER VIII

The Chinese deceived by a prostitute, in the streets of London.

From Lien Chi Altangi, to Fum Hoam, first president of the Ceremonial Academy at Pekin, in China.

How insupportable! oh thou possessor of heavenly wisdom, would be this separation, this immeasurable distance from my friends, were I not able thus to delineate my heart upon paper, and to send thee daily a map of my mind.

I am every day better reconciled to the people among whom I reside, and begin to fancy that in time I shall find them more opulent, more charitable, and more hospitable than I at first imagined. I begin to learn somewhat of their manners and customs, and to see reasons for several deviations which they make from us, from whom all other nations derive their politeness as well as their original.

In spite of taste, in spite of prejudice, I now begin to think their women tolerable; I can now look on a languishing blue eye without disgust, and pardon a set of teeth, even though whiter than ivory. I now begin to fancy there is no universal standard for beauty. The truth is, the manners of the ladies in this city are so very open, and so vastly engaging, that I am inclined to pass over the more glaring defects of their persons, since compensated by the more solid, yet latent beauties of the mind; what tho' they want black teeth, or are deprived of the allurements of feet no bigger than their thumbs, yet still they have souls, my friend, such souls, so free, so pressing, so hospitable, and so engaging——I have received more invitations in the streets of London from the sex in one night, than I have met with at Pekin in twelve revolutions of the moon.

Every evening as I return home from my usual solitary excursions, I am met by several of those well disposed daughters of hospitality, at different times and in different streets, richly dressed, and with minds not less noble than their appearance. You know that nature has indulged me with a person by no means agreeable; yet are they too generous to object to my homely appearance; they feel no repugnance at my broad face and flat nose; they perceive me to be a stranger, and that alone is a sufficient recommendation. They even seem to think it their duty to do the honours of the country by every act of complaisance in their power. One takes me under the arm, and in a manner forces me along; another catches me round the neck, and desires to partake in this office of hospitality; while a third kinder still, invites me to refresh my spirits with wine. Wine is in England reserved only for the rich, yet here even wine is given away to the stranger!

A few nights ago, one of those generous creatures, dressed all in white, and flaunting like a meteor by my side, forcibly attended me home to my own apartment. She seemed charmed with the elegance of the furniture, and the convenience of my situation. And well indeed she might, for I have hired an apartment for not less than two shillings of their money every week. But her civility did not rest here; for at parting, being desirous to know the hour, and perceiving my watch out of order, she kindly took it to be repaired by a relation of her own, which you may imagine will save some expence, and she assures me that it will cost her nothing. I shall have it back in a few days when mended, and am preparing a proper speech expressive of my gratitude on the occasion: *Celestial excellence*, I intend to say, *happy I am in having found out, after many painful adventures, a land of innocence, and a people of humanity: I may rove into other climes, and converse with nations yet unknown, but where shall I meet a soul of such purity as that which resides in thy breast! Sure thou hast been nurtured by the bill of the Shin Shin, or suck'd the breasts of the provident Gin Hiung. The melody of thy voice could rob the Chong Fou of her whelps, or inveigle the Boh that lives in the midst of the waters. Thy servant shall ever retain a sense of thy favours; and one day boast of thy virtue, sincerity, and truth, among the daughters of China.* Adieu.

LETTER IX

The licentiousness of the English, with regard to women. A character of a woman's man.

To the same.

I HAVE been deceived! she whom I fancied a daughter of Paradise has proved to be one of the infamous disciples of Han! I have lost a trifle, I have gained the consolation of having discovered a deceiver. I once more, therefore, relax into my former indifference with regard to the English ladies, they once more begin to appear disagreeable in my eyes: Thus is my whole time passed in forming conclusions which the next minute's experience may probably destroy; the present moment becomes a comment on the past, and I improve rather in humility than wisdom.

Their laws and religion forbid the English to keep more than one woman, I therefore concluded that prostitutes were banished from society; I was deceived; every man here keeps as many wives as he can maintain; the laws are cemented with blood, praised and disregarded. The very Chinese, whose religion allows him two wives, takes not half the liberties of the English in this particular. Their laws may be compared to the books of the Sybils, they are held in great veneration, but seldom read, or seldomer understood; even those who pretend to be their guardians dispute about the meaning of many of them, and confess their ignorance of others. The law therefore which commands them to have but one wife, is strictly observed only by those for whom one is more than sufficient, or by such as have not money to buy two. As for the rest, they violate it publicly, and some glory in its violation. They seem to think like the Persians, that they give evident marks of manhood by encreasing their seraglio. A mandarine therefore here generally keeps four wives, a gentleman three, and a stage-player two. As for the magistrates, the country justices and squires, they are employed first in debauching young virgins, and then punishing the transgression.

From such a picture you will be apt to conclude, that he who employs four ladies for his amusement, has four times as much constitution to spare as he who is contented with one; that a Mandarin is much cleverer than a gentleman, and a gentleman than a player, and yet it is quite the reverse; a Mandarine is frequently supported on spindle shanks, appears emaciated by luxury, and is obliged to have recourse to variety, merely from the weakness, not the vigour of his constitution, the number of his wives being the most equivocal symptom of his virility.

Beside the country squire, there is also another set of men, whose whole employment consists in corrupting beauty; these the silly part of the fair sex call amiable; the more sensible part of them, however, give them the title of abominable. You will probably demand what are the talents of a man thus caressed by the majority of the opposite sex; what talents, or what beauty is he possessed of superior to the rest of his fellows. To answer you directly, he has neither talents nor beauty, but then he is possessed of impudence and assiduity. With assiduity and impudence, men of all ages, and all figures, may commence admirers. I have even been told of some who made professions of expiring for love, when all the world could perceive they were going to die of old age: and what is more surprising still, such batter'd beaus are generally most infamously successful.

A fellow of this kind employs three hours every morning in dressing his head, by which is understood only his hair.

He is a professed admirer, not of any particular lady, but of the whole sex.

He is to suppose every lady has caught cold every night, which gives him an opportunity of calling to see how she does the next morning.

He is upon all occasions to shew himself in very great pain for the ladies; if a lady drops even a pin, he is to fly in order to present it.

He never speaks to a lady without advancing his mouth to her ear, by which he frequently addresses more senses than one.

Upon proper occasions he looks excessively tender. This is performed by laying his hand upon his heart, shutting his eyes, and showing his teeth.

He is excessively fond of dancing a minuet with the ladies, by which is only meant walking round the floor eight or ten times with his hat on, affecting great gravity, and sometimes looking tenderly on his partner.

He never affronts any man himself, and never resents an affront from another.

He has an infinite variety of small talk upon all occasions, and laughs when he has nothing more to say.

Such is the killing creature who prostrates himself to the sex till he has undone them; all whose submissions are the effects of design, and who to please the ladies almost becomes himself a lady.

From LETTER X

The journey of the Chinese from Pekin to Moscow. The customs of the Daures.

To the same.

I HAVE hitherto given you no account of my journey from China to Europe, of my travels through countries, where nature sports in primeval rudeness, where she pours forth her wonders in solitude; countries, from whence the rigorous climate, the sweeping inundation, the drifted desart, the howling forest, and mountains of immeasurable height banish the husbandman, and spread extensive desolation; countries where the brown Tartar wanders for a precarious subsistence, with an heart that never felt pity, himself more hideous than the wilderness he makes.

You will easily conceive the fatigue of crossing vast tracts of land, either desolate, or still more dangerous by its inhabitants. The retreat of men, who seem driven from society, in order to make war upon all the human race; nominally professing a subjection to Moscovy or China, but without any resemblance to the countries on which they depend.

After I had crossed the great wall, the first objects that presented were the remains of desolated cities, and all the magnificence of venerable ruin. There were to be seen temples of beautiful structure, statues wrought by the hand of a master, and around a country of luxuriant plenty; but not one single inhabitant to reap the bounties of nature. These were prospects that might humble the pride of kings, and repress human vanity. I ask'd my guide the cause of such desolation. These countries, says he, were once the dominions of a Tartar prince; and these ruins the seat of arts, elegance, and ease. This prince waged an unsuccessful war with one of the emperors of China; he was conquered, his cities plundered, and all his subjects carried into captivity. Such are the effects of the ambition of Kings! Ten Dervises, says the Indian proverb, shall sleep in peace upon a single carpet, while two kings shall quarrel though they have kingdoms to divide them. Sure, my friend, the cruelty and the pride of man have made more desarts than nature ever made! she is kind, but man is ungrateful!

Proceeding in my journey through this pensive scene of desolated beauty, in a few days I arrived among the Daures, a nation still dependent on China.

. . . .

The religion of the Daures is more absurd than even that of the sectaries of Fohi. How would you be surprized. O sage disciple and follower of Confucius! you who believe one eternal intelligent cause of all, should you be present at the barbarous ceremonies of this infatuated people. How would you deplore the blindness and folly of mankind. His boasted reason seems only to light him astray, and brutal instinct more regularly points out the path to happiness. Could you think it? they adore a wicked divinity; they fear him and they worship him; they imagine him a malicious being, ready to injure and ready to be appeased. The men and women assemble at midnight in a hut, which serves for a temple. A priest stretches himself on the ground, and all the people pour forth the most horrid cries, while drums and timbrels swell the infernal concert. After this dissonance, miscalled music, has continued about two hours, the priest rises from the ground, assumes an air of inspiration, grows big with the inspiring dæmon, and pretends to a skill in futurity.

. . . .

The customs of this people correspond to their religion; they keep their dead for three days on the same bed where the person died; after which they bury him in a grave moderately deep, but with the head still uncovered. Here for several days they present him different sorts of meats; which, when they perceive he does not consume, they fill up the grave, and desist from desiring him to eat for the future.

. . . .

Here we observe a whole country adoring a divinity through fear, and attempting to feed the dead. These are their most serious and most religious occupations: are these men rational, or are not the apes of Borneo more wise?

LETTER XII

The funeral solemnities of the English. Their passion for flattering epitaphs.

To the same.

FROM the funeral solemnities of the Daures, who think themselves the politest people in the world, I must make a transition to the funeral solemnities of the English, who think themselves as polite as they. The numberless ceremonies which are used here when a person is sick, appear to me so many evident marks of fear and apprehension. Ask an Englishman, however, whether he is afraid of death, and he boldly answers in the negative; but observe his behaviour in circumstances of approaching sickness, and you will find his actions give his assertions the lie.

The Chinese are very sincere in this respect; they hate to die, and they confess their terrors: a great part of their life is spent in preparing things proper for their funeral; a poor artizan shall spend half his income in providing himself a tomb twenty years before he wants it; and denies himself the necessaries of life, that he may be amply provided for when he shall want them no more.

But people of distinction in England really deserve pity, for they die in circumstances of the most extreme distress. It is an established rule, never to let a man know that he is dying: physicians are sent for, the clergy are called, and every thing passes in silent solemnity round the sick bed; the patient is in agonies, looks round for pity, yet not a single creature will say that he is dying. If he is possessed of fortune, his relations entreat him to make his will, as it may restore the tranquillity of his mind. He is desired to undergo the rites of the church, for decency requires it. His friends take their leave only because they don't care to see him in pain. In short, an hundred stratagems are used to make him do what he might have been induced to perform only by being told; *Sir, you are past all hopes, and had as good think decently of dying.*

Besides all this, the chamber is darkened, the whole house ecchoes to the cries of the wife, the lamentations of the children, the grief of the servants, and the sighs of friends. The bed is surrounded with priests and doctors in black, and only flambeaux emit a yellow gloom. Where is the man, how intrepid soever, that would not shrink at such a hideous solemnity? For fear of affrighting their expiring friends, the English practise all that can fill them with terror. Strange effect of human prejudice thus to torture merely from mistaken tenderness!

You see, my friend, what contradictions there are in the tempers of those islanders; when prompted by ambition, revenge, or disappointment, they meet death with the utmost resolution; the very man who in his bed would have trembled at the aspect of a doctor, shall go with intrepidity to attack a bastion, or deliberately nooze himself up in his garters.

The passion of the Europeans for magnificent interments, is equally strong with that of the Chinese. When a tradesman dies, his frightful face is painted up by an undertaker, and placed in a proper situation to receive company; this is called lying in state. To this disagreeable spectacle all the idlers in town flock, and learn to loath the wretch dead, whom they despised when living. In this manner you see some who would have refused a shilling to save the life of their dearest friend, bestow thousands on adorning their putrid corpse. I have been told of a fellow, who grown rich by the price o blood, left it in his will that he should lie in state, and thus unknowingly gibbeted himself into infamy, when he might have otherwise quietly retired into oblivion.

When the person is buried, the next care is to make his epitaph; they are generally reckoned best which flatter most; such Relations therefore as have received most benefits from the defunct, discharge this friendly office; and generally flatter in proportion to their joy. When we read those monumental histories of the dead, it may be justly said, that *all men are equal in the dust*; for they all appear equally remarkable for being the most sincere Christians, the most benevolent neighbours, and the honestest men of their time. To go through an European cemetery, one would be apt to wonder how mankind could have so basely degenerated from such excellent ancestors; every tomb pretends to claim your reverence and regret; some are praised for piety in those inscriptions who never entered the temple until they were dead; some are praised for being excellent poets, who were never mentioned, except for their dulness, when living: others for sublime orators, who were never noted except for their impudence; and others still for military achievements, who were never in any other skirmishes but with the watch. Some even make epitaphs for themselves, and bespeak the readers good will. It were indeed to be wished, that every man would early learn in this manner to make his own; that he would draw it up in terms as flattering as possible; and that he would make it the employment of his whole life to deserve it!

I have not yet been in a place called Westminster Abbey, but soon intend to visit it. There I am told I shall see justice done to deceased merit; none, I am told, are permitted to be buried there, but such as have adorned as well as improved mankind. There no intruders by the influence of friends or fortune, presume to mix their unhallowed ashes with philosophers, heroes, and poets. Nothing but true merit has a place in that awful sanctuary: the guardianship of the tombs is committed to several reverend priests, who are never guilty for a superior reward of taking down the names of good men, to make room for others of equivocal character, nor ever prophane the sacred walls with pageants, that posterity cannot know, or shall blush to own.

I always was of opinion, that sepulchral honours of this kind should be considered as a national concern, and not trusted to the care of the priests of any country, how respectable soever; but from the conduct of the reverend personages, whose disinterested patriotism I shall shortly be able to discover, I am taught to retract my former sentiments. It is true, the Spartans and the Persians made a fine political use of sepulchral vanity; they permitted none to be thus interred, who had not fallen in the vindication of their country; a monument thus became a real mark of distinction, it nerved the heroe's arm with tenfold vigour; and he fought without fear, who only fought for a grave. Farewell.

LETTER XIII

An account of Westminster Abbey.

From the same.

I AM just returned from Westminster-abbey, the place of sepulture for the philosophers, heroes, and kings of England. What a gloom do monumental inscriptions and all the venerable remains of deceased merit inspire! Imagine a temple marked with the hand of antiquity, solemn as religious awe, adorned with all the magnificence of barbarous profusion, dim windows, fretted pillars, long colonades, and dark cielings. Think then, what were my sensations at being introduced to such a scene. I stood in the midst of the temple, and threw my eyes round on the walls filled with the statues, the inscriptions, and the monuments of the dead.

Alas, I said to myself, how does pride attend the puny child of dust even to the grave! Even humble as I am, I possess more consequence in the present scene than the greatest heroe of them all; they have toiled for an hour to gain a transient immortality, and are at length retired to the grave, where they have no attendant but the worm, none to flatter but the epitaph.

As I was indulging such reflections, a gentleman dressed in black, perceiving me to be a stranger, came up, entered into conversation, and politely offered to be my instructor and guide through the temple. If any monument, said he, should particularly excite your curiosity, I shall endeavour to satisfy your demands. I accepted with thanks the gentleman's offer, adding, that " I was come to observe the policy, the wisdom, and the justice of the English, in conferring rewards upon deceased merit. If adulation like this, continued I, be properly conducted, as it can no ways injure those who are flattered, so it may be a glorious incentive to those who are now capable of enjoying it. It is the duty of every good government to turn this monumental pride to its own advantage; to become strong in the aggregate from the weakness of the individual. If none but the truly great have a place in this awful repository, a temple like this will give the finest lessons of morality, and be a strong incentive to true ambition. I am told, that none have a place here but characters of the most distinguished merit." The man in black seemed impatient at my observations, so I discontinued my remarks, and we walked on together to take a view of every particular monument in order as it lay.

As the eye is naturally caught by the finest objects, I could not avoid being particularly curious about one monument which appeared more beautiful than the rest; that, said I to my guide, I take to be the tomb of some very great man. By the peculiar excellence of the workmanship, and the magnificence of the design, this must be a trophy raised to the memory of some king who has saved his country from ruin, or law-giver, who has reduced his fellow-citizens from anarchy into just subjection——It is not requisite, replied my companion smiling, to have such qualifications in order to have a very fine monument here. More humble abilities will suffice. *What, I suppose then, the gaining two or three battles, or the taking half a score towns, is thought a sufficient qualification?* Gaining battles, or taking towns, replied the man in black, may be of service; but a gentleman may have a very fine monument here without ever seeing a battle or a siege. *This then is the monument of some poet, I presume, of one whose wit has gained him immortality?* No, sir, replied my guide, the gentleman who lies here never made verses; and as for wit, he despised it in others, because he had none himself. *Pray tell me then in a word*, said I peevishly, *what is the great man who lies here particularly remarkable for?* Remarkable, sir! said my companion; why, sir, the gentleman that lies here is remarkable, very remarkable——for a tomb in Westminster-abbey. *But, head of my Ancestors! how has he got here? I fancy he could never bribe the guardians of the temple to give him a place: Should he not be ashamed to be seen among company, where even moderate merit would look like infamy?* I suppose, replied the man in black, the gentleman was rich, and his friends, as is usual in such a case, told him he was great. He readily believed them; the guardians of the temple, as they got by the self-delusion, were ready to believe him too; so he paid his money for a fine monument; and the workman, as you see, has made him one the most beautiful. Think not, however, that this gentleman is singular in his desire of being buried among the great, there are several others in the temple, who, hated and shunned by the great while alive, have come here, fully resolved to keep them company now they are dead.

As we walked along to a particular part of the temple, there, says the gentleman, pointing with his finger, that is the poets corner; there you see the monuments of Shakespear, and Milton and Prior, and Drayton. Drayton, I replied, I never heard of him before, but I have been told of one Pope, is he there?[1] It is time enough, replied my guide, these hundred years, he is not long dead, people have not done hating him yet. Strange, cried I, can any be found to hate a man, whose life was wholly spent in entertaining and instructing his fellow creatures! Yes, says my guide, they hate him for that very reason. There are a set of men called answerers of books, who take upon them to watch the republic of letters, and distribute reputation by the sheet; they somewhat resemble the eunuchs in a seraglio, who are incapable of giving pleasure themselves, and hinder those that would. These answerers have no other employment but to cry out Dunce, and Scribbler, to praise the dead, and revile the living, to grant a man of confessed abilities some small share of merit, to applaud twenty blockheads in order to gain the reputation of candour, and to revile the moral character of the man whose writings they cannot injure. Such wretches are kept in pay by

[1] [Pope was buried at his own desire at Twickenham in 1744. A monument to him was erected on the North Wall of Westminster Abbey in 1761 by William Warburton.]

some mercenary bookseller, or more frequently, the bookseller himself takes this dirty work off their hands, as all that is required is to be very abusive and very dull; every Poet of any genius is sure to find such enemies, he feels, though he seems to despise their malice, they make him miserable here, and in the pursuit of empty fame, at last he gains solid anxiety.

Has this been the case with every poet I see here? cried I—Yes, with every mother's son of them, replied he, except he happened to be born a mandarine. If he has much money, he may buy reputation from your book answerers, as well as a monument from the guardians of the temple.

But are there not some men of distinguished taste, as in China, who are willing to patronize men of merit and soften the rancour of malevolent dulness?

I own there are many, replied the man in black, but, alas! Sir, the book answerers croud about them, and call themselves the writers of books; and the patron is too indolent, to distinguish; thus poets are kept at a distance, while their enemies eat up all their rewards at the mandarine's table.

Leaving this part of the temple, we made up to an iron gate, through which my companion told me we were to pass in order to see the monuments of the kings. Accordingly I marched up without further ceremony, and was going to enter, when a person who held the gate in his hand, told me I must pay first. I was surprised at such a demand; and asked the man whether the people of England kept a *shew*? Whether the paltry sum he demanded was not a national reproach? Whether it was not more to the honour of the country to let their magnificence or their antiquities be openly seen, than thus meanly to tax a curiosity which tended to their own honour? As for your questions, replied the gate-keeper, to be sure they may be very right, because I don't understand them, but as for that there three-pence, I farm it from one, who rents it from another, who hires it from a third, who leases it from the guardians of the temple, and we all must live. I expected upon paying here to see something extraordinary, since what I had seen for nothing filled me with so much surprize; but in this I was disappointed; there was little more within than black coffins, rusty armour, tatter'd standards, and some few slovenly figures in wax. I was sorry I had paid, but I comforted myself by considering it would be my last payment. A person attended us, who, without once blushing, told an hundred lies, he talked of a lady who died by pricking her finger, of a king with a golden head, and twenty such pieces of absurdity; Look ye there, gentlemen, says he, pointing to an old oak chair, there's a curiosity for ye; in that chair the kings of England were crowned, you see also a stone underneath, and that stone is Jacob's pillow. I could see no curiosity either in the oak chair or the stone; could I, indeed, behold one of the old kings of England seated in this, or Jacob's head laid upon the other, there might be something curious in the sight; but in the present case, there was no more reason for my surprize than if I should pick a stone from their streets, and call it a curiosity, merely because one of their kings happened to tread upon it as he passed in a procession.

From hence our conductor led us through several dark walks and winding ways, uttering lies, talking to himself, and flourishing a wand which he held in his hand. He reminded me of the black magicians of Kobi. After we had been almost fatigued with a variety of objects, he, at last, desired me to consider attentively a certain suit of armour, which seemed to shew nothing remarkable. This armour, said he, belonged to general Monk. *Very surprising, that a general should wear armour.* And pray, added he, observe this cap, this is general Monk's cap. *Very strange, indeed, very strange, that general should have a cap also! Pray friend, what might this cap have cost originally?* That, Sir, says he, I don't know, but this cap is all the wages I have for my trouble. *A very small recompence, truly,* said I. Not so very small, replied he, for every gentleman puts some money into it, and I spend the money. *What, more money! still more money!* Every gentleman gives something, sir. I'll give thee nothing, returned I; the guardians of the temple should pay you your wages, friend, and not permit you to squeeze thus from every spectator. When we pay our money at the door to see a shew, we never give more as we are going out. Sure the guardians of the temple can never think they get enough. Shew me the gate; if I stay longer, I may probably meet with more of those ecclesiastical beggars.

Thus leaving the temple precipitately, I returned to my lodgings, in order to ruminate over what was great, and to despise what was mean in the occurrences of the day.

LETTER XIV

The reception of the Chinese from a lady of distinction.

From the same.

I WAS some days ago agreeably surprised by a message from a lady of distinction, who sent me word, that she most passionately desired the pleasure of my acquaintance; and, with the utmost impatience, expected an interview. I will not deny, my dear Fum Hoam, but that my vanity was raised at such an invitation, I flattered myself that she had seen me in some public place, and had conceived an affection for my person, which thus induced her to deviate from the usual decorums of the sex. My imagination painted her in all the bloom of youth and beauty. I fancied her attended by the loves and graces, and I set out with the most pleasing expectations of seeing the conquest I had made.

When I was introduced into her apartment, my expectrtions were quickly at an end; I perceived a little shrivelled figure indolently reclined on a sofa, who nodded by way of approbation at my approach. This, as I was afterwards informed, was the lady herself, a woman equally distinguished for rank, politeness, taste, and understanding. As I was dressed after the fashion of Europe, she had taken me for an Englishman, and consequently saluted me in her ordinary manner; but when the footman informed her grace that I was the gentleman from China, she instantly lifted herself from the couch, while her eyes sparkled with unusual vivacity. "Bless me! can this be the gentleman that was born so far from home? What an unusual share of *somethingness* in his whole appearance. Lord how I am charmed with the outlandish cut of his face; how bewitching the exotic breadth of his forehead. I would give the world to see him in his own country dress. Pray turn about, Sir, and let me see you behind. There! there's a travell'd air for you. You that attend there, bring up a plate of beef cut into small pieces; I have a violent passion to see him eat. Pray, Sir, have you got your chop sticks about you? It will be so pretty to see the meat carried to the mouth with a jerk. Pray speak a little Chinese: I have learned some of the language myself. Lord, have you nothing pretty from China about you; something that one does not know what to do with? I have got twenty things from China that are of no use in the world. Look at those jars, they are of the right pea-green: these are the furniture." *Dear madam*, said I, *those, though they may appear fine in your eyes, are but paltry to a Chinese; but, as they are useful utensils, it is proper they should have a place in every apartment.* Useful! Sir, replied the lady; sure you mistake, they are of no use in the world. *What! are they not filled with an infusion of tea as in China?* replied I. Quite empty and useless upon my honour, Sir. *Then they are the most cumbrous and clumsy furniture in the world, as nothing is truly elegant but what unites use with beauty.* I protest, says the lady, I shall begin to suspect thee of being an actual barbarian. I suppose also you hold my two beautiful pagods in contempt. *What!* cried I, *has Fohi spread his gross superstitions here also? Pagods of all kinds are my aversion.* A Chinese, a traveller, and want taste! it surprises me. Pray, sir, examine the beauties of that Chinese temple which you see at the end of the garden. Is there any thing in China more beautiful? *Where I stand I see nothing, madam, at the end of the garden that may not as well be called an Egyptian pyramid as a Chinese temple; for that little building in view is as like the one as t'other.* What! Sir, is not that a Chinese temple? you must surely be mistaken. Mr. Freeze, who designed it, calls it one, and nobody disputes his pretensions to taste. I now found it vain to contradict the lady in any thing she thought fit to advance: so was resolved rather to act the disciple than the instructor. She took me through several rooms all furnished, as she told me, in the Chinese manner; sprawling dragons, squatting pagods, and clumsy mandarines, were stuck upon every shelf: In turning round one must have used caution not to demolish a part of the precarious furniture.

In a house like this, thought I, one must live continually upon the watch; the inhabitant must resemble a knight in an enchanted castle, who expects to meet an adventure at every turning. *But, Madam,* said I, *do no accidents ever happen to all this finery?* Man, Sir, replied the lady, is born to misfortunes, and it is but fit I should have a share. Three weeks ago, a careless servant snapp'd off the head of a favourite mandarine: I had scarce done grieving for that, when a monkey broke a beautiful jar; this I took the more to heart, as the injury was done me by a friend: however, I survived the calamity; when yesterday crash went half a dozen dragons upon the marble hearth stone; and yet I live; I survive it all: you can't conceive what comfort I find under afflictions from philosophy. There is Seneca, and Bolingbroke,[1] and some others, who guide me through life, and teach me to support its calamities.—I could not but smile at a woman who makes her own misfortunes,

[1] [Henry St. John, Lord Bolingbroke (1678–1751), whose philosophy Pope versified in his *Essay on Man.* Goldsmith wrote his biography. Johnson dealt with Bolingbroke more summarily, defining *Irony* in his Dictionary as, "A mode of speech in which the meaning is contrary to the words: as, *Bolingbroke was a holy man.*"

and then deplores the miseries of her situation. Wherefore, tired of acting with dissimulation, and willing to indulge my meditations in solitude, I took leave just as the servant was bringing in a plate of beef, pursuant to the directions of his mistress. Adieu.

From LETTER XVI

Of falshood propagated by books seemingly sincere.

From the same.

A CHRISTIAN doctor in one of his principal performances* says, that it was not impossible for a whole nation to have but one eye in the middle of the forehead. He is not satisfied with leaving it in doubt; but in another work† assures us, that the fact was certain, and that he himself was an eye-witness of it. *When*, says he, *I took a journey into Ethiopia in company with several other servants of Christ, in order to preach the gospel there; I beheld in the southern provinces of that country a nation which had only one eye in the midst of their foreheads.*

. . . .

One would think that these authors had an antipathy to the human form, and were resolved to make a new figure of their own: but let us do them justice; though they sometimes deprive us of a leg, an arm, an head, or some such trifling part of the body, they often as liberally bestow upon us something that we wanted before. Simon Mayole[1] seems our particular friend in this respect: if he has denied heads to one part of mankind, he has given tails to another. He describes many of the English of his time, which is not more than an hundred years ago, as having tails. His own words are as follow. *In England there are some families which have tails, as a punishment for deriding an Augustin Friar sent by St. Gregory, and who preached in Dorsetshire. They sewed the tails of different*

* Augustin. de Civit. Dei, lib. xvi. p. 412.

† Id. ad fratres in Eremo, Serm. xxxvii.

[1] [Simon Maiolo (1520–97), an Italian bishop.]

animals to his cloaths; but soon they found those tails entailed on them and their posterity for ever. It is certain, the author had some ground for this description; many of the English wear tails to their wigs to this very day, as a mark, I suppose, of the antiquity of their families, and perhaps as a symbol of those tails with which they were formerly distinguished by nature.

You see, my friend, there is nothing so ridiculous that has not at some time been said by some philosopher. The writers of books in Europe seem to think themselves authorised to say what they please; and an ingenious philosopher among them* has openly asserted, that he would undertake to persuade the whole republic of readers to believe that the sun was neither the cause of light nor heat; if he could only get six philosophers on his side. Farewell.

LETTER XVII

Of the war now carried on between France and England, with its frivolous motives.

From the same.

WERE an Asiatic politician to read the treaties of peace and friendship that have been annually making for more than an hundred years among the inhabitants of Europe, he would probably be surpriz'd how it should ever happen that christian princes could quarrel among each other. Their compacts for peace are drawn up with the utmost precision, and ratified with the greatest solemnity; to these each party promises a sincere and inviolable obedience, and all wears the appearance of open friendship and unreserved reconciliation.

Yet, notwithstanding those treaties, the people of Europe are almost continually at war. There is nothing more easy than to break a treaty ratified in all the usual forms, and yet neither party be the aggressor. One side, for instance, breaks a

* Fontenelle.

trifling article by mistake; the opposite party upon this makes a small but premeditated reprisal; this brings on a return of greater from the other; both sides complain of injuries and infractions; war is declar'd; they beat, are beaten; some two or three hundred thousand men are killed, they grow tired, leave off just where they began; and so sit cooly down to make new treaties.

The English and French seem to place themselves foremost among the champion states of Europe. Though parted by a narrow sea, yet are they entirely of opposite characters; and from their vicinity are taught to fear and admire each other. They are at present engaged in a very destructive war, have already spilled much blood, are excessively irritated; and all upon account of one side's desiring to wear greater quantities of *furs* than the other.

The pretext of the war is about some lands a thousand leagues off; a country cold, desolate, and hideous; a country belonging to a people who were in possession for time immemorial. The savages of Canada claim a property in the country in dispute; they have all the pretensions which long possession can confer. Here they had reigned for ages without rivals in dominion, and knew no enemies but the prowling bear or insidious tyger;[1] their native forests produced all the necessaries of life, and they found ample luxury in the enjoyment. In this manner they might have continued to live to eternity, had not the English been informed that those countries produced furs in great abundance. From that moment the country became an object of desire; it was found that furs were things very much wanted in England; the ladies edged some of their cloaths with furs, and muffs were worn both by gentlemen and ladies. In short, furs were found

[1] [Goldsmith is still ridiculed, even in the *Oxford Companion to English Literature*, for putting tigers in America. This seems to me unjust; there are several species of larger cats in North America, and the usual eighteenth century name for the puma, "tyger," is at least as reasonable as the modern "mountain lion."]

indispensably necessary for the happiness of the state: and the king was consequently petitioned to grant not only the country of Canada, but all the savages belonging to it to the subjects of England, in order to have the people supplied with proper quantities of this necessary commodity.

So very reasonable a request was immediately complied with, and large colonies were sent abroad to procure furs, and take possession. The French who were equally in want of furs (for they were as fond of muffs and tippets as the English) made the very same request to their monarch, and met with the same gracious reception from their king, who generously granted what was not his to give. Wherever the French landed, they called the country their own; and the English took possession wherever they came, upon the same equitable pretensions. The harmless savages made no opposition; and could the intruders have agreed together, they might peaceably have shared this desolate country between them. But they quarrelled about the boundaries of their settlements, about grounds and rivers to which neither side could shew any other right than that of power, and which neither could occupy but by usurpation. Such is the contest, that no honest man can heartily wish success to either party.

The war has continued for some time with various success. At first the French seemed victorious; but the English have of late dispossessed them of the whole country in dispute. Think not, however, that success on one side is the harbinger of peace: on the contrary, both parties must be heartily tired to effect even a temporary reconciliation. It should seem the business of the victorious party to offer terms of peace; but there are many in England, who, encouraged by success, are for still protracting the war.

The best English politicians, however, are sensible, that to keep their present conquests, would be rather a burthen than an advantage to them, rather a diminution of their strength than an encrease of power. It is in the politic as in the human constitution; if the limbs grow too large for the body, their size, instead of improving, will diminish the vigour of the whole. The colonies should always bear an exact proportion to the mother country; when they grow populous, they grow powerful, and by becoming powerful, they become independent also; thus subordination is destroyed, and a country swallowed up in the extent of its own dominions. The Turkish empire would be more formidable, were it less extensive: Were it not for those countries, which it can neither command, nor give entirely away, which it is obliged to protect, but from which it has no power to exact obedience.

Yet, obvious as these truths are, there are many Englishmen who are for transplanting new colonies into this late acquisition, for peopling the desarts of America with the refuse of their countrymen, and (as they express it) with the waste of an exuberant nation. But who are those unhappy creatures who are to be thus drained away? Not the sickly, for they are unwelcome guests abroad as well as at home; nor the idle, for they would starve as well behind the Appalachian mountains as in the streets of London. This refuse is composed of the laborious and enterprising, of such men as can be serviceable to their country at home, of men who ought to be regarded as the sinews of the people, and cherished with every degree of political indulgence. And what are the commodities which this colony, when established, are to produce in return? Why, raw silk, hemp, and tobacco. England, therefore, must make an exchange of her best and bravest subjects for raw silk, hemp, and tobacco; her hardy veterans and honest tradesmen, must be truck'd for a box of snuff or a silk petticoat. Strange absurdity! Sure the politics of the Daures are not more strange, who sell their religion, their wives, and their liberty for a glass bead, or a paltry penknife. Farewell.

LETTER XIX

The English method of treating women caught in adultery. The Russian method.

To the same.

THE gentleman dressed in black, who was my companion through Westminster Abbey, came yesterday to pay me a visit; and after drinking tea, we both resolved to take a walk together, in order to enjoy the freshness of the country, which now begins to resume its verdure. Before we got out of the suburbs, however, we were stopped in one of the streets by a crowd of people, gathered in a circle round a man and his wife, who seemed too loud and too angry to be understood. The people were highly pleased with the dispute, which upon enquiry we found to be between Dr. Cacafogo an apothecary, and his wife. The doctor, it seems, coming unexpectedly into his wife's apartment, found a gentleman there in circumstances not in the least equivocal.

The doctor, who was a person of nice honour, resolving to revenge the flagrant insult, immediately flew to the chimney-piece, and taking down a rusty blunderbuss, drew the trigger upon the defiler of his bed; the delinquent would certainly have been shot through the head, but that the piece had not been charged for many years. The gallant made a shift to escape through the window, but the lady still remained; and as she well knew her husband's temper, undertook to manage the quarrel without a second. He was furious, and she loud; their noise had gathered all the mob who charitably assembled on the occasion, not to prevent, but to enjoy the quarrel.

Alas, said I to my companion, what will become of this unhappy creature thus caught in adultery! Believe me, I pity her from my heart; her husband, I suppose, will shew her no mercy. Will they burn her as in India, or behead her as in Persia; will they load her with stripes as in Turkey, or keep her in perpetual imprisonment, as with us in China! Prythee, what is the wife's punishment in England for such offences? When a lady is thus caught tripping, replied my companion, they never punish her, but the husband. You surely jest, interrupted I; I am a foreigner, and you would abuse my ignorance! I am really serious, returned he; Dr. Cacafogo has caught his wife in the act; but as he had no witnesses, his small testimony goes for nothing; the consequence therefore of his discovery will be, that she may be packed off to live among her relations, and the doctor must be obliged to allow her a separate maintenance. Amazing, cried I! is it not enough that she is permitted to live separate from the object she detests, but must he give her money to keep her in spirits too? That he must, says my guide; and be called a cuckold by all his neighbours into the bargain. The men will laugh at him, the ladies will pity him; and all that his warmest friends can say in his favour, will be, that the *poor good soul has never had any harm in him*. I want patience, interrupted I; what! are there no private chastisements for the wife; no schools of penitence to shew her her folly; no rods for such delinquents? Psha, man, replied he smiling; if every delinquent among us were to be treated in your manner, one half of the kingdom would flog the other.

I must confess, my dear Fum, that if I were an English husband, of all things I would take care not to be jealous, nor busily pry into these secrets my wife was pleased to keep from me. Should I detect her infidelity, what is the consequence? If I calmly pocket the abuse, I am laughed at by her and her gallant; if I talk my griefs aloud like a tragedy heroe, I am laughed at by the whole world. The course then I'd take would be, whenever I went out, to tell my wife where I was going, lest I should unexpectedly meet her abroad in company with some dear deceiver. Whenever I returned, I would use a peculiar rap at the door, and give four loud hems as I walked deliberately up the stair-case. I would never inquisitively peep under her bed, or look behind the curtains. And even though

I knew the captain was there, I would calmly take a dish of my wife's cool tea, and talk of the army with reverence.

Of all nations, the Russians seem to me to behave most wisely in such circumstances. The wife promises her husband never to let him see her transgressions of this nature; and he as punctually promises, whenever she is so detected, without the least anger, to beat her without mercy: so they both know what each has to expect; the lady transgresses, is beaten, taken again into favour, and all goes on as before.

When a Russian young lady, therefore, is to be married, her father, with a cudgel in his hand, asks the bridegroom, whether he chuses this virgin for his bride? to which the other replies in the affirmative. Upon this, the father turning the lady three times round, and giving her three strokes with his cudgel on the back; *my dear*, cries he, *these are the last blows you are ever to receive from your tender father, I resign my authority, and my cudgel to your husband; he knows better than me the use of either.* The bridegroom knows decorums too well to accept of the cudgel abruptly; he assures the father that the lady will never want it, and that he would not for the world make any use of it. But the father, who knows what the lady may want better than he, insists upon his acceptance. Upon this, there follows a scene of Russian politeness, while one refuses, and the other offers the cudgel. The whole, however, ends with the bridegroom's taking it, upon which the lady drops a courtesy in token of obedience, and the ceremony proceeds as usual.

There is something excessively fair and open in this method of courtship. By this, both sides are prepared for all the matrimonial adventures that are to follow. Marriage has been compared to a game of skill for life; it is generous thus in both parties to declare they are sharpers in the beginning. In England, I am told both sides use every art to conceal their defects from each other before marriage, and the rest of their lives may be regarded as doing penance for their former dissimulation. Farewell.

LETTER XXI

The Chinese goes to see a play.

To the same.

THE English are as fond of seeing plays acted as the Chinese; but there is a vast difference in the manner of conducting them. We play our pieces in the open air, the English theirs under cover; we act by day-light, they by the blaze of torches. One of our plays continues eight or ten days successively; an English piece seldom takes up above four hours in the representation.

My companion in black, with whom I am now beginning to contract an intimacy, introduced me a few nights ago to the play-house, where we placed ourselves conveniently at the foot of the stage. As the curtain was not drawn before my arrival, I had an opportunity of observing the behaviour of the spectators, and indulging those reflections which novelty generally inspires.

The rich in general were placed in the lowest seats, and the poor rose above them in degrees proportioned to their poverty. The order of precedence seemed here inverted; those who were undermost all the day, now enjoyed a temporary eminence, and became masters of the ceremonies. It was they who called for the music, indulging every noisy freedom, and testifying all the insolence of beggary in exaltation.

They who held the middle region seemed not so riotous as those above them, nor yet so tame as those below; to judge by their looks, many of them seem'd strangers there as well as myself. They were chiefly employed during this period of expectation in eating oranges, reading the story of the play, or making assignations.

Those who sat in the lowest rows, which are called the pit, seemed to consider themselves as judges of the merit of the poet and the performers; they were assembled partly to be amused, and partly to shew their taste; appearing to labour under that restraint which an affectation of superior discernment generally produces. My companion, however, informed me, that not one in an hundred of them knew even the first principles of criticism; that they assumed the right of being censors because there was none to contradict their pretensions; and that every man who now called himself a connoisseur, became such to all intents and purposes.

Those who sat in the boxes appeared in the most unhappy situation of all. The rest of the audience came merely for their own amusement; these rather to furnish out a part of the entertainment themselves. I could not avoid considering them as acting parts in dumb shew, not a curtesy or nod, that was not the result of art; not a look nor a smile that was not designed for murder. Gentlemen and ladies ogled each other through spectacles; for my companion observed, that blindness was of late become fashionable, all affected indifference and ease, while their hearts at the same time burned for conquest. Upon the whole, the lights, the music, the ladies in their gayest dresses, the men with chearfulness and expectation in their looks, all conspired to make a most agreeable picture, and to fill an heart that sympathises at human happiness with inexpressible serenity.

The expected time for the play[1] to begin at last arrived, the curtain was drawn, and the actors came on. A woman, who personated a queen, came in curtesying to the audience, who clapped their hands upon her appearance. Clapping of hands is, it seems, the manner of applauding in England: the manner is absurd; but every country, you know, has its peculiar absurdities. I was equally surprised, however, at the submission of the actress, who should have considered herself as a queen, as at the little discernment of the audience who gave her such marks of applause before she attempted to deserve them. Preliminaries between her and the audience being thus adjusted,

[1] [Possibly *Douglas* by John Home (1722–1808), which Goldsmith had reviewed in the *Monthly Review* of May, 1757.]

the dialogue was supported between her and a most hopeful youth, who acted the part of her confidant. They both appeared in extreme distress, for it seems the queen had lost a child some fifteen years before, and still kept its dear resemblance next her heart, while her kind companion bore a part in her sorrows.

Her lamentations grew loud. Comfort is offered, but she detests the very sound. She bids them preach comfort to the winds. Upon this her husband comes in, who, seeing the queen so much afflicted, can himself hardly refrain from tears or avoid partaking in the soft distress. After thus grieving through three scenes, the curtain dropped for the first act.

Truly, said I to my companion, these kings and queens are very much disturbed at no very great misfortune; certain I am were people of humbler stations to act in this manner, they would be thought divested of common sense. I had scarce finished this observation, when the curtain rose, and the king came on in a violent passion. His wife had, it seems, refused his proffered tenderness, had spurned his royal embrace; and he seemed resolved not to survive her fierce disdain. After he had thus fretted, and the queen had fretted through the second act, the curtain was let down once more.

Now, says my companion, you perceive the king to be a man of spirit, he feels at every pore; one of your phlegmatic sons of clay would have given the queen her own way, and let her come to herself by degrees; but the king is for immediate tenderness, or instant death: death and tenderness are leading passions of every modern buskin'd heroe; this moment they embrace, and the next stab, mixing daggers and kisses in every period.

I was going to second his remarks, when my attention was engrossed by a new object; a man came in balancing a straw upon his nose, and the audience were clapping their hands in all the raptures of applause. To what purpose, cried I, does this unmeaning figure make his appearance; is he a part of the plot? Unmeaning do you call him, replied my friend in black; this is one of the most important characters of the whole play; nothing pleases the people more than the seeing a straw balanced; there is a great deal of meaning in the straw; there is something suited to every apprehension in the sight; and a fellow possessed of talents like these is sure of making his fortune.

The third act now began with an actor, who came to inform us that he was the villain of the play, and intended to shew strange things before all was over. He was joined by another, who seem'd as much disposed for mischief as he; their intrigues continued through this whole division. If that be a villain, said I, he must be a very stupid one, to tell his secrets without being ask'd; such soliloquies of late are never admitted in China.

The noise of clapping interrupted me once more; a child of six years old was learning to dance on the stage, which gave the ladies and mandarines infinite satisfaction. I am sorry, said I, to see the pretty creature so early learning so very bad a trade. Dancing being, I presume, as contemptible here as it is in China. Quite the reverse, interrupted my companion; dancing is a very reputable and genteel employment here; men have a greater chance for encouragement from the merit of their heels than their heads. One who jumps up and flourishes his toes three times before he comes to the ground, may have three hundred a year; he who flourishes them four times, gets four hundred; but he who arrives at five is inestimable, and may demand what salary he thinks proper. The female dancers too are valued for this sort of jumping and crossing; and 'tis a cant word among them, that she deserves most who shews highest. But the fourth act is begun, let us be attentive.

In the fourth act the queen finds her long lost child, now grown up into a youth of smart parts and great qualifications; wherefore she wisely considers that the crown will fit his head better than that of her husband, whom she knows to be a driveler. The king discovers her design, and here comes on the deep distress; he loves the queen, and he loves the kingdom; he resolves therefore, in order to possess both, that her son must die. The queen exclaims at his barbarity; is frantic with rage, and at length overcome with sorrow, falls into a fit; upon which the curtain drops, and the act is concluded.

Observe the art of the poet, cries my companion; when the queen can say no more, she falls into a fit. While thus her eyes are shut, while she is supported in the arms of Abigail, what horrors do we not fancy, we feel it in every nerve; take my word for it, that fits are the true aposiopesis of modern tragedy.

The fifth act began, and a busy piece it was. Scenes shifting, trumpets sounding, mobs hallooing, carpets spreading, guards bustling from one door to another; gods, dæmons, daggers, racks and ratsbane. But whether the king was killed, or the queen was drowned, or the son was poisoned, I have absolutely forgotten.

When the play was over, I could not avoid observing, that the persons of the drama appeared in as much distress in the first act as the last: how is it possible, said I, to sympathize with them through five long acts; pity is but a short-lived passion; I hate to hear an actor mouthing trifles, neither startings, strainings, nor attitudes affect me unless there be cause: after I have been once or twice deceived by those unmeaning alarms, my heart sleeps in peace, probably unaffected by the principal distress. There should be one great passion aimed at by the actor as well as the poet, all the rest should be subordinate, and only contribute to make that the greater; if the actor therefore exclaims upon every occasion in the tones of despair, he attempts to move us too soon; he anticipates the blow, he ceases to affect though he gains our applause.

I scarce perceived that the audience were almost all departed; wherefore, mixing with the crowd, my companion and I got into the street; where essaying an hundred obstacles from coach wheels and palanquin poles, like birds in their flight through the branches of a forest, after various turnings, we both at length got home in safety. Adieu.

From LETTER XXII

The Chinese philosopher's Son made a slave in Persia.

From the same.

THE letter which came by the way of Smyrna, and which you sent me unopened, was from my son. As I have permitted you to take copies of all those I send to China, you might have made no ceremony in opening those directed to me. Either in joy or sorrow, my friend should participate in my feelings. *It would give pleasure to see a good man pleased at my success; it would give almost equal pleasure to see him sympathise at my disappointment.*

Every account I receive from the east seems to come loaded with some new affliction. My wife and daughter were taken from me, and yet I sustained the loss with intrepidity; my son is made a slave among barbarians, which was the only blow that could have reached my heart: yes, I will indulge the transports of nature for a little, in order to shew I can overcome them in the end. *True magnanimity consists not in* NEVER *falling, but in* RISING *every time we fall.*

When our mighty emperor had published his displeasure at my departure, and seized upon all that was mine, my son was privately secreted from his resentment. Under the protection and guardianship of Fum Hoam, the best and the wisest of all the inhabitants of China; he was for some time instructed in the learning of the missionaries, and the wisdom of the east. But hearing of my adventures, and incited by filial piety, he was resolved to follow my fortunes, and share my distress.

He passed the confines of China in disguise; hired himself as a camel-driver to a caravan that was crossing the desarts of Thibet, and was within one day's journey of the river Laur, which divides that country from India; when a body of wandering Tartars falling unexpectedly upon the caravan, plundered it and made those who escaped their first fury slaves. By those he was led into the extensive and desolate regions that border on the shores of the Aral lake.

Here he lived by hunting; and was obliged to supply every day a certain proportion of the spoil to regale his savage masters; his learning, his virtues, and even his beauty were qualifications that no way served to recommend him; they knew no merit but that of providing large quantities of milk and raw flesh; and were sensible of no happiness but that of rioting on the undressed meal.

Some merchants from Mesched, however, coming to trade with the Tartars, for slaves, he was sold among the number, and led into the kingdom of Persia, where he is now detained. He is there obliged to watch the looks of a voluptuous and cruel master, a man fond of pleasure yet incapable of refinement, whom many years service in war has taught pride, but not bravery.

LETTER XXIV

The venders of quack medicines and nostrums, ridiculed.

To the same.

WHATEVER may be the merits of the English in other sciences, they seem peculiarly excellent in the art of healing. There is scarcely a disorder incident to humanity, against which they are not possessed with a most infallible antidote. The professors of other arts confess the inevitable intricacy of things; talk with doubt, and decide with hesitation; but doubting is entirely unknown in medicine; the advertising professors here delight in cases of difficulty; be the disorder never so desperate or radical, you will find numbers in every street, who, by leveling a pill at the part affected, promise a certain cure without loss of time, knowledge of a bedfellow, or hindrance of business.

When I consider the assiduity of this profession, their

benevolence amazes me. They not only in general give their medicines for half value, but use the most persuasive remonstrances to induce the sick to come and be cured. Sure there must be something strangely obstinate in an English patient, who refuses so much health upon such easy terms; does he take a pride in being bloated with a dropsy? Does he find pleasure in the alternations of an intermittent fever? Or feel as much satisfaction in nursing up his gout, as he found pleasure in acquiring it? He must, otherwise he would never reject such repeated assurances of instant relief. What can be more convincing than the manner in which the sick are invited to be well? The doctor first begs the most earnest attention of the public to what he is going to propose; he solemnly affirms the pill was never found to want success; he produces a list of those who have been rescued from the grave by taking it. Yet, notwithstanding all this, there are many here who now and then think proper to be sick; only sick did I say? There are some who even think proper to die! Yes, by the head of Confucius they die; though they might have purchased the health-restoring specific for half a crown at every corner.

I am amazed, my dear Fum Hoam, that these doctors who know what an obstinate set of people they have to deal with, have never thought of attempting to revive the dead. When the living are found to reject their prescriptions, they ought in conscience to apply to the dead, from whom they can expect no such mortifying repulses; they would find in the dead the most complying patients imaginable; and what gratitude might they not expect from the patient's son, now no longer an heir, and his wife, now no longer a widow.

Think not, my friend, that there is any thing chimerical in such an attempt; they already perform cures equally strange: What can be more truly astonishing than to see old age restored to youth, and vigour to the most feeble constitutions; yet this is performed here every day; a simple electuary effects these wonders, even without the bungling ceremonies of having the patient boiled up in a kettle, or ground down in a mill.

Few physicians here go through the ordinary courses of education, but receive all their knowledge of medicine by immediate inspiration from heaven. Some are thus inspired even in the womb; and what is very remarkable, understand their profession as well at three years old as at threescore. Others have spent a great part of their lives unconscious of any latent excellence, till a bankruptcy, or a residence in gaol, have called their miraculous powers into exertion. And others still there are indebted to their superlative ignorance alone for success. The more ignorant the practitioner, the less capable is he thought of deceiving. The people here judge, as they do in the east; where it is thought absolutely requisite that a man should be an ideot before he pretend to be either a conjuror or a doctor.

When a physician by inspiration is sent for, he never perplexes the patient by previous examination; he asks very few questions, and those only for form sake. He knows every disorder by intuition. He administers the pill or drop for every distemper; nor is more inquisitive than the farrier while he drenches an horse. If the patient lives, then has he one more to add to the surviving list; if he dies, then it may be justly said of the patient's disorder, *that as it was not cured, the disorder was incurable.*

LETTER XXVI

The character of the man in black; with some instances of his inconsistent conduct.

From the same.

THO' fond of many acquaintances, I desire an intimacy only with a few. The man in black whom I have often mentioned, is one whose friendship I cou'd wish to acquire, because he possesses my esteem. His manners it is true, are tinctured with some strange inconsistencies; and he may be justly termed an humourist in a nation of humourists. Tho' he is generous even to profusion, he affects to be thought a prodigy of parsimony and prudence; though his conversation be replete with the most sordid and selfish maxims, his heart is dilated with the most unbounded love. I have known him profess himself a man-hater, while his cheek was glowing with compassion; and while his looks were softened into pity, I have heard him use the language of the most unbounded ill nature. Some affect humanity and tenderness, others boast of having such dispositions from nature; but he is the only man I ever knew who seemed ashamed of his natural benevolence. He takes as much pains to hide his feelings as any hypocrite would to conceal his indifference; but on every unguarded moment the mask drops off, and reveals him to the most superficial observer.

In one of our late excursions into the country, happening to discourse upon the provision that was made for the poor in England, he seemed amazed how any of his countrymen could be so foolishly weak as to relieve occasional objects of charity, when the laws had made such ample provision for their support. In every parish house, says he, the poor are supplied with food, cloaths, fire, and a bed to lie on; they want no more, I desire no more my self; yet still they seem discontented. I'm surprized at the inactivity of our magistrates, in not taking up such vagrants who are only a weight upon the industrious; I'm surprized that the people are found to relieve them, when they must be at the same time sensible that it, in some measure, encourages idleness, extravagance, and imposture. Were I to advise any man for whom I had the least regard, I would caution him by all means not to be imposed upon by their false pretences: let me assure you, Sir, they are impostors, every one of them; and rather merit a prison than relief.

He was proceeding in this strain earnestly, to dissuade me

from an imprudence of which I am seldom guilty; when an old man who still had about him the remnants of tattered finery, implored our compassion. He assured us that he was no common beggar, but forced into the shameful profession, to support a dying wife and five hungry children. Being prepossessed against such falshoods, his story had not the least influence upon me; but it was quite otherwise with the man in black; I could see it visibly operate upon his countenance, and effectually interrupt his harangue. I could easily perceive that his heart burned to relieve the five starving children, but he seemed ashamed to discover his weakness to me. While he thus hesitated between compassion and pride, I pretended to look another way, and he seized this opportunity of giving the poor petitioner a piece of silver, bidding him at the same time, in order that I should hear, go work for his bread, and not teize passengers with such impertinent falsehoods for the future.

As he had fancied himself quite unperceived, he continued, as we proceeded, to rail against beggars with as much animosity as before; he threw in some episodes on his own amazing prudence and œconomy, with his profound skill in discovering impostors; he explained the manner in which he would deal with beggars were he a magistrate, hinted at enlarging some of the prisons for their reception, and told two stories of ladies that were robbed by beggarmen. He was beginning a third to the same purpose, when a sailor with a wooden leg once more crossed our walks, desiring our pity, and blessing our limbs. I was for going on without taking any notice, but my friend looking wishfully upon the poor petitioner, bid me stop, and he would shew me with how much ease he could at any time detect an impostor.

He now therefore assumed a look of importance, and in an angry tone began to examine the sailor, demanding in what engagement he was thus disabled and rendered unfit for service. The sailor replied in a tone as angrily as he, that he had been an officer on board a private ship of war, and that he had lost his leg abroad in defence of those who did nothing at home. At this reply, all my friend's importance vanished in a moment; he had not a single question more to ask; he now only studied what method he should take to relieve him unobserved. He had however no easy part to act, as he was obliged to preserve the appearance of ill nature before me, and yet relieve himself by relieving the sailor. Casting therefore a furious look upon some bundles of chips which the fellow carried in a string at his back, my friend demanded how he sold his matches; but not waiting for a reply, desired, in a surly tone, to have a shilling's worth. The sailor seemed at first surprised at his demand, but soon recollecting himself, and presenting his whole bundle, Here, master, says he, take all my cargo, and a blessing into the bargain.

It is impossible to describe with what an air of triumph my friend marched off with his new purchase, he assured me that he was firmly of opinion that those fellows must have stolen their goods, who could thus afford to sell them for half value; he informed me of several different uses to which those chips might be applied; he expatiated largely upon the savings that would result from lighting candles with a match instead of thrusting them into the fire. He averred, that he would as soon have parted with a tooth as his money to those vagabonds, unless for some valuable consideration. I cannot tell how long this panegyric upon frugality and matches might have continued, had not his attention been called off by another object more distressful than either of the former. A woman in rags, with one child in her arms, and another on her back, was attempting to sing ballads, but with such a mournful voice that it was difficult to determine whether she was singing or crying. A wretch, who, in the deepest distress still aimed at good humour, was an object my friend was by no means capable of withstanding: his vivacity, and his discourse were instantly interrupted; upon this occasion his very dissimulation had forsaken him. Even in my presence, he immediately applied his hands to his pockets, in order to relieve her; but guess his confusion, when he found he had already given away all the money he carried about him to former objects. The misery painted in the woman's visage, was not half so strongly expressed as the agony in his. He continued to search for some time, but to no purpose, till, at length, recollecting himself, with a face of ineffable good-nature, as he had no money, he put into her hands his shilling's worth of matches.

LETTER XXVII

The history of the man in black.

To the same.

As there appeared something reluctantly good in the character of my companion, I must own it surprized me what could be his motives for thus concealing virtues which others take such pains to display. I was unable to repress my desire of knowing the history of a man who thus seemed to act under continual restraint, and whose benevolence was rather the effect of appetite than reason.

It was not however till after repeated solicitations he thought proper to gratify my curiosity. "If you are fond, says he, of hearing *hair breadth 'scapes*, my history must certainly please; for I have been for twenty years upon the very verge of starving, without ever being starved.

"My father, the younger son of a good family, was possessed of a small living in the church. His education was above his fortune, and his generosity greater than his education. Poor as he was, he had his flatterers still poorer than himself; for every dinner he gave them, they returned him an equivalent in praise; and this was all he wanted; the same ambition that actuates a monarch at the head of an army, influenced my father at the head of his table: he told the story of the ivy-tree, and that was laughed at; he repeated the jest of the two scholars and one pair of breeches, and the company laughed at that; but the story of Taffy in the sedan chair was sure to set the table in a roar;[1] thus his pleasure encreased in proportion to the pleasure he gave; he loved all the world, and he fancied all the world loved him.

"As his fortune was but small, he lived up to the very extent of it; he had no intentions of leaving his children money, for that was dross; he was resolved they should have learning; for learning, he used to observe, was better than silver or gold. For this purpose he undertook to instruct us himself; and took as much pains to form our morals, as to improve our understanding. We were told that universal benevolence was what first cemented society; we were taught to consider all the wants of mankind as our own; to regard the *human face divine* with affection and esteem; he wound us up to be mere machines of pity, and rendered us incapable of withstanding the slightest impulse made either by real or fictitious distress; in a word, we were perfectly instructed in the art of *giving away* thousands, before we were taught the more necessary qualifications of *getting* a farthing.

"I cannot avoid imagining, that, thus refined by his lessons out of all my suspicion, and divested of even all the little cunning which nature had given me, I resembled, upon my first entrance into the busy and insidious world, one of those gladiators who were exposed without armour in the amphitheatre at Rome. My father, however, who had only seen the world on one side, seemed to triumph in my superior discernment; though my whole stock of wisdom consisted in being able to talk like himself upon subjects that once were useful, because they were then topics of the busy world; but that now were utterly useless, because connected with the busy world no longer.

[1] [Goldsmith was fond of these now unidentifiable and perhaps mythical chestnuts. There is also Hardcastle's "Ould Grouse in the gun-room" (see p. 766).]

"The first opportunity he had of finding his expectations disappointed, was at the very middling figure I made in the university: he had flattered himself that he should soon see me rising into the foremost rank in literary reputation, but was mortified to find me utterly unnoticed and unknown. His disappointment might have been partly ascribed to his having over-rated my talents, and partly to my dislike of mathematical reasonings at a time, when my imagination and memory yet unsatisfied, were more eager after new objects, than desirous of reasoning upon those I knew. This did not, however, please my tutors, who observed, indeed, that I was a little dull; but at the same time allowed, that I seemed to be *very good natured*, and had no harm in me.

"After I had resided at college seven years, my father died, and left me—his blessing. Thus shoved from shore without ill-nature to protect, or cunning to guide, or proper stores to subsist me in so dangerous a voyage, I was obliged to embark in the wide world at twenty-two. But, in order to settle in life, my friends *advised* (for they always advise when they begin to despise us) they advised me, I say, to go into orders.

"To be obliged to wear a long wig, when I liked a short one, or a black coat, when I generally dressed in brown, I thought was such a restraint upon my liberty, that I absolutely rejected the proposal. A priest in England, is not the same mortified creature with a bonze in China; with us, not he that fasts best, but eats best, is reckoned the best liver; yet I rejected a life of luxury, indolence, and ease, from no other consideration but that boyish one of dress.[1] So that my friends were now perfectly satisfied I was undone; and yet they thought it a pity for one who had not the least harm in him, and was so very good-natured.

"Poverty naturally begets dependance, and I was admitted

[1] [Dress, according to Dr. Strean, prevented Goldsmith from becoming a priest; the Bishop of Elphin refused to ordain him when he presented himself in scarlet breeches.]

as flatterer to a great man. At first I was surprised, that the situation of a flatterer at a great man's table could be thought disagreeable; there was no great trouble in listening attentively when his lordship spoke, and laughing when he looked round for applause. This even good-manners might have obliged me to perform. I found, however, too soon, that his lordship was a greater dunce than myself; and from that very moment my power of flattery was at an end. I now rather aimed at setting him right, than at receiving his absurdities with submission: to flatter those we do not know is an easy task; but to flatter our intimate acquaintances, all whose foibles are strongly in our eye, is drudgery insupportable. Every time I now opened my lips in praise, my falshood went to my conscience; his lordship soon perceived me to be unfit for service; I was therefore discharged; my patron at the same time being graciously pleased to observe, that he believed I was tolerably good-natured, and had not the least harm in me.

"Disappointed in ambition I had recourse to love. A young lady, who lived with her aunt, and was possessed of a pretty fortune in her own disposal, had given me, as I fancied, some reasons to expect success. The symptoms by which I was guided were striking; she had always laughed with me at her aukward acquaintance, and at her aunt among the number; she always observed, that a man of sense would make a better husband than a fool, and I as constantly applied the observation in my own favour. She continually talked in my company of friendship and the beauties of the mind, and spoke of Mr. Shrimp my rival's high-heel'd shoes with detestation. These were circumstances which I thought strongly in my favour; so after resolving, and re-resolving, I had courage enough to tell her my mind. Miss heard my proposal with serenity, seeming at the same time to study the figures of her fan. Out at last it came. There was but one small objection to complete our happiness, which was no more, than——that she was married three months before to Mr. Shrimp with high-heel'd shoes! By way of consolation however she observed, that tho' I was disappointed in her, my addresses to her aunt would probably kindle her into sensibility; as the old lady always allowed me to be very good natured, and not to have the least share of harm in me.

"Yet still I had friends, numerous friends, and to them I was resolved to apply. O friendship! thou fond soother of the human breast, to thee we fly in every calamity; to thee the wretched seek for succour; on thee the care-tired son of misery fondly relies; from thy kind assistance the unfortunate always hopes relief, and may be ever sure of——disappointment! My first application was to a city scrivener, who had frequently offered to lend me money when he knew I did not want it. I informed him, that now was the time to put his friendship to the test; that I wanted to borrow a couple of hundreds for a certain occasion, and was resolved to take it up from him. And pray, Sir, cried my friend, do you want all this money?[1] Indeed I never wanted it more, returned I. I am sorry for that, cries the scrivener, with all my heart; for they who want money when they come to borrow, will always want money when they should come to pay.

"From him I flew with indignation to one of the best friends I had in the world, and made the same request. Indeed, Mr. Dry-bone, cries my friend, I always thought it would come to this. You know, sir, I would not advise you but for your own good; but your conduct has hitherto been ridiculous in the highest degree, and some of your acquaintance always thought you a very silly fellow; let me see, you want two hundred pounds; do you want only two hundred, sir, exactly? To confess a truth, returned I, I shall want three hundred; but then I have another friend from whom I can borrow the rest. Why then, replied my friend, if you would take my advice; and you know I should not presume to advise

[1] [This passage, down to "serve for all, you know," is closely paralleled in *On the Use of Language* (see p. 242).]

you but for your own good, I would recommend it to you to borrow the whole sum from that other friend; and then one note will serve for all, you know.

"Poverty now began to come fast upon me, yet instead of growing more provident or cautious as I grew poor, I became every day more indolent and simple. A friend was arrested for fifty pounds, I was unable to extricate him except by becoming his bail. When at liberty he fled from his creditors, and left me to take his place.[1] In prison I expected greater satisfactions than I had enjoyed at large. I hoped to converse with men in this new world simple and believing like myself, but I found them as cunning and as cautious as those in the world I had left behind. They spunged up my money whilst it lasted, borrowed my coals and never paid them, and cheated me when I played at cribbage. All this was done because they believed me to be very good-natured, and knew that I had no harm in me.

"Upon my first entrance into this mansion, which is to some the abode of despair, I felt no sensations different from those I experienced abroad. I was now on one side the door, and those who were unconfined were on the other; this was all the difference between us. At first indeed I felt some uneasiness, in considering how I should be able to provide this week for the wants of the week ensuing; but after some time, if I found myself sure of eating one day, I never troubled my head how I was to be supplied another. I seized every precarious meal with the utmost good humour, indulged no rants of spleen at my situation, never called down heaven and all the stars to behold me dining upon an halfpenny-worth of radishes; my very companions were taught to believe that I liked sallad better than mutton. I contented myself with thinking, that all my life I should either eat white bread or brown; considered that all that happened was best, laughed when I was not in pain, took the world as it went, and read Tacitus often, for want of more books and company.

[1] [This probably happened to Goldsmith (see the footnote on p. 837).]

"How long I might have continued in this torpid state of simplicity I cannot tell, had I not been rouzed by seeing an old acquaintance, whom I knew to be a prudent blockhead preferred to a place in the government. I now found that I had pursued a wrong track, and that the true way of being able to relieve others, was first to aim at independance myself. My immediate care, therefore, was to leave my present habitation, and make an entire reformation in my conduct and behaviour. For a free, open, undesigning deportment, I put on that of closeness, prudence and œconomy. One of the most heroic actions I ever performed, and for which I shall praise myself as long as I live, was the refusing half a crown to an old acquaintance, at the time when he wanted it, and I had it to spare; for this alone I deserve to be decreed an ovation.

"I now therefore pursued a course of uninterrupted frugality, seldom wanted a dinner, and was consequently invited to twenty. I soon began to get the character of a saving hunks that had money; and insensibly grew into esteem. Neighbours have asked my advice in the disposal of their daughters, and I have always taken care not to give any. I have contracted a friendship with an alderman, only by observing, that if we take a farthing from a thousand pound it will be a thousand pound no longer. I have been invited to a pawnbroker's table, by pretending to hate gravy; and am now actually upon treaty of marriage with a rich widow, for only having observed that the bread was rising. If ever I am asked a question, whether I know it or not, instead of answering, I only smile and look wise. If a charity is proposed, I go about with the hat, but put nothing in myself. If a wretch solicits my pity, I observe that the world is filled with impostors, and take a certain method of not being deceived by never relieving. In short, I now find the truest way of finding esteem even from the indigent, is *to give away nothing, and thus have much in our power to give.*"

LETTER XXX

The proceedings of the club of authors.

From the same.

By my last advices from Moscow, I find the caravan has not yet departed for China: I still continue to write, expecting that you may receive a large number of my letters at once. In them you will find rather a minute detail of English peculiarities, than a general picture of their manners or disposition. Happy it were for mankind if all travellers would thus, instead of characterising a people in general terms, lead us into a detail of those minute circumstances which first influenced their opinion: the genius of a country should be investigated with a kind of experimental enquiry: by this means we should have more precise and just notions of foreign nations, and detect travellers themselves when they happened to form wrong conclusions.

My friend and I repeated our visit to the club of authors; where, upon our entrance, we found the members all assembled and engaged in a loud debate.

The poet, in shabby finery, holding a manuscript in his hand, was earnestly endeavouring to persuade the company to hear him read the first book of an heroic poem, which he had composed the day before. But against this, all the members very warmly objected. They knew no reason why any member of the club should be indulged with a particular hearing, when many of them had published whole volumes which had never been looked in. They insisted that the law should be observed, where reading in company was expresly noticed. It was in vain that the plaintiff pleaded the peculiar merit of his piece; he spoke to an assembly insensible to all his remonstrances; the book of laws was opened, and read by the secretary, where it was expresly enacted, "That whatsoever poet, speech-maker, critic, or historian, should presume to engage the company by reading his own works, he was to lay down sixpence previous to opening the manuscript, and should be charged one shilling an hour while he continued reading; the said shilling to be equally distributed among the company as a recompence for their trouble."

Our poet seemed at first to shrink at the penalty, hesitating for some time whether he should deposit the fine, or shut up the poem; but looking round, and perceiving two strangers in the room, his love of fame out-weighed his prudence, and laying down the sum by law established, he insisted on his prerogative.

A profound silence ensuing, he began by explaining his design. "Gentlemen, says he, the present piece is not one of your common epic poems, which come from the press like paper kites in summer; there are none of your Turnuses or Dido's in it; it is an heroical description of nature. I only beg you'll endeavour to make your soul's unison with mine, and hear with the same enthusiasm with which I have written. The poem begins with the description of an author's bed-chamber: the picture was sketched in my own apartment; for you must know, gentlemen, that I am myself the heroe. Then putting himself into the attitude of an orator, with all the emphasis of voice and action, he proceeded.

"Where the Red Lion flaring o'er the way,
Invites each passing stranger that can pay;
Where Calvert's butt, and Parson's black champaign,
Regale the drabs and bloods of Drury lane;
There in a lonely room, from bailiffs snug,
The muse found Scroggen stretch'd beneath a rug,
A window patch'd with paper lent a ray,
That dimly shew'd the state in which he lay;
The sanded floor that grits beneath the tread;
The humid wall with paltry pictures spread:
The royal game of goose was there in view,
And the twelve rules the royal martyr drew;

The seasons fram'd with listing found a place,
And brave prince William shew'd his lamp-black face:
The morn was cold, he views with keen desire
The rusty grate unconscious of a fire:
With beer and milk arrears the frieze was scor'd,
And five crack'd tea cups dress'd the chimney board,
A night cap deck'd his brows instead of bay,
A cap by night——a stocking all the day!"[1]

With this last line he seemed so much elated, that he was unable to proceed: "There gentlemen, cries he, there is a description for you; Rablais's bed-chamber is but a fool to it:

A cap by night—a stocking all the day!

There is sound and sense, and truth, and nature in the trifling compass of ten little syllables."

He was too much employed in self-admiration to observe the company: who by nods, winks, shrugs, and stifled laughter, testified every mark of contempt. He turned severally to each for their opinion, and found all however ready to applaud. One swore it was inimitable; another said it was damn'd fine; and a third cried out in rapture, Carissimo. At last addressing himself to the president, and pray, Mr. Squint, says he, let us have your opinion. Mine, answered the president, (taking the manuscript out of the author's hands) may

[1] [In a letter of January, 1759 to his brother Henry, Goldsmith quoted lines 7–18 as part of a "heroicomical poem." "Brave prince William" (the Duke of Cumberland) had originally been "Prussia's Monarch" (Frederick the Great). The letter continues:

And Now immagine after his soliloquy the landlord to make his appearance in order to Dun him for the reckoning,

Not with that face so servile and so gay
That welcomes every stranger that can pay,
With sulky eye he smoak'd the patient man
Then pull'd his breeches tight, and thus began, &c.

All this is taken you see from Nature.

There is a somewhat similar passage in *The Deserted Village* (lines 227–36, pp. 613–4).]

this glass suffocate me, but I think it equal to any thing I have seen; and I fancy, (continued he, doubling up the poem, and forcing it into the author's pocket) that you will get great honour when it comes out; so I shall beg leave to put it in. We will not intrude upon your good-nature, in desiring to hear more of it at present; *ex ungue Herculem*, we are satisfied, perfectly satisfied. The author made two or three attempts to pull it out a second time, and the president made as many to prevent him. Thus though with reluctance he was at last obliged to sit down, contented with the commendations for which he had paid.

When this tempest of poetry and praise was blown over, one of the company changed the subject, by wondering how any man could be so dull as to write poetry at present, since prose itself would hardly pay. Would you think it, gentlemen, continued he, I have actually written last week sixteen prayers, twelve bawdy jests, and three sermons, all at the rate of sixpence a-piece; and what is still more extraordinary, the bookseller has lost by the bargain. Such sermons would once have gain'd me a prebend's stall; but now alas we have neither piety, taste, nor humour among us. Positively if this season does not turn out better than it has begun, unless the ministry commit some blunders to furnish us with a new topic of abuse, I shall resume my old business of working at the press, instead of finding it employment.

The whole club seem to join in condemning the season, as one of the worst that had come for some time; a gentleman particularly observed that the nobility were never known to subscribe worse than at present. "I know not how it happens, said he, though I follow them up as close as possible, yet I can hardly get a single subscription in a week. The houses of the great are as inaccessible as a frontier garrison at mid-night. I never see a nobleman's door half opened that some surly porter or footman does not stand full in the breach. I was yesterday to wait with a subscription proposal upon my lord

Squash the creolian. I had posted myself at his door the whole morning, and just as he was getting into his coach, thrust my proposal snugg into his hand folded up in the form of a letter from myself. He just glanced at the superscription, and, not knowing the hand, consigned it to his valet de chambre; this respectable personage treated it as his master, and put it into the hands of the porter. The porter grasped my proposal frowning; and, measuring my figure from top to toe, put it back into my own hands unopened."

"To the devil I pitch all the nobility, cries a little man, in a peculiar accent, I am sure they have of late used me most scurvily. You must know, gentlemen, some time ago, upon the arrival of a certain noble duke from his travels, I set myself down, and vamped up a fine flaunting, poetical panegyric, which I had written in such a strain, that I fancied it would have even wheedled milk from a mouse. In this I represented the whole kingdom welcoming his grace to his native soil, not forgetting the loss France and Italy would sustain in their arts by his departure. I expected to touch for a bank bill at least; so folding up my verses in gilt paper, I gave my last half crown to a genteel servant to be the bearer. My letter was safely conveyed to his grace, and the servant after four hours absence, during which time I led the life of a fiend, returned with a letter four times as big as mine. Guess my extasy at the prospect of so fine a return. I eagerly took the pacquet into my hands, that trembled to receive it. I kept it some time unopened before me, brooding over the expected treasure it contained; when opening it, as I hope to be saved, gentlemen, his grace had sent me in payment for my poem no Bank bills, but six copies of verse, each longer than mine, addressed to him upon the same occasion."

"A nobleman, cries a member, who had hitherto been silent, is created as much for the confusion of us authors as the catch-pole. I'll tell you a story, gentlemen, which is as true as that this pipe is made of clay. When I was delivered of my first book, I owed my taylor for a suit of cloaths, but that is nothing new, you know, and may be any man's case as well as mine. Well, owing him for a suit of cloaths, and hearing that my book took very well, he sent for his money, and insisted upon being paid immediately: though I was at that time rich in fame, for my book run like wild-fire, yet I was very short in money, and being unable to satisfy his demand, prudently resolved to keep my chamber, preferring a prison of my own chusing at home, to one of my taylor's chusing abroad. In vain the bailiffs used all their arts to decoy me from my citadel, in vain they sent to let me know that a gentleman wanted to speak with me at the next tavern, in vain they came with an urgent message from my aunt in the country; in vain I was told that a particular friend was at the point of death, and desired to take his last farewell; I was deaf, insensible, rock, adamant, the bailiffs could make no impression on my hard heart, for I effectually kept my liberty by never stirring out of the room.

"This was very well for a fortnight; when one morning I received a most splendid message from the earl of Doomsday, importing, that he had read my book, and was in raptures with every line of it; he impatiently longed to see the author, and had some designs which might turn out greatly to my advantage. I paused upon the contents of this message, and found there could be no deceit, for the card was gilt at the edges, and the bearer, I was told, had quite the looks of a gentleman. Witness ye powers, how my heart triumphed at my own importance; I saw a long perspective of felicity before me, I applauded the taste of the times, which never saw genius forsaken; I had prepared a set introductory speech for the occasion, five glaring compliments for his lordship, and two more modest for myself. The next morning, therefore, in order to be punctual to my appointment, I took coach, and ordered the fellow to drive to the street and house mentioned in his lordship's address. I had the precaution to pull up the windows as I went along to keep off the busy part of mankind, and, big with expectation, fancied the coach never went fast enough. At length, however, the wish'd for moment of its stopping arrived, this for some time I impatiently expected, and letting down the door in a transport, in order to take a previous view of his lordship's magnificent palace and situation, I found—poison to my sight! I found myself, not in an elegant street, but a paltry lane, not at a nobleman's door, but the door of a spunging-house; I found the coachman had all this while been driving me to jail, and I saw the bailiff with a devil's face, coming out to secure me."

To a philosopher, no circumstance, however trifling, is too minute; he finds instruction and entertainment in occurrences, which are passed over by the rest of mankind as low, trite, and indifferent; it is from the number of these particulars, which, to many, appear insignificant, that he is at last enabled to form general conclusions; this, therefore, must be my excuse for sending so far as China accounts of manners and follies, which, though minute in their own nature, serve more truly to characterise this people than histories of their public treaties, courts, ministers, negotiations, and ambassadors. Adieu.

LETTER XXXII

Of the degeneracy of some of the English nobility. A Mushroom feast among the Tartars.

From the same.

IN a late excursion with my friend into the country, a gentleman with a blue ribbon tied round his shoulder, and in a chariot drawn by six horses passed swiftly by us, attended with a numerous train of captains, lacquies, and coaches filled with women. When we were recovered from the dust raised by his cavalcade, and could continue our discourse without danger of suffocation, I observed to my companion, that all this state and equipage which he seemed to despise, would in China be regarded with the utmost reverence, because such distinctions were always the reward of merit; the greatness of a Mandarine's retinue being a most certain mark of the superiority of his abilities or virtue.

The gentleman who has now passed us, replied my companion, has no claims from his own merit to distinction; he is possessed neither of abilities nor virtue; it is enough for him that one of his ancestors was possessed of these qualities two hundred years before him. There was a time, indeed, when his family deserved their titles, but they are long since degenerated, and his ancestors for more than a century have been more and more solicitous to keep up the breed of their dogs and horses than that of their children. This very nobleman, simple as he seems, is descended from a race of statesmen and heroes; but unluckily his great grandfather marrying a cook maid, and she having a trifling passion for his lordship's groom, they some-how crossed the strain, and produced an heir, who took after his mother in his great love to *good eating*, and his father in a violent affection for *horse flesh*. These passions have for some generations passed on from father to son, and are now become the characteristics of the family, his present lordship being equally remarkable for his kitchen and his stable.

But such a nobleman, cried I, deserves our pity thus placed in so high a sphere of life, which only the more exposes to contempt. A king may confer titles, but it is personal merit alone that insures respect. I suppose, added I, that such men who are so very unfit to fill up their dignity, are despised by their equals, neglected by their inferiors, and condemned to live among involuntary dependants in irksome solitude?

You are still under a mistake, replied my companion, for though this nobleman is a stranger to generosity; though he takes twenty opportunities in a day of letting his guests know how much he despises them; though he is possessed neither of taste, wit, nor wisdom; though incapable of improving others by his conversation, and never known to enrich any by his bounty, yet for all this, his company is eagerly sought after: he is a lord, and that is as much as most people desire in a companion. Quality and title have such allurements, that hundreds are ready to give up all their own importance, to cringe, to flatter, to look little, and to pall every pleasure in constraint, merely to be among the great, though without the least hopes of improving their understanding or sharing their generosity: they might be happy among their equals, but those are despised for company, where they are despised in turn. You saw what a crowd of humble cousins, card-ruined beaus, and captains on half pay, were willing to make up this great man's retinue down to his country seat. Not one of all these that could not lead a more comfortable life at home in their little lodging of three shillings a week, with their lukewarm dinner, served up between two pewter plates from a cook's shop. Yet poor devils, they are willing to undergo the impertinence and pride of their entertainer, merely to be thought to live among the great: they are willing to pass the summer in bondage, though conscious they are taken down only to approve his lordship's taste upon every occasion, to tag all his stupid observations with a *very true*, to praise his stable, and descant upon his claret and cookery.

The pitiful humiliations of the gentlemen you are now describing, said I, puts me in mind of a custom among the Tartars of Koreki, not entirely dissimilar to this we are now considering.* The Russians, who trade with them carry thither a kind of mushrooms, which they exchange for furrs of squirrels, ermins, sables, and foxes. These mushrooms the rich Tartars lay up in large quantities for the winter; and

* Van Stralenberg, a writer of credit, gives the same account of this people. Vid. an Historico Geographical Description of the north eastern parts of Europe and Asia, p. 397.

when a nobleman makes a mushroom feast, all the neighbours around are invited. The mushrooms are prepared by boiling, by which the water acquires an intoxicating quality, and is a sort of drink which the Tartars prize beyond all other. When the nobility and ladies are assembled, and the ceremonies usual between people of distinction over, the mushroom broth goes freely round; they laugh, talk double entendre, grow fuddled, and become excellent company. The poorer sort, who love mushroom broth to distraction as well as the rich, but cannot afford it at the first hand, post themselves on these occasions round the huts of the rich, and watch the opportunity of the ladies and gentlemen as they come down to pass their liquor, and holding a wooden bowl, catch the delicious fluid, very little altered by filtration, being still strongly tinctured with the intoxicating quality. Of this they drink with the utmost satisfaction, and thus they get as drunk and as jovial as their betters.[1]

Happy nobility, cries my companion, who can fear no diminution of respect, unless by being seized with a strangury; and who when most drunk are most useful; though we have not this custom among us, I foresee, that if it were introduced, we might have many a toad-eater in England ready to drink from the wooden bowl on these occasions, and to praise the flavour of his lordship's liquor: As we have different classes of gentry, who knows but we might see a lord holding the bowl to a minister, a knight holding it to his lordship, and a simple

[1] [The mushrooms were fly agaric (*Amanita muscaria*). Mr. John Ramsbottom's delicate reference to this practice (*Poisonous Fungi*, King Penguin, 1945) confirms Van Stralenberg's account, even to the possibility of intoxication at second hand:

> Amongst the Koryak tribes of north-east Siberia the fungus is eaten to produce a state of excessive emotion on occasions which seem to warrant it. For over two centuries it has been known that to prolong the festivities use is made of the fact that the stimulant is eliminated by the kidneys. According to Scandinavian tradition the Vikings ate *Amanita muscaria* to go berserk . . . the price in the barren Steppes, three or four reindeer for a single specimen, suggests considerable potency.]

'squire drinking it double distilled from the loins of knighthood. For my part, I shall never for the future hear a great man's flatterers haranguing in his praise that I shall not fancy I behold the wooden bowl; for I can see no reason why a man, who can live easily and happily at home, should bear the drudgery of decorum and the impertinence of his entertainer, unless intoxicated with a passion for all that was quality; unless he thought that whatever came from the great was delicious, and had the tincture of the mushroom in it. Adieu.

LETTER XXXV

The Philosopher's son describes a lady, his fellow captive.

From Hingpo, a slave in Persia, to Altangi, a travelling philosopher of China, by the way of Moscow.

FORTUNE has made me the slave of another, but nature and inclination render me entirely subservient to you; a tyrant commands my body, but you are master of my heart. And yet let not thy inflexible nature condemn me when I confess that I find my soul shrink with my circumstances. I feel my mind not less than my body, bend beneath the rigours of servitude, the master whom I serve grows every day more formidable. In spite of reason which should teach me to despise him, his hideous image fills even my dreams with horror.

A few days ago a christian slave, who wrought in the gardens, happening to enter an arbour where the tyrant was entertaining the ladies of his Haram with coffee, the unhappy captive was instantly stabbed to the heart for his intrusion. I have been preferred to his place, which tho' less laborious than my former station, is yet more ungrateful, as it brings me nearer him whose presence excites sensations at once of disgust and apprehension.

Into what a state of misery are the modern Persians fallen!

A nation once famous for setting the world an example of freedom, is now become a land of tyrants, and a den of slaves. The houseless Tartar of Kamkatska, who enjoys his herbs and his fish in unmolested freedom, may be envied, if compared to the thousands who pine here in hopeless servitude, and curse the day that gave them being. Is this just dealing, heaven! to render millions wretched to swell up the happiness of a few; cannot the powerful of this earth be happy without our sighs and tears; must every luxury of the great be woven from the calamities of the poor! It must, it must surely be, that this jarring discordant life is but the prelude to some future harmony; the soul attuned to virtue here, shall go from hence to fill up the universal choir where Tien presides in person, where there shall be no tyrants to frown, no shackles to bind, nor no whips to threaten, where I shall once more meet my father with rapture, and give a loose to filial piety, where I shall hang on his neck, and hear the wisdom of his lips, and thank him for all the happiness to which he has introduced me.

The wretch whom fortune has made my master, has lately purchased several slaves of both sexes; among the rest I hear a christian captive talked of with admiration. The eunuch who bought her, and who is accustomed to survey beauty with indifference, speaks of her with emotion! Her pride, however, astonishes her attendant slaves not less than her beauty; it is reported that she refuses the warmest solicitations of her haughty lord; he has even offered to make her one of his four wives upon changing her religion, and conforming to his. It is probable she cannot refuse such extraordinary offers, and her delay is perhaps intended to enhance her favours.

I have just now seen her, she inadvertently approached the place without a veil, where I sat writing. She seemed to regard the heavens alone with fixed attention; there her most ardent gaze was directed. Genius of the sun! what unexpected softness! what animated grace! her beauty seemed the transparent covering of virtue. Celestial beings could not wear a look of more perfection while sorrow humanized her form, and mixed my admiration with pity. I rose from the bank on which I sat, and she retired; happy that none observed us, for such an interview might have been fatal.

I have regarded, till now, the opulence and the power of my tyrant, without envy; I saw him with a mind incapable of enjoying the gifts of fortune, and consequently regarded him as one loaded, rather than enriched with its favours. But at present, when I think that so much beauty is reserved only for him, that so many charms shall be lavished on a wretch incapable of feeling the greatness of the blessing, I own I feel a reluctance to which I have hitherto been a stranger.

But let not my father impute those uneasy sensations to so trifling a cause as love. No, never let it be thought that *your* son, and the pupil of the wise Fum Hoam could stoop to so degrading a passion. I am only displeased at seeing so much excellence so unjustly disposed of.

The uneasiness which I feel is not for myself, but for the beautiful christian. When I reflect on the barbarity of him for whom she is designed, I pity, indeed I pity her. When I think that she must only share one heart, who deserves to command a thousand, excuse me, if I feel an emotion, which universal benevolence extorts from me. As I am convinced, that you take a pleasure in those sallies of humanity, and are particularly pleased with compassion, I could not avoid discovering the sensibility with which I felt this beautiful stranger's distress. I have for a while forgot in hers, the miseries of my own hopeless situation. Our tyrant grows every day more severe, and love which softens all other minds into tenderness, seems only to have encreased his severity. Adieu.

LETTER XXXVI

A continuance of his correspondence. The beautiful captive consents to marry her lord.

From the same.

THE whole Haram is filled with a tumultuous joy; Zelis, the beautiful captive, has consented to embrace the religion of Mahomet, and become one of the wives of the fastidious Persian. It is impossible to describe the transport that sits on every face on this occasion. Music and feasting fill every apartment, the most miserable slave seems to forget his chains, and sympathizes with the happiness of Mostadad. The herb we tread beneath our feet is not made more for our use, than every slave around him for their imperious master; mere machines of obedience they wait with silent assiduity, feel his pains, and rejoice in his exultation. Heavens! how much is requisite to make one man happy!

Twelve of the most beautiful slaves, and I among the number, have got orders to prepare for carrying him in triumph to the bridal apartment. The blaze of perfumed torches are to imitate the day; the dancers and singers are hired at a vast expense. The nuptials are to be celebrated on the approaching feast of Barboura, when an hundred taels in gold are to be distributed among the barren wives, in order to pray for fertility from the approaching union.

What will not riches procure! an hundred domestics, who curse the tyrant in their souls, are commanded to wear a face of joy, and they are joyful. An hundred flatterers are ordered to attend, and they fill his ears with praise. Beauty, all commanding beauty, sues for admittance, and scarcely receives an answer; even love itself seems to wait upon fortune, or though the passion be only feigned, yet it wears every appearance of sincerity; and what greater pleasure can even true sincerity confer, or what would the rich have more?

Nothing can exceed the intended magnificence of the bridegroom, but the costly dresses of the bride, six eunuchs in the most sumptuous habits are to conduct him to the nuptial couch, and wait his orders. Six ladies, in all the magnificence of Persia, are directed to undress the bride. Their business is to assist, to encourage her, to divest her of every encumbering part of her dress, all but the last covering, which, by an artful complication of ribbons, is purposely made difficult to unloose, and with which she is to part reluctantly even to the joyful possessor of her beauty.

Mostadad, O my father, is no philosopher; and yet he seems perfectly contented with his ignorance. Possessed of numberless slaves, camels, and women, he desires no greater possession. He never opened the page of Mentius, and yet all the slaves tell me that he is happy.

Forgive the weakness of my nature, if I sometimes feel my heart rebellious to the dictates of wisdom, and eager for happiness like his. Yet why wish for his wealth with his ignorance; to be like him, incapable of sentimental pleasures, incapable of feeling the happiness of making others happy, incapable of teaching the beautiful Zelis philosophy.

What, shall I in a transport of passion give up the golden mean, the universal harmony, the unchanging essence for the possession of an hundred camels; as many slaves, thirty-five beautiful horses, and seventy-three fine women: first blast me to the centre! Degrade me beneath the most degraded! Pare my nails, ye powers of heaven! ere I would stoop to such an exchange. What, part with philosophy, which teaches me to suppress my passions instead of gratifying them, which teaches me even to divest my soul of passion, which teaches serenity in the midst of tortures; philosophy, by which even now I am so very serene, and so very much at ease, to be persuaded to part with it for any other enjoyment! Never, never, even though persuasion spoke in the accents of Zelis!

A female slave informs me that the bride is to be arrayed in a tissue of silver, and her hair adorned with the largest pearls of Ormus; but why teize you with particulars, in which we both are so little concerned; the pain I feel in separation throws a gloom over my mind, which in this scene of universal joy I fear may be attributed to some other cause; how wretched are those who are like me, denied even the last resource of misery, their tears. Adieu.

LETTER XXXIX

The description of true politeness. Two letters of different countries, by ladies falsely thought polite at home.

*From Lien Chi Altangi to ***, Merchant in Amsterdam.*

CEREMONIES are different in every country, but true politeness is every where the same. Ceremonies, which take up so much of our attention, are only artificial helps which ignorance assumes, in order to imitate politeness, which is the result of good sense and good-nature. A person possessed of those qualities, though he had never seen a court, is truly agreeable; and if without them, would continue a clown, though he had been all his life a gentleman usher.

How would a Chinese, bred up in the formalities of an eastern court, be regarded, should he carry all his good manners beyond the Great Wall? How would an Englishman, skilled in all the decorums of western good breeding, appear at an eastern entertainment? Would he not be reckoned more fantastically savage than even his unbred footman!

Ceremony resembles that base coin which circulates through a country by the royal mandate; it serves every purpose of real money at home, but is entirely useless if carried abroad; a person who should attempt to circulate his native trash in another country, would be thought either ridiculous or culpable. He is truly well bred who knows when to value and when to despise those national peculiarities which are regarded by some with so much observance, a traveller of taste at once perceives that the wise are polite all the world over; but that fools are polite only at home.

I have now before me two very fashionable letters upon the same subject, both written by ladies of distinction; one of whom leads the fashion in England, and the other sets the ceremonies of China: they are both regarded in their respective countries by all the beau monde, as standards of taste, and models of true politeness, and both give us a true idea of what they imagine elegant in their admirers; which of them understands true politeness, or whether either, you shall be at liberty to determine: the English lady writes thus to her female confidant.

As I live, my dear Charlotte, I believe the colonel will carry it at last; he is a most irresistable fellow, that's flat. So well dress'd, so neat, so sprightly, and plays about one so agreeably, that I vow, he has as much spirits as the marquis of Monkeyman's Italian greyhound. I first saw him at Renelagh; he shines there; he's nothing without Renelagh, and Renelagh nothing without him. The next day he sent a card, and compliments, desiring to wait on mamma and me to the music subscription. He looked all the time with such irresistable impudence, that positively he had something in his face gave me as much pleasure as a pair-royal of naturals in my own hand. He waited on mamma and me the next morning to know how we got home: you must know the insidious devil makes love to us both. Rap went the footman at the door; bounce went my heart; I thought he would have rattled the house down. Chariot drove up to the window, with his footmen in the prettiest liveries: he has infinite taste, that's flat. Mamma had spent all the morning at her head; but for my part, I was in an undress to receive him; quite easy, mind that; no way disturbed at his approach: mamma pretended to be as degagée as I, and yet I saw her blush in spite of her. Positively he is a most killing devil! We did nothing but laugh all the time he staid with us; I never heard so many very good things before; at first he mistook mamma for my sister; at which she laughed: then he mistook my natural complection for paint; at which I laugh'd: and then he shewed us a picture in the lid of his snuff-box, at which we all laughed. He plays picquet so very ill, and is so very fond of cards, and loses with such a grace, that positively he has won me; I have got a cool hundred, but have lost my heart. I need not tell you that he is only a colonel of the train-bands.

I am, dear Charlotte,
Yours for ever,
BELINDA.

The Chinese lady addresses her confidant, a poor relation of the family, upon the same occasion; in which she seems to understand decorums even better than the western beauty. You who have resided so long in China will readily acknowledge the picture to be taken from nature; and, by being acquainted with the Chinese customs, will better apprehend the lady's meaning.

From YAOUA *to* YAYA

Papa insists upon one, two, three, four hundred taels from the colonel my lover, before he parts with a lock of my hair. Ho, how I wish the dear creature may be able to produce the money, and pay papa my fortune. The colonel is reckoned the politest man in all Shensi. The first visit he paid at our house; mercy, what stooping, and cringing, and stopping, and figeting, and going back, and creeping forward, there was between him and papa, one would have thought he had got the seventeen books of ceremonies all by heart. When he was come into the hall he flourished his hands three times in a very graceful manner. Papa, who would not be out-done, flourished his four times; upon this the colonel began again, and both thus continued flourishing for some minutes in the politest manner imaginable. I was posted in the usual place behind the screen, where I saw the whole ceremony through a slit. Of this the colonel was sensible, for papa informed him. I would have given the world to have shewn him my little shoes, but had no opportunity. It was the first time I had ever the happiness of seeing any man but papa, and I vow my dear Yaya, I thought my three souls would have actually have fled from my lips. Ho, but he looked most charmingly, he is reckoned the best shaped man in the whole province, for he is very fat, and very short; but even those natural advantages are improved by his dress, which is fashionable past description. His head was close shaven, all but the crown, and the hair of that was braided into a most beautiful tail, that reaching down to his heels, was terminated by a bunch of yellow roses. Upon his first entering the room, I could easily perceive he had been highly perfumed with assafœtida. But then his looks, his looks, my dear Yaya, were irresistible. He kept his eyes stedfastly fixed on the wall during the whole ceremony, and I sincerely believe no accident could have discomposed his gravity, or drawn his eyes away. After a polite silence of two hours, he gallantly begged to have the singing women introduced, purely for my amusement. After one of them had for some time entertained us with her voice, the colonel and she retired for some minutes together. I thought they would never have come back; I must own he is a most agreeable creature. Upon his return, they again renewed the concert, and he continued to gaze upon the wall as usual, when, in less than half an hour more! Ho, but he retired out of the room with another. He is indeed a most agreeable creature.

When he came to take his leave, the whole ceremony began afresh; papa would see him to the door, but the colonel swore he would rather see the earth turned upside down than permit him to stir a single step, and papa was at last obliged to comply. As soon as he was got to the door, papa went out to see him on horseback; here they continued half an hour bowing and cringing, before one would mount or the other go in, but the colonel was at last victorious. He had scarce gone an hundred paces from the house when papa running out halloo'd after him, A good journey. Upon which the colonel returned, and would see papa into his house before ever he would depart. He was no sooner got home than he sent me a very fine present of duck eggs painted of twenty different colours. His generosity I own has won me. I have ever since been trying over the eight letters of good fortune, and have great hopes. All I have to apprehend is that after he has married me, and that I am carried to his house close shut up in my chair, when he comes to have the first sight of my face, he may shut me up a second time and send me back to papa. However I shall appear as fine as possible; Mamma, and I have been to buy the cloaths for my wedding. I am to have a new *fong whang*[1] in my hair, the beak of which will reach down to my nose; the milaner from whom we bought that and our ribbons cheated us as if she had no conscience, and so to quiet mine I cheated her. All this is fair you know. I remain, my dear Yaya,

Your ever faithful,

YAOUA.

LETTER XLI

The behaviour of the congregation in St. Paul's church at prayers.

From Lien Chi Altangi, to Fum Hoam, first president of the Ceremonial Academy at Pekin, in China.[2]

SOME time since I sent thee, oh holy disciple of Confucius, an account of the grand abbey or mausoleum of the kings and heroes of this nation. I have since been introduced to a

[1] [An ornament representing the Chinese phoenix.]

[2] [In the first edition the address is *To the same*; that of the previous letter (here omitted) is *From the same*, which begs the question. But it is obvious from the first line that this letter is addressed to Fum Hoam and not the Amsterdam merchant.]

temple not so ancient, but far superior in beauty and magnifi cence. In this, which is the most considerable of the empire, there are no pompous inscriptions, no flattery paid the dead, but all is elegant and awfully simple. There are however a few rags hung round the walls, which have at a vast expence been taken from the enemy in the present war. The silk of which they are composed when new, might be valued at half a string of copper money in China; yet this wise people fitted out a fleet and an army in order to seize them; though now grown old, and scarce capable of being patched up into a handkerchief. By this conquest the English are said to have gained, and the French to have lost, much honour. Is the honour of European nations placed only in tattered silk?

In this temple I was permitted to remain during the whole service; and were you not already acquainted with the religion of the English, you might, from my description, be inclined to believe them as grosly idolatrous as the disciples of Lao. The idol which they seem to address, strides like a colossus over the door of the inner temple, which here, as with the Jews, is esteemed the most sacred part of the building. Its oracles are delivered in an hundred various tones, which seem to inspire the worshippers with enthusiasm and awe: an old woman who appeared to be the priestess, was employed in various attitudes, as she felt the inspiration. When it began to speak, all the people remained fixed in silent attention, nodding assent, looking approbation, appearing highly edified by those sounds, which to a stranger might seem inarticulate and unmeaning.

When the idol had done speaking, and the priestess had locked up its lungs with a key, observing almost all the company leaving the temple, I concluded the service was over, and taking my hat, was going to walk away with the crowd, when I was stopt by the man in black, who assured me that the ceremony had scarcely yet begun! What, cried I, do I not see almost the whole body of the worshippers leaving the church? Would you persuade me that such numbers who profess religion and morality, would in this shameless manner quit the temple before the service was concluded? you surely mistake; not even the Kalmouks would be guilty of such an indecency, tho' all the object of their worship was but a joint stool. My friend seemed to blush for his countrymen, assuring me that those whom I saw running away, were only a parcel of musical blockheads, whose passion was merely for sounds, and whose heads were as empty as a fiddle case; those who remain behind, says he, are the true Religious; they make use of music to warm their hearts, and to lift them to a proper pitch of rapture; examine their behaviour, and you will confess there are some among us who practise true devotion.

I now looked round me as he directed, but saw nothing of that fervent devotion, which he had promised; one of the worshippers appeared to be ogling the company through a glass; another was fervent not in addresses to heaven, but to his mistress; a third whispered, a fourth took snuff, and the priest himself, in a drowsy tone, read over the *duties* of the day.

Bless my eyes, cried I, as I happened to look towards the door, what do I see; one of the worshippers fallen fast asleep, and actually sunk down on his cushion: is he now enjoying the benefit of a trance, or does he receive the influence of some mysterious vision! *Alas, alas*, replied my companion, *no such thing; he has only had the misfortune of eating too hearty a dinner, and finds it impossible to keep his eyes open.* Turning to another part of the temple, I perceived a young lady just in the same circumstances and attitude; strange, cried I, can she too have over-eaten herself? *O, fie*, replied my friend, *you now grow censorious. She grow drowsy from eating too much; that would be profanation! She only sleeps now from having sat up all night at a brag party.* Turn me where I will then, says I, I can perceive no single symptom of devotion among the worshippers, except from that old woman in the corner, who sits groaning behind the long sticks of a mourning fan; she indeed seems greatly edified with what she hears. *Aye*, replied my friend, *I knew we should find some to catch you; I know her; that is the Deaf lady who lives in the cloysters.*

In short, the remissness of behaviour in almost all the worshippers, and some even of the guardians, struck me with surprize; I had been taught to believe that none were ever promoted to offices in the temple, but men remarkable for their superior sanctity, learning, and rectitude; that there was no such thing heard of as persons being introduced into the church merely to oblige a senator, or provide for the younger branch of a noble family: I expected, as their minds were continually set upon heavenly things, to see their eyes directed there also, and hoped from their behaviour to perceive their inclinations corresponding with their duty. But I am since informed, that some are appointed to preside over temples they never visit; and, while they receive all the money, are contented with letting others do all the good. Adieu.

LETTER XLIII

An apostrophe on the supposed death of Voltaire.

To the same.

WE have just received accounts here, that Voltaire the poet and philosopher of Europe is dead![1] He is now beyond the reach of the thousand enemies, who while living, degraded his writings, and branded his character. Scarce a page of his latter productions that does not betray the agonies of an heart bleeding under the scourge of unmerited reproach. Happy therefore at last in escaping from calumny, happy in leaving a world that was unworthy of him and his writings.

[1] [These accounts were mistaken. Voltaire did not die until 30 May, 1778. While most of his English contemporaries regarded Voltaire as a monster, Goldsmith admired him ungrudgingly and wrote a flattering, if hasty, sketch of his life which was published in the *Lady's Magazine* in 1761.]

Let others, my friend, bestrew the hearses of the great with panegyric; but such a loss as the world has now suffered affects me with stronger emotions. When a philosopher dies, I consider myself as losing a patron, an instructor, and a friend. I consider the world as losing one who might serve to console her amidst the desolations of war and ambition. Nature every day produces in abundance men capable of filling all the requisite duties of authority; but she is niggard in the birth of an exalted mind, scarcely producing in a century a single genius to bless and enlighten a degenerate age. Prodigal in the production of kings, governors, mandarines, chams, and courtiers, she seems to have forgotten for more than three thousand years, the manner in which she once formed the brain of a Confucius; and well it is she has forgotten, when a bad world gave him so very bad a reception.

Whence, my friend, this malevolence which has ever pursued the great even to the tomb; whence this more than fiend-like disposition of embittering the lives of those who would make us more wise and more happy?

When I cast my eye over the fates of several philosophers, who have at different periods enlightened mankind, I must confess it inspires me with the most degrading reflections on humanity. When I read of the stripes of Mentius, the tortures of Tchin, the bowl of Socrates, and the bath of Seneca; when I hear of the persecutions of Dante, the imprisonment of Galileo, the indignities suffered by Montagne, the banishment of Cartesius, the infamy of Bacon; and that even Locke himself escaped not without reproach; when I think on such subjects, I hesitate whether most to blame the ignorance or the villany of my fellow creatures.

Should you look for the character of Voltaire among the journalists and illiterate writers of the age; you will there find him characterized as a monster, with a head turned to wisdom, and an heart inclining to vice; the powers of his mind and the baseness of his principles forming a detestable contrast. But seek for his character among writers like himself, and you find him very differently described. You perceive him in their accounts possessed of good nature, humanity, greatness of soul, fortitude, and almost every virtue; in this description those who might be suppos'd best acquainted with his character are unanimous. The royal Prussian,* Dargens,† Diderot,‡ D'alambert, and Fontenelle conspire in drawing the picture, in describing the friend of man and the patron of every rising genius.

An inflexible perseverance in what he thought was right, and a generous detestation of flattery, formed the ground-work of this great man's character. From these principles many strong virtues and few faults arose; as he was warm in his friendship, and severe in resentment, all that mention him seem possessed of the same qualities, and speak of him with rapture or detestation. A person of his eminence can have few indifferent as to his character; every reader must be an enemy or an admirer.

This poet began the course of glory so early as the age of eighteen, and even then was author of a tragedy which deserves applause; possessed of a small patrimony he preserved his independance, in an age of venality, and supported the dignity of learning, by teaching his cotemporary writers to live like him, above the favours of the great. He was banished his native country for a satire upon the royal concubine. He had accepted the place of historian to the French king, but refused to keep it, when he found it was presented only in order that he should be the first flatterer of the state.

The great Prussian received him as an ornament to his kingdom, and had sense enough to value his friendship, and profit by his instructions. In this court he continued till an intrigue, with which the world seems hitherto unacquainted, obliged him to quit that country. His own happiness, the

* Philosophe sans souci. † Let. Chin. ‡ Encycloped.

happiness of the monarch, *of his sister*,[1] of a part of the court, rendered his departure necessary.

Tired at length of courts, and all the follies of the great, he retired to Switzerland, a country of liberty, where he enjoyed tranquility and the muse. Here, though without any taste for magnificence himself, he usually entertained at his table the learned and polite of Europe, who were attracted by a desire of seeing a person from whom they had received so much satisfaction. The entertainment was conducted with the utmost elegance, and the conversation was that of philosophers. Every country that at once united liberty and science, were his peculiar favourites. The being an Englishman was to him a character that claimed admiration and respect.

Between Voltaire and the disciples of Confucius, there are many differences; however, being of a different opinion does not in the least diminish my esteem; I am not displeased with my brother, because he happens to ask our father for favours in a different manner from me. Let his errors rest in peace, his excellencies deserve admiration; let me with the wise admire his wisdom; let the envious and the ignorant ridicule his foibles; the folly of others is ever most ridiculous to those who are themselves most foolish. Adieu.

LETTER XLV

The ardour of the people of London, in running after sights and monsters.

To the same.

THO' the frequent invitations I receive from men of distinction here might excite the vanity of some, I am quite mortified

[1] [Frederick's sister, Wilhelmina, Margravine of Bayreuth. In a letter to M. D'Arget, translated in the first number of *The Bee*, Voltaire says that she "ever preserved a friendship" for him. I can find no other hint of this intrigue, with which the world seems likely to remain unacquainted. In *A Short Account of the Late Mr. Maupertuis* in *The Bee*, Goldsmith attributes Voltaire's quarrel with Frederick to one of the known causes, "the preference which this royal scholar gave to Maupertuis."]

however when I consider the motives that inspire their civility. I am sent for not to be treated as a friend, but to satisfy curiosity; not to be entertained so much as wondered at; the same earnestness which excites them to see a Chinese, would have made them equally proud of a visit from the rhinoceros.

From the highest to the lowest, this people seem fond of sights and monsters. I am told of a person here who gets a very comfortable livelihood by making wonders, and then selling or shewing them to the people for money; no matter how insignificant they were in the beginning, by locking them up close, and shewing for money, they soon became prodigies! His first essay in this way was to exhibit himself as a wax-work figure behind a glass door at a puppet show. Thus keeping the spectators at a proper distance, and having his head adorned with a copper crown, he looked extreamly *natural, and very like the life itself.* He continued this exhibition with success, till an involuntary fit of sneezing brought him to life before all the spectators, and consequently rendered him for that time as entirely useless, as the peaceable inhabitant of a catacomb.

Determined to act the statue no more, he next levied contributions under the figure of an Indian king; and by painting his face, and counterfeiting the savage howl, he frighted several ladies and children with amazing success: in this manner therefore he might have lived very comfortably, had he not been arrested for a debt that was contracted when he was the figure in wax-work: thus his face underwent an involuntary ablution, and he found himself reduced to his primitive complexion and indigence.

After some time, being freed from gaol, he was now grown wiser, and instead of making himself a wonder, was resolved only to make wonders. He learned the art of pasting up mummies; was never at a loss for an artificial *lusus naturæ*; nay, it has been reported, that he has sold seven petrified lobsters of his own manufacture to a noted collector of rarities; but this the learned Cracovius Putridus has undertaken to refute in a very elaborate dissertation.

His last wonder was nothing more than an halter, yet by this halter he gained more than by all his former exhibitions. The people, it seems, had got it in their heads, that a certain noble criminal[1] was to be hanged with a silken rope. Now there was nothing they so much desired to see as this very rope; and he was resolved to gratify their curiosity: he therefore got one made, not only of silk, but to render it the more striking, several threads of gold were intermixed. The people paid their money only to see silk, but were highly satisfied when they found it was mixed with gold into the bargain. It is scarce necessary to mention, that the projector sold his silken rope for almost what it had cost him, as soon as the criminal was known to be hanged in hempen materials.

By the fondness of sights, one would be apt to imagine, that instead of desiring to see things as they should be, they are rather solicitous of seeing them as they ought not to be. A cat with four legs is disregarded, though never so useful; but if it has but two, and is consequently incapable of catching mice, it is reckoned inestimable, and every man of taste is ready to raise the auction. A man, though in his person faultless as an aerial genius, might starve; but if stuck over with hideous warts like a porcupine, his fortune is made for ever, and he may propagate the breed with impunity and applause.

A good woman in my neighbourhood, who was bred an habit-maker, though she handled her needle tolerably well, could scarcely get employment. But being obliged by an accident to have both her hands cut off from the elbows, what would in another country have been her ruin, made her fortune here, she now was thought more fit for her trade than before; business flowed in apace, and all people paid for seeing the mantua-maker who wrought without hands.

[1] [Laurence Shirley, fourth Earl Ferrers (1720–60), hanged on 5 May 1760 for murder by the "new drop just then introduced."]

A gentleman shewing me his collection of pictures, stopped at one with peculiar admiration; there, cries he, is an inestimable piece. I gazed at the picture for some time, but could see none of those graces with which he seemed enraptured; it appeared to me the most paltry piece of the whole collection: I therefore demanded where those beauties lay, of which I was yet insensible. Sir, cries he, the merit does not consist in the piece, but in the manner in which it was done. The painter drew the whole with his foot, and held the pencil between his toes: I bought it at a very great price; for peculiar merit should ever be rewarded.

But these people are not more fond of wonders than liberal in rewarding those who shew them. From the wonderful dog of knowledge at present under the patronage of the nobility, down to the man with the box, who professes to shew *the most imitation of nature that was ever seen*; they all live in luxury. A singing woman shall collect subscriptions in her own coach and six; a fellow shall make a fortune by tossing a straw from his toe to his nose; one in particular has found that eating fire was the most ready way to live; and another who gingles several bells fixed to his cap, is the only man that I know of who has received emolument from the labours of his head.

A young author, a man of good nature and learning, was complaining to me some nights ago of this misplaced generosity of the times. Here, says he, have I spent part of my youth in attempting to instruct and amuse my fellow creatures, and all my reward has been solitude, poverty, and reproach; while a fellow, possessed of even the smallest share of fidling merit, or who has perhaps learned to whistle double, is rewarded, applauded, and caressed! Prythee, young man, says I to him, are you ignorant, that in so large a city as this, it is better to be an amusing than an useful member of society? Can you leap up, and touch your feet four times before you come to the ground? *No, Sir.* Can you pimp for a man of quality? *No, Sir.* Can you stand upon two horses at full speed? *No, Sir.* Can you swallow a pen-knife? *I can do none of these tricks.* Why then, cried I, there is no other prudent means of subsistence left but to apprize the town that you speedily intend to eat up your own nose, by subscription.

I have frequently regretted that none of our eastern posture masters or show men have ever ventured to England. I should be pleased to see that money circulate in Asia, which is now sent to Italy and France, in order to bring their vagabonds hither. Several of our tricks would undoubtedly give the English high satisfaction. Men of fashion would be greatly pleased with the postures as well as the condescention of our dancing girls; and ladies would equally admire the conductors of our fire-works. What an agreeable surprize would it be to see a huge fellow with whiskers flash a charged blunderbuss full in a lady's face, without singing her hair, or melting her pomatum. Perhaps when the first surprize was over, she might then grow familiar with danger; and the ladies might vie with each other in standing fire with intrepidity.

But of all the wonders of the east, the most useful, and I should fancy, the most pleasing, would be the looking-glass of Lao, which reflects the mind as well as the body. It is said that the emperor Chusi used to make his concubines dress their heads and their hearts in one of these glasses every morning; while the lady was at her toilet, he would frequently look over her shoulder; and it is recorded that among the three hundred which composed his seraglio, not one was found whose mind was not even more beautiful than her person.

I make no doubt but a glass in this country would have the very same effect. The English ladies, concubines and all, would undoubtedly cut very pretty figures in so faithful a monitor. There, should we happen to peep over a lady's shoulder while dressing, we might be able to see neither gaming nor ill-nature; neither pride, debauchery, nor a love of gadding. We should find her, if any sensible defect appeared in the mind, more careful in rectifying it, than plaistering up the irreparable decays of the person; nay, I am even apt to fancy, that ladies would find more real pleasure in this utensil in private, than in any other bauble imported from China, though never so expensive, or amusing.

LETTER XLVI

A dream.

To the same.

UPON finishing my last letter I retired to rest, reflecting upon the wonders of the glass of Lao, wishing to be possessed of one here, and resolved in such a case to oblige every lady with a sight of it for nothing. What fortune denied me waking, fancy supplied in a dream; the glass, I know not how, was put into my possession, and I could perceive several ladies approaching, some voluntarily, others driven forward against their wills by a set of discontented genii, whom by intuition I knew were their husbands.

The apartment in which I was to show away was filled with several gaming tables, as if just forsaken; the candles were burnt to the socket, and the hour was five o'clock in the morning. Placed at one end of the room, which was of prodigious length, I could more easily distinguish every female figure as she marched up from the door; but guess my surprize, when I could scarce perceive one blooming or agreeable face among the number. This, however, I attributed to the early hour, and kindly considered that the face of a lady just risen from bed ought always to find a compassionate advocate.

The first person who came up in order to view her intellectual face was a commoner's wife, who, as I afterwards found, being bred during her virginity in a pawn-broker's shop, now attempted to make up the defects of breeding and sentiment by the magnificence of her dress, and the expensiveness of her amusements. "Mr. Showman, cried she, approaching, I am told you *has* something to shew in *that there* sort of magic lanthorn, by which folks can see themselves on the inside; I protest, as my lord Beetle says, I am sure it will be vastly pretty, for I have never seen any thing like it before. But how; are we to strip off our cloaths and be turned inside out? if so, as lord Beetle says, I absolutely declare off; for I would not strip for the world before a man's face, and so I *tells* his lordship almost every night of my life." I informed the lady that I would dispense with the ceremony of stripping, and immediately presented my glass to her view.

As when a first-rate beauty, after having with difficulty escaped the small pox, revisits her favourite mirror, that mirror which had repeated the flattery of every lover, and even added force to the compliment; expecting to see what had so often given her pleasure, she no longer beholds the cherried lip, the polished forehead, and speaking blush, but an hateful phyz, quilted into a thousand seams by the hand of deformity; grief, resentment, and rage fill her bosom by turns; she blames the fates and the stars, but most of all the unhappy glass feels her resentment. So it was with the lady in question; she had never seen her own mind before, and was now shocked at its deformity. One single look was sufficient to satisfy her curiosity; I held up the glass to her face, and she shut her eyes; no entreaties could prevail upon her to gaze once more! she was even going to snatch it from my hands, and break it in a thousand pieces. I found it was time therefore to dismiss her as incorrigible, and shew away to the next that offered.

This was an unmarried lady, who continued in a state of virginity till thirty-six, and then admitted a lover when she despaired of an husband. No woman was louder at a revel than she, perfectly free-hearted, and almost in every respect a man; she understood ridicule to perfection, and was once known even to sally out in order to beat the watch. "Here, you my dear with the outlandish face, (said she addressing me) let me take a single peep. Not that I care three dams what figure I may cut in the glass of such an old fashioned creature; if I am allowed the beauties of the face by people of fashion, I know the world will be complaisant enough to toss me the beauties of the mind into the bargain." I held my glass before her as she desired, and must confess, was shocked with the reflection. The lady, however, gazed for some time with the utmost complacency; and at last turning to me with the most satisfied smile said, she never could think she had been half so handsome.

Upon her dismission a lady of distinction was reluctantly hawled along to the glass by her husband; in bringing her forward, as he came first to the glass himself, his mind appeared tinctured with immoderate jealousy, and I was going to reproach him for using her with such severity; but when the lady came to present herself, I immediately retracted; for alas it was seen that he had but too much reason for his suspicions.

The next was a lady who usually teized all her acquaintance in desiring to be told of her faults, and then never mended any. Upon approaching the glass, I could readily perceive vanity, affectation, and some other ill-looking blots on her mind; wherefore by my advice she immediately set about mending. But I could easily find she was not earnest in the work; for as she repaired them on one side, they generally broke out on another. Thus, after three or four attempts, she began to make the ordinary use of the glass in settling her hair.

The company now made room for a woman of learning, who approached with a slow pace and a solemn countenance, which, for her own sake, I could wish had been cleaner. "Sir, cried the lady, flourishing her hand, which held a pinch of snuff, I shall be enraptured by having presented to my view a mind with which I have so long studied to be acquainted: but, in order to give the sex a proper example, I must insist, that all the company be permitted to look over my shoulder." I bowed assent, and presenting the glass, shewed the lady a mind by no means so fair as she had expected to see. Ill-nature, ill placed pride, and spleen, were too legible to be mistaken. Nothing could be more amusing than the mirth of her female companions who had looked over. They had hated her from the beginning, and now the apartment ecchoed with an universal laugh. Nothing but a fortitude like her's could have withstood their raillery: she stood it however; and when the burst was exhausted, with great tranquility she assured the company, that the whole was a deceptio visus, and that she was too well acquainted with her own mind to believe any false representations from another. Thus saying, she retired with a sullen satisfaction, resolved not to mend her faults, but to write a criticism on the mental reflector.

I must own, by this time I began myself to suspect the fidelity of my mirror; for as the ladies appeared at least to have the merit of rising early, since they were up at five, I was amazed to find nothing of this good quality pictured upon their minds in the reflection; I was resolved therefore to communicate my suspicions to a lady, whose intellectual countenance appeared more fair than any of the rest, not having above seventy-nine spots in all, besides slips and foibles. "I own, young woman, said I, that there are some virtues upon that mind of your's; but there is still one which I do not see represented; I mean that of rising betimes in the morning; I fancy the glass false in that particular." The young lady smiled at my simplicity; and, with a blush, confessed, that she and the whole company had been up all night gaming.

By this time all the ladies, except one, had seen themselves successively, and disliked the show, or scolded the showman; I was resolved, however, that she who seemed to neglect herself, and was neglected by the rest, should take a view; and going up to a corner of the room, where she still continued sitting, I presented my glass full in her face. Here it was that I exulted in my success; no blot, no stain, appeared on any part of the faithful mirror. As when the large, unwritten page presents its snowy spotless bosom to the writer's hand; so appeared the glass to my view. Here, O ye daughters of English ancestors, cried I, turn hither, and behold an object worthy imitation: look upon the mirror now, and acknowledge its justice, and this woman's pre-eminence! The ladies obeying the summons, came up in a groupe, and, looking on, acknowledged there was some truth in the picture, as the person now represented had been deaf, dumb, and a fool from her cradle.

Thus much of my dream I distinctly remember; the rest was filled with chimæras, enchanted castles, and flying dragons as usual. As you, my dear Fum Hoam, are particularly versed in the interpretation of those midnight warnings, what pleasure should I find in your explanation: but that our distance prevents; I make no doubt, however, but that from my description you will very much venerate the good qualities of the English ladies in general, since dreams, you know, go always by contraries. Adieu.

LETTER XLVIII

The absurdity of persons in high station pursuing employments beneath them, exemplified in a fairy tale.

*From Lien Chi Altangi to ***** merchant in Amsterdam.*

HAPPENING some days ago to call at a painter's to amuse my self in examining some pictures (I had no design to buy) it surprised me to see a young Prince in the working room, dressed in a painter's apron, and assiduously learning the trade. We instantly remembered to have seen each other; and, after the usual compliments, I stood by while he continued to paint on. As every thing done by the rich is praised, as princes here, as well as in China, are never without followers, three or four persons, who had the appearance of gentlemen, were placed behind to comfort and applaud him at every stroke.

Need I tell, that it struck me with very disagreeable sensations *to see a youth, who by his station in life, had it in his power to be useful to thousands, thus letting his mind run to waste upon canvas, at the same time fancying himself improving in taste, and filling his rank with proper decorum.*

As seeing an error, and attempting to redress it, are only one and the same with me, I took occasion, upon his lordship's desiring my opinion of a Chinese scroll, intended for the frame of a picture, to assure him, that a mandarine of China thought a minute acquaintance with such mechanical trifles below his dignity.

This reply raised the indignation of some, and the contempt of others: I could hear the names of Vandal, Goth, taste, polite arts, delicacy, and fire, repeated in tones of ridicule or resentment. But considering that it was vain to argue against people who had so much to say, without contradicting them, I begged leave to repeat a fairy tale. This request redoubled their laughter; but not easily abashed at the raillery of boys, I persisted, observing that it would set the absurdity of placing our affections upon trifles, in the strongest point of view, and adding that it was hoped the moral would compensate for its stupidity. For heaven's sake, cried the great man, washing his brush in water, let us have no morality at present; if we must have a story, let it be without any moral. I pretended not to hear; and while he handled the brush, proceeded as follows.

In the kingdom of Bonbobbin, which, by the Chinese annal, appears to have flourished twenty thousand years ago, there reigned a prince, endowed with every accomplishment which generally distinguishes the sons of kings. His beauty was brighter than the sun. The sun, to which he was nearly related, would sometimes stop his course in order to look down and admire him.

His mind was not less perfect than his body: he knew all things without having ever read; philosophers, poets, and historians, submitted their works to his decision; and so penetrating was he, that he could tell the merit of a book by looking on the cover. He made epic poems, tragedies, and pastorals, with surprising facility; song, epigram, or rebus, was all one to him, tho' it is observed he could never finish an acrostic. In short, the fairy, who presided at his birth, had endowed him with almost every perfection, or what was just the same, his subjects were ready to acknowledge he possessed them all; and, for his own part, he knew nothing to the contrary. A prince so accomplished, received a name suitable to his merit; and he was called Bonbenin bonbobbin bonbobbinet, which signifies *Enlightener of the Sun.*

As he was very powerful, and yet unmarried, all the neighbouring kings earnestly sought his alliance. Each sent his daughter, dressed out in the most magnificent manner, and with the most sumptuous retinue imaginable, in order to allure the prince: so that at one time there were seen at his court not less than seven hundred foreign princesses of exquisite sentiment and beauty, each alone sufficient to make seven hundred ordinary men happy.

Distracted in such a variety, the generous Bonbenin, had he not been obliged by the laws of the empire to make choice of one, would very willingly have married them all, for none understood gallantry better. He spent numberless hours of solicitude in endeavouring to determine whom he should chuse; one lady was possessed of every perfection, but he disliked her eyebrows; another was brighter than the morning star, but he disapproved her fong whang; a third did not lay white enough on her cheek; and a fourth did not sufficiently blacken her nails. At last after numberless disappointments on the one side and the other, he made choice of the incomparable Nanhoa, queen of the scarlet dragons.

The preparations for the royal nuptials, or the envy of the

disappointed ladies, needs no description; both the one and the other were as great as they could be; the beautiful princess was conducted amidst admiring multitudes to the royal couch, where after being divested of every encumbering ornament, she was placed, in expectance of the youthful bridegroom, who did not keep her long in expectation. He came more chearful than the morning, and printing on her lips a burning kiss, the attendants took this as a proper signal to withdraw.

Perhaps I ought to have mentioned in the beginning that, among several other qualifications, the prince was fond of collecting and breeding mice, which being an harmless pastime, none of his counsellors thought proper to dissuade him from: he therefore kept a great variety of these pretty little animals in the most beautiful cages enriched with diamonds, rubies, emeralds, pearls, and other precious stones: thus he *innocently* spent four hours each day, in contemplating their innocent little pastimes.

But to proceed, the Prince and Princess were now in bed; one with all the love and expectation, the other with all the modesty and fear, which is natural to suppose, both willing, yet afraid to begin; when the Prince happening to look towards the outside of the bed, perceived one of the most beautiful animals in the world, a white mouse with green eyes, playing about the floor, and performing an hundred pretty tricks. He was already master of blue mice, red mice, and even white mice with yellow eyes; but a white mouse with green eyes, was what he long endeavoured to possess: wherefore leaping from bed with the utmost impatience and agility, the youthful Prince attempted to seize the little charmer, but it was fled in a moment; for alas! the mouse was sent by a discontented Princess, and was itself a fairy.

It is impossible to describe the agony of the Prince upon this occasion. He sought round and round every part of the room, even the bed where the Princess lay was not exempt from the enquiry: he turned the Princess on one side and t'other, stripped her quite naked, but no mouse was to be found; the Princess herself was kind enough to assist, but still to no purpose.

Alas, cryed the young Prince in an agony, how unhappy am I to be thus disapointed; never sure was so beautiful an animal seen, I would give half my kingdom and my princess, to him that would find it. The Princess, though not much pleased with the latter part of his offer, endeavoured to comfort him as well as she could; she let him know that he had an hundred mice already, which ought to be at least sufficient to satisfy any philosopher like him. Tho' none of them had green eyes, yet he should learn to thank heaven that they had eyes. She told him, (for she was a profound moralist) that incurable evils must be born, and that useless lamentations were vain, and that man was born to misfortunes; she even entreated him to return to bed, and she would endeavour to lull him on her bosom to repose; but still the Prince continued inconsolable; and regarding her with a stern air, for which his family was remarkable, he vowed never to sleep in the royal palace, or indulge himself in the innocent pleasures of matrimony, till he had found the white mouse with the green eyes.

Prythee, Col. Leech, cried his Lordship, interrupting me, how do you like that nose; don't you think there is something of the manner of Rembrandt in it? A prince in all this agony for a white mouse, O ridiculous! Don't you think, Major Vampyre, that eye-brow stippled very prettily? but pray what are the green eyes to the purpose, except to amuse children? I would give a thousand guineas to lay on the colouring of this cheek more smoothly. But I ask pardon, pray Sir, proceed.

LETTER XLIX

The fairy tale continued.

From the same.

KINGS, continued I, at that time were different from what they are now; they then never engaged their word for any thing which they did not rigorously intend to perform. This was the case of Bonbenin, who continued all night to lament his misfortunes to the Princess, who ecchoed groan for groan. When morning came, he published an edict, offering half his kingdom, and his Princess, to the person who should catch and bring him the white mouse with green eyes.

The edict was scarce published, when all the traps in the kingdom were baited with cheese; numberless mice were taken and destroyed; but still the much wished for mouse was not among the number. The privy council were assembled more than once to give their advice; but all their deliberations came to nothing; even though there were two complete vermin-killers and three professed rat-catchers of the number. Frequent addresses, as is usual on extraordinary occasions, were sent from all parts of the empire; but though these promised well, though in them he received an assurance, that his faithful subjects would assist in his search with ther lives and fortunes, yet, with all their loyalty, they failed when the time came that the mouse was to be caught.

The Prince therefore was resolved to go himself in search, determined never to lie two nights in one place till he had found what he sought for. Thus quitting his palace without attendants, he set out upon his journey, and travelled through many a desert, and crossed many a river, high over hills, and down along vales, still restless, still enquiring wherever he came; but no white mouse was to be found.

As one day, fatigued with his journey, he was shading himself from the heat of the mid-day sun, under the arching branches of a banana tree, meditating on the object of his pursuit, he perceived an old woman, hideously deformed, approaching him; by her stoop, and the wrinkles of her visage, she seemed at least five hundred years old; and the spotted toad was not more freckled than was her skin. "Ah! prince Bonbenin-bonbobbin-bonbobbinet, cried the creature, what has led you so many thousand miles from your own kingdom; what is it you look for, and what induces you to travel into the Kingdom of Emmets?" The prince, who was excessively complaisant, told her the whole story three times over; for she was hard of hearing. "Well, says the old fairy, for such she was, I promise to put you in possession of the white mouse with green eyes, and that immediately too, upon one condition." "One condition, cried the prince in a rapture, name a thousand; I shall undergo them all with pleasure." "Nay, interrupted the old fairy, I ask but one, and that not very mortifying neither; it is only that you instantly consent to marry me."

It is impossible to express the prince's confusion at this demand; he loved the mouse, but he detested the bride; he hesitated; he desired time to think upon the proposal; he would have been glad to consult his friends on such an occasion. "Nay, nay, cried the odious fairy, if you demur, I retract my promise; I do not desire to force my favours on any man. Here, you my attendants, cried she, stamping with her foot, let my machine be driven up; Barbacela, Queen of Emmets, is not used to contemptuous treatment." She had no sooner spoken than her fiery chariot appeared in the air, drawn by two snails; and she was just going to step in, when the prince reflected, that now or never was the time to be possessed of the white mouse; and quite forgetting his lawful princess Nanhoa, falling on his knees, he implored forgiveness for having rashly rejected so much beauty. This well-timed compliment instantly appeased the angry fairy. She affected an hideous leer of approbation, and, taking the young prince by the hand, conducted him to a neighbouring church, where they were married together in a moment. As soon as the ceremony was performed, the prince, who was to the last degree desirous of seeing his favourite mouse, reminded the bride of her promise. "To confess a truth, my prince, cried she, I myself am that very white mouse you saw on your wedding night in the royal apartment. I now therefore give you the choice, whether you would have me a mouse by day, and a woman by night, or a mouse by night and a woman by day." Tho' the prince was an excellent casuist, he was quite at a loss how to determine, but at last thought it most prudent to have recourse to a blue cat that had followed him from his own dominions, and frequently amused him with its conversation, and assisted him with its advice; in fact this cat was no other than the faithful Princess Nanhoa herself, who had shared with him all his hardships in this disguise.

By her instructions he was determined in his choice, and returning to the old fairy, prudently observed that as she must have been sensible he had married her *only for the sake of what she had*, and not for her personal qualifications, he thought it would for several reasons be most convenient, if she continued a woman by day and appeared a mouse by night.

The old fairy was a good deal mortified at her husband's want of gallantry, though she was reluctantly obliged to comply; the day was therefore spent in the most polite amusements, the gentlemen talked smut, the ladies laughed, and were angry. At last the happy night drew near, the blue cat still stuck by the side of its master, and even followed him to the bridal apartment. Barbacela entered the chamber, wearing a train fifteen yards long, supported by porcupines, and all over beset with jewels, which served to render her more detestable. She was just stepping into bed to the Prince, forgetting her promise, when he insisted upon seeing her in the shape of a mouse. She had promised, and no fairy can break her word; wherefore assuming the figure of the most beautiful mouse in the world, she skipped and play'd about with an infinity of amusement. The Prince in an agony of rapture, was desirous of seeing his pretty playfellow move a slow dance about the floor to his own singing; he began to sing, and the mouse immediately to perform with the most perfect knowledge of time, and the finest grace and greatest gravity imaginable; it only began, for Nanhoa, who had long waited for the opportunity in the shape of a cat, flew upon it instantly without remorse, and eating it up in the hundredth part of a moment, broke the charm, and then resumed her natural figure.

The Prince now found that he had all along been under the power of enchantment, that his passion for the white mouse was entirely fictitious, and not the genuine complexion of his soul; he now saw that his earnestness after mice was an illiberal amusement, and much more becoming a ratcatcher than a Prince. All his meannesses now stared him in the face, he begged the discreet Princesses pardon an hundred times. The Princess very readily forgave him; and both returning to their palace in Bonbobbin, lived very happily together, and reigned many years with all that wisdom, which, by the story, they appear to have been possessed of. Perfectly convinced by their former adventures, that *they who place their affections on trifles at first for amusement, will find those trifles at last become their most serious concern.* Adieu.

LETTER LI

A Bookseller's visit to the Chinese.

From Lien Chi Altangi, to Fum Hoam, first president of the Ceremonial Academy at Pekin, in China.

As I was yesterday seated at breakfast over a pensive dish of tea, my meditations were interrupted by my old friend and companion, who introduced a stranger, dressed pretty much like himself. The gentleman made several apologies for his visit, begged of me to impute his intrusion to the sincerity of his respect, and the warmth of his curiosity.

As I am very suspicious of my company, when I find them very civil, without any apparent reason, I answered the stranger's caresses at first with reserve; which my friend perceiving, instantly let me into my visitant's trade and character, asking Mr. Fudge, whether he had lately published any thing new? I now conjectured that my guest was no other than a bookseller, and his answer confirmed my suspicions.

"Excuse me, Sir, says he, it is not the season; books have their time as well as cucumbers. I would no more bring out a new work in summer, than I would sell pork in the dog-days. Nothing in my way goes off in summer, except very light goods indeed. A review, a magazine, or a sessions paper, may amuse a summer reader; but all our stock of value we reserve for a spring and winter trade." *I must confess, Sir*, says I, *a curiosity to know what you call a valuable stock, which can only bear a winter perusal.* "Sir, replied the bookseller, it is not my way to cry up my own goods; but without exaggeration I will venture to shew with any of the trade; my books at least have the peculiar advantage of being always new; and it is my way to clear off my old to the trunkmakers every season. I have ten new title pages now about me, which only want books to be added to make them the finest things in nature. Others may pretend to direct the vulgar; but that is not my way; I always let the vulgar direct me; wherever popular clamour arises, I always eccho the million. For instance, should the people in general say that such a man is a rogue, I instantly give orders to set him down in print a villain; thus every man buys the book, not to learn new sentiments, but to have the pleasure of seeing his own reflected." *But Sir*, interrupted I, *you speak as if you yourself wrote the books you publish; may I be so bold as to ask a sight of some of those intended publications which are shortly to surprize the world?* "As to that, Sir, replied the talkative bookseller, I only draw out the plans myself; and though I am very cautious of communicating them to any, yet, as in the end I have a favour to ask, you shall see a few of them. Here, Sir, here they are, diamonds of the first water, I assure you. Imprimis, a translation of several medical precepts for the use of such physicians as do not understand Latin. Item, the young clergyman's art of placing patches regularly, with a dissertation on the different manners of smiling without distorting the face. Item, the whole art of love made perfectly easy by a broker of 'Change Alley. Item, the proper manner of cutting black-lead pencils, and making crayons; by the Right Hon. the Earl of ***. Item, the muster master general, or the review of reviews—" *Sir*, cried I, interrupting him, *my curiosity with regard to title pages is satisfied, I should be glad to see some longer manuscript, an history, or an epic poem.*—"Bless me, cries the man of industry, now you speak of an epic poem, you shall see an excellent farce. Here it is; dip into it where you will, it will be found replete with true modern humour. Strokes, Sir; it is filled with strokes of wit and satire in every line." *Do you call these dashes of the pen strokes*, replied I, *for I must confess I can see no other?*" And pray Sir, returned he, what do you call them? Do you see any thing good now a-days that is not filled with strokes—and dashes?—Sir, a well placed dash makes half the wit of our writers of modern humour. I bought last season a piece that had no other merit upon earth than nine hundred and ninety-five breaks, seventy-two ha ha's, three good things, and a garter. And yet it played off, and bounced, and cracked, and made more sport than a fire work." *I fancy then, Sir, you were a considerable gainer?* "It must be owned the piece did pay; but upon the whole I cannot much boast of last winter's success; I gained by two murders, but then I lost by an ill timed charity sermon. I was a considerable sufferer by my Direct road to an estate, but the Infernal Guide brought me up again. Ah, Sir, that was a piece touched off by the hands of a master, filled with good things from one end to the other. The author had nothing but the jest in view; no dull moral lurking beneath, nor ill-natured satyr to sour the reader's good humour; he wisely considered that moral and humour at the same time were quite overdoing the business." *To what purpose was the book then published?* cried I. "Sir, the book was published in order to be sold; and no book sold better, except the criticisms upon it, which came out soon after. Of all kinds of writing that goes off best at present; and I generally fasten a criticism upon every selling book that is published.

"I once had an author who never left the least opening for the critics: close was the word, always very right, and very dull, ever on the safe side of an argument; yet, with all his qualifications, incapable of coming into favour. I soon perceived that his bent was for criticism; and as he was good for nothing else, supplied him with pens and paper, and planted him at the beginning of every month as a censor on the works of others. In short, I found him a treasure; no merit could escape him: but what is most remarkable of all, he ever wrote best and bitterest when drunk." *But are there not some works,* interrupted I, *that from the very manner of their composition must be exempt from criticism; particularly such as profess to disregard its laws.* "There is no work whatsoever but he can criticise, replied the bookseller; even though you wrote in Chinese he would have a pluck at you. Suppose you should take it into your head to publish a book, let it be a volume of Chinese letters for instance; write how you will, he shall shew the world you could have written better. Should you, with the most local exactness, stick to the manners and customs of the country from whence you come; should you confine yourself to the narrow limits of eastern knowledge, and be perfectly simple, and perfectly natural, he has then the strongest reason to exclaim. He may with a sneer send you back to China for readers. He may observe, that after the first or second letter the iteration of the same simplicity is insupportably tedious; but the worst of all is, the public in such a case will anticipate his censures, and leave you with all your uninstructive simplicity to be mauled at discretion."

Yes, cried I, *but, in order to avoid his indignation, and what I should fear more, that of the public, I would in such a case write with all the knowledge I was master of. As I am not possessed of much learning, at least I would not suppress what little I had; nor would I appear more stupid than nature made me.* "Here then, cries the bookseller, we should have you entirely in our power; unnatural, uneastern; quite out of character; erroneously sensible would be the whole cry; Sir, we should then hunt you down like a rat." *Head of my father!* said I, *sure there are but the two ways; the door must either be shut, or it must be open. I must either be natural or unnatural.* "Be what you will, we shall criticise you, returned the bookseller, and prove you a dunce in spite of your teeth. But, Sir, it is time that I should come to business. I have just now in the press an history of China; and if you will but put your name to it as the author, I shall repay the obligation with gratitude." *What, Sir,* replied I, *put my name to a work which I have not written! Never while I retain a proper respect for the public and myself.* The bluntness of my reply quite abated the ardour of the bookseller's conversation; and, after about half an hour's disagreeable reserve, he with some ceremony took his leave and withdrew. Adieu.

LETTER LII

The impossibility of distinguishing men in England, by their dress. Two instances of this.

To the same.

IN all other countries, my dear Fum Hoam, the rich are distinguished by their dress. In Persia, China, and most parts of Europe, those who are possessed of much gold or silver, put some of it upon their cloaths; but in England, those who carry much upon their cloaths, are remarked for having but little in their pockets. A tawdry outside is regarded as a badge of poverty, and those who can sit at home, and glote over their thousands in silent satisfaction, are generally found to do it in plain cloaths.

This diversity of thinking from the rest of the world which prevails here, I was first at a loss to account for; but am since informed that it was introduced by an intercourse between them and their neighbours the French; who, whenever they came in order to pay those islanders a visit, were generally very well dressed, and very poor, daubed with lace, but all the gilding on the outside. By this means laced cloaths have been brought so much into contempt, that at present even their Mandarines are ashamed of finery.

I must own myself a convert to English simplicity; I am no more for ostentation of wealth than of learning; the person who in company should pretend to be wiser than others, I am apt to regard as illiterate and ill bred; the person whose cloaths are extremely fine, I am too apt to consider as not being possessed of any superiority of fortune, but resembling those Indians who are found to wear all the gold they have in the world in a bob at the nose.

I was lately introduced into a company of the best dressed men I have seen since my arrival. Upon entering the room, I was struck with awe at the grandeur of the different dresses. That personage, thought I, in blue and gold, must be some Emperor's son; that, in green and silver, a Prince of the blood; he, in embroidered scarlet, a prime minister; all first rate noblemen, I suppose, and well looking noblemen too. I sate for some time with that uneasiness which conscious inferiority produces in the ingenuous mind, all attention to their discourse. However, I found their conversation more vulgar than I could have expected from personages of such distinction: if these, thought I to myself, be Princes, they are the most stupid Princes I have ever conversed with: yet still I continued to venerate their dress; for dress has a kind of mechanical influence on the mind.

My friend in black indeed did not behave with the same deference, but contradicted the finest of them all in the most peremptory tones of contempt. But I had scarce time to wonder at the imprudence of his conduct, when I found occasion to be equally surprized at the absurdity of theirs; for upon the entry of a middle-aged man, dressed in a cap, dirty shirt and boots, the whole circle seemed diminished of their former importance, and contended who should be first to pay their obeysance to the stranger. They somewhat resembled a circle of Kalmucs offering incense to a bear.

Eager to know the cause of so much seeming contradiction, I whispered my friend out of the room, and found that the august company consisted of no other than a dancing master, two fiddlers, and a third rate actor, all assembled in order to make a set at country dances, as the middle-aged gentleman whom I saw enter was a squire from the country, and desirous of learning the new manner of footing, and smoothing up the rudiments of his rural minuet.

I was no longer surprized at the authority which my friend assumed among them, nay, was even displeased (pardon my eastern education) that he had not kicked every creature of them down stairs. "What, said I, shall a set of such paltry fellows dress themselves up like sons of kings, and claim even the transitory respect of half an hour. There should be some law to restrain so manifest a breach of privilege; they should go from house to house, as in China, with the instruments of their profession strung round their necks; by this means we might be able to distinguish and treat them in a stile of becoming contempt." Hold, my friend, replied my companion, were your reformation to take place, as dancing masters and fiddlers now mimic gentlemen in appearance, we should then find our fine gentlemen conforming to theirs. A beau might be introduced to a lady of fashion with a fiddle case hanging at his neck by a red ribbon; and, instead of a cane, might carry a fiddle stick. Tho' to be as dull as a first rate dancing master might be used with proverbial justice; yet, dull as he is, many a fine gentleman sets him up as the proper standard of politeness, copies not only the pert vivacity of his air, but the flat insipidity of his conversation. In short, if you make a law against dancing masters imitating the fine gentleman, you should with as much reason enact, That no fine gentleman shall imitate the dancing master.

After I had left my friend, I made towards home, reflecting as I went upon the difficulty of distinguishing men by their appearance. Invited, however, by the freshness of the evening, I did not return directly, but went to ruminate on what had passed in a public garden belonging to the city. Here, as I sate upon one of the benches, and felt the pleasing sympathy which nature in bloom inspires, a disconsolate figure, who sate on the other end of the seat, seemed no way to enjoy the serenity of the season.

His dress was miserable beyond description; a thread-bare coat of the rudest materials; a shirt, though clean, yet extremely coarse; hair that seemed to have been long unconscious of the comb; and all the rest of his equipage impressed with the marks of genuine poverty.

As he continued to sigh, and testify every symptom of despair, I was naturally led, from a motive of humanity, to offer comfort and assistance. You know my heart; and that all who are miserable may claim a place there. The pensive stranger at first declined any conversation; but at last perceiving a peculiarity in my accent and manner of thinking, he began to unfold himself by degrees.

I now found that he was not so very miserable as he at first appeared; upon my offering him a small piece of money, he refused my favour, yet without appearing displeased at my intended generosity. It is true he sometimes interrupted the conversation with a sigh, and talked pathetically of neglected merit; yet still I could perceive a serenity in his countenance, that, upon a closer inspection, bespoke inward content.

Upon a pause in the conversation I was going to take my leave, when he begged I would favour him with my company home to supper. I was surprized at such a demand from a person of his appearance; but willing to indulge curiosity, I accepted his invitation; and though I felt some repugnance at being seen with one who appeared so very wretched, went along with seeming alacrity.

Still as he approached nearer home, his good humour proportionably seemed to encrease. At last he stopped, not at the gate of an hovel, but of a magnificent palace! When I cast my eyes upon all the sumptuous elegance which every where presented upon entering, and then when I looked at my seeming miserable conductor, I could scarce think that all this finery belonged to him; yet in fact it did. Numerous servants ran through the apartments with silent assiduity; several ladies of beauty and magnificently dressed came to welcome his return; a most elegant supper was provided; in short, I found the person, whom a little before I had sincerely pitied, to be in reality a most refined epicure; *One who courted contempt abroad, in order to feel with keener gust the pleasure of preeminence at home.* Adieu.

LETTER LIV

The character of an important trifler.

From the same.

THO' naturally pensive, yet I am fond of gav company, and take every opportunity of thus dismissing the mind from duty. From this motive I am often found in the centre of a crowd; and wherever pleasure is to be sold, am always a purchaser. In those places, without being remarked by any, I join in whatever goes forward, work my passions into a similitude of frivolous earnestness, shout as they shout, and condemn as they happen to disapprove. A mind thus sunk for a while below its natural standard, is qualified for stronger flights, as those first retire who would spring forward with greater vigour.

Attracted by the serenity of the evening, my friend and I lately went to gaze upon the company in one of the public walks near the city. Here we sauntred together for some time, either praising the beauty of such as were handsome, or the dresses of such as had nothing else to recommend them. We had gone thus deliberately forward for some time, when stopping on a sudden, my friend caught me by the elbow, and led me out of the public walk; I could perceive by the quickness of his pace, and by his frequently looking behind, that he was attempting to avoid somebody who followed; we now turned to the right, then to the left; as we went forward he still went faster, but in vain; the person whom he attempted to escape, hunted us through every doubling, and gained upon us each moment; so that at last we fairly stood still, resolving to face what we could not avoid.

Our pursuer soon came up, and joined us with all the familiarity of an old acquaintance. *My dear Drybone*, cries he, shaking my friend's hand, *where have you been hiding this half a century? Positively I had fancied you were gone down to cultivate matrimony and your estate in the country*. During the reply, I had an opportunity of surveying the appearance of our new companion; his hat was pinch'd up with peculiar smartness; his looks were pale, thin, and sharp; round his neck he wore a broad black ribbon, and in his bosom a buckle studded with glass; his coat was trimmed with tarnish'd twist; he wore by his side a sword with a black hilt, and his stockings of silk, though newly wash'd, were grown yellow by long service. I was so much engaged with the peculiarity of his dress, that I attended only to the latter part of my friend's reply, in which he complimented Mr. Tibbs on the taste of his cloaths, and the bloom in his countenance, *Psha, psha, Will,* cried the figure, *no more of that if you love me, you know I hate flattery, on my soul I do; and yet to be sure an intimacy with the great will improve one's appearance, and a course of venison will fatten; and yet faith I despise the great as much as you do; but there are a great many damn'd honest fellows among them; and we must not quarrel with one half, because the other wants weeding. If they were all such as my lord Mudler, one of the most good-natured creatures that ever squeezed a lemon, I should myself be among the number of their admirers. I was yesterday to dine at the Duchess of Piccadilly's, My lord was there. Ned, says he to me, Ned, says he, I'll hold gold to silver I can tell where you were poaching last night. Poaching my lord, says I; faith you have missed already; for I staid at home, and let the girls poach for me. That's my way; I take a fine woman as some animals do their prey; stand still, and swoop, they fall into my mouth.*

Ah, Tibbs, thou art an happy fellow, cried my companion with looks of infinite pity, I hope your fortune is as much improved as your understanding in such company? *Improved,* reply'd the other; *You shall know,—but let it go no further,—a great secret——five hundred a year to begin with.——My Lord's word of honour for it—His Lordship took me down in his own Chariot yesterday, and we had a tete-a-tete dinner in the country; where we talked of nothing else.* I fancy you forget, sir, cried I, you told us but this moment of your dining yesterday in town! *Did I say so,* replied he, cooly, *to be sure if I said so; it was so—Dined in town: egad now I do remember, I did dine in town; but I dined in the country too; for you must know, my boys, I eat two dinners. By the bye, I am grown as nice as the Devil in my eating. I'll tell you a pleasant affair about that, we were a select party of us to dine at Lady Grogram's, an affected piece, but let it go no farther; a secret: well, there happened to be no Assafœtida in the sauce to a turkey, upon which, says I, I'll hold a thousand guineas, and say done first, that—But dear Dry-*

bone, you are an honest creature, lend me half-a-crown for a minute or two, or so, just till—But hearkee, ask me for it the next time we meet, or it may be twenty to one but I forget to pay you.

When he left us, our conversation naturally turned upon so extraordinary a character. His very dress, cries my friend, is not less extraordinary than his conduct. If you meet him this day you find him in rags, if the next in embroidery. With those persons of distinction, of whom he talks so familiarly, he has scarce a coffee-house acquaintance. However, both for interests of society, and perhaps for his own, heaven has made him poor, and while all the world perceive his wants, he fancies them concealed from every eye. An agreeable companion because he understands flattery, and all must be pleased with the first part of his conversation, though all are sure of its ending with a demand on their purse. While his youth countenances the levity of his conduct, he may thus earn a precarious subsistance, but when age comes on, the gravity of which is incompatible with buffoonery, then will he find himself forsaken by all. Condemned in the decline of life to hang upon some rich family whom he once despised, there to undergo all the ingenuity of studied contempt, to be employed only as a spy upon the servants, or a bug-bear to fright the children into obedience. Adieu.

LETTER LV

His character continued: With that of his wife, his house, and furniture.

To the Same.

I AM apt to fancy I have contracted a new acquaintance whom it will be no easy matter to shake off. My little beau yesterday overtook me again in one of the publick walks, and slapping me on the shoulder, saluted me with an air of the most perfect familiarity. His dress was the same as usual, except that he had more powder in his hair, wore a dirtier shirt, a pair of temple spectacles,[1] and his hat under his arm.

As I knew him to be an harmless amusing little thing, I could not return his smiles with any degree of severity; so we walked forward on terms of the utmost intimacy, and in a few minutes discussed all the usual topics preliminary to particular conversation.

The oddities that marked his character, however, soon began to appear; he bowed to several well dressed persons, who, by their manner of returning the compliment, appeared perfect strangers. At intervals he drew out a pocket book, seeming to take memorandums before all the company, with much importance and assiduity. In this manner he led me through the length of the whole walk, fretting at his absurdities, and fancying myself laughed at not less than him by every spectator.

When we were got to the end of our procession, *Blast me*, cries he, with an air of vivacity, *I never saw the park so thin in my life before; there's no company at all to day. Not a single face to be seen.* No company, interrupted I peevishly; no company where there is such a crowd; why man, there's too much. What are the thousand that have been laughing at us but company! *Lord, my dear*, returned he with the utmost good humour, *you seem immensely chagrined; but, blast me, when the world laughs at me, I laugh at the world, and so we are even. My Lord Trip, Bill Squash, the Creolian, and I sometimes make a party at being ridiculous; and so we say and do a thousand things for the joke sake. But I see you are grave, and if you are for a fine grave sentimental companion, you shall dine with me and my wife to day, I must insist on 't; I'll introduce you to Mrs. Tibbs, a Lady of as elegant qualifications as any in nature; she was bred, but that's between ourselves, under the inspection of the Countess of All-night. A charming body of voice, but no more of*

[1] [Spectacles with side pieces that gripped the temples instead of hooking over the ears.]

that, she shall give us a song. You shall see my little girl too, Carolina Wilhelma Amelia Tibbs, a sweet pretty creature; I design her for my Lord Drumstick's eldest son, but that's in friendship, let it go no farther; she's but six years old, and yet she walks a minuet, and plays on the guittar immensely already. I intend she shall be as perfect as possible in every accomplishment. In the first place I'll make her a scholar; I'll teach her Greek myself, and learn that language purposely to instruct her; but let that be a secret.

Thus saying, without waiting for a reply, he took me by the arm and hauled me along. We passed through many dark alleys and winding ways; for, from some motives to me unknown, he seemed to have a particular aversion to every frequented street; at last, however, we got to the door of a dismal looking house in the outlets of the town, where he informed me he chose to reside for the benefit of the air.

We entered the lower door, which ever seemed to lie most hospitably open; and I began to ascend an old and creaking stair-case, when, as he mounted to shew me the way, he demanded, whether I delighted in prospects, to which answering in the affirmative, *Then*, says he, *I shall shew you one of the most charming in the world out of my windows; we shall see the ships sailing, and the whole country for twenty miles round, tip top, quite high. My Lord Swamp would give ten thousand guineas for such a one; but as I sometimes pleasantly tell him, I always love to keep my prospects at home, that my friends may see me the oftener.*

By this time we were arrived as high as the stairs would permit us to ascend, till we came to what he was facetiously pleased to call the first floor down the chimney; and knocking at the door, a voice from within demanded, who's there? My conductor answered, that it was him. But this not satisfying the querist, the voice again repeated the demand: to which he answered louder than before; and now the door was opened by an old woman with cautious reluctance.

When we were got in, he welcomed me to his house with great ceremony, and turning to the old woman, asked where was her lady? "Good troth, replied she, in a peculiar dialect, she's washing your twa shirts at the next door, because they have taken an oath against lending out the tub any longer." *My two shirts*, cries he in a tone that faultered with confusion, *what does the ideot mean?* "I ken what I mean well enough, replied the other, she's washing your twa shirts at the next door, because——" *Fire and fury, no more of thy stupid explanations*, cried he.—*Go and inform her we have got company. Were that Scotch hag to be for ever in my family, she would never learn politeness, nor forget that absurd poisonous accent of hers, or testify the smallest specimen of breeding or high life; and yet it is very surprizing too, as I had her from a parliament man, a friend of mine, from the highlands, one of the politest men in the world; but that's a secret.*

We waited some time for Mrs. Tibbs's arrival, during which interval I had a full opportunity of surveying the chamber and all its furniture; which consisted of four chairs with old wrought bottoms, that he assured me were his wife's embroidery; a square table that had been once japanned, a cradle, in one corner, a lumbering cabinet in the other; a broken shepherdess, and a mandarine without an head, were stuck over the chimney; and round the walls several paltry, unframed pictures, which he observed, were all his own drawing: *What do you think, Sir, of that head in the corner, done in the manner of Grisoni? there's the true keeping in it; its my own face, and though there happens to be no likeness, a countess offered me an hundred for its fellow; I refused her, for, hang it, that would be mechanical, you know.*

The wife at last made her appearance, at once a slattern and a coquet; much emaciated, but still carrying the remains of beauty. She made twenty apologies for being seen in such an odious dishabille, but hoped to be excused, as she had staid out all night at the gardens with the countess, who was excessively fond of the *horns*. "And, indeed, my dear, added she, turning to her husband, his lordship drank your health in a bumper." *Poor Jack*, cries he, *a dear good-natured creature, I know he loves me; but I hope, my dear, you have given orders for dinner; you need make no great preparations neither, there are but three of us, something elegant, and little will do; a turbot, an ortolan, or a ——. Or what do you think, my dear*, interrupts the wife, *of a nice pretty bit of ox cheek, piping hot, and dressed with a little of my own sauce.—The very thing*, replies he, *it will eat best with some smart bottled beer; but be sure to let's have the sauce his Grace was so fond of. I hate your immense loads of meat, that is country all over; extreme disgusting to those who are in the least acquainted with high life.*

By this time my curiosity began to abate, and my appetite to encrease; the company of fools may at first make us smile, but at last never fails of rendering us melancholy. I therefore pretended to recollect a prior engagement, and after having shewn my respect to the house, according to the fashion of the English, by giving the old servant a piece of money at the door, I took my leave. Mr. Tibbs assuring me, that dinner, if I staid, would be ready at least in less than two hours.

LETTER LVIII

A Visitation dinner described.

To the same.

As the man in black takes every opportunity of introducing me to such company as may serve to indulge my speculative temper, or gratify my curiosity; I was by his influence lately invited to a *visitation* dinner. To understand this term, you must know, that it was formerly the custom here for the principal priests to go about the country once a year, and examine upon the spot whether those of subordinate orders did their duty, or were qualified for the task; whether their temples were kept in proper repair, or the laity pleased with their administration.

Though a visitation of this nature was very useful, yet it was found to be extremely troublesome, and for many reasons utterly inconvenient; for as the principal priests were obliged to attend at court, in order to solicit preferment, it was impossible they could at the same time attend in the country, which was quite out of the road to promotion: if we add to this the gout, which has been time immemorial a clerical disorder here, together with the bad wine, and ill dressed provisions that must infallibly be served up by the way, it was not strange that the custom has been long discontinued. At present, therefore, every head of the church, instead of going about to visit his priests, is satisfied if his priests come in a body once a year to visit him; by this means the duty of half a year is dispatched in a day. When assembled, he asks each in his turn how they have behaved, and are liked; upon which, those who have neglected their duty, or are disagreeable to their congregation, no doubt accuse themselves, and tell him all their faults; for which he reprimands them most severely.

The thoughts of being introduced into a company of philosophers and learned men, (for as such I conceived them) gave me no small pleasure; I expected our entertainment would resemble those sentimental banquets so finely described by Xenophon and Plato; I was hoping some Socrates would be brought in from the door, in order to harangue upon divine love; but as for eating and drinking I had prepared myself to be disappointed in that particular. I was apprized, that fasting and temperance were tenets strongly recommended to the professors of Christianity; and I had seen the frugality and mortification of the priests of the east: so that I expected an entertainment where we should have much reasoning, and little meat.

Upon being introduced, I confess I found no great signs of

mortification in the faces or persons of the company. However, I imputed their florid looks to temperance, and their corpulency to a sedentary way of living. I saw several preparations indeed for dinner, but none for philosophy. The company seemed to gaze upon the table with silent expectation; but this I easily excused. Men of wisdom, thought I, are ever slow of speech; they deliver nothing unadvisedly. *Silence*, says Confucius, *is a friend that will never betray*. They are now probably inventing maxims, or hard sayings, for their mutual instruction, when some one shall think proper to begin.

My curiosity was now wrought up to the highest pitch; I impatiently looked round to see if any were going to interrupt the mighty pause; when, at last, one of the company declared, that there was a sow in his neighbourhood that farrowed fifteen pigs at a litter. This I thought a very preposterous beginning: but just as another was going to second the remark, dinner was served, which interrupted the conversation for that time.

The appearance of dinner, which consisted of a variety of dishes, seemed to diffuse new chearfulness upon every face; so that I now expected the philosophical conversation to begin, as they improved in good humour. The principal priest, however, opened his mouth, with only observing, that the venison had not been kept enough, though he had given strict orders for having it killed ten days before. *I fear*, continued he, *it will be found to want the true heathy flavour; you will find nothing of the original wildness in it.* A priest, who sate next him, having smelt it and wiped his nose: "Ah, my good lord, cries he, you are too modest, it is perfectly fine; every body knows that no body understands keeping venison with your Lordship." "Ay, and partridges too, interrupted another; I never find them right any where else." His Lordship was going to reply, when a third took off the attention of the company, by recommending the pig as inimitable. "I fancy, my Lord, continues he, it has been smothered in its own blood." "If it has been smothered in its blood, cried a facetious member, helping himself, we'll now smother it in egg sauce." This poignant piece of humour produced a long loud laugh, which the facetious brother observing, and now that he was in luck, willing to second his blow, assured the company he would tell them a good story about that: "As good a story, cries he, bursting into a violent fit of laughter himself, as ever you heard in your lives; there was a farmer of my parish, who used to sup upon wild ducks and flummery; so this farmer—*Doctor Marrowfat*, cries his Lordship, interrupting him, *give me leave to drink your health*—so being fond of wild ducks and flummery—*Doctor*, adds a gentleman who sate next him, *let me advise you to a wing of this turkey;*—so this farmer being fond —*Hob nob*, *Doctor*, *which do you chuse*, *white or red?*—So being fond of wild ducks and flummery;—*take care of your band*, *Sir*, *it may dip in the gravy*. The Doctor, now looking round, found not a single *eye* disposed to listen; wherefore calling for a glass of wine, he gulped down the disappointment and the tale in a bumper.

The conversation now began to be little more than a rhapsody of exclamations; as each had pretty well satisfied his own appetite, he now found sufficient time to press others. *Excellent*, *the very thing; let me recommend the pig*, *do but taste the bacon; never eat a better thing in my life; exquisite*, *delicious*. This edifying discourse continued thro' three courses, which lasted as many hours, till every one of the company were unable to swallow or utter any thing more.

It is very natural for men who are abridged in one excess, to break into some other. The clergy here, particularly those who are advanced in years, think if they are abstemious with regard to women and wine, they may indulge their other appetites without censure. Thus some are found to rise in the morning only to a consultation with their cook about dinner, and when that has been swallowed, make no other use of their faculties (if they have any) but to ruminate on the succeeding meal.

A debauch in wine is even more pardonable than this, since one glass insensibly leads on to another, and instead of sateing whets the appetite. The progressive steps to it are chearful and seducing; the grave are animated, the melancholy relieved, and there is even classic authority to countenance the excess. But in eating after nature is once satisfied every additional morsel brings stupidity and distempers with it, and as one of their own poets expresses it,

> The soul subsides, and wickedly inclines,
> To seem but mortal, even in sound divines.[1]

Let me suppose, after such a meal as this I have been describing, while all the company are sitting in lethargic silence round the table, grunting under a load of soup, pig, pork, and bacon; let me suppose, I say, some hungry beggar, with looks of want, peeping through one of the windows, and thus addressing the assembly, *Prithee, pluck those napkins from your chins; after nature is satisfied all that you eat extraordinary is my property, and I claim it as mine. It was given you in order to relieve me, and not to oppress yourselves. How can they comfort or instruct others who can scarce feel their own existence, except from the unsavoury returns of an ill digested meal. But though neither you nor the cushions you sit upon will hear me, yet the world regards the excesses of its teachers with a prying eye, and notes their conduct with double severity.* I know no other answer any one of the company could make to such an expostulation, but this: "Friend, you talk of our losing a character, and being disliked by the world; well, and supposing all this to be true, what then! who cares for the world? We'll preach for the world, and the world shall pay us for preaching, whether we like each other or not."

[1] [Pope's *Second Satire of the Second Book of Horace Paraphrased*, lines 79–80.]

LETTER LIX

The Chinese philosopher's son escapes with the beautiful captive from slavery.

From Hingpo to Lien Chi Altangi, by the way of Moscow.

You will probably be pleased to see my letter dated from Terki, a city which lies beyond the bounds of the Persian empire: here, blessed with security, with all that is dear, I double my raptures, by communicating them to you; the mind sympathizing with the freedom of the body, my whole soul is dilated in gratitude, love, and praise.

Yet were my own happiness all that inspired my present joy, my raptures might justly merit the imputation of self-interest; but when I think that the beautiful Zelis is also free, forgive my triumph when I boast of having rescued from captivity the most deserving object upon earth.

You remember the reluctance she testified at being obliged to marry the tyrant she hated. Her compliance at last was only feigned, in order to gain time to try some future means of escape. During the interval between her promise and the intended performance of it, she came undiscovered one evening to the place where I generally retired after the fatigues of the day; her appearance was like that of an aerial genius, when it descends to minister comfort to undeserved distress; the mild lustre of her eye served to banish my timidity; her accents were sweeter than the eccho of some distant symphony. "Unhappy stranger, said she, in the Persian language, you here perceive one more wretched than thyself; all this solemnity of preparation, this elegance of dress, and the number of my attendants, serve but to encrease my miseries; if you have courage to rescue an unhappy woman from approaching ruin, and our detested tyrant, you may depend upon my future gratitude." I bowed to the ground, and she left me filled with rapture and astonishment. Night brought no rest, nor could the ensuing morning calm the anxieties of my mind. I projected a thousand methods for her delivery; but each, when strictly examined, appeared impracticable; in this uncertainty the evening again arrived, and I placed myself on my former station in hopes of a repeated visit. After some short expectation, the bright perfection again appeared; I bowed, as before, to the ground; when raising me up she observed, that the time was not to be spent in useless ceremony; she observed that the day following was appointed for the celebration of her nuptials, and that something was to be done that very night for our mutual deliverance. I offered with the utmost humility to pursue whatever scheme she should direct; upon which she proposed that instant to scale the garden wall, adding, that she had prevailed upon a female slave, who was now waiting at the appointed place, to assist her with a ladder.

Pursuant to this information I led her trembling to the place appointed; but instead of the slave we expected to see, Mostadad himself was there awaiting our arrival; the wretch in whom we confided, it seems, had betrayed our design to her master, and he now saw the most convincing proofs of her information. He was just going to draw his sabre, when a principle of avarice repressed his fury, and he resolved, after a severe chastisement, to dispose of me to another master, in the mean time ordering me to be confined in the strictest manner, and the next day to receive an hundred blows on the soles of my feet.

When the morning came I was led out in order to receive the punishment, which, from the severity with which it is generally inflicted upon slaves, is worse even than death.

A trumpet was to be a signal for the solemnization of the nuptials of Zelis, and for the infliction of my punishment. Each ceremony to me equally dreadful were just going to begin, when we were informed that a large party of Circassian Tartars had invaded the town, and were laying all in ruin. Every person now thought only of saving himself; I instantly unloosed the cords with which I was bound, and seizing a scymetar from one of the slaves who had not courage to resist me, flew to the women's apartment where Zelis was confined, dressed out for the intended nuptials. I bade her follow me without delay; and going forward, cut my way through eunuchs, who made but a faint resistance. The whole city was now a scene of conflagration and terror; every person was willing to save himself, unmindful of others. In this confusion seizing upon two of the fleetest coursers in the stables of Mostadad, we fled northward towards the kingdom of Circassia. As there were several others flying in the same manner, we passed without notice, and in three days arrived at Terki, a city that lies in a valley within the bosom of the frowning mountains of Caucasus.

Here, free from every apprehension of danger, we enjoy all those satisfactions which are consistent with virtue; though I find my heart at intervals give way to unusual passions, yet such is my admiration for my fair companion, that I lose even tenderness in distant respect. Though her person demands particular regard even among the beauties of Circassia, yet is her mind far more lovely. How very different is a woman who thus has cultivated her understanding, and been refined into delicacy of sentiment, from the daughters of the east, whose education is only formed to improve the person, and make them more tempting objects of prostitution! Adieu.

LETTER LX

The history of the beautiful captive.

From Hingpo to Lien Chi Altangi, by the way of Moscow.

WHEN sufficiently refreshed after the fatigues of our precipitate flight, my curiosity, which had been restrained by the appearance of immediate danger, now began to revive: I longed to know by what distressful accidents my fair fugitive became a captive, and could not avoid testifying a surprize how so much beauty could be involved in the calamities from whence she had been so lately rescued.

Talk not of personal charms, cried she with emotion, since to them I owe every misfortune: look round on the numberless beauties of the country where we are; and see how nature has poured its charms upon every face, and yet by this profusion heaven would seem to shew how little it regards such a blessing, since the gift is lavished upon a nation of prostitutes.

I perceive you desire to know my story, and your curiosity is not so great as my impatience to gratify it: I find a pleasure in telling past misfortunes to any, but when my deliverer is pleased with the relation, my pleasure is prompted by duty.

"I* was born in a country far to the west, where the men are braver, and the women more fair than those of Circassia; where the valour of the hero is guided by wisdom, and where delicacy of sentiment points the shafts of female beauty. I was the only daughter of an officer in the army, the child of his age, and as he used fondly to express it, the only chain that bound him to the world, or made his life pleasing. His station procured him an acquaintance with men of greater rank or fortune than himself, and his regard for me induced him to bring me into every family where he was acquainted: Thus I was early taught all the elegancies and fashionable foibles of such as the world calls polite, and though without fortune myself, was taught to despise those who lived as if they were poor.

My intercourse with the great, and my affectation of

* This story bears a striking similitude to the real history of Miss S——d who accompanied Lady W——e, in her retreat near Florence, and which the editor had from her own mouth. [Lady W——e is almost certainly Lady Walpole, the wife of Horace Walpole's elder brother, Robert. She was later divorced, and married to Sewallis Shirley, whose father, Earl Ferrers, was hanged for the murder of his steward. She spent most of her life in Italy, entertaining as her lovers a succession of distinguished Italians and Frenchmen. She died at Pisa in 1781. I have been unable to identify Miss S——d.]

grandeur procured me many lovers; but want of fortune deterred them all from any other views than those of passing the present moment agreeably, or of meditating my future ruin. In every company I found myself addressed in a warmer strain of passion, than other ladies who were superior in point of rank and beauty; and this I imputed to an excess of respect, which in reality proceeded from very different motives.

Among the number of such as paid me their addresses, was a gentleman, a friend of my father, rather in the decline of life, with nothing remarkable either in his person or address to recommend him. His age which was about forty, his fortune which was moderate, and barely sufficient to support him, served to throw me off my guard, so that I considered him as the only sincere admirer I had.

Designing lovers in the decline of life are ever most dangerous. Skilled in all the weaknesses of the sex, they seize each favourable opportunity and by having less passion than youthful admirers, have less real respect, and therefore less timidity. This insidious wretch used a thousand arts to succeed in his base designs, all which I saw, but imputed to different views, because I thought it absurd to believe the real motives.

As he continued to frequent my father's, the friendship between them became every day greater; and at last from the intimacy with which he was received, I was taught to look upon him as a guardian and a friend. Though I never loved, yet I esteemed him; and this was enough to make me wish for an union, for which he seemed desirous, but to which he feigned several delays; while in the mean time, from a false report of our being married, every other admirer forsook me.

I was at last however awakened from the delusion, by an account of his being just married to another young lady with a considerable fortune. This was no great mortification to me, as I had always regarded him merely from prudential motives; but it had a very different effect upon my father, who, rash and passionate by nature, and besides stimulated by a mistaken notion of military honour, upbraided his friend in such terms, that a challenge was soon given and accepted.

It was about midnight when I was awakened by a message from my father, who desired to see me that moment. I rose with some surprize, and following the messenger, attended only by another servant, came to a field not far from the house, where I found him, the assertor of my honour, my only friend and supporter, the tutor and companion of my youth, lying on one side covered over with blood, and just expiring. No tears streamed down my cheeks, nor sigh escaped from my breast, at an object of such terror. I sat down, and supporting his aged head in my lap, gazed upon the gastly visage with an agony more poignant even than despairing madness. The servants were gone for more assistance. In this gloomy stillness of the night no sounds were heard but his agonizing respirations; no object was presented but his wounds, which still continued to stream. With silent anguish I hung over his dear face, and with my hands strove to stop the blood as it flowed from his wounds; he seemed at first insensible, but at last turning his dying eyes upon me, "*My dear*, *dear child*, cried he, *dear*, *though you have forgotten your own honour and stained mine*, *I will yet forgive you; by abandoning virtue you have undone me and yourself*, *yet take my forgiveness with the same compassion I wish heaven may pity me*." He expired. All my succeeding happiness fled with him. Reflecting that I was the cause of his death whom only I loved upon earth, accused of betraying the honour of his family with his latest breath: conscious of my own innocence, yet without even a possibility of vindicating it; without fortune or friends to relieve or pity me, abandoned to infamy and the wide censuring world, I called out upon the dead body that lay stretched before me, and in the agony of my heart asked why he could have left me thus? Why, my dear, my only pappa, why could you ruin me thus and yourself for ever! O pity, and return, since there is none but you to comfort me.

I soon found that I had real cause for sorrow; that I was to expect no compassion from my own sex, nor assistance from the other; and that reputation was much more useful in our commerce with mankind than really to deserve it. Wherever I came, I perceived myself received either with contempt or detestation; or whenever I was civilly treated, it was from the most base and ungenerous motives.

Thus driven from the society of the virtuous, I was at last, in order to dispell the anxieties of insupportable solitude, obliged to take up with the company of those whose characters were blasted like my own; but who perhaps deserved their infamy. Among this number was a lady of the first distinction, whose character the public thought proper to brand even with greater infamy than mine. A similitude of distress soon united us; I knew that general reproach had made her miserable; and I had learned to regard misery as an excuse for guilt. Though this lady had not virtue enough to avoid reproach, yet she had too much delicate sensibility not to feel it. She therefore proposed our leaving the country where we were born, and going to live in Italy, where our characters and misfortunes would be unknown. With this I eagerly complied, and we soon found ourselves in one of the most charming retreats in the most beautiful province of that inchanting country.

Had my companion chosen this as a retreat for injured virtue, an harbour where we might look with tranquility on the distant angry world, I should have been happy; but very different was her design; she had pitch'd upon this situation only to enjoy those pleasures in private, which she had not sufficient effrontery to satisfy in a more open manner. A nearer acquaintance soon shewed me the vicious part of her character; her mind as well as her body seemed formed only for pleasure; she was sentimental only as it served to protract the immediate enjoyment. Formed for society alone, she spoke infinitely better than she wrote, and wrote infinitely better than she lived. A person devoted to pleasure often leads the most miserable life imaginable; such was her case; she considered the natural moments of languor as insupportable, passed all her hours between rapture and anxiety; ever in an extreme of agony or of bliss. She felt a pain as sincere for want of appetite, as the starving wretch who wants a meal. In those intervals she usually kept her bed, and rose only when in expectation of some new enjoyment. The luxuriant air of the country, the romantic situation of her palace, and the genius of a people whose only happiness lies in sensual refinement, all contributed to banish the remembrance of her native country.

But tho' such a life gave her pleasure, it had a very different effect upon me; I grew every day more pensive, and my melancholy was regarded as an insult upon her good humour: I now perceived myself entirely unfit for all society; discarded from the good, and detesting the infamous, I seemed in a state of war with every rank of people: that virtue which should have been my protection in the world, was here my crime: in short, detesting life, I was determined to become a recluse, to leave a world where I found no pleasure that could allure me to stay. Thus determined, I embarked in order to go by sea to Rome, where I intended to take the veil; but even in so short a passage my hard fortune still attended me; our ship was taken by a Barbary corsair; the whole crew, and I among the number, being made slaves. It carries too much the air of romance to inform you of my distresses or obstinacy in this miserable state; it is enough to observe that I have been bought by several masters, each of whom perceiving my reluctance, rather than use violence, sold me to another, till it was my happiness to be at last rescued by you."

Thus ended her relation, which I have abridg'd, but as soon as we are arrived at Moscow, for which we intend to set out shortly, you shall be informed of all more particularly. In the mean time, the greatest addition to my happiness will be to hear of yours. Adieu.

LETTER LXVIII

Quacks ridiculed. Some particularly mentioned.

From Lien Chi Altangi, to Fum Hoam, first president of the Ceremonial Academy at Pekin, in China.

I FORMERLY acquainted thee, most grave *Fum*, with the excellence of the *English* in the art of healing. The *Chinese* boast their skill in pulses, the *Siamese* their botanical knowledge, but the *English* advertising physicians alone, of being the great restorers of health, the dispensers of youth, and the insurers of longevity. I can never enough admire the sagacity of this country for the encouragement given to the professors of this art; with what indulgence does she foster up those of her own growth, and kindly cherish those that come from abroad. Like a skilful gardener she invites them from every foreign climate to herself. Here every great exotic strikes root as soon as imported, and feels the genial beam of favour; while the mighty metropolis, like one vast munificent dunghill, receives them indiscriminately to her breast, and supplies each with more than native nourishment.

In other countries the physician pretends to cure disorders in the lump; the same doctor who combats the gout in the toe, shall pretend to prescribe for a pain in the head, and he who at one time cures a consumption, shall at another give drugs for a dropsy. How absurd and ridiculous! this is being a mere jack of all trades. Is the animal machine less complicated than a brass pin? Not less than ten different hands are required to make a pin; and shall the body be set right by one single operator?

The *English* are sensible of the force of this reasoning; they have therefore one doctor for the eyes, another for the toes; they have their sciatica doctors, and inoculating doctors; they have one doctor who is modestly content with securing them from bugbites, and five hundred who prescribe for the bite of mad dogs.

The learned are not here retired with vicious modesty from public view; for every dead wall is covered with their names, their abilities, their amazing cures, and places of abode. Few patients can escape falling into their hands, unless blasted by lightening, or struck dead with some sudden disorder: it may sometimes happen, that a stranger who does not understand *English*, or a countryman who cannot read, dies without ever hearing of the vivifying drops, or restorative electuary; but for my part, before I was a week in town, I had learned to bid the whole catalogue of disorders defiance, and was perfectly acquainted with the names and the medicines of every great man, or great woman of them all.

But as nothing pleases curiosity more than anecdotes of the great, however minute or trifling, I must present you, inadequate as my abilities are to the subject, with some account of those personages who lead in this honourable profession.

The first upon the list of glory is doctor *Richard Rock*, F. U. N. This great man is short of stature, is fat, and waddles as he walks. He always wears a white three-tailed wig nicely combed, and frizzed upon each cheek. Sometimes he carries a cane, but a hat never; it is indeed very remarkable, that this extraordinary personage should never wear an hat, but so it is he never wears an hat. He is usually drawn at the top of his own bills, sitting in his arm-chair, holding a little bottle between his finger and thumb, and surrounded with rotten teeth, nippers, pills, pacquets, and gallypots. No man can promise fairer nor better than he; for, as he observes, *Be your disorder never so far gone, be under no uneasiness, make yourself quite easy, I can cure you.*

The next in fame, though by some reckoned of equal pretensions, is doctor *Timothy Franks*, F. O. G. H. living in a place called the *Old Bailey*. As *Rock* is remarkably squab, his great rival *Franks* is as remarkably tall. He was born in the year of the christian æra 1692, and is, while I now write, exactly sixty-eight years, three months, and four days old. Age, however, has no ways impaired his usual health and vivacity, I am told, he generally walks with his breast open. This gentleman, who is of a mixed reputation, is particularly remarkable for a becoming assurance, which carries him gently through life; for, except doctor *Rock*, none are more blest with the advantages of face than doctor *Franks*.

And yet the great have their foibles as well as the little. I am almost ashamed to mention it. Let the foibles of the great rest in peace. Yet I must impart the whole to my friend. These two great men are actually now at variance; yes, my dear *Fum Hoam*, by the head of our grandfather, they are now at variance like mere men, mere common mortals. The champion *Rock* advises the world to beware of bog trotting quacks, while *Franks* retorts the wit and the sarcasm (for they have both a world of wit) by fixing on his rival the odious appellation of *Dumplin Dick*. He calls the serious doctor *Rock*, *Dumplin Dick!* Head of *Confucius*, what profanation! *Dumplin Dick!* What a pity, ye powers, that the learned, who were born mutually to assist in enlightening the world, should thus differ among themselves, and make even the profession ridiculous! Sure the world is wide enough, at least, for two great personages to figure in; men of science should leave controversy to the little world below them; and then we might see *Rock* and *Franks* walking together hand in hand, smiling onward to immortality.

Next to these is doctor *Walker*, preparator of his own medicines. This gentleman is remarkable for an aversion to quacks; frequently cautioning the public to be careful into what hands they commit their safety: by which he would insinuate that if they do not employ him alone, they must be undone. His public spirit is equal to his success. Not for himself, but his country, is the gally-pot prepared and the drops sealed up with proper directions for any part of the town or country. All this is for his country's good: so that he is now grown old in the practice of physic and virtue; and to use his own elegance of expression, *There is not such another medicine as his in the world again.*

This, my friend, is a formidable triumvirate; and yet, formidable as they are, I am resolved to defend the honour of *Chinese* physic against them all. I have made a vow to summon doctor *Rock* to a solemn disputation in all the mysteries of the profession, before the face of every *Philomath*, student in astrology, and member of the learned societies. I adhere to, and venerate the doctrines of old *Wang-shu-ho*. In the very teeth of opposition I will maintain,* *That the heart is the son of the liver, which has the kidneys for its mother, and the stomach for its wife.* I have therefore drawn up a disputation challenge, which is to be sent speedily, to this effect:

I, *Lien Chi Altangi*, **D. M. R. P.** native of *Honan* in *China*, to *Richard Rock*, F. U. N. native of *Garbage-alley* in *Wapping*, defiance. Though, Sir, I am perfectly sensible of your importance, though no stranger to your studies in the paths of nature, yet there may be many things in the art of physic with which you are yet unacquainted. I know full well a doctor thou art, great *Rock*, and so am I. Wherefore I challenge, and do hereby invite you to a trial of learning upon hard problems, and knotty physical points. In this debate we will calmly investigate the whole theory and practice of medicine, botany and chymistry; and I invite all the philomaths, with many of the lecturers in medicine, to be present at the dispute: which, I hope, will be carried on with due decorum, with proper gravity, and as befits men of erudition and science, among each other. But before we meet face to face, I would thus publickly, and in the face of the whole world, desire you to answer me one question; I ask it with the same earnestness with which you have often solicited the public; answer me, I say, at once, without having recourse to your physical dictionary, which of those three disorders, incident to the human

* See Du Halde, vol. II. fol. p. 185.

body, is the most fatal, the *syncope*, *parenthesis*, or *apoplexy*? I beg your reply may be as public as this my demand.* I am, as hereafter may be, your admirer, or your rival. Adieu.

LETTER LXIX

The fear of mad dogs ridiculed.

To the same.

INDULGENT nature seems to have exempted this island from many of those epidemic evils which are so fatal in other parts of the world. A want of rain but for a few days beyond the expected season in China, spreads famine, desolation, and terror, over the whole country; the winds that blow from the brown bosom of the western desart are impregnated with death in every gale; but in this fortunate land of Britain, the husbandman ever sows in joyful expectation.

But tho' the nation be exempt from real evils, think not, my friend, that it is more happy on this account than others. They are afflicted, it is true, with neither famine nor pestilence, but then there is a disorder peculiar to the country, which every season makes strange ravages among them; it spreads with pestilential rapidity, and infects almost every rank of people; what is still more strange the natives have no name for this peculiar malady, tho' well known to foreign physicians by the appellation of *Epidemic terror*.

A season is never known to pass in which the people are not visited by this cruel calamity in one shape or another, seemingly different, tho' ever the same; one year it issues from a baker's shop in the shape of a sixpenny loaf, the next it takes the appearance of a comet with a fiery tail, a third it threatens like a flat-bottomed boat, and a fourth it carries consternation at the bite of a mad dog. The people, when once infected,

* The day after this was published the editor received an answer, in which the doctor seems to be of opinion, that the apoplexy is most fatal.

lose their relish for happiness, saunter about with looks of despondence, ask after the calamities of the day, and receive no comfort but in heightening each others distress. It is insignificant how remote or near, how weak or powerful the object of terror may be, when once they resolve to fright and be frighted, the meerest trifles sow consternation and dismay, each proportions his fears not to the object, but to the dread he discovers in the countenance of others; for when once the fermentation is begun, it goes on of itself, tho' the original cause be discontinued which first set it in motion.

A dread of mad dogs is the *epidemic terror* which now prevails, and the whole nation is at present actually groaning under the malignity of its influence. The people sally from their houses with that circumspection which is prudent in such as expect a mad dog at every turning. The physician publishes his prescription, the beadle prepares his halter, and a few of unusual bravery arm themselves with boots and buff gloves, in order to face the enemy if he should offer to attack them. In short, the whole people stand bravely upon their defence, and seem by their present spirit to shew a resolution of not being tamely bit by mad dogs any longer.

Their manner of knowing whether a dog be mad or no, somewhat resembles the ancient European custom of trying witches. The old woman suspected was tied hand and foot and thrown into the water. If she swam, then she was instantly carried off to be burnt for a witch, if she sunk, then indeed she was acquitted of the charge, but drown'd in the experiment. In the same manner a crowd gather round a dog suspected of madness, and they begin by teizing the devoted animal on every side; if he attempts to stand upon the defensive and bite, then is he unanimously found guilty, for *a mad dog always snaps at every thing*; if, on the contrary, he strives to escape by running away, then he can expect no compassion, *for mad dogs always run straight forward before them.*

It is pleasant enough for a neutral being like me, who have no share in those ideal calamities, to mark the stages of this national disease. The terror at first feebly enters with a disregarded story of a little dog, that had gone through a neighbouring village, that was thought to be mad by several that had seen him. The next account comes, that a mastiff ran through a certain town, and had bit five geese, which immediately run mad, foamed at the bill, and died in great agonies soon after. Then comes an affecting history of a little boy bit in the leg, and gone down to be dipt in the salt water; when the people have sufficiently shuddered at that, they are next congealed with a frightful account of a man who was said lately to have died from a bite he had received some years before. This relation only prepares the way for another, still more hideous, as how the master of a family, with seven small children, were all bit by a mad lap dog, and how the poor father first perceived the infection by calling for a draught of water, where he saw the lap dog swimming in the cup.

When epidemic terror is thus once excited, every morning comes loaded with some new disaster; as in stories of ghosts each loves to hear the account, though it only serves to make him uneasy, so here each listens with eagerness, and adds to the tidings with new circumstances of peculiar horror. A lady for instance, in the country, of very weak nerves has been frighted by the barking of a dog; and this, alas! too frequently happens. The story soon is improved and spreads, that a mad dog had frighted a lady of distinction. These circumstances begin to grow terrible before they have reached the neighbouring village, and there the report is, that a lady of quality was *bit* by a mad mastiff. This account every moment gathers new strength and grows more dismal as it approaches the capital, and by the time it has arrived in town the lady is described, with wild eyes, foaming mouth, running mad upon all four, barking like a dog, biting her servants, and at last smothered between two beds by the advice of her doctors: while the mad mastiff is in the mean time ranging the whole country over, slavering at the mouth, and seeking whom he may devour.

My landlady, a good natured woman, but a little credulous, waked me some mornings ago before the usual hour with horror and astonishment in her looks; she desired me if I had any regard for my safety, to keep within; for a few days ago so dismal an accident had happened, as to put all the world upon their guard. A mad dog down in the country, she assured me, had bit a farmer, who soon becoming mad ran into his own yard, and bit a fine brindled cow; the cow quickly became as mad as the man, began to foam at the mouth, and raising herself up, walked about on her hind legs, sometimes barking like a dog, and sometimes attempting to talk like the farmer. Upon examining the grounds of this story, I found my landlady had it from one neighbour, who had it from another neighbour, who heard it from very good authority.

Were most stories of this nature thoroughly examined, it would be found that numbers of such as have been said to suffer were no way injured, and that of those who have been actually bitten, not one in a hundred was bit by a mad dog. Such accounts in general therefore only serve to make the people miserable by false terrors, and sometimes fright the patient into actual phrenzy, by creating those very symptoms, they pretended to deplore.

But even allowing three or four to die in a season of this terrible death (and four is probably too large a concession) yet still it is not considered, how many are preserved in their health and in their property by this devoted animal's services. The midnight robber is kept at a distance; the insidious thief is often detected, the healthful chace repairs many a worn constitution, and the poor man finds in his dog a willing assistant, eager to lessen his toil, and content with the smallest retribution.

A dog, says one of the English poets,[1] "is an honest creature, and I am a friend to dogs." Of all the beasts that graze the lawn or hunt the forest, a dog is the only animal, that leaving his fellows, attempts to cultivate the friendship of man; to man he looks in all his necessities with a speaking eye for assistance; exerts for him all the little service in his power with chearfulness and pleasure; for him bears famine and fatigue with patience and resignation; no injuries can abate his fidelity, no distress induce him to forsake his benefactor, studious to please, and fearing to offend, he is still an humble stedfast dependant, and in him alone fawning is not flattery. How unkind then to torture this faithful creature who has left the forest, to claim the protection of man; how ungrateful a return to the trusty animal for all its services. Adieu.

LETTER LXXI

The shabby beau, the man in black, the Chinese philosopher, &c. at Vaux-hall.

To the same.

THE People of *London* are as fond of walking as our friends at *Pekin* of riding; one of the principal entertainments of the citizens here in summer is to repair about nightfall to a garden not far from town, where they walk about, shew their best cloaths and best faces, and listen to a concert provided for the occasion.

I accepted an invitation a few evenings ago from my old friend, the man in black, to be one of a party that was to sup there, and at the appointed hour waited upon him at his lodgings. There I found the company assembled and expecting

[1] [Otway in *Venice Preserv'd*:

Jaffier. What's he that asks the Question?
Pierre. A Friend to Dogs, for they are honest Creatures,
And ne're betray their Masters; never fawn
On any that they love not.]

my arrival. Our party consisted of my friend in superlative finery, his stockings rolled, a black velvet waistcoat which was formerly new, and his grey wig combed down in imitation of hair. A pawn-broker's widow, of whom, by the bye, my friend was a professed admirer, dressed out in green damask, with three gold rings on every finger. Mr. *Tibbs* the second-rate beau, I have formerly described, together with his lady, in flimsy silk, dirty gauze instead of linnen, and an hat as big as an umbrello.

Our first difficulty was in settling how we should set out. Mrs. *Tibbs* had a natural aversion to the water, and the widow being a little in flesh, as warmly protested against walking, a coach was therefore agreed upon; which being too small to carry five, Mr. *Tibbs* consented to sit in his wife's lap.

In this manner therefore we set forward, being entertained by the way with the bodings of Mr. *Tibbs*, who assured us, he did not expect to see a single creature for the evening above the degree of a cheesemonger; that this was the last night of the gardens, and that consequently we should be pestered with the nobility and gentry from *Thames-street* and *Crooked-lane*, with several other prophetic ejaculations probably inspired by the uneasiness of his situation.

The illuminations began before we arrived, and I must confess, that upon entring the gardens, I found every sense overpaid with more than expected pleasure; the lights every where glimmering through the scarcely moving trees; the full-bodied consort bursting on the stillness of the night, the natural consort of the birds, in the more retired part of the grove, vying with that which was formed by art; the company gayly dressed looking satisfaction, and the tables spread with various delacacies, all conspired to fill my imagination with the visionary happiness of the *Arabian* lawgiver, and lifted me into an extasy of admiration. Head of *Confucius*, cried I to my friend, this is fine! this unites rural beauty with courtly magnificence, if we except the virgins of immortality that hang on every tree, and may be plucked at every desire, I don't see how this falls short of *Mahomet*'s *Paradise*! As for virgins, cries my friend, it is true, they are a fruit that don't much abound in our gardens here; but if ladies as plenty as apples in autumn, and as complying as any *hoüry* of them all can content you, I fancy, we have no need to go to heaven for Paradise.

I was going to second his remarks, when we were called to a consultation by Mr. *Tibbs* and the rest of the company, to know in what manner we were to lay out the evening to the greatest advantage. Mrs. *Tibbs* was for keeping the genteel walk of the garden, where she observed there was always the very best company; the widow, on the contrary, who came but once a season, was for securing a good standing place to see the water-works,[1] which she assured us would begin in less than an hour at farthest; a dispute therefore began, and as it was managed between two of very opposite characters, it threatned to grow more bitter at every reply. Mrs. *Tibbs* wondered how people could pretend to know the polite world who had received all their rudiments of breeding behind a compter; to which the other replied, that tho' some people sat behind compters, yet they could sit at the head of their own tables too, and carve three good dishes of hot meat whenever they thought proper, which was more than some people could say for themselves, that hardly knew a rabbet and onions from a green goose and gooseberries.

It is hard to say where this might have ended, had not the husband, who probably knew the impetuosity of his wife's disposition, proposed to end the dispute by adjourning to a

[1] [Not, apparently, fountains. Austin Dobson quotes the *Gentleman's Magazine* of August, 1765:

> A curious piece of machinery . . . representing a beautiful landscape in perspective, with a miller's house, a water-mill, and a cascade. The exact appearance of water is seen flowing down a declivity; and turning the wheel of the mill, it rises up in a foam at the bottom, and then glides away.]

box, and try if there was any thing to be had for supper that was supportable. To this we all consented, but here a new distress arose, Mr. and Mrs. *Tibbs* would sit in none but a genteel box, a box where they might see and be seen, one, as they expressed it, in the very focus of public view; but such a box was not easy to be obtained, for tho' we were perfectly convinced of our own gentility, and the gentility of our appearance, yet we found it a difficult matter to persuade the keepers of the boxes to be of our opinion; they chose to reserve genteel boxes for what they judged more genteel company.

At last however we were fixed, tho' somewhat obscurely, and supplied with the usual entertainment of the place. The widow found the supper excellent, but Mrs. *Tibbs* thought every thing detestable: come, come, my dear, cries the husband, by way of consolation, to be sure we can't find such dressing here as we have at lord Crump's or lady Crimp's; but for Vauxhall dressing it is pretty good; it is not their victuals indeed I find fault with, but their wine; their wine, cries he, drinking off a glass, indeed, is most abominable.

By this last contradiction the widow was fairly conquered in point of politeness. She perceived now that she had no pretensions in the world to taste, her very senses were vulgar, since she had praised detestable custard, and smacked at wretched wine; she was therefore content to yield the victory, and for the rest of the night to listen and improve. It is true, she would now and then forget herself, and confess she was pleased, but they soon brought her back again to miserable refinement. She once praised the painting of the box in which we were sitting, but was soon convinced that such paltry pieces ought rather to excite horror than satisfaction; she ventured again to commend one of the singers, but Mrs. *Tibbs* soon let her know, in the style of a connoisseur, that the singer in question had neither ear, voice, nor judgment.

Mr. *Tibbs* now willing to prove that his wife's pretensions to music were just, entreated her to favour the company with a song; but to this she gave a positive denial, for you know very well, my dear, says she, that I am not in voice to day, and when one's voice is not equal to one's judgment, what signifies singing; besides as there is no accompanyment, it would be but spoiling music. All these excuses however were over-ruled by the rest of the company, who, though one would think they already had music enough, joined in the intreaty. But particularly the widow, now willing to convince the company of her breeding, pressed so warmly that she seemed determined to take no refusal. At last then the lady complied, and after humming for some minutes, began with such a voice and such affectation, as I could perceive gave but little satisfaction to any except her husband. He sat with rapture in his eye, and beat time with his hand on the table.

You must observe, my friend, that it is the custom of this country, when a lady or gentleman happens to sing, for the company to sit as mute and motionless as statues. Every feature, every limb must seem to correspond in fixed attention, and while the song continues, they are to remain in a state of universal petrefaction. In this mortifying situation we had continued for some time, listening to the song, and looking with tranquility, when the master of the box came to inform us, that the water-works were going to begin. At this information I could instantly perceive the widow bounce from her seat; but correcting herself, she sat down again, repressed by motives of good breeding. Mrs. *Tibbs*, who had seen the water-works an hundred times, resolving not to be interrupted, continued her song without any share of mercy, nor had the smallest pity on our impatience. The widow's face, I own, gave me high entertainment; in it I could plainly read the struggle she felt between good breeding and curiosity; she talked of the water-works the whole evening before, and seemed to have come merely in order to see them; but then she could not bounce out in the very middle of a song, for that would be forfeiting all pretensions to high life, or high-lived company ever after: Mrs. *Tibbs* therefore kept on singing, and we continued to listen, till at last, when the song was just concluded, the waiter came to inform us that the water-works were over!

The water-works over, cried the widow! the water-works over already, that's impossible, they can't be over so soon! It is not my business, replied the fellow, to contradict your ladyship, I'll run again and see; he went, and soon returned with a confirmation of the dismal tidings. No ceremony could now bind my friend's disappointed mistress, she testified her displeasure in the openest manner; in short, she now began to find fault in turn, and at last, insisted upon going home, just at the time that Mr. and Mrs. *Tibbs* assured the company, that the polite hours were going to begin, and that the ladies would instantaneously be entertained with the horns. Adieu.

LETTER LXXVII

The behaviour of a shop keeper and his journeyman.

To the same.

THE Shops of London are as well furnished as those of Pekin. Those of London have a picture hung at their door, informing the passengers what they have to sell, as those at Pekin have a board to assure the buyer, that they have no intentions to cheat him.

I was this morning to buy silk for a night-cap; immediately upon entering the mercer's shop, the master and his two men, with wigs plaistered with powder, appeared to ask my commands. They were certainly the civillest people alive; if I but looked, they flew to the place, where I cast my eye; every motion of mine sent them running round the whole shop for my satisfaction. I informed them that I wanted what was good, and they shewed me not less than forty pieces, and each was better than the former; the prettiest pattern in nature, and the fittest in the world for night-caps. My very good friend, said I to the mercer, you must not pretend to instruct me in silks, I know these in particular to be no better than your mere flimsy *Bungees*. *That may be*, cried the mercer, who I afterwards found had never contradicted a man in his life, *I can't pretend to say but they may; but I can assure you, my Lady Trail has had a sacque from this piece this very morning*. But friend, said I, though my Lady has chosen a sacque from it, I see no necessity that I should wear it for a night-cap. *That may be*, returned he again, *yet what becomes a pretty Lady, will at any time look well on a handsome Gentleman*. This short compliment was thrown in so very seasonably upon my ugly face, that even tho' I disliked the silk, I desired him to cut me off the pattern of a night-cap.

While this business was consigned to his journeyman, the master himself took down some pieces of silk still finer than any I had yet seen, and spreading them before me, *There*, cries he, *there's beauty, my Lord Snakeskin has bespoke the fellow to this for the birth-night this very morning; it would look charmingly in waistcoats*. But I don't want a waistcoat, replied I: *Not want a waistcoat*, returned the mercer; *then I would advise you to buy one; when waistcoats are wanted, you may depend upon it they will come dear. Always buy before you want, and you are sure to be well used, as they say in Cheapside*. There was so much justice in his advice, that I could not refuse taking it; besides, the silk, which was really a good one, encreased the temptation, so I gave orders for that too.

As I was waiting to have my bargains measured and cut, which I know not how, they executed but slowly; during the interval, the mercer entertained me with the modern manner of some of the nobility receiving company in their morning gowns; *Perhaps, Sir*, adds he, *you have a mind to see what kind of silk is universally worn*. Without waiting for my reply, he spreads a piece before me, which might be reckoned beautiful even in China. *If the nobility*, continues he, *were to know I sold this to any, under a Right Honourable, I should certainly lose their custom; you see, my Lord, it is at once rich, tastey, and quite the thing*. I am no Lord, interrupted I.—*I beg pardon*, cried he, *but be pleased to remember, when you intend buying a morning gown, that you had an offer from me of something worth money. Conscience, Sir, conscience is my way of dealing; you may buy a morning gown now, or you may stay till they become dearer and less fashionable, but it is not my business to advise.* In short, most reverend *Fum*, he persuaded me to buy a morning gown also, and would probably have persuaded me to have bought half the goods in his shop, if I had stayed long enough, or was furnished with sufficient money.

Upon returning home, I could not help reflecting with some astonishment, how this very man with such a confined education and capacity, was yet capable of turning me as he thought proper, and molding me to his inclinations! I knew he was only answering his own purposes, even while he attempted to appear solicitous about mine; yet by a voluntary infatuation, a sort of passion compounded of vanity and good nature, I walked into the snare with my eyes open, and put myself to future pain in order to give him immediate pleasure. The wisdom of the ignorant, somewhat resembles the instinct of animals; it is diffused in but a very narrow sphere, but within that circle it acts with vigour, uniformity, and success. Adieu.

LETTER LXXXVIII

The ladies advised to get husbands. A story to this purpose.

To the same.

As the instruction of the fair sex in this country is entirely committed to the care of foreigners, as their language-masters, music-masters, hair-frizzers, and governesses, are all from abroad, I had some intentions of opening a female academy myself, and made no doubt, as I was quite a foreigner, of meeting a favourable reception.

In this I intended to instruct the ladies in all the conjugal mysteries; wives should be taught the art of managing husbands, and maids the skill of properly chusing them; I would teach a wife how far she might venture to be sick without giving disgust, she should be acquainted with the great benefits of the cholic in the stomach, and all the thorough-bred insolence of fashion; maids should learn the secret of nicely distinguishing every competitor; they should be able to know the difference between a pedant and a scholar, a citizen and a prig, a squire and his horse, a beau and his monkey; but chiefly they should be taught the art of managing their smiles, from the contemptuous simper to the long laborious laugh.

But I have discontinued the project; for what would signify teaching ladies the manner of governing or chusing husbands, when marriage is at present so much out of fashion, that a lady is very well off, who can get any husband at all. Celibacy now prevails in every rank of life, the streets are crouded with old bachelors, and the houses with ladies who have refused good offers, and are never likely to receive any for the future.

The only advice, therefore, I could give the fair sex, as things stand at present, is to get husbands as fast as they can. There is certainly nothing in the whole creation, not even Babylon in ruins, more truly deplorable than a lady in the virgin bloom of sixty-three, or a battered unmarried beau, who squibs about from place to place, shewing his pig-tail wig and his ears. The one appears to my imagination in the form of a double night-cap, or a roll of pomatum, the other in the shape of an electuary, or a box of pills.

I would once more therefore advise the ladies to get husbands. I would desire them not to discard an old lover without very sufficient reasons, nor treat the new with ill-nature till they know him false; let not prudes alledge the falseness of the sex, coquets the pleasures of long courtship, or parents the necessary preliminaries of penny for penny. I have reasons that would silence even a casuist in this particular. In the first place, therefore, I divide the subject into fifteen heads, and then *sic argumentor*—but not to give you and myself the spleen, be contented at present with an Indian tale.

In a winding of the river Amidar, just before it falls into the Caspian sea, there lies an island unfrequented by the inhabitants of the Continent. In this seclusion, blest with all that wild uncultivated nature could bestow, lived a princess and her two daughters. She had been wrecked upon the coast while her children as yet were infants, who of consequence, though grown up, were entirely unacquainted with man. Yet, unexperienced as the young ladies were in the opposite sex, both early discovered symptoms, the one of prudery, the other of being a coquet. The eldest was ever learning maxims of wisdom and discretion from her mamma, while the youngest employed all her hours in gazing at her own face in a neighbouring fountain.

Their usual amusement in this solitude was fishing: Their mother had taught them all the secrets of the art; she shewed them which were the most likely places to throw out the line, what baits were most proper for the various seasons, and the best manner to draw up the finny prey, when they had hooked it. In this manner they spent their time, easy and innocent, till one day, the Princess being indisposed, desired them to go and catch her a sturgeon or a shark for supper, which she fancied might sit easy on her stomach. The daughters obeyed, and clapping on a gold fish, the usual bait, on those occasions, went and sat upon one of the rocks, letting the gilded hook glide down with the stream.

On the opposite shore, farther down, at the mouth of the river, lived a diver for pearls; a youth, who, by long habit in his trade, was almost grown amphibious; so that he could remain whole hours at the bottom of the water, without ever fetching breath. He happened to be at that very instant diving when the ladies were fishing with the gilded hook. Seeing therefore the bait, which to him had the appearance of real gold, he was resolved to seize the prize, but both his hands being already filled with pearl oysters, he found himself obliged to snap at it with his mouth: The consequence is easily imagined; the hook, before unperceived, was instantly fastened in his jaw, nor could he, with all his efforts, or his floundering, get free.

"Sister, cries the youngest Princess, I have certainly caught a monstrous fish; I never perceived any thing struggle so at the end of my line before; come, and help me to draw it in." They both now therefore assisted in fishing up the Diver on shore; but nothing could equal their surprize upon seeing him. "Bless my eyes, cries the prude, what have we got here; this is a very odd fish to be sure; I never saw any thing in my life look so queer; what eyes, what terrible claws, what a monstrous snout; I have read of this monster somewhere before, it certainly must be a *Tanlang* that eats women; let us throw it back into the sea where we found it."

The Diver in the mean time stood upon the beach, at the end of the line, with the hook in his mouth, using every art that he thought could best excite pity, and particularly looking extremely tender, which is usual in such circumstances. The coquet therefore, in some measure influenced by the innocence of his looks, ventured to contradict her companion. "Upon my word, sister, says she, I see nothing in the animal so very terrible as you are pleased to apprehend; I think it may serve well enough for a change. Always sharks, and sturgeons, and lobsters, and crawfish, make me quite sick. I fancy a slice of this nicely grilladed, and dressed up with shrimp sauce, would be very pretty eating. I fancy mamma would like a bit with pickles above all things in the world; and if it should not sit easy on her stomach, it will be time enough to discontinue it when found disagreeable, you know." "Horrid, cries the prude, would the girl be poisoned; I tell you it is a *Tanlang*; I have read of it in twenty places. It is every where described as the most pernicious animal that ever infested the ocean. I am certain it is the most insidious, ravenous creature in the world; and is certain destruction if taken internally." The youngest sister was now therefore obliged to submit: both assisted in drawing the hook with some violence from the Diver's jaw; and he finding himself at liberty, bent his breast against the broad wave and disappeared in an instant.

Just at this juncture the mother came down to the beach, to know the cause of her daughter's delay; they told her every circumstance, describing the monster they had caught. The old lady was one of the most discreet women in the world; she was called the black-eyed Princess, from two black eyes she had received in her youth, being a little addicted to boxing in her liquor. "Alas, my children, cries she, what have you done? the fish you caught was a man-fish; one of the most tame domestic animals in the world. We could have let him run and play about the garden, and he would have been twenty times more entertaining than our squirrel or monkey." "If that be all, says the young coquet, we will fish for him again. If that be all, I'll hold three tooth-picks to one pound of snuff, I catch him whenever I please." Accordingly they threw in their line once more, but, with all their gilding, and padling, and assiduity, they could never after catch the Diver. In this state of solitude and disappointment they continued for many years, still fishing, but without success; till, at last, the genius of the place, in pity to their distresses, changed the prude into a shrimp, and the coquet into an oyster. Adieu.

LETTER XC

The English subject to the spleen.

From the same.

WHEN the men of this country are once turned of thirty, they regularly retire every year at proper intervals to lie in of the *spleen*. The vulgar, unfurnished with the luxurious comforts of the soft cussion, down bed, and easy-chair, are obliged when the fit is on them, to nurse it up by drinking, idleness and ill-humour. In such dispositions, unhappy is the foreigner who happens to cross them; his long chin, tarnished coat, or pinched hat, are sure to receive no quarter. If they meet no foreigner however to fight with, they are in such cases generally content with beating each other.

The rich, as they have more sensibility, are operated upon with greater violence by this disorder. Different from the poor, instead of becoming more insolent, they grow totally unfit for opposition. A general here, who would have faced a culverin when well, if the fit be on him, shall hardly find courage to snuff a candle. An admiral, who could have opposed a broadside without shrinking, shall sit whole days in his chamber, mobbed up in double night-caps, shuddering at the intrusive breeze, and distinguishable from his wife only by his black beard and heavy eyebrows.

In the country this disorder mostly attacks the fair sex, in town it is most unfavourable to the men. A lady, who has pined whole years amidst cooing doves and complaining nightingales, in rural retirement, shall resume all her vivacity in one night at a city gaming-table; her husband who roar'd, hunted, and got drunk at home, shall grow splenetic in town in proportion to his wife's good humour. Upon their arrival in London, they exchange their disorders. In consequence of her parties and excursions, he puts on the furred cap and scarlet stomacher, and perfectly resembles an Indian husband, who when his wife is safely delivered, permits her to transact business abroad, while he undergoes all the formality of keeping his bed, and receiving all the condolence in her place.

But those who reside constantly in town, owe this disorder mostly to the influence of the weather. It is impossible to describe what a variety of transmutations an east wind shall produce; it has been known to change a Lady of fashion into a parlour couch; an Alderman into a plate of custards, and a dispenser of justice into a rat trap. Even Philosophers themselves are not exempt from its influence; it has often converted a Poet into a coral and bells, and a patriot Senator into a dumb waiter.

Some days ago I went to visit the man in black, and entered his house with that chearfulness, which the certainty of a favourable reception always inspires. Upon opening the door of his apartment, I found him with the most rueful face imaginable in a morning gown and flannel night-cap, earnestly employed in learning to blow the German flute. Struck with the absurdity of a man in the decline of life, thus blowing away all his constitution and spirits, even without the consolation of being musical; I ventured to ask what could induce him to attempt learning so difficult an instrument so late in life. To this he made no reply, but groaning, and still holding the flute to his lip, continued to gaze at me for some moments very angrily, and then proceeded to practise his gammut as before. After having produced a variety of the most hideous tones in nature; at last turning to me, he demanded, whether I did not think he had made a surprizing progress in two days? You see, continues he, I have got the Ambusheer[1] already, and as for fingering, my master tells me, I shall have that in a few lessons more. I was so much astonished with this instance of inverted ambition, that I knew not what to reply, but soon discerned the cause of all his absurdities; my friend was under

[1] [The *embouchure* or "mouthing" as distinct from the fingering of a wind instrument. This insular spelling of Goldsmith's seems to be unique.]

a metamorphosis by the power of spleen, and flute-blowing was unluckily become his adventitious passion.

In order therefore to banish his anxiety imperceptibly, by seeming to indulge it, I began to descant on those gloomy topics by which Philosophers often get rid of their own spleen, by communicating it; the wretchedness of a man in this life, the happiness of some wrought out of the miseries of others, the necessity that wretches should expire under punishment, that rogues might enjoy affluence in tranquility; I led him on from the inhumanity of the rich to the ingratitude of the beggar; from the insincerity of refinement to the fierceness of rusticity; and at last had the good fortune to restore him to his usual serenity of temper, by permitting him to expatiate upon all the modes of human misery.

"Some nights ago, says my friend, sitting alone by my fire, I happened to look into an account of the detection of a set of men called the thief-takers. I read over the many hideous cruelties of those haters of mankind, of their pretended friendship to wretches they meant to betray, of their sending men out to rob and then hanging them. I could not avoid sometimes interrupting the narrative by crying out, *Yet these are men!* As I went on, I was informed that they had lived by this practice several years, and had been enriched by the price of blood, *and yet*, cried I, *I have been sent into this world, and am desired to call these men my brothers!* I read that the very man who led the condemned wretch to the gallows, was he who falsely swore his life away; *and yet*, continued I, *that perjurer had just such a nose, such lips, such hands and such eyes as Newton.* I at last came to the account of the wretch that was searched after robbing one of the thief-takers of half a crown. Those of the confederacy knew that he had got but that single half crown in the world; after a long search therefore, which they knew would be fruitless, and taking from him the half crown, which they knew was all he had, one of the gang compassionately cried out, *Alas, poor creature let him keep all the rest he has got, it will do him service in Newgate, where we are sending him.* This was an instance of such complicated guilt and hypocrisy, that I threw down the book in an agony of rage, and began to think with malice of all the human kind. I sat silent for some minutes, and soon perceiving the ticking of my watch beginning to grow noisy and troublesome, I quickly placed it out of hearing, and strove to resume my serenity. But the watch-man soon gave me a second alarm. I had scarcely recovered from this, when my peace was assaulted by the wind at my window; and when that ceased to blow, I listened for death-watches in the wainscot. I now found my whole system discomposed, I strove to find a resource in philosophy and reason; but what could I oppose, or where direct my blow, when I could see no enemy to combat. I saw no misery approaching, nor knew any I had to fear, yet still I was miserable. Morning came, I sought for tranquility in dissipation, sauntered from one place of public resort to another, but found myself disagreeable to my acquaintance, and ridiculous to others. I tried at different times dancing, fencing, and riding, I solved geometrical problems, shaped tobacco-stoppers, wrote verses and cut paper. At last I placed my affections on music, and find, that earnest employment if it cannot cure, at least will palliate every anxiety." Adieu.

LETTER XCIII

The fondness of some, to admire the writings of lords, &c.

To the same.

It is surprizing what an influence titles shall have upon the mind, even though these titles be of our own making. Like children we dress up the puppets in finery, and then stand in astonishment at the plastic wonder. I have been told of a rat-catcher here, who strolled for a long time about the villages near town, without finding any employment; at last, however, he thought proper to take the title of his Majesty's Rat-catcher in ordinary, and this succeeded beyond his expectations; when it was known that he caught rats at court, all were ready to give him countenance and employment.

But of all the people, they who make books seem most perfectly sensible of the advantage of titular dignity. All seem convinced, that a book written by vulgar hands, can neither instruct nor improve; none but Kings, Chams, and Mandarines, can write with any probability of success. If the titles inform me right, not only Kings and Courtiers, but Emperors themselves in this country, periodically supply the press.

A man here who should write, and honestly confess that he wrote for bread, might as well send his manuscript to fire the baker's oven; not one creature will read him; all must be court-bred poets, or pretend at least to be court-bred, who can expect to please. Should the caitiff fairly avow a design of emptying our pockets and filling his own, every reader would instantly forsake him; even those, who write for bread themselves, would combine to worry him, perfectly sensible, that his attempts only served to take the bread out of their mouths.

And yet this silly prepossession the more amazes me, when I consider, that almost all the excellent productions in wit that have appeared here, were purely the offspring of necessity; their Drydens, Butlers, Otways, and Farquhars, were all writers for bread. Believe me, my friend, hunger has a most amazing faculty of sharpening the genius; and he who with a full belly, can think like a hero, after a course of fasting, shall rise to the sublimity of a demi-god.

But what will most amaze, is, that this very set of men, who are now so much depreciated by fools, are however the very best writers they have among them at present. For my own part, were I to buy an hat, I would not have it from a stocking-maker, but an hatter; were I to buy shoes, I should not go to the taylor's for that purpose. It is just so with regard to wit: did I, for my life, desire to be well served, I would apply only to those who made it their trade, and lived by it. You smile at the oddity of my opinion; but be assured, my friend, that wit is in some measure mechanical; and that a man long habituated to catch at even its resemblance, will at last be happy enough to possess the substance: by a long habit of writing he acquires a justness of thinking, and a mastery of manner, which holiday-writers, even with ten times his genius, may vainly attempt to equal.

How then are they deceived, who expect from title, dignity, and exterior circumstance, an excellence, which is in some measure acquired by habit, and sharpened by necessity; you have seen, like me, many literary reputations promoted by the influence of fashion, which have scarce survived the possessor; you have seen the poor hardly earn the little reputation they acquired, and their merit only acknowledged when they were incapable of enjoying the pleasures of popularity; such, however, is the reputation worth possessing, that which is hardly earned is hardly lost. Adieu.

LETTER XCIV

The philosopher's son is again separated from his beautiful companion.

From Hingpo in Moscow, to Lien Chi Altangi in London.

WHERE will my disappointments end? Must I still be doomed to accuse the severity of my fortune, and shew my constancy in distress rather than moderation in prosperity? I had at least hopes of conveying my charming companion safe from the reach of every enemy, and of again restoring her to her native soil. But those hopes are now no more.

Upon leaving Terki, we took the nearest road to the dominions of Russia. We passed the Ural mountains covered in eternal snow, and traversed the forests of Ufa, where the prowling bear and shrieking hyena keep an undisputed possession. We next embarked upon the rapid river Bulija, and made the best of our way to the banks of the Wolga, where it waters the fruitful valleys of Casan.

There were two vessels in company properly equipped and armed in order to oppose the Wolga pyrates, who we were informed infested this river. Of all mankind these pyrates are the most terrible. They are composed of the criminals and outlawed peasants of Russia, who fly to the forests that lie along the banks of the Wolga for protection. Here they join in parties, lead a savage life, and have no other subsistence but plunder. Being deprived of houses, friends, or a fixed habitation, they become more terrible even than the tyger, and as insensible to all the feelings of humanity. They neither give quarter to those they conquer, nor receive it when overpowered themselves. The severity of the laws against them serve to encrease their barbarity, and seem to make them a neutral species of beings between the wildness of the lion and the subtilty of the man. When taken alive their punishment is hideous. A floating gibbet is erected, which is let run down with the stream; here upon an iron hook stuck under their ribs, and upon which the whole weight of their body depends, they are left to expire in the most terrible agonies; some being thus found to linger several days successively.

We were but three days voyage from the confluence of this river into the Wolga, when we perceived at a distance behind us an armed barque coming up with the assistance of sails and oars, in order to attack us. The dreadful signal of death was hung upon the mast, and our captain with his glass could easily discern them to be pyrates. It is impossible to express our consternation on this occasion; the whole crew instantly came together to consult the properest means of safety. It was therefore soon determined to send off our women and valuable commodities in one of our vessels, and that the men should stay in the other and boldly oppose the enemy. This resolution was soon put into execution, and I now reluctantly parted from the beautiful Zelis for the first time since our retreat from

Persia. The vessel in which she was disappeared to my longing eyes, in proportion as that of the pyrates approached us: They soon came up; but, upon examining our strength, and perhaps sensible of the manner in which we had sent off our most valuable effects, they seemed more eager to pursue the vessel we had sent away than attack us. In this manner they continued to harrass us for three days; still endeavouring to pass us without fighting. But, on the fourth day, finding it entirely impossible, and despairing to seize the expected booty, they desisted from their endeavours, and left us to pursue our voyage without interruption.

Our joy on this occasion was great; but soon a disappointment more terrible, because unexpected, succeeded. The barque, in which our women and treasure were sent off, was wrecked upon the banks of the Wolga, for want of a proper number of hands to manage her, and the whole crew carried by the peasants up the country. Of this however we were not sensible till our arrival at Moscow; where expecting to meet our separated barque, we were informed of its misfortune, and our loss. Need I paint the situation of my mind on this occasion? Need I describe all I feel, when I despair of beholding the beautiful Zelis more! Fancy had dressed the future prospect of my life in the gayest colouring; but one unexpected stroke of fortune has robbed it of every charm. Her dear idea mixes with every scene of pleasure, and without her presence to enliven it, the whole becomes tedious, insipid, insupportable. I will confess, now that she is lost, I will confess, I loved her; nor is it in the power of time, or of reason, to erase her image from my heart. Adieu.

LETTER XCVII

Almost every subject of literature, has been already exhausted.

From Lien Chi Altangi, to Fum Hoam, first president of the Ceremonial Academy at Pekin, in China.

It is usual for the booksellers here, when a book has given universal pleasure upon one subject, to bring out several more upon the same plan; which are sure to have purchasers and readers from that desire which all men have to view a pleasing object on every side. The first performance serves rather to awake than satisfy attention; and when that is once moved, the slightest effort serves to continue its progression; the merit of the first diffuses a light sufficient to illuminate the succeeding efforts; and no other subject can be relished, till that is exhausted. A stupid work coming thus immediately in the train of an applauded performance, weans the mind from the object of its pleasure; and resembles the sponge thrust into the mouth of a discharged culverin, in order to adapt it for a new explosion.

This manner, however, of drawing off a subject, or a peculiar mode of writing to the dregs, effectually precludes a revival of that subject or manner for some time for the future; the sated reader turns from it with a kind of literary nausea; and though the titles of books are the part of them most read, yet he has scarce perseverance enough to wade through the title page.

Of this number I own myself one; I am now grown callous to several subjects, and different kinds of composition: whether such originally pleased I will not take upon me to determine; but at present I spurn a new book merely upon seeing its name in an advertisement; nor have the smallest curiosity to look beyond the first leaf, even though in the second the author promises his own face neatly engraved on copper.

I am become a perfect Epicure in reading; plain beef or

solid mutton will never do. I am for a Chinese dish of bear's claws and bird's nests. I am for sauce strong with assafœtida, or fuming with garlic. For this reason there are an hundred very wise, learned, virtuous, well-intended productions that have no charms for me. Thus, for the soul of me, I could never find courage nor grace enough to wade above two pages deep into *Thoughts upon God and Nature*, or *Thoughts upon Providence*, or *Thoughts upon Free Grace*, or indeed into Thoughts upon any thing at all. I can no longer meditate with Meditations for every day in the year; Essays upon divers subjects cannot allure me, though never so interesting; and as for Funeral Sermons, or even Thanksgiving Sermons, I can neither weep with the one, nor rejoice with the other.

But it is chiefly in gentle poetry, where I seldom look farther than the title. The truth is, I take up books to be told something new; but here, as it is now managed, the reader is told nothing. He opens the book, and there finds very good words, truly, and much exactness of rhyme, but no information. A parcel of gaudy images pass on before his imagination like the figures in a dream; but curiosity, induction, reason, and the whole train of affections are fast asleep. The *jocunda et idonea vitæ*; those sallies which mend the heart while they amuse the fancy, are quite forgotten: so that a reader who would take up some modern applauded performances of this kind, must, in order to be pleased, first leave his good sense behind him, take for his recompence and guide bloated and compound epithet, and dwell on paintings, just indeed, because laboured with minute exactness.

If we examine, however, our internal sensations, we shall find ourselves but little pleased with such laboured vanities; we shall find that our applause rather proceeds from a kind of contagion caught up from others, and which we contribute to diffuse, than from what we privately feel. There are some subjects of which almost all the world perceive the futility; yet all combine in imposing upon each other, as worthy of praise. But chiefly this imposition obtains in literature, where men publicly contemn what they relish with rapture in private, and approve abroad what has given them disgust at home. The truth is, we deliver those criticisms in public which are supposed to be best calculated not to do justice to the author, but to impress others with an opinion of our superior discernment.

But let works of this kind, which have already come off with such applause, enjoy it all. It is neither my wish to diminish, as I was never considerable enough to add to their fame. But for the future I fear there are many poems, of which I shall find spirits to read but the title. In the first place, all odes upon winter, or summer, or autumn; in short all odes, epodes, and monodies whatsoever, shall hereafter be deemed too polite, classical, obscure, and refined, to be read, and entirely above human comprehension. Pastorals are pretty enough—for those that like them—but to me Thyrsis is one of the most insipid fellows I ever conversed with; and as for Corridon, I do not chuse his company. Elegies and epistles are very fine to those to whom they are addressed; and as for epic poems, I am generally able to discover the whole plan in reading the two first pages.

Tragedies, however, as they are now made, are good instructive moral *sermons* enough; and it would be a fault not to be pleased with *good things*. There I learn several great truths; as, that it is impossible to see into the ways of futurity; that punishment always attends the villain, that love is the fond soother of the human breast, that we should not resist heaven's will, for in resisting heaven's will, heaven's will is resisted; with several other sentiments equally new, delicate and striking. Every new tragedy therefore I shall go to see; for reflections of this nature make a tolerable harmony, when mixed up with a proper quantity of drum, trumpet, thunder, lightening, or the scene shifter's whistle. Adieu.

LETTER XCIX

A visit from the little Beau. The indulgence with which the fair sex are treated, in several parts of Asia.

From the same.

I LATELY received a visit from the little beau, who I found had assumed a new flow of spirits with a new suit of cloaths. Our discourse happened to turn upon the different treatment of the fair sex here and in Asia, with the influence of beauty in refining our manners and improving our conversation.

I soon perceived he was strongly prejudiced in favour of the Asiatic method of treating the sex, and that it was impossible to persuade him, but that a man was happier who had four wives at his command, than he who had only one. "It is true, cries he, your men of fashion in the East are slaves, and under some terrors of having their throats squeezed by a bow-string; but what then, they can find ample consolation in a seraglio; they make indeed an indifferent figure in conversation abroad, but then they have a seraglio to console them at home. I am told they have no balls, drums, nor operas, but then they have got a seraglio; they may be deprived of wine and French cookery, but they have a seraglio; a seraglio, a seraglio, my dear creature, wipes off every inconvenience in the world.

"Besides, I am told, your Asiatic beauties are the most convenient women alive, for they have no souls; positively there is nothing in nature I should like so much as ladies without souls; soul, here, is the utter ruin of half the sex. A girl of eighteen shall have soul enough to spend an hundred pounds in the turning of a trump. Her mother shall have soul enough to ride a sweepstake match at an horse-race; her maiden aunt shall have soul enough to purchase the furniture of a whole toy shop, and others shall have soul enough to behave as if they had no souls at all."

With respect to the soul, interrupted I, the Asiatics are much kinder to the fair sex than you imagine; instead of one soul,

Fohi the idol of China gives every woman three, the Bramines give them fifteen; and even Mahomet himself, no where excludes the sex from Paradise. Abulfeda reports, that an old woman one day importuning him to know what she ought to do in order to gain Paradise? *My good Lady*, answered the Prophet, *old women never get there*; what, never get to Paradise, returned the matron, in a fury! Never, says he, for they always grow young by the way.

No, Sir, continued I, the men of Asia behave with more deference to the sex than you seem to imagine. As you of Europe say grace, upon sitting down to dinner, so it is the custom in China to say grace, when a man goes to bed to his wife, *And may I die*, returned my companion, *but a very pretty ceremony; for seriously, Sir, I see no reason why a man should not be as grateful in one situation as in the other. Upon honour, I always find myself much more disposed to gratitude, on the couch of a fine woman, than upon sitting down to a sirloin of beef.*

Another ceremony, said I, resuming the conversation, in favour of the sex amongst us, is the bride's being allowed after marriage, *her three days of freedom*. During this interval a thousand extravagancies are practised by either sex. The lady is placed upon the nuptial bed, and numberless monkey tricks are played round to divert her. One gentleman smells her perfumed handkerchief, another attempts to untie her garters, a third pulls off her shoe to play hunt the slipper, another pretends to be an ideot, and endeavours to raise a laugh by grimacing; in the mean time, the glass goes briskly about, till ladies, gentlemen, wife, husband, and all are mixed together in one inundation of arrack punch.

"Strike me dumb, deaf, and blind, cried my companion, but very pretty; there's some sense in your Chinese ladies condescentions; but among us, you shall scarce find one of the whole sex that shall hold her good humour for three days together. No later than yesterday I happened to say some civil things to a citizen's wife of my acquaintance, not because I loved, but because I had charity; and what do you think was the tender creature's reply! Only that she detested my pigtail wig, high heeled shoes, and sallow complexion. That is all. Nothing more! Yes, by the heavens, though she was more ugly than an unpainted actress, I found her more insolent than a thorough bred woman of quality."

He was proceeding in this wild manner, when his invective was interrupted, by the man in black, who entered the apartment, introducing his neice, a young lady of exquisite beauty. Her very appearance was sufficient to silence the severest satyrist of the sex; easy without pride, and free without impudence, she seemed capable of supplying every sense with pleasure; her looks, her conversation were natural and unconstrained; she had neither been taught to languish nor ogle, to laugh without a jest, or sigh without sorrow. I found that she had just returned from abroad, and had been conversant in the manners of the world. Curiosity prompted me to ask several questions, but she declined them all. I own I never found myself so strongly prejudiced in favour of apparent merit before; and could willingly have prolonged our conversation, but the company after some time withdrew. Just, however, before the little beau took his leave he called me aside, and requested I would change him a twenty pound bill, which as I was incapable of doing, he was contented with borrowing half a crown. Adieu.

LETTER CIII

The Chinese Philosopher begins to think of quitting England.

*From Lien Chi Altangi to ***, Merchant in Amsterdam.*

I HAVE just received a letter from my son, in which he informs me of the fruitlessness of his endeavours to recover the lady with whom he fled from Persia. He strives to cover under the appearance of fortitude a heart torn with anxiety and disappointment. I have offered little consolation; since that but too frequently feeds the sorrow which it pretends to deplore, and strengthens the impression, which nothing but the external rubs of time and accident can thoroughly efface.

He informs me of his intentions of quitting Moscow the first opportunity, and travelling by land to Amsterdam. I must therefore, upon his arrival, entreat the continuance of your friendship; and beg of you to provide him with proper directions for finding me in London. You can scarcely be sensible of the joy I expect upon seeing him once more: the ties between the father and the son among us of China are much more closely drawn than with you of Europe.

The remittances sent me from Argun to Moscow came in safety, I cannot sufficiently admire that spirit of honesty, which prevails through the whole country of Siberia: perhaps the savages of that desolate region are the only untutored people of the globe, that cultivate the moral virtues, even without knowing that their actions merit praise. I have been told surprising things of their goodness, benevolence, and generosity; and the uninterrupted commerce between China and Russia serves as a collateral confirmation.

Let us, says the Chinese law-giver, *admire the rude virtues of the ignorant, but rather imitate the delicate morals of the polite*. In the country where I reside, though honesty and benevolence be not so congenial: yet art supplies the place of nature. Though here every vice is carried to excess; yet every virtue is practised also with unexampled superiority. A city like this is the soil for great virtues and great vices; the villain can soon improve here in the deepest mysteries of deceiving; and the practical philosopher can every day meet new incitements to mend his honest intentions. There are no pleasures, sensual or sentimental, which this city does not produce; yet, I know not how, I could not be content to reside here for life. There is something so seducing in that spot in which we first had existence, that nothing but it can please; whatever vicissitudes we experience in life, however we toil, or wheresoever we wander, our fatigued wishes still recur to home for tranquillity, we long to die in that spot which first gave us birth, and in that pleasing expectation opiate every calamity.

You now therefore perceive that I have some intentions of leaving this country; and yet my designed departure fills me with reluctance and regret. Though the friendships of travellers are generally more transient than vernal snows, still I feel an uneasiness at breaking the connections I have formed since my arrival; particularly I shall have no small pain in leaving my usual companion, guide, and instructor.

I shall wait for the arrival of my son before I set out. He shall be my companion in every intended journey for the future; in his company I can support the fatigues of the way with redoubled ardour, pleased at once with conveying instruction, and exacting obedience. Adieu.

LETTER CVI

Funeral elegies written upon the great, ridiculed. A specimen of one.

From Lien Chi Altangi, to Fum Hoam, first president of the Ceremonial Academy at Pekin, in China.

IT was formerly the custom here, when men of distinction died, for their surviving acquaintance to throw each a slight present into the grave. Several things of little value were made use of for that purpose; perfumes, reliques, spices, bitter herbs, camomile, wormwood, and verses. This custom however is almost discontinued; and nothing but verses alone are now lavished on such occasions; an oblation which they suppose may be interred with the dead, without any injury to the living.

Upon the death of the great therefore, the poets and undertakers are sure of employment. While one provides the long cloak, black staff, and mourning coach, the other produces the pastoral or elegy, the monody or apotheosis. The nobility need be under no apprehensions, but die as fast as they think proper, the poet and undertaker are ready to supply them; these can find metaphorical tears and family escutcheons at half an hour's warning; and when the one has soberly laid the body in the grave, the other is ready to fix it figuratively among the stars.

There are several ways of being poetically sorrowful on such occasions. The bard is now some pensive youth of science, who sits deploring among the tombs; again he is Thyrsis, complaining in a circle of harmless sheep. Now Britannia sits upon her own shore, and gives a loose to maternal tenderness; at another time, Parnassus, even the mountain Parnassus, gives way to sorrow, and is bathed in tears of distress.

But the most usual manner is this: Damon meets Menalcas, who has got a most gloomy countenance. The shepherd asks his friend, whence that look of distress? to which the other replies, that Pollio is no more. If that be the case then, cries Damon, let us retire to yonder bower at some distance off, where the cypress and the jessamine add fragrance to the breeze; and let us weep alternately for Pollio, the friend of shepherds, and the patron of every muse. Ah, returns his fellow shepherd, what think you rather of that grotto by the fountain side; the murmuring stream will help to assist our complaints, and a nightingale on a neighbouring tree will join her voice to the concert. When the place is thus settled, they begin: the brook stands still to hear their lamentations; the cows forget to graze; and the very tygers start from the forest with sympathetic concern. By the tombs of our ancestors, my dear Fum, I am quite unaffected in all this distress: the whole is liquid laudanum to my spirits; and a tyger of common sensibility has twenty times more tenderness than I.

But though I could never weep with the complaining shepherd, yet I am sometimes induced to pity the poet, whose trade is thus to make Demigods and Heroes for a dinner. There is not in nature a more dismal figure than a man who sits down to premeditated flattery; every stanza he writes tacitly reproaches the meanness of his occupation, till at last his stupidity becomes more stupid, and his dullness more diminutive.

I am amazed therefore that none have yet found out the secret of flattering the worthless, and yet of preserving a safe conscience. I have often wished for some method by which a man might do himself and his deceased patron justice, without being under the hateful reproach of self-conviction. After long lucubration, I have hit upon such an expedient; and send you the specimen of a poem upon the decease of a great man, in which the flattery is perfectly fine, and yet the poet perfectly innocent.

*On the Death of the Right Honourable ****

Ye muses, pour the pitying tear
For Pollio snatch'd away:
O had he liv'd another year!
——*He had not dy'd to-day.*

O, were he born to bless mankind,
In virtuous times of yore,
Heroes themselves had fallen behind!
——*Whene'er he went before.*

How sad the groves and plains appear,
And sympathetic sheep;
Even pitying hills would drop a tear!
——*If hills could learn to weep.*

His bounty in exalted strain
Each bard might well display:
Since none implor'd relief in vain!
——*That went reliev'd away.*

And hark! I hear the tuneful throng;
His obsequies forbid.
He still shall live, shall live as long
——*As ever dead man did.*

LETTER CVII

The English too fond of believing every report, without examination. A story of an incendiary to this purpose.

To the same.

It is the most usual method in every report, first to examine its probability, and then act as the conjuncture may require. The English, however, exert a different spirit in such circumstances; they first act, and, when too late, begin to examine. From a knowledge of this disposition, there are several here who make it their business to frame new reports at every convenient interval, all tending to denounce ruin both on their cotemporaries and their posterity. This denunciation is eagerly caught up by the public; away they fling to propagate the distress; sell out at one place, buy in at another, grumble at their governors, shout in mobs, and when they have thus, for some time, behaved like fools, sit down coolly to argue and talk wisdom, to puzzle each other with syllogism, and prepare for the next report that prevails, which is always attended with the same success.

Thus are they ever rising above one report only to sink into another. They resemble a dog in a well, pawing to get free. When he has raised his upper parts above water, and every spectator imagines him disengaged, his lower parts drag him down again and sink him to the nose; he makes new efforts to emerge, and every effort increasing his weakness, only tends to sink him the deeper.

There are some here, who, I am told, make a tolerable subsistence by the credulity of their countrymen: as they find the public fond of blood, wounds and death, they contrive political ruins suited to every month in the year; this month the people are to be eaten up by the French in flat-bottomed boats; the next by the soldiers, designed to beat the French back; now the people are going to jump down the gulph of luxury; and now nothing but an herring subscription can fish them up again. Time passes on; the report proves false; new circumstances produce new changes, but the people never change, they are persevering in folly.

In other countries those boding politicians would be left to fret over their own schemes alone, and grow splenetic without hopes of infecting others: But England seems to be the very region where spleen delights to dwell; a man not only can give an unbounded scope to the disorder in himself, but may, if he pleases, propagate it over the whole kingdom, with a certainty of success. He has only to cry out, that the government, the government is all wrong, that their schemes are leading to ruin, that Britons are no more, every good member of the commonwealth thinks it his duty, in such a case, to deplore the universal decadence with sympathetic sorrow, and, by fancying the constitution in a decay, absolutely to impair its vigour.

This people would laugh at my simplicity, should I advise them to be less sanguine in harbouring gloomy predictions, and examine cooly before they attempted to complain. I have just heard a story, which, though transacted in a private family, serves very well to describe the behaviour of the whole nation, in cases of threatened calamity. As there are public, so there are private incendiaries here. One of the last, either for the amusement of his friends, or to divert a fit of the spleen, lately sent a threatening letter to a worthy family in my neighbourhood, to this effect.

"SIR,

Knowing you to be very rich, and finding myself to be very poor, I think proper to inform you, that I have learned the secret of poisoning man, woman, and child, without danger of detection. Don't be uneasy, Sir, you may take your choice of being poisoned in a fortnight, or poisoned in a month, or poisoned in six weeks; you shall have full time to settle all your affairs. Though I'm poor, I love to do things like a gentleman. But, Sir, you must die; I have determined it within my own breast that you must die. Blood, Sir, blood is my trade; so I could wish you would this day six weeks take leave of your friends, wife, and family, for I cannot possibly allow you longer time. To convince you more certainly of the power of my art, by which you may know I speak truth, take this letter; when you have read it, tear off the seal, fold it up, and give it to your favourite Dutch mastiff that sits by the fire, he will swallow it, Sir, like a butter'd toast; in three hours four minutes after he has taken it, he will attempt to bite off his own tongue, and half an hour after burst asunder in twenty pieces. Blood, blood, blood; so no more at present from, Sir, your most obedient, most devoted humble servant to command till death."

You may easily imagine the consternation into which this letter threw the whole good-natured family. The poor man, to whom it was addressed, was the more surprised, as not knowing how he could merit such inveterate malice. All the friends of the family were convened; it was universally agreed, that it was a most terrible affair, and that the government should be solicited to offer a reward and a pardon: a fellow of this kind would go on poisoning family after family; and it was impossible to say where the destruction would end. In pursuance of these determinations the government was applied to; strict search was made after the incendiary, but all in vain. At last, therefore, they recollected that the experiment was not yet tried upon the dog; the Dutch mastiff was brought up, and placed in the midst of the friends and relations, the seal was torn off, the pacquet folded up with care, and soon they found to the great surprize of all——that the dog would not eat the letter. Adieu.

LETTER CVIII

The utility and entertainment which might result from a journey into the East.

To the same.

I HAVE frequently been amazed at the ignorance of almost all the European travellers, who have penetrated any considerable way eastward into Asia. They have been influenced either by motives of commerce or piety, and their accounts are such as might reasonably be expected from men of very narrow or very prejudiced education, the dictates of superstition or the result of ignorance. Is it not surprizing, that in such a variety of adventurers not one single philosopher should be found; for as to the travels of Gemelli, the learned are long agreed that the whole is but an imposture.[1]

There is scarce any country how rude or incultivated soever, where the inhabitants are not possessed of some peculiar secrets, either in nature or art, which might be transplanted with success; in Siberian Tartary, for instance, the natives extract a strong spirit from milk, which is a secret probably unknown to the chymists of Europe. In the most savage parts of India, they are possessed of the secret of dying vegetable substances scarlet; and of refining lead into a metal which, for hardness and colour, is little inferior to silver; not one of which secrets but would in Europe make a man's fortune. The power of the Asiatics in producing winds, or bringing down rain, the Europeans are apt to treat as fabulous, because they have no instances of the like nature among themselves; but they would have treated the secrets of gunpowder, and the mariner's compass, in the same manner, had they been told the Chinese used such arts before the invention was common with themselves at home.

Of all the English philosophers I most reverence *Bacon*,

[1] [Giovanni Francesco Gemelli-Careri (1651–1725). He travelled round the world at the age of forty. On his return he published an account of his travels, *Giro del Mondo* (Naples, 1699–1700), which was discredited by the Jesuits. Humboldt did not consider him an impostor.]

that great and hardy genius; he it is who allows of secrets yet unknown; who, undaunted by the seeming difficulties that oppose, prompts human curiosity to examine every part of nature, and even exhorts man to try whether he cannot subject the tempest, the thunder, and even earthquakes to human controll: O did a man of his daring spirit, of his genius, penetration, and learning travel to those countries which have been visited only by the superstitious and mercenary, what might not mankind expect: how would he enlighten the regions to which he travelled! And what a variety of knowledge and useful improvement would he not bring back in exchange!

There is probably no country so barbarous, that would not disclose all it knew, if it received from the traveller equivalent information; and I am apt to think, that a person, who was ready to give more knowledge than he received, would be welcome wherever he came. All his care in travelling should only be to suit his intellectual banquet to the people with whom he conversed; he should not attempt to teach the unlettered Tartar astronomy, nor yet instruct the polite Chinese in the ruder arts of subsistence; he should endeavour to improve the Barbarian in the secrets of living comfortably; and the inhabitant of a more refined country in the speculative pleasures of science. How much more nobly would a philosopher thus employed spend his time, than by sitting at home earnestly intent upon adding one star more to his catalogue; or one monster more to his collection; or still, if possible, more triflingly sedulous in the incatenation of fleas, or the sculpture of a cherry-stone.

I never consider this subject, without being surprized how none of those societies so laudably established in England for the promotion of arts and learning, have never thought of sending one of their members into the most eastern parts of Asia, to make what discoveries he was able. To be convinced of the utility of such an undertaking, let them but read the relations of their own travellers. It will be there found, that they are as often deceived themselves, as they attempt to deceive others. The merchant tells us perhaps the price of different commodities, the methods of baling them up, and the properest manner for an European to preserve his health in the country. The missioner, on the other hand, informs us, with what pleasure the country to which he was sent embraced christianity, and the numbers he converted; what methods he took to keep Lent in a region where there was no fish, or the shifts he made to celebrate the rites of his religion, in places where there was neither bread nor wine; such accounts, with the usual appendage of marriages and funerals, inscriptions, rivers, and mountains, make up the whole of an European traveller's diary; but as to all the secrets of which the inhabitants are possessed, those are universally attributed to magic; and when the traveller can give no other account of the wonders he sees performed, he very contentedly ascribes them to the power of the devil.

It was an usual observation of *Boyle*, the English chymist, that if every artist would but discover what new observations occurred to him in the exercise of his trade, philosophy would thence gain innumerable improvements. It may be observed, with still greater justice, that if the useful knowledge of every country, howsoever barbarous, was gleaned by a judicious observer, the advantages would be inestimable. Are there not even in Europe, many useful inventions known or practised, but in one place? The instrument, as an example, for cutting down corn in Germany, is much more handy and expeditious, in my opinion, than the sickle used in England. The cheap and expeditious manner of making vinegar without previous fermentation, is known only in a part of France. If such discoveries therefore, remain still to be known at home; what funds of knowledge might not be collected, in countries yet unexplored, or only passed through by ignorant travellers in hasty caravans.

The caution with which foreigners are received in Asia, may be alledged as an objection to such a design. But how readily have several European merchants found admission into regions the most suspecting, under the character of *Sanjapins*, or northern pilgrims; to such not even China itself denies access.

To send out a traveller, properly qualified for these purposes, might be an object of national concern; it would in some measure repair the breaches made by ambition; and might shew that there were still some who boasted a greater name than that of patriots, who professed themselves lovers of men. The only difficulty would remain in chusing a proper person, for so arduous an enterprize. He should be a man of a philosophical turn, one apt to deduce consequences of general utility from particular occurrences, neither swollen with pride, nor hardened by prejudice, neither wedded to one particular system, nor instructed only in one particular science; neither wholly a botanist, nor quite an antiquarian; his mind should be tinctured with miscellaneous knowledge, and his manners humanized by an intercourse with men. He should be, in some measure, an enthusiast to the design; fond of travelling, from a rapid imagination, and an innate love of change; furnished with a body capable of sustaining every fatigue, and an heart not easily terrified at danger.[1] Adieu.

[1] [Goldsmith seriously considered undertaking this project and addressed a minute upon the subject to the Prime Minister, Lord Bute.

> When this was talked of in Dr. Johnson's company, he said, "Of all men Goldsmith is the most unfit to go out upon such an inquiry; for he is utterly ignorant of such arts as we already possess, and consequently could not know what would be accessions to our present stock of mechanical knowledge. Sir, he would bring home a grinding-barrow, which you see in every street in London, and think he had furnished a wonderful improvement."
>
> Bennett Langton, as quoted in Boswell's *Life of Johnson*.]

LETTER CXII

An election described.

To the same.

THE English are at present employed in celebrating a feast which becomes general every seventh year; the Parliament of the nation being then dissolved and another appointed to be chosen. This solemnity falls infinitely short of our feast of the lanthorns in magnificence and splendour; it is also surpassed by others of the East in unanimity and pure devotion, but no festival in the world can compare with it for eating. Their eating indeed amazes me: Had I five hundred heads, and were each head furnished with brains, yet would they all be insufficient to compute the number of cows, pigs, geese and turkies, which upon this occasion die for the good of their country!

To say the truth, eating seems to make a grand ingredient in all English parties of zeal, business or amusement. When a Church is to be built, or an Hospital endowed, the Directors assemble, and instead of consulting upon it, they eat upon it, by which means the business goes forward with success. When the Poor are to be relieved, the officers appointed to dole out public charity, assemble and eat upon it: Nor has it ever been known, that they filled the bellies of the poor till they had previously satisfied their own. But in the election of Magistrates the people seem to exceed all bounds; the merits of a candidate are often measured by the number of his treats; his constituents assemble, eat upon him, and lend their applause, not to his integrity or sense, but the quantities of his beef and brandy.

And yet I could forgive this people their plentiful meals on this occasion, as it is extremely natural for every man to eat a great deal when he gets it for nothing; but what amazes me is, that all this good living no way contributes to improve their good humour. On the contrary, they seem to lose their temper as they lose their appetites; every morsel they swallow, and every glass they pour down serves to encrease their animosity. Many an honest man, before as harmless as a tame rabbit, when loaded with a single election dinner, has become more dangerous than a charged culverin. Upon one of these occasions, I have actually seen a bloody minded Man Milliner sally forth at the head of a mob, determined to face a desperate Pastry Cook, who was General of the opposite party.

But you must not suppose they are without a pretext for thus beating each other. On the contrary, no man here is so uncivilized as to beat his neighbour without producing very sufficient reasons. One candidate, for instance, treats with gin, a spirit of their own manufacture; another, always drinks brandy imported from abroad. Brandy is a wholesome liquor; gin a liquor wholly their own. This then furnishes an obvious cause of quarrel, Whether it be most reasonable to get drunk with gin, or get drunk with brandy? The mob meet upon the debate; fight themselves sober; and then draw off to get drunk again, and charge for another encounter. So that the English may now properly be said to be engaged in war; since while they are subduing their enemies abroad, they are breaking each other's heads at home.

I lately made an excursion to a neighbouring village, in order to be a spectator of the ceremonies practised upon this occasion. I left town in company with three fidlers, nine dozen of hams, and a corporation poet, which were designed as reinforcements to the gin drinking party. We entered the town with a very good face; the fidlers, no way intimidated by the enemy, kept handling their arms up the principal street. By this prudent manœuvre they took peaceable possession of their head-quarters, amidst the shouts of multitudes, who seemed perfectly rejoiced at hearing their music, but above all at seeing their bacon.

I must own I could not avoid being pleased to see all ranks of people on this occasion, levelled into an equality, and the poor, in some measure, enjoying the primitive privileges of nature. If there was any distinction shewn, the lowest of the people seemed to receive it from the rich. I could perceive a cobler with a levee at his door, and an haberdasher giving audience from behind his counter. But my reflections were soon interrupted by a mob, who demanded whether I was for the Distillery, or the Brewery? as these were terms with which I was totally unacquainted, I chose at first to be silent; however, I know not what might have been the consequence of my reserve, had not the attention of the mob been called off to a skirmish between a brandy-drinker's cow, and a gin-drinker's mastiff, which turned out, greatly to the satisfaction of the mob, in favour of the mastiff.

This spectacle, which afforded high entertainment, was at last ended by the appearance of one of the candidates; who came to harangue the mob; he made a very pathetic speech upon the late excessive importation of foreign drams; and the downfall of the distillery: I could see some of the audience shed tears. He was accompanied in his procession by Mrs. Deputy and Mrs. Mayoress. Mrs. Deputy was not in the least in liquor; and for Mrs. Mayoress, one of the spectators assured me in my ear that,—She was a very fine woman before she had the small-pox.

Mixing with the croud, I was now conducted to the hall where the magistrates are chosen; but what tongue can describe this scene of confusion; the whole crowd seemed equally inspired with anger, jealousy, politics, patriotism and punch: I remarked one figure that was carried up by two men upon this occasion. I at first began to pity his infirmities as natural, but soon found the fellow so drunk that he could not stand; another made his appearance to give his vote, but though he could stand, he actually lost the use of his tongue, and remained silent; a third, who though excessively drunk could both stand and speak, being asked the Candidate's name for whom he voted, could be prevailed upon to make no other answer, but Tobacco and Brandy. In short, an election-hall seems to be a theatre where every passion is seen without disguise; a school where fools may readily become worse, and where philosophers may gather wisdom. Adieu.

LETTER CXIV

Against the marriage act. A Fable.

To the same.

THE Formalities, delays and disappointments, that precede a treaty of marriage here, are usually as numerous as those previous to a treaty of peace. The laws of this country are finely calculated to promote all commerce, but the commerce between the sexes. Their encouragements for propagating hemp, madder and tobacco, are indeed admirable. Marriages are the only commodity that meet with none!

Yet from the vernal softness of the air, the verdure of the fields, the transparency of the streams, and the beauty of the women, I know few countries more proper to invite to courtship. Here love might sport among painted lawns and warbling groves, and revel upon gales, wafting at once both fragrance and harmony. Yet it seems he has forsaken the island; and when a couple are now to be married, mutual love or an union of minds is the last and most trifling consideration. If their goods and chattles can be brought to unite, their sympathetic souls are ever ready to guarantee the treaty. The gentleman's mortgaged lawn becomes enamoured of the ladies marriagable grove; the match is struck up, and both parties are piously in love——according to act of Parliament.

Thus they, who have fortune, are possessed at least of something that is lovely; but I actually pity those that have none. I am told there was a time, when Ladies with no other merit but youth, virtue and beauty, had a chance for husbands, at least, among the ministers of the church, or the officers of the army. The blush and innocence of sixteen was said to have a powerful influence over these two professions. But of late, all the little traffic of blushing, ogling, dimpling, and smiling, has been forbidden by an act in that case wisely made and provided.[1] A Lady's whole cargo of smiles, sighs and whispers, is declared utterly contraband, till she arrives in the warm latitudes of twenty-two, where commodities of this nature are too often found to decay. She is then permitted to dimple and smile, when the dimples and smiles begin to forsake her; and when perhaps grown ugly, is charitably entrusted with an unlimited use of her charms. Her lovers, however, by this time have forsaken her; the captain has changed for another mistress; the priest himself leaves her in solitude, to bewail her virginity, and she dies even without benefit of clergy.

Thus you find the Europeans discouraging love with as much earnestness as the rudest savage of Sofala. The Genius is surely now no more. In every region I find enemies in arms to oppress him. Avarice in Europe, jealousy in Persia, ceremony in China, poverty among the Tartars, and lust in Circassia, are all prepared to oppose his power. The Genius is certainly banished from earth, though once adored under such a variety of forms. He is no where to be found; and all that the Ladies of each country can produce, are but a few trifling reliques as instances of his former residence and favour.

The genius of Love, says the eastern Apologue, had long resided in the happy plains of Abra, where every breeze was health, and every sound produced tranquility. His temple at first was crowded, but every age lessened the number of his votaries, or cooled their devotion. Perceiving, therefore, his altars at length quite deserted, he was resolved to remove to some more propitious region, and he apprized the fair sex of every country, where he could hope for a proper reception, to assert their right to his presence among them. In return to

[1] [The Marriage Act of 1753 which included measures to prevent clandestine marriages and the marriage of minors without their parents' consent.]

this proclamation, embassies were sent from the Ladies of every part of the world to invite him, and to display the superiority of their claims.

And first the beauties of China appeared. No country could compare with them for modesty, either of look, dress, or behaviour; their eyes were never lifted from the ground; the robes of the most beautiful silk hid their hands, bosom and neck, while their faces only were left uncovered. They indulged no airs that might express loose desire, and they seemed to study only the graces of inanimate beauty. Their black teeth and plucked eyebrows were, however, alledged by the Genius against them, but he set them entirely aside when he came to examine their little feet.

The beauties of Circassia next made their appearance. They advanced hand in hand, singing the most immodest airs, and leading up a dance in the most luxurious attitudes. Their dress was but half a covering; the neck, the left breast, and all the limbs, were exposed to view, which after some time seemed rather to satiate than inflame desire. The lily and the rose contended in forming their complexions; and a soft sleepiness of eye added irresistible poignance to their charms: but their beauties were obtruded, not offered to their admirers; they seemed to give rather than receive courtship; and the genius of Love dismissed them as unworthy his regard, since they exchanged the duties of love, and made themselves not the pursued, but the pursuing sex.

The kingdom of Kashmire next produced its charming deputies. This happy region seemed peculiarly sequestered by nature for his abode. Shady mountains fenced it on one side from the scorching sun; and seaborn breezes, on the other, gave peculiar luxuriance to the air. Their complexions were of a bright yellow, that appeared almost transparent, while the crimson tulip seemed to blossom on their cheeks. Their features and limbs were delicate beyond the statuary's power to express; and their teeth whiter than their own ivory. He was almost persuaded to reside among them, when unfortunately one of the ladies talked of appointing his seraglio.

In this procession the naked inhabitants of Southern America would not be left behind: their charms were found to surpass whatever the warmest imagination could conceive; and served to shew, that beauty could be perfect, even with the seeming disadvantage of a brown complexion. But their savage education rendered them utterly unqualified to make the proper use of their power, and they were rejected as being incapable of uniting mental with sensual satisfaction. In this manner the deputies of other kingdoms had their suits rejected: the black beauties of Benin, and the tawny daughters of Borneo, the women of Wida with well scarred faces, and the hideous virgins of Cafraria; the squab ladies of Lapland, three feet high, and the giant fair ones of Patagonia.

The beauties of Europe at last appeared: grace was in their steps, and sensibility sate smiling in every eye. It was the universal opinion, while they were approaching, that they would prevail; and the Genius seemed to lend them his most favourable attention. They opened their pretensions with the utmost modesty; but unfortunately as their orator proceeded she happened to let fall the words *house in town*, *settlement and pin-money*. These seemingly harmless terms had instantly a surprising effect: the Genius with ungovernable rage burst from amidst the circle; and waving his youthful pinions, left this earth, and flew back to those etherial mansions from whence he descended.

The whole assembly was struck with amazement: they now justly apprehended, that female power would be no more, since love had forsaken them. They continued some time thus in a state of torpid despair, when it was proposed by one of the number, that, since the real Genius had left them, in order to continue their power, they should set up an idol in his stead; and that the ladies of every country should furnish him with what each liked best. This proposal was instantly relished and agreed to. An idol was formed by uniting the capricious gifts of all the assembly, tho' no way resembling the departed Genius. The ladies of China furnished the monster with wings; those of Kashmire supplied him with horns; the dames of Europe clapped a purse in his hand; and the virgins of Congo furnished him with a tail. Since that time, all the vows addressed to love are in reality paid to the idol; but, as in other false religions, the adoration seems most fervent, where the heart is least sincere. Adieu.

LETTER CXIX

On the distresses of the poor, exemplified in the life of a private centinel.

To the same.

THE misfortunes of the great, my friend, are held up to engage our attention, are enlarged upon in tones of declamation, and the world is called upon to gaze at the noble sufferers; they have at once the comfort of admiration and pity.

Yet where is the magnanimity of bearing misfortunes when the whole world is looking on? Men in such circumstances can act bravely even from motives of vanity. He only who, in the vale of obscurity, can brave adversity, who without friends to encourage, acquaintances to pity, or even without hope to alleviate his distresses, can behave with tranquility and indifference, is truly great: whether peasant or courtier, he deserves admiration, and should be held up for our imitation and respect.

The miseries of the poor are however entirely disregarded; tho' some undergo more real hardships in one day, than the great in their whole lives. It is indeed inconceiveable what difficulties the meanest English sailor or soldier endures without murmuring or regret. Every day is to him a day of misery, and yet he bears his hard fate without repining.

With what indignation do I hear the heroes of tragedy

complain of misfortunes and hardships, whose greatest calamity is founded in arrogance and pride. Their severest distresses are pleasures, compared to what many of the adventuring poor every day sustain, without murmuring. These may eat, drink, and sleep, have slaves to attend them, and are sure of subsistence for life, while many of their fellow-creatures are obliged to wander, without a friend to comfort or to assist them, find enmity in every law, and are too poor to obtain even justice.

I have been led into these reflections from accidentally meeting some days ago a poor fellow begging at one of the outlets of this town, with a wooden leg. I was curious to learn what had reduced him to his present situation; and after giving him what I thought proper, desired to know the history of his life and misfortunes, and the manner in which he was reduced to his present distress. The disabled soldier, for such he was, with an intrepidity truly British, leaning on his crutch, put himself into an attitude to comply with my request, and gave me his history as follows:

"As for misfortunes, Sir, I can't pretend to have gone through more than others. Except the loss of my limb, and my being obliged to beg, I don't know any reason, thank heaven, that I have to complain: there are some who have lost both legs, and an eye; but, thank heaven, it is not quite so bad with me.

"My father was a labourer in the country, and died when I was five years old; so I was put upon the parish. As he had been a wandering sort of a man, the parishioners were not able to tell to what parish I belonged, or where I was born; so they sent me to another parish, and that parish sent me to a third; till at last it was thought I belonged to no parish at all. At length, however, they fixed me. I had some disposition to be a scholar, and had actually learned my letters; but the master of the workhouse put me to business as soon as I was able to handle a mallet.

"Here I lived an easy kind of a life for five years. I only wrought ten hours in the day, and had my meat and drink provided for my labour. It is true, I was not suffered to stir far from the house, for fear I should run away: but what of that, I had the liberty of the whole house, and the yard before the door, and that was enough for me.

"I was next bound out to a farmer, where I was up both early and late, but I ate and drank well, and liked my business well enough, till he died. Being then obliged to provide for myself, I was resolved to go and seek my fortune. Thus I lived, and went from town to town, working when I could get employment, and starving when I could get none, and might have lived so still: But happening one day to go through a field belonging to a magistrate, I spy'd a hare crossing the path just before me. I believe the devil put it in my head to fling my stick at it: well, what will you have on't? I killed the hare, and was bringing it away in triumph, when the justice himself met me: he called me a villain, and collaring me, desired I would give an account of myself. I began immediately to give a full account of all that I knew of my breed, seed, and generation: but though I gave a very long account, the justice said, I could give no account of myself; so I was indicted, and found guilty of being poor, and sent to Newgate, in order to be transported to the plantations.

"People may say this and that of being in jail; but for my part, I found Newgate as agreeable a place as ever I was in, in all my life. I had my belly full to eat and drink, and did no work; but alas, this kind of life was too good to last for ever! I was taken out of prison, after five months, put on board of a ship, and sent off with two hundred more. Our passage was but indifferent, for we were all confined in the hold, and died very fast, for want of sweet air and provisions; but for my part, I did not want meat, because I had a fever all the way: providence was kind, when provisions grew short, it took away my desire of eating. When we came ashore, we were sold to the planters. I was bound for seven years, and as I was no scholar, for I had forgot my letters, I was obliged to work among the negroes; and served out my time, as in duty bound to do.

"When my time was expired, I worked my passage home, and glad I was to see Old England again, because I loved my country. O liberty, liberty, liberty! that is the property of every Englishman, and I will die in its defence: I was afraid, however, that I should be indicted for a vagabond once more, so did not much care to go into the country, but kept about town, and did little jobs when I could get them. I was very happy in this manner for some time; till one evening, coming home from work, two men knocked me down, and then desired me to stand still. They belonged to a press-gang; I was carried before the justice, and as I could give no account of my self, (that was the thing that always hobbled me,) I had my choice left, whether to go on board a man of war, or list for a soldier. I chose to be a soldier; and in this post of a gentleman I served two campaigns, was at the battles in Flanders, and received but one wound through the breast, which is troublesome to this day.

"When the peace came on, I was discharged; and as I could not work, because my wound was sometimes painful, I listed for a landman in the East India company's service. I here fought the French in six pitched battles; and verily believe, that if I could read or write, our captain would have given me promotion, and made me a corporal. But that was not my good fortune, I soon fell sick, and when I became good for nothing, got leave to return home again with forty pounds in my pocket, which I saved in the service. This was at the beginning of the present war, so I hoped to be set on shore, and to have the pleasure of spending my money; but the government wanted men, and I was pressed again, before ever I could set foot on shore.

"The boatswain found me, as he said, an obstinate fellow:

he swore that I understood my business perfectly well, but that I pretended sickness merely to be idle: God knows, I knew nothing of sea-business: He beat me without considering what he was about. But still my forty pounds was some comfort to me under every beating; the money was my comfort, and the money I might have had to this day; but that our ship was taken by the French, and so I lost it all!

"Our crew was carried into a French prison, and many of them died, because they were not used to live in a jail; but for my part it was nothing to me, for I was seasoned. One night however, as I was sleeping on the bed of boards, with a warm blanket about me, (for I always loved to lie well,) I was awaked by the boatswain, who had a dark lanthorn in his hand. 'Jack, says he to me, will you knock out the French centry's brains?' 'I don't care, says I, striving to keep myself awake, if I lend a hand.' 'Then follow me, says he, and I hope we shall do business.' So up I got, and tied my blanket, which was all the cloaths I had, about my middle, and went with him to fight the Frenchmen: we had no arms; but one Englishman is able to beat five French at any time; so we went down to the door, where both the centries were posted, and rushing upon them, seized their arms in a moment, and knocked them down. From thence, nine of us ran together to the key, and seizing the first boat we met, got out of the harbour, and put to sea: we had not been here three days before we were taken up by an English privateer, who was glad of so many good hands; and we consented to run our chance. However, we had not so much luck as we expected. In three days we fell in with a French man of war, of forty guns, while we had but twenty three; so to it we went. The fight lasted for three hours, and I verily believe we should have taken the Frenchman, but unfortunately, we lost almost all our men, just as we were going to get the victory. I was once more in the power of the French, and I believe it would have gone hard with me, had I been brought back to my old jail in Brest: but by good fortune, we were re-taken, and carried to England once more.

"I had almost forgot to tell you, that in this last engagement I was wounded in two places; I lost four fingers of the left hand, and my leg was shot off. Had I the good fortune to have lost my leg and use of my hand on board a king's ship, and not a privateer, I should have been entitled to cloathing and maintenance during the rest of my life, but that was not my chance; one man is born with a silver spoon in his mouth, and another with a wooden ladle. However, blessed be God, I enjoy good health, and have no enemy in this world that I know of, but the French, and the Justice of Peace."

Thus saying, he limped off, leaving my friend and me in admiration of his intrepidity and content; nor could we avoid acknowledging, that an habitual acquaintance with misery, is the truest school of fortitude and philosophy. Adieu.

LETTER CXXIII

The Conclusion.

To the same.

After a variety of disapointments, my wishes are at length fully satisfied. My son so long expected is arrived; at once, by his presence banishing my anxiety, and opening a new scene of unexpected pleasure. His improvements in mind and person have far surpass'd even the sanguine expectations of a father. I left him a boy, but he is returned a man; pleasing in his person, hardened by travel, and polished by adversity. His disappointment in love, however, had infused an air of melancholy into his conversation, which seemed at intervals to interrupt our mutual satisfaction. I expected that this could find a cure only from time; but fortune, as if willing to load us with her favours, has in a moment repaid every uneasiness with rapture.

Two days after his arrival, the man in black with his beautiful niece, came to congratulate us upon this pleasing occasion: but, guess our surprize, when my friend's lovely kinswoman was found to be the very captive my son had rescued from Persia, and who had been wreck'd on the Wolga, and was carried by the Russian peasants to the port of Archangel. Were I to hold the pen of a novelist, I might be prolix in describing their feelings, at so unexpected an interview; but you may conceive their joy, without my assistance, words were unable to express their transports, then how can words describe it?

When two young persons are sincerely enamoured of each other, nothing can give me such pleasure as seeing them married: whether I know the parties or not, I am happy at thus binding one link more in the universal chain. Nature has, in some measure, formed me for a match-maker, and given me a soul to sympathize with every mode of human felicity. I instantly therefore consulted the man in black, whether we might not crown their mutual wishes by marriage; his soul seems formed of similar materials with mine, he instantly gave his consent, and the next day was appointed for the solemnization of their nuptials.

All the acquaintances which I had made since my arrival, were present at this gay solemnity. The little beau was constituted master of the ceremonies, and his wife Mrs. Tibbs conducted the entertainment with proper decorum. The man in black and the pawn-broker's widow, were very sprightly and tender upon this occasion. The widow was dressed up under the direction of Mrs. Tibbs; and as for her lover, his face was set off by the assistance of a pig-tail wig, which was lent by the little beau, to fit him for making love with proper formality. The whole company easily perceived, that it would be a double wedding before all was over, and indeed my friend and the widow seemed to make no secret of their passion; he even called me aside, in order to know my candid opinion, whether I did not think him a little too old to be married. As for my own part, continued he, I know I am going to play the fool, but all my friends will praise my wisdom, and produce me as the very pattern of discretion to others.

At dinner, every thing seemed to run on with good humour, harmony, and satisfaction. Every creature in company thought themselves pretty, and every jest was laught at: the man in black sat next his mistress, helped her plate, chimed her glass, and jogging her knees and her elbow, he whispered something arch in her ear, on which she patted his cheek; never was antiquated passion so playful, so harmless, and amusing, as between this reverend couple.

The second course was now called for, and among a variety of other Dishes, a fine turkey was placed before the widow. The Europeans, you know, carve as they eat; my friend therefore begged his mistress to help him to a part of the turkey. The widow, pleased with an opportunity of shewing her skill in carving; an art, upon which it seems, she picqued herself; began to cut it up by first taking off the leg. *Madam*, cries my friend, *if I might be permitted to advise, I would begin by cutting off the wing, and then the Leg will come off more easily.* Sir, replies the widow, give me leave to understand cutting up a fowl, I always begin with the leg. *Yes Madam*, replies the lover, *but if the wing be the most convenient manner, I would begin with the wing.* Sir, interrupts the lady, when you have fowls of your own, begin with the wing if you please; but give me leave to take off the leg, I hope I am not to be taught at this time of day. *Madam*, interrupts he, *we are never too old to be instructed.* Old, Sir! interrupts the other, who is old, Sir? when I die of age, I know of some that will quake for fear; if the leg does not come off, take the turkey to yourself. *Madam*, replied the man in black, *I don't care a farthing whether the leg or the wing comes off; if you are for the leg first, why you shall have the argument, even though it be as I say.* As for the matter of that, cries the widow, I don't care a fig, whether you are for the leg off, or on; and friend, for the future keep your distance. O, replied the other, *that is easily done, it is only removing to the other end of the table, and so, madam, your most obedient humble servant.*

Thus, was this courtship of an age destroyed in one moment; for this dialogue effectually broke off the match between this respectable couple, that had been but just concluded. The smallest accidents disappoint the most important treaties: However, though it in some measure interrupted the general satisfaction, it no ways lessened the happiness of the youthful couple; and by the young lady's looks I could perceive, she was not entirely displeased with this interruption.

In a few hours the whole transaction seemed entirely forgotten, and we have all since, enjoyed those satisfactions which result from a consciousness of making each other happy. My son and his fair partner are fixed here for life; the man in black, has given them up a small estate in the country, which added to what I was able to bestow, will be capable of supplying all the real, but not the fictitious demands of happiness. As for myself, the world being but one city to me, I don't much care in which of the streets I happen to reside; I shall therefore spend the remainder of life, in examining the manners of different countries, and have prevailed upon the man in black to be my companion. *They must often change, says* Confucius, *who would be constant in happiness or wisdom.* Adieu.

[1] ["I am not offended by a few faults." *Ars Poetica*, 351–2.]

THE LIFE OF

RICHARD NASH, Esq;

LATE MASTER OF THE CEREMONIES
AT BATH

[*ABRIDGED*]

EXTRACTED PRINCIPALLY
FROM HIS ORIGINAL PAPERS

Non ego paucis
Offendar Maculis. Hor.[1]

The Life of Richard Nash, of Bath, Esq; Extracted principally from his Original Papers was first published on 14 October, 1762, *Printed for J. Newbery, in St. Paul's Church-yard; W. Frederick, at Bath.* Apart from a hasty life of Voltaire published in 1761, it is the first and much the best of Goldsmith's biographies. The others are lives of Parnell and Bolingbroke; they did not appear until 1770. *The Life of Richard Nash* still remains the chief source for the article on Nash in the *Dictionary of National Biography*, although Goldsmith as an historian was more concerned to be entertaining than accurate. Later in 1762 a second edition was published with a slightly altered title: *The Life of Richard Nash, Esq; Late Master of the Ceremonies at Bath.* The list of booksellers was increased by the name of *G. Faulkener, in Dublin*; and Goldsmith added several new passages to the text and a number of footnotes. The text of the second edition is used here.

I have been forced by lack of space to reduce the text by about a quarter. Goldsmith printed a number of Nash's papers in the *Life*. Some of these, such as the letters of the Duchess of Marlborough, are included only to show "what a parcel of stupid trifles the world is ready to admire." Others merely repeat material which Goldsmith had worked into his own narrative. The chief matters I have omitted are: several letters written to Nash; a lengthy and involved account of Nash's attempts to evade the gaming laws; a long extract from a book on cheating by a pickpocket; a panegyric on Nash in verse; and two epitaphs on him, one running to some hundred and fifty lines of English, the other to a hundred lines of Latin, which Goldsmith translates in full. I have included the letter inveighing against gaming (p. 546), as I feel convinced, though without any evidence except the style, that it is by Goldsmith himself.

PREFACE

THE following memoir is neither calculated to enflame the reader's passions with descriptions of gallantry, nor to gratify his malevolence with details of scandal. The amours of coxcombs, and the pursuits of debauchees, are as destitute of novelty to attract us, as they are of variety to entertain, they still present us but the same picture, a picture we have seen a thousand times repeated. The life of Mr. *Nash* is incapable of supplying any entertainment of this nature to a prurient curiosity. Tho' it was passed in the very midst of debauchery, he practised but few of those vices he was often obliged to assent to. Tho' he lived where gallantry was the capital pursuit, he was never known to favour it by his example, and what authority he had was set to oppose it. Instead therefore of a romantic history, filled with warm pictures and fanciful adventures, the reader of the following account must rest satisfied with a genuine and candid recital compiled from the papers he left behind, and others equally authentic; a recital neither written with a spirit of satire nor panegyric, and with scarce any other art, than that of arranging the materials in their natural order.

But tho' little art has been used, it is hoped that some entertainment may be collected from the life of a person so much talked of, and yet so little known as Mr. *Nash*. The history of a man, who for more than fifty years presided over the pleasures of a polite kingdom, and whose life, tho' without anything to surprise, was ever marked with singularity, deserves the attention of the present age; the pains he took in pursuing pleasure, and the solemnity he assumed in adjusting trifles, may one day claim the smile of posterity. At least such an history is well enough calculated to supply a vacant hour with innocent amusement, however it may fail to open the heart, or improve the understanding.

Yet his life, how trifling soever it may appear to the inattentive, was not without its real advantages to the public. He was the first who diffused a desire of society, and an easiness of address among a whole people who were formerly censured by foreigners for a reservedness of behaviour, and an aukward timidity in their first approaches. He first taught a familiar intercourse among strangers at *Bath* and *Tunbridge*, which still subsists among them. That ease and open access first acquired there, our gentry brought back to the metropolis, and thus the whole kingdom by degrees became more refined by lessons originally derived from him.

Had it been my design to have made this history more pleasing at the expence of truth, it had been easily performed; but I chose to describe the man as he was, not such as imagination could have helped in compleating his picture; he will be found to be a weak man, governing weaker subjects, and may be considered as resembling a monarch of *Cappadocia*, whom *Cicero* somewhere calls, *the little king of a little people*.

But while I have been careful in describing the monarch, his dominions have claimed no small share of my attention; I have given an exact account of the rise, regulation, and nature of the amusements of the city of *Bath*, how far Mr. *Nash* contributed to establish and refine them, and what pleasure a stranger may expect there upon his arrival. Such anecdotes as are at once true and worth preserving are produced in their order, and some stories are added, which, tho' commonly known, more necessarily belong to this history, than to the places from whence they have been extracted. But it is needless to point out the pains that have been taken, or the entertainment that may be expected from the perusal of this performance. It is but an indifferent way to gain the reader's esteem, to be my own panegyrist, nor is this preface so much designed to lead him to beauties, as to demand pardon for defects.

THE LIFE OF RICHARD NASH, ESQ;

HISTORY owes its excellence more to the writer's manner than the materials of which it is composed. The intrigues of courts, or the devastation of armies, are regarded by the remote spectator with as little attention as the squabbles of a village, or the fate of a malefactor, that fall under his own observation. The great and the little, as they have the same senses, and the same affections, generally present the same picture to the hand of the draughtsman; and whether the heroe or the clown be the subject of the memoir, it is only man that appears with all his native minuteness about him; for nothing very great was ever yet formed from the little materials of humanity.

Thus none can properly be said to write history, but he who understands the human heart, and its whole train of affections and follies. Those affections and follies are properly the materials he has to work upon. The relations of great events may surprize indeed; they may be calculated to instruct those very few, who govern the million beneath, but the generality of mankind find the most real improvement from relations which are levelled to the general surface of life; which tell, not how men learned to conquer, but how they endeavoured to live; not how they gained the shout of the admiring crowd, but how they acquired the esteem of their friends and acquaintance.

Every man's own life would perhaps furnish the most pleasing materials for history, if he only had candour enough to be sincere, and skill enough to select such parts as once making him more prudent, might serve to render his readers more cautious. There are few who do not prefer a page of *Montaigne* or *Colley Cibber*, who candidly tell us what they thought of the world, and the world thought of them, to the more stately memoirs and transactions of *Europe*, where we see Kings pretending to immortality, that are now almost forgotten, and statesmen planning frivolous negociations, that scarce outlive the signing.

It were to be wished that ministers and Kings were left to write their own histories; they are truly useful to few but themselves; but for men who are contented with more humble stations, I fancy such truths only are serviceable as may conduct them safely through life. That knowledge which we can turn to our real benefit should be most eagerly pursued. Treasures which we cannot use but little encrease the happiness or even the pride of the possessor.

I profess to write the history of a man placed in the middle ranks of life; of one, whose vices and virtues were open to the eye of the most undiscerning spectator, who was placed in public view, without power to repress censure, or command adulation, who had too much merit not to become remarkable, yet too much folly to arrive at greatness. I attempt the character of one, who was just such a man as probably you or I may be, but with this difference, that he never performed an action which the world did not know, or ever formed a wish which he did not take pains to divulge. In short, I have chosen to write the life of the noted Mr. *Nash*, as it will be the delineation of a mind without disguise, of a man ever assiduous without industry, and pleasing to his superiors, without any superiority of genius or understanding.

Yet if there be any who think the subject of too little importance to command attention, and had rather gaze at the actions of the great, than be directed in guiding their own, I have one undeniable claim to their attention. Mr. *Nash* was himself a king. In this particular, perhaps no Biographer has been so happy as I. They who are for a delineation of men and manners may find some satisfaction that way, and those who delight in adventures of Kings and Queens, may perhaps find their hopes satisfied in another.

It is a matter of very little importance who were the

parents, or what was the education of a man who owed so little of his advancement to either. He seldom boasted of family or learning, and his father's name and circumstances were so little known, that Doctor *Cheyne* used frequently to affirm, that *Nash* had no father. The Dutchess of *Marlborough* one day rallying him in public company upon the obscurity of his birth, compared him to *Gil Blas*, who was ashamed of his father: No, Madam, replied *Nash*, I seldom mention my father in company, not because I have any reason to be ashamed of him; but because he has some reason to be ashamed of me.

However, though such anecdotes be immaterial, to go on in the usual course of history, it may be proper to observe that *Richard Nash*, Esq., the subject of this memoir, was born in the town of *Swansea*, in *Glamorganshire*, on the 18th of *October*, in the year 1674. His father was a gentleman, whose principal income arose from a partnership in a glass-house; his mother was niece to Colonel *Poyer*, who was killed by *Oliver Cromwell*, for defending *Pembroke* castle against the rebels. He was educated under Mr. *Maddocks* at *Carmarthan* school, and from thence sent to *Jesus* college, in *Oxford*, in order to prepare him for the study of the law. His father had strained his little income to give his son such an education, but from the boy's natural vivacity, he hoped a recompence from his future preferment. In college, however, he soon shewed that though much might be expected from his genius, nothing could be hoped from his industry. A mind strongly turned to pleasure, always is first seen at the university: there the youth first finds himself freed from the restraint of tutors, and being treated by his friends in some measure as a man, assumes the passions and desires of riper age, and discovers in the boy, what are likely to be the affections of his maturity.

The first method Mr. *Nash* took to distinguish himself at college was not by application to study, but by his assiduity in intrigue. In the neighbourhood of every university there are girls who with some beauty, some coquetry, and little fortune, lie upon the watch for every raw amorous youth, more inclined to make love than to study. Our Heroe was quickly caught, and went through all the mazes and adventures of a college intrigue, before he was seventeen; he offered marriage, the offer was accepted, but the whole affair coming to the knowledge of his tutor, his happiness, or perhaps his future misery, was prevented, and he was sent home from college, with necessary advice to him, and proper instructions to his father.

When a man knows his power over the fair sex, he generally commences their admirer for the rest of life. That triumph which he obtains over one, only makes him the slave of another; and thus he proceeds, conquering and conquered, to the closing of the scene. The army seemed the most likely profession in which to display this inclination for gallantry; he therefore purchased a pair of colours, commenced a professed admirer of the sex, and dressed to the very edge of his finances. But the life of a soldier is more pleasing to the spectator at a distance than to the person who makes the experiment. Mr. *Nash* soon found that a red coat alone would never succeed, that the company of the fair sex is not to be procured without expence, and that his scanty commission could never procure him the proper reimbursements. He found too that the profession of arms required attendance and duty, and often encroached upon those hours he could have wished to dedicate to softer purposes. In short, he soon became disgusted with the life of a soldier, quitted the army, entered his name as a student in the temple books, and here went to the very summit of second-rate luxury. Though very poor he was very fine; he spread the little gold he had, in the most ostentatious manner, and though the gilding was but thin, he laid it on as far as it would go. They who know the town, cannot be unacquainted with such a character as I describe; one, who, though he may have dined in private upon a banquet served cold from a cook's shop, shall dress at six for the side box; one of those, whose wants are only known to their laundress and tradesmen, and their fine cloaths to half the nobility; who spend more in chair hire, than housekeeping; and prefer a bow from a Lord, to a dinner from a Commoner.

In this manner Mr. *Nash* spent some years about town, till at last his genteel appearance, his constant civility, and still more, his assiduity, gained him the acquaintance of several persons qualified to lead the fashion both by birth and fortune. To gain the friendship of the young nobility little more is requisite than much submission and very fine cloaths; dress has a mechanical influence upon the mind, and we naturally are awed into respect and esteem at the elegance of those, whom even our reason would teach us to contemn. He seemed early sensible of human weakness in this respect, he brought a person genteelly dressed to every assembly, he always made one of those who are called very good company, and assurance gave him an air of elegance and ease.

When King *William* was upon the throne, Mr. *Nash* was a member of the *Middle Temple*. It had been long customary for the Inns of court to entertain our Monarchs upon their accession to the crown, or some such remarkable occasion, with a revel and pageant. In the earlier periods of our history, Poets were the conductors of these entertainments; plays were exhibited, and complimentary verses were then written; but by degrees the pageant alone was continued, Sir *John Davis* being the last poet that wrote verses upon such an occasion in the reign of *James* I.

This ceremony, which has been at length totally discontinued, was last exhibited in honour of King *William*, and Mr. *Nash* was chosen to conduct the whole with proper decorum. He was then but a very young man, but we see at how early an age he was thought proper to guide the amusements of his country, and be the *Arbiter Elegantiarum* of his time; we see how early he gave proofs of that spirit of regularity, for which he afterwards became famous, and shewed an attention to those little circumstances, of which, tho' the observance be trifling, the neglect has often interrupted men of the greatest abilities in the progress of their fortunes.

In conducting this entertainment, *Nash* had an opportunity of exhibiting all his abilities, and King *William* was so well satisfied with his performance, that he made him an offer of knighthood. This, however, he thought proper to refuse, which in a person of his disposition seems strange. *Please your Majesty*, replied he, when the offer was made him, *if you intend to make me a Knight*, *I wish it may be one of your poor Knights of* Windsor, *and then I shall have a fortune at least able to support my title.* Yet we do not find, that the King took the hint of encreasing his fortune, perhaps he could not, he had at that time numbers to oblige, and he never cared to give money without important services.

But though *Nash* acquired no riches by his late office, yet he gained many friends, or what is more easily obtained, many acquaintance, who often answer the end as well. In the populous city where he resided, to be known was almost synonimous with being in the road to fortune. How many little Things do we see, without merit, or without friends, push themselves forward into public notice, and by self-advertizing, attract the attention of the day. The wise despise them, but the public are not all wise. Thus they succeed, rise upon the wing of folly, or of fashion, and by their success give a new sanction to effrontery.

But beside his assurance, Mr. *Nash* had in reality some merit and some virtues. He was, if not a brilliant, at least an easy companion. He never forgot good manners, even in the highest warmth of familiarity, and, as I hinted before, never went in a dirty shirt to disgrace the table of his patron or his friend. These qualifications might make the furniture of his head; but for his heart, that seemed an assemblage of the virtues which display an honest benevolent mind; with the vices which spring from too much good nature. He had pity for every creature's distress, but wanted prudence in the application of his benefits. He had generosity for the wretched in the highest degree, at a time when his creditors complained of his justice. He often spoke falshoods, but never had any of his harmless tales tinctured with malice.

An instance of his humanity is told us in the Spectator,[1] though his name is not mentioned. When he was to give in his accompts to the masters of the temple, among other articles, he charged *For making one man happy* 10*l.* Being questioned about the meaning of so strange an item, he frankly declared, that happening to over-hear a poor man declare to his wife and a large family of children, that 10*l.* would make him happy, he could not avoid trying the experiment. He added, that if they did not chuse to acquiesce in his charge, he was ready to refund the money. The masters, struck with such an uncommon instance of good nature, publicly thanked him for his benevolence, and desired that the sum might be doubled as a proof of their satisfaction.

Another instance of his unaccountable generosity, and I shall proceed. In some transactions with one of his friends, Mr. *Nash* was brought in debtor twenty pounds. His friend frequently asked for the money, and was as often denied. He found at last, that assiduity was likely to have no effect, and therefore contrived an honourable method of getting back his money without dissolving the friendship that subsisted between them. One day, returning from *Nash*'s chamber with the usual assurance of being paid to morrow, he went to one of their mutual acquaintance, and related the frequent disappointments he had received, and the little hopes he had of being ever paid. "My design, continues he, is that you should go, and try to borrow twenty pounds from *Nash*, and bring me the money. I am apt to think he will lend to you, though

[1] [Number 248.]

he will not pay me. Perhaps we may extort from his generosity, what I have failed to receive from his justice." His friend obeys, and going to Mr. *Nash*, assured him, that, unless relieved by his friendship, he should certainly be undone; he wanted to borrow twenty pounds, and had tried all his acquaintance without success. Mr. *Nash*, who had, but some minutes before, refused to pay a just debt, was in raptures at thus giving an instance of his friendship, and instantly lent what was required. Immediately upon the receipt, the pretended borrower goes to the real creditor, and gives him the money, who met Mr. *Nash* the day after; our heroe upon seeing him, immediately began his usual excuses, that the billiard room had stript him, that he was never so damnably out of cash, but that in a few days—My dear Sir, be under no uneasiness, replied the other, I would not interrupt your tranquillity for the world, you lent twenty pounds yesterday to our friend of the back stairs, and he lent it to me, give him your receipt, and you shall have mine. "Perdition seize thee, cried *Nash*, thou hast been too many for me. You demanded a debt, he asked a favour; to pay thee, would not encrease our friendship, but to lend him was procuring a new friend, by conferring a new obligation."

Whether men, at the time I am now talking of, had more wit than at present, I will not take upon me to determine; but certain it is, they took more pains to shew what they had. In that age, a fellow of high humour would drink no wine, but what was strained through his mistress's smock. He would eat a pair of her shoes tossed up in a fricasee. He would swallow tallow-candles instead of toasted cheese, and even run naked about town, as it was then said, to divert the ladies. In short, that was the age of such kind of wit as is the most distant of all others from wisdom.

Mr. *Nash*, as he sometimes played tricks with others, upon certain occasions, received very severe retaliations. Being at *York*, and having lost all his money; some of his companions agreed to equip him with fifty guineas, upon this proviso, that he would stand at the great door of the Minster, in a blanket, as the people were coming out of church. To this proposal he readily agreed, but the Dean passing by unfortunately knew him. What, cried the Divine, Mr. *Nash*, in masquerade? *Only a* Yorkshire *penance*, *Mr. Dean*, *for keeping bad company*, says *Nash*, pointing to his companions.

Some time after this, he won a wager of still greater consequence, by riding naked through a village upon a cow. This was then thought an harmless frolic, at present it would be looked upon with detestation.

He was once invited by some gentlemen of the navy, on board a man of war, that had sailing orders for the Mediterranean. This was soon after the affair of the revels, and being ignorant of any design against him, he took his bottle with freedom. But he soon found, to use the expression then in fashion, that he was absolutely *bitten.* The ship sailed away before he was aware of his situation, and he was obliged to make the voyage in the company where he had spent the night.

Many lives are often passed without a single adventure, and I do not know of any in the life of our hero, that can be called such, except what we are now relating. During this voyage, he was in an engagement, in which his particular friend was killed by his side, and he himself wounded in the leg. For the anecdote of his being wounded, we are solely to trust to his own veracity; but most of his acquaintance were not much inclined to believe him, when he boasted on those occasions. Telling one day of the wound he had received for his country, in one of the public rooms at *Bath*, (*Wiltshire*'s if I don't forget) a lady of distinction, that sat by, said it was all false. I protest, Madam, replied he, it is true; and if I cannot be believed, your Ladyship may, if you please, receive farther information, and feel the ball in my leg.

Mr. *Nash* was now fairly for life entered into a new course of gaiety and dissipation, and steady in nothing but in pursuit of variety. He was thirty years old, without fortune, or useful talents to acquire one. He had hitherto only led a life of expedients, he thanked chance alone for his support, and having been long precariously supported, he became, at length, totally a stranger to prudence, or precaution. Not to disguise any part of his character, he was now, by profession, a gamester, and went on from day to day, feeling the vicissitudes of rapture and anguish, in proportion to the fluctuations of fortune.

At this time, *London* was the only theatre in *England*, for pleasure, or intrigue. A spirit of gaming had been introduced in the licentious age of *Charles* II. and had by this time thriven surprizingly. Yet all its devastations were confined to *London* alone. To this great mart of every folly, sharpers from every country daily arrived, for the winter, but were obliged to leave the kingdom at the approach of summer, in order to open a new campaign at *Aix*, *Spaw*, or the *Hague*. *Bath*, *Tunbridge*, *Scarborough*, and other places of the same kind here, were then frequented only by such as really went for relief; the pleasures they afforded were merely rural, the company splenetic, rustic, and vulgar. In this situation of things, people of fashion had no agreeable summer retreat from the town, and usually spent that season amidst a solitude of country squires, parsons wives, and visiting tenants, or farmers; they wanted some place where they might have each others company, and win each others money, as they had done during the winter in town.

To a person, who does not thus calmly trace things to their source, nothing will appear more strange, than how the healthy could ever consent to follow the sick to those places of spleen, and live with those, whose disorders are ever apt to excite a gloom in the spectator. The truth is, the gaming table was properly the salutary font, to which such numbers flocked. Gaming will ever be the pleasure of the rich, while men continue to be men, while they fancy more happiness in being possessed of what they want, than they experience pleasure in the fruition of what they have. The wealthy only stake those riches, which give no real content, for an expectation of riches, in which they hope for satisfaction. By this calculation, they cannot lose happiness, as they begin with none; and they hope to gain it, by being possessed of something they have not had already.

Probably upon this principle, and by the arrival of Queen *Anne* there for her health, about the year 1703, the city of *Bath* became in some measure frequented by people of distinction. The company was numerous enough to form a country dance upon the bowling green; they were amused with a fiddle and hautboy, and diverted with the romantic walks round the city. They usually sauntered in fine weather in the grove, between two rows of sycamore trees. Several learned physicians, Doctor *Jordan*, and others, had even then praised the salubrity of the wells, and the amusements were put under the direction of a master of the ceremonies.

Captain *Webster* was the predecessor of Mr. *Nash*: This I take to be the same gentleman, whom Mr. *Lucas* describes in his history of the lives of the gamesters, by which it appears, that *Bath*, even before the arrival of Mr. *Nash*, was found a proper retreat for men of that profession. This gentleman, in the year 1704, carried the balls to the town hall, each man paying half a guinea each ball.

Still, however, the amusements of this place were neither elegant, nor conducted with delicacy. General society among people of rank or fortune was by no means established. The nobility still preserved a tincture of *Gothic* haughtiness, and refused to keep company with the gentry at any of the public entertainments of the place. Smoaking in the rooms was permitted; gentlemen and ladies appeared in a disrespectful manner at public entertainments in aprons and boots. With an eagerness common to those, whose pleasures come but seldom, they generally continued them too long; and thus they were rendered disgusting by too free an enjoyment. If the company liked each other, they danced till morning; if any person lost at cards, he insisted on continuing the game till luck should turn. The lodgings for visitants were paltry, though expensive, the dining rooms and other chambers were floored with boards, coloured brown with soot and small beer, to hide the dirt; the walls were covered with unpainted wainscot, the furniture corresponded with the meanness of the architecture; a few oak chairs, a small looking glass, with a fender and tongs, composed the magnificence of these temporary habitations. The city was in itself mean and contemptible, no elegant buildings, no open streets, nor uniform squares. The pump-house was without any director; the chairmen permitted no gentlemen or ladies to walk home by night without insulting them; and to add to all this, one of the greatest physicians of his age conceived a design of ruining the city, by writing against the efficacy of the waters. It was from a resentment of some affronts he had received there, that he took this resolution; and accordingly published a pamphlet, by which he said, *he would cast a toad into the spring.*

In this situation of things it was, that Mr. *Nash* first came into that city, and hearing the threat of this physician, he humourously assured the people, that if they would give him leave, he would charm away the poison of the Doctor's toad, as they usually charmed the venom of the Tarantula, by music. He therefore was immediately empowered to set up the force of a band of music, against the poison of the Doctor's reptile; the company very sensibly encreased, *Nash* triumphed, and the sovereignty of the city was decreed to him by every rank of people.

We are now to behold this gentleman as arrived at a new dignity for which nature seemed to have formed him; we are to see him directing pleasures, which none had better learned to share; placed over rebellious and refractory subjects, that were to be ruled only by the force of his address, and governing such as had been accustomed to govern others. We see a kingdom beginning with him, and sending off *Tunbridge* as one of its colonies.

But to talk more simply, when we talk at best of trifles. None could possibly conceive a person more fit to fill this employment than *Nash*: He had some wit, as I have said once or twice before; but it was of that sort which is rather happy than permanent. Once a week he might say a good thing; this the little ones about him took care to divulge; or if they happened to forget the joke, he usually remembered to repeat it himself: In a long intercourse with the world he had acquired an impenetrable assurance; and the freedom with which he was received by the Great, furnished him with vivacity, which could be commanded at any time, and which some mistook for wit. His former intercourse among people of fashion in town, had let him into most of the characters of the nobility; and he was acquainted with many of their private intrigues. He understood rank and precedence with the utmost exactness, was fond of shew and finery himself, and generally set a pattern of it to others. These were his favourite talents, and he was the favourite of such as had no other.

But to balance these, which some may consider as foibles, he was charitable himself, and generally shamed his betters into a similitude of sentiment, if they were not naturally so before. He was fond of advising those young men, who, by youth and too much money, are taught to look upon extravagance as a virtue. He was an enemy to rudeness in others, though in the latter part of his life he did not much seem to encourage a dislike of it by his own example. None talked with more humanity of the foibles of others, when absent, than he, nor kept those secrets with which he was entrusted more inviolably. But above all (if moralists will allow it among the number of his virtues) tho' he gamed high, he always played very fairly. These were his qualifications. Some of the nobility regarded him as an inoffensive, useful companion, the size of whose understanding was, in general, level with their own; but their little imitators admired him as a person of fine sense, and great good breeding. Thus people became fond of ranking him in the number of their acquaintance, told over his jests, and Beau *Nash* at length became the fashionable companion.

His first care, when made master of the ceremonies, or king of *Bath*, as it is called, was to promote a music subscription, of one guinea each, for a band which was to consist of six performers, who were to receive a guinea a week each for their trouble. He allowed also two guineas a week for lighting and sweeping the rooms, for which he accounted to the subscribers by receipt.

The pump-house was immediately put under the care of an officer, by the name of the *Pumper*; for which he paid the corporation an annual rent. A row of new houses was begun on the south side of the gravel walks, before which a handsome pavement was then made for the company to walk on. Not less than seventeen or eighteen hundred pounds was raised this year, and in the beginning of 1706, by subscription, and laid out in repairing the roads near the city. The streets began to be better paved, cleaned and lighted, the licences of the chairmen were repressed, and, by an act of parliament procured on this occasion, the invalids, who came to drink or bathe, were exempted from all manner of toll, as often as they should go out of the city for recreation.

The houses and streets now began to improve, and ornaments were lavished upon them even to profusion. But in the midst of this splendor the company still were obliged to assemble in a booth to drink tea and chocolate, or to game. Mr. *Nash* undertook to remedy this inconvenience. By his direction, one *Thomas Harrison* erected a handsome Assembly-house for these purposes. A better band of music was also procured, and the former subscription of one guinea was raised to two. *Harrison* had three guineas a week for the room and candles, and the music two guineas a man. The money Mr.

Nash received and accounted for with the utmost exactness and punctuality. To this house were also added gardens for people of rank and fashion to walk in; and the beauty of the suburbs continued to encrease, notwithstanding the opposition that was made by the corporation, who, at that time, looked upon every useful improvement, particularly without the walls, as dangerous to the inhabitants within.

His dominion was now extensive and secure, and he determined to support it with the strictest attention. But, in order to proceed in every thing like a king, he was resolved to give his subjects a law, and the following rules were accordingly put up in the pump-room.

RULES *to be observ'd at* BATH

1. That a visit of ceremony at first coming and another at going away, are all that are expected or desired, by ladies of quality and fashion,—except impertinents.

2. That ladies coming to the ball appoint a time for their footmen coming to wait on them home, to prevent disturbance and inconveniencies to themselves and others.

3. That gentlemen of fashion never appearing in a morning before the ladies in gowns and caps, shew breeding and respect.

4. That no person take it ill that any one goes to another's play, or breakfast, and not theirs;—except captious by nature.

5. That no gentleman give his ticket for the balls to any but gentlewomen.—N.B. Unless he has none of his acquaintance.

6. That gentlemen crowding before the ladies at the ball, shew ill manners; and that none do so for the future,—except such as respect nobody but themselves.

7. That no gentleman or lady takes it ill that another dances before them;—except such as have no pretence to dance at all.

8. That the elder ladies and children be content with a second bench at the ball, as being past or not come to perfection.

9. That the younger ladies take notice how many eyes observe them. N.B. This does not extend to the *Have-at-alls.*

10. That all whisperers of lies and scandal, be taken for their authors.

11. That all repeaters of such lies, and scandal, be shun'd by all company;—except such as have been guilty of the same crime.

N.B. Several men of no character, old women and young ones, of questioned reputation, are great authors of lies in these places, being of the sect of levellers.

These laws were written by Mr. *Nash* himself, and, by the manner in which they are drawn up, he undoubtedly designed them for wit. The reader, however, it is feared, will think them dull. Poor *Nash* was not born a writer; for whatever humour he might have in conversation, he used to call a pen his torpedo; whenever he grasped it, it numbed all his faculties.

But were we to give laws to a nursery, we should make them childish laws; his statutes, tho' stupid, were addressed to fine gentlemen and ladies, and were probably received with sympathetic approbation. It is certain, they were in general religiously observed by his subjects, and executed by him with impartiality; neither rank nor fortune shielded the refractory from his resentment.

The balls, by his directions, were to begin at six, and to end at eleven. Nor would he suffer them to continue a moment longer, lest invalids might commit irregularities, to counteract the benefit of the waters. Every thing was to be performed in proper order. Each ball was to open with a minuet, danced by two persons of the highest distinction present. When the minuet concluded, the lady was to return to her seat, and Mr. *Nash* was to bring the gentleman a new partner. This ceremony was to be observed by every succeeding couple, every gentleman being obliged to dance with two ladies till the minuets were over, which generally continued two hours. At eight, the country dances were to begin, ladies of quality, according to their rank, standing up first. About nine o'clock a short interval was allowed for rest, and for the gentlemen to help their partners to tea. That over, the company were to pursue their amusements till the clock struck eleven. Then the master of the ceremonies entering the ballroom, ordered the music to desist, by lifting up his finger. The dances discontinued, and some time allowed for becoming cool, the ladies were handed to their chairs.

Even the royal family themselves had not influence enough to make him deviate from any of these rules. The princess *Amelia* once applying to him for one dance more, after he had given the signal to withdraw, he assured her royal highness, that the established rules of *Bath* resembled the laws of *Lycurgus*, which would admit of no alteration, without an utter subversion of all his authority.

He was not less strict with regard to the dresses, in which ladies and gentlemen were to appear. He had the strongest aversion to a white apron, and absolutely excluded all who ventured to come to the assembly dressed in that manner. I have known him on a ball night strip even the dutchess of *Q[ueensbury]*, and throw her apron at one of the hinder benches among the ladies women; observing, that none but *Abigails* appeared in white aprons. This from another would be insult, in him it was considered as a just reprimand; and the good natured dutchess acquiesced in his censure, and with great good sense, and good humour, begged his *Majesty*'s pardon.

But he found more difficulty in attacking the gentlemen's irregularities; and for some time strove, but in vain, to prohibit the use of swords. Disputes arising from love or play, were sometimes attended with fatal effects. To use his own expression, he was resolved to hinder people from doing, *what they had no mind to*; but for some time without effect. However, there happened about that time, a duel between two gamesters, whose names were *Taylor* and *Clarke*, which helped to promote his peaceable intentions. They fought by torchlight in the grove; *Taylor* was run through the body, but lived seven years after, at which time his wound breaking out afresh, it caused his death. *Clarke* from that time pretended to be a Quaker, but the orthodox brethren never cordially received him among their number; and he died at *London*, about eighteen years after, in poverty and contrition. From that time it was thought necessary to forbid the wearing of swords at *Bath*, as they often tore the ladies' cloaths, and frighted them, by sometimes appearing upon trifling occasions. Whenever therefore *Nash* heard of a challenge given, or accepted, he instantly had both parties arrested. The gentlemen's boots also made a very desperate stand against him, the country 'squires were by no means submissive to his usurpations; and probably his authority alone would never have carried him thro', had he not reinforced it with ridicule. He wrote a song upon the occasion, which, for the honour of his poetical talents, the world shall see.

FRONTINELLA'S *invitation to the Assembly*

Come, one and all, to *Hoyden* Hall,
For there 's the assembly this night;
None but prude fools,
Mind manners and rules;
We *Hoydens* do decency slight.

Come, Trollops and Slatterns,
Cockt hats and white aprons,
This best our modesty suits;
For why should not we
In dress be as free
As *Hogs-Norton* 'squires in boots?

The keenness, severity, and particularly the good rhymes of this little *morçeau*, which was at that time highly relished by many of the nobility at *Bath*, gained him a temporary triumph. But to push his victories, he got up a puppet-shew, in which Punch came in booted and spurred, in the character of a country 'squire. He was introduced as courting his mistress, and having obtained her consent to comply with his wishes, upon going to bed, he is desired to pull off his boots. My boots, replies Punch, why, madam, you may as well bid me pull off my legs. I never go without boots, I never ride, I never dance without them; and this piece of politeness is quite the thing at *Bath*. We always dance at our town in boots, and the ladies often move minuets in riding-hoods. Thus he goes on, till his mistress, grown impatient, kicks him off the stage.

From that time few ventured to appear at the assemblies in *Bath* in a riding-dress; and whenever any gentleman, thro' ignorance, or haste, appeared in the rooms in boots, *Nash* would make up to him, and, bowing in an arch manner, would tell him, that he had forgot his horse. Thus he was at last completely victorious.

Dolisque coacti
Quos neque Tydides nec Larissaeus Achilles
Non anni domuere decem.[1]

He began therefore to reign without a rival, and like other kings had his mistresses, flatterers, enemies and calumniators. The amusements of the place however wore a very different aspect from what they did formerly. Regularity repressed pride, and that lessened, people of fortune became fit for society. Let the morose and grave censure an attention to forms and ceremonies, and rail at those, whose only business it is to regulate them; but tho' ceremony is very different from

[1] ["They succumbed to guile whom neither the son of Tydeus nor Achilles nor even ten years of war could conquer." Virgil, *Æneid*, 2. 197.]

politeness, no country was ever yet polite, that was not first ceremonious. The natural gradation of breeding begins in savage disgust, proceeds to indifference, improves into attention, by degrees refines into ceremonious observance, and the trouble of being ceremonious at length produces politeness, elegance and ease. There is therefore some merit in mending society, even in one of the inferior steps of this gradation; and no man was more happy in this respect than Mr. *Nash.* In every nation there are enough who have no other business or care, but that of buying pleasure; and he taught them, who bid at such an auction, the art of procuring what they sought without diminishing the pleasure of others.

The city of *Bath*, by such assiduity, soon became the theatre of summer amusements for all people of fashion; and the manner of spending the day there must amuse any, but such as disease or spleen had made uneasy to themselves. The following is a faint picture of the pleasures that scene affords. Upon a stranger's arrival at *Bath*, he is welcomed by a peal of the Abbey bells, and in the next place, by the voice and music of the city waits. For these civilities the ringers have generally a present made them of half a guinea; and the waits of half a crown, or more, in proportion to the person's fortune, generosity, or ostentation. These customs, tho' disagreeable are however generally liked, or they would not continue. The greatest incommodity attending them is the disturbance the bells must give the sick. But the pleasure of knowing the name of every family that comes to town recompences the inconvenience. Invalids are fond of news, and upon the first sound of the bells, every body sends out to enquire for whom they ring.

After the family is thus welcomed to *Bath*, it is the custom for the master of it to go to the public places, and subscribe two guineas at the assembly-houses towards the balls and music in the pump-house, for which he is entitled to three tickets every ball night. His next subscription is a crown, half a guinea, or a guinea, according to his rank and quality, for the liberty of walking in the private walks belonging to *Simpson*'s assembly-house; a crown or half a guinea is also given to the booksellers, for which the gentleman is to have what books he pleases to read at his lodgings. And at the coffee-house another subscription is taken for pen, ink and paper, for such letters as the subscriber shall write at it during his stay. The ladies too may subscribe to the booksellers, and to an house by the pump-room, for the advantage of reading the news, and for enjoying each other's conversation.

Things being thus adjusted, the amusements of the day are generally begun by bathing, which is no unpleasing method of passing away an hour, or so.

The baths are five in number. On the south-west side of the abbey church is the King's Bath; which is an oblong square, the walls are full of niches, and at every corner are steps to descend into it: this bath is said to contain 427 tons and 50 gallons of water; and on its rising out of the ground over the springs, it is sometimes too hot to be endured by those who bathe therein. Adjoining to the King's Bath there is another, called the Queen's Bath; this is of a more temperate warmth, as borrowing its water from the other.

In the south-west part of the city are three other baths, viz. The Hot Bath, which is not much inferior in heat to the King's Bath, and contains 53 tons 2 hogsheads, and 11 gallons of water. The Cross Bath, which contains 52 tons 3 hogsheads, and 11 gallons; and the Leper's Bath, which is not so much frequented as the rest.

The King's Bath (according to the best observations) will fill in about nine hours and a half; the Hot Bath in about eleven hours and a half; and the Cross Bath in about the same time.

The hours for bathing are commonly between six and nine in the morning; and the Baths are every morning supplied with fresh water; for when the people have done bathing, the sluices in each Bath are pulled up, and the water is carried off by drains into the river Avon.

In the morning the lady is brought in a close chair, dressed in her bathing cloaths, to the Bath; and, being in the water, the woman who attends, presents her with a little floating dish like a bason; into which the lady puts a handkerchief, a snuff-box, and a nosegay. She then traverses the Bath; if a novice with a guide, if otherwise by herself; and having amused herself thus while she thinks proper, calls for her chair, and returns to her lodgings.

The amusement of bathing is immediately succeeded by a general assembly of people at the pump-house, some for pleasure, and some to drink the hot waters. Three glasses, at three different times, is the usual portion for every drinker; and the intervals between every glass are enlivened by the harmony of a small band of music, as well as by the conversation of the gay, the witty, or the forward.

From the pump-house the ladies, from time to time, withdraw to a female coffee-house, and from thence return to their lodgings to breakfast. The gentlemen withdraw to their coffee-houses, to read the papers, or converse on the news of the day, with a freedom and ease not to be found in the metropolis.

People of fashion make public breakfasts at the assembly-houses, to which they invite their acquaintances, and they sometimes order private concerts; or when so disposed, attend lectures upon the arts and sciences, which are frequently taught there in a pretty superficial manner, so as not to teize the understanding, while they afford the imagination some amusement. The private concerts are performed in the ball-rooms, the tickets a crown each.

Concert breakfasts at the assembly-house, sometimes make also a part of the morning's amusement here, the expences of which are defrayed by a subscription among the men. Persons of rank and fortune who can perform are admitted into the orchestra, and find a pleasure in joining with the performers.

Thus we have the tedious morning fairly over. When noon approaches, and church (if any please to go there) is done, some of the company appear upon the parade, and other public walks, where they continue to chat and amuse each other, 'till they have formed parties for the play, cards, or dancing for the evening. Another part of the company divert themselves with reading in the booksellers shops, or are generally seen tasting the air and exercise, some on horseback, some in coaches. Some walk in the meadows round the town, winding along the side of the river Avon, and the neighbouring canal; while others are seen scaling some of those romantic precipices that overhang the city.

When the hour of dinner draws nigh, and the company is returned from their different recreations, the provisions are generally served with the utmost elegance and plenty. Their mutton, butter, fish, and fowl, are all allowed to be excellent, and their cookery still exceeds their meat.

After dinner is over, and evening prayers ended, the company meet a second time at the pump-house. From this they retire to the walks, and from thence go to drink tea at the assembly-houses, and the rest of the evenings are concluded either with balls, plays or visits. A theatre was erected in the year 1705 by subscription, by people of the highest rank, who permitted their arms to be engraven on the inside of the house, as a public testimony of their liberality towards it. Every tuesday and friday evening is concluded with a public ball, the contributions to which are so numerous, that the price of each ticket is trifling. Thus Bath yields a continued rotation of diversions, and people of all ways of thinking, even from the libertine to the methodist, have it in their power to complete the day with employments suited to their inclinations.

In this manner every amusement soon improved under Mr. *Nash*'s administration. The magistrates of the city found, that he was necessary and useful, and took every opportunity of paying the same respect to his fictitious royalty, that is generally extorted by real power. The same satisfaction a young lady finds upon being singled out at her first appearance; or an applauded poet, on the success of his first tragedy, influenced him. All admired him as an extraordinary character; and some who knew no better, as a very fine gentleman; he was perfectly happy in their little applause, and affected at length something particular in his dress, behaviour and conversation.

His equipage was sumptuous, and he usually travelled to *Tunbridge*, in a post chariot and six greys, with out-riders, foot-men, *French* horns, and every other appendage of expensive parade. He always wore a white hat, and, to apologize for this singularity, said, he did it purely to secure it from being stolen; his dress was tawdry, tho' not perfectly genteel; he might be considered as a beau of several generations, and in his appearance he, in some measure, mixed the fashions of the last age with those of the present. He perfectly understood elegant expence, and generally passed his time in the very best company, if persons of the first distinction deserve that title.

But I hear the reader now demand, what finances were to support all this finery, or where the treasures, that gave him such frequent opportunities of displaying his benevolence, or his vanity? To answer this, we must now enter upon another part of his character, his talents as a gamester; for by gaming alone at that period, of which I speak, he kept up so very genteel an appearance. When he first figured at *Bath*, there were few laws against this destructive amusement. The gaming-table was the constant resource of despair and indigence, and the frequent ruin of opulent fortunes. Wherever people of fashion came, needy adventurers were generally found in waiting. With such *Bath* swarmed, and among this class Mr. *Nash* was certainly to be numbered in the beginning, only with this difference, that he wanted the corrupt heart, too commonly attending a life of expedients; for he was generous, humane and honourable, even tho' by profession a gamester.

A thousand instances might be given of his integrity, even in this infamous profession; where his generosity often impelled him to act in contradiction to his interest. Wherever he found a novice in the hands of a sharper, he generally forewarned him of the danger; whenever he found any inclined to play, yet ignorant of the game, he would offer his services, and play for them. I remember an instance to this effect, tho' too nearly concerned in the affair to publish the gentleman's name of whom it is related. In the year 1725, there came to *Bath* a giddy youth, who had just resigned his fellowship at *Oxford.* He brought his whole fortune with him there, it was but a trifle, however, he was resolved to venture it all. Good fortune seemed kinder than could be expected. Without the smallest skill in play, he won a sum sufficient to make any unambitious man happy. His desire of gain encreasing with his gains, in the *October* following he was *at all*, and added four thousand pounds to his former capital. Mr. *Nash* one night, after losing a considerable sum to this undeserving son of fortune, invited him to supper. Sir, cried this honest, tho' veteran gamester, perhaps you may imagine I have invited you, in order to have my revenge at home; but, sir! I scorn so inhospitable an action. I desired the favour of your company to give you some advice, which you will pardon me, Sir, you seem to stand in need of. You are now high in spirits, and drawn away by a torrent of success. But there will come a time, when you will repent having left the calm of a college life for the turbulent profession of a gamester. Ill runs will come, as sure as day and night succeed each other. Be therefore advised, remain content with your present gains; for be persuaded, that had you the bank of *England*, with your present ignorance of gaming, it would vanish like a fairy dream. You are a stranger to me, but to convince you of the part I take in your welfare, I'll give you fifty guineas, to forfeit twenty, every time you lose two hundred at one sitting. The young gentleman refused his offer, and was at last undone!

The late duke of *B*[*olton*] being chagrined at losing a considerable sum, pressed Mr. *Nash* to tie him up for the future from playing deep. Accordingly, the beau gave his grace an hundred guineas to forfeit ten thousand, whenever he lost a sum to the same amount at play, in one sitting. The duke loved play to distraction, and soon after at hazard lost eight thousand guineas, and was going to throw for three thousand more; when *Nash*, catching hold of the dice-box, entreated his Grace to reflect upon the penalty if he lost: the Duke for that time desisted; but so strong was the furor of play upon him, that soon after, losing a considerable sum at *New-market*, he was contented to pay the penalty.

When the late earl of *T——d* was a youth, he was passionately fond of play, and never better pleased than with having Mr. *Nash* for his antagonist. *Nash* saw with concern his lordship's foible, and undertook to cure him, tho' by a very disagreeable remedy. Conscious of his own superior skill, he determined to engage him in single play for a very considerable sum. His lordship, in proportion as he lost his game, lost his temper too; and as he approached the gulph, seemed still more eager for ruin. He lost his estate; some writings were put into the winner's possession; his very equipage was deposited as a last stake, and he lost that also. But, when our generous gamester had found his lordship sufficiently punished for his temerity, he returned all; only stipulating, that he should be paid five thousand pounds whenever he should think proper to make the demand. However, he never made any such demand during his lordship's life; but some time after his decease, Mr. *Nash*'s affairs being in the wane, he demanded the money of his lordship's heirs, who honourably paid it without any hesitation.

But whatever skill *Nash* might have acquired by long practice in play, he was never formed by nature for a successful gamester. He was constitutionally passionate and generous. To acquire a perfection in that art, a man must be naturally phlegmatic, reserved and cool; every passion must learn to obey controul; but he frequently was unable to restrain the violence of his, and was often betrayed by this means into unbecoming rudeness, or childish impertinence; was sometimes a minion of fortune, and as often deprest by adversity. While others made considerable fortunes at the gaming-table, he was ever in the power of chance; nor did even the intimacy with which he was received by the great, place him in a state of independance.

The considerable inconveniences that were found to result from a permission of gaming, at length attracted the attention of the legislature, and in the twelfth year of his late majesty, the most prevalent games at that time were declared fraudulent and unlawful. Every age has had its peculiar modes of gaming. The games of Gleek, Primero, In and In, and several others now exploded, employed our sharping ancestors; to these succeeded the Ace of hearts, Pharaoh, Basset, and Hazard, all games of chance like the former. But tho' in these the chances seemed equal to the novice; in general those who kept the bank were considerable winners. The act therefore, passed upon this occasion, declared all such games and lotteries illicit, and directed, that all who should set up such games, should forfeit two hundred pounds, to be levied by distress on the offender's goods; one third to go to the informer, the residue to the poor.

The act further declared, that every person who played in any place, except in the royal palace where his majesty resided, should forfeit fifty pounds, and should be condemned to pay treble costs in case of an appeal.

. . . .

But now that we have viewed his conduct as a gamester, and seen him on that side of his character, which is by far the most unfavourable, seen him declining from his former favour and esteem, the just consequence of his quitting, tho' but ever so little, the paths of honour; let me turn to those brighter parts of his life and character, which gained the affection of his friends, the esteem of the corporation which he assisted, and may possibly attract the attention of posterity. By his successes we shall find, that figuring in life, proceeds less from the possession of great talents, than from the proper application of moderate ones. Some great minds are only fitted to put forth their powers in the storm; and the occasion is often wanting during a whole life for a great exertion: but trifling opportunities of shining, are almost every hour offered to the little sedulous mind; and a person thus employed, is not only more pleasing, but more useful in a state of tranquil society.

Tho' gaming first introduced him into polite company, this alone could hardly have carried him forward, without the assistance of a genteel address, much vivacity, some humour, and some wit. But once admitted into the circle of the Beau Monde, he then laid claim to all the privileges by which it is distinguished. Among others, in the early part of his life, he entered himself professedly into the service of the fair sex; he set up for a man of gallantry and intrigue; and if we can credit the boasts of his old age, he often succeeded. In fact, the business of love somewhat resembles the business of physic; no matter for qualifications, he that makes vigorous pretensions to either is surest of success. Nature had by no means formed Mr. *Nash* for a Beau Garçon; his person was clumsey, too large and aukward, and his features harsh, strong, and peculiarly irregular; yet even, with those disadvantages, he made love, became an universal admirer of the sex, and was universally admired. He was possessed, at least, of some requisites of a lover. He had assiduity, flattery, fine cloaths, and as much wit as the ladies he addressed. Wit, flattery, and fine cloaths, he used to say, were enough to debauch a nunnery. But my fair readers of the present day are exempt from this scandal; and it is no matter now, what he said of their grandmothers.

As *Nestor* was a man of three ages, so *Nash* sometimes humorously called himself a beau of three generations. He had seen flaxen bobs succeeded by majors, which in their turn gave way to negligents, which were at last totally routed by bags and ramilees. The manner in which gentlemen managed their amours, in these different ages of fashion, were not more different than their perriwigs. The lover in the reign of king *Charles* was solemn, majestic, and formal. He visited his mistress in state: Languished for the favour, kneeled when he toasted his goddess, walked with solemnity, performed the most trifling things with decorum, and even took snuff with a flourish. The beau of the latter part of queen *Ann*'s reign was disgusted with so much formality, he was pert, smart and lively; his billet-doux were written in a quite different stile from that of his antiquated predecessor; he was ever laughing at his own ridiculous situation; till at last, he persuaded the lady to become as ridiculous as himself. The beau of the third age, in which Mr. *Nash* died, was still more extraordinary than either; his whole secret in intrigue consisted in perfect indifference. The only way to make love now, I have heard Mr. *Nash* say, was to take no manner of notice of the lady, which method was found the surest way to secure her affections.

However these things be, this gentleman's successes in amour were in reality very much confined in the second and third age of intrigue; his character was too public for a lady to consign her reputation to his keeping. But in the beginning of life it is said, he knew the secret history of the times, and contributed himself to swell the page of scandal. Were I upon the present occasion to hold the pen of a novelist, I could recount some amours, in which he was successful. I could fill a volume with little anecdotes, which contain neither pleasure nor instruction; with histories of professing lovers, and poor believing girls deceived by such professions. But such adventures are easily written, and as easily atchieved. The plan even of fictitious novel is quite exhausted; but truth, which I have followed here, and ever design to follow, presents in the affair of love scarce any variety. The manner in which one reputation is lost, exactly resembles that by which another is taken away. The gentleman begins at timid distance, grows more bold, becomes rude, till the lady is married or undone; such is the substance of every modern novel; nor will I gratify the pruriency of folly, at the expence of every other pleasure my narration may afford.

Mr. *Nash* did not long continue an universal gallant; but in the earlier years of his reign, entirely gave up his endeavours to deceive the sex, in order to become the honest protector of their innocence, the guardian of their reputation, and a friend to their virtue.

This was a character he bore for many years, and supported it with integrity, assiduity and success. It was his constant practice to do every thing in his power to prevent the fatal consequences of rash and inconsiderate love; and there are many persons now alive, who owe their present happiness to his having interrupted the progress of an amour, that threatened to become unhappy, or even criminal, by privately making their guardians or parents acquainted with what he could discover. And his manner of disconcerting these schemes was such as generally secured him from the rage and resentment of the disappointed. One night, when I was in *Wiltshire*'s room, *Nash* came up to a lady and her daughter, who were people of no inconsiderable fortune, and bluntly told the mother, *she had better be at home*: this was at that time thought an audacious piece of impertinence, and the lady turned away piqued and disconcerted. *Nash*, however, pursued her, and repeated the words again; when the old lady, wisely conceiving there might be some hidden meaning couched under this seeming insolence, retired, and coming to her lodgings, found a coach and six at the door, which a sharper had provided to carry off her eldest daughter.

I shall beg leave to give some other instances of Mr. *Nash*'s good-sense and good-nature on these occasions, as I have had the accounts from himself. At the conclusion of the treaty of peace at *Utrecht*, colonel *M*—— was one of the thoughtless, agreeable, gay creatures, that drew the attention of the company at *Bath*. He danced and talked with great vivacity; and when he gamed among the ladies, he shewed, that his attention was employed rather upon their hearts than their fortunes. His own fortune however was a trifle, when compared to the elegance of his expence; and his imprudence at last was so great, that it obliged him to sell an annuity, arising from his commission, to keep up his splendor a little longer.

However thoughtless he might be, he had the happiness of gaining the affections of Miss *L*——, whose father designed her a very large fortune. This lady was courted by a nobleman of distinction, but she refused his addresses, resolved upon gratifying rather her inclinations than her avarice. The intrigue went on successfully between her and the colonel, and they both would certainly have been married, and been undone, had not Mr. *Nash* apprized her father of their intentions. The old gentleman recalled his daughter from *Bath*, and offered Mr. *Nash* a very considerable present, for the care he had taken, which he refused.

In the mean time colonel *M*—— had an intimation how his intrigue came to be discovered; and by taxing Mr. *Nash*, found that his suspicions were not without foundation. A challenge was the immediate consequence, which the king of *Bath*, conscious of having only done his duty, thought proper to decline. As none are permitted to wear swords at *Bath*, the colonel found no opportunity of gratifying his resentment, and waited with impatience to find Mr. *Nash* in town, to require proper satisfaction.

During this interval, however, he found his creditors

became too importunate for him to remain longer at *Bath*; and his finances and credit being quite exhausted, he took the desperate resolution of going over to the *Dutch* army in *Flanders*, where he enlisted himself a volunteer. Here he underwent all the fatigues of a private centinel, with the additional misery of receiving no pay, and his friends in *England* gave out, that he was shot at the battle of ——.

In the mean time the nobleman pressed his passion with ardour, but during the progress of his amour, the young lady's father died, and left her heiress to a fortune of fifteen hundred a year. She thought herself now disengaged from her former passion. An absence of two years had in some measure abated her love for the colonel; and the assiduity, the merit, and real regard of the gentleman who still continued to solicit her, were almost too powerful for her constancy. Mr. *Nash*, in the mean time, took every opportunity of enquiring after colonel *M*——, and found, that he had for some time been returned to *England*, but changed his name, in order to avoid the fury of his creditors; and that he was entered into a company of strolling players, who were at that time exhibiting at *Peterborough*.

He now therefore thought he owed the colonel, in justice, an opportunity of promoting his fortune, as he had once deprived him of an occasion of satisfying his love. Our Beau therefore invited the lady to be of a party to *Peterborough*, and offered his own equipage, which was then one of the most elegant in *England*, to conduct her there. The proposal being accepted, the lady, the nobleman, and Mr. *Nash*, arrived in town just as the players were going to begin.

Colonel *M*——, who used every means of remaining *incognito*, and who was too proud to make his distresses known to any of his former acquaintance, was now degraded into the character of *Tom* in the *Conscious Lovers*.[1] Miss *L*—— was placed in the foremost row of the spectators, her lord on one

[1] [By Richard Steele, first produced 7 November, 1722, at Drury Lane.]

side, and the impatient *Nash* on the other; when the unhappy youth appeared in that despicable situation upon the stage. The moment he came on, his former mistress struck his view, but his amazement was encreased, when he saw her fainting away in the arms of those who sate behind her. He was incapable of proceeding, and scarce knowing what he did, he flew and caught her in his arms.[1]

Colonel, cried *Nash*, when they were in some measure recovered, you once thought me your enemy, because I endeavoured to prevent you both from ruining each other, you were then wrong, and you have long had my forgiveness. If you love well enough now for matrimony, you fairly have my consent, and d——n him, say I, that attempts to part you. Their nuptials were solemnized soon after, and affluence added a zest to all their future enjoyments. Mr. *Nash* had the thanks of each, and he. afterwards spent several agreeable days in that society, which he had contributed to render happy.

I shall beg the reader's patience, while I give another instance, in which he ineffectually offered his assistance and advice. This story is not from himself; but told us partly by Mr. *Wood*, the architect of *Bath*, as it fell particularly within his own knowledge; and partly from another memoir, to which he refers.[2]

Miss *Sylvia S*—— was descended from one of the best families in the kingdom, and was left a large fortune upon her Sister's decease. She had early in life been introduced into the best company, and contracted a passion for elegance and

[1] [Compare George Primrose's experiences (p. 115).]

[2] [Almost all the details of Sylvia's acquaintance with Dame Lindsey and her tragic death are to be found in John Wood's *An Essay Towards a Description of Bath*, 1749 (p. 446 ff.). There is no mention of her affair with "the good-natured man" nor of any connection with Nash except that her old maid was "sirnamed . . . Nash after the proper Name of the Beau, and titular King of the City." The other memoir to which Wood refers is *New Court Tales: Or, Modern Amours*. I have not seen a copy. Sylvia's real name was Fanny Braddock (see *Gentleman's Magazine*, September, 1731).]

expence. It is usual to make the heroine of a story very witty, and very beautiful, and such circumstances are so surely expected, that they are scarce attended to. But whatever the finest poet could conceive of wit, or the most celebrated painter imagine of beauty, were excelled in the perfections of this young lady. Her superiority in both was allowed by all, who either heard, or had seen her. She was naturally gay, generous to a fault, good-natured to the highest degree, affable in conversation, and some of her letters, and other writings, as well in verse as prose, would have shone amongst those of the most celebrated wits of this, or any other age, had they been published.

But these great qualifications were marked by another, which lessened the value of them all. She was imprudent! But let it not be imagined, that her reputation or honour suffered by her imprudence; I only mean, she had no knowledge of the use of money, she relieved distress, by putting herself into the circumstances of the object whose wants she supplied.

She was arrived at the age of nineteen, when the croud of her lovers, and the continual repetition of new flattery, had taught her to think she could never be forsaken, and never poor. Young ladies are apt to expect a certainty of success, from a number of lovers; and yet I have seldom seen a girl courted by an hundred lovers, that found a husband in any. Before the choice is fixed, she has either lost her reputation, or her good sense; and the loss of either is sufficient to consign her to perpetual virginity.

Among the number of this young lady's lovers was the celebrated *S*——, who, at that time, went by the name of *the good-natured man.* This gentleman, with talents that might have done honour to humanity, suffered himself to fall at length into the lowest state of debasement. He followed the dictates of every newest passion, his love, his pity, his generosity, and even his friendships were all in excess; he was unable to make head against any of his sensations or desires, but they were in general worthy wishes and desires; for he was constitutionally virtuous. This gentleman, who at last died in a gaol, was at that time this lady's envied favourite.

It is probable that he, thoughtless creature, had no other prospect from this amour, but that of passing the present moments agreeably. He only courted dissipation, but the lady's thoughts were fixed on happiness. At length, however, his debts amounting to a considerable sum, he was arrested, and thrown into prison. He endeavoured at first to conceal his situation from his beautiful mistress; but she soon came to a knowledge of his distress, and took a fatal resolution of freeing him from confinement by discharging all the demands of his creditors.

Mr. *Nash* was at that time in *London*, and represented to the thoughtless young lady, that such a measure would effectually ruin both; that so warm a concern for the interests of Mr. *S*——, would in the first place quite impair her fortune, in the eyes of our sex; and what was worse, lessen her reputation in those of her own. He added, that thus bringing Mr. *S*—— from prison, would be only a temporary relief; that a mind so generous as his, would become bankrupt under the load of gratitude; and instead of improving in friendship or affection, he would only study to avoid a creditor he could never repay; that tho' small favours produce good-will, great ones destroy friendship. These admonitions however were disregarded, and she too late found the prudence and truth of her adviser. In short, her fortune was by this means exhausted, and, with all her attractions, she found her acquaintance began to dis-esteem her, in proportion as she became poor.

In this situation she accepted Mr. *Nash*'s invitation of returning to *Bath*; he promised to introduce her to the best company there, and he was assured that her merit would do the rest; upon her very first appearance, ladies of the highest distinction courted her friendship and esteem; but a settled melancholy had taken possession of her mind, and no amusements that they could propose were sufficient to divert it. Yet still, as if from habit, she followed the crowd in its levities, and frequented those places, where all persons endeavour to forget themselves in the bustle of ceremony and shew.

Her beauty, her simplicity, and her unguarded situation, soon drew the attention of a designing wretch, who at that time kept one of the rooms at *Bath*, and who thought, that this lady's merit, properly managed, might turn to good account. This woman's name was dame *Lindsey*, a creature, who, though vicious, was in appearance sanctified; and, though designing, had some wit and humour. She began by the humblest assiduity to ingratiate herself with miss *S*——; shewed that she could be amusing as a companion, and by frequent offers of money, proved, that she could be useful as a friend. Thus, by degrees, she gained an entire ascendant over this poor, thoughtless, deserted girl; and, in less than one year, namely about 1727, miss *S*, without ever transgressing the laws of virtue, had entirely lost her reputation. Whenever a person was wanting to make up a party for play at dame *Lindsey*'s, *Sylvia*, as she was then familiarly called, was sent for, and was obliged to suffer all those slights, which the rich but too often let fall upon their inferiors in point of fortune.

In most, even the greatest, minds, the heart at last becomes level with the meanness of its condition; but, in this charming girl, it struggled hard with adversity, and yielded to every encroachment of contempt with sullen reluctance.

But though in the course of three years she was in the very eye of public inspection, yet Mr. *Wood* the architect, avers, that he could never, by the strictest observations, perceive her to be tainted with any other vice, than that of suffering herself to be decoyed to the gaming-table, and, at her own hazard, playing for the amusement and advantage of others. Her friend, Mr. *Nash*, therefore, thought proper to induce her to break off all connections with dame *Lindsey*, and to rent part of Mr. *Wood*'s house, in *Queen square*, where she behaved with the utmost complaisance, regularity, and virtue.

In this situation her detestation of life still continued; she found, that time would infallibly deprive her of part of her attractions, and that continual solicitude would impair the rest. With these reflections she would frequently entertain herself, and an old faithful maid in the vales of *Bath*, whenever the weather would permit them to walk out. She would even sometimes start questions in company, with seeming unconcern, in order to know what act of suicide was easiest, and which was attended with the smallest pain. When tired with exercise, she generally retired to meditation, and she became habituated to early hours of sleep and rest. But when the weather prevented her usual exercise, and her sleep was thus more difficult, she made it a rule to rise from her bed, and walk about her chamber, till she began to find an inclination for repose.

This custom made it necessary for her to order a burning candle to be kept all night in her room. And the maid usually, when she withdrew, locked the chamber door, and pushing the key under it beyond reach, her mistress by that constant method lay undisturbed till seven o'clock in the morning, then she arose, unlocked the door, and rang the bell, as a signal for the maid to return.

This state of seeming piety, regularity, and prudence, continued for some time, till the gay, celebrated, toasted miss *Sylvia* was sunk into an housekeeper to the gentleman at whose house she lived. She was unable to keep company for want of the elegancies of dress, that are the usual passport among the polite, and she was too haughty to seem to want them. The fashionable, the amusing, and the polite in society now seldom visited her, and from being once the object of every eye, she was now deserted by all, and preyed upon by the bitter reflections of her own imprudence.

Mr. *Wood*, and part of his family, were gone to *London*.

Miss *Sylvia* was left with the rest as a governess at *Bath.* She sometimes saw Mr. *Nash*, and acknowledged the friendship of his admonitions, though she refused to accept any other marks of his generosity, than that of advice. Upon the close of the day, in which Mr. *Wood* was expected to return from *London*, she expressed some uneasiness at the disappointment of not seeing him; took particular care to settle the affairs of his family, and then as usual sate down to meditation. She now cast a retrospect over her past misconduct, and her approaching misery; she saw, that even affluence gave her no real happiness, and from indigence she thought nothing could be hoped but lingering calamity. She at length conceived the fatal resolution of leaving a life, in which she could see no corner for comfort, and terminating a scene of imprudence in suicide.

Thus resolved, she sate down at her dining-room window, and with cool intrepidity, wrote the following elegant lines on one of the panes of the window.

O death; thou pleasing end of human woe!
Thou cure for life! Thou greatest good below!
Still may'st thou fly the coward, and the slave,
And thy soft slumbers only bless the brave.

She then went into company with the most chearful serenity; talked of indifferent subjects till supper, which she ordered to be got ready in a little library belonging to the family. There she spent the remaining hours, preceding bed-time, in dandling two of Mr. *Wood*'s children on her knees. In retiring from thence to her chamber, she went into the nursery, to take her leave of another child, as it lay sleeping in the cradle. Struck with the innocence of the little babe's looks, and the consciousness of her meditated guilt, she could not avoid bursting into tears, and hugging it in her arms; she then bid her old servant a good night, for the first time she had ever done so, and went to bed as usual.

It is probable she soon quitted her bed, and was seized with an alternation of passions, before she yielded to the impulse of despair. She dressed herself in clean linen, and white garments of every kind, like a bride-maid. Her gown was pinned over her breast, just as a nurse pins the swaddling cloaths of an infant. A pink silk girdle was the instrument with which she resolved to terminate her misery, and this was lengthened by another made of gold thread. The end of the former was tied with a noose, and the latter with three knots, at a small distance from one another.

Thus prepared, she sate down again, and read; for she left the book open at that place, in the story of *Olympia*, in the *Orlando Furioso* of *Ariosto*, where, by the perfidy and ingratitude of her bosom friend, she was ruined, and left to the mercy of an unpitying world. This tragical event gave her fresh spirits to go through her fatal purpose; so standing upon a stool, and flinging the girdle, which was tied round her neck, over a closet-door that opened into her chamber, she remained suspended. Her weight however broke the girdle, and the poor despairer fell upon the floor with such violence, that her fall awakened a workman that lay in the house about half an hour after two o'clock.

Recovering herself, she began to walk about the room, as her usual custom was when she wanted sleep; and the workman imagining it to be only some ordinary accident, again went to sleep. She once more, therefore, had recourse to a stronger girdle made of silver thread; and this kept her suspended till she died.

Her old maid continued in the morning to wait as usual for the ringing of the bell, and protracted her patience, hour after hour, till two o'clock in the afternoon; when the workmen at length entering the room through the window, found their unfortunate mistress still hanging, and quite cold. The coroner's jury being impanelled, brought in their verdict lunacy; and her corpse was next night decently buried in her father's grave, at the charge of a female companion, with whom she had for many years an inseparable intimacy.

Thus ended a female wit, a toast, and a gamester; loved, admired, and forsaken. Formed for the delight of society, fallen by imprudence into an object of pity. Hundreds in high life lamented her fate, and wished, when too late, to redress her injuries. They who once had helped to impair her fortune, now regretted that they had assisted in so mean a pursuit. The little effects she had left behind were bought up with the greatest avidity, by those who desired to preserve some token of a companion, that once had given them such delight. The remembrance of every virtue she was possessed of was now improved by pity. Her former follies were few, but the last swelled them to a large amount. As she remains the strongest instance to posterity, that want of prudence alone, almost cancels every other virtue.

In all this unfortunate lady's affairs Mr. *Nash* took a peculiar concern, he directed her when they played, advised her when she deviated from the rules of caution, and performed the last offices of friendship after her decease, by raising the auction of her little effects.

But he was not only the assistant and the friend of the fair sex, but also their defender. He secured their persons from insult, and their reputations from scandal. Nothing offended him more, than a young fellow's pretending to receive favours from ladies he probably never saw; nothing pleased him so much, as seeing such a piece of deliberate mischief punished. Mr. *Nash* and one of his friends, being newly arrived at *Tunbridge* from *Bath*, were one day on the walks, and seeing a young fellow of fortune, with whom they had some slight acquaintance, joined him. After the usual chat and news of the day was over, Mr. *Nash* asked him, how long he had been at the wells, and what company was there? The other replied, he had been at *Tunbridge* a month; but as for company, he could find as good at a *Tyburn* ball. Not a soul was to be seen, except a parcel of gamesters and whores, who would grant the last favour, for a single stake at the Pharaoh bank. "Look you there," continued he, "that Goddess of midnight, so fine, at t'other end of the walks, by Jove, she was mine this morning for half a guinea. And she there, who brings up the rear with powdered hair and dirty ruffles, she's pretty enough, but cheap, perfectly cheap; why, my boys, to my own knowledge, you may have her for a crown, and a dish of chocolate into the bargain. Last *Wednesday* night we were happy." "Hold there, sir," cried the gentleman; "as for your having the first lady, it is possible it may be true, and I intend to ask her about it, for she is my sister; but as to your lying with the other last *Wednesday*, I am sure you are a lying rascal—she is my wife, and we came here but last night." The Buck vainly asked pardon; the gentleman was going to give him proper chastisement; when Mr. *Nash* interposed in his behalf, and obtained his pardon, upon condition that he quitted *Tunbridge* immediately.

But Mr. *Nash* not only took care, during his administration, to protect the ladies from the insults of our sex, but to guard them from the slanders of each other. He, in the first place, prevented any animosities that might arise from place and precedence, by being previously acquainted with the rank and quality of almost every family in the *British* dominions. He endeavoured to render scandal odious, by marking it as the result of envy and folly united. Not even *Solon* could have enacted a wiser law in such a society as *Bath*. The gay, the heedless, and the idle, which mostly compose the groupe of water-drinkers, seldom are at the pains of talking upon universal topics, which require comprehensive thought, or abstract reasoning. The adventures of the little circle of their own acquaintance, or of some names of quality and fashion, make up their whole conversation. But it is too likely, that when we mention those, we wish to depress them, in order to render ourselves more conspicuous; scandal must therefore have fixed her throne at *Bath*, preferable to any other part of the kingdom. However, tho' these endeavours could not totally suppress this custom among the fair, yet they gained him the friendship of several ladies of distinction, who had smarted pretty severely under the lash of censure. Among this number was the old duchess of *Marlborough*, who conceived a particular friendship for him, and which continued during her life. She frequently consulted him in several concerns of a private nature. Her letting leases, building bridges, or forming canals, were often carried on under his guidance; but she advised with him particularly in purchasing liveries for the footmen; a business to which she thought his genius best adapted.

. . . .

Whatever might have been Mr. *Nash*'s other excellencies, there was one in which few exceeded him; I mean his extensive humanity. None felt pity more strongly, and none made greater efforts to relieve distress. If I were to name any reigning and fashionable virtue in the present age, I think it should be charity. The numberless benefactions privately given, the various public solicitations for charity, and the success they meet with, serve to prove, that though we may fall short of our ancestors in other respects, yet in this instance we greatly excel them. I know not whether it may not be spreading the influence of Mr. *Nash* too widely to say, that he was one of the principal causes of introducing this noble emulation among the rich; but certain it is, no private man ever relieved the distresses of so many as he did.

Before gaming was suppressed, and in the meridian of his life and fortune, his benefactions were generally found to equal his other expences. The money he got without pain, he gave away without reluctance; and whenever unable to relieve a wretch who sued for assistance, he has been often seen to shed tears. A gentleman of broken fortune, one day standing behind his chair, as he was playing a game of picquet for two hundred pounds, and observing with what indifference he won the money, could not avoid whispering these words to another who stood by; "Heavens! how happy would all that money make me!" *Nash*, overhearing him, clapped the money into his hand; and cried, *Go and be happy*.

About six and thirty years ago, a clergyman brought his family to *Bath* for the benefit of the waters. His wife laboured under a lingering disorder, which it was thought nothing but the Hot Wells could remove. The expences of living there soon lessened the poor man's finances; his cloaths were sold, piece by piece, to provide a temporary relief for his little family; and his appearance was at last so shabby, that, from the number of holes in his coat and stockings, *Nash* gave him the name of doctor *Cullender*. Our beau, it seems, was rude enough to make a jest of poverty, though he had sensibility enough to relieve it. The poor clergyman combated his distresses with fortitude; and, instead of attempting to solicit relief, endeavoured to conceal them. Upon a living of thirty pounds a year he endeavoured to maintain his wife and six children; but all his resources at last failed him, and nothing but famine was seen in the wretched family. The poor man's circumstances were at last communicated to *Nash*; who, with his usual chearfulness, undertook to relieve him. On a sunday evening, at a public tea-drinking at *Harrison*'s, he went about to collect a subscription, and began it himself, by giving five guineas. By this means, two hundred guineas were collected in less than two hours, and the poor family raised from the lowest despondence into affluence and felicity. A bounty so unexpected had a better influence even upon the woman's constitution, than all that either the physicians or the waters of *Bath* could produce, and she recovered. But his good offices did not rest here. He prevailed upon a nobleman of his acquaintance, to present the Doctor with a living of an hundred and sixty pounds a year, which made that happiness, he had before produced, in some measure permanent.

In the severe winter, which happened in the year 1739, his charity was great, useful, and extensive. He frequently, at that season of calamity, entered the houses of the poor, whom he thought too proud to beg, and generously relieved them. The colliers were at this time peculiarly distressed; and, in order to excite compassion, a number of them yoaked themselves to a waggon loaded with coals, and drew it into *Bath*, and presented it to Mr. *Nash*. Their scheme had the proper effect. Mr. *Nash* procured them a subscription, and gave ten guineas towards it himself. The weavers also shared his bounty at that season. They came begging in a body into *Bath*, and he provided a plentiful dinner for their entertainment, and gave each a week's subsistence at going away.

. . . .

It may not be known to the generality of my readers, that the last act of the comedy, called *Esop*, which was added to the *French* plot of *Boursault*, by Mr. *Vanbrugh*, was taken from a story told of Mr. *Nash*, upon a similar occasion. He had in the early part of life made proposals of marriage to miss *V*——, of *D*——; his affluence at that time, and the favour which he was in with the nobility, readily induced the young lady's father to favour his addresses. However, upon opening the affair to herself, she candidly told him, her affections were placed upon another, and that she could not possibly comply. Though this answer satisfied Mr. *Nash*, it was by no means sufficient to appease the father; and he peremptorily insisted upon her obedience. Things were carried to the last extremity; when Mr. *Nash* undertook to settle the affair; and desiring his favoured rival to be sent for, with his own hand presented his mistress to him, together with a fortune equal to what her father intended to give her. Such an uncommon instance of generosity had an instant effect upon the severe parent; he considered such disinterestedness as a just reproach to his own mercenary disposition, and took his daughter once more into favour. I wish, for the dignity of history, that the sequel could be concealed, but the young lady ran away with her footman, before half a year was expired; and her husband died of grief.

In general, the benefactions of a generous man are but ill bestowed. His heart seldom gives him leave to examine the real distress of the object which sues for pity; and good-nature takes the alarm too soon, and he bestows his fortune on only apparent wretchedness. The man naturally frugal, on the other hand, seldom relieves, but when he does, his reason, and not his sensations, generally find out the object. Every instance of his bounty is therefore permanent, and bears witness to his benevolence.

Of all the immense sums which *Nash* lavished upon real or apparent wretchedness, the effects, after a few years, seemed to disappear. His money was generally given to support immediate want, or to relieve improvident indolence, and therefore it vanished in an hour. Perhaps towards the close of life, were he to look round on the thousands he had relieved, he would find but few made happy, or fixed by his bounty in a state of thriving industry; it was enough for him, that he gave to those that wanted; he never considered, that charity to some might impoverish himself without relieving them; he seldom considered the merit or the industry of the petitioner; or he rather fancied, that misery was an excuse for indolence and guilt. It was an usual saying of his, when he went to beg for any person in distress, that they who could stoop to the meanness of solicitation, must certainly *want* the favour for which they petitioned.

In this manner therefore he gave away immense sums of his own, and still greater, which he procured from others. His way was, when any person was proposed to him as an object of charity, to go round with his hat, first among the nobility, according to their rank, and so on, till he left scarce a single person unsolicited. They who go thus about to beg for others, generally find a pleasure in the task. They consider, in some measure, every benefaction they procure, as given by themselves, and have at once the pleasure of being liberal, without the self reproach of being profuse.

But of all the instances of Mr. *Nash*'s bounty, none does him more real honour, than the pains he took in establishing an hospital at *Bath*, in which benefaction, however, Doctor *Oliver* had a great share. This was one of those well guided charities, dictated by reason, and supported by prudence. By this institution the diseased poor might recover health, when incapable of receiving it in any other part of the kingdom. As the disorders of the poor, who could expect to find relief at *Bath*, were mostly chronical, the expence of maintaining them there was found more than their parishes thought proper to afford. They therefore chose to support them in a continual state of infirmity, by a small allowance at home, rather than be at the charge of an expensive cure. An hospital therefore at *Bath* it was thought would be an assylum, and a place of relief to those disabled creatures, and would, at the same time, give the physician more thorough insight into the efficacy of the waters, from the regularity with which such patients would be obliged to take them. These inducements therefore influenced Doctor *Oliver*, and Mr. *Nash*, to promote a subscription towards such a benefaction. The design was set on foot so early as the year 1711, but not completed till the year 1742. This delay, which seems surprizing, was in fact owing to the want of a proper fund for carrying the work into execution. What I said above, of charity being the characteristic virtue of the present age, will be more fully evinced, by comparing the old and new subscriptions for this hospital. These will shew the difference between ancient and modern benevolence. When I run my eye over the list of those who subscribed in the year 1723, I find the subscription in general seldom rise above a guinea each person; so that, at that time, with all their efforts, they were unable to raise four hundred pounds; but in about twenty years after, each particular subscription was greatly encreased, ten, twenty, thirty pounds, being the most ordinary sums subscribed, and they soon raised above two thousand pounds for the purpose.

Thus chiefly by the means of Doctor *Oliver* and Mr. *Nash*, but not without the assistance of the good Mr. *Allen*, who gave them the stone for building and other benefactions, this hospital was erected, and it is at present fitted up for the reception of patients, the cases most paralytic or leprous. The following conditions are observed previous to admittance.

"I. The case of the patient must be described by some physician, or person of skill, in the neighbourhood of the place where the patient has resided for some time; and this description, together with a certificate of the poverty of the patient, attested by some persons of credit, must be sent in a letter post-paid, directed to the register of the *General Hospital at Bath*.

II. After the patient's case has been thus described, and sent, he must remain in his usual place or residence 'till he has notice of a vacancy, signified by a letter from the register.

III. Upon the receipt of such a letter, the patient must set forward for *Bath*, bringing with him this letter, the parish certificate duly executed, and allowed by two justices, and three pounds caution-money, if from any part of *England* or *Wales*; but if the patient comes from *Scotland* or *Ireland*, then the caution-money, to be deposited before admission, is the sum of five pounds.

IV. Soldiers may, instead of parish certificates, bring a certificate from their commanding officers, signifying to what corps they belong, and that they shall be received into the same corps, when discharged from the Hospital, in whatever condition they are. But it is necessary that their cases be described, and sent previously, and that they bring with them three pounds caution-money.

Note, The intention of the caution-money is to defray the expences of returning the patients after they are discharged from the Hospital, or of their burial in case they die there. The remainder of the caution-money, after these expences are defrayed, will be returned to the person who made the deposit."

I am unwilling to leave this subject of his benevolence, because it is a virtue in his character which must stand almost single against an hundred follies; and it deserves the more to be insisted on, because it was large enough to outweigh them all. A man may be an hypocrite safely in every other instance, but in charity; there are few who will buy the character of benevolence at the rate for which it must be acquired. In short, the sums he gave away were immense; and, in old age, when at last grown too poor to give relief, *he gave*, as the poet has it, *all he had*, *a tear*; when incapable of relieving the agonies of the wretched, he attempted to relieve his own by a flood of sorrow.

The sums he gave and collected for the hospital, were great, and his manner of doing it was no less admirable. I am told that he was once collecting money in *Wiltshire*'s room for that purpose, when a lady entered who is more remarkable for her wit than her charity, and not being able to pass by him unobserved, she gave him a pat with her fan, and said, *You must put down a trifle for me*, Nash, *for I have no money in my pocket*. Yes, madam, says he, that I will with pleasure, if your grace will tell me when to stop: then taking a handful of guineas out of his pocket, he began to tell them into his white hat, one, two, three, four, five. *Hold*, *hold*, says the dutchess, *consider what you are about*. Consider your rank and fortune, madam, says *Nash*, and continued telling, six, seven, eight, nine, ten. Here the dutchess called again, and seemed angry. Pray compose yourself, *madam*, cried *Nash*, and don't interrupt the work of charity; eleven, twelve, thirteen, fourteen, fifteen. Here the dutchess stormed, and caught hold of his hand. Peace, *madam*, says *Nash*; you shall have your name written in letters of gold, *madam*, and upon the front of the building, *madam.* Sixteen, seventeen, eighteen, nineteen, twenty. *I won't pay a farthing more*, says the dutchess. Charity hides a multitude of sins, replies *Nash.* Twenty-one, twenty-two, twenty-three, twenty-four, twenty-five. *Nash*, says she, *I protest you frighten me out of my wits. L——d, I shall die!* Madam, you will never die with doing good; and if you do, it will be the better for you, answered *Nash*, and was about to proceed; but perceiving her grace had lost all patience, a parley ensued, when he, after much altercation, agreed to stop his hand, and compound with her grace for thirty guineas. The dutchess, however, seemed displeased the whole evening; and when he came to the table where she was playing, bid him *stand farther, an ugly devil, for she hated the sight of him.* But her grace afterwards, having a run of good luck, called *Nash* to her. *Come*, says she, *I will be friends with you, though you are a fool; and to let you see I am not angry, there is ten guineas more for your charity. But this I insist on, that neither my name, nor the sum, shall be mentioned.*

From the hospital erected for the benefit of the poor, it is an easy transition to the monuments erected by him in honour of the great. Upon the recovery of the Prince of *Orange*, by drinking the *Bath* waters, Mr. *Nash* caused a small obelisk, thirty feet high, to be erected in a grove near the Abbey church, since called *Orange Grove.* This Prince's arms adorn the west side of the body of the pedestal. The inscription is on the opposite side, in the following words:

In memoriam
Sanitatis
Principi Auriaco
Aquarum thermalium potu.
Favente Deo,
Ovante Britannia,
Feliciter restitutæ,
M. DCC. XXXIV.

In English thus.

In memory
Of the happy restoration
Of the health of the
Prince of *Orange*,
Through the favour of God,
And to the great joy of Britain,
By drinking the *Bath* waters.
1734.

I find it a general custom, at all Baths and Spaws, to erect monuments of this kind to the memory of every Prince, who has received benefit from the waters. *Aix*, *Spaw* and *Pisa*, abound with inscriptions of this nature, apparently doing honour to the Prince, but in reality celebrating the efficacy of their springs. It is wrong, therefore, to call such monuments instances of gratitude, though they may wear that appearance.

In the year 1738, the Prince of *Wales* came to *Bath*, who presented Mr. *Nash* with a large gold enamelled snuff-box; and upon his departure, *Nash*, as King of *Bath*, erected an obelisk in honour of this Prince, as he had before done for the Prince of *Orange*. This handsome memorial in honour of that good-natured Prince is erected in *Queen square*. It is enclosed with a stone balustrade, and in the middle of every side there are large iron gates. In the centre is the obelisk, seventy feet high, and terminating in a point. The expences of this were eighty pounds; and Mr. *Nash* was determined, that the inscription should answer the magnificence of the pile. With this view he wrote to Mr. *Pope*, at *London*, requesting an inscription. I should have been glad to have given Mr. *Nash*'s letter upon this occasion; the reader, however, must be satisfied with *Pope*'s reply; which is as follows.

SIR

I have received yours, and thank your partiality in my favour. You say words cannot express the gratitude you feel for the favour of his R. H. and yet you would have me express what you feel, and in a few words. I own myself unequal to the task; for even, granting it possible to express an inexpressible idea, I am the worst person you could have pitched upon for this purpose, who have received so few favours from the great myself, that I am utterly unacquainted with what kind of thanks they like best. Whether the P—— most loves poetry or prose, I protest I do not know; but this I dare venture to affirm, that you can give him as much satisfaction in either as I can.

I am,

SIR,

Your affectionate Servant,

A. POPE.

What Mr. *Nash*'s answer to this billet was, I cannot take upon me to ascertain, but it was probably a perseverance in his former request. The following is the copy of Mr. *Pope*'s reply to his second letter.

SIR

I had sooner answered yours, but in the hope of procuring a properer hand than mine; and then in consulting with some, whose office about the P—— might make them the best judges, what sort of inscription to set up. Nothing can be plainer than the inclosed; it is nearly the common sense of the thing, and I do not know how to flourish upon it. But this you would do as well, or better yourself, and I dare say may mend the expression. I am truly,

Dear SIR,

Your affectionate Servant,

A. POPE.

I think I need not tell you my name should not be mentioned.

Such a letter as this was what might naturally be expected from Mr. *Pope*. Notwithstanding the seeming modesty towards the conclusion, the vanity of an applauded writer bursts through every line of it. The difficulty of concealing his hand from the clerks at the Post-office, and the solicitude to have his name concealed, were marks of the consciousness of his own importance. It is probable, his hand was not so very well known, nor his letters so eagerly opened by the clerks of the Office, as he seems always to think. But in all his letters, as well as those of *Swift*, there runs a strain of pride, as if the world talked of nothing but themselves. *Alass*, says he, in one of them, *the day after I am dead, the sun will shine as bright as the day before, and the world will be as merry as usual!* Very strange, that neither an eclipse nor an earthquake should follow the loss of a Poet!

The inscription referred to in this letter, was the same which was afterwards engraved on the obelisk; and is as follows.

In memory of honours bestow'd,
And in gratitude for benefits conferred in this city,
By his Royal Highness
Frederick, Prince of *Wales*,
And his Royal Consort,
In the Year 1738,
This obelisk is erected by
Richard Nash, Esq;

I dare venture to say, there was scarce a common-councilman in the corporation of *Bath*, but could have done this as well. Nothing can be more frigid; though the subject was worthy of the utmost exertions of Genius.

About this period every season brought some new accession of honour to Mr. *Nash*; and the corporation now universally found, that he was absolutely necessary for promoting the welfare of the city; so that this year seems to have been the meridian of his glory. About this time he arrived at such a pitch of authority, that I really believe *Alexander* was not greater at *Persepolis*. The countenance he received from the Prince of *Orange*, the favour he was in with the Prince of *Wales*, and the caresses of the nobility, all conspired to lift him to the utmost pitch of vanity. The exultation of a little mind, upon being admitted to the familiarity of the Great, is inexpressible. The prince of *Orange* had made him a present of a very fine snuff-box. Upon this some of the nobility thought it would be proper to give snuff-boxes too; they were quickly imitated by the middling gentry, and it soon became the fashion to give Mr. *Nash* snuff-boxes; who had in a little time a number sufficient to have furnished a good toy-shop.

To add to his honours, there was placed a full-length picture of him, in *Wiltshire*'s-*Ball-room*, between the busts of *Newton* and *Pope*. It was upon this occasion that the Earl of *Chesterfield* wrote the following severe but witty epigram.

Immortal *Newton* never spoke
More truth than here you'll find;
Nor *Pope* himself e'er pen'd a joke
Severer on mankind.

This picture placed these busts between,
Gives satire its full strength;
Wisdom and *Wit* are little seen,
But Folly at full length.

There is also a full length picture of Mr. *Nash* in *Simpson*'s *Ball-room*; and his Statue at full length in the *Pump-room*, with a plan of the *Bath-Hospital* in his hand. He was now treated in every respect like a great man; he had his levee, his flatterers, his buffoons, his good-natured creatures, and even his dedicators. A trifling ill supported vanity was his foible, and while he received the homage of the vulgar, and enjoyed the familiarity of the great, he felt no pain for the unpromising view of poverty that lay before him; he enjoyed the world as it went, and drew upon content for the deficiencies of fortune. If a cringing wretch called him his Honour, he was pleased; internally conscious, that he had the justest pretensions to the title. If a beggar called him my Lord, he was happy, and generally sent the flatterer off happy too. I have known him, in *London*, wait a whole day at a window in the *Smyrna* coffee-house, in order to receive a bow from the Prince, or the Dutchess of *Marlborough*,[1] as they passed by where he was standing; and he would then look round upon the company for admiration and respect.

But perhaps the reader desires to know, who could be low enough to flatter a man, who himself lived in some measure by dependance. Hundreds are ready upon those occasions. The very needy are almost ever flatterers. A man in wretched circumstances forgets his own value, and feels no pain in giving up superiority to every claimant. The very vain are ever flatterers; as they find it necessary to make use of all their arts, to keep company with such as are superior to themselves. But particularly the prodigal are prone to adulation, in order to open new supplies for their extravagance. The poor, the vain, and extravagant, are chiefly addicted to this vice; and such hung upon his good nature. When these three characters are found united in one person, the composition generally becomes a great man's favourite. It was not difficult to collect such a groupe in a city that was the center of pleasure. *Nash* had them of all sizes, from the half pay captain in laced cloaths, to the humble boot-catcher at the *Bear*.

. . . .

The man, who is constantly served up with adulation, must be a first-rate philosopher, if he can listen without contracting new affectations. The opinion we form of ourselves, is generally measured by what we hear from others; and when they conspire to deceive, we too readily concur in the delusion. Among the number of much applauded men in the circle of

[1] [The Duchess died in 1744 when Goldsmith was still in Ireland.]

our own friends, we can recollect but few that have heads quite strong enough to bear a loud acclamation of public praise in their favour; among the whole list, we shall scarce find one, that has not thus been made, on some side of his character, a coxcomb.

When the best head turns and grows giddy with praise, is it to be wondered that poor *Nash* should be driven by it almost into a phrenzy of affectation? Towards the close of life he became affected. He chiefly laboured to be thought a sayer of good things; and by frequent attempts was now and then successful, for he ever lay upon the lurch.

There never perhaps was a more silly passion, than this desire of having a man's jests recorded. For this purpose, it is necessary to keep ignorant or ill-bred company, who are only fond of repeating such stories; in the next place, a person must tell his own jokes, in order to make them more universal; but what is worst of all, scarce a joke of this kind succeeds, but at the expence of a man's good nature; and he who exchanges the character of being thought agreeable, for that of being thought witty, makes but a very bad bargain.

The success *Nash* sometimes met with led him on, when late in life, to mistake his true character. He was really agreeable, but he chose to be thought a wit. He therefore indulged his inclination, and never mattered how rude he was, provided he was thought comical. He thus got the applause he sought for, but too often found enemies, where he least expected to find them. Of all the jests recorded of him, I scarce find one that is not marked with petulance; he said whatever came uppermost, and in the number of his remarks it might naturally be expected that some were worth repeating; he threw often, and sometimes had a lucky cast.

In a life of almost ninety years, spent in the very point of public view, it is not strange, that five or six sprightly things of his have been collected, particularly as he took every opportunity of repeating them himself. His usual way, when he thought he said any thing clever, was to strengthen it with an oath, and to make up its want of sentiment by asseveration and grimace. For many years he thus entertained the company at the coffee-house with old stories, in which he always made himself the principal character. Strangers liked this well enough; but they who were used to his conversation found it insupportable. One story brought on another, and each came in the same order that it had the day preceding. But this custom may be rather ascribed to the peculiarity of age, than a peculiarity of character; it seldom happens, that old men allure, at least by novelty; age that shrivels the body contracts the understanding; instead of exploring new regions, they rest satisfied in the old, and walk around the circle of their former discoveries. His manner of telling a story, however, was not displeasing, but few of those he told are worth transcribing. Indeed it is the manner, which places the whole difference between the wit of the vulgar, and of those who assume the name of the polite; one has in general as much good sense as the other; a story transcribed from the one, will be as entertaining as that copied from the other; but in conversation, the manner will give charms even to stupidity. The following is the story which he most frequently told, and pretty much in these words. Suppose the company to be talking of a *German* war, or *Elizabeth Canning*, he would begin thus: "I'll tell you something to that purpose that I fancy will make you laugh. A covetous old parson, as rich as the Devil, scraped a fresh acquaintance with me several years ago at *Bath*. I knew him when he and I were students at *Oxford*, where we both studied damnationly hard, but that's neither here nor there. Well. Very well. I entertained him at my house in *John*'s *Court*. (No, my house in *John*'s *Court* was not built then) but I entertained him with all that the city could afford; the rooms, the music, and every thing in the world. Upon his leaving *Bath*, he pressed me very hard to return the visit; and desired me to let him have the pleasure of seeing me at his house in *Devonshire*. About six months after, I happened to be in that neighbourhood, and was resolved to see my old friend, from whom I expected a very warm reception. Well: I knocks at his door, when an old queer creature of a maid, came to the door, and denied him. I suspected, however, that he was at home; and going into the parlour, what should I see, but the Parson's legs up the chimney, where he had thrust himself to avoid entertaining me. This was very well. My dear, says I to the maid, it is very cold, extreme cold indeed, and I am afraid I have got a touch of my ague, light me the fire, if you please. La, Sir, says the maid, who was a modest creature to be sure, the chimney smokes monstrously; you could not bear the room for three minutes together. By the greatest good luck there was a bundle of straw in the hearth, and I called for a candle. The candle came. Well, good woman, says I, since you won't light me a fire, I'll light one for myself, and in a moment the straw was all in a blaze. This quickly unkennelled the old fox; there he stood in an old rusty night gown, blessing himself, and looking like—a—hem—egad."

He used to tell surprizing stories of his activity when young. "Here I stand, gentlemen, that could once leap forty two feet upon level ground, at three standing jumps, backward or forward. One, two, three, dart like an arrow out of a bow. But I am old now. I remember I once leaped for three hundred guineas with Count *Klopstock*, the great leaper, leaping-master to the Prince of *Passau*; you must all have heard of him. First he began with the running jump, and a most damnable bounce it was, that's certain: Every body concluded that he had the match hollow; when only taking off my hat, stripping off neither coat, shoes, nor stockings, mind me, I fetches a run, and went beyond him one foot, three inches and three quarters, measured, upon my soul, by Captain *Pately*'s own standard."

But in this torrent of insipidity, there sometimes were found very severe satire, strokes of true wit, and lines of humour, *cum fluerent lutulentus, &c.*[1] He rallied very successfully, for he never felt another's joke; and drove home his own without pity. With his superiors he was familiar and blunt, the inferiority of his station secured him from their resentment; but the same bluntness which they laughed at, was by his equals regarded as insolence. Something like a familiar boot-catcher at an inn, a gentleman would bear that joke from him, for which a brother boot-catcher would knock him down.

Among other stories of *Nash*'s telling, I remember one, which I the more chearfully repeat, as it tends to correct a piece of impertinence that reigns in almost every country assembly. The principal inhabitants of a market-town, at a great distance from the capital, in order to encourage that harmony which ought to subsist in society, and to promote a mutual intercourse between the sexes, so desirable to both, and so necessary for all, had established a monthly assembly in the Town Hall, which was conducted with such decency, decorum, and politeness, that it drew the attention of the gentlemen and ladies in the neighbourhood; and a nobleman and his family continually honoured them with their presence. This naturally drew others, and in time the room was crouded with, what the world calls, good company, and the assembly prospered, till some of the new admitted ladies took it into their heads, that the tradesmen's daughters were unworthy of their notice, and therefore refused to join hands with them in the dance. This was complained of by the town ladies, and that complaint was resented by the country gentlemen, who, more pert than wise, publickly advertised, that they would not dance with tradesmen's daughters. This the most eminent tradesmen considered as an insult on themselves, and being men of worth, and able to live independently, they in return advertised that they would give no credit out of their town, and desired all others to discharge their accounts. A general

[1] ["In the turbid stream." Horace, *Satires*, I. 4. 11.]

uneasiness ensued; some writs were actually issued out, and much distress would have happened, had not my Lord, who sided with no party, kindly interfered and composed the difference. The assembly however was ruined, and the families, I am told, are not friends yet, though this affair happened thirty years ago.

Nothing debases human nature so much as pride—This *Nash* knew, and endeavoured to stifle every emotion of it at *Bath.* When he observed any ladies so extremely delicate and proud of a pedigree, as to only touch the back of an inferior's hand in the dance, he always called to order, and desired them to leave the room, or behave with common decency; and when any Ladies and Gentlemen drew off, after they had gone down a dance, without standing up till the dance was finished, he made up to them, and after asking whether they had done dancing, told them, they should dance no more unless they stood up for the rest; and on these occasions he always was as good as his word.

Nash, tho' no great wit, had the art of sometimes saying rude things with decency, and rendering them pleasing by an uncommon turn.—But most of the good things attributed to him, which have found their way into the jest books, are no better than puns; the smartest things I have seen are against him. One day in the grove, he joined some ladies, and asking one of them, who was crooked, whence she came? she replied, strait from *London.* Confound me, madam, said he, then you must have been damnably warpt by the way.

She soon, however, had ample revenge. Sitting the following evening in one of the rooms, he once more joined her company, and with a sneer and a bow, asked her, if she knew her Catechism, and could tell the name of *Tobit*'s dog? His name, Sir, was *Nash*, replied the lady, and an impudent dog he was. This story is told in a celebrated romance;[1] I only repeat

[1] [Smollett's *Roderick Random*, Chapter LV. Only the latter part of the story is told.]

it here to have an opportunity of observing, that it actually happened.

Queen *Anne* once asked him, why he would not accept of knighthood? To which he replied, lest Sir *William Read*, the mountebank, who had been just knighted, should call him brother.

A house in *Bath* was said to be haunted by the Devil, and a great noise was made about it, when *Nash*, going to the minister of St. *Michael*'s, intreated him to drive the Devil out of *Bath* for ever, if it were only to oblige the ladies.

Nash used sometimes to visit the great Doctor *Clarke*. The Doctor was one day conversing with *Locke*, and two or three more of his learned and intimate companions, with that freedom, gaiety and chearfulness, which is ever the result of innocence. In the midst of their mirth and laughter, the Doctor, looking from the window, saw *Nash*'s chariot stop at the door. Boys, boys, cried the philosopher, to his friends, let us now be wise, for here is a fool coming.

Nash was one day complaining in the following manner to the Earl of *Chesterfield* of his bad luck at play. Would you think it, my Lord, that damned bitch fortune, no later than last night, tricked me out of 500. Is it not surprizing, continued he, that my luck should never turn, that I should thus eternally be mauled? I don't wonder at your losing money *Nash*, says his lordship, but all the world is surprized where you get it to lose.

Doctor *Cheney* once, when *Nash* was ill, drew up a prescription for him, which was sent in accordingly. The next day the Doctor coming to see his patient, found him up and well; upon which he asked, if he had followed his prescription? Followed your prescription, cried *Nash*, No.—Egad, if I had, I should have broke my neck, for I flung it out of the two pair stairs window.

It would have been well, had he confined himself to such sallies; but as he grew old he grew insolent, and seemed, in some measure, insensible of the pain his attempts to be a wit gave others. Upon asking a lady to dance a minuet; if she refused, he would often demand, if she had got bandy legs. He would attempt to ridicule natural defects; he forgot the deference due to birth and quality, and mistook the manner of settling rank and precedence upon many occasions. He now seemed no longer fashionable among the present race of gentry, he grew peevish and fretful, and they who only saw the remnant of a man, severely returned that laughter upon him, which he had once lavished upon others.

Poor *Nash* was no longer the gay, thoughtless, idly industrious creature he once was; he now forgot how to supply new modes of entertainment, and became too rigid, to wind with ease through the vicissitudes of fashion. The evening of his life began to grow cloudy. His fortune was gone, and nothing but poverty lay in prospect. To embitter his hopes, he found himself abandoned by the great, whom he had long endeavoured to serve; and was obliged to fly to those of humbler stations for protection, whom he once affected to despise. He now began to want that charity, which he had never refused to any; and to find, that a life of dissipation and gaiety, is ever terminated by misery and regret.

. . . .

He found poverty now denied him the indulgence not only of his favourite follies, but of his favourite virtues. The poor now solicited him in vain; he was himself a more pitiable object than they. The child of the public seldom has a friend, and he who once exercised his wit at the expence of others, must naturally have enemies. Exasperated at last to the highest degree, an unaccountable whim struck him; poor *Nash* was resolved to become an author; he who, in the vigour of manhood, was incapable of the task, now at the impotent age of eighty-six, was determined to write his own history! From the many specimens already given of his style, the reader will not much regret that the historian was interrupted in his design. Yet as *Montaigne* observes, as the adventures of an infant, if an infant could inform us of them, would be pleasing; so the life of a Beau, if a beau could write, would certainly serve to regale curiosity.

Whether he really intended to put this design in execution, or did it only to alarm the nobility, I will not take upon me to determine; but certain it is, that his friends went about collecting subscriptions for the work, and he received several encouragements from such as were willing to be politely charitable. It was thought by many, that this history would reveal the intrigues of a whole age; that he had numberless secrets to disclose; but they never considered, that persons of public character, like him, were the most unlikely in the world to be made partakers of those secrets which people desired the public should not know. In fact, he had few secrets to discover, and those he had, are now buried with him in the grave.

He was now past the power of giving or receiving pleasure, for he was poor, old and peevish; yet still he was incapable of turning from his former manner of life to pursue his happiness. The old man endeavoured to practise the follies of the boy, he spurred on his jaded passions after every trifle of the day; tottering with age he would be ever an unwelcome guest in the assemblies of the youthful and gay; and he seemed willing to find lost appetite among those scenes where he was once young.

An old man thus striving after pleasure is indeed an object of pity; but a man at once old and poor, running on in this pursuit, might excite astonishment. To see a Being both by fortune and constitution rendered incapable of enjoyment, still haunting those pleasures he was no longer to share in; to see one of almost ninety settling the fashion of a lady's cap, or assigning her place in a country dance; to see him unmindful of his own reverend figure, or the respect he should have for himself, toasting demireps, or attempting to entertain the lewd and idle; a sight like this might well serve as a satire on humanity; might shew that man is the only preposterous creature alive, who pursues the shadow of pleasure without temptation.

But he was not permitted to run on thus without severe and repeated reproof. The clergy sent him frequent calls to reformation; but the asperity of their advice in general abated its intended effects; they threatened him with fire and brimstone, for what he had long been taught to consider as foibles, and not vices; so, like a desperate debtor, he did not care to settle an account, that, upon the first inspection, he found himself utterly unable to pay.

. . . .

Thus we see a variety of causes concurred to embitter his departing life. The weakness and infirmities of exhausted nature, the admonitions of the grave, who aggravated his follies into vices; the ingratitude of his dependants, who formerly flattered his fortunes; but particularly the contempt of the great, many of whom quite forgot him in his wants; all these hung upon his spirits and soured his temper, and the poor man of pleasure might have terminated his life very tragically, had not the corporation of *Bath* charitably resolved to grant him ten guineas the first *Monday* of every month. This bounty served to keep him from actual necessity, though far too trifling, to enable him to support the character of a gentleman. Habit, and not nature, makes almost all our wants; and he who had been accustomed in the early parts of life to affluence and prodigality, when reduced to an hundred and twenty-six pounds a year, must pine in actual indigence.

In this variety of uneasiness his health began to fail. He had received from nature a robust and happy constitution, that was scarce even to be impaired by intemperance. He even pretended, among his friends, that he never followed a single prescription in his life; however, in this he was one day detected on the parade; for boasting there of his contempt and utter disuse of medicine, unluckily the water of two blisters, which Dr. *Oliver* had prescribed, and which he then had upon each leg, ouzed through his stockings, and betrayed him. His aversion to physic, however, was frequently a topic of raillery between him and Doctor *Cheney*, who was a man of some wit and breeding. When *Cheney* recommended his vegetable diet, *Nash* would swear, that his design was to send half the world grazing like *Nebuchadnezzar*. Ay, *Cheney* would reply, *Nebuchadnezzar* was never such an infidel as thou art. It was but last week, gentlemen, that I attended this fellow in a fit of sickness; there I found him rolling up his eyes to heaven, and crying for mercy; he would then swallow my drugs like breast-milk, yet you now hear him, how the old dog blasphemes the faculty. What *Cheney* said in jest was true, he feared the approaches of death more than the generality of mankind, and was generally very devout while it threatened him. Though he was somewhat the libertine in action, none believed or trembled more than he; for a mind neither schooled by philosophy, nor encouraged by conscious innocence, is ever timid at the appearance of danger.

For some time before his decease nature gave warning of his approaching dissolution. The worn machine had run itself down to an utter impossibility of repair; he saw, that he must die, and shuddered at the thought. His virtues were not of the great, but the amiable kind; so that fortitude was not among the number. Anxious, timid, his thoughts still hanging on a receding world, he desired to enjoy a little longer that life, the miseries of which he had experienced so long. The poor unsuccessful gamester husbanded the wasting moments, with an encreased desire to continue the game, and to the last eagerly wished for one yet more happy throw. He died at his house in St. *John*'s *Court*, *Bath*, on the 12th of *February*, 1761, aged eighty-seven years, three months, and some days.

His death was sincerely regretted by the city, to which he had been so long, and so great a benefactor. The day after he died, the Mayor of *Bath* called the corporation together, where they granted fifty pounds towards burying their sovereign with proper respect. After the corpse had lain four days, it was conveyed to the abbey church in that city, with a solemnity somewhat peculiar to his character. About five the procession moved from his house; the charity girls two and two preceded, next the boys of the charity school singing a solemn occasional hymn. Next marched the city music, and his own band sounding at proper intervals a dirge. Three clergymen immediately preceded the coffin, which was adorned with sable plumes, and the pall supported by the six senior aldermen. The masters of the assembly-rooms followed as chief mourners; the beadles of that hospital, which he had contributed so largely to endow, went next; and last of all, the poor patients themselves, the lame, the emaciated, and the feeble, followed their old benefactor to his grave, shedding unfeigned tears, and lamenting themselves in him.

The crowd was so great, that not only the streets were filled, but, as one of the journals in a *Rant* expresses it, "even the tops of the houses were covered with spectators, each thought the occasion affected themselves most; as when a real king dies, they asked each other, *where shall we find such another*; sorrow sate upon every face, and even children lisped that their Sovereign was no more. The awfulness of the solemnity made the deepest impression on the minds of the distressed inhabitants. The peasant discontinued his toil, the ox rested from the plough, all nature seemed to sympathize with their loss, and the muffled bells rung a peal of Bob Major."

Our deepest solemnities have something truly ridiculous in them: there is somewhat ludicrous in the folly of historians, who thus declaim upon the death of kings and princes, as if there was any thing dismal, or any thing unusual in it. "For my part," says *Poggi*, the *Florentine*, "I can no more grieve for another's death, than I could for my own. I have ever regarded death as a very trifling affair; nor can black staves, long cloaks, or mourning coaches, in the least influence my spirits. Let us live here as long, and as merrily as we can, and when we must die, why, let us die merrily too, but die so as to be happy."

The few things he was possessed of were left to his relations. A small library of well chosen books, some trinkets and pictures, were his only inheritance. Among the latter (besides the box given him by the prince of *Wales*), were a gold box, which was presented to him by the countess of *Burlington*, with lady *Euston*'s picture in the lid; an etui, mounted in gold, with a diamond to open it, and ornamented with another diamond at the top, given him by the princess dowager of *Wales*. He had also a silver terene, which was given him by the princess *Amelia*; and some other things of no great value. The rings, watches, and pictures, which he formerly received from others, would have come to a considerable amount; but these his necessities had obliged him to dispose of: some family pictures, however, remained, which were sold by advertisement, for five guineas each, after Mr. *Nash*'s decease.

It was natural to expect, that the death of a person so long in the eye of the public, must have produced a desire in several to delineate his character, or deplore his loss. He was scarce dead, when the public papers were filled with elegies, groans and characters; and before he was buried, there were epitaphs ready made to inscribe on his stone. I remember one of those character writers, and a very grave one too, after observing, alas! that *Richard Nash*, Esq. was no more, went on to assure us, that he was *sagacious*, *debonair*, *and commode*; and concluded with gravely declaring, *that impotent posterity would in vain fumble to produce his fellow*. Another, equally sorrowful, gave us to know, *that he was indeed a man*; an assertion, which I fancy none will be so hardy as to contradict. But the merriest of all the lamentations made upon this occasion was that where he is called, *A constellation of the heavenly sphere*.

One thing, however, is common almost with each of them, and that is, that *Venus*, *Cupid*, and the *Graces*, are commanded to weep; and that *Bath* shall never find such another.

. . . .

Whatever might have been justly observed of Mr. *Nash*'s superiority as a governor, at least it may be said, that few cotemporary kings have met with such able panegyrists. The former enumerates all his good qualities with tenderness; and the latter enforces them with impetuosity. They both seem to have loved him, and honourably paid his remains the last debt of friendship. But a cool biographer, unbiased by resentment or regard, will probably find nothing in the man either truly great, or strongly vicious. His virtues were all amiable, and more adapted to procure friends than admirers, they were more capable of raising love than esteem. He was naturally endued with good sense; but by having been long accustomed to pursue trifles, his mind shrunk to the size of the little objects on which it was employed. His generosity was boundless, because his tenderness and his vanity were in equal proportion; the one impelling him to relieve misery, and the other to make his benefactions known. In all his actions, however virtuous, he was guided by sensation, and not by reason; so that the uppermost passion was ever sure to prevail. His being constantly in company had made him an easy tho' not a polite companion. He chose to be thought rather an odd fellow, than a well-bred man; perhaps that mixture of respect and ridicule, with which his mock royalty was treated, first inspired him with this resolution. The foundations of his empire were laid in vicious compliance, the continuance of his reign was supported by a virtuous impartiality. In the beginning of his authority, he in reality obeyed those whom he pretended to govern; towards the end, he attempted to extort a real obedience from his subjects, and supported his right by prescription. Like a monarch *Tacitus* talks of; they complied with him at first because they loved, they obeyed at last because they feared him. He often led the rich into new follies, in order to promote the happiness of the poor, and served the one at the expence of the other. Whatever his vices were, they were of use to society; and this neither Petronius, nor Apicius, nor Tigellius, nor any other professed voluptuary, could say. To set him up, as some do, for a pattern of imitation, is wrong, since all his virtues received a tincture from the neighbouring folly; to denounce peculiar judgments against him, is equally unjust, as his faults raise rather our mirth than our detestation. He was fitted for the station in which fortune placed him. It required no great abilities to fill it, and few of great abilities, but would have disdained the employment. He led a life of vanity, and long mistook it for happiness. Unfortunately he was taught at last to know, that a man of pleasure leads the most unpleasant life in the world.

A Letter from Mr. **** *in* Tunbridge, *to Lord*—— *in* London; *found among the Papers of Mr.* Nash, *and prepared by him for the press.*

My Lord,

What I foresaw has arrived, poor *Jenners*, after losing all his fortune, has shot himself through the head. His losses to *Bland* were considerable, and his playing soon after with *Spedding* contributed to hasten his ruin. No man was ever more enamour'd of play, or understood it less. At whatever game he ventured his money, he was most usually the dupe, and still foolishly attributed to his bad luck, those misfortunes that entirely proceeded from his want of judgment.

After finding that he had brought on himself irreparable indigence and contempt, his temper, formerly so sprightly, began to grow gloomy and unequal; he grew more fond of solitude, and more liable to take offence at supposed injuries; in short, for a week before he shot himself, his friends were of opinion that he meditated some such horrid design. He was found in his chamber fallen on the floor, the bullet having glanced on the bone, and lodged behind his right eye.

You remember my Lord, what a charming fellow this deluded man was once. How benevolent, just, temperate, and every way virtuous; the only faults of his mind arose from motives of humanity; he was too easy, credulous and good-natured, and unable to resist temptation, when recommended by the voice of friendship. These foibles the vicious and the needy soon perceived, and what was at first a weakness they soon perverted into guilt; he became a gamester, and continued the infamous profession, till he could support the miseries it brought with it no longer.

I have often been not a little concerned to see the first introduction of a young man of fortune to the gaming-table. With what eagerness his company is courted by the whole fraternity of sharpers; how they find out his most latent wishes, in order to make way to his affections by gratifying them; and continue to hang upon him with the meanest degree of condescension. The youthful dupe no way suspecting, imagines himself surrounded by friends and gentlemen, and incapable of even suspecting that men of such seeming good sense, and so genteel an appearance, should deviate from the laws of honour, walks into the snare, nor is he undeceived till schooled by the severity of experience.

As I suppose no man would be a gamester unless he hoped to win, so I fancy it would be easy to reclaim him, if he was once effectually convinced, that by continuing to play he must certainly lose. Permit me, my Lord, to attempt this task, and to shew, that no young gentleman by a year's run of play, and in a mixed company, can possibly be a gainer.

Let me suppose in the first place, that the chances on both sides are equal, that there are no marked cards, no pinching, shuffling, nor hiding; let me suppose that the players also have no advantage of each other in point of judgment, and still further let me grant, that the party is only formed at home, without going to the usual expensive places of resort frequented by gamesters. Even with all these circumstances in the young gamester's favour, it is evident he cannot be a gainer. With equal players after a year's continuance of any particular game it will be found, that, whatever has been played for, the winnings on either side are very inconsiderable, and most commonly nothing at all. Here then is a year's anxiety, pain, jarring, and suspense, and nothing gained; were the parties to sit down and professedly play for nothing, they would contemn the proposal; they would call it trifling away time, and one of the most insipid amusements in nature; yet in fact, how do equal players differ? it is allowed that little or nothing can be gained; but much is lost; our youth, our time, those moments that may be laid out in pleasure or improvement, are foolishly squandered away, in tossing cards, fretting at ill luck, or, even with a run of luck in our favour, fretting that our winnings are so small.

I have now stated gaming in that point of view in which it is alone defensible, as a commerce carried on with equal advantage and loss to either party, and it appears, that the loss is great, and the advantage but small. But let me suppose the players not to be equal, but the superiority of judgment in our own favour. A person who plays under this conviction, however, must give up all pretensions to the approbation of his own mind, and is guilty of as much injustice, as the thief who robbed a blind man, because he knew he could not swear to his person.

But in fact, when I allowed the superiority of skill on the young beginner's side, I only granted an impossibility. Skill in gaming, like skill in making a watch, can only be acquired by long and painful industry. The most sagacious youth alive was never taught at once all the arts and all the niceties of gaming. Every passion must be schooled by long habit into caution, and phlegm; the very countenance must be taught proper discipline; and he who would practice this art with success, must practice on his own constitution all the severities of a martyr, without any expectation of the reward. It is evident therefore every beginner must be a dupe, and can only be expected to learn his trade by losses, disappointments, and dishonour.

If a young gentleman therefore begins to game, the commencements are sure to be to his disadvantage; and all that he can promise himself is, that the company he keeps, though superior in skill, are above taking advantage of his ignorance, and unacquainted with any sinister arts to correct fortune. But this, however, is but a poor hope at best, and what is worse, most frequently a false one. In general, I might almost have said always, those who live by gaming, are not beholding to chance alone for their support, but take every advantage which they can practise without danger of detection. I know many are apt to say, and I have once said so myself, that after I have shuffled the cards, it is not in the power of a sharper to pack them; but at present I can confidently assure your Lordship, that such reasoners are deceived. I have seen men, both in *Paris*, the *Hague*, and *London*, who, after three deals, could give whatever hands they pleased to all the company. However, the usual way with sharpers is to correct fortune thus but once in a night, and to play in other respects without blunder or mistake, and a perseverance in this practice always balances the year in their favour.

It is impossible to enumerate all the tricks and arts practised upon cards; few but have seen those bungling poor fellows who go about at coffee-houses perform their clumsy feats, and yet, indifferently as they are versed in the trade, they often deceive us; when such as these are possessed of so much art, what must not those be, who have been bred up to gaming from their infancy, whose hands are not like those mentioned above, rendered callous by labour, who have continual practice in the trade of deceiving, and where the eye of the spectator is less upon its guard.

Let the young beginner only reflect by what a variety of methods it is possible to cheat him, and perhaps it will check his confidence. His antagonists may act by signs and confederacy, and this he can never detect; they may cut to a particular card after three or four hands have gone about, either by having that card pinched, or broader than the rest, or by having an exceeding fine wire thrust between the folds of the paper, and just peeping out at the edge. Or the cards may be chalked with particular marks, which none but the sharper can understand, or a new pack may be slipped in at a proper opportunity. I have known myself in *Paris*, a fellow thus detected with a tin case, containing two packs of cards concealed within his shirt sleeve, and which, by means of a spring, threw the cards ready packed into his hands. These and an hundred other arts may be practised with impunity, and escape detection.

The great error lies in imagining every fellow with a laced coat to be a gentleman. The address and transient behaviour of a man of breeding are easily acquired, and none are better qualified than gamesters in this respect. At first, their complaisance, civility, and apparent honour is pleasing, but upon examination, few of them will be found to have their minds sufficiently stored with any of the more refined accomplishments, which truly characterize the man of breeding. This will commonly serve as a criterion to distinguish them, though there are other marks which every young gentleman of fortune should be apprized of. A sharper, when he plays, generally handles and deals the cards aukwardly like a bungler; he advances his bets by degrees, and keeps his antagonist in spirits by small advantages and alternate success at the beginning; to shew all his force at once, would but fright the bird he intends to decoy; he talks of honour and virtue, and his being a gentleman, and that he knows great men, and mentions his coal mines, and his estate in the country; he is totally divested of that masculine confidence, which is the attendant of real fortune; he turns, yields, assents, smiles, as he hopes will be most pleasing to his destined prey; he is afraid of meeting a shabby acquaintance, particularly if in better company; as he grows richer, he wears finer cloaths; and if ever he is seen in an undress, it is most probable he is without money; so that seeing a gamester growing finer each day, is a certain symptom of his success.

The young gentleman who plays with such men for considerable sums, is sure to be undone, and yet we seldom see even the rook himself make a fortune. A life of gaming must necessarily be a life of extravagance: parties of this kind are formed in houses, where the whole profits are consumed; and while those who play mutually ruin each other, they only who keep the house or the table acquire fortunes. Thus gaming may readily ruin a fortune, but has seldom been found to retrieve it. The wealth which has been acquired with industry and hazard, and preserved for ages by prudence and foresight, is swept away on a sudden; and when a besieging sharper sits down before an estate, the property is often transferred in less time, than the writings can be drawn to secure the possession. The neglect of business, and the extravagance of a mind which has been taught to covet precarious possession, brings on premature destruction; though poverty may fetch a compass and go somewhat about, yet will it reach the gamester at last; and though his ruin be slow, yet it is certain.

A thousand instances could be given of the fatal tendency of this passion, which first impoverishes the mind, and then perverts the understanding. Permit me to mention one, not caught from report, or dressed up by fancy, but such as has actually fallen under my own observation, and of the truth of which, I beg your Lordship may rest satisfied.

At *Tunbridge*, in the year 1715, Mr. *J. Hedges* made a very brilliant appearance; he had been married about two years to a young lady of great beauty and large fortune; they had one child, a boy, on whom they bestowed all that affection which they could spare from each other. He knew nothing of gaming, nor seemed to have the least passion for play; but he was unacquainted with his own heart; he began by degrees to bett at the tables for trifling sums, and his soul took fire at the prospect of immediate gain; he was soon surrounded with sharpers, who with calmness lay in ambush for his fortune, and cooly took advantage of the precipitancy of his passions.

His lady perceived the ruin of her family approaching, but, at first, without being able to form any scheme to prevent it. She advised with his brother, who, at that time, was possessed of a small fellowship in *Cambridge*. It was easily seen, that whatever passion took the lead in her husband's mind, seemed to be there fixed unalterably; it was determined therefore, to let him pursue fortune, but previously take measures, to prevent the pursuits being fatal.

Accordingly every night this gentleman was a constant attender at the hazard table; he understood neither the arts of sharpers, nor even the allowed strokes of a connoisseur, yet still he played. The consequence is obvious; he lost his estate, his equipage, his wife's jewels, and every other moveable that could be parted with, except a repeating watch. His agony upon this occasion was inexpressible; he was even mean enough to ask a gentleman, who sate near, to lend him a few pieces, in order to turn his fortune; but this prudent gamester, who plainly saw there were no expectations of being repaid, refused to lend a farthing, alledging a former resolution against lending. *Hedges* was at last furious with the continuance of ill success, and pulling out his watch, asked if any person in company would set him sixty guineas upon it: the company were silent; he then demanded fifty, still no answer; he sunk to forty, thirty, twenty; finding the company still without answering, he cried out, by *G—d*, it shall never go for less, and dashed it against the floor, at the same time, attempting to dash out his brains against the marble chimney-piece.

This last act of desperation immediately excited the attention of the whole company; they instantly gathered round, and prevented the effects of his passion; and after he again became cool, he was permitted to return home, with sullen discontent, to his wife. Upon his entering her apartment, she received him with her usual tenderness and satisfaction; while he answered her caresses with contempt and severity; his disposition being quite altered with his misfortunes. But, my dear *Jemmy*, says his wife, perhaps you don't know the news I have to tell; *My Mamma's old uncle is dead, the messenger is now in the house, and you know his estate is settled upon you.* This account seemed only to encrease his agony, and looking angrily at her, he cried, there you lie, my dear, his estate is not settled upon me. *I beg your pardon*, says she, *I really thought it was, at least you have always told me so.* No, returned he, as sure as you and I are to be miserable here, and our children beggars hereafter, I have sold the reversion of it this day, and have lost every farthing I got for it at the hazard table. *What all!* replied the lady. Yes, every farthing, returned he, and I owe a thousand pounds more than I have to pay. Thus speaking, he took a few frantic steps across the room. When the lady had a little enjoyed his perplexity. *No, my dear*, cried she, *you have lost but a trifle, and you owe nothing. Our brother and I have taken care to prevent the effects of your rashness, and are actually the persons, who have won your fortune; we employed proper persons for this purpose, who brought their winnings to me; your money, your equipage, are in my possession, and here I return them to you, from whom they were unjustly taken. I only ask permission to keep my jewels, and to keep you, my greatest jewel, from such dangers for the future.* Her prudence had the proper effect, he ever after retained a sense of his former follies, and never played for the smallest sums, even for amusement.

Not less than three persons in one day, fell a sacrifice at *Bath*, to this destructive passion. Two gentlemen fought a duel, in which one was killed, and the other desperately wounded; and a youth of great expectation, and excellent disposition, at the same time ended his own life by a pistol. If there be any state that deserves pity, it must be that of a gamester; but the state of a dying gamester is of all situations the most deplorable.

There is another argument which your lordship, I fancy, will not entirely despise; beauty, my lord, I own is at best but a trifle, but such as it is, I fancy few would willingly part with what little they have. A man with a healthful complexion, how great a philosopher soever he be, would not willingly exchange it for a sallow hectic phyz, pale eyes, and sharp wrinkled visage. I entreat you only to examine the faces of all the noted gamblers round one of our public tables; have you ever seen any thing more haggard, pinched, and miserable? and it is but natural that it should be so. The succession of passions flush the cheek with red, and all such flushings are ever succeeded by consequent paleness; so that a gamester contracts the sickly hue of a student, while he is only acquiring the stupidity of a fool.

Your good sense, my lord, I have often had an occasion of knowing, yet how miserable is it to be in a set of company where the most sensible is ever the least skilful: your footman, with a little instruction, would, I dare venture to affirm, make a better and more successful gamester than you; want of passions, and low cunning, are the two great arts; and it is peculiar to this science alone, that they who have the greatest passion for it, are of all others the most unfit to practise it.

Of all the men I ever knew, *Spedding* was the greatest blockhead, and yet the best gamester: he saw almost intuitively the advantage on either side, and ever took it; he could calculate the odds in a moment, and decide upon the merits of a cock or a horse, better than any man in *England*; in short, he was such an adept in gaming, that he brought it up to a pitch of sublimity it had never attained before; yet, with all this, *Spedding* could not write his own name. What he died worth, I cannot tell; but of this I am certain, he might have possessed a ministerial estate, and that won from men, famed for their sense, literature, and patriotism.

If, after this description, your Lordship is yet resolved to hazard your fortune at gaming, I beg you would advert to the situation of an old and luckless gamester. Perhaps there is not in nature a more deplorable being, his character is too well marked, he is too well known to be trusted. A man that has been often a bankrupt, and renewed trade upon low compositions, may as well expect extensive credit as such a man. His reputation is blasted, his constitution worn, by the extravagance and ill hours of his profession, he is now incapable of alluring his dupes, and like a superannuated savage of the forest, he is starved for want of vigour to hunt after prey.

Thus gaming is the source of poverty, and still worse, the parent of infamy and vice. It is an inlet to debauchery; for the money thus acquired is but little valued. Every gamester is a rake, and his morals worse than his mystery. It is his interest to be exemplary in every scene of debauchery, his prey is to be courted with every guilty pleasure; but these are to be changed, repeated, and embellished, in order to employ his imagination, while his reason is kept asleep; a young mind is apt to shrink at the prospect of ruin, care must be taken to harden his courage, and make him keep his rank; he must be either found a libertine, or he must be made one. And when a man has parted with his money like a fool, he generally sends his conscience after it like a villain, and the nearer he is to the brink of destruction, the fonder does he grow of ruin.

Your friend and mine, my Lord, had been thus driven to the last reserve: he found it impossible to disentangle his affairs, and look the world in the face; impatience at length threw him into the abyss he feared, and life became a burthen, because he feared to die. But I own that play is not always attended with such tragical circumstances, some have had courage to survive their losses, and go on content with beggary; and sure those misfortunes, which are of our own production, are of all others most pungent. To see such a poor disbanded being an unwelcome guest at every table, and often flapped off like a fly is affecting; in this case the closest alliance is forgotten, and contempt is too strong for the ties of blood to unbind.

But however fatal this passion may be in its consequence, none allures so much in the beginning, the person once listed as a gamester, if not soon reclaimed, pursues it through his whole life; no loss can retard, no danger awaken him to common sense; nothing can terminate his career but want of money to play, or of honour to be trusted.

Among the number of my acquaintance, I knew but of two who succeeded by gaming; the one a phlegmatic heavy man, who would have made a fortune in whatever way of life he happened to be placed; the other who had lost a fine estate in his youth by play, and retrieved a greater at the age of sixty-five, when he might be justly said, to be past the power of enjoying it. One or two successful gamesters are thus set up in an age to allure the young beginner; we all regard such, as the highest prize in a lottery, unmindful of the numerous losses that go to the accumulation of such infrequent success.

Yet I would not be so morose, as to refuse your youth all kinds of play: the innocent amusements of a family, must often be indulged, and cards allowed to supply the intervals of more real pleasure; but the sum played for in such cases should always be a trifle; something to call up attention, but not engage the passions. The usual excuse for laying large sums is, to make the players attend to their game; but in fact, he that plays only for shillings, will mind his cards equally well, with him that betts guineas; for the mind, habituated to stake large sums, will consider them as trifles at last; and if one shilling could not exclude indifference at first, neither will an hundred in the end.

I have often asked myself, how it is possible that he who is possessed of competence, can ever be induced to make it precarious, by beginning play with the odds against him; for wherever he goes to sport his money, he will find himself overmatched and cheated. Either at *White*'s, *New-market*, the *Tennis-Court*, the *Cock-Pit*, or the *Billiard-Table*, he will find numbers who have no other resource, but their acquisitions there; and if such men live like gentlemen, he may readily conclude it must be on the spoils of his fortune, or the fortunes of ill judging men like himself. Was he to attend but a moment to their manner of betting at those places he would readily find the gamester seldom proposing betts, but with the advantage in his own favour. A man of honour continues to lay on the side on which he first won; but gamesters shift, change, lie upon the lurch, and take every advantage, either of our ignorance or neglect.

In short, my Lord, if a man designs to lay out his fortune in quest of pleasure, the gaming table is, of all other places, that where he can have least for his money. The company are superficial, extravagant, and unentertaining; the conversation flat, debauched, and absurd; the hours unnatural, and fatiguing; the anxiety of losing is greater than the pleasure of winning; friendship must be banished from that society, the members of which are intent only on ruining each other; every other improvement, either in knowledge or virtue, can scarce find room in that breast, which is possessed by the spirit of play; the spirits become vapid, the constitution is enfeebled, the complexion grows pale; till, in the end, the mind, body, friends, fortune, and even the hopes of futurity sink together! Happy, if nature terminates the scene, and neither justice nor suicide are called in to accelerate her tardy approach.

I am,

my Lord, &c.

. . . .

As the heart of a man is better known by his private than public actions, let us take a view of *Nash* in domestick life; among his servants and dependants where no gloss was required to colour his sentiments and disposition, nor any mask necessary to conceal his foibles. Here we shall find him the same open-hearted, generous, good-natured man we have already described; one who was ever fond of promoting the interests of his friends, his servants, and dependants, and making them happy. In his own house no man perhaps was more regular, chearful, and beneficent than Mr. *Nash*. His table was always free to those who sought his friendship, or wanted a dinner; and after grace was said, he usually accosted the company in the following extraordinary manner, to take off all restraint and ceremony. "Come, gentlemen, eat and welcome; spare, and the Devil choak you." I mention this circumstance for no other reason, but because it is well known, and is consistent with the singularity of his character and behaviour.

As Mr. *Nash*'s thoughts were entirely employed in the affairs of his government, he was seldom at home but at the time of eating or of rest. His table was well served, but his entertainment consisted principally of plain dishes. Boiled chicken and roast mutton were his favourite meats, and he was so fond of the small sort of potatoes, that he called them *English* pine-apples, and generally eat them as others do fruit, after dinner. In drinking he was altogether as regular and abstemious. Both in this, and in eating, he seemed to consult nature, and obey only her dictates. Good small beer, with or without a glass of wine in it, and sometimes wine and water, was his drink at meals, and after dinner he generally drank one glass of wine. He seemed fond of hot suppers, usually supped about nine or ten o'clock, upon roast breast of mutton and his potatoes, and soon after supper went to bed; which induced Dr. *Cheney* to tell him jestingly, *that he behaved like other brutes, and lay down as soon as he had filled his belly. Very true*, replied Nash, *and this prescription I had from my neighbour's Cow, who is a better physician than you, and a superior judge of plants, notwithstanding you have written so learnedly on the vegetable diet.*

Nash generally arose early in the morning, being seldom in bed after five; and to avoid disturbing the family, and depriving his servants of their rest, he had the fire laid after he was in bed, and in the morning lighted it himself, and sat down to read some of his few, but well chosen books. After reading some time, he usually went to the pump-room and drank the waters; then took a walk on the parade, and went to the coffee-house to breakfast; after which, till two o'clock (his usual time of dinner) his hours were spent in arbitrating differences amongst his neighbours, or the company resorting to the wells; directing the diversions of the day, in visiting the new comers, or receiving friends at his own house, of which there were a great concourse till within six or eight years before his death.

His generosity and charity in private life, though not so conspicuous, was as great as that in publick, and indeed far more considerable than his little income would admit of. He could not stifle the natural impulse which he had to do good, but frequently borrowed money to relieve the distressed; and when he knew not conveniently where to borrow, he has been often observed to shed tears, as he passed through the wretched supplicants who attended his gate.

This sensibility, this power of feeling the misfortunes of the miserable, and his address and earnestness in relieving their wants, exalts the character of Mr. *Nash*, and draws an impenetrable veil over his foibles. His singularities are forgotten when we behold his virtues, and he who laughed at the whimsical character and behaviour of this Monarch of *Bath*, now laments that he is no more.

EXTRACTS FROM

AN HISTORY

OF THE EARTH AND

ANIMATED NATURE

In February, 1765, Goldsmith contracted with Griffin to compile a "New Natural History of Animals" at a hundred guineas a volume. In September, 1771 he wrote to Bennet Langton,

> The natural History is about half finished and I will shortly finish the rest. God knows Im tired of this kind of finishing, which is but bungling work, and that not so much my fault as the fault of my scurvy circumstances.

But he did not complete the task until early in 1774.

An History of the Earth and Animated Nature was published on 30 June, 1774, almost three months after Goldsmith's death. It ran to eight quarto volumes, *Printed for J. Nourse, in the Strand, Bookseller to His Majesty.*

Very little of this vast work was original; most of it was compiled from Buffon, Ulloa, Krantz and the *Transactions of the Philosophical Society*. Goldsmith was no natural historian, and his work has been much abused for its ignorance and credulity. But in fact his own commonsense judgments were often sounder than those of the theorists from whom he was compiling. The two fantastic anecdotes which I have included here, of floating islands and nautical squirrels, though delightful, are not representative. *Animated Nature* is of interest for two reasons: occasional passages are very well and wittily written; and the work as a whole gives a remarkably complete picture of the ideas about the world which an ordinary man of the eighteenth century took for granted, but which we have since forgotten or rejected.

AN HISTORY
OF THE EARTH AND ANIMATED NATURE

From the PREFACE

THE delight which I found in reading Pliny, first inspired me with the idea of a work of this nature. Having a taste rather classical than scientific, and having but little employed myself in turning over the dry labours of modern system-makers, my earliest intention was to translate this agreeable writer, and by the help of a commentary to make my work as amusing as I could. Let us dignify natural history never so much with the grave appellation of a useful science, yet still we must confess that it is the occupation of the idle and the speculative, more than of the busy and the ambitious part of mankind. My intention therefore was to treat what I then conceived an idle subject, in an idle manner; and not to hedge round plain and simple narratives with hard words, accumulated distinctions, ostentatious learning, and disquisitions that produced no conviction. Upon the appearance however of Mr. Buffon's work, I dropped my former plan, and adopted the present, being convinced by his manner, that the best imitation of the ancients was to write from our own feelings, and to imitate nature.

It will be my chief pride therefore, if this work may be found an innocent amusement for those who have nothing else to employ them, or who require a relaxion from labour. Professed naturalists will, no doubt, find it superficial; and yet I should hope that even these will discover hints, and remarks, gleaned from various reading, not wholly trite or elementary. I would wish for their approbation. But my chief ambition is to drag up the obscure and gloomy learning of the cell to open inspection; to strip it from its garb of austerity, and to shew the beauties of that form, which only the industrious and the inquisitive have been hitherto permitted to approach.

OF THE APPEARANCE OF NEW ISLANDS, AND TRACTS; AND OF THE DISAPPEARING OF OTHERS

Mariners assure us, that there are sometimes whole plains uprooted from the main lands, by floods and tempests. These being carried out to sea, with all their trees and animals upon them, are frequently seen floating in the ocean, and exhibiting a surprizing appearance of rural tranquillity in the midst of danger. The greatest part, however, having the earth at their roots at length washed away, are dispersed, and their animals drowned; but now and then some are found to brave the fury of the ocean, till being stuck either among rocks or sands, they again take firm footing, and become permanent islands.

OF THE GENERATION OF ANIMALS

In this manner the polypus multiplies naturally; but, one may take a much readier and shorter way to encrease them, and this only by cutting them in pieces. Though cut into thousands of parts, each part still retains its vivacious quality, each shortly becomes a distinct and a complete polypus; whether cut lengthways, or crossways, it is all the same; this extraordinary creature seems a gainer by our endeavours, and multiplies by apparent destruction. The experiment has been tried, times without number, and still attended with the same success. Here, therefore, naturalists who have been blamed for the cruelty of their experiments upon living animals, may now boast of their encreasing animal life, instead of destroying it. The production of the polypus is a kind of philosophical generation. The famous Sir Thomas Brown hoped one day to be able to produce children by the same method as trees are produced;[1] the polypus is multiplied in this manner;

[1] [*Religio Medici, The Second Part.*]

and every philosopher may thus, if he pleases, boast of a very numerous, though, I should suppose, a very useless progeny.

ON THE EDUCATION OF CHILDREN

ALMOST every philosopher who has written on the education of children, has been willing to point out a method of his own, chiefly professing to advance the health, and improve the intellects at the same time. These are usually found to begin with finding nothing right in the common practice; and by urging a total reformation. In consequence of this, nothing can be more wild or imaginary than their various systems of improvement. Some will have the children every day plunged in cold water, in order to strengthen their bodies; they will have them converse with the servants in nothing but the Latin language, in order to strengthen their minds; every hour of the day must be appointed for its own studies, and the child must learn to make these very studies an amusement; till about the age of ten or eleven it becomes a prodigy of premature improvement. Quite opposite to this, we have others, whom the courtesy of mankind also calls philosophers: and they will have the child learn nothing till the age of ten or eleven, at which the former has attained so much perfection; with them the mind is to be kept empty, until it has a proper distinction of some metaphysical ideas about truth; and the promising pupil is debarred the use of even his own faculties, lest they should conduct him into prejudice and error. In this manner, some men, whom fashion has celebrated for profound and fine thinkers, have given their hazarded and untried conjectures, upon one of the most important subjects in the world, and the most interesting to humanity. When men speculate at liberty upon innate ideas, or the abstracted distinctions between will and power, they may be permitted to enjoy their systems at pleasure, as they are harmless, although they may be wrong;

but when they alledge that children are to be every day plunged in cold water, and, whatever be their constitution, indiscriminately enured to cold and moisture; that they are to be kept wet in the feet, to prevent their catching cold; and never to be corrected when young, for fear of breaking their spirits when old; these are such noxious errors, that all reasonable men should endeavour to oppose them. Many have been the children whom these opinions, begun in speculation, have injured or destroyed in practice; and I have myself seen many a little philosophical martyr, whom I wished, but was unable to relieve.

OF MONSTERS

THIS race of giants [the Patagonians] are described as possessed of great strength; and, no doubt, they must be very different from those accidental giants that are to be seen in different parts of Europe. Stature with these, seems rather their infirmity than their pride; and adds to their burthen, without encreasing their strength. Of those I have seen, the generality were ill-formed and unhealthful; weak in their persons, or incapable of exerting what strength they were possessed of. The same defects of understanding that attended those of suppressed stature, were found in those who were thus overgrown: they were heavy, phlegmatic, stupid, and inclined to sadness. Their numbers, however, are but few; and it is thus kindly ordered by Providence, that as the middle state is the best fitted for happiness, so the middle ranks of mankind are produced in the greatest variety.

However, mankind seems naturally to have a respect for men of extraordinary stature; and it has been a supposition of long standing, that our ancestors were much taller, as well as much more beautiful than we. This has been, indeed, a theme of poetical declamation from the beginning; and man was scarce formed, when he began to deplore an imaginary decay.

Nothing is more natural than this progress of the mind, in looking up to antiquity with reverential wonder. Having been accustomed to compare the wisdom of our fathers, with our own early imbecillity, the impression of their superiority remains when they no longer exist, and when we cease to be inferior. Thus the men of every age consider the past as wiser than the present; and the reverence seems to accumulate as our imaginations ascend. For this reason, we allow remote antiquity many advantages, without disputing their title: the inhabitants of uncivilized countries represent them as taller and stronger; and the people of a more polished nation, as more healthy and more wise. Nevertheless, these attributes seem to be only the prejudices of ingenuous minds; a kind of gratitude, which we hope in turn to receive from posterity. The ordinary stature of men, Mr. Derham observes, is, in all probability, the same now as at the beginning. The oldest measure we have of the human figure, is in the monument of Cheops, in the first pyramid of Egypt. This must have subsisted many hundred years before the times of Homer, who is the first that deplores the decay. This monument, however, scarce exceeds the measure of our ordinary coffins: the cavity is no more than six feet long, two feet wide, and deep in about the same proportion. Several mummies also, of a very early age, are found to be only of the ordinary stature; and shew that, for these three thousand years at least, men have not suffered the least diminution. We have many corroborating proofs of this, in the ancient pieces of armour which are dug up in different parts of Europe. The brass helmet dug up at Medauro, fits one of our men, and yet is allowed to have been left there at the overthrow of Asdrubal. Some of our finest antique statues, which we learn from Pliny, and others, to be exactly as big as the life, still continue to this day, remaining monuments of the superior excellènce of their workmen indeed, but not of the superiority of their stature. We may conclude, therefore, that men have been, in all ages, pretty much of the same size they are at present; and that the only difference must have been accidental, or perhaps national.

As to the superior beauty of our ancestors, it is not easy to make the comparison; beauty seems a very uncertain charm; and frequently is less in the object, than in the eye of the beholder. Were a modern lady's face formed exactly like the Venus of Medicis, or the sleeping vestal, she would scarce be considered beautiful, except by the lovers of antiquity, whom, of all her admirers, perhaps, she would be least desirous of pleasing. It is true, that we have some disorders among us that disfigure the features, and from which the ancients were exempt; but it is equally so, that we want some which were common among them, and which were equally deforming. As for their intellectual powers, these also were probably the same as ours: we excel them in the sciences, which may be considered as an history of accumulated experience; and they excel us in the poetic arts, as they had the first rifling of all the striking images of Nature.

THE POOR MAN'S COW

THERE are many of our peasantry that have no other possession but a cow; and even of the advantages resulting from this most useful creature, the poor are but the nominal possessors. Its flesh they cannot pretend to taste, since then their whole riches are at once destroyed; its calf they are obliged to fatten for sale, since veal is a delicacy they could not make any pretensions to; its very milk is wrought into butter and cheese for the tables of their masters; while they have no share even in their own possession, but the choice of their market. I cannot bear to hear the rich crying out for liberty, while they thus starve their fellow creatures, and feed them up with an imaginary good, while they monopolize the real benefits of nature.

In those countries where the men are under better subordination, this excellent animal is of more general advantage. In Germany, Poland, and Switzerland, every peasant keeps two or three cows, not for the benefit of his master, but for himself. The meanest of the peasants there kills one cow at least for his own table, which he salts and hangs up, and thus preserves as a delicacy all the year round. There is scarce a cottage in those countries that is not hung round with these marks of hospitality; and which often make the owner better contented with hunger, since he has it in his power to be luxurious when he thinks proper. A piece of beef hung up there, is considered as an elegant piece of furniture, which, though seldom touched, at least it argues the possessor's opulence and ease. But it is very different, for some years past, in this country, where our lower rustics at least are utterly unable to purchase meat any part of the year, and by them even butter is considered as an article of extravagance.

THE CAT

CERTAIN it is, the cat was an animal much higher in esteem among our ancestors than it is at present. By the laws of Howel, the price of a kitten, before it could see, was to be a penny; till it caught a mouse, two pence; and, when it commenced mouser, four pence: it was required, besides, that it should be perfect in its senses of hearing and seeing, be a good mouser, have the claws whole, and be a good nurse. If it failed in any of these qualities, the seller was to forfeit to the buyer the third part of its value. If any one stole or killed the cat that guarded the prince's granary, he was to forfeit a milch ewe, its fleece and lamb, or as much wheat as, when poured on the cat suspended by the tail (the head touching the floor) would form an heap high enough to cover the tip of the former. From hence we discover, besides a picture of the simplicity of the times, a strong argument that cats were not naturally bred in our forests. An animal that could be so easily taken, could never have been rated so highly; and the precautions laid down to improve the breed, would have been superfluous, in a creature that multiplies to such an amazing degree.

THE DOG

WITH regard to the dogs of our country in particular, the varieties are very great, and the number every day encreasing. And this must happen in a country so open by commerce to all others, and where wealth is apt to produce capricious predilection. Here the ugliest and the most useless of their kinds will be entertained merely for their singularity; and, being imported only to be looked at, they will lose even that small degree of sagacity which they possessed in their natural climates. From this importation of foreign useless dogs, our own native breed is, I am informed, greatly degenerated, and the varieties now to be found in England much more numerous than they were in the times of Queen Elizabeth, when Doctor Caius attempted their natural history. Some of these he mentions are no longer to be found among us, although many have since been introduced, by no means so serviceable as those which have been suffered to decay.

THE MIGRATION OF SQUIRRELS

IN Lapland, and the extensive forests to the north, the squirrels are observed to change their habitation, and to remove in vast numbers from one country to another. In these migrations they are generally seen by thousands, travelling directly forward; while neither rocks, forests, nor even the broadest waters can stop their progress. What I am going to relate, appears so extraordinary, that were it not attested by numbers of the most credible historians, among whom are Klein and Linnæus, it might be rejected, with that scorn with which we treat imposture or credulity: however, nothing can be more true than, that when these animals, in their progress, meet with broad rivers, or extensive lakes, which abound in Lapland, they take a very extraordinary method of crossing them. Upon approaching the banks, and perceiving the breadth of the water, they return as if by common consent, into the neighbouring forest, each in quest of a piece of bark, which answers all the purposes of boats for wafting them over. When the whole company are fitted in this manner, they boldly commit their little fleet to the waves; every squirrel sitting on its own piece of bark, and fanning the air with its tail, to drive the vessel to its desired port. In this orderly manner they set forward, and often cross lakes several miles broad. But it too often happens that the poor mariners are not aware of the dangers of their navigation; for although at the edge of the water it is generally calm, in the midst it is always more turbulent. There the slightest additional gust of wind oversets the little sailor and his vessel together. The whole navy, that but a few minutes before rode proudly and securely along, is now overturned, and a shipwreck of two or three thousand sail ensues. This, which is so unfortunate for the little animal, is generally the most lucky accident in the world for the Laplander on the shore; who gathers up the dead bodies as they are thrown in by the waves, eats the flesh, and sells the skins for about a shilling the dozen.

THE MOLE

THE smallness of its eyes, which induced the ancients to think it was blind, is, to this animal, a peculiar advantage. A small degree of vision is sufficient for a creature that is ever destined to live in darkness. A more extensive sight would only have served to shew the horrors of its prison, while Nature had denied it the means of an escape. Had this organ been larger, it would have been perpetually liable to injuries, by the falling of the earth into it; but Nature, to prevent the inconvenience, has not only made them very small, but very closely covered them with hair. Anatomists mention, beside these advantages, another, that contributes to their security; namely, a certain muscle, by which the animal can draw back the eye whenever it is necessary or in danger.

As the eye is thus perfectly fitted to the animal's situation, so also are the senses of hearing and smelling. The first gives it notice of the most distant appearance of danger; the other directs it, in the midst of darkness, to its food. The wants of a subterraneous animal can be but few; and these are sufficient to supply them: to eat, and to produce its kind, are the whole employments of such a life; and for both these purposes it is wonderfully adapted by Nature.

THE LLAMA

THIS animal, as was said before, is above three feet high, and the neck is three feet long, the head is small and well proportioned, the eyes large, the nose long, the lips thick, the upper divided, and the lower a little depending; like all those animals that feed upon grass, it wants the upper cutting teeth; the ears are four inches long, and move with great agility; the tail is but five inches long, it is small, strait, and a little turned up at the end; it is cloven footed, like the ox, but it has a kind of spear-like appendage behind, which assists it in moving over precipices and rugged ways; the wool on the back is short, but long on the sides and the belly; it resembles the camel in the formation of the genital parts in the male, so that it makes urine backwards; it couples also in the same manner, and though it finds much difficulty in the action, it is said to be much inclined to venery. A whole day is often passed, before this necessary business can be compleated, which is spent in growling, quarrelling, and spitting at each other; they seldom produce above one at a time, and their age never extends above ten or twelve years at farthest.

OF THE GENERATION, NESTING AND INCUBATION OF BIRDS

THE return of spring is the beginning of pleasure. Those vital spirits which seemed locked up during the winter, then begin to expand; vegetables and insects supply abundance of food; and the bird having more than a sufficiency for its own subsistence, is impelled to transfuse life as well as to maintain it. Those warblings which had been hushed during the colder seasons, now begin to animate the fields; every grove and bush resounds with the challenge of anger, or the call of allurement. This delightful concert of the grove, which is so much admired by man, is no way studied for his amusement: it is usually the call of the male to the female; his efforts to sooth her during the times of incubation: or it is a challenge between two males, for the affections of some common favourite.

It is by this call that birds begin to pair at the approach of spring, and provide for the support of a future progeny. The loudest notes are usually from the male; while the hen seldom expresses her consent, but in a short, interrupted twittering. This compact, at least for the season, holds with unbroken faith: many birds live with inviolable fidelity together for a constancy; and when one dies, the other is always seen to share the same fate soon after. We must not take our idea of the conjugal fidelity of birds from observing the poultry in our yards, whose freedom is abridged, and whose manners are totally corrupted by slavery. We must look for it in our fields and our forests, where nature continues in unadulterated simplicity; where the number of males is generally equal to that of females; and where every little animal seems prouder of his progeny than pleased with his mate. Were it possible to compare sensations, the male of all wild birds seems as happy in the young brood as the female; and all his former caresses, all his soothing melodies, seem only aimed at that important occasion when they are both to become parents, and to educate a progeny of their own producing. The pleasures of love appear dull in their effects, when compared to the interval immediately after the exclusion of their young. They both seem, at that season, transported with pleasure; every action testifies their pride, their importance, and tender solicitude.

THE PARTRIDGE

In England, where the partridge is much scarcer [than in France], and a great deal dearer, it is still a favourite delicacy at the tables of the rich; and the desire of keeping it to themselves, has induced them to make laws for its preservation, no way harmonizing with the general spirit of English legislation. What can be more arbitrary than to talk of preserving the game; which, when defined, means no more than that the poor shall abstain from what the rich have taken a fancy to keep for themselves? If these birds could, like a cock or a hen, be made legal property, could they be taught to keep within certain districts, and only feed on those grounds that belong to the man whose entertainments they improve, it then might, with some shew of justice, be admitted, that as a man fed them so he might claim them. But this is not the case; nor is it in any man's power to lay a restraint upon the liberty of these birds, that, when let loose, put no limits to their excursions. They feed every where; upon every man's ground; and no man can say, these birds are fed only by me. Those birds which are nourished by all, belong to all; nor can any one man, or any set of men, lay claim to them, when still continuing in a state of nature.

I never walked out about the environs of Paris, that I did not consider the immense quantity of game that was running almost tame on every side of me, as a badge of the slavery of the people; and what they wished me to observe as an object of triumph, I always regarded with a kind of secret compassion: yet this people have no game-laws for the remoter parts of the kingdom; the game is only preserved in a few places for the king; and is free in most places else. In England, the prohibition is general; and the peasant has not a right to what even slaves, as he is taught to call them, are found to possess.

A TRANSLATION OF ADDISON

ADDISON, in some beautiful Latin lines, inserted in the Spectator,[1] is entirely of opinion that birds observe a strict chastity of manners, and never admit the caresses of a different tribe.

Chaste are their instincts, faithful is their fire,
No foreign beauty tempts to false desire:
The snow-white vesture, and the glittering crown,
The simple plumage, or the glossy down,
Prompt not their love. The patriot bird pursues
His well acquainted tints, and kindred hues.
Hence through their tribes no mix'd polluted flame,
No monster breed to mark the groves with shame:
But the chaste blackbird, to its partner true,
Thinks black alone is beauty's favourite hue:

[1] [Number 421.]

The nightingale, with mutual passion blest,
Sings to its mate, and nightly charms the nest:
While the dark owl, to court his partner flies,
And owns his offspring in their yellow eyes.

But whatever may be the poet's opinion, the probability is against this fidelity among the smaller tenants of the grove. The great birds are much more true to their species than these; and, of consequence, the varieties among them are more few.... But it is otherwise with the small birds we are describing; it requires very little trouble to make a species between a goldfinch and a canary-bird, between a linnet and a lark.

THE ROOK

THE rook, as is well known, builds in woods and forests in the neighbourhood of man, and sometimes makes choice of groves in the very midst of cities for the place of its retreat and security. In these it establishes a kind of legal constitution, by which all intruders are excluded from coming to live among them, and none suffered to build but acknowledged natives of the place. I have often amused myself with observing their plan of policy from my window in the Temple, that looks upon a grove where they have made a colony in the midst of the city. At the commencement of spring, the rookery, which during the continuance of winter seemed to have been deserted, or only guarded by about five or six, like old soldiers in a garrison, now begins to be once more frequented; and in a short time all the bustle and hurry of business is fairly commenced. Where these numbers resided during the winter is not easy to guess; perhaps in the trees of hedge-rows to be nearer their food. In spring, however, they cultivate their native trees; and, in the places where they were themselves hatched, they prepare to propagate a future progeny.

They keep together in pairs; and when the offices of courtship are over, they prepare for making their nests and laying. The old inhabitants of the place are all already provided; the nest which served them for years before, with a little trimming and dressing will serve very well again; the difficulty of nestling lies only upon the young ones who have no nest, and must therefore get up one as well as they can. But not only the materials are wanting, but also the place in which to fix it. Every part of a tree will not do for this purpose, as some branches may not be sufficiently forked; others may not be sufficiently strong; and still others may be too much exposed to the rockings of the wind. The male and female upon this occasion are, for some days, seen examining all the trees of the grove very attentively; and when they have fixed upon a branch that seems fit for their purpose, they continue to sit upon and observe it very sedulously for two or three days longer. The place being thus determined upon, they begin to gather the materials for their nest; such as sticks and fibrous roots, which they regularly dispose in the most substantial manner. But here a new and unexpected obstacle arises. It often happens that the young couple have made choice of a place too near the mansion of an older pair, who do not chuse to be incommoded by such troublesome neighbours. A quarrel therefore instantly ensues; in which the old ones are always victorious.

The young couple, thus expelled, are obliged again to go through the fatigues of deliberating, examining, and chusing; and having taken care to keep their due distance, the nest begins again, and their industry deserves commendation. But their alacrity is often too great in the beginning; they soon grow weary of bringing the materials of their nest from distant places; and they very easily perceive that sticks may be provided nearer home, with less honesty indeed, but some degree of address. Away they go, therefore, to pilfer as fast as they can; and wherever they see a nest unguarded, they take care to rob it of the very choicest sticks of which it is composed. But these thefts never go unpunished; and probably upon complaint being made there is a general punishment inflicted. I have seen eight or ten rooks come upon such occasions, and setting upon the new nest of the young couple all at once, tear it in pieces in a moment.

At length, therefore, the young pair find the necessity of going more regularly and honestly to work. While one flies to fetch the materials, the other sits upon the tree to guard it; and thus in the space of three or four days, with a skirmish now and then between, the pair have fitted up a commodious nest composed of sticks without, and of fibrous roots and long grass within. From the instant the female begins to lay, all hostilities are at an end; not one of the whole grove, that a little before treated her so rudely, will now venture to molest her; so that she brings forth her brood with patient tranquility. Such is the severity with which even native rooks are treated by each other; but if a foreign rook should attempt to make himself a denizen of their society, he would meet with no favour; the whole grove would at once be up in arms against him, and expel him without mercy.

OF THE BITTERN OR MIRE-DRUM

THOSE who have walked in an evening by the sedgy sides of unfrequented rivers, must remember a variety of notes from different water-fowl: the loud scream of the wild goose, the croaking of the mallard, the whining of the lapwing, and the tremulous neighing of the jack-snipe. But of all those sounds, there is none so dismally hollow as the booming of the bittern. It is impossible for words to give those who have not heard this evening-call an adequate idea of its solemnity. It is like the interrupted bellowing of a bull, but hollower and louder, and is heard at a mile's distance, as if issuing from some formidable being that resided at the bottom of the waters.

The bird, however, that produces this terrifying sound is not so big as an heron, with a weaker bill, and not above four inches long. It differs from the heron chiefly in its colour, which is in general of a paleish yellow, spotted and barred with black. Its wind-pipe is fitted to produce the sound for which it is remarkable; the lower part of it dividing into the lungs is supplied with a thin loose membrane, that can be filled with a large body of air and exploded at pleasure. These bellowing explosions are chiefly heard from the beginning of spring to the end of autumn; and, however awful they may seem to us, are the calls to courtship, or of connubial felicity.

. . . .

I remember in the place where I was a boy with what terror this bird's note affected the whole village; they considered it as the presage of some sad event; and generally found or made one to succeed it. I do not speak ludicrously; but if any person in the neighbourhood died, they supposed it could not be otherwise, for the night-raven had foretold it; but if nobody happened to die, the death of a cow or a sheep gave completion to the prophecy.

THE LAPWING

THE place these birds chiefly chuse to breed in, is in some island surrounded with sedgy moors, where men seldom resort; and in such situations I have often seen the ground so strewed with eggs and nests, that one could scarce take a step, without treading upon some of them. As soon as a stranger intrudes upon these retreats, the whole colony is up, and an hundred different screams are heard from every quarter. The arts of the lapwing to allure men or dogs from her nest, are perfectly amusing. When she perceives the enemy approaching, she never waits till they arrive at her nest, but boldly runs to meet them: when she has come as near them as she dares venture, she then rises with a loud screaming before them, seeming as if she were just flushed from hatching; while she is then probably a hundred yards from the nest. Thus she flies, with great clamour and anxiety, whining and screaming round the invaders, striking at them with her wings, and fluttering as if she were wounded. To add to this deceit, she appears still more clamorous, as more remote from the nest. If she sees them very near, she then seems to be quite unconcerned, and her cries cease, while her terrors are really augmenting. If there be dogs, she flies heavily at a little distance before them, as if maimed; still vociferous and still bold, but never offering to move towards the quarter where her treasure is deposited. The dog pursues, in hopes every moment of seizing the parent, and by this means actually loses the young; for the cunning bird, when she has thus drawn him off to a proper distance, then puts forth her powers, and leaves her astonished pursuer to gaze at the rapidity of her flight. The eggs of all these birds are highly valued by the luxurious; they are boiled hard, and thus served up, without any further preparation.

THE TOAD

If we regard the figure of the Toad, there seems nothing in it that should disgust more than that of a frog. Its form and proportions are nearly the same; and it chiefly differs in colour, which is blacker; and its slow and heavy motion, which exhibits nothing of the agility of the frog: yet such is the force of habit, begun in early prejudice, that those who consider the one as an harmless, playful animal, turn from the other with horror and disgust. The frog is considered as a useful assistant, in ridding our grounds of vermin; the toad, as a secret enemy, that only wants an opportunity to infect us with its venom.

The imagination, in this manner biassed by its terrors, paints out the toad in the most hideous colouring, and cloaths it in more than natural deformity. Its body is broad; its back flat, covered with a dusky, pimpled hide; the belly is large and swagging; the pace laboured and crawling; its retreat gloomy and filthy; and its whole appearance calculated to excite disgust and horror: yet upon my first seeing a toad, none of all these deformities in the least affected me with sensations of loathing: born, as I was, in a country where there are no toads, I had prepared my imagination for some dreadful object; but there seemed nothing to me more alarming in the sight, than in that of a common frog; and indeed, for some time, I mistook and handled the one for the other. When first informed of my mistake, I very well remember my sensations: I wondered how I had escaped with safety, after handling and dissecting a toad, which I had mistaken for a frog. I then began to lay in a fund of horror against the whole tribe, which, though convinced they are harmless, I shall never get rid of. My first imaginations were too strong not only for my reason, but for the conviction of my senses.

POETRY

THE TRAVELLER

OR

A PROSPECT OF SOCIETY

In February, 1755, Goldsmith left Leyden where he had been studying medicine and spent a year as a "philosophic vagabond" wandering about Europe. Nine years later *The Traveller; or, A Prospect of Society* was the result.

The earliest text was discovered by Bertram Dobell, and is now in the British Museum. It is an unique copy of the page proofs, printed in 1764 but undated, of *A Prospect of Society*; it consists of batches of about forty lines of *The Traveller*, arranged in the reverse order. Sir Arthur Quiller-Couch suggested that Goldsmith, or someone else copying out the poem, laid each completed page face upwards on top of the previous one, and the printer set it up as it stood. The *Cambridge Bibliography of English Literature* puts forward the equally likely, if less attractive theory that it was a printer's fault in make-up. The first seventy-two lines of *The Traveller* are not represented.

The first edition of *The Traveller; or, A Prospect of Society. Printed for J. Newbery in St. Paul's Church-Yard* was published on 19 December, 1764, dated 1765. A few copies have occurred in the sale rooms dated 1764 and with a much shorter dedication. The text of *A Prospect of Society* had been much revised, mainly under the influence of Dr. Johnson, who wrote the last ten lines, except for the penultimate couplet, and supplied the line

> To stop too fearful, and too faint to go,

in place of Goldsmith's

> And faintly fainter, fainter seems to go;

The second, third and fourth editions appeared in 1765, the fifth in 1768 and the sixth "corrected" in 1770. The sixth edition represents Goldsmith's last revision, and is the text here used.

TO THE REV. HENRY GOLDSMITH

DEAR SIR,

I AM sensible that the friendship between us can acquire no new force from the ceremonies of a Dedication; and perhaps it demands an excuse thus to prefix your name to my attempts, which you decline giving with your own. But as a part of this Poem was formerly written to you from Switzerland, the whole can now, with propriety, be only inscribed to you. It will also throw a light upon many parts of it, when the reader understands, that it is addressed to a man, who, despising Fame and Fortune, has retired early to Happiness and Obscurity, with an income of forty pounds a year.

I now perceive, my dear brother, the wisdom of your humble choice. You have entered upon a sacred office, where the harvest is great, and the labourers are but few; while you have left the field of Ambition, where the labourers are many, and the harvest not worth carrying away. But of all kinds of ambition, what from the refinement of the times, from different systems of criticism, and from the divisions of party, that which pursues poetical fame is the wildest.

Poetry makes a principal amusement among unpolished nations; but in a country verging to the extremes of refinement, Painting and Music come in for a share. As these offer the feeble mind a less laborious entertainment, they at first rival Poetry, and at length supplant her; they engross all that favour once shewn to her, and though but younger sisters, seize upon the elder's birthright.

Yet, however this art may be neglected by the powerful, it is still in greater danger from the mistaken efforts of the learned to improve it. What criticisms have we not heard of late in favour of blank verse, and Pindaric odes, chorusses, anapests and iambics, alliterative care and happy negligence! Every absurdity has now a champion to defend it, and as he is generally much in the wrong, so he has always much to say; for error is ever talkative.

But there is an enemy to this art still more dangerous, I mean Party. Party entirely distorts the judgment, and destroys the taste. When the mind is once infected with this disease, it can only find pleasure in what contributes to increase the distemper. Like the tyger, that seldom desists from pursuing man after having once preyed upon human flesh, the reader, who has once gratified his appetite with calumny, makes, ever after, the most agreeable feast upon murdered reputation. Such readers generally admire some half-witted thing, who wants to be thought a bold man, having lost the character of a wise one. Him they dignify with the name of poet; his tawdry lampoons are called satires, his turbulence is said to be force, and his phrenzy fire.[1]

What reception a Poem may find, which has neither abuse, party, nor blank verse to support it, I cannot tell nor am I sollicitous to know. My aims are right. Without espousing the cause of any party, I have attempted to moderate the rage of all. I have endeavoured to shew, that there may be equal happiness in states, that are differently governed from our own; that every state has a particular principle of happiness, and that this principle in each may be carried to a mischievous excess. There are few can judge, better than yourself, how far these positions are illustrated in this Poem.

I am, dear Sir,

Your most affectionate Brother,

OLIVER GOLDSMITH

[1] [This attack was aimed at Charles Churchill (1731–64) the author of the *Rosciad.*]

THE TRAVELLER

OR A PROSPECT OF SOCIETY

Remote, unfriended, melancholy, slow,
Or by the lazy Scheld, or wandering Po;
Or onward, where the rude Carinthian boor,
Against the houseless stranger shuts the door;
Or where Campania's plain forsaken lyes,
A weary waste expanding to the skies:
Where'er I roam, whatever realms to see,
My heart untravell'd fondly turns to thee;
Still to my brother turns, with ceaseless pain,
And drags at each remove a lengthening chain.
Eternal blessings crown my earliest friend,
And round his dwelling guardian saints attend;
Blest be that spot, where chearful guests retire
To pause from toil, and trim their ev'ning fire;
Blest that abode, where want and pain repair,
And every stranger finds a ready chair;
Blest be those feasts with simple plenty crown'd,
Where all the ruddy family around,
Laugh at the jests or pranks that never fail,
Or sigh with pity at some mournful tale,
Or press the bashful stranger to his food,
And learn the luxury of doing good.
But me, not destin'd such delights to share,
My prime of life in wand'ring spent and care,
Impell'd, with steps unceasing, to pursue
Some fleeting good, that mocks me with the view;
That, like the circle bounding earth and skies,

Allures from far, yet, as I follow, flies;
My fortune leads to traverse realms alone,
And find no spot of all the world my own.
   Even now, where Alpine solitudes ascend,
I sit me down a pensive hour to spend;
And, plac'd on high above the storm's career,
Look downward where an hundred realms appear;
Lakes, forests, cities, plains extending wide,
The pomp of kings, the shepherd's humbler pride.
   When thus Creation's charms around combine,
Amidst the store, should thankless pride repine?
Say, should the philosophic mind disdain
That good, which makes each humbler bosom vain?
Let school-taught pride dissemble all it can,
These little things are great to little man;
And wiser he, whose sympathetic mind
Exults in all the good of all mankind.
Ye glitt'ring towns, with wealth and splendour crown'd,
Ye fields, where summer spreads profusion round,
Ye lakes, whose vessels catch the busy gale,
Ye bending swains, that dress the flow'ry vale,
For me your tributary stores combine;
Creation's heir, the world, the world is mine.
   As some lone miser visiting his store,
Bends at his treasure, counts, recounts it o'er;
Hoards after hoards his rising raptures fill,
Yet still he sighs, for hoards are wanting still:
Thus to my breast alternate passions rise,
Pleas'd with each good that heaven to man supplies:
Yet oft a sigh prevails, and sorrows fall,
To see the hoard of human bliss so small;
And oft I wish, amidst the scene, to find
Some spot to real happiness consign'd,
Where my worn soul, each wand'ring hope at rest,
May gather bliss to see my fellows blest.

But where to find that happiest spot below,
Who can direct, when all pretend to know?
The shudd'ring tenant of the frigid zone
Boldly proclaims that happiest spot his own,
Extols the treasures of his stormy seas,
And his long nights of revelry and ease;
The naked negroe, panting at the line,
Boasts of his golden sands and palmy wine,
Basks in the glare, or stems the tepid wave,
And thanks his Gods for all the good they gave.
Such is the patriot's boast, where'er we roam,
His first, best country ever is, at home.
And yet, perhaps, if countries we compare,
And estimate the blessings which they share;
Tho' patriots flatter, still shall wisdom find
An equal portion dealt to all mankind,
As different good, by Art or Nature given,
To different nations makes their blessings even.
Nature, a mother kind alike to all,
Still grants her bliss at Labour's earnest call;
With food as well the peasant is supply'd
On Idra's[1] cliffs as Arno's shelvy side;
And though the rocky crested summits frown,
These rocks, by custom, turn to beds of down.
From Art more various are the blessings sent;
Wealth, commerce, honour, liberty, content.
Yet these each other's power so strong contest,
That either seems destructive of the rest.
Where wealth and freedom reign contentment fails,
And honour sinks where commerce long prevails.
Hence every state to one lov'd blessing prone,
Conforms and models life to that alone.
Each to the favourite happiness attends,
And spurns the plan that aims at other ends;

[1] [Probably Lake Idro near Lake Garda in Northern Italy.]

'Till, carried to excess in each domain,
This favourite good begets peculiar pain.
  But let us try these truths with closer eyes,
And trace them through the prospect as it lies:
Here for a while my proper cares resign'd,
Here let me sit in sorrow for mankind,
Like yon neglected shrub at random cast,
That shades the steep, and sighs at every blast.
  Far to the right where Appennine ascends,
Bright as the summer, Italy extends;
Its uplands sloping deck the mountain's side,
Woods over woods in gay theatric pride;
While oft some temple's mould'ring tops between,
With venerable grandeur mark the scene.
  Could Nature's bounty satisfy the breast,
The sons of Italy were surely blest.
Whatever fruits in different climes were found,
That proudly rise, or humbly court the ground;
Whatever blooms in torrid tracts appear,
Whose bright succession decks the varied year;
Whatever sweets salute the northern sky
With vernal lives that blossom but to die;
These here disporting own the kindred soil,
Nor ask luxuriance from the planter's toil;
While sea-born gales their gelid wings expand
To winnow fragrance round the smiling land.
  But small the bliss that sense alone bestows,
And sensual bliss is all the nation knows.
In florid beauty groves and fields appear,
Man seems the only growth that dwindles here.
Contrasted faults through all his manners reign,
Though poor, luxurious, though submissive, vain,
Though grave, yet trifling, zealous, yet untrue,
And ev'n in penance planning sins anew.
All evils here contaminate the mind,

That opulence departed leaves behind;
For wealth was theirs, not far remov'd the date,
When commerce proudly flourished through the state;
At her command the palace learnt to rise,
Again the long-fallen column sought the skies;
The canvass glow'd beyond e'en Nature warm,
The pregnant quarry teem'd with human form.
Till, more unsteady than the southern gale,
Commerce on other shores display'd her sail;
While nought remain'd of all that riches gave,
But towns unman'd, and lords without a slave:
And late the nation found with fruitless skill
Its former strength was but plethoric ill.
Yet, still the loss of wealth is here supplied
By arts, the splendid wrecks of former pride;
From these the feeble heart and long-fall'n mind
An easy compensation seem to find.
Here may be seen, in bloodless pomp array'd,
The paste-board triumph and the cavalcade;
Processions form'd for piety and love,
A mistress or a saint in every grove.
By sports like these are all their cares beguil'd,
The sports of children satisfy the child;
Each nobler aim represt by long controul,
Now sinks at last, or feebly mans the soul;
While low delights, succeeding fast behind,
In happier meanness occupy the mind:
As in those domes, where Cæsars once bore sway,
Defac'd by time and tottering in decay,
There in the ruin, heedless of the dead,
The shelter-seeking peasant builds his shed,
And, wond'ring man could want the larger pile,
Exults, and owns his cottage with a smile.
My soul turn from them, turn we to survey
Where rougher climes a nobler race display,

Where the bleak Swiss their stormy mansions tread,
And force a churlish soil for scanty bread;
No product here the barren hills afford,
But Man and steel, the soldier and his sword.
No vernal blooms their torpid rocks array,
But winter ling'ring chills the lap of May;
No Zephyr fondly sues the mountain's breast,
But meteors glare, and stormy glooms invest.
  Yet still, even here, content can spread a charm,
Redress the clime, and all its rage disarm.
Though poor the peasant's hut, his feasts though small,
He sees his little lot the lot of all;
Sees no contiguous palace rear its head
To shame the meanness of his humble shed;
No costly lord the sumptuous banquet deal
To make him loath his vegetable meal;
But calm, and bred in ignorance and toil,
Each wish contracting, fits him to the soil.
Chearful at morn he wakes from short repose,
Breasts the keen air, and carrols as he goes;
With patient angle trolls the finny deep,
Or drives his venturous plow-share to the steep;
Or seeks the den where snow-tracks mark the way,
And drags the struggling savage into day.
At night returning, every labour sped,
He sits him down the monarch of a shed;
Smiles by his chearful fire, and round surveys
His childrens looks, that brighten at the blaze;
While his lov'd partner, boastful of her hoard,
Displays her cleanly platter on the board:
And haply too some pilgrim, thither led,
With many a tale repays the nightly bed.
  Thus every good his native wilds impart,
Imprints the patriot passion on his heart,
And even those ills, that round his mansion rise,

Enhance the bliss his scanty fund supplies.
Dear is that shed to which his soul conforms,
And dear that hill which lifts him to the storms;
And as a child, when scaring sounds molest,
Clings close and closer to the mother's breast,
So the loud torrent, and the whirlwind's roar,
But bind him to his native mountains more.
  Such are the charms to barren states assign'd;
Their wants but few, their wishes all confin'd.
Yet let them only share the praises due,
If few their wants, their pleasures are but few;
For every want that stimulates the breast,
Becomes a source of pleasure when redrest.
Whence from such lands each pleasing science flies,
That first excites desire, and then supplies;
Unknown to them, when sensual pleasures cloy,
To fill the languid pause with finer joy;
Unknown those powers that raise the soul to flame,
Catch every nerve, and vibrate through the frame.
Their level life is but a smould'ring fire,
Unquench'd by want, unfann'd by strong desire;
Unfit for raptures, or, if raptures cheer
On some high festival of once a year,
In wild excess the vulgar breast takes fire,
Till, buried in debauch, the bliss expire.
  But not their joys alone thus coarsely flow:
Their morals, like their pleasures, are but low,
For, as refinement stops, from sire to son
Unalter'd, unimprov'd the manners run,
And love's and friendship's finely pointed dart
Fall blunted from each indurated heart.
Some sterner virtues o'er the mountain's breast
May sit, like falcons cow'ring on the nest;
But all the gentler morals, such as play
Through life's more cultur'd walks, and charm the way,

These far dispers'd, on timorous pinions fly,
To sport and flutter in a kinder sky.
To kinder skies, where gentler manners reign,
I turn; and France displays her bright domain.
Gay sprightly land of mirth and social ease,
Pleas'd with thyself, whom all the world can please,
How often have I led thy sportive choir,
With tuneless pipe, beside the murmuring Loire?
Where shading elms along the margin grew,
And freshen'd from the wave the Zephyr flew;
And haply, though my harsh touch faltering still,
But mock'd all tune, and marr'd the dancer's skill;
Yet would the village praise my wonderous pow'r,
And dance, forgetful of the noon-tide hour.
Alike all ages. Dames of ancient days
Have led their children through the mirthful maze,
And the gay grandsire, skill'd in gestic lore,
Has frisk'd beneath the burthen of threescore.
So blest a life these thoughtless realms display,
Thus idly busy rolls their world away:
Theirs are those arts that mind to mind endear,
For honour forms the social temper here.
Honour, that praise which real merit gains,
Or even imaginary worth obtains,
Here passes current; paid from hand to hand,
It shifts in splendid traffic round the land:
From courts, to camps, to cottages it strays,
And all are taught an avarice of praise;
They please, are pleas'd, they give to get esteem,
Till, seeming blest, they grow to what they seem.
But while this softer art their bliss supplies,
It gives their follies also room to rise;
For praise too dearly lov'd, or warmly sought,
Enfeebles all internal strength of thought.
And the weak soul, within itself unblest,

Leans for all pleasure on another's breast.
Hence ostentation here, with tawdry art,
Pants for the vulgar praise which fools impart;
Here vanity assumes her pert grimace,
And trims her robes of frize with copper lace,
Here beggar pride defrauds her daily cheer,
To boast one splendid banquet once a year;
The mind still turns where shifting fashion draws,
Nor weighs the solid worth of self applause.
To men of other minds my fancy flies,
Embosom'd in the deep where Holland lies,
Methinks her patient sons before me stand,
Where the broad ocean leans against the land,
And, sedulous to stop the coming tide,
Lift the tall rampire's artificial pride.
Onward methinks, and diligently slow
The firm connected bulwark seems to grow;
Spreads its long arms amidst the watry roar,
Scoops out an empire, and usurps the shore.
While the pent ocean rising o'er the pile,
Sees an amphibious world beneath him smile;
The slow canal, the yellow blossom'd vale,
The willow tufted bank, the gliding sail,
The crowded mart, the cultivated plain,
A new creation rescu'd from his reign.
Thus, while around the wave-subjected soil
Impels the native to repeated toil,
Industrious habits in each bosom reign,
And industry begets a love of gain.
Hence all the good from opulence that springs,
With all those ills superfluous treasure brings,
Are here display'd. Their much-lov'd wealth imparts
Convenience, plenty, elegance, and arts;
But view them closer, craft and fraud appear,
Even liberty itself is barter'd here.

At gold's superior charms all freedom flies,
The needy sell it, and the rich man buys;
A land of tyrants, and a den of slaves,
Here wretches seek dishonourable graves,
And calmly bent, to servitude conform,
Dull as their lakes that slumber in the storm.
   Heavens! how unlike their Belgic sires of old!
Rough, poor, content, ungovernably bold;
War in each breast, and freedom on each brow;
How much unlike the sons of Britain now!
   Fir'd at the sound my genius spreads her wing,
And flies where Britain courts the western spring;
Where lawns extend that scorn Arcadian pride,
And brighter streams than fam'd Hydaspis glide.
There all around the gentlest breezes stray,
There gentle music melts on every spray;
Creation's mildest charms are there combin'd,
Extremes are only in the master's mind!
Stern o'er each bosom reason holds her state,
With daring aims irregularly great,
Pride in their port, defiance in their eye,
I see the lords of human kind pass by,
Intent on high designs, a thoughtful band,
By forms unfashion'd, fresh from Nature's hand;
Fierce in their native hardiness of soul,
True to imagin'd right, above controul,
While even the peasant boasts these rights to scan,
And learns to venerate himself as man.
   Thine, Freedom, thine the blessings pictur'd here,
Thine are those charms that dazzle and endear;
Too blest indeed, were such without alloy,
But foster'd even by Freedom ills annoy:
That independence Britons prize too high,
Keeps man from man, and breaks the social tie;
The self-dependent lordlings stand alone,

All claims that bind and sweeten life unknown;
Here by the bonds of nature feebly held,
Minds combat minds, repelling and repell'd.
Ferments arise, imprison'd factions roar,
Represt ambition struggles round her shore,
Till over-wrought, the general system feels
Its motions stop, or phrenzy fire the wheels.
  Nor this the worst. As nature's ties decay,
As duty, love, and honour fail to sway,
Fictitious bonds, the bonds of wealth and law,
Still gather strength, and force unwilling awe.
Hence all obedience bows to these alone,
And talent sinks, and merit weeps unknown;
Till time may come, when stript of all her charms,
The land of scholars, and the nurse of arms;
Where noble stems transmit the patriot flame,
Where kings have toil'd, and poets wrote for fame;
One sink of level avarice shall lie,
And scholars, soldiers, kings, unhonour'd die.
  Yet think not, thus when Freedom's ills I state,
I mean to flatter kings, or court the great;
Ye powers of truth that bid my soul aspire,
Far from my bosom drive the low desire;
And thou fair Freedom, taught alike to feel
The rabble's rage, and tyrant's angry steel;
Thou transitory flower, alike undone
By proud contempt, or favour's fostering sun,
Still may thy blooms the changeful clime endure,
I only would repress them to secure:
For just experience tells, in every soil,
That those who think must govern those that toil
And all that freedom's highest aims can reach,
Is but to lay proportion'd loads on each.
Hence, should one order disproportion'd grow,
Its double weight must ruin all below.

O then how blind to all that truth requires,
Who think it freedom when a part aspires!
Calm is my soul, nor apt to rise in arms,
Except when fast approaching danger warms:
But when contending chiefs blockade the throne,
Contracting regal power to stretch their own,
When I behold a factious band agree
To call it freedom when themselves are free;
Each wanton judge new penal statutes draw,
Laws grind the poor, and rich men rule the law;
The wealth of climes, where savage nations roam,
Pillag'd from slaves to purchase slaves at home;
Fear, pity, justice, indignation start,
Tear off reserve, and bare my swelling heart;
'Till half a patriot, half a coward grown,
I fly from petty tyrants to the throne.
Yes, brother, curse with me that baleful hour,
When first ambition struck at regal power;
And thus polluting honour in its source,
Gave wealth to sway the mind with double force.
Have we not seen, round Britain's peopled shore,
Her useful sons exchang'd for useless ore?
Seen all her triumphs but destruction haste,
Like flaring tapers brightening as they waste;
Seen opulence, her grandeur to maintain,
Lead stern depopulation in her train,
And over fields where scatter'd hamlets rose,
In barren solitary pomp repose?
Have we not seen at pleasure's lordly call,
The smiling long-frequented village fall?
Beheld the duteous son, the sire decay'd,
The modest matron, and the blushing maid,
Forc'd from their homes, a melancholy train,
To traverse climes beyond the western main;
Where wild Oswego spreads her swamps around,

And Niagara[1] stuns with thund'ring sound?
  Even now, perhaps, as there some pilgrim strays
Through tangled forests, and through dangerous ways;
Where beasts with man divided empire claim,
And the brown Indian marks with murderous aim;
There, while above the giddy tempest flies,
And all around distressful yells arise,
The pensive exile, bending with his woe,
To stop too fearful, and too faint to go,
Casts a long look where England's glories shine,
And bids his bosom sympathize with mine.
  Vain, very vain, my weary search to find
That bliss which only centers in the mind:
Why have I stray'd, from pleasure and repose,
To seek a good each government bestows?
In every government, though terrors reign,
Though tyrant kings, or tyrant laws restrain,
How small of all that human hearts endure,
That part which laws or kings can cause or cure.
Still to ourselves in every place consign'd,
Our own felicity we make or find:
With secret course, which no loud storms annoy,
Glides the smooth current of domestic joy.
The lifted ax, the agonizing wheel,
Luke's[2] iron crown, and Damien's[3] bed of steel,
To men remote from power but rarely known,
Leave reason, faith, and conscience, all our own.

[1] [Stressed "Nìagàra" by Goldsmith and subsequently by other writers, but apparently with no authority of Indian usage. See the long controversy in *Notes and Queries*, beginning I. vi. 555, especially I. ix. 533.]

[2] [Luke Dosa and his brother George led a popular revolt in Hungary. George (not Luke) was proclaimed king by the peasants, for which, in 1514, he was tortured in a red-hot crown.]

[3] [See footnote, p. 296.]

THE DESERTED VILLAGE

The Deserted Village, A Poem was first published in quarto on 26 May, 1770, *Printed for W. Griffin, at Garrick's Head, in Catharine-street, Strand.* Second, third, fourth and fifth editions were published in the next month, and Goldsmith made considerable revisions in the text up to and including the fourth edition.

There are also several very rare privately printed duodecimo editions. They may have preceded the first quarto. The two in the Ashley Collection in the British Museum are printed from different settings of type and vary in spelling and punctuation, but do not otherwise differ from the first quarto, from which they probably derive. The present text is that of the fourth quarto edition.

Goldsmith probably took about two years writing the poem and, as with *The Traveller*, had difficulty in finishing it. The last four lines are by Johnson.

TO SIR JOSHUA REYNOLDS

Dear Sir,

I can have no expectations in an address of this kind, either to add to your reputation, or to establish my own. You can gain nothing from my admiration, as I am ignorant of that art in which you are said to excel; and I may lose much by the severity of your judgment, as few have a juster taste in poetry than you. Setting interest therefore aside, to which I never paid much attention, I must be indulged at present in following my affections. The only dedication I ever made was to my brother, because I loved him better than most other men. He is since dead. Permit me to inscribe this Poem to you.

How far you may be pleased with the versification and mere mechanical parts of this attempt, I don't pretend to enquire; but I know you will object (and indeed several of our best and wisest friends concur in the opinion) that the depopulation it deplores is no where to be seen, and the disorders it laments are only to be found in the poet's own imagination. To this I can scarce make any other answer than that I sincerely believe what I have written; that I have taken all possible pains, in my country excursions, for these four or five years past, to be certain of what I alledge; and that all my views and enquiries have led me to believe those miseries real, which I here attempt to display. But this is not the place to enter into an enquiry, whether the country be depopulating, or not; the discussion would take up much room, and I should prove myself, at best, an indifferent politician, to tire the reader with a long preface, when I want his unfatigued attention to a long poem.

In regretting the depopulation of the country, I inveigh against the encrease of our luxuries; and here also I expect the shout of modern politicians against me. For twenty or thirty years past, it has been the fashion to consider luxury as one of the greatest national advantages; and all the wisdom of antiquity in that particular, as erroneous. Still however, I must remain a professed ancient on that head, and continue to think those luxuries prejudicial to states, by which so many vices are introduced, and so many kingdoms have been undone. Indeed so much has been poured out of late on the other side of the question, that, merely for the sake of novelty and variety, one would sometimes wish to be in the right.

I am,

Dear Sir,

Your sincere friend,

and ardent admirer,

OLIVER GOLDSMITH

THE DESERTED VILLAGE

Sweet Auburn, loveliest village of the plain,
Where health and plenty cheared the labouring swain,
Where smiling spring its earliest visit paid,
And parting summer's lingering blooms delayed,
Dear lovely bowers of innocence and ease,
Seats of my youth, when every sport could please,
How often have I loitered o'er thy green,
Where humble happiness endeared each scene;
How often have I paused on every charm,
The sheltered cot, the cultivated farm,
The never failing brook, the busy mill,
The decent church that topt the neighbouring hill,
The hawthorn bush, with seats beneath the shade,
For talking age and whispering lovers made;
How often have I blest the coming day,
When toil remitting lent its turn to play,
And all the village train from labour free
Led up their sports beneath the spreading tree;
While many a pastime circled in the shade,
The young contending as the old surveyed;
And many a gambol frolicked o'er the ground,
And slights of art and feats of strength went round;
And still as each repeated pleasure tired,
Succeeding sports the mirthful band inspired;
The dancing pair that simply sought renown
By holding out to tire each other down;
The swain mistrustless of his smutted face,
While secret laughter tittered round the place;

The bashful virgin's side-long looks of love,
The matron's glance that would those looks reprove:
These were thy charms, sweet village; sports like these,
With sweet succession, taught even toil to please;
These round thy bowers their chearful influence shed,
These were thy charms—But all these charms are fled.
  Sweet smiling village, loveliest of the lawn,
Thy sports are fled, and all thy charms withdrawn;
Amidst thy bowers the tyrant's hand is seen,
And desolation saddens all thy green:
One only master grasps the whole domain,
And half a tillage stints thy smiling plain;
No more thy glassy brook reflects the day,
But choaked with sedges, works its weedy way.
Along thy glades, a solitary guest,
The hollow sounding bittern guards its nest;
Amidst thy desert walks the lapwing flies,
And tires their ecchoes with unvaried cries.[1]
Sunk are thy bowers, in shapeless ruin all,
And the long grass o'ertops the mouldering wall,
And trembling, shrinking from the spoiler's hand,
Far, far away thy children leave the land.
  Ill fares the land, to hastening ills a prey,
Where wealth accumulates, and men decay:
Princes and lords may flourish, or may fade;
A breath can make them, as a breath has made;
But a bold peasantry, their country's pride,
When once destroyed, can never be supplied.
  A time there was, ere England's griefs began,
When every rood of ground maintained its man;
For him light labour spread her wholesome store,
Just gave what life required, but gave no more:
His best companions, innocence and health;

[1] [See Goldsmith's description of the bittern and the lapwing in the extract from *An History of the Earth and Animated Nature* on pp. 578–9.]

And his best riches, ignorance of wealth.
But times are altered; trade's unfeeling train
Usurp the land and dispossess the swain;
Along the lawn, where scattered hamlets rose,
Unwieldy wealth, and cumbrous pomp repose;
And every want to oppulence allied,
And every pang that folly pays to pride.
These gentle hours that plenty bade to bloom,
Those calm desires that asked but little room,
Those healthful sports that graced the peaceful scene,
Lived in each look, and brightened all the green;
These far departing seek a kinder shore,
And rural mirth and manners are no more.
Sweet AUBURN! parent of the blissful hour,
Thy glades forlorn confess the tyrant's power.
Here as I take my solitary rounds,
Amidst thy tangling walks, and ruined grounds,
And, many a year elapsed, return to view
Where once the cottage stood, the hawthorn grew,
Remembrance wakes with all her busy train,
Swells at my breast, and turns the past to pain.
In all my wanderings round this world of care,
In all my griefs—and GOD has given my share—
I still had hopes my latest hours to crown,
Amidst these humble bowers to lay me down;
To husband out life's taper at the close,
And keep the flame from wasting by repose.
I still had hopes, for pride attends us still,
Amidst the swains to shew my book-learned skill,
Around my fire an evening groupe to draw,
And tell of all I felt, and all I saw;
And, as an hare whom hounds and horns pursue,
Pants to the place from whence at first she flew,
I still had hopes, my long vexations past,
Here to return—and die at home at last.

O blest retirement, friend to life's decline,
Retreats from care that never must be mine,
How happy he who crowns in shades like these,
A youth of labour with an age of ease;
Who quits a world where strong temptations try,
And, since 'tis hard to combat, learns to fly.
For him no wretches, born to work and weep,
Explore the mine, or tempt the dangerous deep;
No surly porter stands in guilty state
To spurn imploring famine from the gate,
But on he moves to meet his latter end,
Angels around befriending virtue's friend;
Bends to the grave with unperceived decay,
While resignation gently slopes the way;
And all his prospects brightening to the last,
His Heaven commences ere the world be past!
Sweet was the sound when oft at evening's close,
Up yonder hill the village murmur rose;
There as I past with careless steps and slow,
The mingling notes came softened from below;
The swain responsive as the milk-maid sung,
The sober herd that lowed to meet their young,
The noisy geese that gabbled o'er the pool,
The playful children just let loose from school,
The watch-dog's voice that bayed the whispering wind,
And the loud laugh that spoke the vacant mind,
These all in sweet confusion sought the shade,
And filled each pause the nightingale had made.
But now the sounds of population fail,
No chearful murmurs fluctuate in the gale,
No busy steps the grass-grown foot-way tread,
For all the bloomy flush of life is fled.
All but yon widowed, solitary thing
That feebly bends beside the plashy spring;
She, wretched matron, forced, in age, for bread,

To strip the brook with mantling cresses spread,
To pick her wintry faggot from the thorn,
To seek her nightly shed, and weep till morn;
She only left of all the harmless train,
The sad historian of the pensive plain.
    Near yonder copse, where once the garden smil'd,
And still where many a garden flower grows wild;
There, where a few torn shrubs the place disclose,
The village preacher's modest mansion rose.
A man he was, to all the country dear,
And passing rich with forty pounds a year;
Remote from towns he ran his godly race,
Nor e'er had changed, nor wished to change his place;
Unpractised he to fawn, or seek for power,
By doctrines fashioned to the varying hour;
Far other aims his heart had learned to prize,
More skilled to raise the wretched than to rise.
His house was known to all the vagrant train,
He chid their wanderings, but relieved their pain;
The long remembered beggar was his guest,
Whose beard descending swept his aged breast;
The ruined spendthrift, now no longer proud,
Claimed kindred there, and had his claims allowed;
The broken soldier, kindly bade to stay,
Sate by his fire, and talked the night away;
Wept o'er his wounds, or tales of sorrow done,
Shouldered his crutch, and shewed how fields were won.
Pleased with his guests, the good man learned to glow,
And quite forgot their vices in their woe;
Careless their merits, or their faults to scan,
His pity gave ere charity began.
    Thus to relieve the wretched was his pride,
And even his failings leaned to Virtue's side;
But in his duty prompt at every call,
He watched and wept, he prayed and felt, for all.

And, as a bird each fond endearment tries,
To tempt its new fledged offspring to the skies;
He tried each art, reproved each dull delay,
Allured to brighter worlds, and led the way.
  Beside the bed where parting life was layed,
And sorrow, guilt, and pain, by turns dismayed,
The reverend champion stood. At his control,
Despair and anguish fled the struggling soul;
Comfort came down the trembling wretch to raise,
And his last faultering accents whispered praise.
  At church, with meek and unaffected grace,
His looks adorned the venerable place;
Truth from his lips prevailed with double sway,
And fools, who came to scoff, remained to pray.
The service past, around the pious man,
With steady zeal each honest rustic ran;
Even children followed with endearing wile,
And plucked his gown, to share the good man's smile.
His ready smile a parent's warmth exprest,
Their welfare pleased him, and their cares distrest;
To them his heart, his love, his griefs were given,
But all his serious thoughts had rest in Heaven.
As some tall cliff that lifts its awful form,
Swells from the vale, and midway leaves the storm,
Tho' round its breast the rolling clouds are spread,
Eternal sunshine settles on its head.
  Beside yon straggling fence that skirts the way,
With blossomed furze unprofitably gay,
There, in his noisy mansion, skill'd to rule,
The village master taught his little school;
A man severe he was, and stern to view,
I knew him well, and every truant knew;
Well had the boding tremblers learned to trace
The day's disasters in his morning face;
Full well they laugh'd with counterfeited glee,

At all his jokes, for many a joke had he;
Full well the busy whisper circling round,
Conveyed the dismal tidings when he frowned;
Yet he was kind, or if severe in aught,
The love he bore to learning was in fault;
The village all declared how much he knew;
'Twas certain he could write, and cypher too;
Lands he could measure, terms and tides presage,
And even the story ran that he could gauge.
In arguing too, the parson owned his skill,
For even tho' vanquished, he could argue still;
While words of learned length, and thundering sound,
Amazed the gazing rustics ranged around;
And still they gazed, and still the wonder grew,
That one small head could carry all he knew.
    But past is all his fame. The very spot
Where many a time he triumphed, is forgot.
Near yonder thorn, that lifts its head on high,
Where once the sign-post caught the passing eye,
Low lies that house where nut-brown draughts inspired,
Where grey-beard mirth and smiling toil retired,
Where village statesmen talked with looks profound,
And news much older than their ale went round.
Imagination fondly stoops to trace
The parlour splendours of that festive place;
The white-washed wall, the nicely sanded floor,
The varnished clock that clicked behind the door;
The chest contrived a double debt to pay,
A bed by night, a chest of drawers by day;
The pictures placed for ornament and use,
The twelve good rules,[1] the royal game of goose;[2]
The hearth, except when winter chill'd the day,

[1] [A set of maxims "found in the study of King Charles the First, of Blessed Memory," which were frequently printed as a broadside.]

[2] [A very simple board game not unlike ludo. It is still popular in France.]

With aspen boughs, and flowers, and fennel gay,
While broken tea-cups, wisely kept for shew,
Ranged o'er the chimney, glistened in a row.[1]
  Vain transitory splendours! Could not all
Reprieve the tottering mansion from its fall!
Obscure it sinks, nor shall it more impart
An hour's importance to the poor man's heart;
Thither no more the peasant shall repair
To sweet oblivion of his daily care;
No more the farmer's news, the barber's tale,
No more the wood-man's ballad shall prevail;
No more the smith his dusky brow shall clear,
Relax his ponderous strength, and lean to hear;
The host himself no longer shall be found
Careful to see the mantling bliss go round;
Nor the coy maid, half willing to be prest,
Shall kiss the cup to pass it to the rest.
  Yes! let the rich deride, the proud disdain,
These simple blessings of the lowly train;
To me more dear, congenial to my heart,
One native charm, than all the gloss of art;
Spontaneous joys, where Nature has its play,
The soul adopts, and owns their first born sway;
Lightly they frolic o'er the vacant mind,
Unenvied, unmolested, unconfined.
But the long pomp, the midnight masquerade,
With all the freaks of wanton wealth arrayed,
In these, ere triflers half their wish obtain,
The toiling pleasure sickens into pain;
And, even while fashion's brightest arts decoy,
The heart distrusting asks, if this be joy.
  Ye friends to truth, ye statesmen, who survey
The rich man's joys encrease, the poor's decay,
'Tis yours to judge, how wide the limits stand

[1] [Compare the *Description of an Author's Bedchamber* on p. 345.]

Between a splendid and an happy land.
Proud swells the tide with loads of freighted ore,
And shouting Folly hails them from her shore;
Hoards, even beyond the miser's wish abound,
And rich men flock from all the world around.
Yet count our gains. This wealth is but a name
That leaves our useful products still the same.
Not so the loss. The man of wealth and pride,
Takes up a space that many poor supplied;
Space for his lake, his park's extended bounds,
Space for his horses, equipage, and hounds;
The robe that wraps his limbs in silken sloth,
Has robbed the neighbouring fields of half their growth;
His seat, where solitary sports are seen,
Indignant spurns the cottage from the green;
Around the world each needful product flies,
For all the luxuries the world supplies.
While thus the land adorned for pleasure, all
In barren splendour feebly waits the fall.
As some fair female unadorned and plain,
Secure to please while youth confirms her reign,
Slights every borrowed charm that dress supplies,
Nor shares with art the triumph of her eyes.
But when those charms are past, for charms are frail,
When time advances, and when lovers fail,
She then shines forth, sollicitous to bless,
In all the glaring impotence of dress.
Thus fares the land, by luxury betrayed;
In nature's simplest charms at first arrayed;
But verging to decline, its splendour rise,
Its vistas strike, its palaces surprize;
While scourged by famine from the smiling land,
The mournful peasant leads his humble band;
And while he sinks without one arm to save,
The country blooms—a garden, and a grave.

Where then, ah where, shall poverty reside,
To scape the pressure of contiguous pride?
If to some common's fenceless limits strayed,
He drives his flock to pick the scanty blade,
Those fenceless fields the sons of wealth divide,
And even the bare-worn common is denied.
If to the city sped—What waits him there?
To see profusion that he must not share;
To see ten thousand baneful arts combined
To pamper luxury, and thin mankind;
To see those joys the sons of pleasure know,
Extorted from his fellow-creature's woe.
Here, while the courtier glitters in brocade,
There the pale artist plies the sickly trade;
Here, while the proud their long-drawn pomps display,
There the black gibbet glooms beside the way.
The dome where Pleasure holds her midnight reign,
Here, richly deckt, admits the gorgeous train;
Tumultuous grandeur crowds the blazing square,
The rattling chariots clash, the torches glare.
Sure scenes like these no troubles e'er annoy!
Sure these denote one universal joy!
Are these thy serious thoughts?—Ah, turn thine eyes
Where the poor houseless shivering female lies.
She once, perhaps, in village plenty blest,
Has wept at tales of innocence distrest;
Her modest looks the cottage might adorn,
Sweet as the primrose peeps beneath the thorn;
Now lost to all; her friends, her virtue fled,
Near her betrayer's door she lays her head,
And pinch'd with cold, and shrinking from the shower,
With heavy heart deplores that luckless hour
When idly first, ambitious of the town,
She left her wheel and robes of country brown.
Do thine, sweet AUBURN, thine, the loveliest train,

Do thy fair tribes participate her pain?
Even now, perhaps, by cold and hunger led,
At proud men's doors they ask a little bread!
  Ah, no. To distant climes, a dreary scene,
Where half the convex world intrudes between,
Through torrid tracts with fainting steps they go,
Where wild Altama[1] murmurs to their woe.
Far different there from all that charm'd before,
The various terrors of that horrid shore;
Those blazing suns that dart a downward ray,
And fiercely shed intolerable day;
Those matted woods where birds forget to sing,
But silent bats in drowsy clusters cling,
Those poisonous fields with rank luxuriance crowned,
Where the dark scorpion gathers death around;
Where at each step the stranger fears to wake
The rattling terrors of the vengeful snake;
Where crouching tigers wait their hapless prey,
And savage men, more murderous still than they;
While oft in whirls the mad tornado flies,
Mingling the ravaged landschape with the skies.
Far different these from every former scene,
The cooling brook, the grassy vested green,
The breezy covert of the warbling grove,
That only sheltered thefts of harmless love.
  Good Heaven! what sorrows gloom'd that parting day,
That called them from their native walks away;
When the poor exiles, every pleasure past,
Hung round their bowers, and fondly looked their last,
And took a long farewell, and wished in vain
For seats like these beyond the western main;
And shuddering still to face the distant deep,
Returned and wept, and still returned to weep.
The good old sire, the first prepared to go

[1] [Alatamaha, in Georgia, U.S.A.]

To new found worlds, and wept for others woe.
But for himself, in conscious virtue brave,
He only wished for worlds beyond the grave.
His lovely daughter, lovelier in her tears,
The fond companion of his helpless years,
Silent went next, neglectful of her charms,
And left a lover's for a father's arms.
With louder plaints the mother spoke her woes,
And blest the cot where every pleasure rose;
And kist her thoughtless babes with many a tear,
And claspt them close in sorrow doubly dear;
Whilst her fond husband strove to lend relief
In all the silent manliness of grief.
O luxury! Thou curst by Heaven's decree,
How ill exchanged are things like these for thee!
How do thy potions, with insidious joy,
Diffuse their pleasures only to destroy!
Kingdoms, by thee, to sickly greatness grown,
Boast of a florid vigour not their own;
At every draught more large and large they grow,
A bloated mass of rank unwieldy woe;
Till sapped their strength, and every part unsound,
Down, down they sink, and spread a ruin round.
Even now the devastation is begun,
And half the business of destruction done;
Even now, methinks, as pondering here I stand,
I see the rural virtues leave the land:
Down where yon anchoring vessel spreads the sail,
That idly waiting flaps with every gale,
Downward they move, a melancholy band,
Pass from the shore, and darken all the strand.
Contented toil, and hospitable care,
And kind connubial tenderness, are there;
And piety, with wishes placed above,
And steady loyalty, and faithful love:

And thou, sweet Poetry, thou loveliest maid,
Still first to fly where sensual joys invade;
Unfit in these degenerate times of shame,
To catch the heart, or strike for honest fame;
Dear charming nymph, neglected and decried,
My shame in crowds, my solitary pride;
Thou source of all my bliss, and all my woe,
That found'st me poor at first, and keep'st me so;
Thou guide by which the nobler arts excell,
Thou nurse of every virtue, fare thee well.
Farewell, and O where'er thy voice be tried,
On Torno's[1] cliffs, or Pambamarca's[2] side,
Whether where equinoctial fervours glow,
Or winter wraps the polar world in snow,
Still let thy voice prevailing over time,
Redress the rigours of the inclement clime;
Aid slighted truth, with thy persuasive strain,
Teach erring man to spurn the rage of gain;
Teach him, that states of native strength possest,
Tho' very poor, may still be very blest;
That trade's proud empire hastes to swift decay,
As ocean sweeps the labour'd mole away;
While self-dependent power can time defy,
As rocks resist the billows and the sky.

[1] [Usually identified with River Torne, on the border between Sweden and Finland. But Torno, near Como on the shore of Lake Como in Italy, seems more likely.]

[2] [A mountain near Quito, in Ecuador.]

THE HAUNCH OF VENISON

A POETICAL EPISTLE TO LORD CLARE

The Haunch of Venison, A Poetical Epistle to Lord Clare was first published in 1776, two years after Goldsmith's death. It was *Printed for G. Kearsley, in Fleet Street; and J. Ridley, in St. James's Street*, and had as frontispiece an engraving of Goldsmith after a drawing by Henry Bunbury, which Mary Horneck said "gives the head with admirable fidelity as he actually lived among us." It was probably written in 1771. Robert Nugent, Lord Clare, was Goldsmith's friend and patron; he was a large Rabelaisian Irishman and something of a poet. *The Haunch of Venison*, for all its freshness and spontaneity of style, is not original in theme, but is modelled on Boileau's third Satire, which, in its turn, probably derives from Horace.

A New Edition, With considerable Additions and Corrections, "taken from the Author's *last* Transcript," appeared later in 1776. This text, which the present edition follows, is a considerable improvement on the first edition.

THE HAUNCH OF VENISON
A POETICAL EPISTLE TO LORD CLARE

THANKS, my Lord, for your Venison, for finer or fatter
Never rang'd in a forest, or smoak'd in a platter;
The Haunch was a picture for Painters to study,
The fat was so white, and the lean was so ruddy.
Tho' my stomach was sharp, I could scarce help regretting
To spoil such a delicate picture by eating;
I had thoughts, in my Chambers, to place it in view,
To be shewn to my Friends as a piece of *Virtu*;
As in some *Irish* houses, where things are so so,
One Gammon of Bacon hangs up for a show:
But for eating a Rasher of what they take pride in,
They'd as soon think of eating the Pan it is fry'd in.
But hold—let me pause—Don't I hear you pronounce
This tale of the Bacon a damnable Bounce?
Well, suppose it a Bounce—sure a Poet may try,
By a Bounce now and then, to get Courage to fly:
But, my Lord, it's no Bounce: I protest in my Turn,
It's a Truth—and your Lordship may ask Mr. *Burn*.[1]
To go on with my Tale—as I gaz'd on the Haunch,
I thought of a Friend that was trusty and staunch;
So I cut it, and sent it to *Reynolds* undrest,
To paint it, or eat it, just as he lik'd best.
Of the Neck and the Breast I had next to dispose;
'Twas a Neck and a Breast that might rival *M*[*on*]*r*[*o*]*se*:[2]
But in parting with these I was puzzled again,
With the how, and the who, and the where, and the when.

[1] [Lord Clare's nephew.]
[2] [Dorothy Monroe, a famous beauty.]

There's *H*[*owar*]*d*, and *C*[*ole*]*y*, and *H—rth*,[1] and *H*[*i*]*ff*,[2]
I think they love Venison—I know they love Beef;
There's my Countryman *H*[*i*]*gg*[*i*]*ns*—Oh! let him alone,
For making a Blunder, or picking a Bone.
But hang it—to Poets who seldom can eat,
Your very good Mutton's a very good Treat;
Such Dainties to them their Health it might hurt,
It's like sending them Ruffles, when wanting a Shirt.
While thus I debated, in Reverie center'd,
An Acquaintance, a Friend as he call'd himself, enter'd;
An under-bred, fine-spoken Fellow was he,
And he smil'd, as he look'd at the Venison and me.
What have we got here?—Why this is good eating!
Your own, I suppose—or is it in waiting?
Why whose should it be? cried I, with a Flounce,
I get these Things often;—but that was a Bounce:
Some Lords, my acquaintance, that settle the nation,
Are pleas'd to be kind—but I hate ostentation.
  If that be the case, then, cried he, very gay,
I'm glad I have taken this House in my Way.
To-morrow you take a poor dinner with me;
No Words—I insist on't—precisely at three:
We'll have *Johnson*, and *Burke*, all the Wits will be there,
My acquaintance is slight, or I'd ask my *Lord Clare*.[3]
And now that I think on't, as I am a sinner!
We wanted this Venison to make out the Dinner.
What say you—a pasty—it shall, and it must,
And my Wife, little *Kitty*, is famous for crust.

[1] ["H—rth" has not been definitely identified. Bolton Corney suggested Hogarth, "the surgeon of Golden Square," and Mr. Arthur Friedman thinks he may possibly be John Hawkesworth, Ll.D. (1715?–73).]

[2] [Paul Hiffernan, M.D., an Irish practitioner and journalist.]

[3] [Compare,

Moliere avec Tartuffe y doit jouër son rôle:
Et Lambert, qui plus est, m'a donné sa parole.
Boileau, *Satires*, 3. 25–6.]

The Haunch of Venison

Here, Porter—this venison with me to *Mile-end*;
No stirring—I beg—my dear friend—my dear friend!
Thus snatching his hat, he brusht off like the wind,
And the porter and eatables follow'd behind.
  Left alone to reflect, having emptied my shelf,
And no body with me at sea but myself;[1]
Tho' I could not help thinking my gentleman hasty,
Yet *Johnson*, and *Burke*, and a good venison pasty,
Were things that I never dislik'd in my life,
Tho' clogg'd with a coxcomb, and *Kitty* his Wife.
So next Day in due splendor to make my approach,
I drove to his door in my own Hackney-coach.
  When come to the place where we all were to dine,
(A chair lumber'd closet just twelve feet by nine:)
My friend bade me welcome, but struck me quite dumb,
With tidings that *Johnson*, and *Burke* would not come.[2]
For I knew it, he cried, both eternally fail,
The one with his speeches, and t'other with *Thrale*;
But no matter, I'll warrant we'll make up the party,
With two full as clever, and ten times as hearty.
The one is a Scotchman, the other a Jew,
They['re] both of them merry, and authors like you;
The one writes the *Snarler*, the other the *Scourge*;
Some think he writes *Cinna*—he owns to *Panurge*.[3]
While thus he describ'd them by trade, and by name,

[1] [A quotation from the Duke of Cumberland's love-letters to Lady Grosvenor, published in 1769.]

[2] [Compare,

> A peine estois-je entré, que ravi de me voir,
> Mon homme en m'embrassant, m'est venu recevoir:
> Et montrant à mes yeux une allegresse entière,
> Nous n'avons, m'a-t-il dit, ni Lambert ni Molière.
>
> Boileau, *Satires*, 3. 31–4.]

[3] [Pseudonyms of Dr. W. Scott who was chaplain to Lord Sandwich whom he championed in the press. In 1767 Goldsmith refused to be a similar political propagandist for Sandwich.]

They enter'd, and dinner was serv'd as they came.
 At the top a fried liver, and bacon were seen,
At the bottom was tripe, in a swingeing tureen;
At the Sides there was spinnage and pudding made hot;
In the middle a place where the pasty—was not.
Now, my Lord, as for Tripe it's my utter aversion,
And your Bacon I hate like a *Turk* or a *Persian*;
So there I sat stuck, like a horse in a pound,
While the bacon and liver went merrily round:
But what vex'd me most was that d—'d *Scottish* Rogue,
With his long-winded speeches, his smiles and his brogue.
And Madam, quoth he, may this bit be my poison,
A prettier dinner I never set eyes on;
Pray a slice of your liver, tho' may I be curst,
But I've eat of your tripe, till I'm ready to burst.
The Tripe, quoth the *Jew*, with his chocolate cheek,
I could dine on this tripe seven days in the week:
I like these here dinners, so pretty and small;
But your Friend there, the Doctor, eats nothing at all.
O—Oh! quoth my Friend, he'll come on in a trice,
He's keeping a corner for something that's nice:
There's a Pasty—A Pasty! repeated the *Jew*,
I don't care, if I keep a corner for't too.
What the De'il, Mon, a Pasty! re-echoed the *Scot*;
Though splitting, I'll still keep a corner for that.
We'll all keep a corner, the Lady cried out;
We'll all keep a corner was echoed about.
While thus we resolv'd, and the Pasty delay'd,
With looks that quite petrified, enter'd the Maid;
A visage so sad, and so pale with affright,
Wak'd *Priam* in drawing his curtains by night.[1]
But we quickly found out, for who could mistake her?
That she came with some terrible news from the Baker:
And so it fell out, for that negligent sloven,

[1] [See 2 *Henry IV*, I. I. 92.]

Had shut out the Pasty on shutting his oven.
Sad Philomel thus—but let Similes drop—
And now that I think on't, the Story may stop.
To be plain, my good Lord, it's but labour misplac'd,
To send such good verses to one of your taste;
You've got an odd something—a kind of discerning—
A relish—a taste—sicken'd over by learning;
At least it's your temper, as very well known,
That you think very slightly of all that's your own:
So, perhaps, in your habits of thinking amiss,
You may make a mistake, and think slightly of this.

RETALIATION

A POEM

INCLUDING EPITAPHS

ON SOME OF THE

MOST DISTINGUISHED WITS

OF THIS METROPOLIS

WITH EXPLANATORY NOTES

AND OBSERVATIONS

At a party at St. James's Coffee-house, Goldsmith was rash enough to involve himself in a battle of wits with Garrick. Each was to write the other's epitaph. Garrick lost no time in leading off with the couplet,

> Here lies NOLLY Goldsmith, for shortness call'd Noll,
> Who wrote like an angel, but talk'd like poor Poll.

Goldsmith was worsted, and found himself in his usual predicament where "his person, not his jest, becomes the mirth of the company." But he reserved his defence, and set about writing his *Retaliation.* This was probably early in 1774, and he died on 4 April of the same year, leaving the poem unfinished.

Retaliation: A Poem . . . Including Epitaphs on some of the most Distinguished Wits of this Metropolis was published on 19 April, 1774, *Printed for G. Kearsly, at No. 46, in Fleet-Street*, with a dedication, apparently by Kearsly, to himself. A second edition appeared later in 1774 with four pages of explanatory notes and a list of errata. The third edition, also of 1774, corrects the errata in the text and prints the explanatory notes as footnotes. The punctuation is amended in a few places. I have followed the text of the third edition, but have preferred that of the second edition in one place where the alteration in the third appears to be accidental (see note on p. 636); and I have omitted those footnotes which are merely cross-references to footnotes on other pages.

The fifth edition (also 1774) included for the first time a punning epitaph on one Caleb Whitefoord, a notorious punster. It is much inferior to the rest of the poem and does not seem quite to belong to it; there is, for instance, no mention of Whitefoord in the preliminary bill of fare; and it has been suspected that Whitefoord wrote it himself. I have not included it here.

RETALIATION

Of old, when Scarron his companions invited,
Each guest brought his dish, and the feast was united;
If our landlord (*a*) supplies us with beef, and with fish,
Let each guest bring himself, and he brings the best dish:
Our (*b*) Dean shall be venison, just fresh from the plains;
Our (*c*) Burke shall be tongue, with a garnish of brains;
Our (*d*) Will shall be wild fowl, of excellent flavour,
And (*e*) Dick with his pepper, shall heighten their savour:
Our (*f*) Cumberland's sweet-bread, its place shall obtain,
And (*g*) Douglas is pudding, substantial and plain:
Our (*h*) Garrick's a sallad, for in him we see
Oil, vinegar, sugar, and saltness agree:
To make out the dinner, full certain I am,

(*a*) The Master of the St. James's Coffee-house, where the Doctor, and the Friends he has characterized in this Poem, held an occasional Club.

(*b*) Doctor Barnard, Dean of Derry in Ireland, author of many ingenious pieces.

(*c*) Mr. Edmund Burke, member for Wendover, and one of the greatest orators in this country.

(*d*) Mr. William Burke, late secretary to General Conway, and member for Bedwin.

(*e*) Mr. Richard Burke, collector of Granada, no less remarkable in the walks of wit and humour than his brother Edmund Burke, is justly distinguished in all branches of useful and polite literature.

(*f*) Author of the West Indian, Fashionable Love, The Brothers, and other dramatic pieces.

(*g*) Doctor Douglas, Canon of Windsor, an ingenious Scotch gentleman, who has no less distinguished himself as a *Citizen of the World*, than a *sound Critic* in detecting several literary mistakes (or rather *forgeries*) of his countrymen; particularly Lauder on Milton, and *Bower's History of the Popes*.

(*h*) David Garrick, Esq; joint Patentee and acting Manager of the Theatre-Royal, Drury-lane. For the *other parts* of his character, *vide* the Poem.

That (*i*) Ridge is anchovy, and (*k*) Reynolds is lamb;
That (*l*) Hickey's a capon, and by the same rule,
Magnanimous Goldsmith, a goosberry fool:
At a dinner so various, at such a repast,
Who'd not be glutton, and stick to the last:
Here, waiter, more wine, let me sit while I'm able,
'Till all my companions sink under the table;
Then with chaos and blunders encircling my head,
Let me ponder, and tell what I think of the dead.
Here lies the good Dean, re-united to earth,
Who mixt reason with pleasure, and wisdom with mirth:
If he had any faults, he has left us in doubt,
At least, in six weeks, I could not find 'em out;
Yet some have declar'd, and it can't be denied 'em,
The sly-boots was cursedly cunning to hide 'em.
Here lies our good Edmund, whose genius was such,
We scarcely can praise it, or blame it too much;
Who, born for the Universe, narrow'd his mind,
And to party gave up, what was meant for mankind.
Tho' fraught with all learning, yet straining his throat,
To persuade (*m*) Tommy Townsend to lend him a vote;
Who, too deep for his hearers, still went on refining,
And thought of convincing, while they thought of dining;
Tho' equal to all things, for all things unfit,
Too nice for a statesman, too proud for a wit:
For a patriot too cool; for a drudge, disobedient,
And too fond of the *right* to pursue the *expedient*.
In short, 'twas his fate, unemploy'd, or in place, Sir,
To eat mutton cold, and cut blocks with a razor.

(*i*) Counsellor John Ridge, a gentleman belonging to the Irish bar, the relish of whose agreeable and pointed conversation is admitted, by all his acquaintance, to be very properly compared to the above sauce.

(*k*) Sir Joshua Reynolds, President of the Royal Academy.

(*l*) An eminent Attorney, whose hospitality and good-humour have acquired him, in this Club, the title of "honest Tom Hickey."

(*m*) Mr. T. Townsend, Member for Whitchurch.

Here lies honest William, whose heart was a mint,
While the owner ne'er knew half the good that was in't;
The pupil of impulse, it forced him along,
His conduct still right, with his argument wrong;
Still aiming at honour, yet fearing to roam,
The coachman was tipsy, the chariot drove home;
Would you ask for his merits, alas! he had none,
What was good was spontaneous, his faults were his own.

Here lies honest Richard, whose fate I must sigh at,
Alas, that such frolic should now be so quiet!
What spirits were his, what wit and what whim,
(*n*) Now breaking a jest, and now breaking a limb;
Now wrangling and grumbling to keep up the ball,
Now teazing and vexing, yet laughing at all!
In short so provoking a Devil was Dick,
That we wish'd him full ten times a day at Old Nick,
But missing his mirth and agreeable vein,
As often we wish'd to have Dick back again.

Here Cumberland lies having acted his parts,
The Terence of England, the mender of hearts;
A flattering painter, who made it his care
To draw men as they ought to be, not as they are.
His gallants are all faultless, his women divine,
And comedy wonders at being so fine;
Like a tragedy queen he has dizen'd her out,
Or rather like tragedy giving a rout.
His fools have their follies so lost in a croud
Of virtues and feelings, that folly grows proud,
And coxcombs alike in their failings alone,
Adopting his portraits are pleas'd with their own.
Say, where has our poet this malady caught,
Or wherefore his characters thus without fault?

(*n*) This gentleman having slightly fractured one of his arms and legs, at different times, the Doctor has rallied him upon those accidents, as a kind of *retributive justice* for breaking jests upon other people.

Say was it that vainly directing his view,
To find out men's virtues and finding them few,
Quite sick of pursuing each troublesome elf,
He grew lazy at last and drew from himself?
  Here Douglas retires from his toils to relax,
The scourge of impostors, the terror of quacks:
Come all ye quack bards, and ye quacking divines,
Come and dance on the spot where your tyrant reclines,
When Satire and Censure encircl'd his throne,
I fear'd for your safety, I fear'd for my own;
But now he is gone, and we want a detector,
Our (*o*) Dodds shall be pious, our (*p*) Kenricks shall lecture;
(*q*) Macpherson write bombast, and call it a style,
Our Townshend make speeches, and I shall compile;
New Lauders and Bowers the Tweed shall cross over,
No countryman living their tricks to discover;
Detection her taper shall quench to a spark,
And Scotchman meet Scotchman and cheat in the dark.
  Here lies David Garrick, describe me who can,
An abridgment of all that was pleasant in man;
As an actor, confest without rival to shine,
As a wit, if not first, in the very first line,
Yet with talents like these, and an excellent heart,
The man had his failings, a dupe to his art;
Like an ill-judging beauty, his colours he spread,
And beplaistered with rouge his own natural red.
On the stage he was natural, simple, affecting,
'Twas only that, when he was off, he was acting:
With no reason on earth to go out of his way,
He turn'd and he varied full ten times a-day;

(*o*) The Rev. Dr. Dodd. [Executed for forgery in June, 1777.]

(*p*) Mr. Kenrick lately read lectures at the Devil Tavern, under the Title of "The School of Shakespeare."

(*q*) James Macpherson, Esq; who lately, from the mere *force of his style*, wrote down the first poet of all antiquity. [The translator of *Ossian*. He published a prose translation of Homer in 1773.]

Tho' secure of our hearts, yet confoundedly sick
If they were not his own by finessing and trick,
He cast off his friends, as a huntsman his pack,
For he knew when he pleas'd he could whistle them back.
Of praise a mere glutton, he swallow'd what came,
And the puff of a dunce, he mistook it for fame;
'Till his relish grown callous, almost to disease,
Who pepper'd the highest, was surest to please.
But let us be candid, and speak out our mind,
If dunces applauded, he paid them in kind.
Ye Kenricks, ye (*r*) Kellys, and (*s*) Woodfalls so grave,
What a commerce was yours, while you got and you gave!
How did Grub-street re-echo the shouts that you rais'd,
While he was beroscius'd, and you were beprais'd!
But peace to his spirit, wherever it flies,
To act as an angel, and mix with the skies:
Those poets, who owe their best fame to his skill,
Shall still be his flatterers, go where he will.
Old Shakespeare, receive him, with praise and with love,
And Beaumonts and Bens be his Kellys above.
  Here Hickey reclines, a most blunt, pleasant creature,
And slander itself must allow him good-nature:
He cherish'd a friend, and he relish'd a bumper;
Yet one fault he had, and that one was a thumper:
Perhaps you may ask if the man was a miser?
I answer, no, no, for he always was wiser;
Too courteous, perhaps, or obligingly flat;
His very worst foe can't accuse him of that.
Perhaps he confided in men as they go;
And so was too foolishly honest; ah, no.
Then what was his failing? come tell it, and burn ye,
He was, could he help it? a special attorney.

(*r*) Hugh Kelly, Esq; Author of False Delicacy, Word to the Wise, Clementina, School for Wives, &c. &c.

(*s*) Mr. William Woodfall, Printer of the Morning Chronicle.

Here Reynolds is laid, and, to tell you my mind,
He has not left a better or wiser[1] behind;
His pencil was striking, resistless and grand,
His manners were gentle, complying and bland;
Still born to improve us in every part,
His pencil our faces, his manners our heart:
To coxcombs averse, yet most civilly steering,
When they judg'd without skill he was still hard of hearing:
When they talked of their Raphaels, Corregios and stuff,
He shifted his (*t*) trumpet, and only took snuff.
[By flattery unspoiled . . .][2]

[1] [The third edition altered this to "wiser or better," apparently accidentally, as there is no authority for it in the errata of the second edition. See the note on p. 630.]

(*t*) Sir Joshua Reynolds is so remarkably deaf as to be under the necessity of using an ear trumpet in company; he is, at the same time, equally remarkable for taking a great quantity of snuff: his manner in both of which, taken in the point of time described, must be allowed, by those who have been witnesses of such a scene, to be as happily given on *paper*, as that great Artist himself, perhaps, could have exhibited upon *canvas*.

[2] [According to Prior (*Life of Goldsmith*, 1837) the manuscript ended with this unfinished line.]

MISCELLANEOUS POEMS

Most of Goldsmith's shorter poems were contributed to periodicals.

On a Beautiful Youth Struck Blind with Lightning, *The Gift* and *An Elegy on . . . Mrs. Mary Blaize* first appeared in the first, second and fourth numbers of *The Bee*, dated 6, 13 and 27 October, 1759. These are the texts here used. *A Sonnet* was first printed in the third number of *The Bee*, 20 October, 1759. The fifth line was revised in the posthumous edition of the *Poetical and Dramatic Works*, 1780, and I have preferred the later text.

The Logicians Refuted here follows the first printed text, which appeared in *The Busy Body* of 18 October, 1759 with the heading

> The following poem, written by Dr. Swift, is communicated to the Public by the Busy Body, to whom it was presented by a Nobleman of distinguished Learning and Taste.

But it was attributed to Goldsmith in the *Poetical and Dramatic Works*, 1780, and has been accepted as his ever since.

The Double Transformation first appeared as *The Double Metamorphosis* in the *Weekly Magazine: or, Gentleman and Lady's Polite Companion* on 5 January, 1760. Goldsmith reprinted it in *Essays*, 1765, with *A New Simile in the Manner of Swift*, which may also have previously occurred in a periodical, but I have not discovered where.

Both poems were slightly revised in the second edition of 1766, which I have followed.

The *Song*, intended for *She Stoops to Conquer*, is here printed from the *London Magazine* of June, 1774, where it appeared with a letter from Boswell,

> I send you a small production of the late Dr. *Goldsmith*, which has never been published, and might perhaps have been totally lost had I not secured it. He intended it as a song in the character of Miss *Hardcastle*, in his admirable comedy, *She stoops to conquer*; but it was left out, as Mrs. *Bulkeley* who played the part did not sing. He sung it himself in private parties very agreeably. The tune is a pretty Irish air, called *The Humours of Balamagairy*.

The *Epitaph on Edward Purdon* follows the text of the Dublin edition of the *Poems and Plays*, 1777, where it was first printed. Several poems are included in prose works printed elsewhere in this edition. I have not repeated them here. A list of them will be found on p. 6.

MISCELLANEOUS POEMS

ON A BEAUTIFUL YOUTH STRUCK BLIND WITH LIGHTNING

Imitated from the SPANISH

SURE 'twas by Providence design'd,
  Rather in pity, than in hate,
That he should be, like Cupid, blind,
  To save him from Narcissus' fate.

THE GIFT

TO IRIS, in Bow-Street, Covent-Garden

SAY, cruel IRIS, pretty rake,
  Dear mercenary beauty,
What annual offering shall I make,
  Expressive of my duty?

My heart, a victim to thine eyes,
  Should I at once deliver,
Say, would the angry fair one prize
  The gift, who slights the giver?

A bill, a jewel, watch or toy,
  My rivals give—and let 'em.
If gems, or gold, impart a joy,
  I'll give them—when I get 'em.

I'll give—but not the full-blown rose,
  Or rose-bud more in fashion;
Such short-liv'd offerings but disclose
  A transitory passion.

I'll give thee something yet unpaid,
   Not less sincere, than civil:
I'll give thee——Ah! too charming maid;
   I'll give thee——To the Devil.

THE LOGICIANS REFUTED

LOGICIANS have but ill defin'd
As rational, the human kind;
Reason, they say, belongs to man,
But let them prove it if they can.
Wise Aristotle and Smiglesius,
By ratiocinations specious,
Have strove to prove with great precision,
With definition and division,
Homo est ratione prœditum;
But for my soul I cannot credit 'em;
And must in spite of them maintain,
That man and all his ways are vain;
And that this boasted lord of nature
Is both a weak and erring creature;
That instinct is a surer guide
Than reason-boasting mortals pride;
And that brute beasts are far before 'em,
Deus est anima brutorum.
Who ever knew an honest brute,
At law his neighbour prosecute,
Bring action for assault and battery,
Or friends beguile with lies and flattery?
O'er plains they ramble unconfin'd,
No politics disturb their mind;
They eat their meals, and take their sport,
Nor know who's in or out at court.

They never to the levee go
To treat as dearest friend, a foe:
They never importune his grace,
Nor ever cringe to men in place;
Nor undertake a dirty job,
Nor draw the quill to write for B[o]b.[1]
Fraught with invective they ne'er go,
To folks at Pater-Noster-Row:
No judges, fidlers, dancing-masters,
No pick-pockets, or poetasters,
Are known to honest quadrupeeds,
No single brute his fellow leads.
Brutes never meet in bloody fray,
Nor cut each other's throats for pay.
Of beasts, it is confess'd, the ape
Comes nearest us in human shape,
Like man he imitates each fashion,
And malice is his ruling passion:
But both in malice and grimaces,
A courtier any ape surpasses.
Behold him humbly cringing wait,
Upon a minister of state:
View him soon after to inferiors,
Aping the conduct of superiors:
He promises with equal air,
And to perform takes equal care.
He in his turn finds imitators,
At court the porters, lacquees, waiters,
Their master's manners still contract,
And footmen, lords and dukes can act.
Thus at the court, both great and small
Behave alike, for all ape all.

[1] [Sir Robert Walpole.]

A SONNET

WEEPING, murmuring, complaining,
Lost to every gay delight;
MYRA, too sincere for feigning,
Fears th'approaching bridal night.

Yet why impair thy bright perfection?
Or dim thy beauty with a tear?
Had MYRA follow'd my direction,
She long had wanted cause for fear.

AN ELEGY ON THAT GLORY OF HER SEX MRS. MARY BLAIZE

GOOD people all, with one accord,
Lament for Madam BLAIZE,
Who never wanted a good word—
From those who spoke her praise.

The needy seldom pass'd her door,
And always found her kind;
She freely lent to all the poor,—
Who left a pledge behind.

She strove the neighbourhood to please,
With manners wond'rous winning,
And never follow'd wicked ways,—
Unless when she was sinning.

An Elegy on Mrs. Mary Blaize

At church, in silks and sattins new,
With hoop of monstrous size,
She never slumber'd in her pew,—
But when she shut her eyes.

Her love was sought, I do aver,
By twenty beaus and more;
The king himself has follow'd her,—
When she has walk'd before.

But now her wealth and finery fled,
Her hangers-on cut short all;
The doctors found, when she was dead,—
Her last disorder mortal.

Let us lament, in sorrow sore,
For Kent-street well may say,
That had she liv'd a twelve-month more,—
She had not dy'd to-day.

THE DOUBLE TRANSFORMATION

A Tale

SECLUDED from domestic strife,
Jack Book-worm led a college life;
A fellowship at twenty-five
Made him the happiest man alive;
He drank his glass and crack'd his joke,
And Freshmen wonder'd as he spoke:
Such pleasures unallay'd with care,
Could any accident impair?
Could Cupid's shaft at length transfix,
Our swain arriv'd at thirty-six?
O had the archer ne'er come down
To ravage in a country town!

Or Flavia been content to stop
At triumphs in a Fleet-street shop.
O had her eyes forgot to blaze!
Or Jack had wanted eyes to gaze.
O!——But let exclamation cease,
Her presence banish'd all his peace.
So with decorum all things carry'd;
Miss frown'd, and blush'd, and then was—
married.
Need we expose to vulgar sight
The raptures of the bridal night?
Need we intrude on hallow'd ground,
Or draw the curtains clos'd around?
Let it suffice, that each had charms;
He clasp'd a goddess in his arms;
And, tho' she felt his usage rough,
Yet in a man 'twas well enough.
The honey-moon like light'ning flew,
The second brought its transports too.
A third, a fourth, were not amiss,
The fifth was friendship mix'd with bliss:
But, when a twelvemonth pass'd away,
Jack found his goddess made of clay;
Found half the charms that deck'd her face,
Arose from powder, shreds, or lace;
But still the worst remain'd behind,
That very face had robb'd her mind.
Skill'd in no other arts was she,
But dressing, patching, repartee;
And, just as humour rose or fell,
By turns a slattern or a belle:
'Tis true she dress'd with modern grace,
Half naked at a ball or race;
But when at home, at board or bed,
Five greasy night-caps wrap'd her head.

Could so much beauty condescend
To be a dull domestic friend?
Could any curtain-lectures bring
To decency so fine a thing?
In short, by night, 'twas fits or fretting;
By day, 'twas gadding or coquetting.
Fond to be seen she kept a bevy
Of powder'd coxcombs at her levy;
The 'squire and captain took their stations,
And twenty other near relations;
Jack suck'd his pipe, and often broke
A sigh in suffocating smoke;
While all their hours were pass'd between
Insulting repartee or spleen.
    Thus as her faults each day were known,
He thinks her features coarser grown;
He fancies every vice she shews
Or thins her lip, or points her nose:
Whenever rage or envy rise,
How wide her mouth, how wild her eyes!
He knows not how, but so it is,
Her face is grown a knowing phyz;
And, tho' her fops are wond'rous civil,
He thinks her ugly as the devil.
    Now, to perplex the ravell'd nooze,
As each a different way pursues,
While sullen or loquacious strife
Promis'd to hold them on for life,
That dire disease, whose ruthless power,
Withers the beauty's transient flower:
Lo! the small-pox, whose horrid glare,
Levell'd its terrors at the fair;
And, rifling ev'ry youthful grace,
Left but the remnant of a face.
    The glass, grown hateful to her sight,

Reflected now a perfect fright:
Each former art she vainly tries
To bring back lustre to her eyes.
In vain she tries her paste and creams,
To smooth her skin, or hide its seams;
Her country beaux and city cousins,
Lovers no more, flew off by dozens:
The squire himself was seen to yield,
And even the captain quit the field.
   Poor Madam, now condemn'd to hack
The rest of life with anxious Jack,
Perceiving others fairly flown
Attempted pleasing him alone.
Jack soon was dazzl'd to behold
Her present face surpass the old;
With modesty her cheeks are dy'd,
Humility displaces pride;
For taudry finery is seen,
A person ever neatly clean:
No more presuming on her sway
She learns good nature every day;
Serenely gay, and strict in duty,
Jack finds his wife a perfect beauty.

A NEW SIMILE IN THE MANNER OF SWIFT

Long had I sought in vain to find
A likeness for the scribbling kind;
The modern scribbling kind, who write,
In wit, and sense, and nature's spite:
'Till reading, I forget what day on,
A chapter out of Took's Pantheon,
I think I met with something there,
To suit my purpose to a hair;

But let us not proceed too furious,
First please turn to God Mercurius;
You'll find him pictur'd at full length
In book the second, page the tenth:
The stress of all my proofs on him I lay,
And now proceed we to our simile.
  Imprimis, pray observe his hat
Wings upon either side—mark that.
Well! what is it from thence we gather?
Why these denote a brain of feather.
A brain of feather! very right,
With wit that's flighty, learning light;
Such as to modern bards decreed:
A just comparison,—proceed.
  In the next place, his feet peruse,
Wings grow again from both his shoes;
Design'd, no doubt, their part to bear,
And waft his godship through the air;
And here my simile unites,
For in a modern poet's flights,
I'm sure it may be justly said,
His feet are useful as his head.
  Lastly, vouchsafe t'observe his hand,
Fill'd with a snake incircl'd wand;
By classic authors term'd caducis,
And highly fam'd for several uses.
To wit—most wond'rously endu'd,
No poppy water half so good!
For let folks only get a touch,
Its soporific virtue's such,
Tho' ne'er so much awake before,
That quickly they begin to snore.
Add too, what certain writers tell,
With this he drives men's souls to hell.
  Now to apply, begin we then;

His wand's a modern author's pen;
The serpents round about it twin'd
Denote him of the reptile kind;
Denote the rage with which he writes,
His frothy slaver, venom'd bites;
An equal semblance still to keep,
Alike too both conduce to sleep.
This diff'rence only, as the God
Drove souls to Tart'rus with his rod;
With his goosequill the scribbling elf,
Instead of others, damns himself.
  And here my simile almost tript,
Yet grant a word by way of postscript.
Moreover, Merc'ry had a failing:
Well! what of that? out with it—stealing;
In which all modern bards agree,
Being each as great a thief as he:
But ev'n this deity's existence
Shall lend my simile assistance.
Our modern bards! why what a pox
Are they but senseless stones and blocks?

SONG

[Intended for *She Stoops to Conquer*]

Ah, me! when shall I marry me?
  Lovers are plenty; but fail to relieve me.
He, fond youth, that could carry me,
  Offers to love, but means to deceive me.

But I will rally and combat the ruiner:
  Not a look, not a smile, shall my passion discover.
She that gives all to the false one pursuing her,
  Makes but a penitent, loses a lover.

EPITAPH ON EDWARD PURDON*

HERE lies poor NED PURDON, from misery freed,
Who long was a bookseller's hack;
He led such a damnable life in this world,—
I don't think he'll wish to come back.

* This gentleman was educated at Trinity College, Dublin; but having wasted his patrimony, he enlisted as a foot soldier. Growing tired of that employment, he obtained his discharge, and became a scribbler in the newspapers. He translated Voltaire's *Henriade.*

PROLOGUES AND EPILOGUES

Of the five poems that follow two were written for friends' plays and three for *She Stoops to Conquer*.

Goldsmith's epilogue to *The Sister* by Charlotte Lenox is here printed from the play which was first published in 1769. It was first acted on 18 February, 1769 at Covent Garden.

The prologue to Joseph Cradock's translation of Voltaire's *Zobeide* is also printed from the play, first published in December 1771. It was first acted on 11 December at Covent Garden.

The circumstances in which the first two epilogues for *She Stoops to Conquer* were written and rejected are described on p. 746. The first is printed from the *Miscellaneous Works*, 1801. The second follows the text of a contemporary transcript in the British Museum.

The *Epilogue for Lee Lewes* was written for his benefit night in *She Stoops to Conquer* on 7 May, 1773. Lee Lewes, who had previously been chiefly noted as a Harlequin, stepped into the part of Young Marlow, which no one else would accept, and made it a success. Goldsmith, although he had always despised the character of Harlequin, was very grateful and wrote him this epilogue. It was published in the *Poetical and Dramatic Works*, 1780, from which it is here reprinted.

PROLOGUES AND EPILOGUES

EPILOGUE TO *THE SISTER*

Spoken by Mrs. BULKLEY

WHAT! five long acts—and all to make us wiser!
Our authoress sure has wanted an adviser.
Had she consulted *me*, she should have made
Her moral play a speaking masquerade;
Warm'd up each bustling scene, and in her rage
Have emptied all the Green-room on the stage.
My life on't, this had kept her play from sinking,
Have pleas'd our eyes, and sav'd the pain of thinking.
Well, since she thus has shewn her want of skill,
What if I give a masquerade? I will.
But how! ay, there's the rub! (*pausing*)—I've got my cue:
The world's a masquerade! the maskers, you, you, you.
[*To Boxes*, *Pit*, *Gall.*
Lud! what a groupe the motley scene discloses!
False wits, false wives, false virgins, and false spouses:
Statesmen with bridles on; and, close beside 'em,
Patriots, in party-colour'd suits, that ride 'em.
There Hebes, turn'd of fifty, try once more,
To raise a flame in Cupids of threescore.
These, in their turn, with appetites as keen,
Deserting fifty, fasten on fifteen.
Miss, not yet full fifteen, with fire uncommon,
Flings down her sampler, and takes up the woman:
The little urchin smiles, and spreads her lure,
And tries to kill ere she's got power to cure.
Thus 'tis with all—Their chief and constant care
Is to seem every thing—but what they are.
Yon broad, bold, angry spark, I fix my eye on,

Who seems t' have robb'd his vizor from the lion;
Who frowns, and talks, and swears, with round parade,
Looking, as who should say, *Damme! who's afraid.*
[*mimicking.*

Strip but his vizor off, and sure I am,
You'll find his lionship a very lamb.
Yon politician, famous in debate,
Perhaps to vulgar eyes bestrides the state;
Yet, when he deigns his real shape t' assume,
He turns old woman, and bestrides a broom.
Yon patriot too, who presses on your sight,
And seems to every gazer all in white;
If with a bribe his candour you attack,
He bows, turns round, and whip—the man's a black!
Yon critic too—but whither do I run?
If I proceed, our bard will be undone!
Well then, a truce, since she requests it too;
Do you spare her, and I'll for once spare you.

PROLOGUE TO *ZOBEIDE*

Spoken by Mr. QUICK in the character of a sailor

IN these bold times, when Learning's sons explore
The distant climate and the savage shore;
When wise *Astronomers* to *India* steer,
And quit for *Venus*, many a brighter here;[1]
While *Botanists*, all cold to smiles and dimpling,
Forsake the fair, and patiently—go simpling;
When every bosom swells with wond'rous scenes,
Priests, cannibals, and hoity toity queens:
Our bard into the general spirit enters,
And fits his little frigate for adventures:

[1] [Captain Cook returned from his voyage to Tahiti to observe the transit of Venus on 12 June, 1771, six months before *Zobeide* was acted. He was accompanied by Sir Joseph Banks and Dr. Solander, botanists.]

Prologue to Zobeide

With *Scythian stores*, and trinkets deeply laden,
He this way steers his course, in hopes of trading—
Yet ere he lands he 'as ordered me before,
To make an observation on the shore.
Where are we driven? Our reck'ning sure is lost!
This seems a barren and a dangerous coast.
Lord what a sultry climate am I under!
Yon ill-foreboding cloud seems big with thunder.
(*Upper Gallery.*)
There Mangroves spread, and larger than I've seen 'em—
(*Pit.*)
Here trees of stately size—and turtles in 'em—
(*Balconies.*)
Here ill-condition'd oranges abound— (*Stage.*)
And apples (*takes up one and tastes it*) *bitter* apples strew the ground.
The place is uninhabited, I fear;
I heard a hissing—there are serpents here!
O there the natives are—a dreadful race!
The men have tails, the women paint the face!
No doubt they're all barbarians—Yes, 'tis so,
I'll try to make palaver with them though; (*making signs*)
'Tis best however keeping at a distance.
Good Savages, our Captain craves assistance;
Our ship's well stor'd;—in yonder creek we've laid her,
His honour is no mercenary trader;[1]
This is his first adventure, lend him aid,
Or you may chance to spoil a thriving trade.
His goods he hopes are prime, and brought from far,
Equally fit for gallantry and war.
What no reply to promises so ample?
I'd best step back—and order up a sample.

[1] [Cradock made over his share of the profits to Mrs. Yates, who played the part of Zobeide.]

EPILOGUE

[Intended for *She Stoops to Conquer*]

Spoken by Mrs. BULKLEY and Miss CATLEY[1]

Enter Mrs. Bulkley, who curtsies very low as beginning to speak. Then enter Miss Catley, who stands full before her, and curtsies to the Audience.

Mrs. BULKLEY.

HOLD, Ma'am, your pardon. What's your business here?

Miss CATLEY.

The Epilogue.

Mrs. BULKLEY.

The Epilogue?

Miss CATLEY.

Yes, the Epilogue, my dear.

Mrs. BULKLEY.

Sure you mistake, Ma'am. The Epilogue *I* bring it.

Miss CATLEY.

Excuse me, Ma'am. The Author bid *me* sing it.

RECITATIVE.

Ye beaux and belles, that form this splendid ring,
Suspend your conversation while I sing.

Mrs. BULKLEY.

Why sure the Girl's beside herself: an Epilogue of singing,
A hopeful end indeed to such a blest beginning.
Besides, a singer in a comic set!
Excuse me, Ma'am, I know the etiquette.

Miss CATLEY.

What if we leave it to the House?

Mrs. BULKLEY.

The House!—Agreed.

[1] [See the editorial note on p. 746.]

Miss CATLEY.

Agreed.

Mrs. BULKLEY.

And she, who's party's largest, shall proceed.
And first I hope, you'll readily agree
I've all the critics and the wits for me.
They, I am sure, will answer my commands,
Ye candid judging few, hold up your hands;
What, no return? I find too late, I fear,
That modern judges seldom enter here.

Miss CATLEY.

I'm for a different set.—Old men, whose trade is
Still to gallant and dangle with the ladies.

RECITATIVE.

Who mump their passion, and who, grimly smiling
Still thus address the fair with voice beguiling.

AIR.—COTILLON.

Turn, my fairest, turn, if ever
Strephon caught thy ravish'd eye.
Pity take on your swain so clever,
Who without your aid must die.
Yes, I shall die, hu, hu, hu, hu,
Yes, I must die, ho, ho, ho, ho.

Da Capo.

Mrs. BULKLEY.

Let all the old pay homage to your merit:
Give me the young, the gay, the men of spirit.
Ye travelled tribe, ye macaroni train
Of French friseurs, and nosegays, justly vain,
Who take a trip to Paris once a year
To dress, and look like awkward Frenchmen here.
Lend me your hands.—O fatal news to tell,
Their hands are only lent to the Heinelle.[1]

[1] [Anna-Frederica Heinel, a celebrated Prussian dancer.]

Miss Catley.

Ay, take your travellers, travellers indeed!
Give me the bonny Scot, that travels from the Tweed.
Where are the Cheels? Ah! Ah, I well discern
The smiling looks of each bewitching bairne.
A bonny young lad is my Jockey.

AIR.

I'll sing to amuse you by night and by day,
And be unco merry when you are but gay;
When you with your bagpipes are ready to play,
My voice shall be ready to carol away
With Sandy, and Sawney, and Jockey,
With Sawney, and Jarvie, and Jockey.

Mrs. Bulkley.

Ye Gamesters, who so eager in pursuit,
Make but of all your fortune one *va Toute*:
Ye Jockey tribe whose stock of words are few,
"I hold the odds.—Done, done, with you, with you."
Ye Barristers, so fluent with grimace,
"My Lord,—your Lordship misconceives the case."
Doctors, who cough and answer every misfortuner,
"I wish I'd been call'd in a little sooner."
Assist my cause with hands and voices hearty,
Come end the contest here, and aid my party.

AIR.—BALEINAMONY.

Miss Catley.

Ye brave Irish lads, hark away to the crack,
Assist me, I pray, in this woful attack;
For sure I don't wrong you, you seldom are slack,
When the ladies are calling, to blush, and hang back.
For you're always polite and attentive,
Still to amuse us inventive,
And death is your only preventive.
Your hands and your voices for me.

Mrs. BULKLEY.

Well, Madam, what if, after all this sparring,
We both agree, like friends, to end our jarring?

Miss CATLEY.

And that our friendship may remain unbroken,
What if we leave the Epilogue unspoken?

Mrs. BULKLEY.

Agreed.

Miss CATLEY.

Agreed.

Mrs. BULKLEY.

And now with late repentance,
Un-epilogued the Poet waits his sentence.
Condemn the stubborn fool who can't submit
To thrive by flattery, though he starves by wit.

[*Exeunt.*

EPILOGUE

Intended for Mrs. BULKLEY in *She Stoops to Conquer*

THERE is a place,—so Ariosto sings,[1]
A Treasury for lost and missing things.
Lost human Wits have Places there Assign'd them,
And they who lose their Senses, there may find them,
But where's this place, this Storehouse of the Age?
The Moon, says he: but I affirm the Stage.
At least in many things I think I see
This lunar and our Mimic World agree
Both shine at night For but at Foote's[2] alone,
We scarce exhibit till the sun goes down.
Both prone to change, no settled limits fix,
Tis said the folks of both are lunaticks.

[1] [*Orlando Furioso*, canto 34.]
[2] [Foote gave matinees at the Haymarket.]

But in this paralell my best pretence is,
That mortals visit both to find their Senses.
To this strange spot Rakes, Macaroni's, Cits,
Come thronging to collect their scatter'd Wits.
The gay Coquet, who ogles all the day,
Comes here by night, and goes a prude away.
The Gamester too, who eager in pursuit
Makes but of all his fortunes one *va toute*,
Whose Mind is barren, and whose words are few;
"I take the odds"—"Done, done, with you, and you,"
Comes here to saunter, having made his betts,
Finds his lost Senses out, and pays his Debts.
The Mohawk too—with angry phrases stor'd
As "Damme Sir" and "Sir I wear a Sword:"
Here lessoned for awhile, and hence retreating,
Goes out, affronts his man, and takes a beating.
Here come the Sons of Scandal and of News
But find no Sense—for they had none to lose.
The poet too—comes hither to be wiser,
And so for once I'll be the Man's Adviser.
What could he hope in this lord loving Age,
Without a brace of lords upon the Stage,
In robes and stars, unless the bard adorn us,
You grow familiar, lose respect, and scorn us.
Then not one passion, fury, sentiment,
Sure his poetick fire is wholly spent!
Oh how I love to hear applauses shower
On my fix'd attitude of half an hour
(*Stands in an Attitude*)
And then with their whining, staring, struggling, slapping,
To force their feelings and provoke their clapping.
Hither the affected City Dame advancing,
Who sighs for Opera's, and doats on dancing,
Who hums a favourite Air and spreading wide,

Swings round the room the Heinele[1] of Cheapside,
Taught by our Art her Ridicule to pause on
Quits the *Che faro*[2] and calls for Nancy Dawson.[3]
Of all the tribe here wanting an Adviser
Our Author's the least likely to grow wiser,
Has he not seen how you your favours place
On Sentimental Queens, and Lords in lace;
Without a Star, a coronet or Garter,
How can the piece expect, or hope for Quarter.
No high-life scenes, no sentiment, the creature
Still stoops among the low to copy Nature.
Yes, he's far gone. And yet some pity mix
The English laws forbid to punish Lunaticks.

EPILOGUE

Spoken by Mr. LEE LEWES in the Character of HARLEQUIN,[4]
at his Benefit

HOLD! Prompter, hold! a word before your nonsense;
I'd speak a word or two, to ease my conscience.
My pride forbids it ever should be said,
My heels eclips'd the honours of my head;
That I found humour in a pyeball vest,
Or ever thought that jumping was a jest.
[*Takes off his mask.*
Whence, and what art thou, visionary birth?
Nature disowns, and reason scorns thy mirth,
In thy black aspect every passion sleeps,
The joy that dimples, and the woe that weeps.
How hast thou fill'd the scene with all thy brood,
Of fools pursuing, and of fools pursu'd!
Whose ins and outs no ray of sense discloses,

[1] [See footnote, p. 657.]
[2] [*Che faro senza Eurydice*, in Glück's *Orfeo*, 1764.]
[3] [A popular song named after a famous hornpipe dancer.]
[4] [See Goldsmith's description of Harlequin in the Italian comedy, p. 839.]

Whose only plot it is to break our noses;
Whilst from below the trap-door *Dæmons* rise,
And from above the dangling deities;
And shall I mix in this unhallow'd crew?
May rosin'd lightning blast me, if I do!
No—I will act, I'll vindicate the stage:
Shakespeare himself shall feel my tragic rage.
Off! off! vile trappings! a new passion reigns!
The mad'ning monarch revels in my veins.
Oh! for a Richard's voice to catch the theme:
Give me another horse! bind up my wounds!—soft—
'twas but a dream.
Aye, 'twas but a dream, for now there's no retreating:
If I cease Harlequin, I cease from eating.
'Twas thus that Æsop's stag, a creature blameless,
Yet something vain, like one that shall be nameless,
Once on the margin of a fountain stood,
And cavill'd at his image in the flood.
"The deuce confound," he cries, "these drumstick shanks,
They never have my gratitude nor thanks;
They're perfectly disgraceful! strike me dead!
But for a head, yes, yes, I have a head.
How piercing is that eye! how sleek that brow!
My horns! I'm told that horns are the fashion now."
Whilst thus he spoke, astonish'd! to his view,
Near, and more near, the hounds and huntsmen drew.
Hoicks! hark forward! came thundering from behind,
He bounds aloft, outstrips the fleeting wind:
He quits the woods, and tries the beaten ways;
He starts, he pants, he takes the circling maze.
At length his silly head, so priz'd before,
Is taught his former folly to deplore;
Whilst his strong limbs conspire to set him free,
And at one bound he saves himself, like me.
[*Taking a jump through the stage door.*

PLAYS

THE GOOD NATUR'D MAN

Apart from a possible tragedy which Goldsmith was reputed to have shown to Richardson, *The Good Natur'd Man* was his first play. It was probably finished early in 1767. There were then two chief theatres in London, Drury Lane and Covent Garden. Rich, the manager of Covent Garden, had recently died; and Goldsmith was therefore obliged to approach Garrick who managed Drury Lane. Goldsmith and Garrick, though they were members of the same circle, were not on very friendly terms; each was too apt to hurt the other's feelings. Garrick had taken offence at some remarks in *An Enquiry*, and had helped to prevent Goldsmith's election as Secretary of the Royal Society. Nevertheless he accepted the play against his better judgment, and it was tacitly understood that he would put it on. But he was not particularly anxious to do so; he told Johnson and Reynolds in confidence that he did not care for the play, but still kept Goldsmith in suspense. Finally, after some months had been wasted, he wanted the play altered; it had two star parts, and one of these would have to go. This led to a violent quarrel, which would have ended in blows if Reynolds and Burke had not intervened. Fortunately, however, Covent Garden was now active again, with Colman as one of the patentees, and Goldsmith was able to turn to him. Garrick agreed to let Colman have the play, but there were still further delays. Garrick was putting on Hugh Kelly's *False Delicacy*, a vapid sentimental comedy of the kind that Goldsmith most disliked and; he was preparing careful plans for its success. He therefore privately arranged with Colman, who anyway had no great hopes of *The Good Natur'd Man*, that it should be held up until the other play had been acted. Thus *The Good Natur'd Man* was not produced until 29 January, 1768. Its reception was cold until Shuter's reading of the incendiary letter, which at once settled the success of the play. The bailiffs, however, were far too "low" for the audience, and had to be omitted after the first night. The play ran for ten nights, the fifth being commanded by the King and Queen. Goldsmith earned about £400 from the author's nights, the third, sixth and ninth.

The Good Natur'd Man was first published on 5 February, 1768, exactly a week after its first night. It was *Printed for W. Griffin, in Catharine-Street, Strand.* The text shows signs of being unrevised, and three of its readings could hardly have been included in the acted version. See the notes on pp. 682, 684 and 693.

The publication of a "new" edition, in which some but not all of the mistakes were corrected, was announced on 9 February in the *Public Advertiser*, which, on 22 February, also announced "a new Edition, being the fourth." This "fourth" edition seems to have been only another impression of the "new" edition. For apart from the first edition and the "new" edition, there is no mention of an earlier edition than the fifth in the catalogues of the British Museum, the Bodleian, the Cambridge University Library, the Edinburgh University Library or the John Rylands Library. The text here used is that of the fifth edition, the last to contain any significant corrections.

PREFACE

When I undertook to write a comedy, I confess I was strongly prepossessed in favour of the poets of the last age, and strove to imitate them. The term, *genteel comedy*, was then unknown amongst us, and little more was desired by an audience, than nature and humour, in whatever walks of life they were most conspicuous. The author of the following scenes never imagined that more would be expected of him, and therefore to delineate character has been his principal aim. Those who know anything of composition, are sensible, that in pursuing humour, it will sometimes lead us into the recesses of the mean; I was even tempted to look for it in the master of a spunging-house: but in deference to the public taste, grown of late, perhaps, too delicate, the scene of the bailiffs was retrenched in the representation. In deference also to the judgment of a few friends, who think in a particular way, the scene is here restored. The author submits it to the reader in his closet; and hopes that too much refinement will not banish humour and character from our's, as it has already done from the French theatre. Indeed the French comedy is now become so very elevated and sentimental, that it has not only banished humour and *Moliere* from the stage, but it has banished all spectators too.

Upon the whole, the author returns his thanks to the public for the favourable reception which the Good Natur'd Man has met with: and to Mr. Colman in particular, for his kindness to it. It may not also be improper to assure any, who shall hereafter write for the theatre, that merit, or supposed merit, will ever be a sufficient passport to his protection.

PROLOGUE

Written by Dr. JOHNSON: spoken by Mr. BENSLEY

PREST by the load of life, the weary mind
Surveys the general toil of human kind;
With cool submission joins the labouring train,
And social sorrow loses half it's pain:[1]
Our anxious Bard, without complaint, may share
This bustling season's epidemic care,
Like Cæsar's pilot, dignified by fate,
Tost in one common storm with all the great;
Distrest alike, the statesman and the wit,
When one a borough courts, and one the pit.
The busy candidates for power and fame,
Have hopes, and fears, and wishes, just the same;
Disabled both to combat, or to fly,
Must hear all taunts, and hear without reply.
Uncheck'd on both, loud rabbles vent their rage,
As mongrels bay the lion in a cage.
Th'offended burgess hoards his angry tale,
For that blest year when all that vote may rail;
Their schemes of spite the poet's foes dismiss,
Till that glad night, when all that hate may hiss.
This day the powder'd curls and golden coat,
Says swelling Crispin, begg'd a cobbler's vote,
This night, our wit, the pert apprentice cries,
Lies at my feet, I hiss him, and he dies.

[1] [The text of the Prologue, as first published in the *Public Advertiser* of 3 February, 1768, continued:

Amidst the Toils of this returning Year,
When Senators and Nobles learn to fear;
Our little Bard . . .

This couplet, like the rest of the Prologue, referred to the forthcoming Parliamentary elections; it probably offended the "Senators and Nobles" as the epithet "little" did Goldsmith. There are other slight differences in the texts; and lines 21–24 do not occur in the first version.]

The great, 'tis true, can charm th' electing tribe;
The bard may supplicate, but cannot bribe.
Yet judg'd by those, whose voices ne'er were sold,
He feels no want of ill persuading gold;
But confident of praise, if praise be due,
Trusts without fear, to merit, and to you.

DRAMATIS PERSONÆ

MEN

Mr. Honeywood,	Mr. Powell.
Croaker,	Mr. Shuter.
Lofty,	Mr. Woodward.
Sir William Honeywood,	Mr. Clarke.
Leontine,	Mr. Bensley.
Jarvis,	Mr. Dunstall.
Butler,	Mr. Cushing.
Bailiff,	Mr. R. Smith.
Dubardieu,	Mr. Holtom.
Postboy,	Mr. Quick.

WOMEN

Miss Richland,	Mrs. Bulkley.
Olivia,	Mrs. Mattocks.
Mrs. Croaker,	Mrs. Pitt.
Garnet,	Mrs. Green.
Landlady,	Mrs. White.

Scene London.

THE GOOD NATUR'D MAN

ACT THE FIRST

SCENE, *An Apartment in* YOUNG HONEYWOOD'S *House*

Enter SIR WILLIAM HONEYWOOD, JARVIS

Sir Will. Good Jarvis, make no apologies for this honest bluntness. Fidelity, like yours, is the best excuse for every freedom.

Jarvis. I can't help being blunt, and being very angry too, when I hear you talk of disinheriting so good, so worthy a young gentleman as your nephew, my master. All the world loves him.

Sir Will. Say rather, that he loves all the world; that is his fault.

Jarvis. I'm sure there is no part of it more dear to him than you are, tho' he has not seen you since he was a child.

Sir Will. What signifies his affection to me, or how can I be proud of a place in a heart where every sharper and coxcomb find an easy entrance?

Jarvis. I grant you that he's rather too good natur'd; that he's too much every man's man; that he laughs this minute with one, and cries the next with another; but whose instructions may he thank for all this?

Sir Will. Not mine, sure? My letters to him during my employment in Italy, taught him only that philosophy which might prevent, not defend his errors.

Jarvis. Faith, begging your honour's pardon, I'm sorry they taught him any philosophy at all; it has only serv'd to spoil him. This same philosophy is a good horse in the stable, but an errant jade on a journey. For my own part, whenever I hear him mention the name on't, I'm always sure he's going to play the fool.

Sir Will. Don't let us ascribe his faults to his philosophy, I entreat you. No, Jarvis, his good nature arises rather from his fears of offending the importunate, than his desire of making the deserving happy.

Jarvis. What it rises from, I don't know. But, to be sure, everybody has it, that asks it.

Sir Will. Ay, or that does not ask it. I have been now for some time a concealed spectator of his follies, and find them as boundless as his dissipation.

Jarvis. And yet, faith, he has some fine name or other for them all. He calls his extravagance, generosity; and his trusting every body, universal benevolence. It was but last week he went security for a fellow whose face he scarce knew, and that he call'd an act of exalted mu—mu—munificence; ay, that was the name he gave it.

Sir Will. And upon that I proceed, as my last effort, tho' with very little hopes to reclaim him. That very fellow has just absconded, and I have taken up the security. Now, my intention is to involve him in fictitious distress, before he has plunged himself into real calamity. To arrest him for that very debt, to clap an officer upon him, and then let him see which of his friends will come to his relief.

Jarvis. Well, if I could but any way see him thoroughly vexed, every groan of his would be music to me; yet, faith, I believe it impossible. I have tried to fret him myself every morning these three years; but instead of being angry, he sits as calmly to hear me scold, as he does to his hair-dresser.

Sir Will. We must try him once more, however, and I'll go this instant to put my scheme into execution; and I don't despair of succeeding, as, by your means, I can have frequent opportunities of being about him, without being known. What a pity it is, Jarvis, that any man's good will to others should produce so much neglect of himself, as to require correction.

Yet, we must touch his weaknesses with a delicate hand. There are some faults so nearly allied to excellence, that we can scarce weed out the vice without eradicating the virtue. [*Exit.*

Jarvis. Well, go thy ways, Sir William Honeywood. It is not without reason that the world allows thee to be the best of men. But here comes his hopeful nephew; the strange good natur'd, foolish, open hearted—And yet, all his faults were such that one loves him still the better for them.

Enter HONEYWOOD

Honeyw. Well, Jarvis, what messages from my friends this morning?

Jarvis. You have no friends.

Honeyw. Well; from my acquaintance then?

Jarvis. (*Pulling out bills*) A few of our usual cards of compliment, that's all. This bill from your taylor; this from your mercer; and this from the little broker in Crooked-lane. He says he has been at a great deal of trouble to get back the money you borrowed.

Honeyw. That I don't know; but I'm sure we were at a great deal of trouble in getting him to lend it.

Jarvis. He has lost all patience.

Honeyw. Then he has lost a very good thing.

Jarvis. There's that ten guineas you were sending to the poor gentleman and his children in the Fleet. I believe that would stop his mouth, for a while at least.

Honeyw. Ay, Jarvis, but what will fill their mouths in the mean time? Must I be cruel because he happens to be importunate; and, to relieve his avarice, leave them to insupportable distress?

Jarvis. 'Sdeath! Sir, the question now is how to relieve yourself. Yourself—Hav'nt I reason to be out of my senses, when I see things going at sixes and sevens?

Honeyw. Whatever reason you may have for being out of

your senses, I hope you'll allow that I'm not quite unreasonable for continuing in mine.

Jarvis. You're the only man alive in your present situation that could do so—Every thing upon the waste. There's Miss Richland and her fine fortune gone already, and upon the point of being given to your rival.

Honeyw. I'm no man's rival.

Jarvis. Your uncle in Italy preparing to disinherit you; your own fortune almost spent; and nothing but pressing creditors, false friends, and a pack of drunken servants that your kindness has made unfit for any other family.

Honeyw. Then they have the more occasion for being in mine.

Jarvis. Soh! What will you have done with him that I caught stealing your plate in the pantry? In the fact; I caught him in the fact.

Honeyw. In the fact! If so, I really think that we should pay him his wages, and turn him off.

Jarvis. He shall be turn'd off at Tyburn, the dog; we'll hang him, if it only be to frighten the rest of the family.

Honeyw. No, Jarvis: it's enough that we have lost what he has stolen, let us not add to it the loss of a fellow creature!

Jarvis. Very fine; well, here was the footman just now, to complain of the butler; he says he does most work, and ought to have most wages.

Honeyw. That's but just; tho' perhaps here comes the butler to complain of the footman.

Jarvis. Ay, its the way with them all, from the scullion to the privy-counsellor. If they have a bad master, they keep quarrelling with him; if they have a good master, they keep quarrelling with one another.

Enter BUTLER, *drunk*

Butler. Sir, I'll not stay in the family with Jonathan; you must part with him, or part with me, that's the ex—ex—exposition of the matter, Sir.

Honeyw. Full and explicit enough. But what's his fault, good Philip?

Butler. Sir, he's given to drinking, Sir, and I shall have my morals corrupted, by keeping such company.

Honeyw. Ha! Ha! He has such a diverting way—

Jarvis. O quite amusing.

Butler. I find my wines a going, Sir; and liquors don't go without mouths, Sir; I hate a drunkard, Sir.

Honeyw. Well, well, Philip, I'll hear you upon that another time, so go to bed now.

Jarvis. To bed! Let him go to the devil.

Butler. Begging your honour's pardon, and begging your pardon master Jarvis, I'll not go to bed, nor to the devil neither. I have enough to do to mind my cellar. I forgot, your honour, Mr. Croaker is below. I came on purpose to tell you.

Honeyw. Why didn't you shew him up, blockhead?

Butler. Shew him up, Sir? With all my heart, Sir. Up or down, all's one to me. [*Exit*.

Jarvis. Ay, we have one or other of that family in this house from morning till night. He comes on the old affair I suppose. The match between his son, that's just returned from Paris, and Miss Richland, the young lady he's guardian to.

Honeyw. Perhaps so. Mr. Croaker, knowing my friendship for the young lady, has got it into his head that I can persuade her to what I please.

Jarvis. Ah! If you lov'd yourself but half as well as she loves you, we should soon see a marriage that would set all things to rights again.

Honeyw. Love me! Sure, Jarvis, you dream. No, no; her intimacy with me never amounted to more than friendship—mere friendship. That she is the most lovely woman that ever warm'd the human heart with desire, I own. But never let me harbour a thought of making her unhappy, by a connection with one so unworthy her merits as I am. No, Jarvis, it shall be my study to serve her, even in spite of my wishes; and to secure her happiness, tho' it destroys my own.

Jarvis. Was ever the like! I want patience.

Honeyw. Besides, Jarvis, tho' I could obtain Miss Richland's consent, do you think I could succeed with her guardian, or Mrs. Croaker his wife; who, tho' both very fine in their way, are yet a little opposite in their dispositions you know.

Jarvis. Opposite enough, Heaven knows; the very reverse of each other; she all laugh and no joke; he always complaining, and never sorrowful; a fretful poor soul that has a new distress for every hour in the four and twenty—

Honeyw. Hush, hush, he's coming up, he'll hear you.

Jarvis. One whose voice is a passing bell—

Honeyw. Well, well, go, do.

Jarvis. A raven that bodes nothing but mischief; a coffin and cross bones; a bundle of rue; a sprig of deadly night shade; a—(*Honeywood stopping his mouth at last, pushes him off.*) [*Exit* Jarvis.

Honeyw. I must own my old monitor is not entirely wrong. There is something in my friend Croaker's conversation that quite depresses me. His very mirth is an antidote to all gaiety, and his appearance has a stronger effect on my spirits than an undertaker's shop.—Mr. Croaker, this is such a satisfaction—

Enter CROAKER[1]

Croaker. A pleasant morning to Mr. Honeywood, and many of them. How is this! You look most shockingly to day my dear friend. I hope this weather does not affect your spirits. To be sure, if this weather continues—I say nothing—But God send we be all better this day three months.

Honeyw. I heartily concur in the wish, tho' I own not in your apprehensions.

Croaker. May be not! Indeed what signifies what weather

[1] [The character of Croaker was admitted to have been founded on Johnson's Suspirius (see *Rambler*, No. 59).]

we have in a country going to ruin like ours? Taxes rising and trade falling. Money flying out of the kingdom and Jesuits swarming into it. I know at this time no less than a hundred and twenty-seven Jesuits between Charing-cross and Temple-bar.

Honeyw. The Jesuits will scarce pervert you or me I should hope.

Croaker. May be not. Indeed what signifies whom they pervert in a country that has scarce any religion to lose? I'm only afraid for our wives and daughters.

Honeyw. I have no apprehensions for the ladies I assure you.

Croaker. May be not. Indeed what signifies whether they be perverted or no? The women in my time were good for something. I have seen a lady drest from top to toe in her own manufactures formerly. But now a-days the devil a thing of their own manufactures about them, except their faces.

Honeyw. But, however these faults may be practised abroad, you don't find them at home, either with Mrs. Croaker, Olivia or Miss Richland.

Croaker. The best of them will never be canoniz'd for a saint when she's dead. By the bye, my dear friend, I don't find this match between Miss Richland and my son much relish'd, either by one side or t'other.

Honeyw. I thought otherwise.

Croaker. Ah, Mr. Honeywood, a little of your fine serious advice to the young lady might go far: I know she has a very exalted opinion of your understanding.

Honeyw. But would not that be usurping an authority that more properly belongs to yourself?

Croaker. My dear friend you know but little of my authority at home. People think, indeed, because they see me come out in a morning thus, with a pleasant face, and to make my friends merry, that all's well within. But I have cares that would break an heart of stone. My wife has so encroach'd upon every one of my privileges, that I'm now no more than a mere lodger in my own house.

Honeyw. But a little spirit exerted on your side might perhaps restore your authority.

Croaker. No, tho' I had the spirit of a lion! I do rouze sometimes. But what then! Always hagling and hagling. A man is tired of getting the better before his wife is tired of losing the victory.

Honeyw. It's a melancholy consideration indeed, that our chief comforts often produce our greatest anxieties, and that an encrease of our possessions is but an inlet to new disquietudes.

Croaker. Ah, my dear friend, these were the very words of poor Dick Doleful to me not a week before he made away with himself. Indeed, Mr. Honeywood, I never see you but you put me in mind of poor—Dick. Ah there was merit neglected for you! and so true a friend; we lov'd each other for thirty years, and yet he never asked me to lend him a single farthing.

Honeyw. Pray what could induce him to commit so rash an action at last?

Croaker. I don't know, some people were malicious enough to say it was keeping company with me; because we us'd to meet now and then and open our hearts to each other. To be sure I lov'd to hear him talk, and he lov'd to hear me talk; poor dear Dick. He us'd to say that Croaker rhim'd to joker; and so we us'd to laugh—Poor Dick. (*Going to cry.*)

Honeyw. His fate affects me.

Croaker. Ay, he grew sick of this miserable life, where we do nothing but eat and grow hungry, dress and undress, get up and lie down; while reason, that should watch like a nurse by our side, falls as fast asleep as we do.

Honeyw. To say truth, if we compare that part of life which is to come, by that which we have past, the prospect is hideous.

Croaker. Life at the greatest and best is but a froward child, that must be humour'd and coax'd a little till it falls asleep, and then all the care is over.[1]

Honeyw. Very true, Sir, nothing can exceed the vanity of our existence, but the folly of our pursuits. We wept when we came into the world, and every day tells us why.

Croaker. Ah, my dear friend, it is a perfect satisfaction to be miserable with you. My son Leontine shan't lose the benefit of such fine conversation. I'll just step home for him. I am willing to shew him so much seriousness in one scarce older than himself—And what if I bring my last letter to the Gazetteer on the encrease and progress of earthquakes? It will amuse us I promise you. I there prove how the late earthquake is coming round to pay us another visit from London to Lisbon, from Lisbon to the Canary Islands, from the Canary Islands to Palmyra, from Palmyra to Constantinople, and so from Constantinople back to London again.[2] [*Exit.*

Honeyw. Poor Croaker! His situation deserves the utmost pity. I shall scarce recover my spirits these three days. Sure to live upon such terms is worse than death itself. And yet, when I consider my own situation, a broken fortune, an hopeless passion, friends in distress; the wish but not the power to serve them—(*pausing and sighing.*)

Enter BUTLER

Butler. More company below, Sir; Mrs. Croaker and Miss Richland; shall I shew them up? But they're shewing up themselves. [*Exit.*

[1] [The last sentence of Sir William Temple's *Essay on Poetry*, slightly misquoted. Goldsmith used it in the final chapter of *An Enquiry*.]

[2] [The catastrophic Lisbon earthquake of 1755 (described in Voltaire's *Candide*), and the subsequent minor rumbles of 1756, 1757, 1761, 1763, 1764 and 1765, had made earthquakes a subject for scientific inquiry and philosophical dispute.]

Enter Mrs. CROAKER *and Miss* RICHLAND

Miss Rich. You're always in such spirits.

Mrs. Croaker. We have just come, my dear Honeywood, from the auction. There was the old deaf dowager, as usual, bidding like a fury against herself. And then so curious in antiques! Herself the most genuine piece of antiquity in the whole collection.

Honeyw. Excuse me, ladies, if some uneasiness from friendship makes me unfit to share in this good humour: I know you'll pardon me.

Mrs. Croaker. I vow he seems as melancholy as if he had taken a dose of my husband this morning. Well, if Richland here can pardon you, I must.

Miss Rich. You would seem to insinuate, madam, that I have particular reasons for being dispos'd to refuse it.

Mrs. Croaker. Whatever I insinuate, my dear, don't be so ready to wish an explanation.

Miss Rich. I own I should be sorry Mr. Honeywood's long friendship and mine should be misunderstood.

Honeyw. There's no answering for others, Madam. But I hope you'll never find me presuming to offer more than the most delicate friendship may readily allow.

Miss Rich. And I shall be prouder of such a tribute from you than the most passionate professions from others.

Honeyw. My own sentiments, Madam: friendship is a disinterested commerce between equals; love, an abject intercourse between tyrants and slaves.

Miss Rich. And, without a compliment, I know none more disinterested or more capable of friendship than Mr. Honeywood.

Mrs. Croaker. And indeed I know nobody that has more friends, at least among the ladies. Miss Fruzz, Miss Odbody and Miss Winterbottom, praise him in all companies. As for Miss Biddy Bundle, she's his professed admirer.

Miss Rich. Indeed! an admirer! I did not know, Sir, you were such a favourite there. But is she seriously so handsome? Is she the mighty thing talk'd of?

Honeyw. The town, Madam, seldom begins to praise a lady's beauty, till she's beginning to lose it. (*Smiling.*)

Mrs. Croaker. But she's resolved never to lose it, it seems. For as her natural face decays, her skill improves in making the artificial one. Well, nothing diverts me more than one of those fine old dressy things, who thinks to conceal her age, by everywhere exposing her person; sticking herself up in the front of a side-box; trailing thro' a minuet at Almack's; and then, in the public gardens; looking for all the world like one of the painted ruins of the place.

Honeyw. Every age has its admirers, ladies. While you, perhaps, are trading among the warmer climates of youth; there ought to be some to carry on an useful commerce in the frozen latitudes beyond fifty.

Miss Rich. But then the mortifications they must suffer before they can be fitted out for traffic. I have seen one of them fret an whole morning at her hair-dresser, when all the fault was her face.

Honeyw. And yet I'll engage has carried that face at last to a very good market. This good natur'd town, Madam, has husbands, like spectacles, to fit every age, from fifteen to fourscore.

Mrs. Croaker. Well, you're a dear good-natur'd creature. But you know you're engaged with us this morning upon a stroling party. I want to shew Olivia the town, and the things; I believe I shall have business for you for the whole day.

Honeyw. I am sorry, Madam, I have an appointment with Mr. Croaker, which it is impossible to put off.

Mrs. Croaker. What! with my husband! Then I'm resolved to take no refusal. Nay, I protest you must. You know I never laugh so much as with you.

Honeyw. Why, if I must, I must. I'll swear you have put me into such spirits. Well, do you find jest, and I'll find laugh, I promise you. We'll wait for the chariot in the next room. [*Exeunt.*

Enter LEONTINE *and* OLIVIA

Leont. There they go, thoughtless and happy. My dearest Olivia, what would I give to see you capable of sharing in their amusements, and as chearful as they are.

Olivia. How, my Leontine, how can I be chearful, when I have so many terrors to oppress me? The fear of being detected by this family, and the apprehensions of a censuring world, when I must be detected—

Leont. The world, my love, what can it say? At worst it can only say that, being compelled by a mercenary guardian to embrace a life you disliked, you formed a resolution of flying with the man of your choice; that you confided in his honour, and took refuge in my father's house;[1] the only one where your's could remain without censure.

Olivia. But consider, Leontine, your disobedience and my indiscretion: your being sent to France to bring home a sister; and, instead of a sister, bringing home—

Leont. One dearer than a thousand sisters. One that I am convinc'd will be equally dear, to the rest of the family, when she comes to be known.

Olivia. And that, I fear, will shortly be.

Leont. Impossible, 'till we ourselves think proper to make the discovery. My sister, you know, has been with her aunt, at Lyons, since she was a child, and you find every creature in the family takes you for her.

Olivia. But may'nt she write, may'nt her aunt write?

Leont. Her aunt scarce ever writes, and all my sister's letters are directed to me.

1 [*in this house*: first and "new" editions. As this is spoken in Honeywood's house the correction is plainly necessary, but it is awkwardly made—"his father's house" would be better—and it may not be Goldsmith's.]

Olivia. But won't your refusing Miss Richland, for whom you know the old gentleman intends you, create a suspicion?

Leont. There, there's my master-stroke. I have resolved not to refuse her; nay, an hour hence I have consented to go with my father, to make her an offer of my heart and fortune.

Olivia. Your heart and fortune!

Leont. Don't be alarm'd, my dearest. Can Olivia think so meanly of my honour, or my love, as to suppose I could ever hope for happiness from any but her? No, my Olivia, neither the force, nor, permit me to add, the delicacy of my passion, leave any room to suspect me. I only offer Miss Richland an heart I am convinc'd she will refuse; as I am confident, that, without knowing it, her affections are fixed upon Mr. Honeywood.

Olivia. Mr. Honeywood! You'll excuse my apprehensions; but when your merits come to be put in the ballance—

Leont. You view them with too much partiality. However, by making this offer, I shew a seeming compliance with my father's commands; and perhaps upon her refusal I may have his consent to chuse for myself.

Olivia. Well, I submit. And yet, my Leontine, I own, I shall envy her, even your pretended addresses. I consider every look, every expression of your esteem, as due only to me. This is folly, perhaps: I allow it; but it is natural to suppose, that merit which has made an impression on ones own heart, may be powerful over that of another.

Leont. Don't, my life's treasure, don't let us make imaginary evils, when you know we have so many real ones to encounter. At worst, you know, if Miss Richland should consent, or my father refuse his pardon, it can but end in a trip to Scotland; and————

Enter CROAKER

Croaker. Where have you been, boy? I have been seeking you. My friend Honeywood here, has been saying such comfortable things. Ah! he's an example indeed; where is he? I left him here.

Leont. Sir, I believe you may see him, and hear him too in the next room: he's preparing to go out with the ladies.

Croaker. Good gracious, can I believe my eyes or my ears! I'm struck dumb with his vivacity, and stunn'd with the loudness of his laugh. Was there ever such a transformation! (*A laugh behind the scenes, Croaker mimics it.*) Ha! ha! ha! there it goes, a plague take their balderdash; yet I could expect nothing less, when my precious wife was of the party. On my conscience, I believe, she could spread an horse-laugh thro' the pews of a tabernacle.

Leont. Since you find so many objections to a wife, Sir, how can you be so earnest in recommending one to me?

Croaker. I have told you, and tell you again, boy, that Miss Richland's fortune must not go out of the family; .one may find comfort in the money, whatever one does in the wife.

Leont. But, Sir, tho', in obedience to your desire, I am ready to marry her, it may be possible, she has no inclination to me.

Croaker. I'll tell you once for all how it stands. A good part of Miss Richland's large fortune consists in a claim upon government, which my good friend Mr. Lofty,[1] assures me the Treasury will allow. One half of this she is to forfeit, by her father's will, in case she refuses to marry you. So, if she rejects you, we seize half her fortune; if she accepts you, we seize the whole, and a fine girl into the bargain.

Leont. But, Sir, if you will but listen to reason—

Croaker. Come, then, produce your reasons. I tell you I'm fix'd, determined, so now produce your reasons. When

[1] [*my good friend Mr. Le Bronze*: first edition. As this is the first mention of Lofty in the play, "Mr. Le Bronze" can hardly be a jocular invention of Croaker's; so presumably Goldsmith first intended to call Lofty "Le Bronze" and omitted to correct this passage.]

I'm determined, I always listen to reason, because it can then do no harm.

Leont. You have alledged that a mutual choice was the first requisite in matrimonial happiness.

Croaker. Well, and you have both of you a mutual choice. She has her choice—to marry you, to lose half her fortune; and you have your choice—to marry her, or pack out of doors without any fortune at all.

Leont. An only Son, Sir, might expect more indulgence.

Croaker. An only father, Sir, might expect more obedience; besides, has not your sister here, that never disobliged me in her life, as good a right as you? He's a sad dog, Livy, my dear, and would take all from you. But he shan't, I tell you he shan't, for you shall have your share.

Olivia. Dear Sir, I wish you'd be convinced that I can never be happy in any addition to my fortune, which is taken from his.

Croaker. Well, well, its a good child, so say no more, but come with me, and we shall see something that will give us a great deal of pleasure, I promise you; old Ruggins, the curry-comb-maker, lying in state; I'm told he makes a very handsome corpse, and becomes his coffin prodigiously.[1] He was an intimate friend of mine, and these are friendly things we ought to do for each other. [*Exeunt.*

END OF THE FIRST ACT

[1] [Lying in state had become very much a middle-class custom. "When a tradesman dies, his frightful face is painted up by an undertaker, and placed in a proper position to receive company; this is called lying in state." *The Citizen of the World*, Letter XII (see p. 306) where there are further details of this practice.]

ACT THE SECOND

SCENE, *Croaker's House*

Miss RICHLAND, GARNET

Miss Rich. Olivia not his sister? Olivia not Leontine's sister? You amaze me!

Garnet. No more his sister than I am; I had it all from his own servant; I can get any thing from that quarter.

Miss Rich. But how? Tell me again, Garnet.

Garnet. Why, Madam, as I told you before, instead of going to Lyons to bring home his sister, who has been there with her aunt these ten years; he never went further than Paris; there he saw and fell in love with this young lady; by the bye, of a prodigious family.

Miss Rich. And brought her home to my guardian, as his daughter?

Garnet. Yes, and daughter she will be. If he don't consent to their marriage, they talk of trying what a Scotch parson can do.

Miss Rich. Well, I own they have deceived me—And so demurely as Olivia carried it too!—Would you believe it, Garnet, I told her all my secrets; and yet the sly cheat concealed all this from me?

Garnet. And, upon my word, Madam, I don't much blame her; she was loath to trust one with her secrets, that was so very bad at keeping her own.

Miss Rich. But, to add to their deceit, the young gentleman, it seems, pretends to make me serious proposals. My guardian and he are to be here presently, to open the affair in form. You know I am to lose half my fortune if I refuse him.

Garnet. Yet, what can you do? For being, as you are, in love with Mr. Honeywood, Madam—

Miss Rich. How! ideot; what do you mean? In love with Mr. Honeywood! Is this to provoke me?

Garnet. That is, Madam, in friendship with him; I meant nothing more than friendship, as I hope to be married; nothing more.

Miss Rich. Well, no more of this! As to my guardian, and his son, they shall find me prepared to receive them; I'm resolved to accept their proposal with seeming pleasure, to mortify them by compliance, and so throw the refusal at last upon them.

Garnet. Delicious! and that will secure your whole fortune to yourself. Well, who could have thought so innocent a face could cover so much cuteness!

Miss Rich. Why, girl, I only oppose my prudence to their cunning, and practise a lesson they have taught me against themselves.

Garnet. Then you're likely not long to want employment, for here they come, and in close conference.

Enter CROAKER, LEONTINE

Leont. Excuse me, Sir, if I seem to hesitate upon the point of putting the lady so important a question.

Croaker. Lord! good Sir, moderate your fears; you're so plaguy shy, that one would think you had changed sexes. I tell you we must have the half or the whole. Come, let me see with what spirit you begin? Well, why don't you? Eh! What? Well then—I must, it seems—Miss Richland, my dear, I believe you guess at our business; an affair which my son here comes to open, that nearly concerns your happiness.

Miss Rich. Sir, I should be ungrateful not to be pleased with any thing that comes recommended by you.

Croaker. How, boy, could you desire a finer opening? Why don't you begin, I say? (*To Leont.*)

Leont. 'Tis true, Madam, my father, Madam, has some intentions—hem—of explaining an affair—which—himself—can best explain, Madam.

Croaker. Yes, my dear; it comes intirely from my son;

it's all a request of his own, Madam. And I will permit him to make the best of it.

Leont. The whole affair is only this, Madam; my father has a proposal to make, which he insists none but himself shall deliver.

Croaker. My mind misgives me, the fellow will never be brought on. (*Aside.*) In short, Madam, you see before you one that loves you; one whose whole happiness is all in you.

Miss Rich. I never had any doubts of your regard, Sir; and I hope you can have none of my duty.

Croaker. That's not the thing, my little sweeting; my love! No, no, another guess lover than I; there he stands, Madam; his very looks declare the force of his passion.—Call up a look, you dog—But then, had you seen him, as I have, weeping, speaking soliloquies and blank verse, sometimes melancholy, and sometimes absent—

Miss Rich. I fear, Sir, he's absent now; or such a declaration would have come most properly from himself.

Croaker. Himself! Madam; he would die before he could make such a confession; and if he had not a channel for his passion thro' me, it would ere now have drowned his understanding.

Miss Rich. I must grant, Sir, there are attractions in modest diffidence, above the force of words. A silent address is the genuine eloquence of sincerity.

Croaker. Madam, he has forgot to speak any other language; silence is become his mother tongue.

Miss Rich. And it must be confessed, Sir, it speaks very powerfully in his favour. And yet, I shall be thought too forward in making such a confession; shan't I Mr. Leontine?

Leont. Confusion! my reserve will undo me. But, if modesty attracts her, impudence may disgust her. I'll try. (*Aside.*) Don't imagine from my silence, Madam, that I want a due sense of the honour and happiness intended me. My father,

Madam, tells me, your humble servant is not totally indifferent to you. He admires you; I adore you; and when we come together, upon my soul I believe we shall be the happiest couple in all St. James's.

Miss Rich. If I could flatter myself, you thought as you speak, Sir——

Leont. Doubt my sincerity, Madam? By your dear self I swear. Ask the brave if they desire glory; ask cowards if they covet safety——

Croaker. Well, well, no more questions about it.

Leont. Ask the sick if they long for health, ask misers if they love money, ask——

Croaker. Ask a fool if he can talk nonsense! What's come over the boy? What signifies asking, when there's not a soul to give you an answer? If you would ask to the purpose, ask this lady's consent to make you happy.

Miss Rich. Why, indeed, Sir, his uncommon ardour almost compels me, forces me, to comply. And yet I'm afraid he'll despise a conquest gain'd with too much ease; wont you, Mr. Leontine?

Leont. Confusion! (*Aside*) O by no means, Madam, by no means. And yet, Madam, you talk'd of force. There is nothing I would avoid so much as compulsion in a thing of this kind. No, Madam, I will still be generous, and leave you at liberty to refuse.

Croaker. But I tell you, Sir, the lady is not at liberty. Its a match. You see she says nothing. Silence gives consent.

Leont. But, Sir, she talk'd of force. Consider, Sir, the cruelty of constraining her inclinations.

Croaker. But I say there's no cruelty. Don't you know, blockhead, that girls have always a roundabout way of saying yes before company? So get you both gone together into the next room, and hang him that interrupts the tender explanation. Get you gone, I say; I'll not hear a word.

Leont. But, Sir, I must beg leave to insist——

Croaker. Get off you puppy, or I'll beg leave to insist upon knocking you down. Stupid whelp. But I don't wonder, the boy takes entirely after his mother.

[*Exeunt Miss* Rich. *and* Leont.

Enter Mrs. CROAKER

Mrs. Croaker. Mr. Croaker, I bring you something, my dear, that I believe will make you smile.

Croaker. I'll hold you a guinea of that, my dear.

Mrs. Croaker. A letter; and, as I knew the hand, I ventured to open it.

Croaker. And how can you expect your breaking open my letters should give me pleasure?

Mrs. Croaker. Poo, its from your sister at Lyons, and contains good news: read it.

Croaker. What a Frenchified cover is here! That sister of mine has some good qualities, but I could never teach her to fold a letter.

Mrs. Croaker. Fold a fiddlestick. Read what it contains.

Croaker. (*reading.*)

DEAR NICK,

An English gentleman, of large fortune, has for some time made private, tho' honourable proposals to your daughter Olivia. They love each other tenderly, and I find she has consented, without letting any of the family know, to crown his addresses. As such good offers don't come every day, your own good sense, his large fortune, and family considerations, will induce you to forgive her.

Yours ever,

RACHEL CROAKER.

My daughter, Olivia, privately contracted to a man of large fortune! This is good news indeed. My heart never foretold me of this. And yet, how slily the little baggage has carried it since she came home. Not a word on't to the old ones for the world. Yet, I thought, I saw something she wanted to conceal.

Mrs. Croaker. Well, if they have concealed their amour, they shan't conceal their wedding; that shall be public, I'm resolved.

Croaker. I tell thee, woman, the wedding is the most foolish part of the ceremony. I can never get this woman to think of the more serious part of the nuptial engagement.

Mrs. Croaker. What, would you have me think of their funeral? But come, tell me, my dear, don't you owe more to me than you care to confess? Would you have ever been known to Mr. Lofty, who has undertaken Miss Richland's claim at the Treasury, but for me? Who was it first made him an acquaintance at Lady Shabbaroon's route?[1] Who got him to promise us his interest? Is not he a backstairs favourite, one that can do what he pleases with those that do what they please? Isn't he an acquaintance that all your groaning and lamentations could never have got us?

Croaker. He is a man of importance, I grant you. And yet, what amazes me is, that while he is giving away places to all the world, he can't get one for himself.

Mrs. Croaker. That perhaps may be owing to his nicety. Great men are not easily satisfied.

Enter FRENCH SERVANT

Servant. An expresse from Monsieur Lofty. He vil be vait upon your honour's instrammant. He be only giving four five instruction, read two tree memorial, call upon von ambassadeur. He vil be vid you in one tree minutes.

Mrs. Croaker. You see now, my dear. What an extensive department! Well, friend, let your master know, that we are extremely honoured by this honour. Was there any thing ever

[1] [Rout, a fashionable gathering.]

in a higher style of breeding! All messages among the great are now done by express.

Croaker. To be sure, no man does little things with more solemnity, or claims more respect than he. But he's in the right on't. In our bad world, respect is given, where respect is claim'd.

Mrs. Croaker. Never mind the world, my dear; you were never in a pleasanter place in your life. Let us now think of receiving him with proper respect (*a loud rapping at the door*) and there he is by the thundering rap.

Croaker. Ay, verily, there he is; as close upon the heels of his own express, as an indorsement upon the back of a bill. Well, I'll leave you to receive him, whilst I go to chide my little Olivia for intending to steal a marriage without mine or her aunt's consent. I must seem to be angry, or she too may begin to despise my authority. [*Exit.*

Enter LOFTY, *speaking to his servant*

Lofty. And if the Venetian Ambassador, or that teazing creature the Marquis, should call, I'm not at home. Dam'me, I'll be pack-horse to none of them. My dear Madam, I have just snatched a moment—And if the expresses to his Grace be ready, let them be sent off; they're of importance. Madam, I ask a thousand pardons.

Mrs. Croaker. Sir, this honour——

Lofty. And Dubardieu! If the person calls about the commission, let him know that it is made out. As for Lord Cumbercourt's stale request, it can keep cold: you understand me. Madam, I ask ten thousand pardons.

Mrs. Croaker. Sir, this honour——

Lofty. And Dubardieu! If the man comes from the Cornish borough, you must do him; you must do him, I say. Madam I ask ten thousand pardons. And if the Russian—Ambassador calls: but he will scarce call to-day, I believe. And now, Madam, I have just got time to express my happiness in having the honour of being permitted to profess myself your most obedient humble servant.

Mrs. Croaker. Sir, the happiness and honour are all mine; and yet, I'm only robbing the public while I detain you.

Lofty. Sink the public, Madam, when the fair are to be attended. Ah, could all my hours be so charmingly devouted! Sincerely, don't you pity us poor creatures in affairs? Thus it is eternally; solicited for places here, teized for pensions there, and courted every where. I know you pity me. Yes, I see you do.

Mrs. Croaker. Excuse me, Sir. Toils of empires pleasures are, as Waller[1] says.

Lofty. Waller, Waller; is he of the House?

Mrs. Croaker. The modern poet of that name, Sir.

Lofty. Oh, a modern! We men of business despise the moderns; and as for the ancients, we have no time to read them. Poetry is a pretty thing enough for our wives and daughters; but not for us. Why now, here I stand that know nothing of books. I say, Madam, I know nothing of books; and yet, I believe, upon a land carriage fishery, a stamp act, or a jaghire,[2] I can talk my two hours without feeling the want of them.

Mrs. Croaker. The world is no stranger to Mr. Lofty's eminence in every capacity.

Lofty. I vow to Gad, Madam, you make me blush. I'm nothing, nothing, nothing in the world; a mere obscure gentleman. To be sure, indeed, one or two of the present ministers are pleased to represent me as a formidable man. I

[1] [*Waller Congrave* [sic]: first and "new" editions. The line, which is slightly misquoted, comes from Juno's song in William Congreve's *The Judgment of Paris*, 1701. The manuscript was presumably corrected somewhat casually—not necessarily by Goldsmith—from "Waller" to "Congreve" and then misread and misunderstood by the printer.

[2] ["An assignment of the king's or the government's share of the produce of a district . . . as an annuity, either for private use or for the maintenance of a public (esp. military) establishment." *Oxford English Dictionary*.]

know they are pleased to be-spatter me at all their little dirty levees. Yet, upon my soul, I wonder what they see in me to treat me so! Measures, not men, have always been my mark; and I vow, by all that's honourable, my resentment has never done the men, as mere men, any manner of harm—That is as mere men.

Mrs. Croaker. What importance, and yet what modesty!

Lofty. Oh, if you talk of modesty, Madam! There, I own, I'm accessible to praise: Modesty is my foible: It was so, the Duke of Brentford used to say of me. I love Jack Lofty, he used to say: no man has a finer knowledge of things; quite a man of information; and when he speaks upon his legs, by the lord, he's prodigious, he scouts them; and yet all men have their faults; too much modesty is his, says his Grace.

Mrs. Croaker. And yet, I dare say, you don't want assurance when you come to solicit for your friends.

Lofty. O, there indeed I'm in bronze. Apropos, I have just been mentioning Miss Richland's case to a certain personage; we must name no names. When I ask, I am not to be put off, Madam. No, no, I take my friend by the button. A fine girl, Sir; great justice in her case. A friend of mine. Borough interest. Business must be done, Mr. Secretary. I say, Mr. Secretary, her business must be done, Sir. That's my way, Madam.

Mrs. Croaker. Bless me! you said all this to the Secretary of State, did you?

Lofty. I did not say the Secretary, did I? Well, curse it, since you have found me out I will not deny it. It was to the Secretary.

Mrs. Croaker. This was going to the fountain head at once, not applying to the understrappers, as Mr. Honeywood would have had us.

Lofty. Honeywood! he! he! He was, indeeu, a fine solicitor. I suppose you have heard what has just happened to him?

Mrs. Croaker. Poor dear man; no accident, I hope.

Lofty. Undone, Madam, that's all. His creditors have taken him into custody. A prisoner in his own house.

Mrs. Croaker. A prisoner in his own house! How! At this very time! I'm quite unhappy for him.

Lofty. Why, so am I. The man, to be sure, was immensely good natur'd. But then I could never find that he had any thing in him.

Mrs. Croaker. His manner, to be sure, was excessive harmless; some, indeed, thought it a little dull. For my part, I always concealed my opinion.

Lofty. It can't be conceal'd, Madam; the man was dull, dull as the last new comedy! A poor impracticable creature! I tried once or twice to know if he was fit for business; but he had scarce talents to be groom-porter to an orange barrow.

Mrs. Croaker. How differently does Miss Richland think of him! For, I believe, with all his faults, she loves him.

Lofty. Loves him! Does she? You should cure her of that by all means. Let me see, what if she were sent to him this instant, in his present doleful situation? My life for it that works her cure. Distress is a perfect antidote to love. Suppose we join her in the next room? Miss Richland is a fine girl, has a fine fortune, and must not be thrown away. Upon my honour, Madam, I have a regard for Miss Richland; and, rather than she should be thrown away, I should think it no indignity to marry her myself. [*Exeunt.*

Enter OLIVIA *and* LEONTINE

Leont. And yet, trust me, Olivia, I had every reason to expect Miss Richland's refusal, as I did every thing in my power to deserve it. Her indelicacy surprizes me!

Olivia. Sure, Leontine, there's nothing so indelicate in being sensible of your merit. If so, I fear, I shall be the most guilty thing alive.

Leont. But you mistake, my dear. The same attention I used to advance my merit with you, I practised to lessen it with her. What more could I do?

Olivia. Let us now rather consider what's to be done. We have both dissembled too long—I have always been asham'd—I am now quite weary of it. Sure I could never have undergone so much for any other but you.

Leont. And you shall find my gratitude equal to your kindest compliance. Tho' our friends should totally forsake us, Olivia, we can draw upon content for the deficiencies of fortune.

Olivia. Then why should we defer our scheme of humble happiness, when it is now in our power? I may be the favourite of your father, it is true; but can it ever be thought, that his present kindness to a suppos'd child, will continue to a known deceiver?

Leont. I have many reasons to believe it will. As his attachments are but few, they are lasting. His own marriage was a private one, as our's may be. Besides, I have sounded him already at a distance, and find all his answers exactly to our wish. Nay, by an expression or two that drop'd from him, I am induced to think he knows of this affair.

Olivia. Indeed! But that would be an happiness too great to be expected.

Leont. However it be, I'm certain you have power over him; and am persuaded, if you inform'd him of our situation, that he would be disposed to pardon it.

Olivia. You had equal expectations, Leontine, from your last scheme with Miss Richland, which you find has succeeded most wretchedly.

Leont. And that's the best reason for trying another.

Olivia. If it must be so, I submit.

Leont. As we could wish, he comes this way. Now, my

dearest Olivia, be resolute. I'll just retire within hearing, to come in at a proper time, either to share your danger, or confirm your victory. [*Exit.*

Enter CROAKER

Croaker. Yes, I must forgive her; and yet not too easily, neither. It will be proper to keep up the decorums of resentment a little, if it be only to impress her with an idea of my authority.

Olivia. How I tremble to approach him!—Might I presume, Sir—If I interrupt you—

Croaker. No, child, where I have an affection, it is not a little thing can interrupt me. Affection gets over little things.

Olivia. Sir, you're too kind. I'm sensible how ill I deserve this partiality. Yet, Heaven knows, there is nothing I would not do to gain it.

Croaker. And you have but too well succeeded, you little hussey, you. With those endearing ways of yours, on my conscience, I could be brought to forgive any thing, unless it were a very great offence indeed.

Olivia. But mine is such an offence—When you know my guilt—Yes, you shall know it, tho' I feel the greatest pain in the confession.

Croaker. Why, then, if it be so very great a pain, you may spare yourself the trouble, for I know every syllable of the matter before you begin.

Olivia. Indeed! Then I'm undone.

Croaker. Ay, Miss, you wanted to steal a match, without letting me know it, did you! But I'm not worth being consulted, I suppose, when there's to be a marriage in my own family. No, I'm to have no hand in the disposal of my own children. No, I'm nobody. I'm to be a mere article of family lumber; a piece of crack'd china to be stuck up in a corner.

Olivia. Dear Sir, nothing but the dread of your authority could induce us to conceal it from you.

Croaker. No, no, my consequence is no more; I'm as little minded as a dead Russian in winter, just stuck up with a pipe in his mouth till there comes a thaw—It goes to my heart to vex her.

Olivia. I was prepar'd, Sir, for your anger, and despair'd of pardon, even while I presum'd to ask it. But your severity shall never abate my affection, as my punishment is but justice.

Croaker. And yet you should not despair neither, Livy. We ought to hope all for the best.

Olivia. And do you permit me to hope, Sir! Can I ever expect to be forgiven! But hope has too long deceiv'd me.

Croaker. Why then, child, it shan't deceive you now, for I forgive you this very moment. I forgive you all; and now you are indeed my daughter.

Olivia. O transport! This kindness overpowers me!

Croaker. I was always against severity to our children. We have been young and giddy ourselves, and we can't expect boys and girls to be old before their time.

Olivia. What generosity! But can you forget the many falshoods, the dissimulation——

Croaker. You did indeed dissemble, you urchin you; but where's the girl that won't dissemble for an husband! My wife and I had never been married, if we had not dissembled a little before hand.

Olivia. It shall be my future care never to put such generosity to a second trial. And as for the partner of my offence and folly, from his native honour, and the just sense he has of his duty, I can answer for him that——

Enter LEONTINE

Leont. Permit him thus to answer for himself. (*Kneeling.*) Thus, Sir, let me speak my gratitude for this unmerited forgiveness. Yes, Sir, this even exceeds all your former tenderness: I now can boast the most indulgent of fathers. The life, he gave, compared to this, was but a trifling blessing.

Croaker. And, good Sir, who sent for you, with that fine tragedy face, and flourishing manner? I don't know what we have to do with your gratitude upon this occasion.

Leont. How, Sir! is it possible to be silent when so much oblig'd! Would you refuse me the pleasure of being grateful! Of adding my thanks to my Olivia's! Of sharing in the transports that you have thus occasion'd?

Croaker. Lord, Sir, we can be happy enough, without your coming in to make up the party. I don't know what's the matter with the boy all this day; he has got into such a rhodomontade manner all the morning!

Leont. But, Sir, I that have so large a part in the benefit, is it not my duty to shew my joy? Is the being admitted to your favour so slight an obligation? Is the happiness of marrying my Olivia so small a blessing?

Croaker. Marrying Olivia! marrying Olivia! marrying his own sister! Sure the boy is out of his senses. His own sister!

Leont. My sister!

Olivia. Sister! How have I been mistaken! [*Aside*.

Leont. Some curs'd mistake in all this I find. [*Aside*.

Croaker. What does the booby mean, or has he any meaning. Eh, what do you mean, you blockhead you?

Leont. Mean, Sir—why, Sir—only when my sister is to be married, that I have the pleasure of marrying her, Sir; that is, of giving her away, Sir—I have made a point of it.

Croaker. O, is that all. Give her away. You have made a point of it. Then you had as good make a point of first giving away yourself, as I'm going to prepare the writings between you and Miss Richland this very minute. What a fuss is here about nothing! Why, what's the matter now? I thought I had made you at least as happy as you could wish.

Olivia. O! yes, Sir, very happy.

Croaker. Do you foresee any thing, child? You look as if you did. I think if any thing was to be foreseen, I have as sharp a look out as another: and yet I foresee nothing. [*Exit*.

Leontine, Olivia

Olivia. What can it mean?

Leont. He knows something, and yet for my life, I can't tell what.

Olivia. It can't be the connexion between us, I'm pretty certain.

Leont. Whatever it be, my dearest, I'm resolv'd to put it out of Fortune's power to repeat our mortification. I'll haste, and prepare for our journey to Scotland this very evening. My friend Honeywood has promis'd me his advice and assistance. I'll go to him, and repose our distresses on his friendly bosom: and I know so much of his honest heart, that if he can't relieve our uneasinesses, he will at least share them. [*Exeunt*.

End of the Second Act

ACT THE THIRD

Scene, *Young Honeywood's House*

Bailiff, Honeywood, Follower

Bailiff. Looky, Sir, I have arrested as good men as you in my time: no disparagement of you neither. Men that would go forty guineas on a game of cribbage. I challenge the town to shew a man in more genteeler practice than myself.

Honeyw. Without all question, Mr. ——. I forget your name, Sir?

Bailiff. How can you forget what you never knew? he, he, he.

Honeyw. May I beg leave to ask your name?

Bailiff. Yes, you may.

Honeyw. Then, pray, Sir, what is your name, Sir?

Bailiff. That I didn't promise to tell you. He, he, he. A joke breaks no bones, as we say among us that practice the law.

Honeyw. You may have reason for keeping it a secret perhaps?

Bailiff. The law does nothing without reason. I'm asham'd to tell my name to no man, Sir. If you can shew cause, as why, upon a special capus, that I should prove my name—But, come, Timothy Twitch is my name. And, now you know my name, what have you to say to that?

Honeyw. Nothing in the world, good Mr. Twitch, but that I have a favour to ask, that's all.

Bailiff. Ay, favours are more easily asked than granted, as we say among us that practice the law. I have taken an oath against granting favours. Would you have me perjure myself?

Honeyw. But my request will come recommended in so strong a manner, as, I believe you'll have no scruple (*pulling out his purse*). The thing is only this: I believe I shall be able to discharge this trifle in two or three days at farthest; but as I would not have the affair known for the world, I have thoughts of keeping you, and your good friend here, about me till the debt is discharged; for which, I shall be properly grateful.

Bailiff. Oh! that's another maxum, and altogether within my oath. For certain, if an honest man is to get any thing by a thing, there's no reason why all things should not be done in civility.

Honeyw. Doubtless, all trades must live, Mr. Twitch; and your's is a necessary one. (*Gives him money.*)

Bailiff. Oh! your honour; I hope your honour takes nothing amiss as I does, as I does nothing but my duty in so doing. I'm sure no man can say I ever give a gentleman, that was a gentleman, ill usage. If I saw that a gentleman was a gentleman, I have taken money not to see him for ten weeks together.

Honeyw. Tenderness is a virtue, Mr. Twitch.

Bailiff. Ay, Sir, it's a perfect treasure. I love to see a gentleman with a tender heart. I don't know, but I think I have a tender heart myself. If all that I have lost by my heart was put together, it would make a—but no matter for that.

Honeyw. Don't account it lost, Mr. Twitch. The ingratitude of the world can never deprive us of the conscious happiness of having acted with humanity ourselves.

Bailiff. Humanity, Sir, is a jewel. It's better than gold. I love humanity. People may say, that we, in our way, have no humanity; but I'll shew you my humanity this moment. There's my follower here, little Flanigan, with a wife and four children, a guinea or two would be more to him, than twice as much to another. Now, as I can't shew him any humanity myself, I must beg leave you'll do it for me.

Honeyw. I assure you, Mr. Twitch, your's is a most powerful recommendation. (*Giving money to the follower.*)

Bailiff. Sir, you're a gentleman. I see you know what to do with your money. But, to business: we are to be with you here as your friends, I suppose. But set in case company comes.—Little Flanigan here, to be sure, has a good face; a very good face: but then, he is a little seedy, as we say among us that practice the law. Not well in cloaths. Smoke the pocket holes.

Honeyw. Well, that shall be remedied without delay.

Enter SERVANT

Servant. Sir, Miss Richland is below.

Honeyw. How unlucky. Detain her a moment. We must improve, my good friend, little Mr. Flanigan's appearance first. Here, let Mr. Flanigan have a suit of my cloaths—quick—the brown and silver—Do you hear?

Servant. That your honour gave away to the begging gentleman that makes verses, because it was as good as new.

Honeyw. The white and gold then.

Servant. That your honour, I made bold to sell, because it was good for nothing.

Honeyw. Well, the first that comes to hand then. The blue and gold. I believe Mr. Flanigan will look best in blue.

[*Exit* Flanigan.

Bailiff. Rabbit me, but little Flanigan will look well in any thing. Ah, if your honour knew that bit of flesh as well as I do, you'd be perfectly in love with him. There's not a prettyer scout in the four counties after a shy-cock than he. Scents like a hound; sticks like a weazle. He was master of the ceremonies to the black queen of Moroco when I took him to follow me. (*Re-enter* Flanigan.) Heh, ecod, I think he looks so well, that I don't care if I have a suit from the same place for myself.

Honeyw. Well, well, I hear the lady coming. Dear Mr. Twitch, I beg you'll give your friend directions not to speak. As for yourself, I know you will say nothing without being directed.

Bailiff. Never you fear me, I'll shew the Lady that I have something to say for myself as well as another. One man has one way of talking, and another man has another, that's all the difference between them.

Enter Miss RICHLAND *and her* MAID

Miss Rich. You'll be surprised, Sir, with this visit. But you know I'm yet to thank you for chusing my little library.

Honeyw. Thanks, Madam, are unnecessary, as it was I that was obliged by your commands. Chairs here. Two of my very good friends, Mr. Twitch and Mr. Flanigan. Pray, gentlemen, sit without ceremony.

Miss Rich. Who can these odd looking men be! I fear it is as I was informed. It must be so. [*Aside.*

Bailiff. (*after a pause*) Pretty weather, very pretty weather for the time of the year, Madam.

Follower. Very good circuit weather in the country.

Honeyw. You officers are generally favourites among the ladies. My friends, Madam, have been upon very disagreeable duty, I assure you. The fair should, in some measure, recompence the toils of the brave.

Miss Rich. Our officers do indeed deserve every favour. The gentlemen are in the marine service, I presume, Sir?

Honeyw. Why, Madam, they do—occasionally serve in the Fleet, Madam. A dangerous service.

Miss Rich. I'm told so. And I own, it has often surprised me, that, while we have had so many instances of bravery there, we have had so few of wit at home to praise it.

Honeyw. I grant, Madam, that our poets have not written as our soldiers have fought; but, they have done all they could, and Hawke or Amherst could do no more.

Miss Rich. I'm quite displeased when I see a fine subject spoiled by a dull writer.

Honeyw. We should not be so severe against dull writers, Madam. It is ten to one, but the dullest writer exceeds the most rigid French critic who presumes to despise him.

Follower. Damn the French, the parle vous, and all that belongs to them.

Miss Rich. Sir!

Honeyw. Ha, ha, ha, honest Mr. Flanigan. A true English officer, Madam; he's not contented with beating the French, but he will scold them too.

Miss Rich. Yet, Mr. Honeywood, this does not convince me but that severity in criticism is necessary. It was our first adopting the severity of French taste, that has brought them in turn to taste us.

Bailiff. Taste us! By the Lord, Madam, they devour us! Give Monseers but a taste, and I'll be damn'd, but they come in for a bellyful.

Miss Rich. Very extraordinary this.

Follower. But very true. What makes the bread rising, the parle vous that devour us. What makes the mutton fivepence a pound, the parle vous that eat it up. What makes the beer three pence halfpenny a pot——

Honeyw. Ah; the vulgar rogues, all will be out. Right, gentlemen, very right, upon my word, and quite to the purpose. They draw a parallel, Madam, between the mental taste, and that of our senses. We are injur'd as much by French severity in the one, as by French rapacity in the other. That's their meaning.

Miss Rich. Tho' I don't see the force of the parallel, yet, I'll own, that we should sometimes pardon books, as we do our friends, that have now and then agreeable absurdities to recommend them.

Bailiff. That's all my eye. The King only can pardon, as the law says: for set in case——

Honeyw. I am quite of your opinion, Sir. I see the whole drift of your argument. Yes, certainly our presuming to pardon any work, is arrogating a power that belongs to another. If all have power to condemn, what writer can be free?

Bailiff. By his habus corpus. His habus corpus can set him free at any time. For set in case——

Honeyw. I'm obliged to you, Sir, for the hint. If, Madam, as my friend observes, our laws are so careful of a gentleman's person, sure we ought to be equally careful of his dearer part, his fame.

Follower. Ay, but if so be a man's nabb'd, you know——

Honeyw. Mr. Flanigan, if you spoke for ever, you could not improve the last observation. For my own part, I think it conclusive.

Bailiff. As for the matter of that, mayhap——

Honeyw. Nay, Sir, give me leave in this instance to be positive. For where is the necessity of censuring works without genius, which must shortly sink of themselves: what is it, but aiming our unnecessary blow against a victim already under the hands of justice?

Bailiff. Justice! O, by the elevens, if you talk about justice, I think I am at home there; for, in a course of law——

Honeyw. My dear Mr. Twitch, I discern what you'd be at

perfectly, and I believe the lady must be sensible of the art with which it is introduced. I suppose you perceive the meaning, Madam, of his course of law?

Miss Rich. I protest, Sir, I do not. I perceive only that you answer one gentleman before he has finished, and the other before he has well begun.

Bailiff. Madam, you are a gentlewoman, and I will make the matter out. This here question, is about severity and justice, and pardon, and the like of they. Now to explain the thing—

Honeyw. O! curse your explanations. [*Aside.*

Enter SERVANT

Servant. Mr. Leontine, Sir, below, desires to speak with you upon earnest business.

Honeyw. That's lucky (*aside*). Dear Madam, you'll excuse me, and my good friends here, for a few minutes. There are books, Madam, to amuse you. Come, gentlemen, you know I make no ceremony with such friends. After you, Sir. Excuse me. Well, if I must. But, I know your natural politeness.

Bailiff. Before and behind, you know.

Follower. Aye, aye, before and behind, before and behind.

[*Exeunt* Honeywood, Bailiff *and* Follower.

Miss Rich. What can all this mean, Garnet?

Garnet. Mean, Madam? why, what should it mean, but what Mr. Lofty sent you here to see? These people he calls officers, are officers sure enough: sheriff's officers; bailiffs, Madam.

Miss Rich. Ay, it is certainly so. Well, tho' his perplexities are far from giving me pleasure, yet, I own, there's something very ridiculous in them, and a just punishment for his dissimulation.

Garnet. And so they are. But I wonder, Madam, that the lawyer you just employed to pay his debts, and set him free, has not done it by this time. He ought at least to have been here before now. But lawyers are always more ready to get a man into troubles, than out of them.

Enter SIR WILLIAM

Sir Will. For Miss Richland to undertake setting him free, I own, was quite unexpected. It has totally unhinged my schemes to reclaim him. Yet, it gives me pleasure to find, that, among a number of worthless friendships, he has made one acquisition of real value; for there must be some softer passion on her side that prompts this generosity. Ha! here before me: I'll endeavour to sound her affections. Madam, as I am the person that have had some demands upon the gentleman of this house, I hope you'll excuse me, if, before I enlarged him, I wanted to see yourself.

Miss Rich. The precaution was very unnecessary, Sir. I suppose your wants were only such as my agent had power to satisfy.

Sir Will. Partly, Madam. But I was also willing you should be fully apprized of the character of the gentleman you intended to serve.

Miss Rich. It must come, Sir, with a very ill grace from you. To censure it, after what you have done, would look like malice; and to speak favourably of a character you have oppressed, would be impeaching your own. And sure, his tenderness, his humanity, his universal friendship, may atone for many faults.

Sir Will. That friendship, Madam, which is exerted in too wide a sphere, becomes totally useless. Our bounty, like a drop of water, disappears when diffused too widely. They, who pretend most to this universal benevolence, are either deceivers, or dupes. Men who desire to cover their private ill-nature, by a pretended regard for all; or, men who, reasoning themselves into false feelings, are more earnest in pursuit of splendid, than of useful virtues.

Miss Rich. I am surprised, Sir, to hear one who has probably been a gainer by the folly of others, so severe in his censure of it.

Sir Will. Whatever I may have gained by folly, Madam, you see I am willing to prevent your losing by it.

Miss Rich. Your cares for me, Sir, are unnecessary. I always suspect those services which are denied where they are wanted, and offered, perhaps, in hopes of a refusal. No, Sir, my directions have been given, and I insist upon their being complied with.

Sir Will. Thou amiable woman. I can no longer contain the expressions of my gratitude: my pleasure. You see before you, one who has been equally careful of his interest: one who has for some time been a concealed spectator of his follies, and only punished, in hopes to reclaim them—His uncle.

Miss Rich. Sir William Honeywood! You amaze me. How shall I conceal my confusion? I fear, Sir, you'll think I have been too forward in my services. I confess I——

Sir Will. Don't make any apologies, Madam. I only find myself unable to repay the obligation. And yet, I have been trying my interest of late to serve you. Having learnt, Madam, that you had some demands upon government, I have, tho' unasked, been your solicitor there.

Miss Rich. Sir, I'm infinitely obliged to your intentions. But my guardian has employed another gentleman who assures him of success.

Sir Will. Who, the important little man who visits here! Trust me, Madam, he's quite contemptible among men in power, and utterly unable to serve you. Mr. Lofty's promises are much better known to people of fashion, than his person, I assure you.

Miss Rich. How have we been deceived! As sure as can be, here he comes.

Sir Will. Does he? Remember I'm to continue unknown. My return to England has not as yet been made public. With what impudence he enters!

Enter LOFTY

Lofty. Let the chariot—let my chariot drive off, I'll visit to his Grace's in a chair. Miss Richland here before me! Punctual, as usual, to the calls of humanity. I'm very sorry, Madam, things of this kind should happen, especially to a man I have shewn every where, and carried amongst us as a particular acquaintance.

Miss Rich. I find, Sir, you have the art of making the misfortunes of others your own.

Lofty. My dear Madam, what can a private man like me do? One man can't do every thing; and then, I do so much in this way every day: Let me see, something considerable might be done for him by subscription; it could not fail if I carried the list. I'll undertake to set down a brace of Dukes, two dozen Lords, and half the lower house, at my own peril.

Sir Will. And after all, its more than probable, Sir, he might reject the offer of such powerful patronage.

Lofty. Then, Madam, what can we do? You know I never make promises. In truth, I once or twice tried to do something with him in the way of business; but, as I often told his uncle, Sir William Honeywood, the man was utterly impracticable.

Sir Will. His uncle! Then that gentleman, I suppose, is a particular friend of yours.

Lofty. Meaning me, Sir?—Yes, Madam, as I often said, my dear Sir William, you are sensible I would do any thing as far as my poor interest goes, to serve your family; but what can be done; there's no procuring first rate places, for ninth rate abilities.

Miss Rich. I have heard of Sir William Honeywood; he's abroad in employment; he confided in your judgment, I suppose.

Lofty. Why, yes, Madam; I believe Sir William has some reason to confide in my judgment; one little reason, perhaps.

Miss Rich. Pray, Sir, what was it?

Lofty. Why, Madam—but let it go no further—it was I procured him his place.

Sir Will. Did you, Sir?

Lofty. Either you or I, Sir.

Miss Rich. This, Mr. Lofty, was very kind, indeed.

Lofty. I did love him, to be sure; he had some amusing qualities; no man was fitter to be toast-master to a club, or had a better head.

Miss Rich. A better head?

Lofty. Ay, at a bottle. To be sure, he was as dull as a choice spirit; but hang it, he was grateful, very grateful; and gratitude hides a multitude of faults.

Sir Will. He might have reason, perhaps. His place is pretty considerable, I'm told.

Lofty. A trifle, a mere trifle, among us men of business. The truth is, he wanted dignity to fill up a greater.

Sir Will. Dignity of person, do you mean, Sir? I'm told he's much about my size and figure, Sir.

Lofty. Ay, tall enough for a marching regiment; but then he wanted a something—a consequence of form—a kind of a—I believe the Lady perceives my meaning.

Miss Rich. O perfectly; you courtiers can do any thing, I see.

Lofty. My dear Madam, all this is but a mere exchange; we do greater things for one another every day. Why, as thus, now: let me suppose you the first lord of the treasury, you have an employment in you that I want; I have a place in me that you want; do me here, do you there: interest of both sides, few words, flat, done and done, and its over.

Sir Will. A thought strikes me. (*Aside.*) Now you mention Sir William Honeywood, Madam; and as he seems, Sir, an acquaintance of yours; you'll be glad to hear he's arrived from Italy; I had it from a friend who knows him as well as he does me, and you may depend on my information.

Lofty. The devil he is! If I had known that, we should not have been quite so well acquainted. (*Aside.*)

Sir Will. He is certainly return'd; and as this gentleman is a friend of yours, he can be of signal service to us, by introducing me to him; there are some papers relative to your affairs, that require dispatch and his inspection.

Miss Rich. This gentleman, Mr. Lofty, is a person employed in my affairs: I know you'll serve us.

Lofty. My dear Madam, I live but to serve you. Sir William shall even wait upon him, if you think proper to command it.

Sir Will. That would be quite unnecessary.

Lofty. Well, we must introduce you then. Call upon me—let me see—ay, in two days.

Sir Will. Now, or the opportunity will be lost for ever.

Lofty. Well, if it must be now, now let it be. But, damn it, that's unfortunate; my lord Grig's curs'd Pensacola business comes on this very hour, and I'm engaged to attend—another time——

Sir Will. A short letter to Sir William will do.

Lofty. You shall have it; yet, in my opinion, a letter is a very bad way of going to work; face to face, that's my way.

Sir Will. The letter, Sir, will do quite as well.

Lofty. Zounds, Sir, do you pretend to direct me; direct me in the business of office? Do you know me, Sir? who am I?

Miss Rich. Dear Mr. Lofty, this request is not so much his as mine; if my commands—but you despise my power.

Lofty. Delicate creature! your commands could even controul a debate at midnight; to a power so constitutional, I am all obedience and tranquility. He shall have a letter; where is my secretary? Dubardieu! And yet, I protest I don't like this way of doing business. I think if I spoke first to Sir William—But you will have it so. [*Exit with Miss* Rich.

SIR WILLIAM, *alone*

Sir Will. Ha, ha, ha! This too is one of my nephew's hopeful associates. O vanity, thou constant deceiver, how do all thy efforts to exalt, serve but to sink us. Thy false colourings, like those employed to heighten beauty, only seem to mend that bloom which they contribute to destroy. I'm not displeased at this interview; exposing this fellow's impudence to the contempt it deserves, may be of use to my design; at least, if he can reflect, it will be of use to himself.

Enter JARVIS

Sir Will. How now, Jarvis, where's your master, my nephew?

Jarvis. At his wits end, I believe; he's scarce gotten out of one scrape, but he's running his head into another.

Sir Will. How so?

Jarvis. The house has but just been cleared of the bailiffs, and now he's again engaging tooth and nail in assisting old Croaker's son to patch up a clandestine match with the young lady that passes in the house for his sister.

Sir Will. Ever busy to serve others.

Jarvis. Ay, any body but himself. The young couple, it seems, are just setting out for Scotland, and he supplies them with money for the journey.

Sir Will. Money! how is he able to supply others, who has scarce any for himself?

Jarvis. Why, there it is; he has no money, that's true; but then, as he never said no to any request in his life, he has given them a bill drawn by a friend of his upon a merchant in the city, which I am to get chang'd; for you must know that I am to go with them to Scotland myself.

Sir Will. How!

Jarvis. It seems the young gentleman is obliged to take a different road from his mistress, as he is to call upon an uncle of his that lives out of the way, in order to prepare a place for their reception, when they return; so they have borrowed me from my master, as the properest person to attend the young lady down.

Sir Will. To the land of matrimony! A pleasant journey, Jarvis.

Jarvis. Ay, but I'm only to have all the fatigues on't.

Sir Will. Well, it may be shorter, and less fatiguing than you imagine. I know but too much of the young lady's family and connexions, whom I have seen abroad. I have also discover'd that Miss Richland is not indifferent to my thoughtless nephew; and will endeavour, tho' I fear, in vain, to establish that connexion. But, come, the letter I wait for must be almost finish'd; I'll let you further into my intentions, in the next room. [*Exeunt.*

END OF THE THIRD ACT

ACT THE FOURTH

SCENE, *Croaker's House*

LOFTY

Lofty. Well, sure the devil's in me of late, for running my head into such defiles, as nothing but a genius like my own could draw me from. I was formerly contented to husband out my places and pensions with some degree of frugality; but, curse it, of late I have given away the whole Court Register in less time than they could print the title page; yet, hang it, why scruple a lie or two to come at a fine girl, when I every day tell a thousand for nothing. Ha! Honeywood here before me. Could Miss Richland have set him at liberty?

Enter HONEYWOOD

Mr. Honeywood, I'm glad to see you abroad again. I find my concurrence was not necessary in your unfortunate affairs. I had put things in a train to do your business; but it is not for me to say what I intended doing.

Honeyw. It was unfortunate indeed, Sir. But what adds to my uneasiness is, that while you seem to be acquainted with my misfortune, I, myself, continue still a stranger to my benefactor.

Lofty. How! not know the friend that served you?

Honeyw. Can't guess at the person.

Lofty. Enquire.

Honeyw. I have, but all I can learn is, that he chuses to remain concealed, and that all enquiry must be fruitless.

Lofty. Must be fruitless?

Honeyw. Absolutely fruitless.

Lofty. Sure of that?

Honeyw. Very sure.

Lofty. Then I'll be damn'd if you shall ever know it from me.

Honeyw. How, Sir!

Lofty. I suppose now, Mr. Honeywood, you think my rent-roll very considerable, and that I have vast sums of money to throw away; I know you do. The world to be sure says such things of me.

Honeyw. The world, by what I learn, is no stranger to your generosity. But where does this tend?

Lofty. To nothing; nothing in the world. The town, to be sure, when it makes such a thing as me the subject of conversation, has asserted, that I never yet patronized a man of merit.

Honeyw. I have heard instances to the contrary, even from yourself.

Lofty. Yes, Honeywood, and there are instances to the contrary that you shall never hear from myself.

Honeyw. Ha, dear Sir, permit me to ask you but one question.

Lofty. Sir, ask me no questions: I say, Sir, ask me no questions; I'll be damn'd, if I answer them!

Honeyw. I will ask no further. My friend, my benefactor, it is, it must be here, that I am indebted for freedom, for honour. Yes, thou worthiest of men, from the beginning I suspected it, but was afraid to return thanks; which, if undeserved, might seem reproaches.

Lofty. I protest I don't understand all this, Mr. Honeywood. You treat me very cavalierly. I do assure you, Sir.—Blood, Sir, can't a man be permitted to enjoy the luxury of his own feelings without all this parade?

Honeyw. Nay, do not attempt to conceal an action that adds to your honour. Your looks, your air, your manner, all confess it.

Lofty. Confess it! Sir. Torture itself, Sir, shall never bring me to confess it. Mr. Honeywood, I have admitted you upon terms of friendship. Don't let us fall out; make me happy, and let this be buried in oblivion. You know I hate ostentation; you know I do. Come, come, Honeywood, you know I always lov'd to be a friend, and not a patron. I beg this may make no kind of distance between us. Come, come, you and I must be more familiar—Indeed we must.

Honeyw. Heavens! Can I ever repay such friendship! Is there any way! Thou best of men, can I ever return the obligation?

Lofty. A bagatelle, a mere bagatelle. But I see your heart is labouring to be grateful. You shall be grateful. It would be cruel to disappoint you.

Honeyw. How! Teach me the manner. Is there any way?

Lofty. From this moment you're mine. Yes, my friend, you shall know it—I'm in love.

Honeyw. And can I assist you?

Lofty. Nobody so well.

Honeyw. In what manner? I'm all impatience.

Lofty. You shall make love for me.

Honeyw. And to whom shall I speak in your favour?

Lofty. To a lady with whom you have great interest, I assure you. Miss Richland.

Honeyw. Miss Richland!

Lofty. Yes, Miss Richland. She has struck the blow up to the hilt, in my bosom, by Jupiter.

Honeyw. Heavens! was ever any thing more unfortunate! It is too much to be endur'd.

Lofty. Unfortunate, indeed! And yet I can endure it, till you have opened the affair to her for me. Between ourselves, I think she likes me. I'm not apt to boast, but I think she does.

Honeyw. Indeed! But do you know the person you apply to?

Lofty. Yes, I know you are her friend and mine: that's enough. To you, therefore, I commit the success of my passion. I'll say no more, let friendship do the rest. I have only to add, that if at any time my little interest can be of service—but, hang it, I'll make no promises—you know my interest is your's at any time. No apologies, my friend, I'll not be answered, it shall be so. [*Exit.*

Honeyw. Open, generous, unsuspecting man! He little thinks that I love her too; and with such an ardent passion!—But then it was ever but a vain and hopeless one; my torment, my persecution! What shall I do! Love, friendship, a hopeless passion, a deserving friend! Love, that has been my tormentor; a friend, that has, perhaps, distress'd himself, to serve me. It shall be so. Yes, I will discard the fondling hope from my bosom, and exert all my influence in his favour. And yet to see her in the possession of another!—Insupportable. But then to betray a generous, trusting friend!—Worse, worse. Yes, I'm resolv'd. Let me but be the instrument of their happiness, and then quit a country, where I must for ever despair of finding my own. [*Exit.*

Enter OLIVIA *and* GARNET, *who carries a Milliner's Box*

Olivia. Dear me, I wish this journey were over. No news of Jarvis yet? I believe the old peevish creature delays purely to vex me.

Garnet. Why, to be sure, Madam, I did hear him say, a little snubbing before marriage, would teach you to bear it the better afterwards.

Olivia. To be gone a full hour, tho' he had only to get a bill changed in the city! How provoking!

Garnet. I'll lay my life, Mr. Leontine, that had twice as much to do, is setting off by this time from his inn; and here you are left behind.

Olivia. Well, let us be prepar'd for his coming, however. Are you sure you have omitted nothing, Garnet?

Garnet. Not a stick, Madam—all's here. Yet I wish you could take the white and silver to be married in. It's the worst luck in the world, in any thing but white. I knew one Bett Stubbs, of our town, that was married in red; and, as sure as eggs is eggs, the bridegroom and she had a miff before morning.

Olivia. No matter. I'm all impatience till we are out of the house.

Garnet. Bless me, Madam, I had almost forgot the wedding-ring!—The sweet little thing—I don't think it would go on my little finger. And what if I put in a gentleman's night-cap, in case of necessity, Madam? But here's Jarvis.

Enter JARVIS

Olivia. O, Jarvis, are you come at last? We have been ready this half hour. Now let's be going. Let us fly!

Jarvis. Aye, to Jericho; for we shall have no going to Scotland this bout, I fancy.

Olivia. How! What's the matter?

Jarvis. Money, money, is the matter, Madam. We have got no money. What the plague do you send me of your fool's errand for? My master's bill upon the city is not worth a rush. Here it is; Mrs. Garnet may pin up her hair with it.

Olivia. Undone! How could Honeywood serve us so! What shall we do? Can't we go without it?

Jarvis. Go to Scotland without money! To Scotland without money! Lord how some people understand geography! We might as well set sail for Patagonia upon a cork jacket

Olivia. Such a disappointment! What a base insincere man

was your master, to serve us in this manner. Is this his good nature?

Jarvis. Nay, don't talk ill of my master, Madam. I won't bear to hear any body talk ill of him but myself.

Garnet. Bless us! now I think on't, Madam, you need not be under any uneasiness: I saw Mr. Leontine receive forty guineas from his father just before he set out, and he can't yet have left the inn. A short letter will reach him there.

Olivia. Well remember'd, Garnet; I'll write immediately. How's this! Bless me, my hand trembles so I can't write a word. Do you write, Garnet; and, upon second thought, it will be better from you.

Garnet. Truly, Madam, I write and indite but poorly. I never was kute in my larning. But I'll do what I can to please you. Let me see. All out of my own head, I suppose?

Olivia. Whatever you please.

Garnet. (*Writing.*) Muster Croaker—Twenty guineas, Madam?

Olivia. Ay, twenty will do.

Garnet. At the bar of the Talbot till call'd for. Expedition—will be blown up—All of a flame—Quick, dispatch—Cupid, the little God of Love—I conclude it, Madam, with Cupid; I love to see a love-letter end like poetry.

Olivia. Well, well, what you please, any thing. But how shall we send it? I can trust none of the servants of this family.

Garnet. Odso, Madam, Mr. Honeywood's butler is in the next room; he's a dear, sweet man; he'll do any thing for me.

Jarvis. He! the dog, he'll certainly commit some blunder. He's drunk and sober ten times a day.

Olivia. No matter. Fly, Garnet; any body we can trust will do. [*Exit* Garnet.] Well, Jarvis, now we can have nothing more to interrupt us. You may take up the things, and carry them on to the inn. Have you no hands, Jarvis?

Jarvis. Soft and fair, young lady. You, that are going to be married, think things can never be done too fast: but we that are old, and know what we are about, must elope methodically, Madam.

Olivia. Well, sure, if my indiscretions were to be done over again——

Jarvis. My life for it you would do them ten times over.

Olivia. Why will you talk so? If you knew how unhappy they make me——

Jarvis. Very unhappy, no doubt: I was once just as unhappy when I was going to be married myself. I'll tell you a story about that——

Olivia. A story! when I'm all impatience to be away. Was there ever such a dilatory creature!——

Jarvis. Well, Madam, if we must march, why we will march; that's all. Tho', odds bobs we have still forgot one thing we should never travel without—a case of good razors, and a box of shaving-powder. But no matter, I believe we shall be pretty well shaved by the way. [*Going.*

Enter GARNET

Garnet. Undone, undone, Madam. Ah, Mr. Jarvis, you said right enough. As sure as death Mr. Honeywood's rogue of a drunken butler drop'd the letter before he went ten yards from the door. There's old Croaker has just pick'd it up, and is this moment reading it to himself in the hall.

Olivia. Unfortunate! We shall be discover'd.

Garnet. No, Madam; don't be uneasy, he can make neither head nor tail of it. To be sure he looks as if he was broke loose from Bedlam about it, but he can't find what it means for all that. O Lud, he is coming this way all in the horrors!

Olivia. Then let us leave the house this instant, for fear he should ask further questions. In the mean time, Garnet, do you write and send off just such another. [*Exeunt.*

Enter CROAKER

Croaker. Death and destruction! Are all the horrors of air, fire and water to be levelled only at me? Am I only to be singled out for gunpowder-plots, combustibles and conflagration! Here it is—An incendiary letter drop'd at my door. *To Muster Croaker, these, with speed.* Ay, ay, plain enough the direction: all in the genuine incendiary spelling, and as cramp as the devil. *With speed.* O, confound your speed. But let me read it once more. (*Reads.*)

Mustar Croakar as sone as yoew see this leve twenty gunnes at the bar of the Talboot tell caled for or yowe and yower experetion will be al blown up. Ah, but too plain. Blood and gunpowder in every line of it. Blown up! murderous dog! All blown up! Heavens! what have I and my poor family done, to be all blown up? (*reads.*) *Our pockets are low, and money we must have.* Ay, there's the reason; they'll blow us up, because they have got low pockets. (*Reads.*) *It is but a short time you have to consider; for if this takes wind, the house will quickly be all of a flame.* Inhuman monsters! blow us up, and then burn us. The earthquake at Lisbon was but a bonfire to it. (*Reads.*) *Make quick dispatch, and so no more at present. But may Cupid, the little God of Love, go with you wherever you go.* The little God of Love! Cupid, the little God of Love go with me! Go you to the devil, you and your little Cupid together; I'm so frightned, I scarce know whether I sit, stand, or go. Perhaps this moment I'm treading on lighted matches, blazing brimstone and barrels of gunpowder. They are preparing to blow me up into the clouds. Murder! We shall be all burnt in our beds; we shall be all burnt in our beds.

Enter Miss RICHLAND

Miss Rich. Lord, Sir, what's the matter?

Croaker. Murder's the matter. We shall be all blown up in our beds before morning.

Miss Rich. I hope not, Sir.

Croaker. What signifies what you hope, Madam, when I have a certificate of it here in my hand. Will nothing alarm my family! Sleeping and eating, sleeping and eating is the only work from morning till night in my house. My insensible crew could sleep, tho' rock'd by an earthquake; and fry beef steaks at a volcano.

Miss Rich. But, Sir, you have alarmed them so often already, we have nothing but earthquakes, famines, plagues and mad dogs from year's end to year's end. You remember, Sir, it is not above a month ago, you assur'd us of a conspiracy among the bakers, to poison us in our bread; and so kept the whole family a week upon potatoes.

Croaker. And potatoes were too good for them. But why do I stand talking here with a girl, when I should be facing the enemy without? Here, John, Nicodemus, search the house. Look into the cellars, to see if there be any combustibles below; and above, in the apartments, that no matches be thrown in at the windows. Let all the fires be put out, and let the engine be drawn out in the yard, to play upon the house in case of necessity. [*Exit.*

Miss RICHLAND *alone*

Miss Rich. What can he mean by all this? Yet, why should I enquire, when he alarms us in this manner almost every day! But Honeywood has desired an interview with me in private. What can he mean; or, rather, what means this palpitation at his approach! It is the first time he ever shewed any thing in his conduct that seem'd particular. Sure he cannot mean to——but he's here.

Enter HONEYWOOD

Honeyw. I presum'd to solicit this interview, Madam, before I left town, to be permitted—

Miss Rich. Indeed! Leaving town, Sir?—

Honeyw. Yes, Madam; perhaps the kingdom. I have presumed, I say, to desire the favour of this interview—in order to disclose something which our long friendship prompts. And yet my fears—

Miss Rich. His fears! What are his fears to mine! (*Aside.*)

We have indeed been long acquainted, Sir; very long. If I remember, our first meeting was at the French Ambassador's. —Do you recollect how you were pleas'd to rally me upon my complexion there?

Honeyw. Perfectly, Madam; I presum'd to reprove you for painting: but your warmer blushes soon convinc'd the company that the colouring was all from nature.

Miss Rich. And yet you only meant it, in your good natur'd way, to make me pay a compliment to myself. In the same manner you danc'd that night with the most aukward woman in company, because you saw nobody else would take her out.

Honeyw. Yes; and was rewarded the next night, by dancing with the finest woman in company, whom every body wish'd to take out.

Miss Rich. Well, Sir, if you thought so then, I fear your judgment has since corrected the errors of a first impression. We generally shew to most advantage at first. Our sex are like poor tradesmen, that put all their best goods to be seen at the windows.

Honeyw. The first impression, Madam, did indeed deceive me. I expected to find a woman with all the faults of conscious flattered beauty. I expected to find her vain and insolent. But every day has since taught me that it is possible to possess sense without pride, and beauty without affectation.

Miss Rich. This, Sir, is a style unusual with Mr. Honeywood; and I shall be glad to know why he thus attempts to encrease that vanity, which his own lessons hath taught me to despise.

Honeyw. I ask pardon, Madam. Yet, from our long friendship, I presumed I might have some right to offer, without offence, what you may refuse without offending.

Miss Rich. Sir! I beg you'd reflect; tho', I fear, I shall scarce have any power to refuse a request of yours; yet, you may be precipitate: consider, Sir.

Honeyw. I own my rashness; but, as I plead the cause of friendship, of one who loves—Don't be alarmed, Madam—Who loves you with the most ardent passion; whose whole happiness is placed in you—

Miss Rich. I fear, Sir, I shall never find whom you mean, by this description of him.

Honeyw. Ah, Madam, it but too plainly points him out; tho' he should be too humble himself to urge his pretensions, or you too modest to understand them.

Miss Rich. Well; it would be affectation any longer to pretend ignorance; and, I will own, Sir, I have long been prejudiced in his favour. It was but natural to wish to make his heart mine, as he seem'd himself ignorant of its value.

Honeyw. I see she always lov'd him! (*aside.*) I find, Madam, you're already sensible of his worth, his passion. How happy is my friend, to be the favourite of one with such sense to distinguish merit, and such beauty to reward it.

Miss Rich. Your friend! Sir. What friend?

Honeyw. My best friend—My friend Mr. Lofty, Madam.

Miss Rich. He, Sir!

Honeyw. Yes, he, Madam. He is, indeed, what your warmest wishes might have form'd him. And to his other qualities, he adds that of the most passionate regard for you.

Miss Rich. Amazement!—No more of this, I beg you, Sir.

Honeyw. I see your confusion, Madam, and know how to interpret it. And since I so plainly read the language of your heart, shall I make my friend happy, by communicating your sentiments?

Miss Rich. By no means.

Honeyw. Excuse me; I must; I know you desire it.

Miss Rich. Mr. Honeywood, let me tell you, that you wrong my sentiments and yourself. When I first applied to your friendship, I expected advice and assistance; but now, Sir, I see that it is vain to expect happiness from him, who has been so bad an œconomist of his own; and that I must disclaim his friendship, who ceases to be a friend to himself. [*Exit.*

Honeyw. How is this! she has confessed she lov'd him, and yet she seemed to part in displeasure. Can I have done any thing to reproach myself with? No; I believe not; yet, after all, these things should not be done by a third person; I should have spared her confusion. My friendship carried me a little too far.

Enter CROAKER, *with the Letter in his Hand, and* *Mrs.* CROAKER

Mrs. Croaker. Ha, ha, ha! And so, my dear, it's your supreme wish that I should be quite wretched upon this occasion? Ha, ha.

Croaker. (*Mimicking*) Ha, ha, ha! and so my dear, it's your supreme pleasure to give me no better consolation?

Mrs. Croaker. Positively, my dear, what is this incendiary stuff and trumpery to me? Our house may travel thro' the air like the house of Loretto,[1] for ought I care, if I'm to be miserable in it.

Croaker. Would to Heaven it were converted into an house of correction for your benefit. Have we not every thing to alarm us? Perhaps, this very moment the tragedy is beginning.

Mrs. Croaker. Then let us reserve our distress till the rising of the curtain, or give them the money they want, and have done with them.

Croaker. Give them my money!—And pray, what right have they to my money?

Mrs. Croaker. And pray, what right then have you to my good humour?

Croaker. And so your good humour advises me to part with my money? Why then, to tell your good humour a piece of

[1] [The legendary Santa Casa, or house of the Virgin Mary at Nazareth, which, at the close of the thirteenth century, was miraculously translated to several towns before finally settling at Loretto near Ancona.]

my mind, I'd sooner part with my wife. Here's Mr. Honeywood, see what he'll say to it. My dear Honeywood, look at this incendiary letter dropped at my door. It will freeze you with terror; and yet lovey here can read it—can read it, and laugh.

Mrs. Croaker. Yes, and so will Mr. Honeywood.

Croaker. If he does, I'll suffer to be hanged the next minute in the rogue's place, that's all.

Mrs. Croaker. Speak, Mr. Honeywood; is there any thing more foolish than my husband's fright upon this occasion?

Honeyw. It would not become me to decide, Madam; but doubtless, the greatness of his terrors now, will but invite them to renew their villainy another time.

Mrs. Croaker. I told you, he'd be of my opinion.

Croaker. How, Sir! do you maintain that I should lie down under such an injury, and shew, neither by my tears, or complaints, that I have something of the spirit of a man in me?

Honeyw. Pardon me, Sir. You ought to make the loudest complaints, if you desire redress. The surest way to have redress, is to be earnest in the pursuit of it.

Croaker. Ay, whose opinion is he of now?

Mrs. Croaker. But don't you think that laughing off our fears is the best way?

Honeyw. What is the best, Madam, few can say; but I'll maintain it to be a very wise way.

Croaker. But we're talking of the best. Surely the best way is to face the enemy in the field, and not wait till he plunders us in our very bed-chamber.

Honeyw. Why, Sir, as to the best, that—that's a very wise way too.

Mrs. Croaker. But can any thing be more absurd, than to double our distresses by our apprehensions, and put it in the power of every low fellow, that can scrawl ten words of wretched spelling, to torment us?

Honeyw. Without doubt, nothing more absurd.

Croaker. How! would it not be more absurd to despise the rattle till we are bit by the snake?

Honeyw. Without doubt, perfectly absurd.

Croaker. Then you are of my opinion?

Honeyw. Entirely.

Mrs. Croaker. And you reject mine?

Honeyw. Heavens forbid, Madam. No, sure no reasoning can be more just than yours. We ought certainly to despise malice if we cannot oppose it, and not make the incendiary's pen as fatal to our repose as the highwayman's pistol.

Mrs. Croaker. O! then you think I'm quite right?

Honeyw. Perfectly right.

Croaker. A plague of plagues, we can't be both right. I ought to be sorry, or I ought to be glad. My hat must be on my head, or my hat must be off.

Mrs. Croaker. Certainly, in two opposite opinions, if one be perfectly reasonable, the other can't be perfectly right.

Honeyw. And why may not both be right, Madam: Mr. Croaker in earnestly seeking redress, and you in waiting the event with good humour? Pray let me see the letter again. I have it. This letter requires twenty guineas to be left at the bar of the Talbot inn. If it be indeed an incendiary letter, what if you and I, Sir, go there; and, when the writer comes to be paid his expected booty, seize him?

Croaker. My dear friend, its the very thing; the very thing. While I walk by the door, you shall plant yourself in ambush near the bar; burst out upon the miscreant like a masqued battery; extort a confession at once, and so hang him up by surprise.

Honeyw. Yes; but I would not chuse to exercise too much severity. It is my maxim, Sir, that crimes generally punish themselves.

Croaker. Well, but we may upbraid him a little, I suppose? (*Ironically.*)

Honeyw. Ay, but not punish him too rigidly.

Croaker. Well, well, leave that to my own benevolence.

Honeyw. Well, I do: but remember that universal benevolence is the first law of nature.

[*Exeunt* Honeywood *and Mrs.* Croaker.

Croaker. Yes; and my universal benevolence will hang the dog, if he had as many necks as a hydra.

END OF THE FOURTH ACT

ACT THE FIFTH

SCENE, *An Inn*

Enter OLIVIA, JARVIS

Olivia. Well, we have got safe to the inn, however. Now, if the post-chaise were ready—

Jarvis. The horses are just finishing their oats; and, as they are not going to be married, they chuse to take their own time.

Olivia. You are for ever giving wrong motives to my impatience.

Jarvis. Be as impatient as you will, the horses must take their own time; besides, you don't consider, we have got no answer from our fellow traveller yet. If we hear nothing from Mr. Leontine, we have only one way left us.

Olivia. What way?

Jarvis. The way home again.

Olivia. Not so. I have made a resolution to go, and nothing shall induce me to break it.

Jarvis. Ay; resolutions are well kept when they jump with inclination. However, I'll go hasten things without. And I'll call too at the bar to see if any thing should be left for us there. Don't be in such a plaguy hurry, Madam, and we shall go the faster, I promise you. [*Exit* Jarvis.

Enter LANDLADY

Landlady. What! Solomon; why don't you move? Pipes and tobacco for the Lamb there.—Will no body answer? To the Dolphin; quick. The Angel has been outrageous this half hour. Did your ladyship call, Madam?

Olivia. No, Madam.

Landlady. I find, as you're for Scotland, Madam—But, that's no business of mine; married, or not married, I ask no questions. To be sure, we had a sweet little couple set off from this two days ago for the same place. The Gentleman, for a taylor, was, to be sure, as fine a spoken taylor, as ever blew froth from a full pot. And the young Lady so bashful, it was near half an hour before we could get her to finish a pint of rasberry between us.

Olivia. But this Gentleman and I are not going to be married, I assure you.

Landlady. May be not. That's no business of mine; for certain, Scotch marriages seldom turn out. There was, of my own knowledge, Miss Macfag, that married her father's footman.—Alack-a-day, she and her husband soon parted, and now keep separate cellars in Hedge-Lane.

Olivia. A very pretty picture of what lies before me. [*Aside.*

Enter LEONTINE

Leont. My dear Olivia, my anxiety till you were out of danger, was too great to be resisted. I could not help coming to see you set out, tho' it exposes us to a discovery.

Olivia. May every thing you do prove as fortunate. Indeed, Leontine, we have been most cruelly disappointed. Mr. Honeywood's bill upon the city, has, it seems, been protested, and we have been utterly at a loss how to proceed.

Leont. How! An offer of his own too. Sure, he could not mean to deceive us.

Olivia. Depend upon his sincerity; he only mistook the

desire for the power of serving us. But let us think no more of it. I believe the post-chaise is ready by this.

Landlady. Not quite yet: and, begging your Ladyship's pardon, I don't think your Ladyship quite ready for the post-chaise. The north road is a cold place, Madam. I have a drop in the house of as pretty rasberry as ever was tipt over tongue. Just a thimble full to keep the wind off your stomach. To be sure, the last couple we had here, they said it was a perfect nosegay. Ecod, I sent them both away as good natur'd—Up went the blinds, round went the wheels, and drive away post-boy, was the word.

Enter CROAKER

Croaker. Well, while my friend Honeywood is upon the post of danger at the bar, it must be my business to have an eye about me here. I think I know an incendiary's look; for, wherever the devil makes a purchase, he never fails to set his mark. Ha! who have we here? My son and daughter! What can they be doing here!

Landlady. I tell you, Madam, it will do you good; I think I know by this time what's good for the north road. It's a raw night, Madam—Sir—

Leont. Not a drop more, good Madam. I should now take it as a greater favour, if you hasten the horses, for I am afraid to be seen myself.

Landlady. That shall be done. Wha, Solomon! are you all dead there? Wha, Solomon, I say. [*Exit bawling.*

Olivia. Well; I dread, lest an expedition begun in fear, should end in repentance.—Every moment we stay increases our danger, and adds to my apprehensions.

Leont. There's no danger, trust me, my dear; there can be none: if Honeywood has acted with honour, and kept my father, as he promised, in employment, till we are out of danger, nothing can interrupt our journey.

Olivia. I have no doubt of Mr. Honeywood's sincerity,

and even his desires to serve us. My fears are from your father's suspicions. A mind so disposed to be alarmed without a cause, will be but too ready when there's a reason.

Leont. Why, let him, when we are out of his power. But, believe me, Olivia, you have no great reason to dread his resentment. His repining temper, as it does no manner of injury to himself, so will it never do harm to others. He only frets to keep himself employed, and scolds for his private amusement.

Olivia. I don't know that; but, I'm sure, on some occasions, it makes him look most shockingly.

Croaker. (*Discovering himself*) How does he look now?—How does he look now?

Olivia. Ah!

Leont. Undone!

Croaker. How do I look now? Sir, I am your very humble servant. Madam, I am your's. What, you are going off, are you? Then, first, if you please, take a word or two from me with you before you go. Tell me first where you are going? and when you have told me that, perhaps, I shall know as little as I did before.

Leont. If that be so, our answer might but increase your displeasure, without adding to your information.

Croaker. I want no information from you, puppy: and you, too, good Madam, what answer have you got? Eh (*A cry without, stop him*) I think I heard a noise. My friend, Honeywood, without—has he seized the incendiary? Ah, no, for now I hear no more on't.

Leont. Honeywood, without! Then, Sir, it was Mr. Honeywood that directed you hither.

Croaker. No, sir, it was Mr. Honeywood conducted me hither.

Leont. Is it possible?

Croaker. Possible! Why, he's in the house now, Sir. More anxious about me, than my own son, Sir.

Leont. Then, Sir, he's a villain!

Croaker. How, sirrah! a villain, because he takes most care of your father? I'll not bear it. I tell you I'll not bear it. Honeywood is a friend to the family, and I'll have him treated as such.

Leont. I shall study to repay his friendship as it deserves.

Croaker. Ah, rogue, if you knew how earnestly he entered into my griefs, and pointed out the means to detect them, you would love him as I do. (*A cry without, stop him*) Fire and fury! they have seized the incendiary: they have the villain, the incendiary in view. Stop him, stop an incendiary, a murderer; stop him. [*Exit.*

Olivia. Oh, my terrors! What can this new tumult mean?

Leont. Some new mark, I suppose, of Mr. Honeywood's sincerity. But we shall have satisfaction: he shall give me instant satisfaction.

Olivia. It must not be, my Leontine, if you value my esteem, or my happiness. Whatever be our fate, let us not add guilt to our misfortunes—Consider that our innocence will shortly be all we have left us. You must forgive him.

Leont. Forgive him! Has he not in every instance betrayed us? Forced me to borrow money from him, which appears a mere trick to delay us: promised to keep my father engaged till we were out of danger, and here brought him to the very scene of our escape?

Olivia. Don't be precipitate. We may yet be mistaken.

Enter POSTBOY, *dragging in* JARVIS: HONEYWOOD *entering soon after*

Postboy. Ay, master, we have him fast enough. Here is the incendiary dog. I'm entitled to the reward; I'll take my oath I saw him ask for the money at the bar, and then run for it.

Honeyw. Come, bring him along. Let us see him. Let him learn to blush for his crimes (*discovering his mistake*). Death! what's here! Jarvis, Leontine, Olivia! What can all this mean?

Jarvis. Why, I'll tell you what it means: that I was an old fool, and that you are my master—that's all.

Honeyw. Confusion.

Leont. Yes, Sir, I find you have kept your word with me. After such baseness, I wonder how you can venture to see the man you have injured.

Honeyw. My dear Leontine, by my life, my honour—

Leont. Peace, peace, for shame; and do not continue to aggravate baseness by hypocrisy. I know you Sir, I know you.

Honeyw. Why, wont you hear me! By all that's just, I knew not——

Leont. Hear you, Sir! to what purpose? I now see through all your low arts; your ever complying with every opinion; your never refusing any request; your friendship as common as a prostitute's favours, and as fallacious; all these, Sir, have long been contemptible to the world, and are now perfectly so to me.

Honeyw. Ha! contemptible to the world! That reaches me. (*Aside.*)

Leont. All the seeming sincerity of your professions I now find were only allurements to betray; and all your seeming regret for their consequences, only calculated to cover the cowardice of your heart. Draw, villain!

Enter CROAKER *out of Breath*

Croaker. Where is the villain? Where is the incendiary? (*seizing the post-boy.*) Hold him fast, the dog; he has the gallows in his face. Come, you dog, confess; confess all, and hang yourself.

Post-Boy. Zounds! Master, what do you throttle me for?

Croaker. (*Beating him.*) Dog, do you resist; do you resist?

Post-Boy. Zounds! Master, I'm not he; there's the man that we thought was the rogue, and turns out to be one of the company.

Croaker. How!

Honeyw. Mr. Croaker, we have all been under a strange

mistake here; I find there is nobody guilty; it was all an error; entirely an error of our own.

Croaker. And I say, Sir, that you're in an error: for there's guilt and double guilt, a plot, a damn'd jesuitical pestilential plot, and I must have proof of it.

Honeyw. Do but hear me.

Croaker. What, you intend to bring 'em off, I suppose; I'll hear nothing.

Honeyw. Madam, you seem at least calm enough to hear reason.

Olivia. Excuse me.

Honeyw. Good Jarvis, let me then explain it to you.

Jarvis. What signifies explanations, when the thing is done?

Honeyw. Will nobody hear me? Was there ever such a set, so blinded by passion and prejudice! (*To the Post-Boy.*) My good friend, I believe you'll be surprized when I assure you——

Post-Boy. Sure me nothing—I'm sure of nothing but a good beating.

Croaker. Come then, you, Madam, if you ever hope for any favour or forgiveness, tell me sincerely all you know of this affair.

Olivia. Unhappily, Sir, I'm but too much the cause of your suspicions: you see before you, Sir, one that with false pretences has stept into your family to betray it: not your daughter——

Croaker. Not my daughter!

Olivia. Not your daughter—but a mean deceiver—who—support me, I cannot——

Honeyw. Help, she's going, give her air.

Croaker. Ay, ay, take the young woman to the air; I would not hurt a hair of her head, whose ever daughter she may be—not so bad as that neither. [*Exeunt all but* Croaker.

Croaker. Yes, yes, all's out; I now see the whole affair; my son is either married, or going to be so, to this lady, whom he imposed upon me as his sister. Ay, certainly so; and yet I don't find it afflicts me so much as one might think. There's the advantage of fretting away our misfortunes beforehand, we never feel them when they come.

Enter Miss RICHLAND *and* SIR WILLIAM

Sir Will. But how do you know, Madam, that my nephew intends setting off from this place?

Miss Rich. My maid assured me he was come to this inn, and my own knowledge of his intending to leave the kingdom, suggested the rest. But what do I see, my guardian here before us! Who, my dear Sir, could have expected meeting you here; to what accident do we owe this pleasure?

Croaker. To a fool, I believe.

Miss Rich. But to what purpose did you come?

Croaker. To play the fool.

Miss Rich. But with whom?

Croaker. With greater fools than myself.

Miss Rich. Explain.

Croaker. Why, Mr. Honeywood brought me here, to do nothing now I am here; and my son is going to be married to I don't know who that is here; so now you are as wise as I am.

Miss Rich. Married! to whom, Sir?

Croaker. To Olivia; my daughter, as I took her to be; but who the devil she is, or whose daughter she is, I know no more than the man in the moon.

Sir Will. Then, Sir, I can inform you; and, tho' a stranger, yet you shall find me a friend to your family: it will be enough at present, to assure you, that, both in point of birth and fortune, the young lady is at least your son's equal. Being left by her father, Sir James Woodville—

Croaker. Sir James Woodville! What, of the West?

Sir Will. Being left by him, I say, to the care of a mercenary wretch, whose only aim was to secure her fortune to himself, she was sent into France, under pretence of education;

and there every art was tried to fix her for life in a convent, contrary to her inclinations. Of this I was informed upon my arrival in Paris; and, as I had been once her father's friend, I did all in my power to frustrate her guardian's base intentions. I had even meditated to rescue her from his authority, when your son stept in with more pleasing violence, gave her liberty, and you a daughter.

Croaker. But I intend to have a daughter of my own chusing, Sir. A young lady, Sir, whose fortune, by my interest with those that have interest, will be double what my son has a right to expect. Do you know Mr. Lofty, Sir?

Sir Will. Yes, Sir; and know that you are deceived in him. But step this way, and I'll convince you.

[Croaker *and Sir* William *seem to confer.*

Enter HONEYWOOD

Honeyw. Obstinate man, still to persist in his outrage! Insulted by him, despis'd by all, I now begin to grow contemptible, even to myself. How have I sunk by too great an assiduity to please! How have I overtax'd all my abilities, lest the approbation of a single fool should escape me! But all is now over; I have survived my reputation, my fortune, my friendships, and nothing remains henceforward for me but solitude and repentance.

Miss Rich. Is it true, Mr. Honeywood, that you are setting off, without taking leave of your friends? The report is, that you are quitting England. Can it be?

Honeyw. Yes, Madam; and tho' I am so unhappy as to have fallen under your displeasure, yet, thank Heaven, I leave you to happiness; to one who loves you, and deserves your love; to one who has power to procure you affluence, and generosity to improve your enjoyment of it.

Miss Rich. And are you sure, Sir, that the gentleman you mean is what you describe him?

Honeyw. I have the best assurances of it, his serving me.

He does indeed deserve the highest happiness, and that is in your power to confer. As for me, weak and wavering as I have been, obliged by all, and incapable of serving any, what happiness can I find but in solitude? What hope but in being forgotten?

Miss Rich. A thousand! to live among friends that esteem you, whose happiness it will be to be permitted to oblige you.

Honeyw. No, Madam; my resolution is fix'd. Inferiority among strangers is easy; but among those that once were equals, insupportable. Nay, to shew you how far my resolution can go, I can now speak with calmness of my former follies, my vanity, my dissipation, my weakness. I will even confess, that, among the number of my other presumptions, I had the insolence to think of loving you. Yes, Madam, while I was pleading the passion of another, my heart was tortur'd with its own. But it is over, it was unworthy our friendship, and let it be forgotten.

Miss Rich. You amaze me!

Honeyw. But you'll forgive it, I know you will; since the confession should not have come from me even now, but to convince you of the sincerity of my intention of—never mentioning it more. [*Going.*

Miss Rich. Stay, Sir, one moment—Ha! he here—

Enter LOFTY

Lofty. Is the coast clear? None but friends. I have followed you here with a trifling piece of intelligence: but it goes no farther, things are not yet ripe for a discovery. I have spirits working at a certain board; your affair at the Treasury will be done in less than—a thousand years. Mum!

Miss Rich. Sooner, Sir, I should hope.

Lofty. Why, yes, I believe it may, if it falls into proper hands, that know where to push and where to parry; that know how the land lies—eh, Honeywood?

Miss Rich. It is fallen into yours.

Lofty. Well, to keep you no longer in suspense, your thing is done. It is done, I say—that's all. I have just had assurances from Lord Neverout, that the claim has been examined, and found admissible. *Quietus* is the word, Madam.

Honeyw. But how! his Lordship has been at Newmarket these ten days.

Lofty. Indeed! Then Sir Gilbert Goose must have been most damnably mistaken. I had it of him.

Miss Rich. He! why Sir Gilbert and his family have been in the country this month.

Lofty. This month! It must certainly be so—Sir Gilbert's letter did come to me from Newmarket, so that he must have met his Lordship there; and so it came about. I have his letter about me, I'll read it to you. (*Taking out a large bundle*.) That's from Paoli of Corsica,[1] that from the Marquis of Squilachi.[2]—Have you a mind to see a letter from Count Poniatowski, now King of Poland—Honest Pon—— [*Searching*. O, Sir, what are you here too? I'll tell you what, honest friend, if you have not absolutely delivered my letter to Sir William Honeywood, you may return it. The thing will do without him.

Sir Will. Sir, I have delivered it, and must inform you it was received with the most mortifying contempt.

Croaker. Contempt! Mr. Lofty, what can that mean?

Lofty. Let him go on, let him go on, I say. You'll find it come to something presently.

Sir Will. Yes, Sir, I believe you'll be amazed, if, after waiting some time in the anti-chamber, after being surveyed with insolent curiosity by the passing servants, I was at last assured, that Sir William Honeywood knew no such person, and I must certainly have been imposed upon.

[1] [General Pascal Paoli, the Corsican patriot. Boswell's *An Account of Corsica and Memoirs of Pascal Paoli* was published ten days after *The Good Natur'd Man*.]

[2] [Leopoldo de Gregorio, marquis of Villesanto and Squillace, a Sicilian by birth, who was then Prime Minister at Madrid.]

Lofty. Good; let me die, very good. Ha! ha! ha!

Croaker. Now, for my life, I can't find out half the goodness of it.

Lofty. You can't? Ha! ha!

Croaker. No, for the soul of me; I think it was as confounded a bad answer as ever was sent from one private gentleman to another.

Lofty. And so you can't find out the force of the message? Why I was in the house at that very time. Ha! ha! It was I that sent that very answer to my own letter. Ha! ha!

Croaker. Indeed! How! why!

Lofty. In one word, things between Sir William and me must be behind the curtain. A party has many eyes. He sides with Lord Buzzard, I side with Sir Gilbert Goose. So that unriddles the mystery.

Croaker. And so it does indeed, and all my suspicions are over.

Lofty. Your suspicions! What then, you have been suspecting, you have been suspecting, have you? Mr. Croaker, you and I were friends, we are friends no longer. Never talk to me. It's over; I say, it's over.

Croaker. As I hope for your favour, I did not mean to offend. It escaped me. Don't be discomposed.

Lofty. Zounds, Sir, but I am discomposed, and will be discomposed. To be treated thus! Who am I! Was it for this I have been dreaded both by inns and outs! Have I been libelled in the Gazetteer, and praised in the St. James's; have I been chaired at Wildman's, and a speaker at Merchant Taylor's Hall; have I had my hand to addresses, and my head in the print-shops, and talk to me of suspects!

Croaker. My dear Sir, be pacified. What can you have but asking pardon?

Lofty. Sir, I will not be pacified—Suspects! Who am I! To be used thus, have I paid court to men in favour to serve my friends, the Lords of the Treasury, Sir William Honeywood, and the rest of the gang, and talk to me of suspects! Who am I, I say, who am I!

Sir Will. Since, Sir, you're so pressing for an answer, I'll tell you who you are. A gentleman, as well acquainted with politics, as with men in power: as well acquainted with persons of fashion, as with modesty; with Lords of the Treasury, as with truth; and with all, as you are with Sir William Honeywood. I am Sir William Honeywood.

[*Discovering his ensigns of the Bath.*

Croaker. Sir William Honeywood!

Honeyw. Astonishment! my uncle! [*Aside.*

Lofty. So then my confounded genius has been all this time only leading me up to the garret, in order to fling me out of the window.

Croaker. What, Mr. Importance, and are these your works? Suspect you! You, who have been dreaded by the inns and outs: you, who have had your hand to addresses, and your head stuck up in print-shops. If you were served right, you should have your head stuck up in the pillory.

Lofty. Ay, stick it where you will, for, by the Lord, it cuts but a very poor figure where it sticks at present.

Sir Will. Well, Mr. Croaker, I hope you now see how incapable this gentleman is of serving you, and how little Miss Richland has to expect from his influence.

Croaker. Ay, Sir, too well I see it, and I can't but say I have had some boding of it these ten days. So I'm resolved, since my son has placed his affections on a lady of moderate fortune, to be satisfied with his choice, and not run the hazard of another Mr. Lofty, in helping him to a better.

Sir Will. I approve your resolution, and here they come, to receive a confirmation of your pardon and consent.

Enter Mrs. CROAKER, JARVIS, LEONTINE, OLIVIA

Mrs. Croaker. Where's my husband! Come, come, lovey, you must forgive them. Jarvis here has been to tell me the whole affair: and, I say, you must forgive them. Our own was a stolen match, you know, my dear; and we never had any reason to repent of it.

Croaker. I wish we could both say so: however, this gentleman, Sir William Honeywood, has been beforehand with you, in obtaining their pardon. So, if the two poor fools have a mind to marry, I think we can tack them together without crossing the Tweed for it. [*Joining their hands.*

Leont. How blest, and unexpected! What, what can we say to such goodness! But our future obedience shall be the best reply. And, as for this gentleman, to whom we owe—

Sir Will. Excuse me, Sir, if I interrupt your thanks, as I have here an interest that calls me. (*Turning to Honeywood.*) Yes, Sir, you are surprised to see me; and I own that a desire of correcting your follies led me hither. I saw, with indignation, the errors of a mind that only sought applause from others; that easiness of disposition, which, tho' inclin'd to the right, had not courage to condemn the wrong. I saw with regret those splendid errors, that still took name from some neighbouring duty. Your charity, that was but injustice; your benevolence, that was but weakness; and your friendship but credulity. I saw, with regret, great talents and extensive learning, only employed to add sprightliness to error, and encrease your perplexities. I saw your mind with a thousand natural charms: but the greatness of its beauty served only to heighten my pity for its prostitution.

Honeyw. Cease to upbraid me, Sir; I have for some time but too strongly felt the justice of your reproaches. But there is one way still left me. Yes, Sir, I have determined, this very hour, to quit forever a place where I have made myself the voluntary slave of all; and to seek among strangers that fortitude which may give strength to the mind, and marshal all its dissipated virtues. Yet, ere I depart, permit me to solicit favour for this gentleman; who, notwithstanding what has happened, has laid me under the most signal obligations. Mr. Lofty—

Lofty. Mr. Honeywood, I'm resolv'd upon a reformation, as well as you. I now begin to find, that the man who first invented the art of speaking truth was a much cunninger fellow than I thought him. And to prove that I design to speak truth for the future, I must now assure you, that you owe your late enlargement to another; as, upon my soul, I had no hand in the matter. So now, if any of the company has a mind for preferment, he may take my place. I'm determined to resign. [*Exit*.

Honeyw. How have I been deceived!

Sir Will. No, Sir, you have been obliged to a kinder, fairer friend for that favour. To Miss Richland. Would she complete our joy, and make the man she has honoured by her friendship happy in her love, I should then forget all, and be as blest as the welfare of my dearest kinsman can make me.

Miss Rich. After what is past, it would be but affectation to pretend to indifference. Yes, I will own an attachment, which I find, was more than friendship. And if my intreaties cannot alter his resolution to quit the country, I will even try, if my hand has not power to detain him. [*Giving her hand*.

Honeyw. Heavens! how can I have deserved all this? How express my happiness, my gratitude! A moment like this overpays an age of apprehension!

Croaker. Well, now I see content in every face; but Heaven send we be all better this day three months.

Sir Will. Henceforth, nephew, learn to respect yourself. He who seeks only for applause from without, has all his happiness in another's keeping.

Honeyw. Yes, Sir, I now too plainly perceive my errors. My vanity, in attempting to please all, by fearing to offend any. My meanness in approving folly, lest fools should disapprove. Henceforth, therefore, it shall be my study to reserve my pity for real distress; my friendship for true merit, and my love for her, who first taught me what it is to be happy.

EPILOGUE*

Spoken by Mrs. BULKLEY

As puffing quacks some caitiff wretch procure
To swear the pill, or drop, has wrought a cure;
Thus on the stage, our play-wrights still depend
For Epilogues and Prologues on some friend,
Who knows each art of coaxing up the town,
And make full many a bitter pill go down.
Conscious of this, our bard has gone about,
And teaz'd each rhyming friend to help him out.
An Epilogue, things can't go on without it;
It could not fail, wou'd you but set about it.
Young man, cries one (a bard laid up in clover)
Alas, young man, my writing days are over;
Let boys play tricks, and kick the straw, not I;
Your brother Doctor there, perhaps, may try.
What I! dear Sir, the Doctor interposes;
What, plant my thistle, Sir, among his roses!
No, no, I've other contests to maintain;
To-night I head our troops at Warwick-Lane.[1]
Go, ask your manager—Who, me! Your pardon;
Those things are not our fort at Covent-Garden.
Our Author's friends, thus plac'd at happy distance,
Give him good words indeed, but no assistance.
As some unhappy wight, at some new play,
At the Pit door stands elbowing away,

* The Author, in expectation of an Epilogue from a Friend at Oxford, deferred writing one himself until the very last hour. What is here offered, owes all its success to the graceful manner of the Actress who spoke it.

[1] [There was a dispute between the Licentiates and the Fellows of The Royal College of Physicians in Warwick Lane because some of the Licentiates were excluded from Fellowships. This couplet and the next but one were omitted when the Epilogue was published in the *Public Advertiser* of 3 February, 1768.]

While oft, with many a smile, and many a shrug,
He eyes the centre, where his friends sit snug,
His simpering friends, with pleasure in their eyes,
Sink as he sinks, and as he rises rise:
He nods, they nod; he cringes, they grimace;
But not a soul will budge to give him place.
Since then, unhelp'd, our bard must now conform
To 'bide the pelting of this pittiless storm,[1]
Blame where you must, be candid where you can,
And be each critick the Good-natur'd Man.

[1] [*King Lear*, 3. 4. 32.]

SHE STOOPS TO CONQUER

OR THE MISTAKES OF A NIGHT

In September, 1771 Goldsmith wrote to Bennet Langton,

> Since I had the pleasure of seeing you last I have been almost wholly in the country at a farmer's house quite alone trying to write a Comedy. It is now finished but when or how it will be acted, or whether it will be acted at all are questions I cannot resolve . . . . Every soul is visiting about and merry but myself. And that is hard too as I have been trying these three months to do something to make people laugh. There have I been strolling about the hedges studying jests with a most tragical countenance.

Goldsmith found it no easier to get his second play acted than his first. Eventually Colman was prevailed upon to produce it, but only after what Johnson called "much solicitation, nay, a kind of force." Even so, there were many difficulties to be overcome. The play still had no satisfactory title. Goldsmith had been able to think of nothing better than *The Mistakes of a Night*, which had little to distinguish it from a score of other comedies; and all his friends were in labour to find another. Colman and most of the actors shared the current prejudice against "low" humour; several of the actors threw up their parts; and there is reason to think that Goldsmith was obliged to revise the play considerably. He sent it to Joseph Cradock who wrote an epilogue to be spoken in the character of Tony Lumpkin. The original version of this epilogue included several references which indicate that Tony Lumpkin and his companions of the *Three Pigeons* had once been much more robustious. Cradock says that he struck out some of these "low" passages in Goldsmith's manuscript before returning it to him.

Cradock's epilogue could not be used, and Goldsmith had difficulty getting another. Murphy sent a sketch of an epilogue to be sung by Miss Catley, who was originally cast as Miss Neville. But Mrs. Bulkley objected and threatened to throw up her part unless she were allowed to speak the epilogue. This gave Goldsmith the idea of writing the "quarrelling epilogue" printed on page 656, but Miss Catley refused. He then wrote the epilogue on page 659, which Colman thought too bad to be spoken, and he had to try yet again. He probably did not send this final epilogue off to Colman until late on the day before the first night of the play. With it he sent an additional title that he had just thought of—*She Stoops to Conquer*.

The play, which was first acted on 15 March, 1773, was a great success and thoroughly disappointed Colman's apprehensions. Johnson, who had championed it all along, "sat in the front row in a side box; and when he laughed, every body thought himself warranted to roar." It ran for twelve nights, the tenth being commanded by the King and Queen.

She Stoops to Conquer: or, The Mistakes of a Night. A Comedy. As it is acted at the Theatre-Royal in Covent-Garden was first published on 26 March, 1773, *Printed for F. Newbery, in St. Paul's Church-Yard.* This is the text here used.

TO SAMUEL JOHNSON, L.L.D.

DEAR SIR,

BY inscribing this slight performance to you, I do not mean so much to compliment you as myself. It may do me some honour to inform the public, that I have lived many years in intimacy with you. It may serve the interests of mankind also to inform them, that the greatest wit may be found in a character, without impairing the most unaffected piety.

I have, particularly, reason to thank you for your partiality to this performance. The undertaking a comedy, not merely sentimental, was very dangerous; and Mr. Colman, who saw this piece in its various stages, always thought it so. However I ventured to trust it to the public; and, though it was necessarily delayed till late in the season, I have every reason to be grateful.

I am, Dear Sir,
Your most sincere friend,
And admirer,
OLIVER GOLDSMITH

PROLOGUE

By DAVID GARRICK, Esq;

Enter Mr. WOODWARD, *Dressed in black, and holding a Handkerchief to his Eyes*

EXCUSE me, Sirs, I pray—I can't yet speak—
I'm crying now—and have been all the week!
'*Tis not alone this mourning suit*,[1] good masters;
I've that within—for which there are no plaisters!
Pray wou'd you know the reason why I'm crying?
The Comic muse, long sick, is now a dying!
And if she goes, my tears will never stop;
For as a player, I can't squeeze out one drop:
I am undone, that's all—shall lose my bread—
I'd rather, but that's nothing—lose my head.
When the sweet maid is laid upon the bier,
Shuter and *I* shall be chief mourners here.
To *her* a mawkish drab of spurious breed,
Who deals in *sentimentals* will succeed!
Poor *Ned* and *I* are dead to all intents,
We can as soon speak *Greek* as *sentiments!*
Both nervous grown, to keep our spirits up,
We now and then take down a hearty cup.
What shall we do?—If Comedy forsake us!
They'll turn us out, and no one else will take us,
But why can't I be moral?—Let me try—
My heart thus pressing—fix'd my face and eye—
With a sententious look, that nothing means
(Faces are blocks, in sentimental scenes)
Thus I begin—*All is not gold that glitters*,
Pleasure seems sweet, but proves a glass of bitters.
When ign'rance enters, folly is at hand;
Learning is better far than house and land.

[1] [*Hamlet*, I. 2. 78.]

Let not your virtue trip, who trips may stumble,
And virtue is not virtue, if she tumble.
I give it up—morals won't do for me;
To make you laugh I must play tragedy.
One hope remains—hearing the maid was ill,
A *doctor* comes this night to show his skill.
To cheer her heart, and give your muscles motion,
He in *five draughts* prepar'd, presents a potion:
A kind of magic charm—for be assur'd,
If you will *swallow it*, the maid is cur'd:
But desp'rate the Doctor, and her case is,
If you reject the dose, and make wry faces!
This truth he boasts, will boast it while he lives,
No *pois'nous drugs* are mix'd in what he gives;
Should he succeed, you'll give him his degree;
If not, within he will receive no fee!
The college *you*, must his pretentions back,
Pronounce him *regular*, or dub him *quack*.

EPILOGUE[1]

By Dr. GOLDSMITH

WELL, having stooped to conquer with success,
And gain'd a husband without aid from dress,
Still as a Bar-maid, I could wish it too,
As I have conquer'd him to conquer you:
And let me say, for all your resolution,
That pretty Bar-maids have done execution.
Our life is all a play, compos'd to please,
"We have our exits and our entrances."[2]
The first act shews the simple country maid,
Harmless and young, of ev'ry thing afraid;
Blushes when hir'd, and with unmeaning action,
I hopes as how to give you satisfaction.
Her second act displays a livelier scene,—
Th' unblushing Bar-maid of a country inn.
Who whisks about the house, at market caters,
Talks loud, coquets the guests, and scolds the waiters.
Next the scene shifts to town, and there she soars,
The chop house toast of ogling connoissieurs.
On 'Squires and Cits she there displays her arts,
And on the gridiron broils her lovers' hearts—
And as she smiles, her triumphs to compleat,
Even Common Councilmen forget to eat.
The fourth act shows her wedded to the 'Squire,
And Madam now begins to hold it higher;
Pretends to taste, at Operas cries *caro*,
And quits her Nancy Dawson, for *Che Faro*.[3]
Doats upon dancing, and in all her pride,
Swims round the room, the *Heinel* of Cheapside:

[1] [Spoken by Mrs. Bulkley in the character of Miss Hardcastle. See p. 746.]

[2] [*As You Like It*, 2. 7. 143. The rest of this epilogue is a variation on Jaques's famous speech.]

[3] [See notes on p. 661.]

Ogles and leers with artificial skill,
Till having lost in age the power to kill,
She sits all night at cards, and ogles at spadille.
Such, thro' our lives, the eventful history—
The fifth and last act still remains for me.
The Bar-maid now for your protection prays,
Turns Female Barrister, and pleads for Bayes.

DRAMATIS PERSONÆ

MEN

Sir CHARLES MARLOW,	Mr. GARDNER.
Young MARLOW (his Son)	Mr. LEWES.
HARDCASTLE,	Mr. SHUTER.
HASTINGS,	Mr. DUBELLAMY.
TONY LUMPKIN,	Mr. QUICK.
DIGGORY,	Mr. SAUNDERS.

WOMEN

Mrs. HARDCASTLE,	Mrs. GREEN.
Miss HARDCASTLE,	Mrs. BULKLEY.
Miss NEVILLE,	Mrs. KNIVETON.
MAID,	Miss WILLEMS.

Landlord, Servants &c., &c.

SHE STOOPS TO CONQUER

OR THE MISTAKES OF A NIGHT

ACT I

SCENE, *A* CHAMBER *in an old-fashioned* HOUSE

Enter Mrs. HARDCASTLE *and Mr.* HARDCASTLE

Mrs. Hardcastle. I vow, Mr. Hardcastle, you're very particular. Is there a creature in the whole country, but ourselves, that does not take a trip to town now and then, to rub off the rust a little? There's the two Miss Hoggs, and our neighbour, Mrs. Grigsby, go to take a month's polishing every winter.

Hardcastle. Ay, and bring back vanity and affectation to last them the whole year. I wonder why London cannot keep its own fools at home. In my time, the follies of the town crept slowly among us, but now they travel faster than a stage-coach. Its fopperies come down, not only as inside passengers, but in the very basket.

Mrs. Hardcastle. Ay, *your* times were fine times, indeed; you have been telling us of *them* for many a long year. Here we live in an old rumbling mansion, that looks for all the world like an inn, but that we never see company. Our best visitors are old Mrs. Oddfish, the curate's wife, and little Cripplegate, the lame dancing-master: And all our entertainment your old stories of Prince Eugene and the Duke of Marlborough. I hate such old-fashioned trumpery.

Hardcastle. And I love it. I love every thing that's old: old friends, old times, old manners, old books, old wine; and, I believe, Dorothy (*Taking her hand*) you'll own I have been pretty fond of an old wife.

Mrs. Hardcastle. Lord, Mr. Hardcastle, you're for ever at your Dorothy's and your old wife's. You may be a Darby, but I'll be no Joan, I promise you. I'm not so old as you'd make me, by more than one good year. Add twenty to twenty, and make money of that.

Hardcastle. Let me see; twenty added to twenty, makes just fifty and seven.

Mrs. Hardcastle. It's false, Mr. Hardcastle: I was but twenty when I was brought to bed of Tony, that I had by Mr. Lumpkin, my first husband; and he's not come to years of discretion yet.

Hardcastle. Nor ever will, I dare answer for him. Ay, you have taught *him* finely.

Mrs. Hardcastle. No matter, Tony Lumpkin has a good fortune. My son is not to live by his learning. I don't think a boy wants much learning to spend fifteen hundred a year.

Hardcastle. Learning, quotha! A mere composition of tricks and mischief.

Mrs. Hardcastle. Humour, my dear: nothing but humour. Come, Mr. Hardcastle, you must allow the boy a little humour.

Hardcastle. I'd sooner allow him an horse-pond. If burning the footmens shoes, frighting the maids, and worrying the kittens, be humour, he has it. It was but yesterday he fastened my wig to the back of my chair, and when I went to make a bow, I popt my bald head in Mrs. Frizzle's face.

Mrs. Hardcastle. And am I to blame? The poor boy was always too sickly to do any good. A school would be his death. When he comes to be a little stronger, who know what a year or two's Latin may do for him?

Hardcastle. Latin for him! A cat and fiddle. No, no, the ale-house and the stable are the only schools he'll ever go to.

Mrs. Hardcastle. Well, we must not snub the poor boy now, for I believe we shan't have him long among us. Any body that looks in his face may see he's consumptive.

Hardcastle. Ay, if growing too fat be one of the symptoms.

Mrs. Hardcastle. He coughs sometimes.

Hardcastle. Yes, when his liquor goes the wrong way.

Mrs. Hardcastle. I'm actually afraid of his lungs.

Hardcastle. And truly so am I; for he sometimes whoops like a speaking trumpet—(Tony *hallooing behind the Scenes*)—O there he goes—A very consumptive figure, truly.

Enter TONY, *crossing the Stage*

Mrs. Hardcastle. Tony, where are you going, my charmer? Won't you give papa and I a little of your company, lovee?

Tony. I'm in haste, mother, I cannot stay.

Mrs. Hardcastle. You shan't venture out this raw evening, my dear: You look most shockingly.

Tony. I can't stay, I tell you. The Three Pigeons expects me down every moment. There's some fun going forward.

Hardcastle. Ay; the ale-house, the old place: I thought so.

Mrs. Hardcastle. A low, paltry set of fellows.

Tony. Not so low, neither. There's Dick Muggins the exciseman, Jack Slang the horse doctor, Little Aminadab that grinds the music box, and Tom Twist that spins the pewter platter.

Mrs. Hardcastle. Pray, my dear, disappoint them for one night at least.

Tony. As for disappointing *them*, I should not much mind; but I can't abide to disappoint *myself*.

Mrs. Hardcastle. (*Detaining him*) You shan't go.

Tony. I will, I tell you.

Mrs. Hardcastle. I say you shan't.

Tony. We'll see which is strongest, you or I.

[*Exit, hawling her out.*

HARDCASTLE *Solus*

Hardcastle. Ay, there goes a pair that only spoil each other. But is not the whole age in a combination to drive sense and discretion out of doors? There's my pretty darling Kate; the fashions of the times have almost infected her too.

By living a year or two in town, she is as fond of gauze, and French frippery, as the best of them.

Enter Miss HARDCASTLE

Hardcastle. Blessings on my pretty innocence! Drest out as usual, my Kate. Goodness! What a quantity of superfluous silk hast thou got about thee, girl! I could never teach the fools of this age, that the indigent world could be cloathed out of the trimmings of the vain.

Miss Hardcastle. You know our agreement, Sir. You allow me the morning to receive and pay visits, and to dress in my own manner; and in the evening, I put on my housewife's dress to please you.

Hardcastle. Well, remember, I insist on the terms of our agreement; and, by the bye, I believe I shall have occasion to try your obedience this very evening.

Miss Hardcastle. I protest, Sir, I don't comprehend your meaning.

Hardcastle. Then to be plain with you, Kate, I expect the young gentleman I have chosen to be your husband from town this very day. I have his father's letter, in which he informs me his son is set out, and that he intends to follow himself shortly after.

Miss Hardcastle. Indeed! I wish I had known something of this before. Bless me, how shall I behave? It's a thousand to one I shan't like him; our meeting will be so formal, and so like a thing of business, that I shall find no room for friendship or esteem.

Hardcastle. Depend upon it, child, I'll never controul your choice; but Mr. Marlow, whom I have pitched upon, is the son of my old friend, Sir Charles Marlow, of whom you have heard me talk so often. The young gentleman has been bred a scholar, and is designed for an employment in the service of his country. I am told he's a man of an excellent understanding.

Miss Hardcastle. Is he?

Hardcastle. Very generous.

Miss Hardcastle. I believe I shall like him.

Hardcastle. Young and brave.

Miss Hardcastle. I'm sure I shall like him.

Hardcastle. And very handsome.

Miss Hardcastle. My dear Papa, say no more (*Kissing his hand*) he's mine, I'll have him.

Hardcastle. And, to crown all, Kate, he's one of the most bashful and reserved young fellows in all the world.

Miss Hardcastle. Eh! you have frozen me to death again. That word, reserved, has undone all the rest of his accomplishments. A reserved lover, it is said, always makes a suspicious husband.

Hardcastle. On the contrary, modesty seldom resides in a breast that is not enriched with nobler virtues. It was the very feature in his character that first struck me.

Miss Hardcastle. He must have more striking features to catch me, I promise you. However, if he be so young, so handsome, and so every thing, as you mention, I believe he'll do still. I think I'll have him.

Hardcastle. Ay, Kate, but there is still an obstacle. It is more than an even wager, he may not have *you.*

Miss Hardcastle. My dear papa, why will you mortify one so?—Well, if he refuses, instead of breaking my heart at his indifference, I'll only break my glass for its flattery. Set my cap to some newer fashion, and look out for some less difficult admirer.

Hardcastle. Bravely resolved! In the mean time I'll go prepare the servants for his reception; as we seldom see company they want as much training as a company of recruits the first day's muster. [*Exit.*

Miss HARDCASTLE *Sola*

Miss Hardcastle. Lud, this news of Papa's puts me all in a flutter. Young, handsome; these he put last; but I put them foremost. Sensible, good-natured; I like all that. But then reserved, and sheepish, that's much against him. Yet can't he be cured of his timidity, by being taught to be proud of his wife? Yes, and can't I—But I vow I'm disposing of the husband, before I have secured the lover.

Enter Miss NEVILLE

Miss Hardcastle. I'm glad you're come, Neville, my dear. Tell me, Constance, how do I look this evening? Is there any thing whimsical about me? Is it one of my well looking days, child? Am I in face to day?

Miss Neville. Perfectly, my dear. Yet now I look again—bless me!—sure no accident has happened among the canary birds or the gold fishes. Has your brother or the cat been meddling? Or has the last novel been too moving?

Miss Hardcastle. No; nothing of all this. I have been threatened—I can scarce get it out—I have been threatened with a lover.

Miss Neville. And his name——

Miss Hardcastle. Is Marlow.

Miss Neville. Indeed!

Miss Hardcastle. The son of Sir Charles Marlow.

Miss Neville. As I live, the most intimate friend of Mr. Hastings, *my* admirer. They are never asunder. I believe you must have seen him when we lived in town.

Miss Hardcastle. Never.

Miss Neville. He's a very singular character, I assure you. Among women of reputation and virtue, he is the modestest man alive; but his acquaintance give him a very different character among creatures of another stamp: you understand me?

Miss Hardcastle. An odd character, indeed. I shall never be able to manage him. What shall I do? Pshaw, think no more of him, but trust to occurrences for success. But how goes on your own affair my dear, has my mother been courting you for my brother Tony, as usual?

Miss Neville. I have just come from one of our agreeable tête-à-têtes. She has been saying a hundred tender things, and setting off her pretty monster as the very pink of perfection.

Miss Hradcastle. And her partiality is such, that she actually thinks him so. A fortune like your's is no small temptation. Besides, as she has the sole management of it, I'm not surprized to see her unwilling to let it go out of the family.

Miss Neville. A fortune like mine, which chiefly consists in jewels, is no such mighty temptation. But at any rate if my dear Hastings be but constant, I make no doubt to be too hard for her at last. However, I let her suppose that I am in love with her son, and she never once dreams that my affections are fixed upon another.

Miss Hardcastle. My good brother holds out stoutly. I could almost love him for hating you so.

Miss Neville. It is a good natured creature at bottom, and I'm sure would wish to see me married to any body but himself. But my aunt's bell rings for our afternoon's walk through the improvements. Allons. Courage is necessary, as our affairs are critical.

Miss Hardcastle. Would it were bed time and all were well.[1]

[*Exeunt.*

SCENE, *An Alehouse Room. Several shabby fellows, with Punch and Tobacco.* TONY *at the head of the Table, a little higher than the rest: A mallet in his hand.*

Omnes. Hurrea, hurrea, hurrea, bravo.

First Fellow. Now, gentlemen, silence for a song. The 'Squire is going to knock himself down for a song.

Omnes. Ay, a song, a song.

Tony. Then I'll sing you, gentlemen, a song I made upon this ale-house, the Three Pigeons.

[1] [1 *Henry IV*, 5. 1. 126.]

SONG

Let school-masters puzzle their brain,
With grammar, and nonsense, and learning;
Good liquor, I stoutly maintain,
Gives genus *a better discerning.*
Let them brag of their Heathenish Gods,
Their Lethes, their Styxes, and Stygians;
Their Quis, and their Quæs, and their Quods,
They're all but a parcel of Pigeons.
Toroddle, toroddle, toroll.

When Methodist preachers come down,
A preaching that drinking is sinful,
I'll wager the rascals a crown,
They always preach best with a skinful.
But when you come down with your pence,
For a slice of their scurvy religion,
I'll leave it to all men of sense,
But you, my good friend, are the pigeon.
Toroddle, toroddle, toroll.

Then come, put the jorum about,
And let us be merry and clever,
Our hearts and our liquors are stout,
Here's the Three Jolly Pigeons for ever.
Let some cry up woodcock or hare,
Your bustards, your ducks, and your widgeons;
But of all the birds in the air,
Here's a health to the Three Jolly Pigeons.
Toroddle, toroddle, toroll.

Omnes. Bravo, bravo.

First Fellow. The 'Squire has got spunk in him.

Second Fellow. I loves to hear him sing, bekeays he never gives us nothing that's *low*.

Third Fellow. O damn anything that's *low*, I cannot bear it.

Fourth Fellow. The genteel thing is the genteel thing at any time. If so be that a gentleman bees in a concatenation accordingly.

Third Fellow. I like the maxum of it, Master Muggins. What, tho' I am obligated to dance a bear, a man may be a gentleman for all that. May this be my poison if my bear ever dances but to the very genteelest of tunes. Water Parted,[1] or the minuet in Ariadne.[2]

Second Fellow. What a pity it is the 'Squire is not come to his own. It would be well for all the publicans within ten miles round of him.

Tony. Ecod, and so it would, Master Slang. I'd then show what it was to keep choice of company.

Second Fellow. O, he takes after his own father for that. To be sure old 'Squire Lumpkin was the finest gentleman I ever set my eyes on. For winding the streight horn, or beating a thicket for a hare, or a wench he never had his fellow. It was a saying in the place, that he kept the best horses, dogs, and girls in the whole county.

Tony. Ecod, and when I'm of age I'll be no bastard I promise you. I have been thinking of Bett Bouncer and the miller's grey mare to begin with. But come, my boys, drink about and be merry, for you pay no reckoning. Well Stingo, what's the matter?

Enter LANDLORD

Landlord. There be two gentlemen in a post-chaise at the door. They have lost their way upo' the forest; and they are talking something about Mr. Hardcastle.

Tony. As sure as can be one of them must be the gentleman that's coming down to court my sister. Do they seem to be Londoners?

[1] [Arbaces' song in Arne's *Artaxerxes*, 1762.]
[2] [By Handel.]

Landlord. I believe they may. They look woundily like Frenchmen.

Tony. Then desire them to step this way, and I'll set them right in a twinkling. (*Exit Landlord.*) Gentleman, as they mayn't be good enough company for you, step down for a moment, and I'll be with you in the squeezing of a lemon.

[*Exeunt Mob.*

TONY *solus*

Tony. Father-in-law has been calling me whelp, and hound, this half year. Now, if I pleased, I could be so revenged upon the old grumbletonian. But then I'm afraid—afraid of what! I shall soon be worth fifteen hundred a year, and let him frighten me out of *that* if he can.

Enter LANDLORD, *conducting* MARLOW *and* HASTINGS

Marlow. What a tedious uncomfortable day have we had of it! We were told it was but forty miles across the country, and we have come above threescore.

Hastings. And all Marlow, from that unaccountable reserve of yours, that would not let us enquire more frequently on the way.

Marlow. I own, Hastings, I am unwilling to lay myself under an obligation to every one I meet: and often, stand the chance of an unmannerly answer.

Hastings. At present, however, we are not likely to receive any answer.

Tony. No offence, gentlemen. But I'm told you have been enquiring for one Mr. Hardcastle, in these parts. Do you know what part of the country you are in?

Hastings. Not in the least Sir, but should thank you for information.

Tony. Nor the way you came?

Hastings. No, Sir; but if you can inform us——

Tony. Why, gentlemen, if you know neither the road you

are going, nor where you are, nor the road you came, the first thing I have to inform is, that—You have lost your way.

Marlow. We wanted no ghost to tell us that.[1]

Tony. Pray, gentlemen, may I be so bold as to ask the place from whence you came?

Marlow. That's not necessary towards directing us where we are to go.

Tony. No offence; but question for question is all fair, you know. Pray, gentlemen, is not this same Hardcastle a cross-grain'd, old-fashion'd, whimsical fellow with an ugly face, a daughter, and a pretty son?

Hastings. We have not seen the gentleman, but he has the family you mention.

Tony. The daughter, a tall trapesing, trolloping, talkative maypole——The son, a pretty, well-bred, agreeable youth, that every body is fond of.

Marlow. Our information differs in this. The daughter is said to be well-bred and beautiful; the son, an aukward booby, reared up, and spoiled at his mother's apron-string.

Tony. He-he-hem—Then, gentlemen, all I have to tell you is, that you won't reach Mr. Hardcastle's house this night, I believe.

Hastings. Unfortunate!

Tony. It's a damn'd long, dark, boggy, dirty, dangerous way. Stingo, tell the gentlemen the way to Mr. Hardcastle's; (*Winking upon the Landlord*) Mr. Hardcastle's, of Quagmire Marsh, you understand me.

Landlord. Master Hardcastle's! Lock-a-daisy, my masters, you're come a deadly deal wrong! When you came to the bottom of the hill, you should have cross'd down Squash-lane.

Marlow. Cross down Squash-lane!

Landlord. Then you were to keep streight forward, 'till you came to four roads.

[1] [*Hamlet*, I. 5. 124.]

Marlow. Come to where four roads meet!

Tony. Ay; but you must be sure to take only one of them.

Marlow. O Sir, you're facetious.

Tony. Then keeping to the right, you are to go sideways till you come upon Crack-skull common: there you must look sharp for the track of the wheel, and go forward, 'till you come to farmer Murrain's barn. Coming to the farmer's barn, you are to turn to the right, and then to the left, and then to the right about again, till you find out the old mill——

Marlow. Zounds, man! we could as soon find out the longitude![1]

Hastings. What's to be done, Marlow?

Marlow. This house promises but a poor reception; though, perhaps the Landlord can accommodate us.

Landlord. Alack, master, we have but one spare bed in the whole house.

Tony. And to my knowledge, that's taken up by three lodgers already. (*After a pause, in which the rest seem disconcerted*) I have hit it. Don't you think, Stingo, our landlady could accommodate the gentlemen by the fire-side, with—— three chairs and a bolster?

Hastings. I hate sleeping by the fire-side.

Marlow. And I detest your three chairs and a bolster.

Tony. You do, do you?—then let me see—what—if you go on a mile further, to the Buck's Head; the old Buck's Head on the hill, one of the best inns in the whole county?

Hastings. Oho! so we have escaped an adventure for this night, however.

Landlord. (*Apart to Tony*) Sure, you ben't sending them to your father's as an inn, be you?

Tony. Mum, you fool you. Let *them* find that out. (*To them*)

[1] [This was a topic of the day. An Act of Parliament had been passed in 1713 offering £20,000 for an accurate means of determining the longitude at sea. John Harrison (1693–1776) eventually gained the reward on 14 June, 1773, but only after a special Act of Parliament and the King's personal intervention.]

You have only to keep on streight forward, till you come to a large old house by the road side. You'll see a pair of large horns over the door. That's the sign. Drive up the yard, and call stoutly about you.

Hastings. Sir, we are obliged to you. The servants can't miss the way?

Tony. No, no: But I tell you though, the landlord is rich, and going to leave off business; so he wants to be thought a Gentleman, saving your presence, he! he! he! He'll be for giving you his company, and ecod if you mind him, he'll persuade you that his mother was an alderman, and his aunt a justice of the peace.

Landlord. A troublesome old blade to be sure; but a keeps as good wines and beds as any in the whole country.

Marlow. Well, if he supplies us with these, we shall want no further connexion. We are to turn to the right, did you say?

Tony. No, no; streight forward. I'll just step myself, and shew you a piece of the way. (*To the landlord*) Mum.

Landlord. Ah, bless your heart, for a sweet, pleasant—— damn'd mischievous son of a whore.

[*Exeunt.*

END OF THE FIRST ACT

ACT II

SCENE, *An old-fashioned* HOUSE

Enter HARDCASTLE, *followed by three or four aukward* SERVANTS

Hardcastle. Well, I hope you're perfect in the table exercise I have been teaching you these three days. You all know your posts and your places, and can shew that you have been used to good company, without ever stirring from home.

Omnes. Ay, ay.

Hardcastle. When company comes, you are not to pop out and stare, and then run in again, like frighted rabbits in a warren.

Omnes. No, no.

Hardcastle. You, Diggory, whom I have taken from the barn, are to make a shew at the side-table; and you, Roger, whom I have advanced from the plough, are to place yourself behind *my* chair. But you're not to stand so, with your hands in your pockets. Take your hands from your pockets, Roger; and from your head, you blockhead you. See how Diggory carries his hands. They're a little too stiff, indeed, but that's no great matter.

Diggory. Ay, mind how I hold them. I learned to hold my hands this way, when I was upon drill for the militia. And so being upon drill——

Hardcastle. You must not be so talkative, Diggory. You must be all attention to the guests. You must hear us talk, and not think of talking; you must see us drink, and not think of drinking; you must see us eat, and not think of eating.

Diggory. By the laws, your worship, that's parfectly unpossible. Whenever Diggory sees yeating going forward, ecod he's always wishing for a mouthful himself.

Hardcastle. Blockhead! Is not a belly-full in the kitchen as good as a belly-full in the parlour? Stay your stomach with that reflection.

Diggory. Ecod I thank your worship, I'll make a shift to stay my stomach with a slice of cold beef in the pantry.

Hardcastle. Diggory, you are too talkative. Then if I happen to say a good thing, or tell a good story at table, you must not all burst out a-laughing, as if you made part of the company.

Diggory. Then ecod your worship must not tell the story of Ould Grouse in the gun-room: I can't help laughing at that—he! he! he!—for the soul of me. We have laughed at that these twenty years—ha! ha! ha!

Hardcastle. Ha! ha! ha! The story is a good one. Well, honest Diggory, you may laugh at that—but still remember to be attentive. Suppose one of the company should call for a glass of wine, how will you behave? A glass of wine, Sir, if you please (*to* Diggory)—Eh, why don't you move?

Diggory. Ecod, your worship, I never have courage till I see the eatables and drinkables brought upo' the table, and then I'm as bauld as a lion.

Hardcastle. What, will no body move?

First Servant. I'm not to leave this pleace.

Second Servant. I'm sure it's no pleace of mine.

Third Servant. Nor mine, for sartain.

Diggory. Wauns, and I'm sure it canna be mine.

Hardcastle. You numbskulls! and so while, like your betters, you are quarrelling for places, the guests must be starved. O you dunces! I find I must begin all over again.—But don't I hear a coach drive into the yard? To your posts you blockheads. I'll go in the mean time and give my old friend's son a hearty reception at the gate.

[*Exit* Hardcastle.

Diggory. By the elevens, my pleace is gone quite out of my head.

Roger. I know that my pleace is to be every where.

First Servant. Where the devil is mine?

Second Servant. My pleace is to be no where at all; and so Ize go about my business.

[*Exeunt Servants, running about as if frighted, different ways.*

Enter SERVANTS *with Candles, shewing in* MARLOW *and* HASTINGS

Servant. Welcome, gentlemen, very welcome. This way.

Hastings. After the disappointments of the day, welcome once more, Charles, to the comforts of a clean room and a good fire. Upon my word, a very well-looking house; antique but creditable.

Marlow. The usual fate of a large mansion. Having first ruined the master by good housekeeping, it at last comes to levy contributions as an inn.

Hastings. As you say, we passengers are to be taxed to pay all these fineries. I have often seen a good sideboard, or a marble chimney-piece, tho' not actually put in the bill, enflame a reckoning confoundedly.

Marlow. Travellers, George, must pay in all places. The only difference is, that in good inns, you pay dearly for luxuries; in bad inns, you are fleeced and starved.

Hastings. You have lived pretty much among them. In truth, I have been often surprized, that you who have seen so much of the world, with your natural good sense, and your many opportunities, could never yet acquire a requisite share of assurance.

Marlow. The Englishman's malady. But tell me, George, where could I have learned that assurance you talk of? My life has been chiefly spent in a college, or an inn, in seclusion from that lovely part of the creation that chiefly teach men confidence. I don't know that I was ever familiarly acquainted with a single modest woman—except my mother—But among females of another class you know—

Hastings. Ay, among them you are impudent enough of all conscience.

Marlow. They are of *us*, you know.

Hastings. But in the company of women of reputation I never saw such an ideot, such a trembler; you look for all the world as if you wanted an opportunity of stealing out of the room.

Marlow. Why man that's because I *do* want to steal out of the room. Faith, I have often formed a resolution to break the ice, and rattle away at any rate. But I don't know how, a single glance from a pair of fine eyes has totally overset my resolution. An impudent fellow may counterfeit modesty, but I'll be hanged if a modest man can ever counterfeit impudence.

Hastings. If you could but say half the fine things to them that I have heard you lavish upon the bar-maid of an inn, or even a college bed-maker—

Marlow. Why, George, I can't say fine things to them. They freeze, they petrify me. They may talk of a comet, or a burning mountain, or some such bagatelle. But to me, a modest woman, drest out in all her finery, is the most tremendous object of the whole creation.

Hastings. Ha! ha! ha! At this rate, man, how can you ever expect to marry!

Marlow. Never, unless as among kings and princes, my bride were to be courted by proxy. If, indeed, like an Eastern bridegroom, one were to be introduced to a wife he never saw before, it might be endured. But to go through all the terrors of a formal courtship, together with the episode of aunts, grandmothers and cousins, and at last to blurt out the broad staring question, of, *madam will you marry me?* No, no, that's a strain much above me I assure you.

Hastings. I pity you. But how do you intend behaving to the lady you are come down to visit at the request of your father?

Marlow. As I behave to all other ladies. Bow very low. Answer yes, or no, to all her demands—But for the rest, I don't think I shall venture to look in her face, till I see my father's again.

Hastings. I'm surprized that one who is so warm a friend can be so cool a lover.

Marlow. To be explicit, my dear Hastings, my chief inducement down was to be instrumental in forwarding your happiness, not my own. Miss Neville loves you, the family don't know you, as my friend you are sure of a reception, and let honour do the rest.

Hastings. My dear Marlow! But I'll suppress the emotion. Were I a wretch, meanly seeking to carry off a fortune, you should be the last man in the world I would apply to for assistance. But Miss Neville's person is all I ask, and that is mine, both from her deceased father's consent, and her own inclination.

Marlow. Happy man! You have talents and art to captivate any woman. I'm doom'd to adore the sex, and yet to converse with the only part of it I despise. This stammer in my address, and this aukward prepossessing visage of mine, can never permit me to soar above the reach of a milliner's 'prentice, or one of the dutchesses of Drury-lane. Pshaw! this fellow here to interrupt us.

Enter HARDCASTLE

Hardcastle. Gentlemen, once more you are heartily welcome. Which is Mr. Marlow? Sir, you're heartily welcome. It's not my way, you see, to receive my friends with my back to the fire. I like to give them a hearty reception in the old stile at my gate. I like to see their horses and trunks taken care of.

Marlow. (*Aside*) He has got our names from the servants already. (*To Him.*) We approve your caution and hospitality, Sir. (*To Hastings.*) I have been thinking, George, of changing our travelling dresses in the morning. I am grown confoundedly ashamed of mine.

Hardcastle. I beg, Mr. Marlow, you'll use no ceremony in this house.

Hastings. I fancy, George, you're right: the first blow is half the battle. I intend opening the campaign with the white and gold.

Hardcastle. Mr. Marlow—Mr. Hastings—gentlemen—pray be under no constraint in this house. This is Liberty-hall, gentlemen. You may do just as you please here.

Marlow. Yet, George, if we open the campaign too fiercely at first, we may want ammunition before it is over. I think to reserve the embroidery to secure a retreat.

Hardcastle. Your talking of a retreat, Mr. Marlow, puts me in mind of the Duke of Marlborough, when we went to besiege Denain. He first summoned the garrison.

Marlow. Don't you think the *ventre dor* waistcoat will do with the plain brown?

Hardcastle. He first summoned the garrison, which might consist of about five thousand men——

Hastings. I think not: Brown and yellow mix but very poorly.

Hardcastle. I say, gentlemen, as I was telling you, he summoned the garrison, which might consist of about five thousand men——

Marlow. The girls like finery.

Hardcastle. Which might consist of about five thousand men, well appointed with stores, ammunition, and other implements of war. Now, says the Duke of Marlborough to George Brooks, that stood next to him—You must have heard of George Brooks; I'll pawn my Dukedom, says he, but I take that garrison without spilling a drop of blood. So——

Marlow. What, my good friend, if you gave us a glass of punch in the mean time, it would help us to carry on the siege with vigour.

Hardcastle. Punch, Sir! (*Aside*) This is the most unaccountable kind of modesty I ever met with.

Marlow. Yes, Sir, Punch. A glass of warm punch, after our journey, will be comfortable. This is Liberty-Hall, you know.

Hardcastle. Here's Cup, Sir.

Marlow. (*Aside*) So this fellow, in his Liberty-hall, will only let us have just what he pleases.

Hardcastle. (*Taking the Cup*) I hope you'll find it to your mind. I have prepared it with my own hands, and I believe you'll own the ingredients are tolerable. Will you be so good as to pledge me, Sir? Here, Mr. Marlow, here is our better acquaintance. [*drinks.*

Marlow. (*Aside*) A very impudent fellow this! but he's a

character, and I'll humour him a little. Sir, my service to you. [*drinks.*

Hastings. (*Aside*) I see this fellow wants to give us his company, and forgets that he's an innkeeper, before he has learned to be a gentleman.

Marlow. From the excellence of your cup, my old friend, I suppose you have a good deal of business in this part of the country. Warm work, now and then, at elections, I suppose.

Hardcastle. No, Sir, I have long given that work over. Since our betters have hit upon the expedient of electing each other, there's no business *for us that sell ale.*

Hastings. So, then you have no turn for politics, I find.

Hardcastle. Not in the least. There was a time, indeed, I fretted myself about the mistakes of government, like other people; but finding myself every day grow more angry, and the government growing no better, I left it to mend itself. Since that, I no more trouble my head about *Heyder Ally*,[1] *Ally Cawn*,[2] than about *Ally Croaker*.[3] Sir, my service to you.

Hastings. So that with eating above stairs, and drinking below, with receiving your friends within, and amusing them without, you lead a good pleasant bustling life of it.

Hardcastle. I do stir about a great deal, it's certain. Half the differences of the parish are adjusted in this very parlour.

Marlow. (*After drinking*) And you have an argument in your cup, old gentleman, better than any in Westminster-hall.

Hardcastle. Ay, young gentleman, that, and a little philosophy.

Marlow. (*Aside*) Well, this is the first time I ever heard of an innkeeper's philosophy.

Hastings. So then, like an experienced general, you attack them on every quarter. If you find their reason manageable, you attack it with your philosophy; if you find they have no

[1] [Hyder Ali, Sultan of Mysore (1717–82).]
[2] [Cossim Ali Cawn, Subah of Bengal.]
[3] [A popular Irish song.]

reason, you attack them with this. Here's your health, my philosopher. (*drinks*)

Hardcastle. Good, very good, thank you; ha, ha. Your Generalship puts me in mind of Prince Eugene, when he fought the Turks at the battle of Belgrade. You shall hear.

Marlow. Instead of the battle of Belgrade, I believe it's almost time to talk about supper. What has your philosophy got in the house for supper?

Hardcastle. For supper, Sir! (*Aside*) Was ever such a request to a man in his own house!

Marlow. Yes, Sir, supper, Sir; I begin to feel an appetite. I shall make devilish work to-night in the larder, I promise you.

Hardcastle. (*Aside*) Such a brazen dog sure never my eyes beheld. (*To him*) Why really, Sir, as for supper I can't well tell. My Dorothy, and the cook maid, settle these things between them. I leave these kind of things entirely to them.

Marlow. You do, do you?

Hardcastle. Entirely. By-the-bye, I believe they are in actual consultation upon what's for supper this moment in the kitchen.

Marlow. Then I beg they'll admit *me* as one of their privy council. It's a way I have got. When I travel, I always chuse to regulate my own supper. Let the cook be called. No offence I hope, Sir.

Hardcastle. O no, Sir, none in the least; yet, I don't know how: our Bridget, the cook maid, is not very communicative upon these occasions. Should we send for her, she might scold us all out of the house.

Hastings. Let's see your list of the larder then. I ask it as a favour. I always match my appetite to my bill of fare.

Marlow. (*To Hardcastle, who looks at them with surprize*) Sir, he's very right, and it's my way too.

Hardcastle. Sir, you have a right to command here. Here, Roger, bring us the bill of fare for to night's supper. I believe it's drawn out. Your manner, Mr. Hastings, puts me in mind of my uncle, Colonel Wallop. It was a saying of his, that no man was sure of his supper till he had eaten it.

Hastings. (*Aside*) All upon the high ropes! His uncle a Colonel! We shall soon hear of his mother being a justice of peace. But let's hear the bill of fare.

Marlow. (*Perusing*) What's here? For the first course; for the second course; for the desert. The devil, Sir, do you think we have brought down the whole Joiners Company, or the Corporation of Bedford, to eat up such a supper? Two or three little things, clean and comfortable, will do.

Hastings. But, let's hear it.

Marlow. (*Reading*) For the first course at the top, a pig, and pruin sauce.

Hastings. Damn your pig, I say.

Marlow. And damn your pruin sauce, say I.

Hardcastle. And yet, gentlemen, to men that are hungry, pig, with pruin sauce is very good eating.

Marlow. At the bottom, a calve's tongue and brains.

Hastings. Let your brains be knock'd out, my good Sir; I don't like them.

Marlow. Or you may clap them on a plate by themselves. I do.

Hardcastle. (*Aside*) Their impudence confounds me. (*To them*) Gentlemen, you are my guests, make what alterations you please. Is there any thing else you wish to retrench or alter, gentlemen?

Marlow. Item. A pork pie, a boiled rabbet and sausages, a florentine, a shaking pudding, and a dish of tiff—taff—taffety cream!

Hastings. Confound your made dishes, I shall be as much at a loss in this house as at a green and yellow dinner at the French ambassador's table. I'm for plain eating.

Hardcastle. I'm sorry, gentlemen, that I have nothing you like, but if there be any thing you have a particular fancy to——

Marlow. Why, really, Sir, your bill of fare is so exquisite, that any one part of it is full as good as another. Send us what you please. So much for supper. And now to see that our beds are air'd, and properly taken care of.

Hardcastle. I entreat you'll leave all that to me. You shall not stir a step.

Marlow. Leave that to you! I protest, Sir, you must excuse me, I always look to these things myself.

Hardcastle. I must insist, Sir, you'll make yourself easy on that head.

Marlow. You see I'm resolved on it. (*Aside*) A very troublesome fellow this, as ever I met with.

Hardcastle. Well, Sir, I'm resolved at least to attend you. (*Aside*) This may be modern modesty, but I never saw any thing look so like old-fashioned impudence.

[*Exeunt* Marlow *and* Hardcastle.

HASTINGS *solus*

Hastings. So I find this fellow's civilities begin to grow troublesome. But who can be angry at those assiduities which are meant to please him. Ha! what do I see? Miss Neville, by all that's happy!

Enter Miss NEVILLE

Miss Neville. My dear Hastings! To what unexpected good fortune? to what accident am I to ascribe this happy meeting?

Hastings. Rather let me ask the same question, as I could never have hoped to meet my dearest Constance at an inn.

Miss Neville. An inn! sure you mistake! my aunt, my guardian, lives here. What could induce you to think this house an inn?

Hastings. My friend Mr. Marlow, with whom I came down, and I, have been sent here as to an inn, I assure you. A young fellow whom we accidentally met at a house hard by directed us hither.

Miss Neville. Certainly it must be one of my hopeful cousin's tricks, of whom you have heard me talk so often, ha! ha! ha! ha!

Hastings. He whom your aunt intends for you? He of whom I have such just apprehensions?

Miss Neville. You have nothing to fear from him, I assure you. You'd adore him if you knew how heartily he despises me. My aunt knows it too, and has undertaken to court me for him, and actually begins to think she has made a conquest.

Hastings. Thou dear dissembler! You must know, my Constance, I have just seized this happy opportunity of my friend's visit here to get admittance into the family. The horses that carried us down are now fatigued with their journey, but they'll soon be refreshed; and then if my dearest girl will trust in her faithful Hastings, we shall soon be landed in France, where even among slaves the laws of marriage are respected.[1]

Miss Neville. I have often told you, that though ready to obey you, I yet should leave my little fortune behind with reluctance. The greatest part of it was left me by my uncle, the India Director, and chiefly consists in jewels. I have been for some time persuading my aunt to let me wear them. I fancy I'm very near succeeding. The instant they are put into my possession you shall find me ready to make them and myself yours.

Hastings. Perish the baubles! Your person is all I desire. In the meantime, my friend Marlow must not be let into his mistake. I know the strange reserve of his temper is such, that if abruptly informed of it, he would instantly quit the house before our plan was ripe for execution.

Miss Neville. But how shall we keep him in the deception?

[1] [An allusion to the Duke of Gloucester's marriage to Lady Waldegrave which was one of the causes of the Royal Marriage Act of 1772. According to Sir James Prior's *Life of Goldsmith* the Duke was present at the first night, and was given several rounds of applause when these lines were spoken.]

Miss Hardcastle is just returned from walking; what if we still continue to deceive him?—This, this way—— [*They confer.*

Enter MARLOW

Marlow. The assiduities of these good people teize me beyond bearing. My host seems to think it ill manners to leave me alone, and so he claps not only himself, but his old-fashioned wife on my back. They talk of coming to sup with us too; and then, I suppose, we are to run the gauntlet thro' all the rest of the family.—What have we got here!—

Hastings. My dear Charles! Let me congratulate you!—The most fortunate accident!—Who do you think is just alighted?

Marlow. Cannot guess.

Hastings. Our mistresses, boy, Miss Hardcastle and Miss Neville. Give me leave to introduce Miss Constance Neville to your acquaintance. Happening to dine in the neighbourhood, they called, on their return to take fresh horses, here. Miss Hardcastle has just stept into the next room, and will be back in an instant. Wasn't it lucky? eh!

Marlow. (*Aside*) I have just been mortified enough of all conscience, and here comes something to complete my embarrassment.

Hastings. Well! but wasn't it the most fortunate thing in the world?

Marlow. Oh! yes. Very fortunate—a most joyful encounter——But our dresses, George, you know, are in disorder ——What if we should postpone the happiness 'till to-morrow?——To-morrow at her own house——It will be every bit as convenient——And rather more respectful——To-morrow let it be. [*offering to go.*

Miss Neville. By no means, Sir. Your ceremony will displease her. The disorder of your dress will shew the ardour of your impatience. Besides, she knows you are in the house, and will permit you to see her.

Marlow. O! the devil! how shall I support it? Hem! hem! Hastings, you must not go. You are to assist me, you know. I shall be confoundedly ridiculous. Yet, hang it! I'll take courage. Hem!

Hastings. Pshaw man! it's but the first plunge, and all's over. She's but a woman, you know.

Marlow. And of all women, she that I dread most to encounter!

Enter Miss HARDCASTLE *as returned from walking, a Bonnet, &c.*

Hastings. (*Introducing them*) Miss Hardcastle, Mr. Marlow, I'm proud of bringing two persons of such merit together, that only want to know, to esteem each other.

Miss Hardcastle. (*Aside*) Now, for meeting my modest gentleman with a demure face, and quite in his own manner. (*After a pause, in which he appears very uneasy and disconcerted.*) I'm glad of your safe arrival, Sir——I'm told you had some accidents by the way.

Marlow. Only a few, madam. Yes, we had some. Yes, Madam, a good many accidents, but should be sorry—Madam—or rather glad of any accidents—that are so agreeably concluded. Hem!

Hastings. (*To him*) You never spoke better in your whole life. Keep it up, and I'll insure you the victory.

Miss Hardcastle. I'm afraid you flatter, Sir. You that have seen so much of the finest company can find little entertainment in an obscure corner of the country.

Marlow. (*Gathering courage*) I have lived, indeed, in the world, Madam; but I have kept very little company. I have been but an observer upon life, Madam, while others were enjoying it.

Miss Neville. But that, I am told, is the way to enjoy it at last.

Hastings. (*To him*) Cicero never spoke better. Once more, and you are confirm'd in assurance for ever.

Marlow. (*To him*) Hem! Stand by me then, and when I'm down, throw in a word or two to set me up again.

Miss Hardcastle. An observer, like you, upon life, were, I fear, disagreeably employed, since you must have had much more to censure than to approve.

Marlow. Pardon me, Madam. I was always willing to be amused. The folly of most people is rather an object of mirth than uneasiness.

Hastings. (*To him*) Bravo, bravo. Never spoke so well in your whole life. Well, Miss Hardcastle, I see that you and Mr. Marlow are going to be very good company. I believe our being here will but embarrass the interview.

Marlow. Not in the least, Mr. Hastings. We like your company of all things. (*To him*) Zounds! George, sure you won't go? How can you leave us?

Hastings. Our presence will but spoil conversation, so we'll retire to the next room. (*To him*) You don't consider, man, that we are to manage a little tête-à-tête of our own.

[*Exeunt*.

Miss Hardcastle. (*After a pause*) But you have not been wholly an observer, I presume, Sir: The ladies I should hope have employed some part of your addresses.

Marlow. (*Relapsing into timidity*) Pardon me, Madam, I—I —I—as yet have studied—only—to—deserve them.

Miss Hardcastle. And that some say is the very worst way to obtain them.

Marlow. Perhaps so, madam. But I love to converse only with the more grave and sensible part of the sex.——But I'm afraid I grow tiresome.

Miss Hardcastle. Not at all Sir; there is nothing I like so much as grave conversation myself; I could hear it for ever. Indeed I have often been surprized how a man of *sentiment* could ever admire those light airy pleasures, where nothing reaches the heart.

Marlow. It's—a—disease—of the mind, madam. In the

variety of tastes there must be some who, wanting a relish for —um—a—um.

Miss Hardcastle. I understand you, Sir. There must be some, who wanting a relish for refined pleasures, pretend to despise what they are incapable of tasting.

Marlow. My meaning, madam, but infinitely better expressed. And I can't help observing—a——

Miss Hardcastle. (*Aside*) Who could ever suppose this fellow impudent upon some occasions. (*To him*) You were going to observe, Sir——

Marlow. I was observing, madam——I protest, madam, I forget what I was going to observe.

Miss Hardcastle. (*Aside*) I vow and so do I. (*To him*) You were observing, Sir, that in this age of hypocrisy—something about hypocrisy, Sir.

Marlow. Yes, madam. In this age of hypocrisy there are few who upon strict enquiry do not—a—a—a——

Miss Hardcastle. I understand you perfectly, Sir.

Marlow. (*Aside*) Egad! and that's more than I do myself.

Miss Hardcastle. You mean that in this hypocritical age there are few that do not condemn in public what they practise in private, and think they pay every debt to virtue when they praise it.

Marlow. True, madam; those who have most virtue in their mouths, have least of it in their bosoms. But I'm sure I tire you, madam.

Miss Hardcastle. Not in the least, Sir; there's something so agreeable and spirited in your manner, such life and force—— pray, Sir, go on.

Marlow. Yes, madam. I was saying——that there are some occasions——when a total want of courage, madam, destroys all the——and puts us——upon a——a——a——

Miss Hardcastle. I agree with you entirely, a want of courage upon some occasions assumes the appearance of ignorance, and betrays us when we most want to excel. I beg you'll proceed.

Marlow. Yes, madam. Morally speaking, madam——But I see Miss Neville expecting us in the next room. I would not intrude for the world.

Miss Hardcastle. I protest, Sir, I never was more agreeably entertained in all my life. Pray go on.

Marlow. Yes, madam. I was——But she beckons us to join her. Madam, shall I do myself the honour to attend you?

Miss Hardcastle. Well then, I'll follow.

Marlow. (*Aside*) This pretty, smooth dialogue has done for me. [*Exit.*

Miss HARDCASTLE *Sola*

Miss Hardcastle. Ha! ha! ha! Was there ever such a sober sentimental interview? I'm certain he scarce look'd in my face the whole time. Yet the fellow, but for his unaccountable bashfulness, is pretty well too. He has good sense, but then so buried in his fears, that it fatigues one more than ignorance. If I could teach him a little confidence, it would be doing somebody that I know of a piece of service. But who is that somebody?—that, faith, is a question I can scarce answer.

[*Exit.*

Enter TONY *and Miss* NEVILLE, *followed by Mrs.* HARDCASTLE *and* HASTINGS

Tony. What do you follow me for, cousin Con? I wonder you're not ashamed to be so very engaging.

Miss Neville. I hope, cousin, one may speak to one's own relations, and not be to blame.

Tony. Ay, but I know what sort of a relation you want to make me though; but it won't do. I tell you, cousin Con, it won't do, so I beg you'll keep your distance, I want no nearer relationship.

[*She follows coqueting him to the back scene.*

Mrs. Hardcastle. Well! I vow, Mr. Hastings, you are very entertaining. There's nothing in the world I love to talk of so much as London, and the fashions, though I was never there myself.

Hastings. Never there! You amaze me! From your air and manner, I concluded you had been bred all your life either at Ranelagh, St. James's, or Tower Wharf.

Mrs. Hardcastle. O! Sir, you're only pleased to say so. We Country persons can have no manner at all. I'm in love with the town, and that serves to raise me above some of our neighbouring rustics; but who can have a manner, that has never seen the Pantheon, the Grotto Gardens, the Borough, and such places where the Nobility chiefly resort? All I can do, is to enjoy London at second-hand. I take care to know every tête-à-tête from the Scandalous Magazine,[1] and have all the fashions as they come out, in a letter from the two Miss Rickets of Crooked-lane. Pray how do you like this head, Mr. Hastings?

Hastings. Extremely elegant and degagée, upon my word, Madam. Your Friseur is a Frenchman, I suppose?

Mrs. Hardcastle. I protest I dressed it myself from a print in the Ladies Memorandum-book for the last year.

Hastings. Indeed. Such a head in a side-box, at the Playhouse, would draw as many gazers as my Lady May'ress at a City Ball.

Mrs. Hardcastle. I vow, since inoculation began, there is no such thing to be seen as a plain woman; so one must dress a little particular or one may escape in the crowd.

Hastings. But that can never be your case, Madam, in any dress. (*Bowing*)

Mrs. Hardcastle. Yet, what signifies *my* dressing when I have such a piece of antiquity by my side as Mr. Hardcastle: all I can say will never argue down a single button from his cloaths. I have often wanted him to throw off his great flaxen

[1] [The *Town and Country Magazine* published "Tête-à-têtes," being paired portraits of celebrated couples, among them the Duke of Gloucester and Lady Waldegrave.]

wig, and where he was bald, to plaister it over like my Lord Pately, with powder.

Hastings. You are right, Madam; for, as among the ladies there are none ugly, so among the men there are none old.

Mrs. Hardcastle. But what do you think his answer was? Why, with his usual Gothic vivacity, he said I only wanted him to throw off his wig to convert it into a tête for my own wearing.

Hastings. Intolerable! At your age you may wear what you please, and it must become you.

Mrs. Hardcastle. Pray, Mr. Hastings, what do you take to be the most fashionable age about town?

Hastings. Some time ago, forty was all the mode; but I'm told the ladies intend to bring up fifty for the ensuing winter.

Mrs. Hardcastle. Seriously. Then I shall be too young for the fashion.

Hastings. No lady begins now to put on jewels till she's past forty. For instance, Miss there, in a polite circle, would be considered as a child, as a mere maker of samplers.

Mrs. Hardcastle. And yet Mrs. Niece thinks herself as much a woman, and is as fond of jewels as the oldest of us all.

Hastings. Your niece, is she? And that young gentleman, a brother of yours, I should presume?

Mrs. Hardcastle. My son, Sir. They are contracted to each other. Observe their little sports. They fall in and out ten times a day, as if they were man and wife already. (*To them*) Well Tony, child, what soft things are you saying to your cousin Constance this evening?

Tony. I have been saying no soft things; but that it's very hard to be followed about so. Ecod! I've not a place in the house now that's left to myself but the stable.

Mrs. Hardcastle. Never mind him, Con, my dear. He's in another story behind your back.

Miss Neville. There's something generous in my cousin's manner. He falls out before faces to be forgiven in private.

Tony. That's a damned confounded——crack.

Mrs. Hardcastle. Ah! he's a sly one. Don't you think they're like each other about the mouth, Mr. Hastings? The Blenkinsop mouth to a T. They're of a size too. Back to back, my pretties, that Mr. Hastings may see you. Come Tony.

Tony. You had as good not make me, I tell you. (*Measuring.*)

Miss Neville. O lud! he has almost cracked my head.

Mrs. Hardcastle. O the monster! For shame, Tony. You a man, and behave so!

Tony. If I'm a man, let me have my fortin. Ecod! I'll not be made a fool of no longer.

Mrs. Hardcastle. Is this, ungrateful boy, all that I'm to get for the pains I have taken in your education? I that have rock'd you in your cradle, and fed that pretty mouth with a spoon! Did not I work that waistcoat to make you genteel? Did not I prescribe for you every day, and weep while the receipt was operating?

Tony. Ecod! you had reason to weep, for you have been dosing me ever since I was born. I have gone through every receipt in the complete huswife ten times over; and you have thoughts of coursing me through *Quincy*[1] next spring. But, Ecod! I tell you, I'll not be made a fool of no longer.

Mrs. Hardcastle. Wasn't it all for your good, viper? Wasn't it all for your good?

Tony. I wish you'd let me and my good alone then. Snubbing this way when I'm in spirits. If I'm to have any good, let it come of itself; not to keep dinging it, dinging it into one so.

Mrs. Hardcastle. That's false; I never see you when you're in spirits. No, Tony, you then go to the alehouse or kennel. I'm never to be delighted with your agreeable, wild notes, unfeeling monster!

[1] [John Quincy's popular *Complete English Dispensatory,* which had run to a fourteenth edition by 1772.]

Tony. Ecod! Mamma, your own notes are the wildest of the two.

Mrs. Hardcastle. Was ever the like? But I see he wants to break my heart, I see he does.

Hastings. Dear Madam, permit me to lecture the young gentleman a little. I'm certain I can persuade him to his duty.

Mrs. Hardcastle. Well! I must retire. Come, Constance, my love. You see, Mr. Hastings, the wretchedness of my situation: Was ever poor woman so plagued with a dear, sweet, pretty, provoking, undutiful boy.

[*Exeunt Mrs.* Hardcastle *and Miss* Neville.

HASTINGS, TONY

Tony (*singing*). *There was a young man riding by, and fain would have his will. Rang do didlo dee.* Don't mind her. Let her cry. It's the comfort of her heart. I have seen her and sister cry over a book for an hour together, and they said, they liked the book the better the more it made them cry.

Hastings. Then you're no friend to the ladies, I find, my pretty young gentleman?

Tony. That's as I find 'um.

Hastings. Not to her of your mother's chusing, I dare answer? And yet she appears to me a pretty well-tempered girl.

Tony. That's because you don't know her as well as I. Ecod! I know every inch about her; and there's not a more bitter cantanckerous toad in all Christendom.

Hastings. (*Aside*) Pretty encouragement this for a lover!

Tony. I have seen her since the height of that. She has as many tricks as a hare in a thicket, or a colt the first day's breaking.

Hastings. To me she appears sensible and silent!

Tony. Ay, before company. But when she's with her playmates she's as loud as a hog in a gate.

Hastings. But there is a meek modesty about her that charms me.

Tony. Yes, but curb her never so little, she kicks up, and you're flung in a ditch.

Hastings. Well, but you must allow her a little beauty.—Yes, you must allow her some beauty.

Tony. Bandbox! She's all a made up thing, mun. Ah! could you but see Bet Bouncer of these parts, you might then talk of beauty. Ecod, she has two eyes as black as sloes, and cheeks as broad and red as a pulpit cushion. She'd make two of she.

Hastings. Well, what say you to a friend that would take this bitter bargain off your hands?

Tony. Anon?

Hastings. Would you thank him that would take Miss Neville and leave you to happiness and your dear Betsy?

Tony. Ay; but where is there such a friend, for who would take *her*?

Hastings. I am he. If you but assist me, I'll engage to whip her off to France, and you shall never hear more of her.

Tony. Assist you! Ecod I will, to the last drop of my blood. I'll clap a pair of horses to your chaise that shall trundle you off in a twinkling, and may be get you a part of her fortin beside, in jewels, that you little dream of.

Hastings. My dear squire, this looks like a lad of spirit.

Tony. Come along then, and you shall see more of my spirit before you have done with me. (*Singing*) *We are the boys that fears no noise where the thundering cannons roar.*

[*Exeunt.*

END OF THE SECOND ACT

ACT III

Enter HARDCASTLE *Solus*

Hardcastle. What could my old friend Sir Charles mean by recommending his son as the modestest young man in town? To me he appears the most impudent piece of brass that ever spoke with a tongue. He has taken possession of the easy chair by the fire-side already. He took off his boots in the parlour, and desired me to see them taken care of. I'm desirous to know how his impudence affects my daughter.—She will certainly be shocked at it.

Enter Miss HARDCASTLE, *plainly dress'd*

Hardcastle. Well, my Kate, I see you have changed your dress as I bid you; and yet, I believe, there was no great occasion.

Miss Hardcastle. I find such a pleasure, Sir, in obeying your commands, that I take care to observe them without ever debating their propriety.

Hardcastle. And yet, Kate, I sometimes give you some cause, particularly when I recommended my *modest* gentleman to you as a lover to-day.

Miss Hardcastle. You taught me to expect something extraordinary, and I find the original exceeds the description.

Hardcastle. I was never so surprized in my life! He has quite confounded all my faculties!

Miss Hardcastle. I never saw any thing like it: And a man of the world, too!

Hardcastle. Ay, he learned it all abroad,—what a fool was I, to think a young man could learn modesty by travelling. He might as soon learn wit at a masquerade.

Miss Hardcastle. It seems all natural to him.

Hardcastle. A good deal assisted by bad company and a French dancing-master.

Miss Hardcastle. Sure you mistake, papa! a French dancing-master could never have taught him that timid look,—that aukward address,—that bashful manner——

Hardcastle. Whose look? whose manner? child!

Miss Hardcastle. Mr. Marlow's: his meauvaise honte, his timidity struck me at the first sight.

Hardcastle. Then your first sight deceived you; for I think him one of the most brazen first sights that ever astonished my senses.

Miss Hardcastle. Sure, Sir, you rally! I never saw any one so modest.

Hardcastle. And can you be serious! I never saw such a bouncing swaggering puppy since I was born. Bully Dawson[1] was but a fool to him.

Miss Hardcastle. Surprizing! He met me with a respectful bow, a stammering voice, and a look fixed on the ground.

Hardcastle. He met me with a loud voice, a lordly air, and a familiarity that made my blood freeze again.

Miss Hardcastle. He treated me with diffidence and respect; censured the manners of the age; admired the prudence of girls that never laughed; tired me with apologies for being tiresome; then left the room with a bow, and, madam, I would not for the world detain you.

Hardcastle. He spoke to me as if he knew me all his life before. Asked twenty questions, and never waited for an answer. Interrupted my best remarks with some silly pun, and when I was in my best story of the Duke of Marlborough and Prince Eugene, he asked if I had not a good hand at making punch. Yes, Kate, he ask'd your father if he was a maker of punch!

Miss Hardcastle. One of us must certainly be mistaken.

Hardcastle. If he be what he has shewn himself, I'm determined he shall never have my consent.

Miss Hardcastle. And if he be the sullen thing I take him, he shall never have mine.

Hardcastle. In one thing then we are agreed—to reject him.

Miss Hardcastle. Yes. But upon conditions. For if you should find him less impudent, and I more presuming; if you find him more respectful, and I more importunate—I don't

[1] [A celebrated bully. Sir Roger de Coverley kicked him in a coffee-house. (*Spectator*, No. 2.)]

know—the fellow is well enough for a man—Certainly we don't meet many such at a horse race in the country.

Hardcastle. If we should find him so——But that's impossible. The first appearance has done my business. I'm seldom deceived in that.

Miss Hardcastle. And yet there may be many good qualities under that first appearance.

Hardcastle. Ay, when a girl finds a fellow's outside to her taste, she then sets about guessing the rest of his furniture. With her, a smooth face stands for good sense, and a genteel figure for every virtue.

Miss Hardcastle. I hope, Sir, a conversation begun with a compliment to my good sense won't end with a sneer at my understanding?

Hardcastle. Pardon me, Kate. But if young Mr. Brazen can find the art of reconciling contradictions, he may please us both, perhaps.

Miss Hardcastle. And as one of us must be mistaken, what if we go to make further discoveries?

Hardcastle. Agreed. But depend on't I'm in the right.

Miss Hardcastle. And depend on't I'm not much in the wrong. [*Exeunt.*

Enter TONY *running in with a Casket*

Tony. Ecod! I have got them. Here they are. My Cousin Con's necklaces, bobs and all. My mother shan't cheat the poor souls out of their fortune neither. O! my genus, is that you?

Enter HASTINGS

Hastings. My dear friend, how have you managed with your mother? I hope you have amused her with pretending love for your cousin, and that you are willing to be reconciled at last? Our horses will be refreshed in a short time, and we shall soon be ready to set off.

Tony. And here's something to bear your charges by the way. (*Giving the casket*) Your sweetheart's jewels. Keep them, and hang those, I say, that would rob you of one of them.

Hastings. But how have you procured them from your mother?

Tony. Ask me no questions, and I'll tell you no fibs. I procured them by the rule of thumb. If I had not a key to every drawer in mother's bureau, how could I go to the ale-house so often as I do? An honest man may rob himself of his own at any time.

Hastings. Thousands do it every day. But to be plain with you; Miss Neville is endeavouring to procure them from her aunt this very instant. If she succeeds, it will be the most delicate way at least of obtaining them.

Tony. Well, keep them, till you know how it will be. But I know how it will be well enough, she'd as soon part with the only sound tooth in her head.

Hastings. But I dread the effects of her resentment, when she finds she has lost them.

Tony. Never you mind her resentment, leave *me* to manage that. I don't value her resentment the bounce of a cracker. Zounds! here they are! Morrice, Prance.

[*Exit* Hastings.

TONY, *Mrs.* HARDCASTLE, *Miss* NEVILLE

Mrs. Hardcastle. Indeed, Constance, you amaze me. Such a girl as you want jewels? It will be time enough for jewels, my dear, twenty years hence, when your beauty begins to want repairs.

Miss Neville. But what will repair beauty at forty, will certainly improve it at twenty, Madam.

Mrs. Hardcastle. Yours, my dear, can admit of none. That natural blush is beyond a thousand ornaments. Besides, child, jewels are quite out at present. Don't you see half the ladies of our acquaintance, my lady Killdaylight, and Mrs. Crump, and the rest of them, carry their jewels to town, and bring nothing but Paste and Marcasites back?

Miss Neville. But who knows, Madam, but somebody that shall be nameless would like me best with all my little finery about me?

Mrs. Hardcastle. Consult your glass, my dear, and then see, if with such a pair of eyes, you want any better sparklers. What do you think, Tony, my dear, does your cousin Con want any jewels, in your eyes, to set off her beauty?

Tony. That's as thereafter may be.

Miss Neville. My dear aunt, if you knew how it would oblige me.

Mrs. Hardcastle. A parcel of old-fashioned rose and table-cut things. They would make you look like the court of king Solomon at a puppet-shew. Besides, I believe I can't readily come at them. They may be missing, for aught I know to the contrary.

Tony. (*Apart to Mrs. Hardcastle*) Then why don't you tell her so at once, as she's so longing for them. Tell her they're lost. It's the only way to quiet her. Say they're lost, and call me to bear witness.

Mrs. Hardcastle. (*Apart to Tony*) You know, my dear, I'm only keeping them for you. So if say I they're gone, you'll bear me witness, will you? He! he! he!

Tony. Never fear me. Ecod! I'll say I saw them taken out with my own eyes.

Miss Neville. I desire them but for a day, Madam. Just to be permitted to shew them as relicks, and then they may be lock'd up again.

Mrs. Hardcastle. To be plain with you, my dear Constance; if I could find them, you should have them. They're missing, I assure you. Lost, for aught I know; but we must have patience wherever they are.

Miss Neville. I'll not believe it; this is but a shallow pretence to deny me. I know they're too valuable to be so slightly kept, and as you are to answer for the loss.

Mrs. Hardcastle. Don't be alarm'd, Constance. If they be lost, I must restore an equivalent. But my son knows they are missing, and not to be found.

Tony. That I can bear witness to. They are missing, and not to be found, I'll take my oath on't.

Mrs. Hardcastle. You must learn resignation, my dear; for tho' we lose our fortune, yet we should not lose our patience. See me, how calm I am.

Miss Neville. Ay, people are generally calm at the misfortunes of others.

Mrs. Hardcastle. Now, I wonder a girl of your good sense should waste a thought upon such trumpery. We shall soon find them; and, in the mean time, you shall make use of my garnets till your jewels be found.

Miss Neville. I detest garnets.

Mrs. Hardcastle. The most becoming things in the world to set off a clear complexion. You have often seen how well they look upon me. You *shall* have them. [*Exit.*

Miss Neville. I dislike them of all things. You shan't stir.—Was ever any thing so provoking to mislay my own jewels, and force me to wear her trumpery.

Tony. Don't be a fool. If she gives you the garnets, take what you can get. The jewels are your own already. I have stolen them out of her bureau, and she does not know it. Fly to your spark, he'll tell you more of the matter. Leave me to manage *her*.

Miss Neville. My dear cousin.

Tony. Vanish. She's here, and has missed them already. Zounds! how she fidgets and spits about like a Catharine wheel.

Enter Mrs. HARDCASTLE

Mrs. Hardcastle. Confusion! thieves! robbers! We are cheated, plundered, broke open, undone.

Tony. What's the matter, what's the matter, mamma? I hope nothing has happened to any of the good family!

Mrs. Hardcastle. We are robbed. My bureau has been broke open, the jewels taken out, and I'm undone.

Tony. Oh! is that all? Ha, ha, ha. By the laws, I never saw it better acted in my life. Ecod, I thought you was ruin'd in earnest, ha, ha, ha.

Mrs. Hardcastle. Why, boy, I *am* ruined in earnest. My bureau has been broke open, and all taken away.

Tony. Stick to that; ha, ha, ha; stick to that. I'll bear witness, you know, call me to bear witness.

Mrs. Hardcastle. I tell you, Tony, by all that's precious, the jewels are gone, and I shall be ruin'd for ever.

Tony. Sure I know they're gone, and I am to say so.

Mrs. Hardcastle. My dearest Tony, but hear me. They're gone, I say.

Tony. By the laws, mamma, you make me for to laugh, ha, ha. I know who took them well enough, ha, ha, ha.

Mrs. Hardcastle. Was there ever such a blockhead, that can't tell the difference between jest and earnest. I tell you I'm not in jest, booby.

Tony. That's right, that's right: You must be in a bitter passion, and then nobody will suspect either of us. I'll bear witness that they are gone.

Mrs. Hardcastle. Was there ever such a cross-grain'd brute, that won't hear me! Can you bear witness that you're no better than a fool? Was ever poor woman so beset with fools on one hand, and thieves on the other!

Tony. I can bear witness to that.

Mrs. Hardcastle. Bear witness again, you blockhead, you, and I'll turn you out of the room directly. My poor niece, what will become of *her*! Do you laugh, you unfeeling brute, as if you enjoy'd my distress?

Tony. I can bear witness to that.

Mrs. Hardcastle. Do you insult me, monster? I'll teach you to vex your mother, I will.

Tony. I can bear witness to that.

[*He runs off, she follows him.*

Enter Miss HARDCASTLE *and* MAID

Miss Hardcastle. What an unaccountable creature is that brother of mine, to send them to the house as an inn, ha, ha. I don't wonder at his impudence.

Maid. But what is more, madam, the young gentleman as you passed by in your present dress, ask'd me if you were the bar maid? He mistook you for the bar maid, madam.

Miss Hardcastle. Did he? Then as I live I'm resolved to keep up the delusion. Tell me, Pimple, how do you like my present dress? Don't you think I look something like Cherry[1] in the Beaux Stratagem?

Maid. It's the dress, madam, that every lady wears in the country, but when she visits or receives company.

Miss Hardcastle. And are you sure he does not remember my face or person?

Maid. Certain of it.

Miss Hardcastle. I vow I thought so; for though we spoke for some time together, yet his fears were such, that he never once looked up during the interview. Indeed, if he had, my bonnet would have kept him from seeing me.

Maid. But what do you hope from keeping him in his mistake?

Miss Hardcastle. In the first place, I shall be *seen*, and that is no small advantage to a girl who brings her face to market. Then I shall perhaps make an acquaintance, and that's no small victory gained over one who never addresses any but the wildest of her sex. But my chief aim is to take my gentleman off his guard, and like an invisible champion of romance examine the giant's force before I offer to combat.

[1] [The landlord's daughter in Farquhar's play.]

Maid. But you are sure you can act your part, and disguise your voice, so that he may mistake that, as he has already mistaken your person?

Miss Hardcastle. Never fear me. I think I have got the true bar cant.—Did your honour call?——Attend the Lion there.——Pipes and tobacco for the Angel.—The Lamb has been outrageous this half hour.

Maid. It will do, madam. But he's here.

[*Exit* Maid.

Enter MARLOW

Marlow. What a bawling in every part of the house; I have scarce a moment's repose. If I go to the best room, there I find my host and his story. If I fly to the gallery, there we have my hostess with her curtesy down to the ground. I have at last got a moment to myself, and now for recollection.

[*Walks and muses.*

Miss Hardcastle. Did you call, Sir? did your honour call?

Marlow (*Musing*). As for Miss Hardcastle, she's too grave and sentimental for me.

Miss Hardcastle. Did your honour call?

[*She still places herself before him, he turning away.*

Marlow. No, child. (*Musing*) Besides from the glimpse I had of her, I think she squints.

Miss Hardcastle. I'm sure, Sir, I heard the bell ring.

Marlow. No. no. (*Musing*) I have pleased my father, however, by coming down, and I'll to-morrow please myself by returning.

[*Taking out his tablets, and perusing.*

Miss Hardcastle. Perhaps the other gentleman called, Sir?

Marlow. I tell you, no.

Miss Hardcastle. I should be glad to know, Sir. We have such a parcel of servants.

Marlow. No, no, I tell you. (*Looks full in her face*) Yes, child, I think I did call. I wanted——I wanted——I vow, child, you are vastly handsome!

Miss Hardcastle. O la, Sir, you'll make one asham'd.

Marlow. Never saw a more sprightly malicious eye. Yes, yes, my dear, I did call. Have you got any of your—a—what d'ye call it in the house?

Miss Hardcastle. No, Sir, we have been out of that these ten days.

Marlow. One may call in this house, I find, to very little purpose. Suppose I should call for a taste, just by way of trial, of the nectar of your lips; perhaps I might be disappointed in that too.

Miss Hardcastle. Nectar! nectar! that's a liquor there's no call for in these parts. French, I suppose. We keep no French wines here, Sir.

Marlow. Of true English growth, I assure you.

Miss Hardcastle. Then it's odd I should not know it. We brew all sorts of wines in this house, and I have lived here these eighteen years.

Marlow. Eighteen years! Why one would think, child, you kept the bar before you were born. How old are you?

Miss Hardcastle. O! Sir, I must not tell my age. They say women and music should never be dated.

Marlow. To guess at this distance, you can't be much above forty. (*Approaching*) Yet nearer I don't think so much. (*Approaching*) By coming close to some women they look younger still; but when we come very close indeed. (*Attempting to kiss her*)

Miss Hardcastle. Pray, Sir, keep your distance. One would think you wanted to know one's age as they do horses, by mark of mouth.

Marlow. I protest, child, you use me extremely ill. If you keep me at this distance, how is it possible you and I can be ever acquainted?

Miss Hardcastle. And who wants to be acquainted with you? I want no such acquaintance, not I. I'm sure you did not treat Miss Hardcastle that was here awhile ago in this obstropalous manner. I'll warrant me, before her you look'd dash'd, and kept bowing to the ground, and talk'd, for all the world, as if you was before a justice of peace.

Marlow. (*Aside*) Egad! she has hit it, sure enough. (*To her*) In awe of her, child? Ha! ha! ha! A mere, aukward, squinting thing, no, no. I find you don't know me. I laugh'd, and rallied her a little; but I was unwilling to be too severe. No, I could not be too severe, *curse me*!

Miss Hardcastle. O! then, Sir, you are a favourite, I find, among the ladies?

Marlow. Yes, my dear, a great favourite. And yet, hang me, I don't see what they find in me to follow. At the Ladies Club[1] in town I'm called their agreeable Rattle. Rattle, child, is not my real name, but one I'm known by. My name is Solomons. Mr. Solomons, my dear, at your service. (*Offering to salute her*)

Miss Hardcastle. Hold, sir; you were introducing me to your club, not to yourself. And you're so great a favourite there you say?

Marlow. Yes, my dear. There's Mrs. Mantrap, Lady Betty Blackleg, the Countess of Sligo, Mrs. Langhorns, old Miss Biddy Buckskin,[2] and your humble servant, keep up the spirit of the place.

Miss Hardcastle. Then it's a very merry place, I suppose.

Marlow. Yes, as merry as cards, suppers, wine, and old women can make us.

Miss Hardcastle. And their agreeable Rattle, ha! ha! ha!

[1] [The Female Coterie in Albemarle Street.]

[2] [Horace Walpole, who was a member of the Female Coterie and thought *She Stoops to Conquer* "a very wretched comedy," wrote to the Countess of Upper Ossory on 27 March, 1773,

> Miss Loyd is in the new play, by the name of Rachael Buckskin, though he has altered it in the printed copies. Somebody wrote for her a very sensible reproof to him, only it ended with an indecent *grossièreté*. However the fool took it seriously, and wrote a most dull and scurrilous answer; but, luckily for him, Mr. Beauclerk and Mr. Garrick intercepted it.]

Marlow. (*Aside*) Egad! I don't quite like this chit. She looks knowing, methinks. You laugh, child!

Miss Hardcastle. I can't but laugh to think what time they all have for minding their work or their family.

Marlow. (*Aside*) All's well, she don't laugh at me. (*To her*) Do *you* ever work, child?

Miss Hardcastle. Ay, sure. There's not a screen or a quilt in the whole house but what can bear witness to that.

Marlow. Odso! Then you must shew me your embroidery. I embroider and draw patterns myself a little. If you want a judge of your work you must apply to me. [*Seizing her hand.*

Miss Hardcastle. Ay, but the colours don't look well by candle light. You shall see all in the morning. [*Struggling.*

Marlow. And why not now, my angel? Such beauty fires beyond the power of resistance.——Pshaw! the father here! My old luck: I never nick'd seven that I did not throw ames ace[1] three times following. [*Exit* Marlow.

Enter HARDCASTLE, *who stands in surprize*

Hardcastle. So, madam! So I find *this* is your *modest* lover. This is your humble admirer that kept his eyes fixed on the ground, and only ador'd at humble distance. Kate, Kate, art thou not asham'd to deceive your father so?

Miss Hardcastle. Never trust me, dear papa, but he's still the modest man I first took him for, you'll be convinced of it as well as I.

Hardcastle. By the hand of my body, I believe his impudence is infectious! Didn't I see him seize your hand? Didn't I see him hawl you about like a milk maid? and now you talk of his respect and his modesty, forsooth!

Miss Hardcastle. But if I shortly convince you of his modesty, that he has only the faults that will pass off with time, and the virtues that will improve with age, I hope you'll forgive him.

[1] [A pair of aces.]

Hardcastle. The girl would actually make one run mad! I tell you I'll not be convinced. I am convinced. He has scarcely been three hours in the house, and he has already encroached on all my prerogatives. You may like his impudence, and call it modesty. But my son-in-law, madam, must have very different qualifications.

Miss Hardcastle. Sir, I ask but this night to convince you.

Hardcastle. You shall not have half the time, for I have thoughts of turning him out this very hour.

Miss Hardcastle. Give me that hour then, and I hope to satisfy you.

Hardcastle. Well, an hour let it be then. But I'll have no trifling with your father. All fair and open, do you mind me?

Miss Hardcastle. I hope, Sir, you have ever found that I considered your commands as my pride; for your kindness is such, that my duty as yet has been inclination. [*Exeunt.*

END OF THE THIRD ACT

ACT IV

Enter HASTINGS *and Miss* NEVILLE

Hastings. You surprise me! Sir Charles Marlow expected here this night? Where have you had your information?

Miss Neville. You may depend upon it. I just saw his letter to Mr. Hardcastle, in which he tells him he intends setting out a few hours after his son.

Hastings. Then, my Constance, all must be completed before he arrives. He knows me; and should he find me here, would discover my name, and perhaps my designs, to the rest of the family.

Miss Neville. The jewels, I hope, are safe.

Hastings. Yes, yes. I have sent them to Marlow, who keeps

the keys of our baggage. In the meantime, I'll go to prepare matters for our elopement. I have had the Squire's promise of a fresh pair of horses; and, if I should not see him again, will write him further directions. [*Exit.*

Miss Neville. Well! success attend you. In the meantime, I'll go amuse my aunt with the old pretence of a violent passion for my cousin. [*Exit.*

Enter MARLOW, *followed by a* SERVANT

Marlow. I wonder what Hastings could mean by sending me so valuable a thing as a casket to keep for him, when he knows the only place I have is the seat of a post-coach at an Inn-door. Have you deposited the casket with the landlady, as I ordered you? Have you put it into her own hands?

Servant. Yes, your honour.

Marlow. She said she'd keep it safe, did she?

Servant. Yes, she said she'd keep it safe enough; she asked me how I came by it? and she said she had a great mind to make me give an account of myself. [*Exit* Servant.

Marlow. Ha! ha! ha! They're safe however. What an unaccountable set of beings have we got amongst! This little bar-maid though runs in my head most strangely, and drives out the absurdities of all the rest of the family. She's mine, she must be mine, or I'm greatly mistaken.

Enter HASTINGS

Hastings. Bless me! I quite forgot to tell her that I intended to prepare at the bottom of the garden. Marlow here, and in spirits too!

Marlow. Give me joy, George! Crown me, shadow me with laurels! Well, George, after all, we modest fellows don't want for success among the women.

Hastings. Some women you mean. But what success has your honour's modesty been crowned with now, that it grows so insolent upon us?

Marlow. Didn't you see the tempting, brisk, lovely little thing that runs about the house with a bunch of keys to its girdle?

Hastings. Well! and what then?

Marlow. She's mine, you rogue you. Such fire, such motion, such eyes, such lips——but egad! she would not let me kiss them though.

Hastings. But are you sure, so very sure of her?

Marlow. Why man, she talk'd of shewing me her work above-stairs, and I am to improve the pattern.

Hastings. But how can *you*, Charles, go about to rob a woman of her honour?

Marlow. Pshaw! pshaw! we all know the honour of the bar-maid of an inn. I don't intend to *rob* her, take my word for it, there's nothing in this house, I shan't honestly *pay* for.

Hastings. I believe the girl has virtue.

Marlow. And if she has, I should be the last man in the world that would attempt to corrupt it.

Hastings. You have taken care, I hope, of the casket I sent you to lock up? It's in safety?

Marlow. Yes, yes. It's safe enough. I have taken care of it. But how could you think the seat of a post-coach at an Inn-door a place of safety? Ah! numbskull! I have taken better precautions for you than you did for yourself.——I have——

Hastings. What!

Marlow. I have sent it to the landlady to keep for you.

Hastings. To the landlady!

Marlow. The landlady.

Hastings. You did.

Marlow. I did. She's to be answerable for its forth-coming, you know.

Hastings. Yes, she'll bring it forth with a witness.

Marlow. Wasn't I right? I believe you'll allow that I acted prudently upon this occasion?

Hastings. (*Aside*) He must not see my uneasiness.

Marlow. You seem a little disconcerted though, methinks. Sure nothing has happened?

Hastings. No, nothing. Never was I in better spirits in all my life. And so you left it with the landlady, who, no doubt, very readily undertook the charge?

Marlow. Rather too readily. For she not only kept the casket; but, thro' her great precaution, was going to keep the messenger too. Ha! ha! ha!

Hastings. He! he! he! They're safe however.

Marlow. As a guinea in a miser's purse.

Hastings. (*Aside*) So now all hopes of fortune are at an end, and we must set off without it. (*To him*) Well, Charles, I'll leave you to your meditations on the pretty bar-maid, and, he! he! he! may you be as successful for yourself as you have been for me. [*Exit.*

Marlow. Thank ye, George! I ask no more. Ha! ha! ha!

Enter HARDCASTLE

Hardcastle. I no longer know my own house. It's turned all topsey-turvey. His servants have got drunk already. I'll bear it no longer, and yet, from my respect for his father, I'll be calm. (*To him*) Mr. Marlow, your servant. I'm your very humble servant. (*Bowing low*)

Marlow. Sir, your humble servant. (*Aside*) What's to be the wonder now?

Hardcastle. I believe, Sir, you must be sensible, Sir, that no man alive ought to be more welcome than your father's son, Sir. I hope you think so?

Marlow. I do, from my soul, Sir. I don't want much intreaty. I generally make my father's son welcome wherever he goes.

Hardcastle. I believe you do, from my soul, Sir. But tho' I say nothing to your own conduct, that of your Servants is insufferable. Their manner of drinking is setting a very bad example in this house, I assure you.

Marlow. I protest, my very good Sir, that's no fault of mine. If they don't drink as they ought *they* are to blame. I ordered them not to spare the cellar. I did, I assure you. (*To the side scene*) Here, let one of my servants come up. (*To him*) My positive directions were, that as I did not drink myself, they should make up for my deficiencies below.

Hardcastle. Then they had your orders for what they do! I'm satisfied!

Marlow. They had, I assure [you]. You shall hear from one of themselves.

Enter SERVANT, *drunk*

Marlow. You, Jeremy! Come forward, sirrah! What were my orders? Were you not told to drink freely, and call for what you thought fit, for the good of the house?

Hardcastle. (*Aside*) I begin to lose my patience.

Jeremy. Please your honour, liberty and Fleet-street for ever! Tho' I'm but a servant, I'm as good as another man. I'll drink for no man before supper, Sir, dammy! Good liquor will sit upon a good supper, but a good supper will not sit upon ——hiccup——upon my conscience, Sir.

Marlow. You see, my old friend, the fellow is as drunk as he can possibly be. I don't know what you'd have more, unless you'd have the poor devil soused in a beer-barrel.

Hardcastle. Zounds! He'll drive me distracted if I contain myself any longer. Mr. Marlow. Sir; I have submitted to your insolence for more than four hours, and I see no likelihood of its coming to an end. I'm now resolved to be master here, Sir, and I desire that you and your drunken pack may leave my house directly.

Marlow. Leave your house!—Sure, you jest, my good friend! What, when I'm doing what I can to please you.

Hardcastle. I tell you, Sir, you don't please me; so I desire you'll leave my house.

Marlow. Sure, you cannot be serious! At this time o'night, and such a night. You only mean to banter me?

Hardcastle. I tell you, Sir, I'm serious; and, now that my passions are rouzed, I say this house is mine, Sir; this house is mine, and I command you to leave it directly.

Marlow. Ha! ha! ha! A puddle in a storm. I shan't stir a step, I assure you. (*In a serious tone*) This your house, fellow! It's my house. This is my house. Mine, while I chuse to stay. What right have you to bid me leave this house, Sir? I never met with such impudence, curse me, never in my whole life before.

Hardcastle. Nor I, confound me if ever I did. To come to my house, to call for what he likes, to turn me out of my own chair, to insult the family, to order his servants to get drunk, and then to tell me *This house is mine, Sir.* By all that's impudent, it makes me laugh. Ha! ha! ha! Pray, Sir, (*Bantering*) as you take the house, what think you of taking the rest of the furniture? There's a pair of silver candlesticks, and there's a fire-screen, and here's a pair of brazen nosed bellows, perhaps you may take a fancy to them?

Marlow. Bring me your bill, Sir, bring me your bill, and let's make no more words about it.

Hardcastle. There are a set of prints too. What think you of the rake's progress for your own apartment?

Marlow. Bring me your bill, I say; and I'll leave you and your infernal house directly.

Hardcastle. Then there's a mahogany table, that you may see your own face in.

Marlow. My bill, I say.

Hardcastle. I had forgot the great chair, for your own particular slumbers, after a hearty meal.

Marlow. Zounds! bring me my bill, I say, and let's hear no more on't.

Hardcastle. Young man, young man, from your father's letter to me, I was taught to expect a well-bred modest man, as a visitor here, but now I find him no better than a coxcomb and a bully; but he will be down here presently, and shall hear more of it. [*Exit.*

Marlow. How's this! Sure, I have not mistaken the house! Every thing looks like an inn. The servants cry, coming. The attendance is aukward; the bar-maid too to attend us. But she's here, and will further inform me. Whither so fast, child. A word with you.

Enter Miss HARDCASTLE

Miss Hardcastle. Let it be short, then. I'm in a hurry. (*Aside*) (I believe he begins to find out his mistake, but it's too soon quite to undeceive him.)

Marlow. Pray, child, answer me one question. What are you, and what may your business in this house be?

Miss Hardcastle. A relation of the family, Sir.

Marlow. What. A poor relation?

Miss Hardcastle. Yes, Sir. A poor relation appointed to keep the keys, and to see that the guests want nothing in my power to give them.

Marlow. That is, you act as the bar-maid of this inn.

Miss Hardcastle. Inn. O law—What brought that in your head. One of the best families in the county keep an inn. Ha, ha, ha, old Mr. Hardcastle's house an inn.

Marlow. Mr. Hardcastle's house! Is this house Mr. Hardcastle's house, child!

Miss Hardcastle. Ay, sure. Whose else should it be.

Marlow. So then all's out, and I have been damnably imposed on. O, confound my stupid head, I shall be laugh'd at over the whole town. I shall be stuck up in caricatura in all the print-shops. The Dullissimo Maccaroni.[1] To mistake this house of all others for an inn, and my father's old friend for an

[1] [The caricatures in the print-shops often had titles of this kind, *e.g. The Southwark Macaroni* (Mr. Thrale) and *The Martial Macaroni* (Goldsmith's friend, Ensign Horneck).]

inn-keeper. What a swaggering puppy must he take me for. What a silly puppy do I find myself. There again, may I be hang'd, my dear, but I mistook you for the bar-maid.

Miss Hardcastle. Dear me! dear me! I'm sure there's nothing in my *behavour* to put me upon a level with one of that stamp.

Marlow. Nothing, my dear, nothing. But I was in for a list of blunders, and could not help making you a subscriber. My stupidity saw every thing the wrong way. I mistook your assiduity for assurance, and your simplicity for allurement. But its over—This house I no more shew *my* face in!

Miss Hardcastle. I hope, Sir, I have done nothing to disoblige you. I'm sure I should be sorry to affront any gentleman who has been so polite, and said so many civil things to me. I'm sure I should be sorry (*Pretending to cry*) if he left the family upon my account. I'm sure I should be sorry, people said any thing amiss, since I have no fortune but my character.

Marlow. (*Aside*) By heaven, she weeps. This is the first mark of tenderness I ever had from a modest woman, and it touches me; (*To her*) Excuse me, my lovely girl, you are the only part of the family I leave with reluctance. But to be plain with you, the difference of our birth, fortune and education, make an honourable connexion impossible; and I can never harbour a thought of seducing simplicity that trusted in my honour, or bringing ruin upon one whose only fault was being too lovely.

Miss Hardcastle. (*Aside*) Generous man! I now begin to admire him. (*To him*) But I'm sure my family is as good as Miss Hardcastle's, and though I'm poor, that's no great misfortune to a contented mind, and, until this moment, I never thought that it was bad to want fortune.

Marlow. And why now, my pretty simplicity?

Miss Hardcastle. Because it puts me at a distance from one, that if I had a thousand pound I would give it all to.

Marlow. (*Aside*) This simplicity bewitches me, so that

if I stay I'm undone. I must make one bold effort, and leave her. (*To her*) Your partiality in my favour, my dear, touches me most sensibly, and were I to live for myself alone, I could easily fix my choice. But I owe too much to the opinion of the world, too much to the authority of a father, so that—I can scarcely speak it—it affects me. Farewell. [*Exit.*

Miss Hardcastle. I never knew half his merit till now. He shall not go, if I have power or art to detain him. I'll still preserve the character in which I stoop'd to conquer, but will undeceive my papa, who, perhaps, may laugh him out of his resolution. [*Exit.*

Enter TONY, *Miss* NEVILLE

Tony. Ay, you may steal for yourselves the next time. I have done my duty. She has got the jewels again, that's a sure thing; but she believes it was all a mistake of the servants.

Miss Neville. But, my dear cousin, sure you won't forsake us in this distress. If she in the least suspects that I am going off, I shall certainly be locked up, or sent to my aunt Pedigree's, which is ten times worse.

Tony. To be sure, aunts of all kinds are damn'd bad things. But what can I do? I have got you a pair of horses that will fly like Whistlejacket,[1] and I'm sure you can't say but I have courted you nicely before her face. Here she comes, we must court a bit or two more, for fear she should suspect us.

[*They retire, and seem to fondle.*

Enter Mrs. HARDCASTLE

Mrs. Hardcastle. Well, I was greatly fluttered, to be sure. But my son tells me it was all a mistake of the servants. I shan't be easy, however, till they are fairly married, and then let her keep her own fortune. But what do I see! Fondling together, as I'm alive. I never saw Tony so sprightly before. Ah! have I caught you, my pretty doves! What, billing, exchanging stolen glances, and broken murmurs. Ah!

[1] [The Marquis of Rockingham's celebrated chestnut horse.]

Tony. As for murmurs, mother, we grumble a little now and then, to be sure. But there's no love lost between us.

Mrs. Hardcastle. A mere sprinkling, Tony, upon the flame, only to make it burn brighter.

Miss Neville. Cousin Tony promises to give us more of his company at home. Indeed, he shan't leave us any more. It won't leave us cousin Tony, will it?

Tony. O! it's a pretty creature. No, I'd sooner leave my horse in a pound, than leave you when you smile upon one so. Your laugh makes you so becoming.

Miss Neville. Agreeable cousin! Who can help admiring that natural humour, that pleasant, broad, red, thoughtless, (*Patting his cheek*) ah! it's a bold face.

Mrs. Hardcastle. Pretty innocence.

Tony. I'm sure I always lov'd cousin Con's hazle eyes, and her pretty long fingers, that she twists this way and that, over the haspicholls, like a parcel of bobbins.

Mrs. Hardcastle. Ah, he would charm the bird from the tree. I was never so happy before. My boy takes after his father, poor Mr. Lumpkin, exactly. The jewels, my dear Con, shall be your's incontinently. You shall have them. Isn't he a sweet boy, my dear? You shall be married to-morrow, and we'll put off the rest of his education, like Dr. Drowsy's sermons, to a fitter opportunity.

Enter DIGGORY

Diggory. Where's the 'Squire? I have got a letter for your worship.

Tony. Give it to my mamma. She reads all my letters first.

Diggory. I had orders to deliver it into your own hands.

Tony. Who does it come from?

Diggory. Your worship mun ask that o' the letter itself.

Tony. I could wish to know, tho'. (*Turning the letter*, *and gazing on it.*)

Miss Neville. (*Aside*) Undone, undone. A letter to him

from Hastings. I know the hand. If my aunt sees it, we are ruined for ever. I'll keep her employ'd a little if I can. (*To Mrs. Hardcastle*) But I have not told you, Madam, of my cousin's smart answer just now to Mr. Marlow. We so laugh'd—You must know, Madam—this way a little, for he must not hear us. [*They confer.*

Tony. (*Still gazing*) A damn'd cramp piece of penmanship, as ever I saw in my life. I can read your print-hand very well. But here there are such handles, and shanks, and dashes, that one can scarce tell the head from the tail. *To Anthony Lumpkin, Esquire.* It's very odd, I can read the outside of my letters, where my own name is, well enough. But when I come to open it, it's all—buzz. That's hard, very hard; for the inside of the letter is always the cream of the correspondence.

Mrs. Hardcastle. Ha, ha, ha. Very well, very well. And so my son was too hard for the philosopher.

Miss Neville. Yes, Madam; but you must hear the rest, Madam. A little more this way, or he may hear us. You'll hear how he puzzled him again.

Mrs. Hardcastle. He seems strangely puzzled now himself, methinks.

Tony. (*Still gazing*) A damned up and down hand, as if it was disguised in liquor. (*Reading*) *Dear Sir.* Ay, that's that. Then there's an *M*, and a *T*, and an *S*, but whether the next be an *izzard* or an *R*, confound me, I cannot tell.

Mrs. Hardcastle. What's that, my dear. Can I give you any assistance?

Miss Neville. Pray, aunt, let me read it. No body reads a cramp hand better than I. (*Twitching the letter from her*) Do you know who it is from?

Tony. Can't tell, except from Dick Ginger the feeder.[1]

Miss Neville. Ay, so it is, (*Pretending to read*) Dear 'Squire, Hoping that you're in health, as I am at this present. The gentlemen of the Shake bag club has cut the gentlemen of

[1] [The feeder of the cocks or the hounds. See the footnote on p. 47.]

goose-green quite out of feather. The odds—um—odd battle —um—long fighting—um here, here, it's all about cocks, and fighting; it's of no consequence, here, put it up, put it up.

[*Thrusting the crumpled letter upon him.*

Tony. But I tell you, Miss, it's of all the consequence in the world. I would not lose the rest of it for a guinea. Here, mother, do you make it out. Of no consequence!

[*Giving Mrs. Hardcastle the letter.*

Mrs. Hardcastle. How's this! (*Reads*) Dear 'Squire, I'm now waiting for Miss Neville, with a post-chaise and pair, at the bottom of the garden, but I find my horses yet unable to perform the journey. I expect you'll assist us with a pair of fresh horses, as you promised. Dispatch is necessary, as the *hag* (ay the hag) your mother, will otherwise suspect us. Your's, Hastings. Grant me patience. I shall run distracted. My rage choaks me.

Miss Neville. I hope, Madam, you'll suspend your resentment for a few moments, and not impute to me any impertinence, or sinister design that belongs to another.

Mrs. Hardcastle. (*Curtesying very low*) Fine spoken, Madam, you are most miraculously polite and engaging, and quite the very pink of curtesy and circumspection, Madam. (*Changing her tone*) And you, you great ill-fashioned oaf, with scarce sense enough to keep your mouth shut. Were you too join'd against me? But I'll defeat all your plots in a moment. As for you, Madam, since you have got a pair of fresh horses ready, it would be cruel to disappoint them. So, if you please, instead of running away with your spark, prepare, this very moment, to run off with *me*. Your old aunt Pedigree will keep you secure, I'll warrant me. You too, Sir, may mount your horse, and guard us upon the way. Here, Thomas, Roger, Diggory, I'll shew you, that I wish you better than you do yourselves. [*Exit.*

Miss Neville. So now I'm completely ruined.

Tony. Ay, that's a sure thing.

Miss Neville. What better could be expected from being connected with such a stupid fool, and after all the nods and signs I made him.

Tony. By the laws, Miss, it was your own cleverness, and not my stupidity, that did your business. You were so nice and so busy with your Shake-bags and Goose-greens, that I thought you could never be making believe.

Enter HASTINGS

Hastings. So, Sir, I find by my servant, that you have shewn my letter, and betray'd us. Was this well done, young gentleman?

Tony. Here's another. Ask Miss there who betray'd you. Ecod, it was her doing, not mine.

Enter MARLOW

Marlow. So I have been finely used here among you. Rendered contemptible, driven into ill manners, despised, insulted, laugh'd at.

Tony. Here's another. We shall have old Bedlam broke loose presently.

Miss Neville. And there, Sir, is the gentleman to whom we all owe every obligation.

Marlow. What can I say to him, a mere boy, an ideot, whose ignorance and age are a protection.

Hastings. A poor contemptible booby, that would but disgrace correction.

Miss Neville. Yet with cunning and malice enough to make himself merry with all our embarrassments.

Hastings. An insensible cub.

Marlow. Replete with tricks and mischief.

Tony. Baw! damme, but I'll fight you both one after the other,——with baskets.[1]

Marlow. As for him, he's below resentment. But your

[1] [Basket-hilted swords.]

conduct, Mr. Hastings, requires an explanation. You knew of my mistakes, yet would not undeceive me.

Hastings. Tortured as I am with my own disappointments, is this a time for explanations? It is not friendly, Mr. Marlow.

Marlow. But, Sir—

Miss Neville. Mr. Marlow, we never kept on your mistake, till it was too late to undeceive you. Be pacified.

Enter SERVANT

Servant. My mistress desires you'll get ready immediately, Madam. The horses are putting to. Your hat and things are in the next room. We are to go thirty miles before morning. [*Exit* Servant.

Miss Neville. Well, well; I'll come presently.

Marlow. (*To Hastings*) Was it well done, Sir, to assist in rendering me ridiculous? To hang me out for the scorn of all my acquaintance. Depend upon it, Sir, I shall expect an explanation.

Hastings. Was it well done, Sir, if you're upon that subject, to deliver what I entrusted to yourself, to the care of another, Sir?

Miss Neville. Mr. Hastings. Mr. Marlow. Why will you increase my distress by this groundless dispute? I implore, I entreat you——

Enter SERVANT

Servant. Your cloak, Madam. My mistress is impatient.

Miss Neville. I come. Pray be pacified. If I leave you thus, I shall die with apprehension.

Enter SERVANT

Servant. Your fan, muff, and gloves, Madam. The horses are waiting.

Miss Neville. O, Mr. Marlow! if you knew what a scene of constraint and ill-nature lies before me, I'm sure it would convert your resentment into pity.

Marlow. I'm so distracted with a variety of passions, that I don't know what I do. Forgive me, Madam. George, forgive me. You know my hasty temper, and should not exasperate it.

Hastings. The torture of my situation is my only excuse.

Miss Neville. Well, my dear Hastings, if you have that esteem for me that I think, that I am sure you have, your constancy for three years will but encrease the happiness of our future connection. If—

Mrs. Hardcastle. (*Within*) Miss Neville. Constance, why Constance, I say

Miss Neville. I'm coming. Well, constancy. Remember, constancy is the word. [*Exit.*

Hastings. My heart! How can I support this. To be so near happiness, and such happiness.

Marlow. (*To Tony*) You see now, young gentleman the effects of your folly. What might be amusement to you, is here disappointment, and even distress.

Tony (*From a reverie*). Ecod, I have hit it. It's here. Your hands. Yours and yours, my poor Sulky. My boots there, ho. Meet me two hours hence at the bottom of the garden; and if you don't find Tony Lumpkin a more good-natur'd fellow than you thought for, I'll give you leave to take my best horse, and Bet Bouncer into the bargain. Come along. My boots, ho! [*Exeunt.*

END OF THE FOURTH ACT

ACT V

SCENE *Continues*

Enter HASTINGS *and* SERVANT

Hastings. You saw the Old Lady and Miss Neville drive off, you say.

Servant. Yes, your honour. They went off in a post coach,

and the young 'Squire went on horseback. They're thirty miles off by this time.

Hastings. Then all my hopes are over.

Servant. Yes, Sir. Old Sir Charles is arrived. He and the Old Gentleman of the house have been laughing at Mr. Marlow's mistake this half hour. They are coming this way.

Hastings. Then I must not be seen. So now to my fruitless appointment at the bottom of the garden. This is about the time. [*Exit.*

Enter Sir CHARLES *and* HARDCASTLE

Hardcastle. Ha, ha, ha. The peremptory tone in which he sent forth his sublime commands.

Sir Charles. And the reserve with which I suppose he treated all your advances.

Hardcastle. And yet he might have seen something in me above a common inn-keeper, too.

Sir Charles. Yes, Dick, but he mistook you for an uncommon innkeeper, ha, ha, ha.

Hardcastle. Well, I'm in too good spirits to think of anything but joy. Yes, my dear friend, this union of our families will make our personal friendships hereditary; and tho' my daughter's fortune is but small——

Sir Charles. Why, Dick, will you talk of fortune to *me.* My son is possessed of more than a competence already, and can want nothing but a good and virtuous girl to share his happiness and encrease it. If they like each other, as you say they do——

Hardcastle. If, man. I tell you they *do* like each other. My daughter as good as told me so.

Sir Charles. But girls are apt to flatter themselves, you know.

Hardcastle. I saw him grasp her hand in the warmest manner, myself; and here he comes to put you out of your *iffs,* I warrant him.

Enter MARLOW

Marlow. I come, Sir, once more, to ask pardon for my strange conduct. I can scarce reflect on my insolence without confusion.

Hardcastle. Tut, boy, a trifle. You take it too gravely. An hour or two's laughing with my daughter will set all to rights again. She'll never like you the worse for it.

Marlow. Sir, I shall be always proud of her approbation.

Hardcastle. Approbation is but a cold word, Mr. Marlow; if I am not deceived, you have something more than approbation thereabouts. You take me.

Marlow. Really, Sir, I have not that happiness.

Hardcastle. Come, boy, I'm an old fellow, and know what's what, as well as you that are younger. I know what has past between you; but mum.

Marlow. Sure, Sir, nothing has past between us but the most profound respect on my side, and the most distant reserve on her's. You don't think, Sir, that my impudence has been past upon all the rest of the family.

Hardcastle. Impudence! No, I don't say that—Not quite impudence—Though girls like to be play'd with, and rumpled a little too, sometimes. But she has told no tales, I assure you.

Marlow. I never gave her the slightest cause.

Hardcastle. Well, well, I like modesty in its place well enough. But this is over-acting, young gentleman. You *may* be open. Your father and I will like you the better for it.

Marlow. May I die, Sir, if I ever——

Hardcastle. I tell you, she don't dislike you; and as I'm sure you like her——

Marlow. Dear Sir—I protest, Sir——

Hardcastle. I see no reason why you should not be joined as fast as the parson can tie you.

Marlow. But hear me, Sir——

Hardcastle. Your father approves the match, I admire it, every moment's delay will be doing mischief, so——

Marlow. But why won't you hear me? By all that's just and true, I never gave Miss Hardcastle the slightest mark of my attachment, or even the most distant hint to suspect me of affection. We had but one interview, and that was formal, modest and uninteresting.

Hardcastle. (*Aside*) This fellow's formal modest impudence is beyond bearing.

Sir Charles. And you never grasp'd her hand, or made any protestations!

Marlow. As heaven is my witness, I came down in obedience to your commands. I saw the lady without emotion, and parted without reluctance. I hope you'll exact no further proofs of my duty, nor prevent me from leaving a house in which I suffer so many mortifications. [*Exit.*

Sir Charles. I'm astonish'd at the air of sincerity with which he parted.

Hardcastle. And I'm astonish'd at the deliberate intrepidity of his assurance.

Sir Charles. I dare pledge my life and honour upon his truth.

Hardcastle. Here comes my daughter, and I would stake my happiness upon her veracity.

Enter Miss HARDCASTLE

Hardcastle. Kate, come hither, child. Answer us sincerely, and without reserve; has Mr. Marlow made you any professions of love and affection?

Miss Hardcastle. The question is very abrupt, Sir! But since you require unreserved sincerity, I think he has.

Hardcastle. (*To Sir Charles*) You see.

Sir Charles. And pray, madam, have you and my son had more than one interview?

Miss Hardcastle. Yes, Sir, several.

Hardcastle. (*To Sir Charles*) You see.

Sir Charles. But did he profess any attachment?

Miss Hardcastle. A lasting one.

Sir Charles. Did he talk of love?

Miss Hardcastle. Much, Sir.

Sir Charles. Amazing! And all this formally?

Miss Hardcastle. Formally.

Hardcastle. Now, my friend, I hope you are satisfied.

Sir Charles. And how did he behave, madam?

Miss Hardcastle. As most profest admirers do. Said some civil things of my face, talked much of his want of merit, and the greatness of mine; mentioned his heart, gave a short tragedy speech, and ended with pretended rapture.

Sir Charles. Now I'm perfectly convinced, indeed. I know his conversation among women to be modest and submissive. This forward canting ranting manner by no means describes him, and I am confident, he never sat for the picture.

Miss Hardcastle. Then what, Sir, if I should convince you to your face of my sincerity? If you and my papa, in about half an hour, will place yourselves behind that screen, you shall hear him declare his passion to me in person.

Sir Charles. Agreed. And if I find him what you describe, all my happiness in him must have an end. [*Exit*..

Miss Hardcastle. And if you don't find him what I describe —I fear my happiness must never have a beginning.

[*Exeunt*.

SCENE *changes to the Back of the Garden*

Enter HASTINGS

Hastings. What an ideot am I, to wait here for a fellow, who probably takes a delight in mortifying me. He never intended to be punctual, and I'll wait no longer. What do I see. It is he, and perhaps with news of my Constance.

Enter TONY, *booted and spattered*

Hastings. My honest 'Squire! I now find you a man of your word. This looks like friendship.

Tony. Ay, I'm your friend, and the best friend you have in the world, if you knew but all. This riding by night, by the bye, is cursedly tiresome. It has shook me worse than the basket of a stage-coach.

Hastings. But how? Where did you leave your fellow-travellers? Are they in safety? Are they housed?

Tony. Five and twenty miles in two hours and a half is no such bad driving. The poor beasts have smoaked for it: Rabbet me, but I'd rather ride forty miles after a fox, than ten with such *varment.*

Hastings. Well, but where have you left the ladies? I die with impatience.

Tony. Left them? Why, where should I leave them, but where I found them?

Hastings. This is a riddle.

Tony. Riddle me this, then. What's that goes round the house, and round the house, and never touches the house?

Hastings. I'm still astray.

Tony. Why, that's it, mon. I have led them astray. By jingo, there's not a pond or slough within five miles of the place but they can tell the taste of.

Hastings. Ha, ha, ha, I understand; you took them in a round, while they supposed themselves going forward. And so you have at last brought them home again.

Tony. You shall hear. I first took them down Feather-bed-lane, where we stuck fast in the mud. I then rattled them crack over the stones of Up-and-down Hill—I then introduc'd them to the gibbet on Heavy-tree Heath, and from that, with a circumbendibus, I fairly lodged them in the horsepond at the bottom of the garden.

Hastings. But no accident, I hope.

Tony. No, no. Only mother is confoundedly frightened. She thinks herself forty miles off. She's sick of the journey, and the cattle can scarce crawl. So if your own horses be ready, you may whip off with cousin, and I'll be bound that no soul here can budge a foot to follow you.

Hastings. My dear friend, how can I be grateful?

Tony. Ay, now its dear friend, noble 'Squire. Just now, it was all ideot, cub, and run me through the guts. Damn *your* way of fighting, I say. After we take a knock in this part of the country, we kiss and be friends. But if you had run me through the guts, then I should be dead, and you might go kiss the hangman.

Hastings. The rebuke is just. But I must hasten to relieve Miss Neville; if you keep the old lady employed, I promise to take care of the young one. [*Exit* Hastings.

Tony. Never fear me. Here she comes. Vanish. She's got from the pond, and draggled up to the waist like a mermaid.

Enter Mrs. HARDCASTLE

Mrs. Hardcastle. Oh, Tony, I'm killed. Shook. Battered to death. I shall never survive it. That last jolt that laid us against the quickset hedge has done my business.

Tony. Alack, mamma, it was all your own fault. You would be for running away by night, without knowing one inch of the way.

Mrs. Hardcastle. I wish we were at home again. I never met so many accidents in so short a journey. Drench'd in the mud, overturn'd in a ditch, stuck fast in a slough, jolted to a jelly, and at last to lose our way. Whereabouts do you think we are, Tony?

Tony. By my guess we should be upon Crackskull common, about forty miles from home.

Mrs. Hardcastle. O lud! O lud! the most notorious spot in all the country. We only want a robbery to make a complete night on't.

Tony. Don't be afraid, mama, don't be afraid. Two of the five that kept here are hanged, and the other three may not find us. Don't be afraid. Is that a man that's galloping behind us? No; it's only a tree. Don't be afraid.

Mrs. Hardcastle. The fright will certainly kill me.

Tony. Do you see anything like a black hat moving behind the thicket?

Mrs. Hardcastle. O death!

Tony. No, it's only a cow. Don't be afraid, mama; don't be afraid.

Mrs. Hardcastle. As I'm alive, Tony, I see a man coming towards us. Ah! I'm sure on't. If he perceives us, we are undone.

Tony. (*Aside*) Father-in-law, by all that's unlucky, come to take one of his night walks. (*To her*) Ah, it's a highwayman, with pistils as long as my arm. A damn'd ill-looking fellow.

Mrs. Hardcastle. Good heaven defend us! He approaches.

Tony. Do you hide yourself in that thicket, and leave me to manage him. If there be any danger I'll cough and cry hem. When I cough be sure to keep close.

[*Mrs. Hardcastle hides behind a tree in the back scene.*

Enter HARDCASTLE

Hardcastle. I'm mistaken, or I heard voices of people in want of help. Oh, Tony, is that you? I did not expect you so soon back. Are your mother and her charge in safety?

Tony. Very safe, Sir, at my aunt Pedigree's. Hem.

Mrs. Hardcastle. (*From behind*) Ah death! I find there's danger.

Hardcastle. Forty miles in three hours; sure, that's too much, my youngster.

Tony. Stout horses and willing minds make short journeys, as they say. Hem.

Mrs. Hardcastle. (*From behind*) Sure he'll do the dear boy no harm.

Hardcastle. But I heard a voice here; I should be glad to know from whence it came?

Tony. It was I, Sir, talking to myself, Sir. I was saying that forty miles in four hours was very good going. Hem. As to be sure it was. Hem. I have got a sort of cold by being out in the air. We'll go in, if you please. Hem.

Hardcastle. But if you talk'd to yourself, you did not answer yourself. I am certain I heard two voices, and am resolved (*Raising his voice*) to find the other out.

Mrs. Hardcastle. (*From behind*) Oh! he's coming to find me out. Oh!

Tony. What need you go, Sir, if I tell you? Hem. I'll lay down my life for the truth—hem—I'll tell you all, Sir.

[*Detaining him.*

Hardcastle. I tell you I will not be detained. I insist on seeing. It's in vain to expect I'll believe you.

Mrs. Hardcastle. (*Running forward from behind*) O lud, he'll murder my poor boy, my darling. Here, good gentleman, whet your rage upon me. Take my money, my life, but spare that young gentleman, spare my child, if you have any mercy.

Hardcastle. My wife! as I'm a Christian. From whence can she come, or what does she mean!

Mrs. Hardcastle. (*Kneeling*) Take compassion on us, good Mr. Highwayman. Take our money, our watches, all we have, but spare our lives. We will never bring you to justice, indeed we won't, good Mr. Highwayman.

Hardcastle. I believe the woman's out of her senses. What, Dorothy, don't you know *me*?

Mrs. Hardcastle. Mr. Hardcastle, as I'm alive! My fears blinded me. But who, my dear, could have expected to meet you here, in this frightful place, so far from home. What has brought you to follow us?

Hardcastle. Sure, Dorothy, you have not lost your wits! So far from home, when you are within forty yards of your own door! (*To him*) This is one of your old tricks, you graceless rogue you. (*To her*) Don't you know the gate, and the mulberry-tree; and don't you remember the horsepond, my dear?

Mrs. Hardcastle. Yes, I shall remember the horsepond as long as I live; I have caught my death in it. (*To Tony*) And is it to you, you graceless varlet, I owe all this? I'll teach you to abuse your mother, I will.

Tony. Ecod, mother, all the parish says you have spoil'd me, and so you may take the fruits on't.

Mrs. Hardcastle. I'll spoil you, I will.

[*Follows him off the stage. Exit.*

Hardcastle. There's morality, however, in his reply.

[*Exit.*

Enter HASTINGS *and Miss* NEVILLE

Hastings. My dear Constance, why will you deliberate thus? If we delay a moment, all is lost for ever. Pluck up a little resolution, and we shall soon be out of the reach of her malignity.

Miss Neville. I find it impossible. My spirits are so sunk with the agitations I have suffered, that I am unable to face any new danger. Two or three years' patience will at last crown us with happiness.

Hastings. Such a tedious delay is worse than inconstancy. Let us fly, my charmer. Let us date our happiness from this very moment. Perish fortune. Love and content will encrease what we possess beyond a monarch's revenue. Let me prevail.

Miss Neville. No, Mr. Hastings; no. Prudence once more comes to my relief, and I will obey its dictates. In the moment of passion, fortune may be despised, but it ever produces a lasting repentance. I'm resolved to apply to Mr. Hardcastle's compassion and justice for redress.

Hastings. But tho' he had the will, he has not the power to relieve you.

Miss Neville. But he has influence, and upon that I am resolved to rely.

Hastings. I have no hopes. But since you persist, I must reluctantly obey you. [*Exeunt.*

SCENE *Changes*

Enter Sir CHARLES *and Miss* HARDCASTLE

Sir Charles. What a situation am I in! If what you say appears, I shall then find a guilty son. If what he says be true, I shall then lose one that, of all others, I most wished for a daughter.

Miss Hardcastle. I am proud of your approbation, and to shew I merit it, if you place yourselves as I directed, you shall hear his explicit declaration. But he comes.

Sir Charles. I'll to your father, and keep him to the appointment. [*Exit Sir* Charles.

Enter MARLOW

Marlow. Tho' prepared for setting out, I come once more to take leave, nor did I, till this moment, know the pain I feel in the separation.

Miss Hardcastle. (*In her own natural manner*) I believe these sufferings cannot be very great, Sir, which you can so easily remove. A day or two longer, perhaps, might lessen your uneasiness, by shewing the little value of what you think proper to regret.

Marlow. (*Aside*) This girl every moment improves upon me. (*To her*) It must not be, Madam. I have already trifled too long with my heart. My very pride begins to submit to my passion. The disparity of education and fortune, the anger of a parent, and the contempt of my equals, begin to lose their weight; and nothing can restore me to myself, but this painful effort of resolution.

Miss Hardcastle. Then go, Sir. I'll urge nothing more to detain you. Tho' my family be as good as her's you came down to visit, and my education, I hope, not inferior, what are these advantages without equal affluence? I must remain contented with the slight approbation of imputed merit; I must have only the mockery of your addresses, while all your serious aims are fix'd on fortune.

Enter HARDCASTLE *and Sir* CHARLES *from behind*

Sir Charles. Here, behind this screen.

Hardcastle. Ay, ay, make no noise. I'll engage my Kate covers him with confusion at last.

Marlow. By heavens, Madam, fortune was ever my smallest consideration. Your beauty at first caught my eye; for who could see that without emotion? But every moment that I converse with you, steals in some new grace, heightens the picture, and gives it stronger expression. What at first seem'd rustic plainness, now appears refin'd simplicity. What seem'd forward assurance, now strikes me as the result of courageous innocence, and conscious virtue.

Sir Charles. What can it mean! He amazes me!

Hardcastle. I told you how it would be. Hush!

Marlow. I am now determined to stay, Madam, and I have too good an opinion of my father's discernment, when he sees you, to doubt his approbation.

Miss Hardcastle. No, Mr. Marlow, I will not, cannot detain you. Do you think I could suffer a connexion, in which there is the smallest room for repentance? Do you think I would take the mean advantage of a transient passion, to load you with confusion? Do you think I could ever relish that happiness, which was acquired by lessening your's?

Marlow. By all that's good, I can have no happiness but what's in your power to grant me. Nor shall I ever feel repentance, but in not having seen your merits before. I will stay, even contrary to your wishes; and tho' you should persist to shun me, I will make my respectful assiduities atone for the levity of my past conduct.

Miss Hardcastle. Sir, I must entreat you'll desist. As our acquaintance began, so let it end, in indifference. I might have given an hour or two to levity; but, seriously, Mr. Marlow, do you think I could ever submit to a connexion, where *I* must appear mercenary, and *you* imprudent? Do you think I could ever catch at the confident addresses of a secure admirer?

Marlow (*Kneeling*) Does this look like security? Does this look like confidence? No, Madam, every moment that shews me your merit, only serves to encrease my diffidence and confusion. Here let me continue——

Sir Charles. I can hold it no longer. Charles, Charles, how hast thou deceived me! Is this your indifference, your uninteresting conversation!

Hardcastle. Your cold contempt; your formal interview. What have you to say now?

Marlow. That I'm all amazement! What can it mean!

Hardcastle. It means that you can say and unsay things at pleasure. That you can address a lady in private, and deny it in public; that you have one story for us, and another for my daughter.

Marlow. Daughter!—this lady your daughter!

Hardcastle. Yes, Sir, my only daughter. My Kate, whose else should she be?

Marlow. Oh, the devil.

Miss Hardcastle. Yes, Sir, that very identical tall squinting lady you were pleased to take me for. (*Curtseying*) She that you addressed as the mild, modest, sentimental man of gravity, and the bold forward agreeable Rattle of the Ladies Club; ha, ha, ha.

Marlow. Zounds, there's no bearing this; it's worse than death.

Miss Hardcastle. In which of your characters, Sir, will you give us leave to address you? As the faultering gentleman, with looks on the ground, that speaks just to be heard, and hates hypocrisy; or the loud confident creature, that keeps it up with Mrs. Mantrap, and old Miss Biddy Buckskin, till three in the morning; ha, ha, ha.

Marlow. Oh, curse on my noisy head. I never attempted to be impudent yet, that I was not taken down. I must be gone.

Hardcastle. By the hand of my body, but you shall not. I see it was all a mistake, and I am rejoiced to find it. You shall not, Sir, I tell you. I know she'll forgive you. Won't you forgive him, Kate? We'll all forgive you. Take courage, man.

[*They retire, she tormenting him to the back Scene.*

Enter Mrs. HARDCASTLE, TONY

Mrs. Hardcastle. So, so, they're gone off. Let them go, I care not.

Hardcastle. Who gone?

Mrs. Hardcastle. My dutiful niece and her gentleman, Mr. Hastings, from Town. He who came down with our modest visitor here.

Sir Charles. Who, my honest George Hastings? As worthy a fellow as lives, and the girl could not have made a more prudent choice.

Hardcastle. Then, by the hand of my body, I'm proud of the connexion.

Mrs. Hardcastle. Well, if he has taken away the lady, he has not taken her fortune, that remains in this family to console us for her loss.

Hardcastle. Sure, Dorothy, you would not be so mercenary?

Mrs. Hardcastle. Ay, that's my affair, not your's. But you know if your son, when of age, refuses to marry his cousin, her whole fortune is then at her own disposal.

Hardcastle. Ay, but he's not of age, and she has not thought proper to wait for his refusal.

Enter HASTINGS *and Miss* NEVILLE

Mrs. Hardcastle. (*Aside*) What, returned so soon. I begin not to like it.

Hastings. (*To Hardcastle*) For my late attempt to fly off with your niece, let my present confusion be my punishment. We are now come back, to appeal from your justice to your humanity. By her father's consent, I first paid her my addresses, and our passions were first founded in duty.

Miss Neville. Since his death, I have been obliged to stoop to dissimulation to avoid oppression. In an hour of levity, I was ready even to give up my fortune to secure my choice. But I'm now recover'd from the delusion, and hope from your tenderness what is denied me from a nearer connexion.

Mrs. Hardcastle. Pshaw, pshaw, this is all but the whining end of a modern novel.

Hardcastle. Be it what it will, I'm glad they're come back to reclaim their due. Come hither, Tony boy. Do you refuse this lady's hand whom I now offer you?

Tony. What signifies my refusing? You know I can't refuse her till I'm of age, father.

Hardcastle. While I thought concealing your age boy was likely to conduce to your improvement, I concurred with your mother's desire to keep it secret. But since I find she turns it to a wrong use, I must now declare, you have been of age these three months.

Tony. Of age! Am I of age, father?

Hardcastle. Above three months.

Tony. Then you'll see the first use I'll make of my liberty. (*Taking Miss Neville's hand*) Witness all men by these presents, that I, Anthony Lumpkin, Esquire, of BLANK place, refuse you, Constantia Neville, spinster, of no place at all, for my true and lawful wife. So Constance Neville may marry whom she pleases, and Tony Lumpkin is his own man again.

Sir Charles. O brave 'Squire.

Hastings. My worthy friend.

Mrs. Hardcastle. My undutiful offspring.

Marlow. Joy, my dear George, I give you joy sincerely. And could I prevail upon my little tyrant here to be less arbitrary, I should be the happiest man alive, if you would return me the favour.

Hastings. (*To Miss Hardcastle*) Come, madam, you are now driven to the very last scene of all your contrivances. I know you like him, I'm sure he loves you, and you must and shall have him.

Hardcastle. (*Joining their hands*) And I say so too. And Mr. Marlow, if she makes as good a wife as she has a daughter, I don't believe you'll ever repent your bargain. So now to supper, to-morrow we shall gather all the poor of the parish about us, and the Mistakes of the Night shall be crowned with a merry morning; so boy take her; as you have been mistaken in the mistress, my wish is, that you may never be mistaken in the wife.

EPILOGUE*

By J. CRADOCK, Esq.

To be spoken in the character of TONY LUMPKIN

WELL—now all's ended—and my comrades gone,
Pray what becomes of *mother's nonly son?*
A hopeful blade!—in town I'll fix my station,
And try to make a bluster in the nation.
As for my cousin Neville, I renounce her,
Off—in a crack—I'll carry big Bett Bouncer.
Why should not I in the great world appear?
I soon shall have a thousand pounds a year;
No matter what a man may here inherit,
In London—'gad, they've some regard for spirit.
I see the horses prancing up the streets,
And big Bet Bouncer, bobs to all she meets;
Then hoikes to jiggs and pastimes ev'ry night—
Not to the plays—they say it a'n't polite,
To Sadler's-Wells perhaps, or Operas go,
And once by chance, to the roratorio.
Thus here and there, for ever up and down,
We'll set the fashions too, to half the town;
And then at auctions—money ne'er regard,
Buy pictures like the great, ten pounds a yard:
Zounds, we shall make these London gentry say,
We know what's damn'd genteel, as well as they.

* This came too late to be spoken.

LETTERS

"When I taxed little Goldsmith for not writing, as he promised me," wrote Dr. Grainger to Bishop Percy, "his answer was that he never wrote a letter in his life; and 'faith I believe him, unless to a bookseller for money." This was an exaggeration, but not an undue one. All except two of Goldsmith's known letters are included in Miss Balderston's edition[1]; and some of them are of considerable biographical, if little literary importance. One or two, however, are among the best things he wrote. Letter I, in particular, is of especial interest; for it shows that even in 1753, long before he had begun to write for a living, he had already mastered that easy but artful artlessness that is the chief delight of his mature style.

Letters I, II and IV follow Miss Balderston's text, which prints Letter I from a contemporary transcript, and Letters II and IV from the original manuscript. The only authority for the text of Letter III is Sir James Prior's *Life of Goldsmith*, 1837, from which it is here printed.

1 *The Collected Letters of Oliver Goldsmith*, edited by Katharine C. Balderston, Cambridge, 1928.

LETTERS

I

To ROBERT BRYANTON

Edinburgh, Sepr. ye 26th 1753

My Dear Bob

How many good excuses (and you know I was ever good at an excuse) might I call up to vindicate my past shamefull silence. I might tell how I wrote a long letter at my first comeing hither, and seem vastly angry at not receiveing an answer; or I might alledge that business, (with business, you know I was always pester'd) had never given me time to finger a pen; but I supress these and twenty more, equally plausible & as easily invented, since they might all be attended with a slight inconvenience of being known to be lies; let me then speak truth; An hereditary indolence (I have it from the Mothers side)[1] has hitherto prevented my writing to you, and still prevents my writing at least twenty five letters more, due to my friends in Ireland—no turnspit gets up into his wheel with more reluctance, than I sit down to write, yet no dog ever loved the roast meat he turns, better than I do him I now address; yet what shall I say now I am enter'd? Shall I tire you with a description of this unfruitfull country? where I must lead you over their hills all brown with heath, or their valleys scarce able to feed a rabbet? Man alone seems to be the only creature who has arived to the naturall size in this poor soil; every part of the country presents the same dismall landscape, no grove nor brook lend their musick to cheer the stranger, or make the inhabitants forget their poverty; yet with all

[1] [A sarcasm, as Miss Balderston has pointed out. There was little love lost between Goldsmith and his mother.]

these disadvantages to call him down to humility, a scotchman is one of the proudest things alive. The poor have pride ever ready to releive them; if mankind shou'd happen to despise them, they are masters of their own admiration, and that they can plentifully bestow on themselves: from their pride and poverty as I take it results one advantage this country enjoys, namely the Gentlemen here are much better bred then among us; no such character here as our Fox-hunter; and they have expresed great surprize when I informed them that some men of a thousand pound a year in Ireland spend their whole lives in runing after a hare, drinking to be drunk, and geting every Girl with Child, that will let them; and truly if such a being, equiped in his hunting dress, came among a circle of scots Gentlemen, they wou'd behold him with the same astonishment that a Country man does King George on horseback; the men here have Generally high cheek bones, and are lean, and swarthy; fond of action; Danceing in particular: tho' now I have mention'd danceing, let me say something of their balls which are very frequent here; when a stranger enters the danceing-hall he sees one end of the room taken up by the Lady's, who sit dismally in a Groupe by themselves. On the other end stand their pensive partners, that are to be, but no more intercourse between the sexes than there is between two Countrys at war, the Ladies indeed may ogle, and the Gentlemen sigh, but an embargo is laid on any closer commerce; at length, to interrupt hostility's, the Lady directeress or intendant, or what you will pitches on a Gentleman and Lady to walk a minuet, which they perform with a formality that aproaches despondence, after five or six couple have thus walked the Gauntlett, all stand up to country dance's, each gentleman furnished with a partner from the afforesaid Lady directress, so they dance much, say nothing, and thus concludes our assembly; I told a scotch Gentleman that such a profound silence resembled the ancient procession of the Roman Matrons in honour of Ceres and the scotch

Gentleman told me, (and faith I beleive he was right) that I was a very great pedant for my pains: now I am come to the Lady's and to shew that I love scotland and every thing that belongs to so charming a Country Il insist on it and will give him leave to break my head that deny's it that the scotch ladys are ten thousand times finer and handsomer than the Irish. To be sure now I see y^{r}. Sisters Betty & Peggy vastly surprized at my Partiality but tell y^{m} flatly I don't value them or their fine skins or Eyes or good sense or—a potatoe for I say it and will maintain it and as a convinceing proof of (I am in a very great passion) of what I assert the scotch Ladies say it themselves, but to be less serious where will you find a language so prettily become a pretty mouth as the broad scotch and the women here speak it in it's highest purity, for instance teach one of the Young Lady's at home to pronounce the Whoar wull I gong with a beccomeing wideness of mouth and I'll lay my life they'l wound every hearer. We have no such character here as a coquett but alass how many envious prudes. Some days ago I walk'd into My Lord Kill-coubry's[1] don't be surpriz'd my Lord is but a Glover, when the Dutchess of Hamilton (that fair who sacrificed her beauty to ambition and her inward peace to a title and Gilt equipage) pass'd by in her Chariot, her batter'd husband[2] or more properly the Guardian of her charms sat beside her. Strait envy began in the shape of no less than three Lady's who sat with me to find fault's in her faultless form—for my part says the first I think that I always thought that the dutchess has too much of the red in her complexion, Madam I am of your oppinion says the seccond and I think her face has a palish cast too much on the delicate order, and let me tell you adds the third Lady whose mouth was puckerd up to the size of an Issue that the Dutchess has fine lips but she wants a mouth. At this every Lady drew up her mouth as If going to

[1] [William Maclellan; he was merely the claimant to the title.]
[2] [The duke was only twenty-nine.]

pronounce the letter P. But how ill my Bob does it become me to ridicule woman with whom I have scarce any correspondence. There are 'tis certain handsome women here and tis as certain they have handsome men to keep them company. An ugly and a poor man is society only for himself and such society the world lets me enjoy in great abundance. Fortune has given you circumstance's and Nature a person to look charming in the Eyes of the fair world nor do I envy my Dear Bob such blessings while I may sit down and laugh at the world, and at myself—the most ridiculous object in it. But you see I am grown downright splenetick, and perhaps this fitt may continue till I receive an answer to this. I know you cant send much news from Ballymahon, but such as it is send it all everything you write will be agreeable and entertaining to me. Has George Conway put up a signe yet has John Binley left off drinking Drams; or Tom Allen got a new wig? But I leave to your own choice what to write but while Noll Goldsmith lives know you have a Friend.

P.S. Give my sincerest regards not merely my compliments (do you mind) to your agreeable family and Give My service to My Mother if you see her for as you express it in Ireland I have a sneaking kindness for her still. Direct to me, Student of Physick in Edinburgh.

II

To the Reverend THOMAS CONTARINE

Leyden [*c.* May 6, 1754][1]

D^r^ S^r^

I SUPPOSE by this time I am accus'd of Either neglect or ingratitude and my silence imputed to my usual slowness of writing but believe me S^r^ when I say that till now I had not an

[1] [From the date on the postmark.]

opertunity of sitting down with that ease of mind, which writing requird, you may see by the top of this letter that I am at Leyden but of my Journey hither you must be informd. Some time after the receipt of your last I embarkd for Burdeaux on board a scotch ship calld the St Andrew, John Watt Master. The ship made a Tolerable apearance and as another inducement I was let to know that six agreeable passengers were to be my company, well we were but two days at sea when a storm drove us into a Citty of England call'd Newcastle upon Tyne. We all went a-shoar to refresh us after the fatigue of our voyage seven men and me. We were one day on shore and on the following evening as we were all verry merry the room door bursts open enters a Serjeant and twelve Grenadiers with their bayonets screwd and put us all under the Kings arrest, it seems my company were Scotch men in the French service and had been in Scotland to enlist Soldiers for the French King. I endeavourd all I could to prove my inocence however I remain'd in prison with the rest a Fortnight and with difficulty got off even then, D^r^ S^r^ keep this all a secret or at least say it was for debt[1] for if it were once known at the university I shoud hardly get a degree, but hear how providence interposd in my Favour. The ship was gone on to burdeaux before I got from prison and was wreckd at the mouth of the Graronne and every one of the crew were drownd. It happen'd the last great storm. There was a ship at that time ready for Holland. I embarkd and in nine days thank My God arrivd safe at Rotterdam from whence I Traveld by land to Leyden whence I now write.

You may Expect some account of this country and tho I am not as yet well qualified for such an undertaking, yet shall I

[1] [According to Dr. Sleigh, in Glover's *Life of Goldsmith* (1774) Goldsmith was imprisoned in Sunderland for a debt which a fellow student had contracted in Edinburgh. (Compare The Man in Black's misfortunes, p. 341). Both stories can hardly be true, and Dr. Sleigh's seems the more likely. Commander Mead, the Honorary Librarian of Lloyd's, who has kindly made inquiries for me, has been unable to find any record of the wreck of the *St. Andrew*.]

endeavour to satisfie some part of your Expectations, nothing surprizes me more than the books every day publishd, descriptive of the manners of this country. Any young man who takes it into his head to publish his traveles visits the countries he intends to describe passes thro them with as much inattention as his valet de chambre and consequently not having a fund himself to fill a vollume he applies to those who wrote before him and gives us the manners of a country not as he must have seen them but such as they might have been fifty years before, the modern dutch man is quite a different creature from him of former times, he in every thing imitates a French man but in his easy disingagd air which is the result of keeping polite company, the dutch man is vastly ceremonious and is perhaps exactly what a French man might have been in the reign of Lewis the 14th. Such are the better bred but the downright Hollander is one of the oddest figures in Nature. Upon a head of lank hair he wears a half cock'd Narrow leav'd hat lacd with black ribon, no coat but seven waistcoats and nine pairs of breeches so that his hips reach almost up to his arm pits. This well cloathd vegetable is now fit to see company or make love but what a pleasing creature is the object of his apetite why she wears a large friez cap with a deal of flanders lace and for every pair of breeches he carries she puts on two petticoats, is it not surprizing how things shoud ever come close enough to make it a match. When I spoke of love I was to be understood not in a—in short I was not to be understood at all, a Dutch Lady burns nothing about her Phlegmatick admirer but his Tobacco. You must know S^r every woman carries in her hand a Stove with coals in it which when she sits she snugs under her petticoats and at this chimney Dozing Strephon lights his pipe. I take it that this continuall smoaking is what gives the man the ruddy healthfull complexion he generally wears by draining his superfluous moisture while the woman deprivd of this amusement overflows with such visciditys as teint the complexion and gives that paleness of visage which Low fenny grounds and moist air conspire to cause. A dutch woman and a Scotch will well bear an oposition. The one is pale & fat and the other lean and ruddy. The one walks as if she were stradling after a go cart and the other takes too Masculine a stride. I shall not endeavour to deprive either country of its share of beauty but must say that of objects on this earth an English farmers Daughter is most charming. Every woman there is a complete beauty while the higher class of women want many of the requisites to make them even Tolerable.

Their pleasures here are very dull tho very various. You may smoak you may doze: you may go to the Italian comedy as good an amusement as either of the former. This entertainment always brings in Harlequin who is generally a Magician and in consequence of his Diabolicall art performs a thousand Tricks on the rest of the persons of the drama who are all fools. I have seen the pit in a roar of laughter at his humour when with his sword he Touches the glass another was drinking from, 'twas not his face they laughd at for that was maskd, they must have seen something vastly queer in the wooden sword that neither I nor you S^{r} were you there cou'd see. In winter, when their cannalls are frozen every house is forsaken and all People are on the ice. Sleds drawn by horses and skating are at that time the reigning amusements. They have boats here that slide on the ice and are driven by the winds. When they spread all their sails they go more than a mile and a half a minite. Their motion is so rapid that the Eye can scarce accompany them. Their ordinary manner of Travelling is very cheap and very convenient. They sail in coverd boats drawn by horses and in these you are sure to meet people of all nations. Here the Dutch slumber the French chatter and the English play cards, any man who likes company may have them to his Taste. For my part I generally detachd myself from all society and was wholy Taken up in observing the face of the country, nothing can Equall its beauty. Wherever I turn my Eye fine houses elegant gardens statues grottoes vistas present themselvs but enter their Towns and you are charmd beyond description. No nothing can be more clean or beautifull.

Scotland and this country bear the highest contrast. There Hills and rocks intercept every prospect here tis all a continu'd plain there you might see a well dresd Dutchess issuing from a dirty close and here a dirty Dutch man inhabiting a Palace. The S[c]otch may be compard to a Tulip planted in dung but I never see a dutch man in his own house, but I think of a magnificent Egyptian Temple dedicated to an ox.

Physick is by no means Taught here so well as in Edinburgh and in all Leyden there are but four British students all nesesarys being so extreamly Dear and the Professors so very Lazy (the chymicall Professor[1] excepted) that we dont much care to come hither. I am not certain how long my stay may be however I expect to have the happiness of seeing you at Kilmore if I can next March.

Direct to me if I am honourd with a letter from you to Madame De Allion's in Leyden. Thou Best of Men may heaven guard and preserve you and those you Love.

OLIVER GOLDSMITH

III

To ROBERT BRYANTON

London, Temple Exchange Coffee-house,
Temple Bar, Aug. 14, 1758

Dear Sir,

I HAVE heard it remark'd, I believe by yourself, that they who are drunk, or out of their wits, fancy every body else in the same condition: mine is a friendship that neither distance nor

[1] [See footnote on p. 212.]

time can efface, which is probably the reason that, for the soul of me, I can't avoid thinking yours of the same complexion; and yet I have many reasons for being of a contrary opinion, else why in so long an absence was I never made a partner in your concerns? To hear of your successes would have given me the utmost pleasure; and a communication of your very disappointments would divide the uneasiness I too frequently feel for my own. Indeed, my dear Bob, you don't conceive how unkindly you have treated one whose circumstances afford him few prospects of pleasure, except those reflected from the happiness of his friends. However, since you have not let me hear from you, I have in some measure disappointed your neglect by frequently thinking of you. Every day do I remember the calm anecdotes of your life, from the fire-side to the easy chair; recal the various adventures that first cemented our friendship,—the school, the college, or the tavern; preside in fancy over your cards; am displeased at your bad play when the rubber goes against you, though not with all that agony of soul as when I once was your partner.

Is it not strange that two of such like affections should be so much separated and so differently employed as we are? You seem placed at the centre of fortune's wheel, and let it revolve never so fast, seem insensible of the motion. I seem to have been tied to the circumference, and turned disagreeably round like an wh— in a whirligig. I sat down with an intention to chide, and yet methinks I have forgot my resentment already. The truth is, I am a simpleton with regard to you; I may attempt to bluster, but like Anacreon, my heart is respondent only to softer affections. And yet now I think on't again, I will be angry. God's curse, Sir! who am I? Eh! what am I? Do you know whom you have offended? A man whose character may one of these days be mentioned with profound respect in a German comment or Dutch dictionary; whose name you will probably hear ushered in by a Doctissimus Doctissimorum, or heel-pieced with a long Latin termination. Think how Goldsmithius, or Gobblegurchius, or some such sound, as rough as a nutmeg-grater, will become me? Think of that!—God's curse, Sir! who am I? I must own my ill-natured cotemporaries have not hitherto paid me those honours I have had such just reason to expect. I have not yet seen my face reflected in all the lively display of red and white paints on any sign-posts in the suburbs. Your handkerchief weavers seem as yet unacquainted with my merits or physiognomy, and the very snuff-box makers appear to have forgot their respect. Tell them all from me, they are a set of Gothic, barbarous, ignorant scoundrels. There will come a day, no doubt it will—I beg you may live a couple of hundred years longer only to see the day—when the Scaligers and Daciers will vindicate my character, give learned editions of my labours, and bless the times with copious comments on the text. You shall see how they will fish up the heavy scoundrels who disregard me now, or will then offer to cavil at my productions. How will they bewail the times that suffered so much genius to lie neglected. If ever my works find their way to Tartary or China, I know the consequence. Suppose one of your Chinese Owanowitzers instructing one of your Tartarian Chianobacchi—you see I use Chinese names to show my own erudition, as I shall soon make our Chinese talk like an Englishman to show his. This may be the subject of the lecture:—

"Oliver Goldsmith flourished in the eighteenth and nineteenth centuries. He lived to be an hundred and three years old, and in that age may justly be styled the sun of literature and the Confucius of Europe. Many of his earlier writings, to the regret of the learned world, were anonymous, and have probably been lost, because united with those of others. The first avowed piece the world has of his is entitled an "Essay on the Present State of Taste and Literature in Europe,"—a work well worth its weight in diamonds. In this he profoundly explains what learning is, and what learning is not. In this he proves that blockheads are not men of wit, and yet that men of wit are actually blockheads."

But as I choose neither to tire my Chinese Philosopher, nor you, nor myself, I must discontinue the oration, in order to give you a good pause for admiration; and I find myself most violently disposed to admire too. Let me, then, stop my fancy to take a view of my future self; and, as the boys say, light down to see myself on horseback. Well, now I am down, where the d—l *is I*? Oh, Gods! Gods! here in a garret writing for bread, and expecting to be dunned for a milk score! However, dear Bob, whether in penury or affluence, serious or gay, I am ever wholly thine.

OLIVER GOLDSMITH

IV

To Mrs. BUNBURY

[London, *c.* December 25, 1773][1]

Madam.

I READ your letter with all that allowance which critical candour would require, but after all find so much to object to, and so much to raise my indignation, that I cannot help giving it a serious reply. I am not so ignorant madam as not to see there are many sarcasms contain'd in it, and solœcisms also (solœcism is a word that comes from the town of Soleis in Attica[2] among the Greeks, built by Solon, and applied as we use the word kidderminster for curtains from a town also of that name, but this is learning you have no taste for) I say madam there are sarcasms in it and solœcisms also. But not to seem an ill natured critic Ill take leave to quote your own

[1] [Miss Balderston's dating. See her *Collected Letters of Oliver Goldsmith*, p. 128.]

[2] [A solecism. According to the *Oxford English Dictionary*, the town was Soloi in Cilicia.]

words and give you my remarks upon them as they occur. You begin as follows,

> I hope my good Doctor you soon will be here
> And your spring velvet coat very smart will appear
> To open our ball the first day in the year.

Pray madam where did you ever find the Epithet good applied to the title of Doctor? Had you calld me learned Doctor, or grave Doctor, or Noble Doctor it might be allowable because these belong to the profession. But not to cavil at triffles; you talk of my spring velvet coat and advise me to wear it the first day in the year, that is in the middle of winter. A spring velvet in the middle of winter?!! That would be a solœcism indeed. And yet to encrease the inconsistence, in another part of your letter you call me a beau. Now on one side or other you must be wrong. If Im a beau I can never think of wearing a spring velvet in winter, and if I be not a beau—why—then —that explains itself. But let me go on to your next two strange lines

> And bring with you a wig that is modish and gay
> To dance with the girls that are makers of hay.

The absurdity of making hay at Christmass you yourself seem sensible of. You say your sister will laugh, and so indeed she well may—the lattins have an expression for a contemptuous kind of laughter, *naso contemnere adunco* that is to laugh with a crooked nose, she may laugh at you in the manner of the ancients if she thinks fit. But now I come to the most extraordinary of all extraordinary propositions which is to take your and your sister's advice in playing at Loo. The presumption of the offer raises my indignation beyond the bounds of prose it inspires me at once with verse and resentment. I take advice! And from who? You shall hear.

> First let me suppose what may shortly be true
> The company set, and the word to be Loo.

All smirking, and pleasant, and big with adventure
And ogling the stake which is fixd in the center.
Round and round go the cards while I inwardly damn
At never once finding a visit from Pam.[1]
I lay down my stake, apparently cool,
While the harpies about me all pocket the pool.
I fret in my gizzard, yet cautious and sly
I wish all my friends may be bolder than I.
Yet still they sit snugg, not a creature will aim
By losing their money to venture at fame.
Tis in vain that at niggardly caution I scold
Tis in vain that I flatter the brave and the bold
All play in their own way, and think me an ass.
What does Mrs. Bunbury? I sir? I pass.
Pray what does Miss Horneck? Take courage. Come do.
Who I! Let me see sir. Why I must pass too.
Mr. Bunbury frets, and I fret like the devil
To see them so cowardly lucky and civil.
Yet still I sit snugg and continue to sigh on
Till made by my losses as bold as a lion
I venture at all, while my avarice regards
The whole pool as my own. Come give me five cards.
Well done cry the ladies. Ah Doctor that's good.
The pool's very rich. Ah. The Doctor is lood.
Thus foild in my courage, on all sides perplext,
I ask for advice from the lady that's next
Pray mam be so good as to give your advice
Dont you think the best way is venture fort twice.
I advise cries the lady to try it I own.
Ah! The Doctor is lood. Come Doctor, put down.
Thus playing and playing I still grow more eager
And so bold and so bold, Im at last a bold beggar.
Now ladies I ask if law matters youre skilld in

[1] [The knave of clubs, which was higher than the knave of trumps.]

Whether crimes such as yours should not come before Fielding[1]
For giving advice that is not worth a straw
May well be call'd picking of pockets in law
And picking of pockets with which I now charge ye
Is by Quinto Elizabeth[2] death without Clergy.
What justice when both to the Old Baily brought
By the gods Ill enjoy it, tho' 'tis but in thought.
Both are placed at the bar with all proper decorum.
With bunches of Fennel and nosegays before em.
Both cover their faces with mobbs and all that
But the judge bids them angrily take off their hat.
When uncovered a buzz of enquiry runs round
Pray what are their crimes? They've been pilfering found.
But pray who have they pilfered? A Doctor I hear.
What, yon solemn fac'd odd looking man that stands near,
The same. What a pitty. How does it surprize one
Two handsomer culprits I never set eyes on.
Then their friends all come round me with cringing and leering
To melt me to pitty, and soften my swearing.
First Sir Charles[3] advances, with phrases well strung
Consider Dear Doctor the girls are but young.
The younger the worse I return him again.
It shews that their habits are all dy'd in grain.
But then theyre so handsome, one's bosom it grieves.
What signifies handsome when people are thieves.
But where is your justice; their cases are hard.
What signifies justice; I want the reward.—

Theres the parish of Edmonton offers forty pound; there's the parish of St Leonard Shoreditch offers forty pound;

[1] [Sir John Fielding, justice of the peace for Westminster.]
[2] [Actually Octavo Elizabeth.]
[3] [Henry Bunbury's elder brother.]

there's the parish of Tyburn from the hog in the pound to St Giles's watch house offers forty pound, I shall have all that if I convict them.

But consider their case, It may yet be your own
And see how they kneel; is your heart made of stone?
This moves, so at last I agree to relent
For ten pounds in hand, and ten pound to be spent.
The judge takes the hint, having seen what we drive at
And lets them both off with correction in private.

I chalenge you all to answer this. I tell you you cannot. It cuts deep. But now for the rest of the letter, and next—but I want room—so I believe I shall battle the rest out at Barton some day next week. I dont value you all.

THE END

there's the parish [illegible] from [illegible] to the [illegible] Christmas [illegible] I shall have all [illegible] dream.

> But consider their case, [illegible] yet [illegible] your [illegible]
> [illegible]
> His [illegible]
> For ten pounds [illegible] and [illegible] pounds [illegible] present,
> The [illegible]
> And [illegible]

Considering yourself as answered [illegible] until you send [illegible] for the rest of the letter, and now—but [illegible] the rest [illegible] I [illegible] you all.

THE END